𝔓𝔰𝔶𝔠𝔥𝔬𝔅𝔦𝔟𝔩𝔢

presented to

_____

_____

_____

_____

DATE

By

PITCHSTONE PUBLISHING
Charlottesville, Virginia 22901

Advance praise for PsychoBible

"Professor Favazza's text is a challenge for us all to think seriously about how we developed our religious beliefs and how we use God and religion in our personal and professional lives. Cowards need not pick up this brilliantly written book. Only those courageous enough to explore the nature of their connection—or lack of it—to God and religion."
— *Professor Ezra Griffith, Yale University*

"Allow Dr. Favazza to take you on an enlightening tour through the most influential book in the Western world. With his help you will capture its terrible contradictions, its cruel and holy advice. You will learn that its messages often lie in the eyes of its beholders. You will discover another way to cosmic awareness. Dr. Favazza is a modern-day Dante."
— *Dr. Bernard Beitman, national award-winning author of* Learning Psychotherapy

"Dr. Favazza is a prominent psychiatrist who has written a book that examines how stories in both the Old and New Testament of the Bible can be used to explain behavior in today's tumultuous times. Readers will gain insights into their personalities that psychiatry cannot yet provide. I recommend this book highly to all those interested in understanding the complexities of human behavior."
— *Benjamin Sadock, Menas S. Gregory Professor, New York University and Editor of the* Comprehensive Textbook of Psychiatry

"In *PsychoBible*, internationally renowned cultural psychiatrist Dr. Armando Favazza takes an in-depth look at religion and the Holy Bible. He provides important psychological insight into numerous biblical figures and situations, and opens the door to greater understanding of religion from a mental health perspective. This unique and fascinating book is certain to stimulate scholars, benefit laymen, and touch the lives of many people."
— *Professor Wen-Shing Tseng, University of Hawaii and Former Chair of the Transcultural Section of the World Psychiatric Association*

"*PsychoBible* is a very important contribution to the emerging dialogue between psychiatry and religion. Dr. Favazza is a reverent truth-teller. His insights are thought provoking for a wide spectrum of readers."
— *The Rev. Canon John F. Fergueson*

"This is a spectacular book, bold in its theme, comprehensive in its content, and beautifully written. Favazza pulls no punches, yet respectfully makes a case for informed faith as a guide for personal behavior. Everyone from true believers to seekers of wisdom and holiness to confirmed atheists will benefit greatly from reading *PsychoBible*. I recommend it for everyone with utmost enthusiasm."
    —*Chella S. David, Alice Sheets Marriott Professor, Mayo Medical School*

"*PsychoBible* has the potential to touch the lives of many persons. It looks at history in a way that questions how many traditions have evolved and how they are impacted by a new understanding and acceptance of psychiatry today. Hopefully, this book will assist in the reflection on the Bible and theology in order to more fully understand the Christian witness of faith."
    —*Sister Anne Lutz, Congregation of Bon Secours*

"*PsychoBible*, written for the laity, deals with biblical history which is presented from a modern psychological perspective blending theological concepts with psychiatric meaning. The book will be useful for mental health professionals and trainees in understanding the religious culture of their patients, which shapes significant elements of their behavior. Sacrifice and suffering are themes illustrated in their psychological, as well as religious, dimensions demonstrating how some self-destructive acts may be atonement in disguise. Dr. Favazza offers the religious community a bold challenge to examine the basis of their faith."
    —*Professor Arthur Freeman, Louisiana State University*

"Dr. Favazza has comprehensively explored in a scholarly manner a previously neglected area in psychiatry and psychotherapy—the role of the Bible in influencing patients' perceptions of their symptoms, illness, and behavior. By clearly examining, without bias, what the Bible actually says about the full range of human behavior and how these views have been interpreted by Christianity and Judaism over the centuries, he has made an important contribution to the literature on psychiatry and religion."
    —*Professor James Boehnlein, Oregon Health and Science University and Editor,* Psychiatry and Religion

"For more than two decades, Dr. Favazza's insights into the relationship of religion and psychiatry have been recognized by scholars throughout the world. This book promises to be another in his series of outstanding contributions to this field. It will find a place on the shelves of students in anthropology, sociology, psychology/psychiatry, religious studies, and philosophy."
    —*Edward Foulks, Sellar-Polchow Professor, Tulane University*

"*PsychoBible* offers the best ever scientific understanding of the impact of religion on behavior. It is a must read book not only for those interested in the mental health profession but also for members of the religious community and everyone interested in learning more about the Bible and behavior."

—Professor Pedro Ruiz, University of Texas-Houston and
Past President of the American College of Psychiatrists

"*PsychoBible* is an invaluable resource for all who want to understand the biblical underpinnings for certain beliefs and behaviors. Coming at a time of renewed interest in the relationship between religion and psychiatry, it is scholarly and illuminating. I highly recommend it."

—Professor Mary McCarthy, Brigham and Women's Hospital,
Harvard University

"The most important tool for crafting the future is a solid grasp of the past. Conclusions about the roots of contemporary society are often limited, facile, and inaccurate. In this book, Dr. Favazza traces the origins of many of our central beliefs and practices. In a conversational tone and a readable format, he supplies comprehensive, scholarly information to inform our discussions about individual psychology and social policy. *PsychoBible* is a fascinating and monumental work."

—Dr. Nada Stotland, Secretary-elect
American Psychiatric Association

"Dr. Favazza has undertaken an intellectual sojourn that most Judeo-Christian psychiatrists avoid: the integration of our psychiatric science-cum–art with earlier religious training—our own training in many cases, as well as the training of many patients regardless of our own religious training or affiliation. This work should provoke thoughts that aid us in examining this last taboo, our private religious and spiritual thoughts, beliefs, and opinions. It will also greatly facilitate our understanding the religious and spiritual life of numerous patients. Non-psychiatrists who can appreciate the Bible as a learned, but not necessarily literal work, should also find it a fascinating read."

—Professor Joseph Westermeyer, University of Minnesota

"Dr. Favazza makes bold and cogent comments on the Hebrew Bible. He notes that Isaiah's "suffering Servant," for example, refers to the suffering of the people of Israel although centuries later Christians reinterpreted the concept to presage Jesus. In addressing boldly and scholarly such core issues of the Hebrew Bible the author ensures that readers of *PsychoBible* will find it to be both refreshing and thought provoking."

—Rabbi Yossi Feintuch, Ph.D.

PsychoBible

Behavior, Religion & the Holy Book

Armando Favazza

PITCHSTONE PUBLISHING
Charlottesville, Virginia 22901

PITCHSTONE PUBLISHING
Charlottesville, Virginia 22901

Library of Congress Cataloging-in-Publication Data

Favazza, Armando R.
    PsychoBible : behavior, religion & the Holy Book / Armando R. Favazza.
        p. cm.
    Includes bibliographical references and index.
    ISBN 0-9728875-0-4 – ISBN 0-9728875-1-2 (pbk.)
        1. Bible–Psychology. 2. Psychology and religion. I. Title.

BS645.F38 2004
220.6'01'9–dc22
                                                    2003062227

To my lovely wife, Christine,
for providing me with a share of heaven on earth,
and
To Kurt Volkan, my publisher,
for believing.

CONTENTS

FOREWORD

This provocative and thoughtful book can be introduced with some reflections on the importance of spirituality and religion to the mental health field. For a psychiatrist like myself, the book makes clear how a historical and biblical perspective on religion and spirituality has been neglected for too long in the mental health field. Dr. Armando Favazza's valuable contribution certainly underlines the relevance of a religious life to people's psychological well-being.

Patients in therapy, whatever their orientation, need something to strive for and to give meaning to their lives to overcome their troubles. Their goals may be worldly, like a fulfilling relationship, a better job, or simply relief from chronic depression. Spirituality transcends this. The dictionary applies phrases like "not tangible or material," "concerned with or affecting the soul," or "pertaining to God." We can think of spirituality as a search for existential or transcendent meaning that can exist independently of affiliation with a specific religious orientation. This is compatible with the interdenominational pluralism that, as Dr. Favazza makes clear, has emerged in recent decades. Tolerance among diverse religious groups has become increasingly common. Even people who maintain little commitment to formal religious practice are open to a more broadly conceived concept of this state of mind.

A spiritual orientation can be experienced by members of a congregation as part of their life-long membership in a religious denomination. This is the case for most people who have found comfort in this outlook since youth. But for others, it may emerge later in life as an intense personal experience which then yields a new look at their lives, even a turnaround in the way they see the world around them. An example of this is the biblical story of St. Paul, who saw a blinding light while on the way to Damascus, and then underwent baptism, embarking on years of learning about the nascent Christian faith and preaching to converts. The psychological issues we shall consider can be highlighted by such intense, sometimes spontaneous, personal encounters with oneself. Experiences like this, of course, abound through history. They are regularly recounted by people born-again into faith; for them,

xiii

an intense spirituality becomes a central part of their religious life. In fact, fully 40 percent of Americans consider themselves born-again Christians. In the realm of psychology they date back to the very origins of the discipline. William James, said to be the father of modern psychology, wrote in 1902 of personal spiritual revelations in his classical work, *The Varieties of Religious Experience*. He derided a simplistic medical view of such revelatory phenomena: "Medical materialism finishes up St. Paul by calling his vision on the road to Damascus a discharging lesion of the occipital cortex, he being an epileptic. It snuffs out St. Teresa as a hysteric, St. Francis of Assisi as a hereditary degenerate."

James drew on the recounting of spiritual awakenings as evidence of the psychological validity of religious faith and the diversity of religious experience. He posited that introspection into religious experiences could provide evidence of the way the mind operates. In doing this, he valued the introspection of historical characters as well as his students and subjects as a legitimate basis for the study of mental function. The subjective nature of spirituality was therefore considered a legitimate psychological dimension from the outset of this discipline.

Psychoanalysts with a positive attitude toward spirituality have had to work their way around the views of their progenitor, Sigmund Freud. William James was a psychologist and philosopher who championed introspection and formulated his perspective around the meaningfulness of religious experience. Around the same time, Freud, a physician experienced in physiologic research, was developing ideas that would invalidate the meaning of such spiritual experiences. He ascribed religion to a neurotic perspective rooted in unresolved childlike fixations. We do not know with certainty why he was adamant on this issue. Perhaps because of his orientation toward biologic science, perhaps because of his reaction to the Anti-Semitism which he encountered in his native Vienna, or perhaps out of the anti-religious, philosophical writings of Central European philosophers such as Hegel and Schopenhauer, Freud spoke of religion as an illusion that operated outside empirical observation, even a mass delusion. His strongly held views were instrumental for many years in the disavowal of religious experience within the psychoanalytic movement.

Early on, however, views were expressed within the psychoanalytic mainstream that ran contrary to Freud's apparent bias. Oskar Pfister, a Lutheran pastor and psychoanalyst, was a longtime friend of Freud's, but emphasized the meaningful nature of religion as a unifying vision of the world, one that transcended the uncertainties of life, and encouraged ethical responsibility. The most elaborately thought-out and well-developed psychoanalytic alternative to the established Freudian view emerged in the writings of Carl Gustav Jung.

Jung did not ascribe validity to a particular creed or to membership in any specific organized religion, but rather believed that his perspective took into account the full range of spiritual experiences, including people's acceptance of a godhead. He viewed the self as lying midway between the unconscious and conscious, and pointed out that it is virtually impossible for people to fully establish meaning and find comfort in life without coming to peace with their spiritual nature.

Ana-Maria Rizzuto, a psychoanalyst and person of faith, picked up on the conception of transitional objects as a potential source of illusionary experience, namely, symbolic thinking and creativity, and focused on qualities in this transitional realm, pointing out that people's conception of God and spirituality emerged from that realm. She emphasized that the acceptance of this perspective does not necessarily imply either the existence or the non-existence of an actual deity, but only defined a psychological realm in which man's spiritual nature operates.

An implicit struggle between the secular and religious perspectives has taken place in our understanding of spirituality over the course of the past century. The secular perspective is manifest in an emphasis on the place of values within a spiritual orientation, rather than theistic or formally religious beliefs. One early presentation of this secular option was made by James' *Varieties of Religious Experience*, in which the great American poet Walt Whitman is described as "the restorer of the eternal natural religion."

Around the same time, Gordon Allport, respectful of the introspective approach of William James, tried to infuse his scientific approach to personality and social psychology with an understanding of the role of personal values in shaping the diversity of people's beliefs. Allport constructed scales that distinguished between an intrinsic religious orientation, in which the individual employs internalized beliefs to achieve personal fulfillment, and an extrinsic one, in which religion is employed to accomplish more practical ends, such as providing self-justification or social acceptance. For him, the mature individual incorporates religious values and diverse elements of human experience into an intrinsically felt sense of purpose that lends meaning to life.

Allport's influence has been felt by many academic psychologists. Some have pointed out that psychotherapy is never value-neutral, even if its practitioners might think they can operate in that manner independent of their own biases. He observed that these are

inevitably evident in their respective approaches to treatment. Allen
Bergin and others, acknowledging this, have called for a restoration of
a spiritual or theistic orientation in psychotherapy. What Dr. Favazza
offers us here, among other contributions of value, is a basis for providing such a restoration.

Marc Galanter
Department of Psychiatry
New York University

PREFACE

Although the idea of writing *PsychoBible* first entered my mind six years ago, it probably has been within me for most of my life. I grew up in Brooklyn, New York, in a neighborhood that connects the Italian Bensonhurst area with the Jewish Borough Park area. My family members were nominal Catholics; my grandmother was arrested briefly for passing out Margaret Sanger birth control literature in front of St. Bernadette's Church. We didn't have a Bible in our home, and I never saw one in the home of any other Italian family. I learned a little about the Bible from Sunday school and from sermons but was never encouraged to read it.

Because of its strong academic reputation, but mainly because I thought the uniforms were neat, I attended Xavier High School in Manhattan. It's a Jesuit military school where all the students live at home and travel on the subways. In my sophomore year I was allowed to select either a science or a Greek honors track. Thinking of a career in medicine I chose the latter; we were told it was designed for students who wanted to be "priests or physi-cians." This juxtaposition of vocations seemed odd, but we were told it was important for a physician to have a classical education. And so I experienced heavy-duty doses of Latin, Greek, and French. In religion courses we used catechisms of varying sophistication but never the Bible. My education was aug-mented by the soap-box orators that I passed each day in Union Square and by occasional visits to Dorothy Day's Catholic Worker offices.

When I was an undergraduate at Columbia University, all of my friends were Jewish, as were some of my best professors, such as Daniel Bell the sociologist, Meyer Shapiro the art historian, Lionel Trilling the literary critic, and Moses Hadas the classicist. I adored Gilbert Highet, whose lec-tures on world literature were remarkably entertaining and insightful. Margaret Mead let me take her graduate seminar on anthropology. It was a decision that has influenced my profes-sional career ever since. I still have a copy of her final examina-tion, which consisted of just one item: Ask yourself a question based on any topic that was dis-cussed in class and then answer it. I studied Italian for four years

and took a course on the New Testament at the university's Union
Theological Seminary. My rationalization was that it would help me
understand Dante's *Divine Comedy* better. As president of the Pre-
Medical Society I invited the eminent theologian Reinhold Neibuhr
to lecture on medical ethics. Meeting him and introducing his presentation to a large audience was a great moment in my life. My education was enlarged during these years and later by a friendship with
Felix Marti-Ibáñez, the editor of *MD* magazine and, in my opinion,
one of the great Spanish authors of the twentieth century. He was
passionately and incurably in love with literature and with medicine.
Though we never discussed religion, he was the most spiritual person I have ever encountered. Like him, I went on to study psychiatry
and to get a master's degree in public health.

Since I had lived in New York City all my life, I decided to attend
medical school in a different cultural setting. I was particularly interested in meeting people called Protestants. I had read a lot about them but
had never really known any. So I studied medicine at Thomas Jefferson's
academical village, the University of Virginia, and got to interact with a
lot of Protestants. Some were wonderful, some weren't. During my first
year I witnessed racial segregation. There were separate drinking foun-
tains in the clinics. An aging, famous professor refused to make neuro-
surgical rounds on black patients. Blacks had to sit in the balcony at the
local movie theater. During a pathology class in my sophomore year, a
professor sadly announced that President Kennedy had been assassinat-
ed. About half of my classmates greeted the announcement with
cheers and applause. By my senior year official segregation had been
eliminated from the university and the town.

I did my psychiatric training and received my public health degree
in community mental health at the University of Michigan. Much of
my clinical training was psychoanalytic. Religion wasn't discussed
much. I do remember, however, that ministers, priests, and rabbis
needed to obtain permission from a patient's therapist if they wished
to visit him or her on the psychiatric ward.

My academic career as a professor of psychiatry at the University
of Missouri in Columbia has concentrated on developing cultural psychiatry, a discipline that interfaces clinical psychiatry and cultural
anthropology. My paper "Foundations of cultural psychiatry" was featured on the cover of the *American Journal of Psychiatry* and, several years later, I became one of the founders of the Society for the
Study of Psychiatry and Culture. Upon the death of my former
teacher, Margaret Mead, I was asked to take her place in writing the
chapter on anthropology and psychiatry in the prestigious
Comprehensive Textbook of Psychiatry.

While my colleagues in cultural psychiatry worked with various ethnic groups, there was no ethnic group of any size in Columbia. This forced me to look around. What I saw were Christians, lots of them. In 1981 I published a paper on "Modern Christian religious healing." To my surprise it also was selected as a cover article in the *American Journal of Psychiatry*. I planned a research project on distance prayer healing of mental patients but was dissuaded when told that it wasn't hard-core science and might be frowned upon by the medical school research committee. As luck would have it, I stumbled upon deliberate self-harm, a vexing clinical problem about which little was known. I was intrigued with the topic because there are many culturally sanctioned rituals as well as practices (such as ear and other body piercing) that involve the deliberate alteration and destruction of body tissue. I devoted five intense years to gathering data both on patients and on relevant anthropological areas. *Bodies Under Siege* was published in 1986. It was my great work and unique contribution to psychiatry. I thoroughly enjoyed reading the positive reviews and receiving invitations to lecture on the topic both nationally and internationally. Now I can relax, I thought to myself, certain that I would never again write another book. But I was wrong.

Academic life changed greatly starting in the late 1980s. Patient care and the income it produced became the primary focus. In many ways I welcomed the change. Patient care was challenging, but it was a lot easier than writing a book. My patient load quadrupled, but at least most of my evenings and weekends were free. I traveled to rural clinics in towns such as Boonville, Fayette, Moberly, and Sedalia. A therapist that I worked with was the wife of a Baptist minister. We became close friends, and I attended revival luncheons at her husband's church. After several patients spontaneously talked about their churches, I started to ask all my patients about their religious life, and I learned how important it was to them. I was amazed that even in Columbia, a fairly sophisticated small city, about half of my patients had an active, meaningful religious life. When I asked why they had not told me about this earlier in the course of treatment, most replied that they didn't think psychiatrists were interested in religion. Some were fearful that psychiatrists would try to talk them out of going to church.

My interest was heightened by contradictory religious ideas and garbled biblical notions expressed by patients. Some said that drinking alcohol is a sin and referred me to the Bible, while others said that the Bible condoned drinking but not drunkenness. Several couples were at odds over the homosexuality of a son. They couldn't agree on biblical teachings about homosexuality. I distinctly remember a woman who read to me several passages from Leviticus and said,

"Homosexuality is an abomination." Her husband, a minister, gently replied, "Honey, that's Old Testament stuff. All the action is in the New Testament. Jesus preached love and compassion." Some patients said that the Bible was clear: their illness was a punishment from God for their sins. Others did not believe that God caused people to become sick. Some said that their suffering was a Christian duty because, as the Bible says, it gives them a share in Christ's sufferings. But others said that Christ healed people because he didn't want them to suffer. I encountered female patients who endured years of incredibly cruel behavior inflicted by their spouses because "the Bible says that the man is the head of the house and can do whatever he wants." All this moved me to search through a copy of the poems of William Blake (1757–1827) to recover a poem that I remembered vaguely:

> Both read the Bible day and night
> But thou reads't black where I read white.

I was getting hooked. I owed it to myself to study the Bible, I thought. I knew from my undergraduate exposure that it was doctrinally confusing since there are so many different religious groups that claim it as their own. In fact, there are 2,000 religious denominations as well as a large number of independent church groups in the United States, and nearly 500,000 churches and temples. I hadn't given much thought to the idea that it was behaviorally confusing, too. *PsychoBible* sprang into existence, a book that would identify biblical bases of behaviors, examine how Christians and Jews have integrated and utilized this biblical knowledge, and then present the ways that psychiatrists understand the behavior. Something else convinced me that I needed to study the Bible. In order to be an effective clinician I needed to understand the sociocultural world of my patients. The more I asked, the more I learned about how many of my patients read the Bible regularly and found great comfort in it. I thought I owed it to them to learn more about the book that seemed to be an important and abiding part of their lives.

In gathering background material I discovered that the United States is unique in the world for having "at the same time a high level of religious belief and a high level of formal education" (Gallup, 1995). One-third of Americans watch some religious television each week; one-third believe that God speaks to them directly. Seventy percent say that they are church members, while 60 percent attend church in a given month. Half of all Americans say that they read the Bible at least once each week outside of church, and 24 percent attend Bible study groups (Wurthnow, 1994). A recent study commissioned by Tyndale House Publications found that 35 percent of persons read the Bible more than they did five years ago; only 7 percent read it less. Despite these figures there is general agreement that the vast majority of Americans are biblical illiterates. The reasons most commonly cited for being frustrated in trying to read the Bible are, in descending order: hard to understand; too long to get through; contradictory messages; hard to find parts that relate to one's life; hard to find topics of interest; and much of the Bible is boring. Eighty percent of Americans consider the Bible to be the most influential book in human history; in second place is Dr. Spock's *Baby and Child Care* (4.7 percent).

My take on all this information, confirmed by hundreds of conversations with colleagues, friends, patients, and most of all strangers (taxi drivers, people who sat next to me on airplanes, sales clerks—anyone who was willing to talk with me) is that most people revere the Bible but are baffled by it and really don't know much about it. They distrust simplistic religious pamphlets and books about the Bible that reflect one denomination's interpretation. Frustration with the Bible is evidenced by the current huge output of books on so-called spirituality replete with cuddly guardian angels, vibrations of cosmic consciousness, and no-fault salvation.

Because people really do not know much about the Bible, they are uncertain about how to apply it to everyday life. Is it sinful to drink alcohol? Is homosexuality an abomination? Do women really have to obey their husbands all the time? Why do many good persons have a miserable life while many unscrupulous persons prosper? Why bother praying when prayers are almost never answered? Should boys be circumcised? These and many other questions about behavior are dealt with in the Bible. Psychiatrists and psychologists are experts in understanding behavior from a scientific viewpoint. How do their understandings differ from biblical and religious ones?

In ordering my book I begin by presenting basic information about the Bible because almost every person with whom I talk assumes that all Bibles are pretty much alike. They rarely give thought to the fascinating and lengthy process that resulted in their Bible. Who wrote the original text and when? Is there, in fact, an original text, or are there many early texts? Has the Bible been edited over the millennia? Since none of the biblical writers mentioned that their material was to be part of a large book, how did the idea of a Bible emerge? Who decided what should be included and the order of the books? The Bible has been translated into just about every known language, and there are hundreds of English language versions. Surely the translations differ, but by how much?

Because of its complexity and length, it is difficult to read more than a brief section of the Bible at a sitting. Unfortunately readers can get so caught up in details that they fail to appreciate the larger view. As an introduction, I thought it useful to discuss the major divisions of the Old Testament (the Torah or Pentateuch, the Prophets, and the Writings) and of the New Testament (Gospels-Acts, Paul's Epistles, Letters, the General Epistles, and Revelation).

The first chapter begins, "God isn't easy," and goes on to examine God as he is presented in the Bible. The Old Testament God begins his work with vigor but gradually becomes the silent "Ancient of Days" whose message is presented in a holy book. Jesus, the man-god, is the second person of the Trinity. What kind of a man was he and when did he know that he was the Messiah? Did he consciously orchestrate some of the events of his final days? What was different about his crucifixion? Would Christianity be a fraud, as Paul claimed, if Jesus really was not resurrected? What are we to make of activities of the Holy Spirit? Some early psychoanalysts had understandings of God and of the Holy Spirit that seem quite offensive in today's world. It makes for unsettling reading but exemplifies the spirit of those times. If you believe that God made man and that the supernatural exists on its own terms, then psychoanalytic studies of the supernatural are irrelevant. If you believe, however, that Man made god and that the supernatural is a construct that arises from human experiences, then psychoanalytic formulations are worth considering (and maybe rejecting). However, some modern psychiatrists have offered reasonable explanations of how we form our mental representations of God, and I discuss these in detail.

In opposition to God, holiness, goodness, and heaven are Satan, evil, sin, and hell. A chapter is devoted to these negative forces that once were compelling issues in Western life but don't mean much anymore. The psychiatrist William Menninger wrote a book titled *Whatever Became of Sin?* His answer was that it has been reconfigured into either criminal behavior or a symptom of mental illness.

The Bible is about God and the devil but, since it is also a book about the interactions of men and women, the theme of gender is the focus of the next two chapters. Throughout history men have ruled over women. Feminists claim that the Bible is a man's book and that traditional interpretations have denigrated women. In fact, many religious leaders have described women in most unflattering terms. St. Bernard, for example, said that a beautiful woman is like a temple built over a sewer. Mary Magdalen, the first person to see the risen Christ, was falsely made out to be a prostitute. Evidence is presented showing that the high rates of depression, anorexia nervosa, and sexual problems in women may in part stem from biblically inspired attitudes. Likewise, hostility and the attribution of psychopathology to homosexuality are often defended on biblical grounds. But how relevant are Levitical laws today? The destruction of Sodom was not always interpreted as punishment for homosexuality. Psychiatry deleted homosexuality from its list of mental disorders in 1973, but homophobia remains a controversial social issue.

Although the drinking of alcohol is not a controversial issue for society at large, attitudes toward it sharply divide religious groups. The Bible provides contradictory statements about alcohol. On the one hand, it "bites like a serpent and stings like an adder" but, on the other hand, it "cheers both God and man." Baptists won't touch it, but Catholics use wine in the communion rite where they claim that it is transformed into the blood of Christ. The greatest political triumph of Christian conservatives was the passage of a prohibition amendment to the American Constitution. Alcoholics Anonymous is thought by some to be a religion in denial; one of its founders said that, "Before AA, we were trying to find God in a bottle." In some ways alcoholism is religion gone awry. According to psychiatrists there's nothing wrong with the moderate consumption of alcohol. Readers can review the evidence in Chapter Five.

We next turn to consideration of animals in the Bible. When King Nebuchadnezzar was transformed into a strange beast, he exposed the so-called animal side of human nature. From the Middle Ages to the 1870s, psychiatrists encountered persons who supposedly were changed into animals, especially wolves. The serpent who seduced Eve is a major biblical presence. God punished the Israelites by pelting them with fiery snakes, and Jesus reviled the scribes and Pharisees by calling them "Serpents, brood of vipers." But if snakes are so terrible, why did Jesus tell his apostles to "be wise as serpents," and why does a snake appear on the seal of many medical societies? Why are people so phobic of snakes? What motivates some Christian groups to risk their lives by dancing with rattlesnakes and copperheads?

Both the Bible and Judeo-Christian religions decry excessive bodily pleasures and teach control of the flesh. The body is a Temple of the Lord, but it is also a place of sensuality and aggression. The resulting dynamic tension has resulted in strange behaviors such as self-castration, skin-cutting, circumcision, and stigmata. Paul was so angry at agitators who were turning Christians against each other over the issue of circumcision that he wished they would castrate themselves. Psychiatric perspectives on these strange behaviors are presented in the chapter on "Something About The Body." The chapter's title comes from *Thus Spake*

Zarathustra by the German philosopher Friedrich Nietzsche who wrote: "The awakened and knowing say: body am I entirely, and nothing else; and soul is only a word for something about the body."

We now move from the body to consideration of healing of disease. The Old Testament attributes most disease to God's retribution: "I kill and I make alive; I wound and I heal . . . I will render vengeance to my enemies." Jesus was a revolutionary. He healed all persons who needed it and, most importantly, didn't blame them for being sick. The saga of Christian healing, from exorcism to special shrines to modern prayer healing, is reviewed, and some contemporary charlatans exposed. Can God be moved by prayers? Praying may help us feel better, but what evidence is there for the efficacy of prayers in healing illness? I contend that the topic cannot be resolved by scientific experiments because the interpretation of results depends on one's mind set.

Leaving the body, we now enter the world of the spirit and explore the vast new spiritual marketplace, ranging from hard-core Pentecostal worship to the mushy vibrations of *The Celestine Prophecy*. Are meditation and the eating of herbs spiritual acts? If faith in medical treatment can be therapeutic, then does faith in God carry more healing power? Psychiatrists historically have had a difficult time accepting spirituality and religion, although it could be argued that depth psychology, such as psychoanalysis, is a rationalized attempt to reach both. The great nineteenth century English psychiatrist, Henry Maudsley, wrote that "the corporeal or material is the fundamental fact—the mental or the spiritual only its effect." Freud considered religion an illusion. Modern psychiatry, however, has settled into a pragmatic working alliance with religion and recognizes that spirituality and congregational support may help patients. Research on the relationship between religion and mental health is quite difficult, and the results of studies are variable. In fact, there seems to be little relationship except for the findings that religiosity is associated with lower use of alcohol and drugs and possibly is related to lower rates of depression.

The final chapter returns full circle to where we began, to the Bible and to God. Modern theologians are reinterpreting Jesus and the Bible with a goal of reinvigorating Christianity but are upsetting traditionalists in the process. Is the rise of feel-good religions related to the world-wide epidemic of depression? Do the biblical religions of Judaism and Christianity lose their meaning without suffering?

PsychoBible is a weighty book—the theme demands seriousness—but not, I hope, ponderous. It contains light-hearted moments and a great deal of scholarship, but I have not burdened the text with all sorts of footnotes. In order to encourage reading the notes for each chapter, I have included in them a great deal of interesting material. Readers who want to know where quotes in the text come from, as well as important sources, will find this information in the notes along with some anecdotes and commentary.

I have been asked on occasion if too great a familiarity with the Bible will breed contempt. In my case just the opposite happened. The more I learned about the Bible, the greater my respect grew for it. *PsychoBible* may challenge a reader's faith but will not lessen it. The truly faithful person will develop a deeper appreciation of Holy Scripture. Informed faith is always better than blind faith, just as understanding is better than rote memorization. In fact, *PsychoBible* could instigate useful discussions in Bible study groups and among students, as well as among persons who are undecided about what they believe or who are contemplating joining a church. I know that writing the book has helped me to understand my patients better, so I suspect that the knowledge in it will also assist others in the helping professions. Finally, the intellectually curious person who simply wants to know more about the great themes of the Bible, religion, and behavior should find the book well worth reading. It's the sort of book that I wish had been available to me over the years.

THE BOOKS OF THE BIBLE
In the order of their appearance

JEWISH SCRIPTURE (HEBREW BIBLE)

THE LAW
(also known as The Pentateuch, The Books of Moses, The Torah)

Genesis	Gen.
Exodus	Ex.
Leviticus	Lev.
Numbers	Num.
Deuteronomy	Deut.

THE PROPHETS
Former Prophets

Joshua	Josh.
Judges	Judg.
Samuel 1	1 Sam.
Samuel 2	2 Sam.
Kings 1	1 Kin.
Kings 2	2 Kin.

Latter Prophets

Isaiah	Is.
Jeremiah	Jer.
Ezekiel	Ezek.

Book of the Twelve Prophets

Hosea	Hos.
Amos	Amos
Micah	Mic.
Joel	Joel
Obadiah	Obad.
Jonah	Jon.
Nahum	Nah.
Habakkuk	Hab.
Zephaniah	Zeph.
Haggai	Hag.
Zechariah	Zech.
Malachi	Mal.

THE WRITINGS

Psalms	Ps.
Job	Job
Proverbs	Prov.
Ruth	Ruth
Song of Solomon	Song.
Ecclesiastes	Eccl.
Lamentations	Lam.
Esther	Esth.

BOOKS OF THE BIBLE

THE OLD TESTAMENT (CHRISTIAN BIBLE)

Christians refer to Jewish Scripture as the Old Testament. It begins with the Torah but then reverses the order of the Hebrew Bible by placing the Writings next and ends with the Prophets. The Roman Catholic and Greek Orthodox versions contain books that do not appear in Protestant Bibles. The additional books, referred to as the Apochrypha (hidden) by Protestants, include in the Writings the books of Tobit, Judith, additions to Esther, Maccabees 1 and 2, the Wisdom of Solomon, and Ecclesiasticus (also known as the Wisdom of Jesus Ben Sirach); additions to the Prophets are the book of Beruch and additions to the Book of Daniel, namely Prayer of Azareah and Song of the Three Young Men, Susannah, and Bel and the Dragon. The books of Esdras 1 and 2 reproduce material found in Ezra-Nehemiah.

In addition to the accepted (canonical) and apochryphal biblical books, a number of infludential Jewish, non-biblical writings were written between 200 B.C. and 20 A.D. known as the Pseudoepigrapha. This literature includes the Letter of Aristeas, Book of Jubilees, Martyrdom and Ascension of Isaiah, Psalms of Solomon, Maccabees 3 and 4, Sibylline Oracles, Ethiopic Book of Enoch 1, Slavonic Book of Enoch 2, Assumption of Moses, Syriac Apocalypse of Baruch 2, Greek Apocalypse of Baruch 3, and Testaments of the Twelve Patriarchs.

THE NEW TESTAMENT (CHRISTIAN SCRIPTURE)

GOSPELS

HISTORICAL NARRATIVE

PAUL AND LETTERS

BOOKS OF THE BIBLE

Philippians .... Phil.
Colossians .... Col.
Thessalonians 1 .... 1 Thess.
Thessalonians 2 .... 2 Thess

PASTORAL EPISTLES
Timothy 1 .... 1 Tim.
Timothy 2 .... 2 Tim.
Titus .... Titus
Philemon .... Philem.

GENERAL EPISTLES
Hebrews .... Heb.
James .... James
Peter 1 .... 1 Pet.
Peter 2 .... 2 Pet.
John 1 .... 1 John
John 2 .... 2 John
John 3 .... 3 John
Jude .... Jude

THE CHRISTIAN APOCALYPSE
Revelation .... Rev.

Many important early Christian written works such as gospels, epistles, and apocalypses never made it into the official Bible. Among these works are the Gospels of Bartholomew, of Basilides, of the Ebionites, of Marcion, of Mattiahs, of Peter, of Philip, of Thomas, and the Protovangelium of James. Acts include those of Andrew, Andrew and Matthias, Andrew and Paul, John, Paul, Peter, Peter and Andrew, Philip, Pilate, and Thomas. Epistles include those of the Apostles, of Christ and Abganus, of the Third Epistle to the Corinthians, and of Paul and Senca. Apocalypses include those of James, Paul, Peter, Steven, Thomas, and the Virgin Mary. Gnostic writings include Wisdom of Jesus and Dialogue of the Savior.

PsychoBible

INTRODUCTION

The essential messages of the Bible are simple. For Jews seeking holiness the most significant verses are, "Hear O Israel: The Lord our God, the Lord is one! You shall love the Lord your God with all your heart, with all your soul, with all your strength" (Deut. 6:4-5). The counterpart for Christians seeking salvation is, "For the wages of sin is death, but the gift of God is eternal life in Christ Jesus our Lord" (Rom. 6:23). That's it. Everything else is elaboration.

Belief in the verses establishes a person's identity as a Jew or a Christian. It is in the details, however, that problems arise. A person may be an Orthodox, a conservative, a liberal, or even a "cultural" Jew, or a member of a sect such as the Hasidim. The variations among Christians are even greater: Roman Catholic, Eastern Orthodox, Pentecostal, Methodist, Lutheran, Presbyterian, Baptist, Episcopal, American Methodist Episcopal, and so on. The list would fill many pages, especially if all the sects throughout the world were included. So great are the variations that a noted historian considered both Christianity's history and its understanding of Christ's nature and teaching to be a series of facts which have almost nothing in common except the name.

It is not my intent to examine the historical forces that have resulted in differing elaborations of the basic biblical messages. Rather, I will focus on the Bible itself because, in questioning hundreds of people from all walks of life, I have found very few persons who both believe in the Bible and know much about it. In fact, I have encountered an odd passivity when it comes to the Bible. For some people the Bible is the revealed word of God and, therefore, above human critique. For others, the Bible is a point of certainty in an uncertain world; to disturb one's beliefs about it, even if they are erroneous, would be an unwelcome act of destabilization. Most persons, however, express a desire to learn more about the Bible even though they realize that such knowledge might reveal a lifetime of misconceptions. Many persons mistakenly believe it to be true, for example, that there exists an original text of the Bible, that the order of books in the Bible reflects the order in which they were written, and that the authors of the Gospels not only

1

were eyewitnesses to Christ's crucifixion but also that they wrote their accounts shortly after the event. I have even encountered some persons, admittedly poorly educated, who really believe that the Bible was written in English, the language of Christ! (After being challenged on this one clever person said that Jesus could speak all the languages of the world, so why not English?) I was reminded of the story, probably untrue, of a governmental debate that raged in Texas about teaching some public school classes in Spanish instead of English. In great exasperation a Fundamentalist legislator lifted his Bible in the air and loudly proclaimed, "If English was good enough for Jesus then it's good enough for the children of Texas."

In this chapter much basic information about the Bible is presented along with historical and psychiatric material, such as Freud's writings on Moses. Especially for the Old Testament I do not provide a book by book outline but rather deal with the three major groupings of The Torah, The Books of the Prophets, and The Writings. This chapter provides some context for understanding better the many biblical citations in subsequent chapters.

TEXTS, TEXTS, TEXTS

Although the Bible may have been inspired by the Holy Spirit, neither Jews nor Christians believe that it was dictated and copied down word by word. The Old Testament, properly called the Hebrew Scripture, was written by a host of mostly unnamed men (there is no proof of female writers) between about 900 B.C. and 165 B.C. The only author whose name is known is Jesus Ben Sirach, who wrote Ecclesiasticus in about 200 B.C. Moses never wrote any biblical books, nor did David or Solomon; their names were used primarily to give more authority to the texts. The ordering of the books as listed in the Old Testament does not reflect the chronological order in which they were written. The final version of the first five books, for example, was composed between about 540 B.C. and 400 B.C. by editors who gathered material from many old sources and reinterpreted it in light of the traumatic experiences of the Jews who had been exiled in Babylon and who feared the demise of their religion. In truth, most of the biblical Hebrew Scripture as we know it was written during and shortly after the period of exile (587–538 B.C.). One of the oldest Old Testament texts, the Song of Deborah (Judges 5), may have been composed in 1000 B.C. All of the Old Testament books were edited over the centuries (from 900 B.C. to 150 B.C.) until they reached a form that approximates what appears in modern Bibles. The division of Scripture into an Old and New Testament was a second-century Christian idea. Each scriptural entry was written to stand alone; none of the writers mention anything about a compilation that would someday be made into a book. Entries were written on papyrus or parchment scrolls, some of which, when unrolled, measured more than twenty feet. Second-century Christians put together the first compilation of Scripture, although it contained only a small portion of what we consider to be the Bible. "Bible" ultimately derives from Byblos, a Phoenician city which produced a lot of papyrus; "Bible" itself means little books.

Rabbi Yochanon ben Zakkai escaped from Jerusalem when the Jewish Temple was being destroyed by the Romans in 70 A.D. The Romans allowed him to establish a sort of academy in the coastal city of Jamnia to preserve and codify Hebrew Scripture. Supposedly a council of rabbis met there in 90 A.D. and established the list of Hebrew books that eventually became the Old Testament. There was no such council meeting, but rather an ongoing debate about Scripture, such as which books were so holy that persons who touched them had to cleanse their hands immediately afterwards. Books that contained the word God ("YHWH"—no vowels were used) clearly were holy. Books such as Esther, Song of Songs, and Ecclesiastes provoked debate; they didn't contain YHWH, yet they were special. A tradition developed in which twenty-two religious books were considered the holy core of Hebrew Scripture. Why twenty-two? Probably because there are twenty-two letters in the Hebrew alphabet. Which books were they? No one knows for sure, although by 130 A.D. they most likely included the books of the Law and of the Prophets, and other Writings such as books of proverbs and of psalms. Some Jewish groups did not rate the books of the Prophets or other Writings very high, but all agreed on the primacy of the books of the Law (known as the Torah, the Pentateuch, and the five books of Moses: Genesis, Exodus, Leviticus, Numbers, and Deuteronomy). How other books came to be included on the final, exact list (known as a "canon") of Hebrew Scripture is unclear, but eventually the list included, in order, the Pentateuch, the Books of the Prophets (Joshua, Judges, 1 and 2 Samuel, 1 and 2 Kings, Isaiah, Jeremiah, Ezekial, Hosea, Amos, Micah, Joel, Obadiah, Jonah, Nahum, Habakkuk, Zephaniah, Haggai, Zechariah, and Malachi), and the Writings (Psalms, Proverbs, Job, Song of Songs, Ruth, Lamentations, Ecclesiastes, Daniel, Esther, Ezra-Nehemiah, and 1 and 2 Chronicles).

Starting about 250 B.C. Hebrew Scripture was translated into Greek by Jewish scholars in Alexandria, Egypt. The process took two centuries, but legend has it that seventy-two elders of Israel completed the task in seventy-two days. This version, known as the Septuagint (referring to the number seventy) or the LXX (Roman numerals for seventy) Bible, was used by the ever-growing population of Jews who were attracted to Greek culture and who no longer knew Hebrew. Christians came to use the Septuagint Bible; many citations from it are found in the New Testament, and it still is the official text of the Greek Orthodox Church. When Jewish theologians in the second century A.D. attempted to codify Hebrew Scripture, they rejected the Septuagint Bible because its translation was considered imprecise and because it contained books that were not sufficiently holy (Judith, Tobit, 1 and 2 Esdras, Ecclesiasticus, the Wisdom of Solomon, Baruch, the Prayer of Manasseh, 1 and 2 Maccabees, and additions to Esther and Daniel). Additionally, its order was thought incorrect because it put the Writings before the Prophets. The way the Old Testament has developed historically is that Hebrew Scripture lists, in order, the Law, the Prophets, and the Writings; Christian Scripture lists, in order, the Law, the Writings, and the Prophets, but only the Roman Catholic and Greek Orthodox Bibles include the books that were rejected by the Jews as not sufficiently holy. These books are known as the Apochrypha ("hidden") because they supposedly contain secret knowledge. Thus, the Hebrew, Catholic, and Protestant versions of the Old Testament differ in content and in order.

The Hebrew version is easiest to follow because the story develops chronologically. The Christian version is somewhat confusing; it ends with the Prophets probably because this is a better transition to the New Testament in which Christ fulfills the Old Testament prophecies. Many Jewish religious books written between 200 B.C. and 200 A.D. never were included in any version of the Bible. Known as the Pseudepigrapha, these books include Jubilees, Sibylline Oracles, and 1 and 2 Enoch; they were influential in the development of Jewish and Christian theology. The Dead Sea Scrolls, discovered in 1947, were written by a Jewish sect known as the Essenes who lived prior to and in Christ's time. They contain copies of Old Testament books as well as original works, some of whose ideas are echoed in the New Testament.

The oldest existing complete copy of the Hebrew Scripture was written in 1009 A.D. It emerged from Jewish scholars of the preceding three centuries. They were known as Masoretes (traditional transmissionists) who devised a method of writing the Bible that included marginal notes, accent markings, and vowel signs that facilitated accurate transmission of the text. A problem arises, however, because there were two very different traditions (Masoroth) that needed to be considered, one from Babylon and one from Palestine as represented, for example, by the famous rabbis Hillel and Shammai. Also, scholars have found evidence of accidental errors as well as changes that were made to conform with theological views and ritual practices. The Masoretic Text in St. Petersburg, Russia, is the one used in Jewish Bibles. Partial copies and fragments of Old Testament books found in the Dead Sea Scrolls date from the third century B.C. and are the earliest existing sources of biblical literature. They validate the major religious beliefs found in the Masoretic Text but differ on a number of details. Important as they are, the Scrolls show differences in the texts of the same books, and some clearly were changed by later writers.

The Christian theologian Origen (about 185–254 A.D.) provided a large-scale revision of the Septuagint Bible that was truer to the Hebrew text. In the fourth century, St. Jerome translated Origen's version of the Septuagint Bible into Latin. Dissatisfied with his results, Jerome learned Hebrew, consulted with other scholars, and produced the Latin Vulgate Bible. This translation, a truly great accomplishment, rapidly became the official Bible of the Church.

It should be apparent that the original scrolls of the Old Testament books do not exist. In fact, there were many scrolls, each somewhat different; there never was one set of original scrolls. It is probable that by the first century B.C. there existed a standard text of the Torah; the Prophets and the Writings were not nearly as standardized. Modern versions of the Old Testament are approximations of an idealized text and are based primarily on the Masoretic text of the Middle Ages, on an unsatisfactory Greek translation of Hebrew texts (the Septuagint), on a Latin translation of both the Greek translation and some Hebrew texts (the Vulgate), and on portions from the Dead Sea Scrolls. The major messages of the Old Testament are found in all versions, but the details vary, often significantly. A sizeable number of Christians and Jews believe that all the words and verses of the Old Testament (as well as the New Testament) must be absolutely true because they were inspired by God, but even if the Old Testament was inspired by the Holy Spirit, we would have to believe that not only the "original" writers but also all the editors and the composers of the basic texts received this inspiration. We then must grapple with the issue of selecting the one truly inspired Old Testament. Jews, Catholics, and Protestants each make a case for their selection, but they all can't be correct.

FORMATION OF THE NEW TESTAMENT

Knowledge about the text of the New Testament comes from a variety of sources, such as a few pottery remnants and amulets with writing on them; less than a hundred fragmentary second-, third-, and fourth-century Egyptian papyrus manuscripts; about 250 parchments, called uncials because of a particular writing style (fourth to ninth centuries; none is complete); about 2,500 manuscripts, called minuscules, written from the ninth to the eighteenth centuries; quotations of the Church Fathers (the *Index Patristicus* in the British Museum lists over 85,000); translations of the New Testament from the Greek (such as the Vulgate; there are no existing manuscripts of a translation prior to the fourth century); and nearly 5,000 Greek manuscripts, each one different than the other. There are serious problems with all of the sources. The accuracy of the Church Fathers' quotations, for example, is questionable. How accurate were their sources? Did they modify quotes in order to support their point of view? As for the Greek manuscripts, the scholar M. Parvis writes, "It is safe to say that there is not one sentence in the New Testament in which the manuscript tradition is wholly uniform . . . The text of the New Testament contains more variants than that of any other body of ancient literature." The original New Testament books were not valued as Holy Scripture by the early Christians. In copying them, accidental and intentional changes were made, both before and after the establishment of an official canon, since no person or Church organization oversaw the copying of manuscripts. All the evidence from the Greek and translated manuscripts and from the quotations of the Church Fathers, according to Parvis, "represents the various interpretations, the various doctrines and dogmas, the various theological interests, and the various worship habits of many different Christians in many different times and places."

Between 150 B.C. and 50 A.D. no religious material was composed that entered into the Bible. In 50 A.D. the first New Testament entry was written, probably Paul's Letter to the Galatians; the last entry, 2 Peter, was written about 150 A.D., but not by Peter, who had died sixty years earlier. The New Testament authors did not know that their writings would be gathered together into a book known as the Bible. Neither Jesus nor anyone else suggested such an undertaking. In fact, the full Christian Bible would not come into existence for over three hundred years.

Mark's Gospel was written in 65–70 A.D., although most scholars believe that about twenty years after Christ's death a collection of his sayings was compiled (the Q document). In 80–90 A.D. both Matthew's and Luke's Gospels were written, followed by John's a few years later. The authors of these Gospels are anonymous. Sixty years after the first Gospel appeared, a Church Bishop wrote, based on hearsay, that the author was Mark, a follower of Peter. No one knows who Matthew was other than that he was a Jewish Christian who probably lived in Syria; he certainly was not one of Christ's original disciples. Luke may have been the name of the author of the third Gospel; it was not ascribed to him until 180 A.D. It is doubtful that he was a physician; he probably did know Paul, but he doesn't seem to have read any of Paul's letters. The fourth Gospel was not ascribed to John until about 145 A.D. If he was the "beloved disciple" then he would be the only Gospel author who personally knew Christ, but the evidence for this is unclear. Bibles contain the attribution "The Gospel according to . . .," but none of the Gospels originally had an author's name attached to it. Authorship was established by "tradition" in the second century.

From about 100 to 150 A.D. the Church, realizing that oral tradition was open to multiple interpretations as it passed from one generation to the next, began to compile written documents. At first none of these documents was considered Holy Scripture, although writings that contained Christ's words were especially revered and read during church services. The first attempt to declare a canon of true Christian Scripture was by a theologian named Marcion. In the 140s he put together one Gospel (which later was ascribed to Luke) and ten of Paul's letters. He rejected the entire Old Testament and purged the one Gospel he selected and Paul's letters of what he considered to be Jewish characteristics. He believed that Christ had rejected Hebrew Scripture and that Christ's followers, except for Paul, had not understood this. Marcion was declared a heretic. His skimpy and expurgated list of true Christian Scripture, however, stimulated the Church Fathers to produce a legitimate one. They asserted their authority by selecting four Gospels (there were at least a dozen more to choose from), Paul's letters (including 1 and 2 Timothy and Titus, which were written many years after Paul's death), and the Acts of the Apostles (which may have been edited to nullify Marcion's claims that Paul was at odds with the apostles).

The oldest canon in the Roman Church (called the Muratorian Canon because it was published in 1740 by the Italian Ludvico Muratori) was compiled toward the end of the second century. It included the four Gospels, thirteen of Paul's letters, the Epistles of Jude and John 1 and 2, Revelation, the Wisdom of Solomon, and the Apocalypses of John and of Peter. Over the next century and a half, an acceptable list emerged, aided by the invention of the codex. Christian Scripture, like Hebrew Scripture, was written on papyrus sheets that were pasted together to form a scroll. Someone had the bright idea to fold the sheets and sew them together to form a codex, or book. The codex brought about a sense of permanence. Material on a scroll could be changed simply by pasting a new sheet over an old one. Material on a codex page couldn't be changed so easily.

Debate about certain writings (such as Revelation, Hebrews, John 2 and 3, Jude, and 2 Peter) continued. Then, in 367 A.D., the bishop of Alexandria, Athanasius, sent a list of twenty-seven books, which he declared as the final canon of the New Testament, to all the Greek-speaking churches under his supervision. Most of the Eastern Churches accepted this list. Various provincial councils of the Western Church approved the list over the next fifty years. As noted in *The Interpreter's Bible*, "The canon was determined by usage, by the common consent of the Christian community, testing the books in its daily life over the centuries; not by formal authority."

UP-BIBLUM GOD: TRANSLATIONS OF THE BIBLE

No book has been translated into more languages than the Bible. After deciding what material to include and in what order, translators must then decide what basic text to use. We have already discussed some problems with the Old Testament text. Many of the same problems exist with the New Testament text. There is no pure, original New Testament text, and much of the material was edited and rewritten by many hands over the three hundred years before the Bible was put together as a book. When the United Bible Societies issued a "standard" Greek New Testament text in 1966, "this committee considered that there were two thousand places where alternative readings of any significance survived in good manuscripts and then chose between them." By 1975 a new, improved "standard" edition was published.

Translators must decide upon words and phrases that best reflect the original Greek and Hebrew. A scrupulously literal translation would be extremely difficult to read and understand. Poetic passages present a dilemma. Should they be rendered in poetic fashion? Ancient colloquialisms may seem very awkward. Wouldn't it be better to find a modern phrase that gets across the same idea?

The Old Testament book of Nehemiah states that the people of Israel listened while "Ezra read from the Law of God, translating and giving the sense, so that the people understood what was read" (8:8). He read the Hebrew words but explained them to the people in Aramaic. Oral explanations eventually were written in Aramaic and are known as Targums. They are expansive translations of most Old Testament books that include paraphrases, recurrent and stock expressions, and rabbinical teachings. In addition to the Targums, there are scholarly books of biblical commentary known as the *midrashim* that were written from 70 to 500 A.D. The rabbis who composed them venerated the holy words of Hebrew Scripture, discoursed on every imaginable detail, and applied their understandings to everyday life. The rabbis, however, often clashed in their interpretations so that the "game" of midrash became very heated and argumentative.

Until the thirteenth century the Bible, with a few exceptions, was available only in Hebrew, Greek, and Latin. In the Eastern Church, where Greek was spoken, access to the Bible was limited primarily by the cost of production; each edition was written by hand (a process that resulted in copyists' errors). In the Western Church only some priests and scholars understood Latin (very few knew Greek and Hebrew). The overwhelming majority of Christians would not have been able to read the Bible even if they had been able to find one. The Church claimed exclusive control over the production, interpretation, and even reading of the Bible. In fact, Church proclamations forbade the reading of the Bible in its entirety by laymen, and translations in local languages were deemed a challenge to its authority. Mere possession of a Bible could lead to a charge of heresy punishable by death. The invention of the printing press in the fifteenth century along with the increasing number of translations of the Bible into local languages finally allowed for wide distribution. It was also during this period that scholars in the spirit of the Renaissance revived the study of Latin, Greek, and Hebrew. This resulted in textually better versions of the Latin Vulgate and Greek Septuagint Bibles, which were then translated into local languages.

In Germany eighteen editions of the Vulgate were translated into German between 1466–1518. Then Martin Luther, the great reformer, revolutionized biblical translation with his edition of the New Testament in 1522. During his lifetime he translated the entire Bible and undertook eleven revisions. "Luther's Bible established the Reformation, created literary German, and became the model for translations in many other languages." In doing his translations Luther always asked himself, "How does a German speak in such a case? . . . One must ask the mother at home, the children in the alley, and the common man in the market place about it, and translate accordingly." The Catholic Church attacked his translations and accused him of adding words to the text in order to advance his own interpretation. The most famous instance concerns Luther's revelation that a person is saved by faith alone. He translated Romans 8:3, "Therefore we maintain that man is justified without doing the works of the law, through faith *alone*." Critics pointed out that the word "alone" was not in any text of the Bible. Luther responded that in German speech it is proper to add the word "alone" when only one of two items is affirmed, e.g., "The peasants bring grain *alone*, and no money." Against his critics he thundered, "I know how to expound Psalms and Prophets, they do not. I know how to translate, they do not. I know how to read Holy Scripture, they do not." Luther accepted the title "Prophet of the Germans" and his works contributed greatly to the formation of German nationalism.

John Wycliffe (1330–1385), an early leader of the Reformation in England, made the first English translation of the New Testament in 1380 and of the Old Testament in 1382. He closely followed the text of the Latin Vulgate Bible. In 1408 English ecclesiastics forbade both the translation and the reading of the Bible in English. Persons who defied the ban and were caught "shall forfeit land, catle, life, and goods from their heyres for ever." Despite this prohibition hundreds of manuscript copies were produced. The Wycliffe Bible was condemned and burned in 1415, and Wycliffe's body was exhumed and burned thirteen years later.

For a century and a half the Wycliffe version was the only complete English Bible. Then William Tyndale (1494–1536) came onto the scene. He studied classical languages at both Oxford and Cambridge Universities. Among his professors was Erasmus, who in 1516 published an epochal scholarly version of the New Testament in Greek. The printing press had been invented, and the time was right for a new English Bible. Tyndale was ordained a minister and attempted a translation because he "perceaved by experyence how that it was impossible to stablysh the laye people in any truth excepte the scripture were playnly layde before their eyes in their mother tongue."

Both priestly and lay authorities in England disapproved of Tyndale's ideas and his translation work, so he went to Germany, became friends with Luther, and printed his English New Testament He secretly shipped three thousand copies to England, where church officials raised money in order to buy copies and then burn them. So oppositional was the attitude of the Catholic Church that an enemy of both Luther and Tyndale railed, "The New Testament translated into the vulgar tongue is in truth the food of death, the fuel of sin, the veil of malice, the pretext of false liberty, the protection of disobedience, the corruption of discipline, the depravity of words, the termination of Concord, the death of honesty, the wellspring of vices, the disease of virtues, the instigation of rebellion, the milk of pride, the nourishment of contempt, the death of peace, the destruction of charity, the enemy of unity, the murderer of truth." Eighteen thousand copies of Tyndale's New Testament were printed between 1525–1528; only two have escaped destruction.

Tyndale published a translation of the first five books of the Old Testament, but his marginal notes riled the authorities, who tried to trick him into returning to England. He was captured in Belgium, was convicted of heresy, and was both strangled and burned at the stake.

His legacy was great, however; about eighty percent of the King James Bible came directly from Tyndale, and his translation has served as a model for most subsequent translations into English. Moreover, both the church and state authorities felt compelled to authorize a "legal" translation.

In fact, a complete Bible in English was published in 1535 (the year before Tyndale's death) by Miles Coverdale. He dedicated it to King Henry VIII, and the 1537 edition states that it was "set foorth with the Kynges moost gracious license." Coverdale borrowed greatly from Tyndale and Luther but omitted controversy in the marginal notes and restored phrases that were textually inaccurate but which conservative clergy considered dear to their hearts. In 1537, the first fully authorized English translation was published, the "Thomas Matthew" Bible (a pseudonym of Tyndale's friend John Rogers, whose work was essentially a combination of Tyndale's and Coverdale's). Political intrigue surrounded this and several other translations that appeared shortly. In 1543, King Henry VIII banned all Bibles in which Tyndale's name appeared. Commoners were forbidden from reading the Bible; members of the high social classes were allowed to read only one authorized version, the "Great Bible." In 1553, Queen Mary ordered that no English Bibles could be used in Church services or published in England. In 1560, during Queen Elizabeth's reign, the Geneva Bible was published, achieved popular usage, and went through more than a hundred editions. It was Protestant in tone; the note for Rev. 9:11 ("And they had as king over them the angel of the bottomless pit . . .") named the Pope as "the anti-Christ, king of hypocrites, and Satan's ambassador." The Geneva was the first English Bible to assign numbers to verses to be printed in modern type, and to be sold at a low cost to everyone. It was the Bible used by Shakespeare, the Pilgrims, and King James.

Protestant clergy made good use of translations in their sermons, much to the chagrin of the Catholic Church. At a large conclave (the Diet of Worms) in 1540, the theologian Surius said: "The heretics want the Bible to be the authority, but only on condition that it shall be for them to interpret . . . They want to unearth its meaning by aid of their own none too erudite brains; we say that meaning is to be discovered in the perpetual agreement of the Catholic Church. They continue to spread the Bible abroad among the illiterate." The Catholic Church finally heeded the many priests who called for a faithful, pure, and germane translation of the Bible into English. The Latin Vulgate was then translated into English by Church scholars in the cities of Rheims (New Testament) and Douai (Old Testament). The project was begun in the 1570s, but because of political problems and insufficient funds, the Rheims-Douai Bible was not published until 1609–1610. The translation was stiff, literal, and contained an abundance of technical ecclesiastical terms and Latinisms. It was revised a century later (in 1738 and in 1749–52) and in 1810 was approved for Catholics in the United States.

In 1603 King James I called a meeting of churchmen to discuss corruption in the church. To most people's surprise he agreed to the request of Puritans for a new translation of the Bible. He ordered this translation to be "as consonant as can be to the original Hebrew and Greek, and this to be set out and printed without any marginal notes and only to be used in all churches of England in time of divine service." Forty-seven scholars worked on the project; four groups on the Old Testament, two on the New Testament. The Tyndale and Coverdale Bibles were the major sources for the new translation, but many other versions were consulted, including Luther's and the Rheims New Testament Unfortunately, the scholars relied on "originall" Hebrew and Greek texts that were flawed. Additionally, errors were made in translation, the same word was frequently rendered into different English words, identical passages were often translated differently, complex or multiple words were sometimes combined into one English word, and the spelling of names in the Old Testament were not the same as in the New Testament (Old Testament Hosea became New Testament Osee, for example). Somewhat confusing was the printing of each verse as a separate paragraph (this was first done in the Geneva Bible).

It took almost half a century for the King James Version to gain the full acceptance of both clergy and laypersons. What finally won the day was its glorious use of the English language and the humble attitude of the translators who wrote in the Preface about previous translators, "So if we building upon their foundation that went before us, and being holpen by their labours, doe endevour to make that better which they left so good; no man, we are sure hath no cause to mislike us; they, we perswade ourselves if they were alive, would thank us."

Many editions that corrected errors in the King James Version have been published; the first just three years after its original publication. A major revision was authorized by the Church of England in 1870. Thirty thousand changes were made in the New Testament alone, many based on the availability of original texts. The English Revised New Testament was published in 1881, the Old Testament in 1885, and the Apocrypha in 1895. An American Edition, published in 1901, featured words and expressions commonly used in the United States. In 1982 the New King James Version was published and is a favored Bible of conservative Protestants.

The twentieth century has seen a tremendous leap forward in scholarship and knowledge about biblical texts. This has been accompanied by a host of translations. Three of the best English language New Testament translations are those of J.B. Phillips (1992 revised edition), William Barclay (1968–69), and Hugh Schonfield (1985 revised edition). The publication of the Revised Standard Version (New Testament 1946, Old Testament 1952) was a major event. Although it used the King James Version as a foundation, it is more textually and linguistically correct.

The best Catholic Bibles are The New Jerusalem Bible (revised 1985) and The New American Bible (1970). New translations seem to appear almost yearly and often have a special slant, such as elimination of gender or social bias. One of the most controversial of this new breed of publications is *The Five Gospels* (Mark, Matthew, Luke, John, and Thomas) by Willard Funk and the scholars of the Jesus Seminar (1993). It is a lively and skillfully noted version of the Gospels. Subtitled: "What Did Jesus Really Say," it provides color codes for the words of Jesus: an "unofficial but helpful interpretation of the colors" is as follows:

Red: That's Jesus!
Pink: Sure sounds like Jesus
Gray: Well, maybe.
Black: There's been some mistake.

The color system surprisingly, and to the chagrin of traditionalists, reveals that only eighteen percent of the words ascribed to Jesus are coded in pink or red. A simpler system was started by the German-American publisher, Louis Klopsach. In the mid-nineteenth century he published a Bible with the words of Jesus in red to symbolize blood. Klopsach was inspired by Luke 20:20: "This cup is the new covenant in my blood, which is poured out for you."

The 450 currently available English translations of the Bible offer something for everybody. *The New Testament in Basic English* (British American Scientific International Council), originally published in 1941, limits its vocabulary to 950 words plus 50 biblical words. *The New Testament and Psalms: An Inclusive Version* (1995) is politically correct; The Lord's Prayer is translated, "Our Father-Mother in heaven . . . " Christ no longer sits at the righthand of God but rather, in order not to offend southpaws, at "the mighty hand."

Kenneth Taylor's *The Living Bible* (1992) has been a commercial success. It has been aptly described by *Time* magazine as a loose, breezy paraphrase. "You son of a perverse, rebellious woman" (1

Samuel 20:30), for example, becomes "You son of a bitch." A 1996 revised version was published amid great fanfare. It is more textually accurate than the first version, although it still is consciously written at the level of junior high students for whom, apparently "Tears came to Jesus' eyes" is more meaningful than the traditional "Jesus wept."

The first Bible since the eighth century to be translated into a native language as a missionary tool was also the first complete Bible published in America (1661–63). It was titled *Up-Biblum God* in the Natick-Algonquin (Massachusetts) language. Upon its publication the great Protestant preacher Cotton Mather wrote: "Behold, ye Americans, the greatest honor that ever you were partakers of. The Bible was printed here at our Cambridge, and is the only Bible that ever was printed in all America, from the very foundation of the world."

AND NOTHING BUT THE TRUTH

It's one thing to believe that the Bible contains truths, perhaps even eternal truths, but its quite another thing to believe that *everything* in the Bible is true. An obvious example of biblical falsehood is the assertion that the sun revolves around the earth. We still marvel at sunrises and sunsets, but in the sixteenth century we learned that the earth revolves around the sun.

In the year of his death, Copernicus published *Revelations of the Heavenly Bodies* (1543), which described the movement of the earth around the sun. Catholic and Protestant theologians alike attacked this new idea. Martin Luther wrote: "This fool wishes to reverse the entire science of astronomy, but sacred scripture tells us that Joshua commanded the sun to stand still, and not the earth." Quoting the 93rd Psalm ("Surely the world is established so that it cannot be moved"), John Calvin asked, "Who will venture to place the authority of Copernicus above that of the Holy Spirit?" In 1615 Galileo, who advanced the ideas of Copernicus, was denounced by Inquisitors in Rome:" . . . that the sun is the center and does not revolve around the earth, is foolish, absurd, false in theology, and heretical, because it is contrary to Holy Scripture; . . . that the earth is not the center but revolves around the sun, is absurd, false in philosophy, and from a theological standpoint opposed to the true faith." In 1632 Galileo published his *Dialogue Concerning Two Great World Systems* and was again brought before the Inquisitors. He considered himself a pious Catholic but defended scientists by pointing out the differences between theological opinions and demonstrable findings. Commanding scientists to disavow their findings was "to enjoin a thing beyond all possibility of doing." He reminded the "wise and prudent Fathers . . . that there is a great difference between commanding a mathematician or a philosopher, and the disposing of a lawyer or a merchant." Galileo was imprisoned. In declining health and weary spirit he recanted: "I, Galileo, in my seventieth year, being a prisoner and on my knees, and before your Eminences, having before my eyes the Holy Gospel which I touch with my hands, abjure, curse, and detest the error and the heresy of the movement of the earth." Supposedly, he then whispered, "*Eppur si muove*" (and yet it moves).

In 1650 Archbishop James Ussher of Armagh, the ecclesiastical seat of Ireland, counted backwards through the biblical generations and calculated that the earth itself was created by God in 4004 B.C. Reverend John Lightfoot, Vice-Chancellor of Cambridge University, then cleverly found biblical "proof" that the exact moment of creation was at 9A.M. on October 23rd. In 1701 this information was printed in the marginal notes of the Authorized English Bible.

More than a thousand years earlier, Augustine noted that the Bible was about salvation through Christ and not about stars or other things that could be understood by reason or experience and which were not profitable for salvation. He warned against citing the Bible as evidence for observable and scientific phenomena: "No wonder that the critics refuse to believe what scripture has to say about the resurrection, life eternal, and the kingdom of heaven, when they can point out that the Bible is ostensibly wrong about facts which they can see or determine for themselves."

Protestant reformers were attracted to the notion that the Bible was inerrant because it supported their position that every person could understand the Holy Scripture. Such understanding was possible because the Bible supposedly was clearly written and based on common sense. With the publication of Charles Lyell's *Principles of Geology* (1830) and Charles Darwin's *On the Origin of Species* (1859) came new understandings that challenged the biblical accounts of the creation of the earth and of humankind. Fundamentalists were steadfast in their support of biblical inerrancy, and in 1910 the Presbyterian General Assembly declared it to be one of the five essential Christian beliefs. A decade earlier, in a scene reminiscent of a bygone era, several major Presbyterian theologians had been convicted of heresy for challenging biblical inerrancy.

Most modern theologians have reconciled themselves to accepting the fact that literal interpretations of biblical accounts of creation and natural phenomena are flawed in light of scientific findings. The Bible is not a scientific textbook but rather "a living instrument serving God for the proclamation of the message of salvation." It is possible to be a good and faithful Jew or Christian without believing, for example, that Noah's ark really contained a pair of all the animals on earth and that the entire world was flooded. There remains, however, a small group of hard-core conservatives who hold to biblical inerrancy in all matters. Their bitter clashes with moderate colleagues have resulted in denominational fragmentation, especially among Lutherans (Missouri Synod) and Southern Baptists.

Since the mid-nineteenth century archeologists have been at work in the Holy Land attempting to find proofs of biblical events. In part these attempts were spurred on by the successful *Life of Jesus* written by the French scholar Ernest Renan (1863). Renan visited the Holy Land for several weeks and wrote, "The striking agreement of the texts and places, the marvelous harmony of the Gospel Ideal with the countryside which served as its frame were a revelation for me. I had before my eyes a fifth Gospel, tattered but still legible." In 1955, a German journalist, Werner Keller, wrote an international best-seller, *The Bible Is Right: Archeology Confirms the Book of Books* (a second revised edition in 1981 was titled *The Bible As History*). In fact, the book is full of suggestive possibilities. Werner recounts a story, for example, about some soldiers in the Sinai desert who were trying to get at water that was seeping slowly out of a limestone rock. When a shovel hit the rock, the smooth hard limestone crust fell away and a stream of water shot up. For Werner "This is a very illuminating explanation of what happened when Moses struck the rocks at Rephidian." Another example involves the parting of the Reed Sea (the much larger Red Sea was not involved) by Moses when escaping from the Egyptians. Werner claims that the ancient topography differs from today's and that Moses could have forded the waterway: "The flight from Egypt by way of the Sea of Reeds is therefore perfectly credible." This is journalistic hype. Even if there was a passable waterway, this certainly does not prove that Moses ever used it.

Werner could not present hard archeological evidence because, even to this day, there is very little of it. The media are quick to report *initial* claims about finding some remnants from Noah's ark or Abraham's house or the fallen walls of Jericho. Rarely, however, are the final reports of negative results published. The few digs that do have relevance generally indicate that the dating of events in the Bible, such as Joshua's conquests, are so inaccurate as to cast doubt on the events themselves.

An example of recent hyperbole is the December 1996 Associated Press story by David Briggs, who asserted that "a string of recent archeological discoveries has provided the first hard evidence for a number of biblical figures and events." The story accurately reports the discovery in 1993 of a piece of stone from an ancient monument in the Golan Heights on which was written the words "King of Israel" and "House of David." The reporter, however, somehow took this to prove not only that David was a real person but also that he slew Goliath! As an aside, David's slingshot victory over the gigantic Goliath is a terrific story as told in 1 Sam. 17:49–50. Another version can be found in 2 Sam. 20:15–19, wherein David is too tired to fight so Elhanan killed Goliath. Scholars believe that Elhanan killed Goliath and that David killed another, nameless giant. To Briggs's credit he mentions the importance of modern politics in biblical archeology. Any finding that might be interpreted as evidence of ancient Jewish rule over the Holy Land would buttress current claims for continued Jewish control. When politics interferes with scholarship, then scientific archeology is replaced by nationalistic archeology. Briggs's article concludes with mention of a retired Harvard University archeologist who never put much faith in the trustworthiness of ancient Old Testament stories. From his home, "where he is in the debilitating stages of Huntington's disease," the professor now believes that, based on his work and the findings of others, there was a flood in the Middle East that was recorded as the great Old Testament flood. He desires his legacy to be "this evidence that supports the Bible."

MOSES AND MONOTHEISM

For more than a thousand years, everyone assumed that the author of the first five books of the Old Testament, known as the Torah or the Pentateuch, was Moses. Seventeenth century English philosopher Thomas Hobbes challenged this assumption, and most scholars now agree that Moses was not the author. Since Moses was the greatest human figure in Jewish history, his name was attached to the books probably in order to give them more credibility; if Moses wrote them, they must be true. In fact, the Torah attributes only several short sections to Moses himself: Exodus 21–22 (laws concerning servants, violence, animal control, property, and some moral and ceremonial principles), Exodus 24:4–8 (the Book of the Covenant), Numbers 33 (a review of Israel's journey from Egypt), and Deuteronomy 5:6–21 (a review of the Ten Commandments).

In the late nineteenth century Julius Wellinghausen and his German colleagues developed a Documentary Theory that is the foundation for modern understanding of the authorship of the Torah. In its simplest form, this theory lists four major authors or groups of authors with distinct styles and contributions. Using material gathered from oral stories, the first author wrote about the creation in

Genesis 2 as well as Adam and Eve, Noah and the flood, Abraham and the early leaders, the flight out of Egypt, and the battles with Canaan. He lived in southern Israel in about 950 B.C. Scholars call him "J" (Jahweh, the German spelling) because he referred to God as Yahweh. In about 850 B.C. a second author, living in northern Israel, used some very old oral stories as a basis for his history beginning with Abraham and ending with victory over Canaan. Scholars call him "E" because he referred to God by the Hebrew word Elohim (a plural form). About a century later an editor combined the histories of J and E into one document. This editor apparently was unwilling to make choices when the histories of J and E conflicted; he simple included both versions. In about 650 B.C. the book of Deuteronomy was written; its author is known as "D," the Deuteronomist (actually a group of writers). He used J and E as a source, added a second set of laws given by Moses just before the Israelites entered Canaan, and stressed that Israel is one people who should worship only one God at a special altar. Finally, between 550 and 450 B.C. a group of priests (known as 'P") unified and rewrote the J, E, and D histories. P composed the Genesis 1 creation account and developed many of the legal lists that came to dominate Judaism. P worked throughout the traumatic exile of the Jews in Babylon, and his concern was saving the Jewish religion by focusing on ritual purity.

My abbreviated description does not do justice to the complexities regarding the authorship and formation of the Torah. Its origins go back to traditional beliefs that are thousands of years old, and it contains a reworking of ancient myths and folk tales. Each of the four documents that underlie the Torah contains a mixture of ancient and then-current elements. It is generally believed that Adam, Eve, Noah, and others existed as myths, and that the first "real" person was Abraham, who may have lived in the nineteenth century B.C. Unfortunately there is no evidence outside of the Bible itself that Abraham, Joseph, or even Moses himself were real persons. The case of Moses is peculiar in that the most ancient portions of the Torah do not mention him at all. The oldest citation about the exodus, for example, simply states "Sing to Yahweh, for he has triumphed gloriously; the horse and the rider he has thrown into the sea" (Exod. 15:21). Also, in the ancient recounting of the exodus in Deut. 29:5–9 Moses is absent: "But the Egyptians mistreated us . . . So the Lord brought us out of Egypt . . . He has brought us to this place . . ." Jeremiah (15:1) and Micah (6:4) are the only early prophets to even name Moses. It may be, as some scholars believe, that Moses was a real person but that he was enlarged by biblical writers who needed a convenient character in order to present a cohesive story and to link together traditional but unrelated stories about the exodus, the wandering of the Jews in the wilderness, and their arrival at the Promised Land.

The exposure to possible death of the newborn Moses, whose mother placed him in a small ark of bullrushes and set him adrift in the river, is clearly derived from an old and widespread folk tale. The following, for example, was written about Sargon, the founder King of Akhed who lived a thousand years before Moses: "My mother was an Enitu princess, I did not know my father. My mother conceived me and bore me in secret. She put me in a little box made of reeds, sealing its lid with pitch. She put me in the river, the river carried me away . . ." The same sort of exposure, where the life of the infant future ruler is endangered, can be found in such diverse cultures as Cyrus in Persia, the first Greek tyrants, Romulus in Rome, King Arthur in England, and Chandragupta in India.

Sigmund Freud's *Moses and Monotheism* (1939) begins, "To deny a people the man whom it praises as the greatest of its sons is not a deed to be undertaken lightly—especially by one belonging to that people." Freud, himself a Jew, theorized that Moses was an Egyptian who transmitted to the Jews the monotheistic religion founded by Amenhotep IV. According to Freud, the Jews revolted against the spiritualized religion that was imposed upon them and killed Moses. This misdeed supposedly was a repetition of the murder of the primal father by his sons in the earliest days of humankind. The murder of Moses, however, "was a case of acting instead of remembering, something which often happens during analytic work with neurotics. They (the Jews) responded to the doctrine of Moses by denying their act, did not progress beyond the recognition of the great father, and barred the passage to the point where later on Paul started his continuation of primeval history." The violent death of Jesus, the second Moses, was the starting point for the creation of a new religion. "Christianity marked a progress in the history of religion: that is, in regard to the return of the repressed. From now on the Jewish religion was, so to speak, a fossil." Through his death Christ both took on himself the guilt of the murder of the primal father and became "God himself beside the Father and in truth in place of the father. Originally a Father religion, Christianity became a Son religion." For Freud the Jews' stubborn adherence to a Father religion is behind the anti-Semitism of Christians who say, "They will not admit that they killed God, but we do and are cleansed from the guilt of it." Freud, who originally intended to subtitle his book "A Historical Novel," based some of his notions on then-current biblical scholarship, much of which has since been discredited. Other notions were products of Freud's conflicted feelings about his father and of his identification with Moses.

Freud's reference to Amenhotep IV is interesting. In about 1350 B.C. this strange-looking, strange-thinking man became both king of Egypt and the world's first ruler to espouse monotheism. A glandular disease probably was responsible for his elongated, skinny face, enlarged breasts, oversized buttocks, and spindle legs. Though his body was weak, his mind was driven by religious fanaticism and intoxicated by a vision new to the world. He proclaimed that only one god existed, the sun god called Aten whose unique symbol was a sun circle with rays that shone on a human hand. The king changed his name to Akhenaton and utilized his military forces both to wrest power from priests of the other Egyptian gods and to shutter their temples. References to gods other than Aten were obliterated from temples and monuments, and religious rituals and sacrifices to these gods were forbidden. He moved his court from the capital city of Thebes and built a new one where Aten reigned in solitary splendor not in the form of a jackal or a falcon but rather as the glory of the sun that warmed the earth and men's hearts. The people of Egypt, however, choked with resentment at this king who forced the sun god down their throats and invalidated all religious activities in the service of other gods, activities that traditionally had given meaning to the lives of hundreds of generations of believers. Within a decade of his death, Egypt reverted totally back to its old ways and its old gods, the royal court returned to Thebes, and references to Akhenaton were removed from temples and monuments. His monotheistic ideas died with him; they did not affect the Jews or any other group other than a single generation of Egyptians.

Most dictionaries define monotheism as a belief in the existence of one god. This is a misconception when applied to the ancient world. Greek, Egyptian, and Middle Eastern cultures all had a high god as well as a group of subordinate gods. The Greek high god Zeus, for example, directed a host of Olympian gods and goddesses. Among the other high gods of the area were Ashur (Assyrian), Marduk (Babylonian), Chemosh (Moabite), and Baal (Canaanite). Worshippers were monotheists in that they recognized the presence both of false gods and of a supreme true god who reigned over the other true gods. East of Egypt the notion of a single supreme god evolved among an ethnically diverse group of wanderers known to the locals as outsiders or Habiru. Eventually a relative small number of Habiru came to be known as Hebrews. From them emerged the patriarch Abraham (he may have been either a person or a tribe) who migrated from Babylon to Palestine in about 2000 B.C. His grandson, Jacob, sired twelve sons from whom descended the twelve tribes of Israel.

Early on, the Israelites worshiped Yahweh as their supreme God, but they also recognized the existence of and paid homage to a host of lesser gods. The name of God associated with the Ark of the Covenant is Yahweh Seba'ot, Lord God of Hosts. The prophet Micaiah said, "Hear the word of the Lord: I saw the Lord sitting on this throne and all the host of heaven standing by, on his right hand and on his left" (1 Kin. 22:19). The heavenly host was God's astral army: "then the kings of Canaan fought . . . The stars on their course fought against Sisera" (Judg. 5:19-20). The council of gods reported about happenings on earth and even offered advice to Yahweh (see Job 1-2). They also sang God's praises: "Holy, holy, holy is the Lord of hosts" (Is. 6:3). The heavenly host originally were pagan gods. Those who accepted Yahweh's authority were accepted into the council, but those who failed to do his bidding would at the End of Time be banished and punished like men: "It shall come to pass on that day that the Lord will punish on high the host of exalted ones, and on earth the kings of the earth . . . Then the moon will be disgraced and the sun ashamed" (Is. 24:21-23). The presence of multiple gods is obvious by naming practices: one of the sons of Saul, the first Israelite king, was Esh-Baal and his grandson was Menb-Baal. The third king, Solomon (965-928 B.C.), built not only a Temple for Yahweh but also shrines for the gods Chemosh and Molech (1 Kin. 11:7). Because of this as well as his philandering with numerous foreign women, the Lord raised up rebels against Solomon. It was during this period that J, the first author of the Torah, wrote about God as Yahweh and about Yahweh's role as creator and ruler of Israel's destiny. Several generations later, Elijah, the lone prophet of the Lord, stood up to the 450 prophets of Baal and challenged the Israelites: "If Yahweh is God, follow him; but if Baal, follow him" (1 Kin. 18:21).

Hosea (about 740 B.C.) was the first biblical writer to decry Israel's devotion to other gods. He declared that Yahweh will punish Israel for attending to the Baals: "She [Israel] burned incense. She decked herself with her earrings and jewelry, and went after her lovers. But me she forgot, says Yahweh" (Hos. 2:13). A century later, in 621 B.C., King Josiah "brought out of the temple of Yahweh all the articles that were made for Baal, for Asherah and for all the host of heaven, and he burned them" (2 Kin. 23:4). It was about this time that the most important passage in the Old Testament was written: "Hear O Israel: The Lord our God, the Lord is one" (*shema Israel, adonai eloheymu adonai ehad*). The most likely meaning of this phrase is that Yahweh alone is God. Chapter four of Deuteronomy supports this interpretation when Moses is presented as reminding the Israelites of all the wonderful things that Yahweh did for them: "This he showed you so that you might know that Yahweh is God indeed and that there is no other."

The greatest expression of monotheism was written by the prophet known as Second Isaiah (he wrote chapters 40–55 of the book of Isaiah) probably during the exile of the Jews to Babylon (587–538 B.C.):"Thus says the Lord, I am the first and the last; besides me there is no other God" (44:6). Compared to Yahweh, the other gods are impotent weaklings; "I am God, and there is none like me" (Is. 46:9). It was during this time that the present form of the Ten Commandments appeared. The first commandment, contrary to the way most people understand it today, did not deny that other gods existed. It meant that Yahweh, a jealous God, forbade the worship of the other gods by the Israelites.

The concept of monotheism as belief in only one god is really not as meaningful as belief in a supreme God. Yahweh, the supreme God of the biblical Hebrews, was known to them by his activities on their behalf and not merely because he existed. Of all the gods, only he directed their history. Christianity also has a supreme God, although this is complicated by the Trinity of Father, Son, and Holy Spirit, as well as a large number of divine entities such as angels, saints, and demons.

PROPHECY: THEM DRY BONES

For many Christians John the Baptist is the quintessential hair-shirted, locust-eating prophet whose voice cried out from the wilderness, "The time is fulfilled, and the kingdom of God is at hand. Repent, and believe in the gospel." He attracted large crowds that included hated tax collectors and lowly prostitutes. He probably spent many years living with the Jewish Essene sect, but he gave up linen robes and exclusivity to preach in public. The Essenes were fanatical about multiple ritual washings every day, but John said that only one baptismal washing was necessary for salvation. He even baptized Jesus. He was a forceful character who spoke his mind: "You brood of vipers," he said to the Pharisees and Sadducees, "Who warned you to flee from the wrath to come?" He attacked King Herod's morals: "It is not lawful for you to have your brother's wife." Herod beheaded him, albeit reluctantly, in order to honor the wish of Herod's stepdaughter to have John's head on a platter. John prophesied that "the kingdom of heaven is at hand." He was the forerunner of Jesus, who made the same statement in the same words. Both of them prophesied an impending apocalypse and both were wrong. Had we lived back then as believers, we would have expected the abomination of desolation to begin in a few months or a few years. Perhaps the expectations of the faint-hearted would have stretched it to a few decades. But it's been almost two thousand years and still, thank God, no apocalypse. Although prophecy may be a glorious calling, accuracy is not one of its strong suits.

Biblical prophets were people, most often men, who claimed to receive messages from God, which they then divulged to an audience, usually by announcing, "Thus saith the Lord." Sometimes they acted out the message through behaviors whose symbolism then had to be decoded by observers. How did a prophet know that he or she really was a prophet? Isaiah (6:8) reported that an angel touched his mouth with a hot coal and then the Lord asked, "Whom shall I send?" Isaiah replied, "Here I am! Send me." Jeremiah (1:5) reported that the Lord ordained him a prophet even before he was conceived. Later on the Lord touched Jeremiah's mouth and commanded him to go among the nations "and speak to them all that I command you." Ezekiel's call to prophecy was a little odd (1–3). He saw a vision of God, heard God's voice, and then was ordered to eat God's words: "Feed your belly, and fill your stomach with this scroll that I give you." He ate it. "It was sweet like honey in my mouth" and then God told him to "go to the house of Israel and speak with my words to them."

The early biblical prophets were not all cut from the same cloth. Some, for example, were royal retainers. 1 Kings 22 relates that Ahab, the King of Israel, had four hundred male prophets in his court. They prophesied a victory over the Syrians, but the situation got messy when the prophet Micaiah first agreed with his colleagues but then prophesied that Ahab would die in battle. This raised a significant problem: if prophets get their messages from the same God, then how can opposing messages be explained? In this case Micaiah said that God planned to entice Ahab into battle by putting "a lying spirit in the mouth of all his prophets." That God would resort to such chicanery is surprising, especially since the effectiveness of his prophets depended upon the willingness of people to believe them.

In addition to those who served the kings, the Bible also mentions "the sons of the prophets" who lived in autonomous groups. Elisha, himself a prophet, encountered them during a famine and fed them after miraculously purifying a poisonous stew (2 Kings 38–41). Elisha did many good deeds and probably was the leader of a prophetic guild (scholars are fond of describing him as a beloved leader), but he had a dark side too. When some young boys made fun of his bald head, "He cursed them in the name of the Lord. And two she-bears came out of the woods and tore forty-two of the boys" (2 Kings 2:23–25). He was the immediate successor to Elijah, the solitary ninth-century prophet who struggled against the prophets of Baal, denounced kings who did not worship Yahweh exclusively, and was rewarded by riding a chariot of fire that carried him to heaven in a whirlwind (2 Kings 2:11). Elijah's popularity grew over the centuries. The Old Testament book of the prophet Malachi ends with God's promise to send Elijah back to earth to set things right between fathers and their children before "the great and dreadful Day of the Lord" (Mal. 4:5-6). In fact, Christian versions of the Bible conclude the Old Testament with these verses. It is a good introduction to the New Testament, where John the Baptist was thought to be Elijah (Matt. 11:14). In Luke's Gospel an angel said of John that he will prepare the people for the Lord "in the spirit and power of Elijah" (1:17).

In addition to the early prophets the Old Testament has the Latter Prophets (from about 450-750 B.C.), who are divided into major and minor groups based primarily on the length of their writings. Amos was the earliest of the prophets and the first to have a book devoted solely to his ideas; succeeding prophets followed this example. The prophecies of Amos were so distressing that he was thrown out of the sanctuary at Bethel and banned from prophesying there ever again. He chastised all the nations of the area, including Israel, for their inhumanity especially towards the downtrodden: "they trample on the heads of ordinary people and push the poor out of their paths" (2:7). God's message was that he hated the feast days and that he would not accept offerings. Rather, he desired that "justice run down like water, and righteousness like a mighty stream" (5:24). To the Israelites, who eagerly anticipated the glorious Day of the Lord, Amos presented his oracle: "Woe to you who desire the Day of the Lord . . . It will be darkness, and not light . . . very dark, with no brightness in it" (5:18-20). The ending of Amos' book (9:1-10) was so bleak—"Behold, the eyes of the Lord God are on the sinful kingdom, and I will destroy it from the face of the earth"—that an anonymous editor added a brief optimistic epilogue in which God promised to restore Israel to its former glory (9:11-15).

Isaiah is generally regarded as the greatest of the prophets although his book was composed by three persons: The first Isaiah of Jerusalem wrote most of the first 39 chapters in the eighth century, while The Second Isaiah (chapters 40-55) and The Third Isaiah (chapters 56-66) wrote in the sixth century. It is among the grandest, most quotable of biblical books and contains many prophecies. On one occasion Isaiah acted out a prophecy that the Assyrian king would lead away the Egyptians and Ethiopians as captives: he acted like a slave and walked naked and barefoot for three years (20:2-4). Three years of nakedness do seem somewhat excessive, especially since no historical data support a conquest of the Egyptians and Ethiopians by the Assyrians.

On every possible occasion the early Christians sought and claimed to find Old Testament verses that foreshadowed the coming of Christ. One famous example is Isaiah's prophecy (7:10–17) to the Judean King Ahaz about the failure of foreign invaders to overthrow the royal house of David. Ahaz did not possess sufficient faith and was unconvinced. Isaiah then made a second prophecy, namely that "a young woman is with child and shall bear a son, and shall call his name Immanuel" (Immanuel means "God is with us"). In Chapter 9 Isaiah then stated, "For unto us a child is born, unto us a son is given; . . . and his name shall be called Wonderful, Counselor, Mighty God, Everlasting Father, Prince of Peace." Anyone who has ever heard Handel's incomparable oratorio *Messiah* will immediately recognize the words as descriptors of Christ. Handel was following a Christian tradition that began with the Gospel of Matthew (1:23) in which Isaiah's prophecy was considered a reference to Jesus and the Virgin Mary. Matthew quoted the Septuagint Bible where the Jewish word "young woman" (*almah*) was mistakenly translated by the Greek word for "virgin" (*parthenos*). Every scholar agrees that the Septuagint translation is incorrect. In fact, Isaiah was referring to Ahaz's son Hezekiah (or possibly to another royal child). In revised Jewish editions of the Septuagint Bible, "virgin" was changed to "maiden." Christians retorted by noting that Hezekiah was nine years old at the time of the Immanuel prophecy (he became king at age twenty-five while his father, Ahaz, reigned for sixteen years: see 2 Kings 16:2 and 18:2). The Jewish reply was that Isaiah must have been referring to his own son or to the son of another wife of Ahaz.

A companion to the Immanuel prophecy appears in Isaiah 11, which begins, "There shall come forth a shoot from the stem of Jesse, and a branch shall grow out of his roots." The prophecy is about a child who possesses the spirit of the Lord and who will slay the wicked and judge the poor with righteousness. Christians have claimed that this is a statement about Christ, but Isaiah wrote it about the accession to the throne of Hezekiah. The rest of the prophecy describes the peaceable kingdom over which Hezekiah will rule, where wolves and lambs, leopards and goats, cows and bears will lie down together "and a little child shall lead them." It was a lovely prophecy but obviously has been unfulfilled.

Another famous prophecy of Isaiah has been interpreted by Christians as a reference to Christ. Isaiah described a Servant of the Lord, a man of sorrows who was despised and rejected yet who "carried our sorrows, was wounded for our transgressions, was bruised for our iniquities . . . by his wounds we are healed" (53:3–5). Isaiah certainly was describing Israel (see Chapter 43: "O Israel . . . You are my witness, says the Lord, and my servant whom I have chosen") and may have been describing a person who represented Israel. The New Testament book of 1 Peter identified the Suffering Servant as Christ (2:24).

The second of the great prophets was Jeremiah. Often called "the prophet of doom," he appears to have been chronically depressed throughout the forty years of his ministry that began in 627 B.C. He relentlessly prophesied unlamented gruesome deaths, famine-driven cannibalism, pestilence, and broken bones. Instead of God's face the Judeans will be utterly humiliated by seeing God's buttocks (18:17). Little wonder that no one liked Jeremiah (15:10, 14): "Woe is me, my mother, for you have borne me to be a man of strife and of dissension for all the land . . . All men curse me . . . O Lord God . . . why is my pain perpetual and my wound incurable?" He was hard on his fellow prophets, especially those who sugar-coated the state of the nation: "And from the prophet to the priest, everyone deals falsely . . . saying 'Peace, peace!' when there is no peace" (6:13–14). And, "Do not listen to the words of the prophets . . . They speak a vision of their own heart, not from the mouth of the Lord" . . . "Behold, I am against the prophets," says the Lord, "who use their tongues and say, "He says." Behold, I am against those who prophecy false dreams and cause my people to err by their lies and their recklessness" (23:16, 31–33). It must have been confusing for those who heard Jeremiah. How could they know if he was a true or a false prophet? He actually urged them to submit to Bablyonian rule, and when he went to Egypt as an old man he railed against the Judean refugees who burned incense, poured out offerings, and worshiped the Queen of Heaven (43–45). He finally decided that, in the end, God would not completely destroy but rather would preserve Israel: "Jacob shall return; have rest and be at ease . . . [but] I will not leave you wholly unpunished" (46:27–28). A word of caution to the reader: Jeremiah is one of the most confusing books of the Bible. Events, for example, do not occur in chronological order and may even be described more than once, and verses and passages may be repeated but in very different contexts. Most English language Bibles use the Hebrew (Masoretic) text of Jeremiah, but the Greek (Septuagint) text is one-eighth shorter and may be superior.

Ezekiel, the third major prophet, lived among Jewish exiles in Babylon where his career began in 593 B.C. Like Vincent van Gogh, he is a delight for psychiatrists because his behavior and his imagery, although well ordered, are often bizarre and schizophrenic-like.

Ezekiel was one of the last books to be accepted into the canon of Jewish Scripture. The delay was mainly because Ezekiel had his visions of God outside the boundaries of the Holy Land, and in the first and tenth chapters the glory of God was described in strange terms—fiery wheels, wings, animal faces—that were unlike anything that other prophets had proclaimed. In fact, these chapters were not read during religious services, and persons under the age of thirty years were banned from reading them at any time.

Ezekiel had a flair for the dramatic. He acted out his prophecy that the people of Israel will eat defiled food during Nebuchadnezzar's siege of Jerusalem by cooking his food over a fire of human feces. Since the length of the siege would be 430 years, he laid on his side for 430 days while restrained with ropes. He prophesied that the only persons in Jerusalem who would not be hacked apart by the axe-wielding executioners sent by God were those with the Hebrew letter *taw* on their foreheads (the early Christians were thrilled by this prophecy because *taw* is written as a cross). Like other prophets, he described Israel as an unfaithful spouse of God, but only he provided the intimate details: "Thus you longed for the lewdness of your youth, when the Egyptians manhandled your bosom to get at your young breasts" (23:21). He prophesied that God would send a shepherd who descended from David to rule over Israel in a peaceful, prosperous existence (34:11–31). Perhaps his most cited prophecy took place in the valley full of the skeletal remains of Israel (37:1–14). Ezekiel said, "O dry bones, hear the word of the Lord." God breathed life into the dry bones which arose as a great army: "O my people," said the Lord, "I will . . . cause you to come from your graves, and bring you into the land of Israel." This was the first real intimation of the resurrection of the body. A more direct statement did not appear until 168 B.C. when the prophet Daniel prophesied that at the End of Time, "Everyone who is found written in the book, and many of those who sleep in the dust of the earth shall awake, some to everlasting life, some to shame and everlasting contempt" (12:1–2).

Ezekiel, the prophet who lived in exile, was obsessed with the land of Jerusalem. He prophesied about the return of the dispersed Jews and the restoration of the area: "The Lord said, 'This is Jerusalem: I have set her in the center of the nations'" (5:5). It would be "the most glorious of all lands" (20:7) and the temple on Mount Zion would be its holy center. Building on God's promise about land possession to Abraham, Ezekiel extended the boundaries and, in the last words of his book, renamed the New Jerusalem Yahweh Shamah (God is there). Several decades after the return of the exiles, the work of restoration still had not begun. The prophet Haggai observed that the people were too busy building their own houses but prophesied that soon the temple would be built and that God would then send the Messiah called Zerubbabel. Once work began on the temple, Zechariah prophesied that "the Lord will take possession of Judah as his inheritance in the Holy Land, and will again choose Jerusalem" (2:12). The phrase "Holy Land" has endured over the centuries and even today is what most people call the area.

The second half of the book of Zechariah was written by his followers in the sixth, fifth, and possibly the fourth centuries. Many of the prophecies about the battle at the End of Time are difficult to comprehend but several made a great impact on the early Christians. There is a prophecy, inspired by Genesis 49:10-11, of a future king, "triumphant and virtuous is he, humble and riding on an ass, on a colt, the foal of an ass" (9:11). There is a prophecy about thirty shekels of silver (11:12-13), and another about the people of Jerusalem mourning "when they look on him whom they have pierced" (12:10). These appear to be startling and accurate prophecies in light of the events of Christ's life as described in the New Testament

There are, however, other possible interpretations: Jesus could have orchestrated events in order to match the Old Testament prophecies, or the authors of the New Testament could have taken liberty with the facts and added some prophecy-fulfilling details to their writings in order to state their case more forcefully. As for Zechariah, one of his final prophecies (13:1-6) was that God will boot the prophets and the unclean spirit out of the land. These deposed prophets will have to admit their falsehoods and explain, for example, that self-inflicted wounds on their back didn't occur during an ecstatic state while prophesying but rather were the result of drunken brawls. And of those who defy God and continue to prophecy, their mothers and fathers will say, "You shall not live, for you speak lies in the name of the Lord." And then their parents will kill them.

That was the end of prophecy in Israel, except for some visions of the apocalypse, although there was an expectation that the practice would be revived. In the Book of Joel, for example, God said it will come to pass in the time of the Messiah that he will pour out his spirit so that sons and daughters shall prophesy, and old men shall dream dreams, and young men shall see visions (2:28). In the New Testament book of Acts, this passage was quoted verbatim by Peter to indicate the revival of prophecy (2:14-21). John the Baptist was "the prophet of the Most High (Luke 1:76), and in all four Gospels, Jesus was called a prophet.

Paul wrote that, "He who prophesies speaks edification and exhortation and comfort to men" (1 Cor. 14:3). He ranked Christians who had received the gift of prophecy from the Holy Spirit as second in importance to the apostles but above teachers, miracle workers, healers, helpers, and those who speak in tongues (1 Cor. 12:27). Paul encouraged his brethren to desire earnestly to prophesy, prohibited flamboyant, ecstatic practices, and counseled that prophets should be orderly and speak one by one in turn (1 Cor. 14:29-39). The Gospels of Matthew (7:5, 24:11, 24) and Mark warned about what would happen at the apocalypse: "False Christs and false prophets will rise and show signs and wonders to deceive, if possible, even the elect" (Mark 13:22). A passage in 1 John urged the faithful to "test the spirits, whether they are of God; because many false prophets have gone out into the world" (4:1). Revelation 1:20 even railed against the Church in the town of Thyatira "because you allow that woman Jezebel, who calls herself a prophetess, to teach and seduce my [God's] servants to commit sexual immorality and eat things sacrificed to idols."

The last book of the New Testament, Revelation, is composed entirely of prophecy. Nothing is known about the author except that his name was John (definitely not the same John who wrote the fourth Gospel) and that he lived on the island of Patmos where an angel sent by the risen Christ presented him with a vision of the apocalypse, of new heavens, and a new earth. He wrote in about 95 A.D. The Roman emperor, Domition, was demanding that Christians worship him. For John these Roman persecutions signaled the beginning of the apocalypse: "Blessed is he who reads and those who hear the words of this prophecy, and keep those things which are written in it: for the time is near" (1:3).

The prophecy is a dreamy, often nightmarish, vision filled with shifting symbolism whose meaning is still debated. It contains allusions to almost every Old Testament book, with an emphasis on Ezekiel and Daniel. Numbers, especially seven, have great significance: there are seven apocalyptic visions, seven seals, seven bowls of anger, the Antichrist-beast has seven heads, the slain Lamb has seven horns, the book is addressed to seven Asian churches, and so on. The vision of the scroll with seven unbroken seals is a famous one (6:1-8:6). As Christ breaks each seal, the earth is engulfed with different horrors such as war, revolution, famine, and death. John's vision of the horrors includes the four horsemen of the apocalypse. The opening of the seventh seal gives rise to seven angels with trumpets. Each trumpet blast brings yet another calamity. The earth is pelted with bloody fireballs. An angel with a key opens the bottomless pit out of which emerge locusts with women's hair and lion's teeth and stinging tails, which they use to torment men for five months: the only men who are spared have the seal of God on their foreheads. The seventh angel utters seven thunders but orders John to "seal up the things which the seven thunders uttered, and do not write them."

Among the most unforgettable figures in the vision is a woman dressed in scarlet and adorned with jewels who holds a golden cup "full of abominations and the filthiness of her fornication, and on her forehead a name was written: Mystery, Babylon the Great, the Mother of Harlots, and of the Abominations of the Earth" (17:4–5). In the end Christ defeats Satan and establishes a New Jerusalem in the sky that has twelve gates inscribed with the names of the twelve tribes of Israel and a city wall with twelve foundations inscribed with the names of the twelve apostles. Additionally the foundation is adorned with twelve different jewels, just as was the breastplate of the Jewish high priest described in the book of Exodus, but John reverses the order of the jewels. This elaborate symbolism probably was meant to demonstrate that Christianity was the fulfillment of Judaism. At any rate, Christ the Lamb invites the faithful to drink the water of life and to enjoy the tree of life with its twelve kinds of fruit. The book ends with a warning against altering any of the words that John had written (scholars call it a cursing colophon) and a reminder that Christ is "coming quickly."

Once the church became established in the post-apostolic era, prophecy for the most part gradually faded away. There were problems not only with distinguishing between true and false prophecies, but also in interpreting what was said. As the church developed into an organization with well-defined rules, roles, and tradition, there was little tolerance for prophets who could upset the applecart. And once the Bible became codified, there was no need for prophets anymore; everything a person needed to know could be found in its pages.

Over the past two thousand years there have been periods in which Christian prophecy was revived. Nowadays there are televangelists and others who thrive on scaring people about the impending apocalypse (prophecy for profit). Their accuracy rate is not very good, but, then again, neither was that of the biblical prophets. In fact, the only reasonably accurate biblical prophet was Agabus. In Acts 11:28 he prophesied "a great famine over all the world; and this took place in the days of Claudius." Well, maybe there wasn't a world-wide famine, but Roman historians did note famines between 41–54 A.D. In Acts 21:11 he prophesied that Paul would be bound by the Jews and delivered into the hands of the Gentiles. Paul actually was rescued by the Romans when the Jews wanted to lynch him, but, in the end, Paul was executed by the Gentiles. Two out of two isn't much of a track record, but in the world of prophecy it's pretty darn good.

VANITY OF VANITIES: THE WRITINGS

After the books of the Torah and of the prophets, the Old Testament combines diverse books into a grouping known as the Writings. The first entry is Psalms, a collection of 150 songs or hymns. In many Bibles the phrase "A psalm of David" begins a majority (73) of the songs, but the Hebrew text could mean that the songs are by, about, or in the style of David or from David's court. It's possible that some of the songs are truly linked to David, but more likely they were ascribed to him mainly because of his musical ability. It is impossible to date each song, although they were assembled together probably in the third century B.C. Some of the songs refer to God as Yahweh, others use the term Elohim.

Psalms is divided into five sections but within each are contained songs of praise and thanksgiving to God, sadness, personal and group petitions to God, wisdom, blessings, curses, and God's place as ruler of the universe. Some of the verses are majestic: "The earth is the Lord's and all its fulness" (24:1); some are abundant with hope: "The Lord is my shepherd: I shall not want" (32:1); some are heartbreaking: "My God, my God, why have you forsaken me" (22:1); and some are nasty: "O daughter of Babylon who are to be destroyed . . . Happy the one who takes and dashes your infants against the rock" (137:8-9). The Psalms were and continue to be integral to both Jewish and Christian holy services. In them many individuals have found inspiration and through them many have learned to pray.

While Psalms sings about heavenly concerns, The Song of Songs (also known as the Song of Solomon and the Canticles) is a rustic collection of erotic poems about eagerly anticipated sex between a man and a woman. They may be, at least in part, lyrics that were sung at weddings. They certainly weren't written by King Solomon; it's hard to believe that with 1,000 wives and concubines he would have penned such mawkish verses as "Your teeth are like a flock of shorn ewes" or "Your belly is like a heap of wheat." Although several songs may have been written in Solomon's time (950 B.C.), most are later compositions.

The final version of the book was produced in the fifth century. It has neither a plot nor dramatic development nor comprehensible connections between its parts. It definitely has two characters, Solomon and the Shulamite maiden; the "third" character, a shepherd, probably represents Solomon, although some claim that the shepherd is the maiden's real love to whom she remains faithful despite Solomon's attempts to seduce her. The book contains many terms not found elsewhere in the Bible.

No one is sure why The Song of Songs was included in the Hebrew canon of Holy Scripture, especially since God is not mentioned at all. When the rabbis were discussing it in the first century A.D., Rabbi Akiba declared, "For all the world is not as worthy as the day on which the Song of Songs was given to Israel, for all the writings are holy, but the Song of Songs is the Holy of Holies." After the rabbis added it to the canon they probably defended their decision by interpreting the lyrics allegorically, a practice which Christian theologians adopted. Thus, the lover-bridegroom was interpreted as Yahweh or Christ, and the maiden-bride as Israel or the Christian Church or the Virgin Mary or Mary Magdalen or wisdom. In trying to make the best of a sensitive situation, modern clergy sometimes interpret the book as a commentary on the pleasures of a committed marriage.

The Writings contains three books—Proverbs, Ecclesiastes, Job— that are traditionally known as wisdom literature; Ecclesiasticus, also known as the Wisdom of Jesus Ben Sirach, and Wisdom of Solomon are the other wisdom texts, but they appear only in some Christian Bibles as books of the Apocrypha. The biblical wisdom literature was written by sages who did not claim special revelations from God and, thus, is unlike prophecy. It focuses not on societal or tribal but rather on individual concerns about matters such as justice, wealth, children, health, and reputation. Meant to be used especially for educating young men about living properly, it utilizes instructions, proverbs, aphorisms, debates, and concessions to common sense and to life experiences. Conspicuously absent are references to other Old Testament texts (although they appear in the Apocryphal books).

Every culture has sages who leave their wise thoughts and sayings as a legacy. Since the concerns of the biblical wisdom books are universal it is no surprise that they were discussed by sages in Egypt, Mesopotamia, Babylon, Canaan, and other nations. Nor is it surprising that the biblical books often contain the same wisdom found in other cultures. Sometimes this wisdom was borrowed and sometimes it was arrived at independently. What distinguishes biblical wisdom literature is its religiously-based humanism and its ultimate appeals to fear Yahweh and to comport oneself accordingly.

The book of Proverbs is a collection of wisdom gathered over many centuries; verses 22:17–23:14 are almost identical to an ancient Egyptian text. Although attributed to Solomon (who undoubtedly did compose some wise sayings), it was compiled by an anonymous editor in the fifth or fourth century B.C. after the exile. The basic points of Proverbs are "the fear of the Lord is the beginning of knowledge" (1:7); one's parents should be heeded and the enticements of sinners avoided (1:8–10); discretion and understanding from wisdom in your heart and knowledge in your soul will deliver you from the evil way (2:10-12); honor the Lord but remember that he chastens and corrects those whom he loves (3:11-12). Examples of some wise sayings are "Drink water from your own cistern" (sleep only with your own wife);"He who is slow to wrath has great understanding, but he who is impulsive exalts folly"; "Pride goes before destruction, and a haughty spirit before a fall"; "Do not be envious of evil men"; "Eat only as much honey as you need, lest you be filled with it and vomit"; "Do not boast about tomorrow, for you do not know what a day may bring"; "The mouth of an immoral woman is a deep pit"; "Open your mouth, judge righteously, and plead the cause of the poor and needy."

The book of Ecclesiastes was written by a third century B.C. urbane wise man knowledgeable about not only Judaism but also Greek and Roman philosophy. He called himself Koheleth (the leader of a congregation) and pretended to be David's son, Solomon, the better to attract the reader's attention. There is an attitude of world-weariness in the book. The author claims that he has experienced just about everything people consider worthwhile and that he has thought about life carefully. His great discovery is that one should live life to the fullest but also in moderation. The book, like life itself, is filled with paradoxes. "Drink your wine with a merry heart" but also remember, "Better to go to the house of mourning than to go to the house of feasting." "Vanity of vanities," writes the author, "all is vanity . . . There is nothing new under the sun . . . The race is not to the swift, nor the battle to the strong, nor bread to the wise, nor riches to men of understanding, nor favor to men of skill; but time and chance happen to them all . . . A feast is made for laughter, and wine makes merry; but money answers everything . . . What happens to men also happens to animals; one thing befalls them; as one dies so dies the other; all go to one place; all are from dust and all return to dust." Ecclesiastes advocates moderation in all things including righteousness, wisdom, wickedness, and foolishness (7:16-17). To the good person and the wicked person, to the saint and the sinner, "all things come alike to all." As might be expected there was much much bitter debate before the rabbis accepted the book into the canon of the Bible. Perhaps what won the day was the ending of the book, which was added by an orthodox editor: "Let us hear the conclusion of the whole matter: Fear God and keep his commandments, for this is man's all. For God will keep every work into judgement, including every secret, whether good or evil."

Perhaps the most intellectually stimulating and theologically troubling book not only of the Writings but also of the entire Old Testament is the Book of Job. The plot is simple. Although he is not

Jewish, Job is an honest, God-fearing, and moral person about whom God inquires during a heavenly counsel. A satan, a type of prosecutor as well as godly agent, says that Job wouldn't be so righteous if he were stripped of his prosperity. God agrees to the test, but Job remains righteous despite the loss of his possessions and the death of his children. God is pleased, but the satan urges him to "touch his bone and his flesh and he will curse you to your face." God again agrees and he "afflicted Job with loathsome sores from the soul of his foot to the crown of his head." Job sits in a pile of dung ash and is so thoroughly miserable that his wife urges him to "curse God and die!" Three of his friends mourn his plight but believe that he *must* have sinned because God is just and punishes sinners. Job calls them miserable comforters full of windy words, proclaims his innocence, begs for pity, and says that he will hold onto his righteousness even though God has made his soul bitter. A man call Elihu comes along, urges Job to consider the wondrous works of the perfect and just God, and suggests that his punishment is a warning for those who think they are so righteous and wise. God then speaks with Job from a whirlwind and presents a list of his mighty accomplishments. Job is humbled and says, "Behold, I am vile: what shall I answer you?" God again regales Job with examples of his might. Job then says, "I abhor myself, and repent in dust and ashes." God then restores Job's possessions by twofold, allows him to have seven sons and three daughters, and to live for 140 years. All's well that ends well but why Job was punished is never clarified. Why would a just God punish a righteous man? Why wouldn't God explain himself? It puzzled Job and it still puzzles readers.

The author of Job is unknown, as is the date it was written (estimates range widely, but the fifth century B.C. is probable). The book is best regarded as a parable; similar stories about undeserved suffering can be found in the ancient Egyptian, Mesopotamian, and Sumerian literature as well as in Greek tragedies such as *Prometheus Bound* by Aeschylus. The text of Job is problematic; the Hebrew version is longer than the Greek, and the language has so many Aramaic characteristics that the Hebrew transmissionists in the Masoretic text made numerous errors (they may have deliberately tried to soften Job's complaints against God). Job's discourse on wisdom (chapter 28) is unrelated to what precedes or follows it, and Elihu's banal speeches may be the work of a late editor, as certainly is God's curious second speech about Behemoth (a hippopotamus) and Leviathan (a crocodile): "Can you put a reed through his nose? . . . Can you fill his skin with harpoons, or his head with fishing spears?" (41:2, 7). Perhaps the most famous verses from a Christian perspective are

19:15-27, "For I know that my Redeemer [or vindicator] lives, and he shall stand at last upon the earth: And after my skin is destroyed, this I know, that in my flesh I shall see God." How can anyone doubt the meaning of these words, especially as sung in Handel's *Messiah*? Alas, the original text does not justify a messianic interpretation. Scholars agree that Job was referring to his vindication *before* his death, not after it. The verses at any rate are what scholars refer to as "corrupt" (messed up) because of the many differences between the Hebrew and the Greek texts. The Book of Job is the Bible's problem child and, despite many attempts, there is no truly plausible understanding of its meaning. Proverbs asserts that "the righteous person is delivered from trouble, and it comes to the wicked instead" (11:8), yet Job was both totally righteous and in a heap of trouble. Even though the Book of Job ends on a positive note, the misery and suffering that Job endured was neither just nor charitable. If nothing else the story does provide some comfort in situations when bad things happen to good people.

Five books in the Writings are read at the five major Jewish festivals and are referred to as Festival Scrolls or Megillot. The Song of Songs is read during Passover, and Ecclesiastes during the autumnal festival of Tabernacles. Lamentations is read during the Fasting Day of the Ninth of Ab during the summer as a mournful reminder of the destruction of Jerusalem's temple by both the Babylonians (587 B.C.) and the Romans (70 A.D.). It was a terrible time and God was so angry with his people because of the sins of the prophets, the iniquities of the priests, and the transgressions of Jerusalem's inhabitants that he allowed the city and the temple to be sacked and the survivors to starve: "The hands of the compassionate women have cooked their own children; They became food for them in the destruction of the daughters of my people" (4:8). The book of Ruth is read at the harvest festival of Pentecost; Esther is read at the Festival of Lots, or Purim, to celebrate the deliverance of the Israelites from the Persians. Both books are discussed in a later chapter.

THE GOSPEL TRUTH

Hebrew Scripture was appropriated by Christians and renamed the Old Testament. The New Testament, however, is purely Christian Scripture and, although not continuous with the Old Testament, with it comprises a common entity. God acts through the people of Israel in the Old Testament and through the new Israel (Christians and their church) in the New Testament, which does not supercede the Old Testament but rather completes it. The Old Testament was written in Hebrew, a language that belonged to Israel and never really spread geographically. The New Testament was written in koiné Greek, a poetical, precise, and subtle language known throughout the cultures of the Mediterranean and of the ancient Near East. The Old Testament is about one group and their land, with Palestine at its center. The New Testament is not so exclusive and opens up to a multitude of people from Palestine to Rome. The greatest person of the Old Testament is Moses, and of the New Testament, Jesus, the second Moses.

There are scholarly doubts about the existence of the biblical Moses; some believe that he was a folk hero who became a legend and, finally, a convenient character who served to bring together the old stories. Similar doubts have been expressed about Jesus. What is the non-Christian evidence about his existence?

There are no artifacts from the time of Jesus that relate to him: no coins, no monuments, no markers, no public records, no cross of the crucifixion, no shroud, no paintings, no statues.

The Jewish literature is surprisingly devoid of any mention of Jesus for several centuries. In the Babylonian and Palestinian Talmud (collections of Jewish law and rabbinic commentary on it dating from about 250 A.D. to 500 A.D.) there are several mentions of Jesus. The early statements mention that he led Israel astray, mocked the wise, practiced sorcery, had five disciples, and was given a fair trial but was hanged as a false teacher. Later comments, perhaps reflecting Jewish anger with Christian anti-Semitism, accuse Jesus of being the illegitimate son of an adulteress and a Roman soldier. One might argue that it would have been advantageous for the Jews to have denied the existence of Jesus if they had any information on this matter, but since no Jewish source denies the existence of Jesus then he must have existed. It's an intriguing argument but hardly proof positive.

What about Roman sources? In 110 A.D. Pliny the Younger wrote that the "Christians sing a hymn to Christ as to a god." In his *Annals* the historian Tacitus (born about 56 A.D.) wrote that the name of the Christians derives from Christ. Suetonius (200 A.D.), in his *Life of Claudius*, mentions Chrestas but probably was referring to Christ. These one-liners certainly do not establish Christ's existence.

We are left with Flavius Josephus (37–110 A.D.), a Jewish leader who became a Roman court historian and chronicled the period of Roman control over the Holy Land. In his *Antiquities* he wrote the following passage concerning the reign of the Emperor Tiberius when the Governor of Judea was Pontius Pilate: "About this time there lived Jesus, a wise man, if indeed one ought to call him a man. For he was one who wrought surprising feats and was a teacher of such people as accept the truth gladly. He won over many Jews and many of the Greeks. He was Christ. When Pilate, upon hearing him

accused by men of the highest standing among us, had him to be crucified, those who had in the first place come to love him did not give
up their affection for him. On the third day he appeared to them
restored to life, for the prophets of God had prophesied these and
countless other marvelous things about him. And the sect of
Christians, so called after him, has still to this day not disappeared"
(18:3:3). This passage, known as the Flavian Testimony, was accepted
as authentic until the late sixteenth century. Some scholars believe
that Josephus did not write the passage at all, while others believe
that the passage was contaminated by comments written on the mar-
gins of a manuscript in the fourth century and then inserted into the
text of later scribes. Of more significance, because scholars accept it
as being written by Josephus, is a sentence which mentions "a man
named James, the brother of Jesus who was called Christ" (20:9:1).

If Christ existed, then the non-Christian world took little notice of
him. In truth, a first-century Roman or Greek historian would have
had little reason to write about a Jewish religious leader with a tiny
following who was crucified as a false teacher in a relatively remote
provincial city. His brief career and the early activities of his followers were considered quite insignificant events, if they were considered at all.

The historical evidence for Christ's existence comes from
Christian sources, mainly the letters of Paul and the Gospels, although
neither Paul nor the Gospel writers, with the possible exception of
John, knew Christ personally. Their writings are based on what other
people told them and, perhaps, on a lost collection of Christ's sayings
compiled in about 50 A.D. (this hypothetical collection is known as
the Q document from the German word *Quelle* or "source").

In about 130 B.C., Papias, a Christian bishop, wrote that he was
told the following: "Mark, who had been Peter's interpreter, wrote
down carefully, but not in order, all that he remembered of the Lord's
sayings and doings . . . Peter used to adapt his teaching to the occasion, without making a systematic arrangement of the Lord's sayings,
so that Mark was quite justified in writing down some things just as
he remembered them." Even though Mark, the first Gospel writer,
didn't order things properly, the later Gospel writers used his outline of the events of Christ's life.

Mark tells us nothing about Christ except for a crucial few years
between his baptism and his crucifixion. In the first few verses we
learn that Jesus is the Son of God, that he was baptized by John as
foretold in the Old Testament prophecy of Isaiah, and that he was
tempted by Satan in the wilderness. Although readers learn about
Christ as Messiah right away, Christ's twelve disciples (representing

the twelve tribes of Israel) don't really possess this information. It's a dramatic situation. An unclean spirit recognizes Jesus ("I know who you are—the Holy One of God" (1:24)), but the disciples don't get it, and in general don't understand most of what Jesus is about. When they misinterpret a parable, Jesus says to them, "Do you not perceive nor understand? Is your heart still hardened? Having eyes, do you not see? And having ears, do you not hear? And do you not remember? . . . How is it you do not understand?" (8:17-21). They may have been slow on the uptake but, in all fairness, Jesus did not want his messianic secret to become general knowledge. On one occasion, for example, Jesus "did not allow the demons to speak because they knew him" (1:34), and when Peter said that "You are the Christ" in front of the disciples, Jesus "strictly warned them that they should tell no one about him" (8:29-30).

Interestingly enough, Jesus never declares himself to be the Messiah, although he describes himself as the Son of Man. This phrase has been the subject of ardent scholarly debate. In the Old Testament the phrase usually means a human person, but Mark uses it differently. It appears when Jesus talks of his future suffering: "the Son of Man will be betrayed to the chief priests and to the scribes . . . and they will mark him, and scourge him, and spit on him, and kill him" (10:33-34). The phrase also appears when Jesus speaks of a heavenly being, but it is unclear if that being is Jesus himself: "Then they will see the Son of Man coming in the clouds with great power and glory" (13:26).

In many ways Mark portrays Christ as a failure. People said of Jesus, "He is out of his mind" (3:21). Jesus noted that "A prophet is not without honor except in his own country, among his own relatives, and in his own house" (6:4). The Jewish priests and scribes wanted him killed and the populace said "Crucify him" to the Roman governor. He was betrayed by Judas, one of his disciples, and even Peter denied knowing Christ when questioned by the high priests. For Mark the creative act of Christ's crucifixion was a moment of glory. Since he wrote his Gospel primarily for the Gentiles, he has a Roman soldier say as Christ dies, "Truly this man is the Son of God" (15:39). Through Christ's death faith came into the world. And through his resurrection—"He is risen! He is not here." (16:6)—he proved that he was the Messiah. The Gospel story ends at verse 16:8 (verses 9-20 were added centuries later) with three women trembling at the empty tomb of Jesus, "for they were afraid." Their fear stemmed from the strangeness of the situation, but there was another good reason for it: Christ had prophesied the imminent destruction of the temple and the beginning of the abomination of desolation when "there will be tribulation such as has not been seen since the beginning of creation . . ." (13:19). It should be noted that Mark's Gospel was written in about 65–70 A.D. In 66 A.D. some Palestinian Jews revolted against Rome. In 70 A.D. Roman troops, after four years of bitter fighting, sacked Jerusalem, killed thousands of Jews, plundered the temple, and then burned it to the ground. The temple already may have been destroyed while Mark was writing his gospel or, at the very least, was on the verge of being overrun by the Romans: the "prophecy" of Jesus about the imminent fall of the temple may have been Mark's invention.

In the twenty years between the Gospel of Mark and that of Matthew, the community of Christians was developing into a church. Matthew describes these troublesome times through his account of Christ's sermons and predictions: "Blessed are you when they revile and persecute you; and say all kinds of evil against you falsely for my sake . . . Beware of men, for they will deliver you up to councils and scourge you in their synagogues . . . When they persecute you in this city, flee to another . . . And then many will be offended, and will betray one another, and will hate one another. Then many false prophets will rise up and deceive many. And because lawlessness will abound, the love of many will grow cold" (5:11, 10:17, 23; 24:10–12). Christians were looking for guidance and for reassurance. Matthew provided both in his Gospel. He took almost all of Mark's structure and added a great deal of information about Christ's teaching (possibly taken from the Q document). For reassurance he showed that Christ was the new Moses and that Christians were the new children of God and the new chosen people.

Matthew's approach is evident from the start. He begins with a genealogy tracing Christ's roots back through David and Abraham. On more than a hundred occasions he quotes or refers to Hebrew Scripture in order to establish links with Christ. At times he invents or repeats folk stories to fit his needs. It is doubtful, for example, that Christ and his family ever traveled to Egypt, but the story was useful because it recalled both the trip of Moses and the verse of Hosea 11:1, "And out of Egypt I [God] called my son." On the basis of a mistranslated word, Matthew erroneously thought that the virgin birth of Christ exemplified the fulfillment of Isaiah's prophecy. He managed to fit other Old Testament references into the birth story. The selection of Bethlehem as Christ's birthplace was masterful: Bethlehem not only was the home of David but also was mentioned in the Old Testament book of Micah 5:2, "But you, Bethlehem, though you are little among the thousands of Judah, yet out of you shall come forth to me the one to be ruler in Israel." By placing a star in the birth story Matthew was able to refer back to the Old Testament book of

Numbers 17:1, "I see him, but not now; I behold him, but not near. A star shall come out of Jacob, a scepter shall rise out of Israel . . ."

Just as there are five books of Moses (the Torah), so too Matthew presents Christ's teachings in five sections. The Sermon on the Mount teaches that the poor, the weak, and the merciful are blessed, that Jesus does not destroy but rather fulfills the law, that lust itself is as sinful as adultery, that divorce is acceptable only for sexual infidelity, and that prayers such as the "Our Father" should be recited in private. In his instructions Christ tells the disciples to preach that the kingdom of heaven is at hand, to heal the sick, to raise the dead, to cast out demons, and to expect persecution. The third section of teaching is devoted to parables, and the fourth to instructions to the church: ". . . whatever you bind on earth will be bound in heaven, and whatever you loose on earth will be loosed in heaven" (18:18). Christ violently attacks the Jewish scribes and Pharisees and teaches about an impending apocalypse: "This generation will by no means pass away until all these things take place" (24:34).

Matthew adds details to Mark's account of Christ's capture, trial, crucifixion, and resurrection. He writes, for example, that Judas betrayed Christ for thirty pieces of silver, an amount that unsurprisingly corresponds to a verse in the Old Testament book of Zechariah (11:12–13). Matthew concludes with the resurrected Christ's meeting with his disciples in Galilee and his instruction to "make disciples of all the nations," to baptize them and to teach them to observe his teachings; "And lo, I am with you always, even to the end of the age."

Luke's Gospel was written a few years after Matthew's, although neither author seems to have known about the other. It records the life of Jesus, while its sequel, Acts of the Apostles, written by the same author, describes events in the formation of Christianity during the three decades after Christ's death. As sources of information Luke used some material unique to his Gospel, the Q document, and Mark's Gospel. Luke was a first-rate writer, some of whose words, translated into Latin, have made this Gospel the favorite of Christians over the centuries. The Hail Mary, or Ave Maria, is the angel Gabriel's greeting to Mary and the Magnificat (1:46–55) is Mary's song, "My soul magnifies the Lord . . ." Luke's writing ability is also exemplified by his decision to change the sequence of some events in Mark's Gospel. He took the story about Jesus and his relatives (Mark 3:31–35), for example, and placed it after the parable of the revealed light (8:16–21) in order to make the parable more meaningful.

In the preface Luke states his intention "to write an orderly account." He accomplishes this not so much by referring back to Hebrew Scripture but rather by placing Jesus within the current historical context and by emphasizing that Christ fulfills God's promise of providing salvation for humankind. In a dramatic scene Jesus was handed the book of Isaiah at the synagogue in Nazareth. He read aloud: "The spirit of the Lord is upon me, because he has anointed me to preach the gospel to the poor; he has sent me to heal the brokenhearted, to preach deliverance to the captives and recovery of sight to the blind, to set at liberty those who are oppressed, and to proclaim the year of the Lord's favor." He then said to everyone, "Today the Scripture is fulfilled in your hearing."

Luke contains several unique parables and gives women a more significant role than the other Gospels. Luke also has the risen Christ appear before the disciples in Jerusalem, where he says, "See my hands and my feet, that it is I myself; handle me, and see; for a spirit has not flesh and bones as you see that I have" (24:39) and even asks for food to eat. This emphasis on the physical body of Christ probably was included to forestall those believers who claimed that Christ was always and only a spirit who did not truly share in mankind's physical nature. Christ then instructs the disciples that he fulfilled what was "written in the law of Moses, and in the prophets, and in the psalms" (24:44); this is the only time when a New Testament verse places together all three sections of the Old Testament. He also instructs "that repentance and forgiveness of sins should be preached to all nations." The Gospel ends with the departure of Christ. Many Bibles include in verse 51 the words that Christ was "carried up to heaven," but this is a later addition and is not included in most textually accurate modern Bibles. Luke does describe Christ's ascension into heaven in Acts 1:9-11 although he indicates in 1:3 that the risen Christ presented himself and spoke with the disciples for forty days instead of ascending on Easter Sunday as implied by the Gospel account.

John's Gospel, the fourth and last written, is unlike the other three, and there are just a few parallels with Mark's and Luke's Gospels. John may have been the beloved disciple to whom Jesus entrusted the care of his mother Mary (John 19:26-27) and, thus, an eyewitness of many events described in his Gospel. He also utilizes material apparently unknown to the other Gospel writers. It is likely that before becoming a Christian he lived as a member of the Jewish Essene sect associated with the Dead Sea Scrolls. This influence is seen in recurrent emphases on darkness versus light, on worship in spirit and truth, and on Christ as the source of light and of truth. John knew about the work of the Jewish Grecophile scholar, Philo of Alexandria, whose concept of Wisdom (personified as Sophia) was enmeshed in God's creative powers. This influence is seen in John's concept of the Logos, or Word, that "became flesh and dwelled among us" (as Jesus).

John stated the purpose of his Gospel: "that you may believe that Jesus is the Christ, the Son of God, and that believing you may have life in his name." He describes a series of miracles, such as changing water into wine, walking on water, and raising Lazarus from the dead, as proof of Christ's divine power. Just as God said to Moses, "I am who I am" (or "I am the one who is," or "I am what I say I am") (Ex. 3:14), so too John decides to have Christ say "I am . . . the bread of life (6:35) . . . the light of the world (8:12) . . . he who existed before Abraham (8:58) . . . the good shepherd (10:11) . . . resurrection and life (11:25) . . . the way, truth, and life (14:6) . . . the authentic vine" (15:1). John, disliking parables, prefers to present a Christ who delivers thoughtful sermons.

John's description of the Last Supper (13:1–30) differs from the other Gospel writers. They say that it took place on Passover, but John says Passover eve. They write about the blood of the new covenant, but John omits this entirely. They write about the ingestion of bread and wine that was changed into Christ's flesh and blood to establish the sacrament of communion. John omits this, too, although he was aware of the story. Instead, in an earlier section he has Jesus present a discourse to the Jews in the synagogue of Capernaum: "Whoever eats my flesh and drinks my blood has eternal life . . . [and] abides in me, and I in him . . . This is the bread which came down from heaven—not as your fathers ate the manna and are dead. He who eats this bread will live forever" (6:51–59).

John's Gospel most likely had several authors. There are discontinuities in the text, differences in style, and geographical dislocations such as placing Jesus in both Galilee and Jerusalem at the same time. It seems probable that John's followers wrote down what he told them and then edited the Gospel after his death. Chapter 21, an epilogue, clearly is an addition.

The Gospels of Mark, Matthew, and Luke are called synoptic because they "see" the story of Jesus as through the same eyes. John's Gospel presents a very different Jesus who doesn't speak in parables, doesn't cast out any demons, and doesn't seem terribly interested in the poor or the oppressed. The synoptic Gospels' presentation of Christ is probably more accurate than John's, although, paradoxically, John was the only Gospel writer who *may* actually have known Jesus.

According to the scholars of the Jesus Seminar, the only words in Mark's Gospel that unequivocally were spoken by Jesus are, "Pay the emperor what belongs to the emperor, and God what belongs to God" (12:17). This identical verse is found in Matthew 21:21; other legitimate verses from Matthew are 5:39–42 (turn the other cheek), 6:9 ("our Father"), 13:33 (one line parable of the leaven), and 20:1–15 (parable of the vineyard laborers). The authentic verses in Luke are 6:20-21 (congratulations to the poor and hungry), 6:29 (turn the other cheek), 6:30 (give to beggars and forgive borrowers), 10:30-35 (parable of the Samaritan), 13:20 (parable of the leaven), 16:1-8 (parable of the shrewd manager), and 20:25 (pay to the Emperor and to God). No authentic words of Jesus are found in John's Gospel.

Even from this very brief introduction to the Gospels it should be apparent that each has its own focus, emphasis, and order. They differ in so many details that it is impossible to extract with precision the events and words of Jesus. Some historians, especially in the eighteenth and nineteenth centuries, regarded Jesus purely as a mythical figure, but hardly anyone today holds such a belief. A rabbi named Jesus did exist. He most likely was born between 5 and 10 B.C. and was crucified on Friday, March 30, 36 A.D. We know the names of his parents and some things about his disciples and his teachings. Remembering that the Gospels were written thirty to sixty years after Christ's death, persons with great faith still may accept events such as the virgin birth and the resurrection as the Gospel truth. To such persons the discrepancies in the Gospels are of little consequence. However, some contemporary scholars that we will encounter in the last chapter of this book take the position that the Gospels were written by enthusiastic followers of the rabbi Jesus who deified him and fostered legends about him.

THE NEW CREATION: PAUL

A few years after the crucifixion of Christ something powerfully strange and sudden happened on the road near the city of Damascus. A conservative Jew named Paul, a.k.a. Saul, was chasing after some Christians in order to persecute them when a heavenly light flashed around him and he collapsed. There are three somewhat different recordings of what happened next, but what essentially occurred is that Paul heard a voice: "I am Jesus whom you are persecuting." This voice told Paul that he was to become a minister, especially to the Gentiles, "to open their eyes in order to turn them from darkness to light, and from the power of Satan to God, that they may receive forgiveness of sins and an inheritance among those who are sanctified by faith in me" (Acts 26:12-17, also see 9:1-8 and 22:1-16). By one account Paul got up off the ground and was unable to see, eat, or drink for three days. Then a Jewish Christian disciple named Ananias came and said, "Brother Saul, the Lord Jesus who appeared to you on the road by which you came, has sent me that you may regain your sight and be filled with the Holy Spirit." Immediately something like scales fell from Paul's eyes; he regained his sight and was baptized (Acts 9:17-18). Thus did Paul become a Christian and a brilliant evangelist who, more than any other person, was responsible for the propagation of this new religion.

What do we know about Paul? He came from an upper middle class Jewish family, was a Roman citizen, and studied the law in Jerusalem at the feet of Rabbi Gamaliel while working as a tentmaker or leather worker to support himself. He joined in the persecution of Christians and, according to Acts 7:54-8:3, consented to the death by stoning of Stephen the martyr who, as he lay dying, forgave his murderers. Paul had some sort of chronic illness (he called it "a thorn in the flesh") and wrote about his "physical infirmity," his weak bodily presence, and his "contemptible speech" (2 Cor. 10:10 and 12:7; Gal. 4:14). The Athenians mocked him when he spoke about the resurrection of the dead and the Roman procurator, Festus, said, "Paul, you are mad; your great learning is turning you mad." Using the editorial we, Paul admitted that sometimes "we are besides ourselves" (probably referring to strange spiritual experiences such as his conversation with Jesus, his visions and revelations of the Lord, and his capacity to speak in tongues), although he added that "it is for God" (2 Cor. 5:18; Acts 17:32 and 26:24). In a popular second-century novel he was described as "a man little of stature, thin-haired upon the head, crooked in the legs, of good state of body, with eyebrows joining, and nose somewhat hooked, full of grace; for sometimes he appeared like a man and sometimes he had the face of an angel."

Our knowledge of Paul comes from Acts and from his Letters. Each of the sources contains unique information about Paul as well as some discordant information (one records five visits to Jerusalem, for example, while the other records only three). We don't know what happened to him for a decade after his conversion, but he started dictating his letters to a traveling secretary in 50 A.D. He probably wrote many more letters than have survived, and he even warned the brethren about false letters "as if from us" (2 Thess. 2:2). Scholars agree that Paul authored seven Letters: 1 and 2 Corinthians, Galatians, Philemon, Philippians, Romans, and 1 Thessalonians. He probably authored Colossians and 2 Thessalonians. He definitely did not write 1 and 2 Timothy and Titus; they were composed after his death. Ephesians contains certain words and a literary style not seen in any other of Paul's works and makes references to all the other genuine letters; one can conclude reasonably that it was written by someone theologically close to Paul. Paul's Letters were collected some thirty years after his death (he was executed in Rome in about 64 A.D.) to aid the new Christian churches in dealing with problems both of faith and of governance.

Many explanations have been offered over the centuries for Paul's experience on the road to Damascus. Was it a complex seizure and was epilepsy his "thorn in the flesh"? Did he have an acute psychotic reaction that took three days to resolve? Deep within was he dissatisfied with some aspect of his orthodox Jewish religion? Perhaps he was secretly moved by the Greek influences of the city where he was reared; he spoke Greek and used the Greek Septuagint version of the Old Testament. Did he project his discontent onto the Christians whom he then persecuted? Was he so touched by the magnanimous attitude of Stephen towards his murderers that he switched his allegiance and finally came to peace with himself? Paul explained his experience as a unique act of God. He alone was chosen for this experience, which he called "a new creation; old things have passed away; behold, all things have become new" (2 Cor. 5:17). He equated his experience with that of the apostles who witnessed the risen Christ (1 Cor. 15:1–11) and declared that he became an apostle, as did the original twelve apostles, "not from men nor through man, but through Jesus Christ and God the Father" (Gal. 1:1). Paul has no room for any intermediaries between him and his experience with Christ; in his own account of his conversion, for example, he doesn't mention Ananias at all. He would not admit that any person taught him about Christianity; he says he learned directly from Christ even though he never met Christ in the flesh. Paul's teachings stem from two basic events: the death and resurrection of Christ. He makes few references to the other events of Christ's life or to his sermons, parables, or teachings.

After his conversion Paul became totally Christ-centered. He declared, "I have been crucified with Christ; it is no longer I who live, but Christ lives in me" (Gal. 2:20). He was proud of the beatings he endured during his missionary activities and noted that "I bear in my body the marks of the Lord Jesus" (Gal. 6:18). That Paul's mysticism, his intense identification with Christ, and his notion that the members of the Church are the body of Christ are not psychopathological is evident by Paul's generosity; he desires that all humankind come to life in Christ. His statement "We are the circumcision" (Phil. 3:3) is strange by today's standards but back then was easily understandable: true believers in Christ had become the new, central core of Israel. Some Jews already had become Christians, however, and Paul believed that the rest would follow suit in due time: "A hardening has come over part of Israel, until the full numbers of the Gentiles come in, and so all Israel will be saved" (Rom. 11:25).

In Romans Paul declares that salvation is necessary because sin is inherent in the human condition: "All have sinned and fall short of the glory of God" (3:23). We may serve God with our minds but with our flesh we serve the law of sin; indwelling sin prevents us from doing what we know is good so that we are confused by our actions (7:15–25). Christ's death was really a victory and the beginning of a new dawn. Paul believed that the age of the Spirit and the moment of salvation "is nearer to us now than when we first believed; the night is far gone, the day is at hand. Let us then cast off the works of darkness and put on the armor of light."

Paul undeniably urged the brethren to prepare for the imminent end of time: "The time is short, so that from now on even those who have wives should be as though they had none . . . [and] those who buy as though they had no goods . . . for the form of the world is passing away" (1 Cor. 7:29–31). Yet Paul was not a traditional apocalyptic fearmonger. He believed that the day of judgement was breaking forth from heaven and would soon appear in its totality. Christ had given humankind a foretaste of the glories of the age of the Spirit. The best way to prepare for judgement was to abstain from evil, to be steadfast in one's faith, and to "love your neighbors as yourself. Love does no wrong to a neighbor; therefore love is the fulfilling of the law" (Rom: 13:9–10). In 1 Thessalonians we learn that the day of the Lord will come unexpectedly like a thief in the night (5:2) and that the Lord will descend from heaven with the archangel's call and with the blast of God's trumpet, "and the dead in Christ will rise first; then we who are alive, who are left, shall be caught up together with them in the clouds to meet the Lord in the air; and so we shall always be with the Lord" (4:16–17).

It is impossible in this brief introduction to do justice to Paul's teachings. His notion that we are saved through faith rather than good works, for example, was taken up by Martin Luther as a central focus for the Protestant Reformation. We shall encounter Paul frequently throughout this book. Neither the enormity of his influence nor the problems associated with it can be denied.

A BANG, NOT A WHIMPER: HEBREWS AND REVELATION

The New Testament concludes with a group of epistles addressed to the Church in general; the one exception is 3 John, a very brief personal letter to a church elder.

The letter to the Hebrews is intriguing. We don't know who wrote it, when it was written, or to whom it was addressed. It isn't even a typical letter but rather a somewhat unique literary form resembling a type of proclamation. The title "To the Hebrews" did not appear in early manuscripts; early on someone probably assumed it was addressed to Hebrew-Christians and wrote those words on the outside of the papyrus scroll. There was initial debate about authorship until Jerome titled it "The Epistle of Paul to the Hebrews" in his Latin translation of the Bible (400 A.D.). Paul was credited with authorship until theologians of the Protestant Reformation convincingly demonstrated otherwise. The Catholic Council of Trent (1546) stuck with Paul, but a Papal Bible Commission in 1914 judged that Catholics don't have to accept Paul as the author.

Hebrews, set "in these last days" (1:2), has a touch of the apocalyptic. The Jews led by Moses, who wandered in the wilderness for forty years, hardened their hearts towards God, but faithful Christians with Jesus as their leader have the opportunity to come to rest in God. Jesus is the perfection, Judaism the preparation. The old order necessitated repeated sacrifices of animals, and even the high priest had to atone his personal sins: "In these sacrifices there is a reminder of sin year after year. For it is impossible that the blood of bulls and goats should take away sin" (10:3–4). But Christ's single sacrifice "perfected for all time those who are sanctified" (20:15). Many Jews believed in two Messiahs, a king from the house of David and a priest from the order of Levi; in Hebrews Christ is presented as the Davidic Messiah as well as the priestly one, although from the older and superior order of Melchizedek, the priest of God most high who blessed Abraham (Gen. 14:18–20).

Chapter eleven of Hebrews is among the most famous in the New Testament. It begins, "Now faith is the assurance of things hoped for, the conviction of things not seen," and goes on to present a list of persons, such as Moses, Abraham, and the harlot Rahab, who lived in faith. The reader is then exhorted to follow the path to the heavenly Jerusalem and is provided a list of things to do: practice brotherly love, be hospitable to strangers, remember and identify with prisoners and the ill-treated, honor marriage, and don't love money. Seek the city which is to come and remember the timelessness of Jesus who is "the same yesterday, and today, and forever" (13:8).

The Letter of James is problematic as regards authorship and date. Scholars variously regard its composition to be about 65 A.D. or as late as 125–150 A.D. It may be a compilation of the teachings of James the brother of Jesus, or it may have been written by a Greek Christian who used the name of James because of James's favorable connections with Paul. At any rate the author berates both wealthy oppressors of the poor and those who use their tongue both to bless God and to curse men: the tongue "is an unruly evil, full of deadly poison." Verses 2:14–26 discuss the role of good works versus faith as justification for salvation. A subtlety in the argument centers on the Old Testament figure of Abraham who, according to Genesis 15:6,

"believed in the Lord, and He accounted it to him for righteousness."
James esteemed both Abraham's faith and works: "Faith was active
along with his works, and faith was completed by his works . . . For
as the body apart from the spirit is dead, so faith apart from works is
dead" (2:22, 26).

Although not given much emphasis in most books about the Bible,
James 5:14–16 is the classic New Testament healing text: "Is any
among you sick? Let him call for the elders of the church, and let
them pray over him, anointing him with oil in the name of the Lord;
and the prayer of faith will save the sick man, and the Lord will raise
him up [from his sickbed]; and if he has committed sins, he will be
forgiven. Therefore, confess your sins to one another, and pray for one
another, that you may be healed." The healing of illness was a major
focus both of Christ's ministry and of early church activity. Healing
declined, however, as the church overcame Roman persecution and
successfully established itself. This decline in healing was fostered by
Jerome's error in translating James's Letter into Latin. Instead of ". . .
that you may be *healed*," Jerome wrote ". . . that you may be *saved*."
This change from physical healing to spiritual salvation affected
Christianity's approach to illness until the mid-twentieth century and
is covered in detail in my chapter on healing.

Neither of the two letters of Peter was written by him. Peter, originally named Simon, was one of Christ's original apostles; according
to tradition he was martyred by Nero in Rome in 64 A.D. The book of
1 Peter was probably written between 110–120 A.D. during the persecution of Christians by the Roman Emperor Trojan. The letter
attempts to soften the fears of Christians: "You are a chosen race, a
royal priesthood, a holy nation, God's own people" (2:0). Verses
3:18–19 state about Christ, "being put to death in the flesh but made
alive in the spirit; in which he went and preached to the spirits in
prison." Scholars have debated long and hard about the significance
of these verses. They probably mean that during the three days
between Christ's death and resurrection he preached to the spirits
imprisoned in Hell, namely everyone who died during the flood (only
Noah, his wife, their three sons and daughters-in-law escaped) and, possibly, the fallen angels (see Gen. 6:1–4). Christ's descent into the underworld provided an answer to questions about what happened to those
persons who died before the time of Christ: "For this is why the Gospel
was preached even to the dead, that though judged in the flesh like
men, they might live in the spirit like God" (4:6). There is a hint of this
notion in Acts 2:27, where the verse from Ps. 16:10 is applied to Jesus:
"For you will not leave my soul in Hades, nor will you allow your holy
one to see corruption." Also, in Luke's Gospel, Jesus applied a verse

from Isaiah to himself about proclaiming "liberty to the imprisoned" (4:18). From these citations a tradition arose about Christ's voyage to hell and the phrase "He descended into hell" gradually was inserted into the Apostle's Creed (although it was not included in many other important church creeds). The fourth-century Gospel known as the Acts of Pilate (a.k.a. Gospel of Nicodemus) is the most influential and elaborate description of Christ's harrowing of hell. The portrayal of a Christ who was not only spiritually alive after his crucifixion but also capable of defeating Satan on his own turf and willing to rescue the imprisoned spirits there undoubtedly held a popular appeal.

The book of 2 Peter, written a century after Peter's death, is in the form of a testament in which Peter presents his last thoughts. He urges true believers not to pay attention to scoffers who say, "Where is the promise of his [Christ's] coming? For since the fathers [apostles] fell asleep [died], all things continue as they were from the beginning of creation" (3:4). Stay steadfast and look for new heavens and a new earth in which righteousness dwells.

The three brief Letters of John were written by an anonymous church elder in about 105 A.D. Some followers of John the Gospel writer evidently were spreading false teachings: "we have not sinned," [we] "deny Jesus is the Christ" and "that Jesus Christ has come in the flesh" (1 John 1:10, 2:22, 4:2). The Letters warn against heretics and Antichrists. "We know that we are of God, and the whole word lies under the sway of the wicked one . . . We know [that Jesus] is the true God and eternal life. Little children, keep yourselves from idols" (2 John 5:19, 21). The Letter of Jude also warns against false teachers, "ungodly men, who turn the grace of our God into lewdness and deny the only Lord God and our Lord Jesus Christ" (1:4).

The New Testament concludes with the overpowering book of Revelation, which was discussed earlier in this chapter. Revelation is incredibly complex, filled with startling symbolism and mysterious secrets, replete with bewildering bursts of energy and shocking scenes, with juxtaposed love and wrath, inspiration and devastation, evil and godliness, weeping and joy, a glorious angel and a harlot drunk with the blood of the saints, the silence of the lamb and the horrible horsemen of the apocalypse, the water of life and the lake of fire. Little wonder that Revelation is a favorite of intensely devout Christians, mystics, theological novices and seasoned veterans, poets, artists, Swedish cinematographers, fortune tellers, late-night radio preachers, fear-mongering televangelists, cult leaders, insane persons, and serial killers.

GOD BLESS THE GOD WHO HAS HIS OWN

God isn't easy. Some say God created human beings, others that human beings created God. Some say God is alive, others dead. Emerson said that man is a god in ruins. Most say God is a he, a few say God is a she. Buddhists don't believe in God at all while Hindus most likely believe in one god with many manifestations. The Old Testament God reveals himself as a loving father in one chapter and as a baby-killer in the next.

God's behavior in the Bible, like Russia's during World War II, often is a riddle wrapped in a mystery inside an enigma. Why, for example, did he create the universe? Why create vegetation on day three and the sun on day four instead of the other way around since plants wither and die without sunlight? Why create human beings? Surely he didn't need to do so. Why select a tribe of wandering Jews as his chosen people? In the Psalms we read that "God has taken his place in the divine council; in the midst of the gods he holds judgement" (82:1). What happened to the other gods? Did they perish when human beings ceased worshiping them? If human beings can cause a god to die, can they also conceive and give birth to a new one? What did God mean when he said to Adam that "you shall surely die" on the day that he ate the fruit of the special tree in the Garden of Eden. Adam ate the fruit and lived. Did God mean that Adam would die spiritually instead of physically? If so, then what other sections of the Bible should be understood symbolically instead of literally? Did a pair of all the creatures on the earth really assemble on Noah's Ark? Were dinosaurs included? If they weren't, then where did the dinosaurs come from?

The New Testament God sent his son, Jesus, to earth in a human form. Did Jesus have both a human and a divine will, or just one will? Did he have both a human and a divine nature, or just one nature? When did he behave as a god and when as a human? Jesus comes easy to the heart but rankles the intellect. Certainly as a psychiatrist I've seen enough Christ wannabes to populate Disneyland. New York subways incubate sleazy, catecombal Christs, while South Carolina specializes in get-out-of-the-temple, seashore shouting Christs. In Louisiana they hip-hop in sharkskin suits while in Oklahoma they have visions taller than oil rigs. Don't even mention California, where they walk on water with surfboards. To reiterate, God isn't easy.

YO! YAH! YAHU! YHWH!... IS GOD

What we now call the Holy Land was originally Canaan, an area 160 miles long and 50 miles wide bordered by the Mediterranean Sea on the west and the Jordan Valley on the east. Canaan had many gods in biblical days. El was the creator and head of the council of gods. Baal, his son, had a devoted human following because he controlled the rain that brought crops to life. His wife was Asherah (Astarte), the goddess of fertility symbolized by the sacred tree of life which was graphically presented as growing out of her genitalia. Mountains, volcanos and special large, uncut rocks were considered sacred. Biblical comments, such as those found in Isaiah, reflect the earthy origins of God: "The Lord of Hosts dwells in Mount Zion" (8:18). "Behold, the name of the Lord comes from afar, burning in his anger, heavy his burden. His lips brim with fury, his tongue is like a devouring fire. His breath is like an overflowing stream" (30:27–28) describes a volcano spewing lava. Similarly when Moses went to meet God, "The mountain of Sinai was entirely wrapped in smoke because Yahweh had descended on it in the form of fire. Like smoke from a furnace the smoke went up, and the whole mountain shook violently" (Ex. 19:18). Since Canaan was once ruled by Egyptians their gods were present, and the Mesopotamian gods were there too because the only feasible land route between Egypt and Mesopotamia was through Canaan. In the desert area south of Canaan, nomads worshipped Sin, the moon god whose sacred mountain was known as Mount Sinai. The Hebrews in the Holy Land not only encountered these gods but also, according to the prophet Joshua (24:2), served them in the old times of the great patriarchs such as Terah and his sons Abraham and Nahor. Joshua said that they served "other" gods (Elohim) instead of the one, true Jewish God, Yahweh.

Exactly when the God named Yahweh first revealed himself is problematic in the Bible. Genesis states that Enosh, Adam's grandson, was "the first to invoke the name of Yahweh" (4:26). Since Enosh means "man," the implication is that mankind's knowledge of Yahweh occurred at that time. Adam and Enosh lived in mythic times, so no real date can be provided. In human time the Bible presents a different account about the revelation of Yahweh. In about 1500 B.C. Moses encountered an angel of God—probably God himself—in the shape of a flaming bush on Mount Sinai. God told Moses to go to Pharaoh and bring the enslaved sons of Israel out of Egypt. Moses was worried that the sons of Israel would ask about *the name* of the God who had commanded him to lead them to freedom. "God said to Moses, "I Am who I Am . . . You are to say to the sons of Israel that Yahweh, the God of your fathers, the God of Abraham, the God of Isaac, and the God of Jacob, has sent me to you. This is my name for all time; by this name I shall be invoked for all generations to come'" (Ex. 3:14–15). Moses had problems fulfilling this task and complained to God, who then said, "I am Yahweh. To Abraham and Isaac and Jacob I appeared as El Shaddai; I did not make myself known to them by my name Yahweh" (Ex. 6:3). Regardless of which account is closer to the truth, it was through his revelation to Moses that Yahweh became established in Jewish consciousness as the supreme God. Why all the fuss about a name? A rose by any other name may still smell as sweet, but gods aren't flowers. In biblical days a god by any other name was, in fact, another god. Yahweh's name contained his very essence; the second commandment prohibited taking his name in vain, while the Lord's Prayer in the New Testament declared that God's name specifically is hallowed (set apart as holy), and in John 17:6 Jesus said to God his Father that "I have glorified you on earth . . . I have made your name known." Yahweh wouldn't reveal his name to Jacob even after wrestling with him all night, although he changed Jacob's name to Israel " . . . 'because you have been strong against God, you shall pre-vail against me.' Jacob then made this request: 'I beg you, tell me your name,' but he replied, 'Why do you ask my name?' And he blessed him there." (Gen. 32:28–29).

Yahweh's disclosure of his name to Moses was a defining moment in the history of the world. The Psalms tell us that Yahweh will put his anger on the kingdoms that do not call on his name (79:6), but "for his name's sake" the Israelites will be led on the path of righteousness (23:3) and their iniquities will be pardoned (25:11). Because they know the name of Yahweh they can put their trust in him and they will be protected. Without knowledge of God's name, there would have been no triumphant Judaism, no Christ, and probably no Christianity.

Scholars believe that Yahweh's name originally was shorter, e.g., Yo, Yahu, Yah. The name Joel, for example, is a combination of Yo (Jo) and El, and thus means "Yo is God." Yah is still used today, especially while singing Handel's *Messiah*; hallelu-yah means "praise Yah." Since biblical Hebrew was written without vowels, Yahweh appeared as YHWH; no one is totally certain about the correct pronunciation of these four sacred letters. Not willing to take the chance that they might profane the powerful name of God, the Hebrews didn't speak it but rather substituted the work Adonai ("Lord"). In the sixteenth century A.D. a Roman Catholic theologian developed a Latin term for YHWH which was eventually translated into English as Jehovah.

It truly is impossible to appreciate the complexity of the Old Testament without an understanding of God's names. Isaiah, for example, called Yahweh "the everlasting rock" (26:4), while Moses sadly sang about fat, bloated Jeshen who "dishonored the rock, his salvation" and about the Israelites who sacrificed to demons: "You forgot the rock who begot you, unmindful now of the God who fathered you" (Deut. 32:15–18). The road to Yahweh was paved with the stones that the ancient Semites worshipped. Traces of Yahweh's rocky past are found throughout the Bible. When Jacob dreamed of the ladder that reached to heaven and of Yahweh's appearance, for example, his pillow was a stone. When Jacob awoke he said, "Truly Yahweh is in this place and I never knew it." He then "took the stone he had used for his pillow, and set it up as a monument, pouring oil over the top of it. He named the place Bethel" (Gen. 28:16–19). Yahweh told Moses, "In every place where I record my name I will come to you and bless you. And if you make me an altar of stone, you shall not build it of hewn stone; for if you use your tool on it, you shall have profaned it" (Ex. 20:24–25). "My God is a rock where I take shelter" (Ps. 94:22) is a metaphor made more powerful by the historical truth that the ancient Semites might have said, "My rock is a God where I take shelter."

Some scholars believe that the Ark of the Covenant, in which Yahweh was present, contained sacred stones, perhaps phallic representations, that connoted the old worship of fertility gods. "Stones" is a slang word for testicles, and Yahweh certainly was very concerned about the fertility of the Israelites. In the famous covenant he promised Abraham that he would become the father of a multitude of nations with as many descendants as there are stars in the sky. Yahweh even allowed him, at the age of one hundred, to have a child with his ninety-year-old wife, Sarah.

Intimations of ancient rock gods abound in the Old Testament, although the Jewish priestly editors probably expunged many direct references. By the time of the New Testament's writing hints of the old rock gods diminished. On one occasion Paul wrote about parallels between the trials of the Israelites in the wilderness and the trials that awaited his brethren; the Israelites drank water that flowed from the rock that Moses struck with his rod, and since they found water in several places it was supposed that the same rock must have followed them in their wanderings: "For they drank from the supernatural Rock that followed them, and the Rock was Christ" (1 Cor. 10:4). In Acts 4:11 Peter told the elders of Israel that Christ "is the stone which was rejected by your builders, which has become the chief cornerstone." 1 Peter 2:4–6 refers both to Christ and Christians as "living stones." In Matt. 16:18 Christ gave his disciple Simon a new name: "And I tell you that you are Peter, and on this rock I will build my church." In Aramaic Christ's words would have been, "You are *Kêpha*, and on this *kêpha* I will build my church." In Greek the words are *Petros* ("Rocky") and *petra* ("rock").

DADDY DEAREST: GOD THE FATHER

The image of God as a rock is but one of many images and attributes passed down from the Bible that have resulted in the distinctive Western construct of a God who is a judge, a ruler, a king, a shepherd feeding his flock, the first and the last, redeemer, Lord of all the earth, the everlasting God (El Olam), the God of the covenant (El Berith), the Lord of Hosts. Because Babylonians and Canaanites worshipped a Father God, the early Israelites shied away from this image. In fact, Jeremiah the weeping prophet chastised his people for their abandonment of the true God and said that they had become like the worshippers of false gods "who say to a tree, 'You are my father', and to a stone, 'You gave birth to me'" (2:27). It wasn't until around 700 B.C. that the Bible regularly stated that "You, Yahweh, yourself are our Father" (Is. 64:16). The Greeks had their Father Zeus and the Romans their Jupiter (the Latin form of Zeus Pater), but the Jews weren't worried about them.

"Father" was the predominant word used by Jesus when referring to God. Jesus is the only person to use "my Father"; he spoke to his disciples about "your Father." Clearly there was a difference between the relationship of Christ and of everyone else to God the Father, but the sense of it all was that Christ's brethren could learn about and then participate in his special relationship. According to Luke 10:22, only Christ and those persons whom he chooses to tell about it know who the Father is. Participation in Christ's relationship with God the Father is implied in Christ's words to Mary Magdalen on the day of his resurrection: "Go and find the brothers, and tell them: I am ascending to my Father and your Father, to my God and your God" (John 20:17). Similarly, Christ said, "You must call no one on earth your father, since you have only one Father, and he is in heaven" (Matt. 23:8). To whom did Christ refer with the words "your" and "you" in these quotes? Since God created the whole human race from a single stock (Acts 17:26), namely Adam "son of God" (Luke 3:38), everyone has the opportunity to share in Christ's filial relationship with the Father; however, Christ said "no one comes to the Father but by me"

(John 14:6) so that only those persons who are adopted by Christ may take advantage of this opportunity. The adoption process consists of receiving the Holy Spirit: "Everyone moved by the Spirit is a son of God . . . It is the spirit of sons, and it makes us cry out, 'Abba, Father!' The Spirit himself and our spirit bear united witness that we are children of God" (Rom. 8:14–16). There is a biblical continuity to this basic concept. In the Old Testament Yahweh promised that he would preserve David's children and make his royal throne secure forever: "I will be a father to him and he a son to me" (2 Sam. 7:14). In the New Testament God promised to live among men in the heavenly Jerusalem and to provide water from the well of life to the thirsty: "It is the rightful countenance of the victorious person; and I will be his God and he a son to me" (Rev. 21:7).

Sigmund Freud was fascinated by the concept of God the Father and in 1923 offered a literal and historical interpretation: "God is a father-substitute, or, more correctly, an exalted father as seen and met within childhood—as the individual sees him in his own childhood and as mankind saw him in prehistoric times as the father of the primal horde. Later on in life the individual sees his father as something different and lesser, but the childish image is preserved and merges with the inherited memory-traces of the primal father to form the idea of God."

For Freud, God springs into existence as a wish in the minds of children. Every child experiences a "terrifying impression of helplessness" that arouses a need for protection through love; this is provided by the father. As the child matures and comes to realize that the world is inexorably cruel and that lifelong helplessness is inherent in the human condition, the need for an even more powerful father arises. God is the fulfillment of a wish for a consoling protector, a daddy who makes helplessness tolerable. Freud also believed that in prehistoric times humans lived as a horde ruled by a tyrannical father. The horde sons rebelled and killed their primal father because he denied them access to women. Since the children both hated and loved their father, the memory of this crime and the guilt it instilled led them first to venerate an animal (a symbolic father substitute) that they designated as the tribal ancestor. Killing the animal, an expression of hatred towards the father, became a sacrament and eating it together became a communion meal, an expression of love for and identification with the father. Over time the venerated animals were replaced by humans who were sacrificed and eaten; they, in turn, were replaced by the more civilized notion of a god such as Christ who is ceremoniously crucified and who is communally eaten in religious services. The memory traces of the original, powerful primal father supposedly reside in us all and contribute to the child's formulation of God. Thus saith Sigmund whose own ambivalent feelings toward his dead father resulted in survivor-guilt dreams.

Carl Jung (1875-1961), the famous Swiss psychiatrist, had a different twist. He believed that every person's mind contains unconscious memories of ancient, prehistoric experiences that constitute the human heritage. These memories include those of the real Father-God. Thus, a child's biological father is a substitute for God. In the words of one scholar, for Jung, "God is less a Big Father than the physical father is a little god."

So, which is it? Is daddy a substitute for God, or is God a substitute for daddy? The answer depends upon your choice of reality as church or couch, altar or bedroom, heaven or earth.

GOD ON THE MOVE

The God of the Old Testament is not a theological abstraction but rather an historical "figure" who becomes known to us through his interventions in the lives of his chosen people. He assumes a masculine gender and primarily does manly things, but, unlike a god like Zeus, he is asexual. At times he is prone to horrible rages, to changing his mind, to regretting his actions, and to being unfair (from a human perspective). He rests, he curses, he gambles, he gets peeved and refuses to talk—in short, he is very like a man except for his lack of direct sexual activity (although he is quite interested in the procreation of others).

The New Testament verse "Jesus Christ is the same yesterday, today, and forever" (Heb. 13:8) indicates unchangeability, but there is nothing comparable in the Old Testament, where God changes many times. In recent books two scholars, Jack Miles and Richard Friedman, have traced God's changes in the Old Testament. God started out full of youthful enthusiasm and bold deeds. As he matured, however, his actions gave way to words and eventually to silence. God the warrior became the Ancient of Days. An appreciation of this process, however, depends upon use of the Hebrew rather than the Christian Bible, because the order of the two differs. The Hebrew Bible concludes with the Writings. The Christian Bible concludes with the Books of the Prophets, a better lead-in to the New Testament because Jesus fulfilled what the prophets proclaimed.

A nameless narrator begins the Bible by recounting the creation of the universe by God. We aren't told who God is or where he was born or who his parents are or what he looks like. He is defined by his actions. Although he appears to be tremendously powerful—he creates simply by willing creation—he puzzlingly rests after six days of labor. Miles asks, "Has it cost him more than we noticed at the time? Is he weaker than he lets on?"

After creating Adam and Eve, God gave them an order: "Be fruitful and multiply; fill the earth and subdue it." Only one thing was forbidden: "Of the tree of the knowledge of good and evil you shall not eat, for on the day that you eat of it you shall surely die." A serpent came along and told Eve that if she ate the fruit "You will not surely die." Eve ate the fruit and convinced Adam to do likewise. The serpent told the truth while God didn't; no one died on that day (although the entire event could be a metaphorical account of humankind's spiritual death). The human couple, suddenly aware of their nakedness, covered up with fig leaves and hid. Sensing something wrong, God sought them out but, strange for someone so powerful, had to ask "Where are you?" Angrily he sentenced them to miserable lives but took the time and the care to clothe them in animal skins. God then said—to whom is unclear, perhaps to other gods or to the heavenly host—that "the man has become like one of us, to know good and evil" and he booted the couple out of Eden lest they eat of the tree of life and "live forever." Again Miles asks, "If God's only motive in making mankind was that mankind should be in God's image, and if God himself lives forever, then why should mankind not live forever?"

The first parents produced two sons, Cain and Abel. Although God hadn't prohibited murder, he became very upset when Cain killed his brother. Nonetheless life went on for many generations until a most peculiar turn of events occurred: "The sons of God came in to the daughters of men and they bore children." According to Genesis 6, the offspring of the meeting between angels and women were mighty men of renown, but legend has it that they were monstrous demons. Bitter with rage God decided to flood the earth and to destroy all the humans and animals, "for I am sorry that I made them." He spared only Noah, some of his kin, and the creatures on Noah's Ark. When the flood was over, Noah presented the first burnt offering. God smelled the soothing aroma, proclaimed that he would never again destroy every living thing, warned humans against shedding each other's blood (was he jealous that humans had usurped his prerogative to destroy?), and said that mankind's duty was to "be fruitful and multiply."

God became somewhat obsessed with procreation, the only positive human behavior that he demanded. Four times during covenant negotiations God promised Abraham spectacular fertility. When Abraham's old, barren wife laughed upon hearing that she would have a son, God peevishly told Abraham to shape up and fly right or else the promise of fertility might be withdrawn. In addition to the general demand that procreation proceed apace, God even intervened by "opening up the womb" of individuals such as Leah and Rachel. The Israelites fulfilled God's command and multiplied so prolifically in Egypt that the Egyptian king ordered the death of newborn Jewish boys: "Look, the people of the children of Israel are more and mightier than we." (Ex. 9:1). This threat to his chosen people was an unintended consequence of God's fertility program, and it spurred him to develop a new identity. Until now he had been a creator, then a cosmic destroyer, then a personal God. In the past he had been open to bargaining, such as when Jacob promised to accept him as his God only if he agreed to provide Jacob with food, clothing, protection, and a safe return home (Gen. 28:20–22). Now it was time for war and for God to become a warrior who spoke with thunder, exploded like a volcano, and bargained with no one.

He provided Moses with a strategy for getting the Israelites out of Egypt and promised to strike hard and fast. He not only killed all Egyptian first-born children but also sent plagues of boils and lice and locusts and darkness. Additionally he intervened psychologically by hardening the Egyptians' hearts so that they could not act to avoid all the death and misery. The great victory song of Moses proclaimed that, "The Lord is a man of war . . . Your right hand, O Lord, has dashed the enemy in pieces" (Ex.15).

Flush with victory, God decided to impose laws governing the behavior of the Israelites. In the very first commandment he admitted to jealousy and warned that no other gods should be worshipped before him. Within forty days, alas, Moses had to gather the sons of Levi and slaughter some of the Israelites because they had reverted to idol worship. The warrior God spoke: "Let every man put on his sword . . . and let every man kill his brother, his neighbor, and his kin" (Ex. 32:27). God demanded much blood both in ritual sacrifices and on the battle field, even if it meant killing one's family. He was ruthless; after defeating the Amalekites, he boasted of blotting out their memory. Then, amazingly, God passed before Moses and proclaimed that he was "merciful and gracious, longsuffering, and abounding in goodness and truth, keeping mercy for thousands, forgiving iniquity, transgression, and sin; yet he does not clear the guilty, visiting the iniquity of the fathers upon the children and the children's children to the third and fourth generations" (Ex. 34:6–7).

In Genesis and Exodus God passed through a dramatic childhood and turbulent adolescence to establish his identity. Now it was time to pause and consolidate his gains. In Leviticus, the third book of Moses, rules for living a pure life were spelled out in detail. These rules were written after the Israelites' exile in Babylon (587–538 B.C.)

and emphasized that God's protection depended upon adherence to complex rituals and laws. Miles characterizes the fourth book, Numbers, as a book of "mutual irritability . . . Israel complains about Moses, Moses complains about Israel, God complains about Israel, Israel complains about God, God complains about Moses, and Moses complains about God." Balaam even complained about his donkey! Everyone was angry and on edge. God ordered the slaughter of Midianite males because they influenced the Israelites to worship Baal. When the army showed some mercy, Moses ordered the officers to "kill every male among the little ones, and kill every woman who has known a man intimately." The soldiers were allowed to keep the virgins as booty.

In Deuteronomy, the fifth book, Moses followed God's orders and told the Israelites that they must love God with all their heart, soul, and strength, that they must follow his commandments and laws, and that they must demonstrate a proper attitude: "Therefore circumcise the foreskin of your heart, and be stiff-necked no longer." Moses described God as mighty, awesome, impartial, and not given to taking bribes. He administers justice to orphans and widows and gives food and shelter to strangers. Because he loves the Israelites he has chosen them to be "a special treasure above all the peoples on the face of the earth." All in all, God seemed to be nice, loving, and loveable. But he wanted people to fear him too. Forget your place and he'll strike you with plague, consumption, fever, boils, tumors, scabs, blindness, and madness. He'll kill your animals and make sure that other men will sleep with your wife. He'll send such famine that mothers will hide their afterbirth from family members and eat it secretly (28:56–57). Talk about tough love!

Moses then recited the words of a song about God's power to kill and to give life, to wound and to heal, to have compassion on his servants and to render vengeance on his enemies. "He is the Rock, his work is perfect." If the words were meant to sway God to compassion, they didn't work. They were, in fact, Moses' swan song. After having done God's bidding and successfully having led his people through holy hell to the edge of Canaan, the promised land, Moses met an unkind fate. God, who was supposedly merciful, gracious, and forgiving of iniquity, transgression, and sin, decided to punish Moses with death. And what was the terrible sin of Moses? We're back to the rocks again. When the Israelites were dying of thirst in the desert, God had told Moses and Aaron to "gather the congregation and speak to the rock before their eyes, and it will yield its water." Instead of speaking to the rock, Moses struck it with his rod. The miracle happened anyway; the water came out abundantly and the congregation and their animals drank. At that time God spoke to Moses and Aaron: "Because you did not believe me, to hallow me in the eyes of the children of Israel, therefore you shall not bring this assembly into the land which I have given them" (Num 20:12). Shortly afterwards he stripped Aaron of his garments and let him die on a mountaintop. God left Moses to lead the Israelites. Now it was his turn to die at the hands of the Rock whose work was perfect. In the big scheme of things, was Moses' behavior so horrible? Didn't all his subsequent labors for God's sake count for anything? Even the Believer's Study Bible notes: "We are not explicitly told all the details of Moses' and Aaron's sin." Was there more to God's anger than Moses' so-called "rebellion"? Was he threatened because Moses had created a miracle on his own?

We now pass into the books of the former prophets (Joshua, Judges, I and II Samuel, I and II Kings). God was on the warpath and even appeared to Joshua: "A man stood opposite him with His sword drawn in His hand . . . as Commander of the army of the Lord I have now come." The Canaanites didn't stand a chance. In battle after battle they were "exterminated" not because of any harm they had done to the Israelites but simply because they happened to live in the land that God wanted for his chosen people. But then some Israelites took to living with the Canaanites. God was enraged: "You have not obeyed me . . . I am not going to drive out these nations before you. They shall become your oppressors" (Judges 2:2-3). The army broke up into factions, each controlled by a separate leader, and the area sunk into brutal lawlessness.

The books of Samuel and of Kings tell about the establishment of a monarchy with Saul as the first king. He offended God by showing mercy to an enemy king; God had ordered him to kill every "man and woman, infant and nursing child." Saul committed suicide. Then David became king and God showed a new side of himself. He promised to establish and keep David's throne forever. Most amazing was his promise never to withdraw his favor from David: "I will be his father and he will be my son" (2 Sam. 7:14). David proceeded to alienate God in a number of ways, especially by having an affair with Bathsheba, a married Canaanite woman, and arranging for the death of her husband. David's son, Solomon, eventually became king. He built a grand temple but had a thousand wives and concubines, many of whom were foreigners. He turned to the goddess Astarte and built a temple to the abominable god Molech.

What was God to do? Time and time again his chosen people failed to heed warnings to follow his commandments. Instead, they imitated other nations, broke their covenant with him, and worshipped

Baal. Rather than inflicting punishment himself, God tried something different. He allowed the Assyrians and Babylonians to conquer the Israelites and take them into an exile of captivity.

The story temporarily ends at this bleak point as we enter the fifteen books of the latter prophets from Isaiah to Malachi. These writers introduced a new complexity to God. He had had enough of burnt offerings, animal blood, and incense: "Bring no more futile sacrifices." Instead, he wanted his people to "Learn to do good; seek justice, rebuke the aggressor, defend the fatherless, plead for the widow. Come now, and let us reason together" (Is. 1:17–18). Wealth was no longer a sign of godliness, and nose jewels and mirrors now reflected only haughtiness. God had punished the Israelites, and he would punish his agents, the Assyrians and the Babylonians, too. Even Jeremiah with his constant, troublesome questions—"Why does the way of the wicked prosper?"—and self-pity seemed to get on God's nerves. Uniquely he first forbade Jeremiah to marry or have children, and then wouldn't even let him give comfort to mourners. Finally God said that he "was against the prophets who use their tongues and say, 'He says' . . . The oracle of the Lord you shall mention no more" (Jer. 24:31–36). God wanted a peaceable, transformed world where "the wolf shall dwell with the lamb . . . The cow and the bear shall feed and their young shall lie down together." A prince descended from King David will rule and he will judge the poor with righteousness, be equitable with the meek and slay the wicked. He will assemble the outcasts from Israel from the four corners of the earth to conquer all the nations and to teach them: "For out of Zion shall go forth the law, and from Jerusalem the word of the Lord."

OLD SOLDIERS NEVER DIE: GOD LIVES FOREVER

God himself recognized that it was impossible for anyone to know him: "His understanding is unsearchable . . . Truly thou art a God who hides yourself." Yet now he promised to "Comfort, yes, comfort my people! Speak tenderly to Jerusalem, and cry out to her that her warfare is ended, that her iniquity is pardoned . . . You shall no longer be called forsaken . . . and as the bridegroom rejoices over the bride, so shall your God rejoice over you" (Is. 40:1–2;62:4–5). In the process of his maturation God had discovered the redeeming power of suffering and of love, but not without a struggle. Both he and his bride, Israel, had engaged in a vicious duet of taunting and hurting, deceiving and deserting, but now he wanted a stable, I'm-yours-till-I-die, loving relationship. To this end he decided to reveal a secret that must have bothered him. When speaking of the failure of the Israelites to obey his laws, he admitted to the elders of Israel that "I gave them laws that were not good and rules by which they could not live; and I defiled them through their gifts by making them sacrifice by fire all their first born, to make them desolate; I did it that they might know that I am the Lord" (Ezek. 20:25). What a confession! The Israelites had been punished for obeying God's bad laws. In a modern courtroom, especially with a Los Angeles jury, the Israelites would be found "not guilty" and a prosecutor might well consider charging God with entrapment.

The Bible proceeds to the Writings, beginning with Psalms and Proverbs. Prophecy no longer was of much consequence. The time had come for contemplation, "to perceive the words of understanding, to receive the instruction of wisdom, justice, judgement, and equity" (Prov. 1:2–3). One bit of wisdom was that "The Lord made everything for a purpose, even the wicked for an evil day" (Prov. 16:14). God had to confront his own wickedness in the book of Job. For no reason other than a bet with the devil, God allowed Job to suffer. Guiltless, Job was forced to endure a living hell. Job ends up repenting, although why is unclear since he had done nothing wrong. In fact, God may have been the penitent. His last words in the Old Testament were a rebuke to Job's three friends. He ordered them to present a burnt offering together with Job "because you have not spoken of me what is right, as my servant Job has."

God is not only silent from this point on, but he isn't even mentioned in the Song of Songs or Esther, who managed to save the Jews without God's help. In Daniel God becomes "the Ancient of Days" who slowly fades away as angelic figures and a "glorious man" spur on the action.

The Hebrew Bible's dramatic plot, which had been suspended in the book of II Kings when the Israelites were sent into exile, picks up again in Ezra and Nehemiah. God roused the Persian king to allow the return of some Jews to Jerusalem so that they might reconstruct the destroyed Temple. Local laborers who offered to help were rebuffed: "We alone will build it." Ezra persevered against governmental resistance and work stoppages. He had told the king that "The hand of our God is held out in blessing all who seek Him," but it was the hand of the king that allowed Ezra's success. The Jews labored alone and then decided without any prompting from God to divorce and expel their pagan wives and children. Meanwhile Nehemiah, "the king's cupbearer" (male love-toy), convinced the king to allow him to lead a large wave of Jews out of exile in order to fortify the damaged wall of Jerusalem. He arrived and took charge: half of his "servants" worked while the others protected them from possible attack. The job was completed in fifty-two days. Ezra then read aloud the laws of Moses from a holy scroll. The people took an oath to follow God's commandments, ordinances, and statutes. Ezra opened the scroll for everyone to see, "Then they bowed their heads and prostrated themselves before the Lord with their faces to the ground" (Neh. 8:5–6). God did not actually appear before them as he had done with Moses when the law had been first presented on Mount Sinai. This time he didn't need to speak or make an appearance. Everything of importance that he had to say was written on a scroll. In a sense, God himself wasn't needed anymore. Was the Ancient of Days saddened by this turn of events or was he relieved? His response, alas, was not recorded.

As we follow the course of events in the Hebrew Bible, we see a God who started out full of vim and vinegar, who intervened directly in human affairs, and who appeared to Moses at Mount Sinai. After Moses he would only make himself known in visions and dreams (Num. 12:6–8). The biblical choice of verbs is significant: God is revealed to Samuel and he appeared to Solomon, but then he doesn't "reveal" himself or "appear" to anyone else. In the early part of the Bible he was associated with wind, earthquakes, and fire, but in the revelation to Elijah the text specifically notes that "the Lord was not in the wind . . . [or] . . . in the earthquake . . . [or] . . . in the fire" (1 Kin. 19:12). God's process of distancing himself from people was hastened by his decision to have prophets speak for him and was paralleled by an escalating boldness of humans in their behavior towards him and in taking control of their own destiny. Consider the movement in the following chronological events: Adam and Eve meekly submitted to God's commands; Abraham questioned God's decision to destroy Sodom and Gomorrah; Jacob physically wrestled with God and said "I will not let You go unless You bless me"; Moses argued against killing the Israelites who worshipped the statue of the gold calf, "so the Lord relented from the harm which he said he would do to his people"; God allowed royal rulers from the lineage of David to keep their thrones even if they committed iniquities; God was involved in Elisha's early miracles, but after Elisha died a dead man was brought back to life simply by coming into contact with Elisha's bones; Esther saved the Jews without God's help.

In his book, *The Disappearance of God*, Friedman writes, "God cedes (or transfers? or relinquishes?) more and more of the visible control of events to human beings themselves. Or do humans take it? Or is it neither of these; but rather, like children growing and separating from their parents, the biblical story too is about the growing, maturing, and natural separating of humans from their creator and parent."

WHAT'S IN A WORD? GOD'S WORD BECOMES JESUS

The Hebrew Bible begins with the Books of Moses, which contain the holy laws of God regulating human behavior. It concludes with the reading of these laws to the Jews who had returned from captivity in Babylon to Jerusalem. God himself was in hiding or had retired from the scene, but he provided his words on a scroll; obedience to these words became the guiding principle of Jewish life. The old religion of bloody sacrifices was over; not only did God seem not to want them anymore but also, with the destruction of the Temple in Jerusalem by the Romans in 70 A.D., the only site for sacrifices no longer existed.

In the New Testament, God the Father, leery perhaps and tired of dealing with stiff-necked, rebellious humans, sent his energetic son Jesus to earth. Jesus was more than an alternative to God's holy words, rather he was their fulfillment. The Gospel of John begins: "In the beginning was the Word [Logos] and the Word was with God, and the Word was God . . . And the Word became flesh and dwelt among us, and we labeled his glory, the glory as of the only begotten of the Father, full of grace and truth."

How exactly did the "Word become flesh"? Mary was the undisputed mother of Jesus, but who was the biological father? In Jewish history a Messiah was to descend from King David. The Gospel of Matthew begins with the genealogy of Jesus, starting with Abraham who begot Isaac, passing through David who begot Solomon, and ending with "Joseph the husband of Mary, of whom was born Jesus who is called Christ." Matthew doesn't say that Joseph begot Jesus, but at the end of the first chapter he notes that Joseph "called his name Jesus." Legally at that time the man who named a child was considered to be the child's father (although Luke 2:21 states that the name was given by an angel before Jesus even was conceived).

There is something odd about Matthew's genealogical list; over forty male descendants are named but only five females (Tamar, Rahab, Ruth, Bathsheba, and Mary). Why were these women selected? Tamar, posing as a temple prostitute, conceived two children with her father-in-law (Gen. 38). Rahab was a descendant of the incestuous union of Lot and his daughters. Ruth got Boaz to marry her after exposing his genitals and spending the night with him (Ruth 3–4). Bathsheba conceived a child with David while she was married to Uriah (2 Sam. 12:24); Matthew omits her name but refers to her as "the wife of Uriah," the better to call attention to her adultery. While not exactly a rogue's gallery these are hardly the women that come to mind as fitting associates of the mother of God. According to one scholar, Matthew "seems to be telling us in an audible aside that the heir had often been born out of the direct line or irregularly. [The women] are forced upon our attention, as if to prepare us for still greater irregularity in the last stage." In the fourth century, St. Jerome noted, "None of the holy women are mentioned in the Savior's genealogy, but only those whom Scripture censures, so that he who came for the sake of sinners, being born of sinners, might blot out all sin." In fact, the birth of Jesus was irregular; Mary "was found with child of the Holy Spirit." She was censured, too, by those who spread rumors that the father of Jesus really was a Roman soldier named Panthera.

The turning into flesh (incarnation) of God posed all sorts of problems for Christians. If there was one God who had a son, doesn't this mean there were now two Gods? By adding the Holy Spirit to the mix, were there then really three Gods? Various solutions were developed that were ultimately deemed heretical. Some declared that Jesus only seemed to be a man but in reality was a spirit who exhibited an appearance in flesh. These believers held that Jesus did not himself suffer death: "If he suffered he was not God. If he was God, he did not suffer." Moreover, he never moved his bowels or urinated; as a spirit he was incorruptible, and therefore he did not process food and liquid as a human would. Others held that Jesus couldn't be a god because he was begotten by his father and thus did not exist forever. He may have been wise and virtuous, but since he ate, drank, slept, and suffered like a human he couldn't possibly be a god who, by definition, is perfect and unchangeable.

The debate was intense and often practically incomprehensible. Latin and Greek theologians fought with each other both intellectually and physically. At Church Councils mobs of ruffians were hired to intimidate the opposition. Words such as *theotokos, homousios, hypostasis, ousia, persona, essentia,* and *prosperon* flew threw the rarified ecclesiastical air like daggers. In 325 A.D. the Council of Nicea came up with a creed that eventually was accepted: "We believe in one God, the Father almighty . . . And in one Lord Jesus Christ, the Son of God, begotten from the Father, that is, from the substance of the Father, God from God, . . . begotten not made, of one substance with the Father . . . Who . . . becoming man, suffered and rose again on the third day . . . And in the Holy Spirit." Opponents argued that if the Father is unbegotten (a property of God), then how could Jesus be God, since the Bible clearly states that he was begotten by his Father? Also, if the Father and the Son have the same properties, then the Son must beget a Son who, in turn, must beget a Son and so on without end. And where does this leave the Holy Spirit? At the Church Council of Constantinople in 381 A.D., an addition was made to the phrase at the end of the Nicene Creed: to "And in the Holy

Spirit" was added "the Lord and Life-giver, who proceeds from the Father, who with the Father and the Son is worshipped together and glorified together, who spoke through the prophets."

And how was the controversy about Christ's two natures settled? The winning side at the Council of Chalcedon in 451 A.D. declared that Christ was "one substance with us as regarded his manhood; like us in all respects except sin; as regards his Godhead, begotten of the father before the ages ... recognized in two natures without confusion, without change, without separation, the difference of the natures being in no wise taken away by reason of the union, but rather the properties of each being preserved and coming together into one person and one hypostasis—not parted into two persons, but are one and the same Son and only begotten, the divine Logos [Word], the Lord Jesus Christ."

Holy smokes! The words "without confusion" were probably included because everyone was so confused. If you, dear reader, can't fully comprehend the meaning (don't forget that I have presented a fairly clear summary), imagine what the host of relatively uneducated early Christians must have felt. In fact, a major reason why Islam was accepted so readily by the populace of the Middle East, tired of the incessant debates over the Trinity and Christ's nature, was its simplicity: Allah is God, Muhammad is his prophet, and that's all there is to it.

IMAGINE THAT: THE IMAGE OF JESUS, THE PERFECT MAN

What kind of a man was Jesus? Was he tall or short or just about average in height? Was he handsome or ugly or just average in his looks? Isaiah in an Old Testament prefiguration of Jesus described the Suffering Servant as follows: "Like a sapling he grew up in front of us, like a root in arid ground. Without beauty, without majesty we saw him, no looks to attract our eyes; a thing despised and rejected by man, a man of sorrows and familiar with suffering, a man to make people hide their faces; he was despised and we did not esteem him." (53:2-3). Is this how he appeared, or was he more like a "typical" Jewish rabbi of the time? Or, since he was "the second David," was he regal and king-like? Or, perhaps, was he a more cosmopolitan, attractive Greek type of person, maybe even as swashbuckling as Odysseus, the shrewd sailor whose ship's mast was a cross?

Because it takes a certain degree of sophistication to worship and pray to a pure, formless spirit, most religions endorse idols and drawings. The Old Testament God, however, absolutely forbade this practice: "You shall not make for yourself a carved image, or any likeness of anything that is in heaven above, or that is in the earth beneath, or that is in the water beneath the earth" (Ex.20:4). Taking this commandment to heart, the early Christians avoided sacred images. Eventually one image was allowed, the communion wafer. Only the wafer actually contained Christ and, therefore, was a true image of him. Moreover, at the Lord's Supper he told his disciples, "This is my body which is given for you; do this in remembrance of me" (Lk.22:19). All other images were forbidden because Christ was the image of God who was by definition beyond description, comprehension, change, and measure.

Not so fast, said opponents of this policy during arguments that raged especially throughout the eighth and ninth centuries. There's nothing wrong with images because God himself, supposedly in consultation with Jesus and the Holy Spirit, was the original image-maker: "Let us make man in our image" (Gen. 1:26). Since Christ "is the image of the invisible God" (Col. 1:15), a statue or drawing of Christ is simply an image of the Image of the invisible God. Further, Romans 1:19 states that "Ever since God created the world his everlasting power and deity—however invisible—have been there for the mind to see in the things he has made." Pagan idols, of course, were earthly images worth no more than the cost of the materials used to construct them. Christian images, however, were sacred because they depicted Christ, of whom the Gospel of John says, "All things were made through him, and without him was not anything made that was made" (1:3). Christ himself took on human form and thus was a living image. By becoming a man Christ entered into human history and, therefore, could be depicted in images that documented history.

In the earliest representations Christ usually appeared more or less like a Greco-Roman, clean-shaven, muscular, and with curly hair in ringlets. The image that has survived, however, came from the Eastern Church, where he had a beard, moustache, flowing hair, penetrating eyes, and a slim but sturdy body. Over the ages, of course, artists and poets have taken liberties with Christ; he has been depicted as everything from a cosmic king to a slave. In *The Everlasting Gospel,* the poet William Blake (1757–1827) even wrote:

> The Vision of Christ that thou dost see
> Is my Visions Greatest Enemy
> Thine has a great hook nose like thine
> Mine has a snub nose like to mine

In an aside Blake noted that, "I always thought that Jesus Christ was a Snubby or I should not have worshipd him if I had thought he had been one of those long spindle nosed rascals."

Ephesians 4:13 referred to Christ as "the perfect man" and urged everyone to imitate him by walking in love; by avoiding fornication, impurity, promiscuity, coarse talk, and foul jokes; by speaking the truth and helping one another; by not holding grudges or letting the sun set on your anger; by keeping away from bad companions and not getting drunk. In addition men should love their wives (and wives should regard their husbands as they regard the Lord); children should be obedient to their parents, and slaves to their masters. Some final advice: "Put on God's armor . . . with truth buckled around your waist, and integrity for a breast plate . . . carrying the shield of faith . . . accept salvation from God to be your helmet and receive the word of God from the Spirit to use as a sword" (5:19–17). It's not a bad list, unless you happen to be a slave or a teenager with nasty parents. Christ himself kept some bad companions and was evasive about speaking the truth. Also, he was way off the mark on one thing; it's been almost two thousand years and the great tribulation, the abomination of desolation, the great apocalypse that he said was impending has still, fortunately, not occurred. Christ wasn't born perfect; "He learned obedience through suffering" (Heb. 5:7). In conversations with his mother he was brusque, maybe even a little rude. He was snide with the Gentile woman who asked him to heal her sick daughter; he compared them to dogs, but was won over by her quick-witted retort (Mark 7:24–30; Matt. 15:21–28). Christ probably wouldn't have endorsed "perfect" on a psychological profile; when a rich, young ruler addressed him as "Good teacher," Christ said, "Why do you call me good? No one is good but one, that is, God" (Mark 10:18).

WHAT DID JESUS KNOW AND WHEN DID HE KNOW IT?

According to Hebrews 2:17, "In all things he had to be made like his brethren, that he might be a merciful and faithful high priest of God's religion." Since Jesus ate food, it's likely that he felt hunger. He slept, so he must have gotten tired. He displayed his temper when confronting the money-changers, so he must have felt anger. He suffered and must have felt pain during his crucifixion. One emotion never attributed to him in the Bible is laughter (according to one German theologian, this was a sign of Christ's perfection), though it's difficult to believe that he never laughed throughout his life. And then, alas, there is the one emotion that we have been conditioned never to associate with either Jesus or God the Father, namely sexual passion. As a perfect man Jesus presumably would have a perfectly functioning body and, at the least, would have experienced pleasurable, involuntary nocturnal emissions. Why is it almost impossible for a believer not to shudder with distaste upon reading the previous sentence? Hunger, fatigue, anger, and suffering do not diminish Christ's godliness, so why should sexual feelings? The Christian, unspoken shame of sexuality is not, I suspect, a mystery of God but rather the legacy of a few powerful men who succeeded against overwhelming odds in making us all uncomfortable with our bodies.

Some theologians have held that Christ was not only a paragon of virtue but also that he knew everything there was to know about everything. This seems unlikely. It's difficult to imagine that as a newborn infant he knew everything. He had to grow to knowledge intellectually just as he had to grow to maturity physically. The Bible only tells us about Christ's birth, about one incident at age twelve, and then about his last years of life when he was in his thirties. From this scant record it is difficult to know how he grew in knowledge, especially how he knew that he was the Son of God.

One of the most amazing aspects of the life of Jesus as told in the Gospels is its precise correspondence to Old Testament events and prophecies. Matthew, for example, says that baby Jesus and his parents fled from King Herod by traveling to Egypt in order to fulfill the prophecy of Hosea ("Out of Egypt I called my son.") None of the other Gospels contains this episode. So what are we to believe? Either events occurred exactly as Matthew presented them or Matthew invented the story so that Jesus would be thought of as an important person, a second Moses (who also traveled through Egypt to escape persecution). Most scholars believe that the story was invented. There are many other Gospel stories about Jesus that refer back to the Old Testament but that are not so obviously made up. Let us suppose that many of the events really did occur. One explanation would be that Christ's fate was the playing-out of history. Another explanation would be that Christ himself orchestrated the events of the last year of his life in accordance with his knowledge of how the Messiah should behave. Several scholars have hinted at the possibility that Christ, believing himself to be the Messiah, *consciously* behaved in a manner that fulfilled old prophecies. Hugh Schonfield, for example, has written a respectful yet rational account of Christ's life. Although it goes against the grain of two thousand years of supernatural explanations and contains a sensational plot, the book presents some ideas that are worth considering.

Schonfield holds that Christ's birth was quite normal but that there was a state of near hysteria among the Jews at that time. Many thought that Israel was entering into the End of the Days, a period in which the forces of evil would intensify and bring great suffering. Books, many of which contained oracles about the End of the Days and the coming of a Messiah, were in the process of being accepted into the body of holy scriptures known to us as the Old Testament. The temple in Jerusalem had been converted into a shrine to Zeus, and the Maccabees had engaged in a rebellion. King Herod the Great (37–4 B.C.) ruled the area through fear and intimidation. The revolts that followed his death were crushed by Roman soldiers who cruci-fied thousands of insurgent Jews. Jewish sects vied for spiritual preem-inence. "The whole condition of the Jewish people was abnormal. The strangest tales and imaginings could find ready credence . . . People were on edge, neurotic." Expectations were high that an Anointed One, a Messiah, would close out the End of the Days, usher in the Kingdom of God, and save the race of Israel. Jesus would come to think of himself as the fulfillment of the messianic hope. However, "He was no charlatan, willfully and deliberately misleading his people, well knowing that his posing as the Messiah was fraudulent . . . On the contrary, no one could be more sure of his vocation than Jesus . . . but this does not require us to think of him as omniscient and infallible."

We know little about the first thirty years of Christ's life. Luke is the only Gospel to tell the story of the twelve-year-old Jesus who slipped away from his parents for three days while he amazed the teachers in the temple with his questions, answers, and understand-ings. (This story is reminiscent of a passage in the autobiography of Josephus, a Jewish historian with whom the author of Luke was famil-iar, where Josephus recounts that as a boy of fourteen, he was often consulted by the chief priests of Jerusalem.) The Jesus story ends when he chides his parents for worrying about him: "Did you not know that I must be busy with my Father's affairs?" (2:49). His words would seem to indicate that he knew then of his deity. However, if this were the case, we would have to believe that he concealed this fact from everyone, healed no one, and performed no miracles until he was more than thirty years old. Such a scenario doesn't fit right. Jesus was a man of action, and it's difficult to believe that as a deity he would have done nothing of note for so many years.

Joseph, the human father of Jesus, probably died when Jesus was a teenager. Presumably they had worked together as carpenters ever since Jesus was a child. Whatever intimations of deity Jesus had must have been buttressed by a powerful and positive relationship with his human father because the path that Jesus chose was to identify him-self as the Son of a heavenly Father. Indeed, the voice from heaven at Christ's baptism could have been spoken by any proud father to his son: "This is my beloved Son, in whom I am well pleased" (Matt. 3:17). At any rate, these intimations needed time to incubate. If Christ thought that he *might* be the Messiah, he had to find out more about what was expected of him. What exactly does a Messiah do? How should a Messiah behave? To answer these questions he probably listened to priests and others familiar with prophecy. He also probably met some members of an ascetic cult called the Essenes who had established themselves in a desert town where they composed what are now known as the Dead Sea Scrolls. From the Essenes he would have learned about a Teacher of Righteousness to whom God made known all the mysteries of the words of the prophets and who would suffer horrible persecution. Indeed, the Teacher of Righteousness was called the Messiah, and he was persecuted by hostile priests of a competing Jewish sect (the Sadducees). His message was chastity, brotherly love, poverty, and penitence. The Essenes expected him to return from the dead in righteous glory. Jesus may have learned the expression "poor in spirit" from the Essenes as well as the custom of having a special "pure meal" where a priest blessed the bread and the wine that was served to the Messiah and to men of renown.

One can imagine Jesus slowly gathering information and putting the pieces of the puzzle together. He can't have been totally certain of his deity because he did nothing Messiah-like. Perhaps he was waiting for a special revelation or experience. Besides, according to prophecy, the work of the Messiah could not begin until the return of the prophet Elijah, who had been taken up to heaven from the banks of the Jordan River centuries earlier in a chariot of fire. The likelihood of this happening was not very high.

But it did happen! John the Baptist came to the River Jordan wearing a prophet's hair garment and a leather belt like Elijah's. "Repent," he said, "for the kingdom of heaven is at hand!" According to both Matthew and Luke, this was "he who was spoken of by the prophet Isaiah, saying, "The voice of one crying in the wilderness: Prepare the way of the Lord.'" Jesus, edging ever closer to his destiny, was baptized in the river by John: "And behold, the heavens opened and he saw the Spirit of God descending like a dove and coming down on him. And a voice spoke from heaven, 'This is my beloved Son, in whom I am well pleased.'" This was the special something that Jesus had been waiting for. Now he knew he was the Son of God. This moment marked the beginning of his new life and "From that time Jesus began to preach and to say, 'Repent, for the kingdom of heaven is at hand' (Matt. 4:17).

DEATH AND CIRCUMSTANCES: THE RESURRECTION

After Jesus finally knew he was the Messiah, he acted as he imagined a Messiah should act, but he wisely didn't proclaim his status. Such a proclamation would have probably led to his premature arrest by the

Romans who didn't want anyone stirring up the crowds. He spoke in parables so that he couldn't be charged with saying anything directly subversive. He chose some disciples noted for their brawn; he changed Simon's name to Peter (Rocky). He set up shop in Capernaum on the Sea of Galilee and he made sure that his fishermen disciples had boats ready in case a quick escape was called for.

He preached, healed, and performed miracles. And then, one day while walking with his disciples, he asked, "Who do men say I am?" They replied, "John the Baptist; but some say Elijah; and others, one of the prophets." He said to them, "But who do you say I am?" Peter answered, "You are Christ" . . . And he began to teach them that the Son of Man must suffer many things, and be rejected by the elders and chief priests and scribes, and be killed, and after three days rise again."

Christ then carefully developed and executed a plan, paying special attention to important prophecies, that finally resulted in his trial and crucifixion. He was very dramatic, even remembering while on the cross to recite the phrase from Psalm 22, "My God, My God, why have you forsaken me?" So far, so good. But now Schonfield's scenario takes a surprising turn. He would have it that Jesus didn't really die but rather was rescued by Joseph of Arimathea. The details of the "plot" are too complicated and even too fanciful to recount here. The only certain fact in this scenario is that Christ's crucifixion wasn't exactly kosher.

Whether by historical accident, by divine intervention, or by his own plan, Christ agitated the crowds in the temple during the days before Passover but slipped away at night. He was not arrested until Thursday evening. It could not have been planned better, if it was planned, because a quick trial on Friday morning followed by an afternoon crucifixion would maximize Christ's chance for survival. The Sabbath officially started at sunset and it was customary to cease all activities, including crucifixions, in time for the start of the Sabbath. Christ would have to spend only a few hours on the cross. According to Schonfield, this is exactly what happened.

Crucifixion was a slow, agonizing form of execution used by the Romans to deter crime. The Romans were experts and had perfected the methodology through a lot of practice; after Herod died in 4 B.C. two thousand rebel Jews had been crucified. Crosses came in two pieces, each weighing about a hundred pounds. One piece was set upright into the ground at the crucifixion site while the other piece, the horizontal beam, was carried by the condemned man. Upon arrival at the site the condemned man's back was placed over the horizontal beam, which had been attached to the upright beam. His arms were outstretched and nails were pounded between the carpal bones of both wrists (not through the hands as portrayed by most artists). The victim's feet were nailed into the upright beam. Crucifixions could be prolonged by providing a small seat support or could be hastened by breaking the victim's legs with a club. Once the legs were broken the victim's body was supported only by his wrists and upraised arms. Death occurred slowly through asphyxiation. The exhausted victim's head leaned forward and eventually blocked off the air supply. Done properly, a crucifixion could last for several days.

In Christ's case the crucifixion lasted only a few hours. His legs were not broken because the Roman soldiers thought he was already dead. A soldier did, however, stick a spear into his chest and immediately blood and water came out. "For these things were done that the Scripture should be fulfilled, 'Not one of His bones shall be broken,' and another Scripture says, 'They shall look on Him whom they pierced'" (John 19:35). Whether this piercing really occurred or was added to the story in order to fulfill the prophecy is unclear.

Physiologically, Jesus should not have died so quickly. The two thieves who were crucified alongside him didn't die quickly, so the Romans broke their legs. Schonfield proposes that it was a set up and points out that Josephus (him again!) had written about an occasion when he had personally begged the Roman ruler to let him have the bodies of three of his friends who had been crucified; two died, one recovered. Joseph of Arimathea begged the Roman ruler for Christ's body and was given permission to take it away. Here we encounter a curious question of language. According to Mark 15:43, Joseph asked for the body (*soma*) of Christ; *soma* is an ambiguous word. The Roman ruler, told that Christ was already dead, granted the corpse (*ptoma*) to Joseph (15:45). It probably is unfair to make too much of the use of these words, but it does advance the story.

Why would Jesus not want to die? He very well may have considered various scriptural texts: "Though I walk in the midst of trouble, you will revive me . . . and your right hand will save me" (Ps. 138:7); "The pangs of death surrounded me, and the flood of ungodliness made me afraid . . . He sent from above, He took me . . . He delivered me because He delighted in me" (Ps. 18:4, 16, 19); "He asked life from You, and You gave it to him . . . They devised a plot which they are not able to perform" (Ps. 21:4, 11); "After two days he will revive us; on the third day He will rise us up" (Hos. 6:2). As the Messiah it was his duty to be saved! Just as he had carefully planned his ministry to fulfill what had been prefigured in the Holy Books, he also had to carefully plan his "revival" from death. There was no deception in the way that we usually think of deception, just as there was no deception when he arranged to have a donkey on hand for his triumphal ride to Jerusalem (according to Matthew 21:2, he sent two disciples into a nearby village and said that they would conveniently find a donkey and a colt tied there) in order to fulfill the prophecy of Zechariah, "Behold, your King is coming to you . . . Lowly and riding on a donkey, a colt, the foal of a donkey" (9:9). His crucifixion "revival" was just more of the same type of arranging for things to happen.

All of this is impossible to believe and totally preposterous. But, is it any easier to believe that a man actually rose from the dead based on reports that were written several decades after the fact by totally biased authors? Thomas Jefferson wrote that he had experienced difficulty in "reconciling the idea of the Unity and the Trinity" and, as regards the New Testament account of Jesus, in "abstracting what is really his from the rubbish in which it is buried." In 1820 Jefferson clipped and pasted together material from the Bible that he considered to be the truth about Jesus. He omitted all mention of the virgin birth, the annunciation, and the resurrection! His version of the Bible ends "There they laid Jesus and rolled a great stone to the door of the sepulcher, and departed." Paul said that without the resurrection of Christ, Christianity would be a fraud. Many devout, modern scholars hold that this is not necessarily so. It is enough to believe that Christ was resurrected. For two thousand years faith in this belief has nurtured countless Christians despite the lack of proof. Besides, faith is better than proof and far more enduring. Deep and abiding faith is practically indestructible, but proof is always susceptible to future discoveries and to charges of past tampering. Even should Christ's crumbly bones be unearthed some day, the faith of true believers would persevere because, for them, "Jesus Christ is the same yesterday, today, and forever."

WHEN THE WIND BLOWS: THE HOLY SPIRIT

Having considered the Father and the Son, we now must confront the third member of the Trinity, the Holy Spirit. It's a difficult assignment because the Holy Spirit soars from heaven on the wings of a dove and descends deep into the guts of psychoanalytic ponderings. With the Holy Spirit we confront ecstasy, nudity, unintelligible languages, and gastrointestinal distress. It's a bit of a walk on the wild side and not for the meek of mind. Forewarned is forearmed!

The word "spirit" does not appear in the Bible. In Hebrew the word used is "wind," and in Greek, "breath." The Latin translation of the Bible used the word "spiritus," which comes out "spirit" in English. The Old Testament Spirit was more a cosmic wind, first hovering over the dark waters of the formless earth and then buffeting the prophets.The New Testament Spirit was more a breath, a concentrated and focused force of sanctification.The Spirit, however, can be unpredictable.

Man became a human being after the Lord God breathed into his nostrils the spirit-breath of life (Gen. 2:7).When a valley full of dried human bones was filled with God's breath, "They lived, and stood upon their feet, an exceedingly great army" (Ezek. 37:10).The Spirit helped the Israelite judges and kings to be better rulers.According to Isaiah, the Spirit acted as the literal arm of the Lord that allowed Moses to divide the Red Sea by stretching out his hand during the exodus (63:12). Because the Spirit was in him, Daniel was able to explain the mysterious writing on the wall (Dan. 5:14). But what the Spirit did best was to inspire the prophets to do their thing.And what ecstatic and sometimes crazy things they did! When Saul was anointed king, he was told that he would meet a group of prophets prophesying with all sorts of musical instruments; "Then the Spirit of God will come upon you, and you will prophesy with them and be turned into another man" (1 Sam. 10:6). Saul did meet the prophets and became mentally unbalanced; a few chapters later he tried to kill David with a spear. David fled to Samuel's house, but Saul sent men to capture him.The Spirit overcame Saul's men, who started prophesying and were unable to communicate any useful information, so Saul himself went searching. The Spirit overcame him also: "He stripped off his clothes and prophesied before Samuel . . . and lay down naked all that day and all that night.Therefore, they say:'Is Saul also among the prophets?'" (19:24). Saul went on to order the murder of priests, to consult a medium during a seance at En Dor, and finally to commit suicide with his own sword. In a different episode, Ezekiel, the most bizarre of all the prophets, said that "He stretched out what seemed to be a hand and took me by a lock of my hair; and the Spirit lifted me up between heaven and earth and brought me in visions of God to Jerusalem, to the north gate of the inner court, where the seat of the image of jealousy was" (Ezek. 8:3).

In the New Testament the Spirit received the adjective "holy" and did many wondrous things. It filled Zacharias and his wife Elizabeth when she was pregnant with John the Baptist; they prophesied that their child would be a prophet who will go before the face of the Lord to prepare his ways.When Joseph was upset at Mary's pregnancy because he couldn't have been the impregnator, an angel told him in a dream,"Do not be afraid to take Mary for your wife, for that which is conceived in her is of the Holy Spirit."At Christ's baptism the Holy Spirit descended in the form of a dove upon him (Luke 3:22). After his baptism, God anointed Jesus "with the Holy Spirit and with power" (Acts 10:38). Jesus himself said, "All sins will be forgiven the sons of men, and whatever blasphemies they may utter; but he who blasphemes against the Holy Spirit never has forgiveness and is guilty of eternal sin" (Mark 3:28–29). Paul said that a person does not belong to Christ unless he possesses the Spirit of Christ (Rom. 8:7). Additionally the death of Christ freed mankind from the domination of the Laws of Moses "so that we should serve in the newness of the Spirit and not in the oldness of the letter" (Rom. 7:6). "The written code kills, but the Spirit gives life" (2 Cor. 3:6). Anyone who repents and is baptized in the name of Jesus for the remission of sins shall receive the gift of the Holy Spirit (Acts 2:38).

One of the most interesting phenomena associated with the Holy Spirit is the often-misunderstood speaking in tongues (glossolalia) that is mentioned twice in the Bible. In Acts 2, fifty days after Christ's resurrection (the Pentecost), the disciples were all together, "And suddenly a sound came from heaven like the rush of a mighty wind . . . and there appeared to them tongues as of fire, distributed and resting on each one of them. And they were filled with the Holy Spirit and began to speak in other tongues, as the Spirit gave them utterance." Each person spoke in the language of a foreign country. "All were amazed and perplexed, saying to one another, 'What does this mean?' Others mocking said, 'They have been drinking too much new wine.'" Peter then made a long speech declaring that the men weren't drunk but rather were fulfilling the words of the prophet Joel that in the last days God will pour out his Spirit on his servants and handmaidens, who then will prophecy.

The second and much longer mention of tongues is found in 1 Corinthians 12–14, where Paul lists various gifts of the Spirit such as wisdom, faith, healing, miracles, prophecy, and speaking in tongues. Although he wished that everyone could speak in tongues, Paul regarded it as the least of the gifts of the Spirit and certainly well below prophecy: "For he who speaks in a tongue does not speak to men but to God, for no one understands him . . . He who speaks in a tongue edifies himself, but he who prophecies edifies the church" (14:3–4). Paul thanked God that he could speak in tongues but "in church I would rather speak five words with my mind, in order to instruct others, than ten thousand words in tongue" (14:19). He warned that "if the whole church assembles and all speak in tongues, and outsiders or unbelievers enter, will they not say that you are mad?" (14:23).

Paul was absolutely correct in warning about the unsettling effect on an outsider of witnessing people who vocalize strange words that are meaningless to everyone, including themselves. Surely it would scare away potential converts. Glossolalia was de-emphasized by the

Church, and St. Augustine explained it away by relegating it to the early days of the Church when it served as one of the credentials of a rudimentary faith. Except for a few instances, glossolalia disappeared until the nineteenth century. A report by Synan of a 1801 revival meeting at the University of Georgia states: "They swooned away and lay for hours in the straw prepared for those 'smitten of the Lord,' or they started suddenly to flee away and fell prostrate as if shot down by a sniper, or they took suddenly to jerking with apparently every muscle in their body until it seemed they would be torn to pieces or converted into marble, or they shouted and talked in unknown tongues." The Shakers practiced glossolalia in the 1840s, and at the dedication of the Mormon Temple in Salt Lake City, hundreds of the Church Elders spoke in tongues. Glossolalia really came to life at the turn of the twentieth century, especially in the United States and Great Britain, and it is a usual practice in Pentecostal and Holiness Churches. In the 1950s it became a component of the charismatic movement among mainstream Protestant churches and a decade later among Catholics.

The first psychological and psychiatric studies considered glossolalia to be psychopathological. Hysteria was the most cited diagnosis, although some saw it as akin to schizophrenia. It was supposedly associated with low intelligence; in a classic early formulation, an illiterate person is driven by excitement to say something but has a poor power of expression and a limited vocabulary; as the pressure of nervous energy increases, the person's mind becomes confused, the upper centers become clogged, the lower centers take over, and meaningless syllables break forth. We now know that all this is gibberish.

How glossolalia works is unclear. It doesn't appear to be associated with physical health changes. It possibly benefits depressed and anxious persons a little. It often is associated with social settings in that it identifies a person as part of a special group. It can occur in quiet or highly emotional settings, in groups or in solitary privacy, in children as well as in adults, and in upper and lower social class persons. It may occur during an altered state of consciousness but usually not. It rarely is a negative experience; most of the time it is mildly positive and sometimes very positive. It's not as weird as it seems to the outsider, although I must admit that when I saw several physicians and lawyers speaking in tongues at a charismatic church service, it gave me the willies.

The power and the oddness associated with the Holy Spirit are so striking that we rarely step back and notice that the Trinity itself is a problematic concept. The basic human social structure is a family comprised of a father, mother, and child. Psychoanalysts believe that supernatural constructs derive from human experience and that a heavenly trinity should reflect the human family. (We may arrive at the same conclusion if we acknowledge that humankind was created in God's image; the human family should reflect the divine family.) From this perspective there is something wrong about the Trinity: it contains a father God and a son God, but no mother Goddess. How did mother come to be replaced by the Holy Spirit? Dear reader, fasten your mental seat belts and we'll examine what psychoanalysts such as Freud and Ernest Jones had to say about the displacement of mother by a holy wind.

RETALIATION AND RECONCILIATION: PSYCHOANALYSIS AND THE HOLY SPIRIT

Earlier in this chapter we considered Freud's notion of human life in prehistoric times. The sons murdered their tyrannical father who kept the women for himself. They hated their father (he was strong and powerful and could punish them in many ways, including castration), but they also loved and admired him. "After they had satisfied their hate by his removal and had carried out their wish for identification with him, the suppressed tender impulses had to assert themselves. This took place in the form of remorse, a sense of guilt was formed." To assuage their guilt and to undo the murder psychologically, the sons did two things: first, they chose a totem, usually an animal, as a surrogate for the father; they worshipped the animal and protected its life as a kind of reconciliation with their father. Second, they denied themselves sexual access to the liberated women. Each of the sons wanted all of the women for himself, but the sons realized that if they wanted to live together then an incest prohibition had to be instituted. It is this scenario, namely the guilt of the sons and the attempt to assuage this guilt and to conciliate the injured father through subsequent obedience, that forms the backdrop for all religions. In fact all religions "are reactions aiming at the same great event with which culture began and which ever since has not yet let mankind come to rest." The son's ambivalence towards father and the joy in triumphing over him remain, however, and "we shall not be surprised to find that a part of the son's defiance also reappears, often in the most remarkable disguises and envisions, in the formation of later religions."

In Christianity man's original sin was an offense against God the Father. This offence must have been the murder of the Father, because mankind was redeemed by the sacrificial death of the Son. The law of retaliation, deeply rooted in human feeling, demands an eye for an eye, a tooth for tooth, a life for a life. Reconciliation with the Father is made more thorough because simultaneously with this sacrifice there follows the complete renunciation of women, for whose sake mankind rebelled against the Father. But the pride and defiance of the Son asserted itself and the Son himself became a God and his religion (Christianity) displaced the religion of the Father (Judaism). The Father wasn't angry, however, because he received a co-equal place with his Son as Gods of the new religion, and because the Son's crucifixion was a gratifying display of remorseful piety. In fact, the Father's wrath was averted, as well as his threat of castration, and the Son's guilt controlled by the periodic reenactment of the crucifixion in the holy mass. There is no place for a mother atop this religion, her presence would constantly inflame the incestuous desires of the Son and interfere with the Father–Son reconciliation.

The Holy Spirit enters the story during the impregnation of Mary. According to Jones, "The impregnation itself is affected by the angel's word of greeting and the breath of a dove simultaneously entering the Madonna's ear. The Dove itself, which is understood to represent the Holy Ghost, emanates from the Father's mouth. The Holy Ghost, therefore, and His breath play here the part of a sexual agent, and appear where we would logically find a phallus and semen respectively." Superficially this type of impregnation implies a denial of the Father's potency, but at a deeper level it implies an exaggerated sense of the Father's virility because he can make a woman pregnant simply by talking to or breathing on her. The word became flesh.

Jones examines the connection between breath and impregnation. The mouth usually has a feminine significance in that it is a receptive organ but it also can have a masculine significance because it contains a phallus-like tongue and emits fluids such as breath and spit (spitting is a common folkloric symbol for the male sexual act; a boy is "the spitting image" of his father). While we consciously think of breathing in terms of inhaling and exhaling air, respiratory processes tend to be interpreted in the unconscious mind in terms of gastrointestinal processes, especially the passing of gas. Breathing and speaking, for example, are both treated in the unconscious mind as equivalents of the act of passing gas, and there is a corresponding displacement of affect from the gas to the spoken word. This can be demonstrated by phrases such as "He is full of hot air," "a long-winded speech," "He's nothing but a gasbag." In addition to wind and speech, other symbolic equivalents of intestinal gas in the unconscious mind include music, thought, fire, incense, and soul.

Some children have the early fantasy that impregnation occurs mysteriously and that mother's belly swells during pregnancy because father transfers his intestinal gas to mother. At any rate, air

emitted downwards as gas becomes associated with air emitted
upwards as breath, and both breath and wind are closely associated
with impregnation and sexual intercourse. One of the most quoted
brief poems in the English language, for example, is:

> Western wind when will thou blow
> The small rain down shall rain.
> Christ, that my love were in my arms
> And I in my bed again.

Thus, the infantile human experience of passing gas gave rise to
the notion of spirits as well as to a fantasy of impregnation.
Admittedly, it is horribly painful to associate all this with the conception of Jesus but, according to Jones, "this most repellent of sexual
phantasies lends itself better than any other to the conveyance of the
most exalted and spiritual ideas of which the mind is capable."

The Dove, instrumental in effecting Mary's impregnation, is a phallic symbol. In fact, an early legend relates that old man Joseph was
chosen as Mary's husband because a dove flew out of his penis and
landed on his head; the story was changed over the years so that the
dove escaped from Joseph's rod and flew to his head. Either way,
Joseph was approved because he could still get an erection despite
his age. The dove, however, also has a feminine aspect, namely its association with love through the gentle, caressing nature of its wooing.
It is one of the most effeminate phallic symbols.

The Holy Spirit is a composite of the original Mother Goddess along
with the creative essence of the Father God. Jesus said that the one
unpardonable sin was blasphemy against the Holy Spirit. This is perfectly understandable because "such an offence would symbolically be
equivalent to defilement of the Holy Mother and an attempted castration of the Father. It would be a repetition of the primordial sin, the
beginning of all sin, gratification of the Oedipus impulse." The feminine
component of the Holy Spirit is overwhelmed by the masculine component as a means of countering the Son's Oedipal desires for Father-
murder and Mother-incest. Ties to the Mother are cut and a close relationship to the Father established through the fiction that the Son has
been re-born by the Father. "Put in terms of the instincts this means that
an incestuous heterosexual fixation is replaced by a sublimated homosexuality." As a male figure that also has the female capacity to bear children, the Holy Spirit is a hermaphroditic ideal of tremendous importance. "We have in it a great reason for the enormous civilizing influence of Christianity, since the civilizing of primitive man essentially
means the mastery of the Oedipus complex and the transformation of

much of it into sublimated homosexuality (i.e., herd instinct), without which no social community can exist." The Mother Goddess survived with a lowered status in the person of Mary. She could not remain a goddess because she inspired incest wishes in the Son and thus prevented his reconciliation with the Father. In this regard it is interesting that Catholicism places Mary high on a pedestal but requires priests to remain single. Protestantism, however, does not practice Mariolatry and allows its ministers to marry.

Gadzooks! Are these psychoanalytic formulations of the Holy Spirit a sick joke? The ravings of some idiot savants permanently regressed to the junior high school whoopee-cushion level of mental development? Freud's *Totem and Taboo* was written in 1913 and Jones' article was written in 1922, so they represent the thinking of those times when psychoanalysts were making amazing new discoveries about the workings of the unconscious mind. Whether these discoveries can be applied as meaningfully to cultural concepts is debatable. And yet, no matter how outrageous the conclusions appear at first reading, some of them have a resonance of truth. This truth certainly is not perfectly pitched but neither is it total cacophony. If you believe that God made man and that the supernatural exists on its own terms, then psychoanalytic studies of the supernatural are irrelevant. If you believe, however, that Man made god and that the supernatural is a construct that arises from human experiences, then psychoanalytic formulations are worth considering (and maybe rejecting). To associate the human creation of the Holy Spirit with the passing of intestinal gas is close to blasphemy on the one hand, but a more or less rational attempt to provide explanations on the other. The Bible is like a vast verbal Rorschach test. Perhaps there are no "correct" interpretations. Perhaps what we uncover in the Bible are truths about ourselves and the times in which we live. Freud and Jones earnestly looked for the Holy Spirit but through the wrong end of a telescope. What they saw was a nugget of the truth that resides deep within our physical being. Had they peered outward they might have seen a larger truth or, then again, at that moment they may have seen nothing but the movement of wind-tossed clouds.

DOES HE OR DOESN'T HE? DOES GOD REALLY EXIST?

In history gods die and then are resurrected in a new guise or configuration. When much of the Old Testament was being written the Greek Olympian gods were on the decline. In the fifth century B.C. a chap named Diagoras gained a measure of fame by declaring that god didn't exist and then by chopping up a wooden statue of Hercules in order to boil his turnips. The great plays of Sophocles and Euripides were tragic because their heroes could no longer count on divine order and justice. Lamenting this fact the chorus in *Oedipus Rex* asked, "Why should I dance before the gods?" When the army and navy of Athens were totally destroyed in Sicily, the great historian Thucydides did not blame this failure on the gods even though the statues of the city's protective god had been mutilated on the eve of the ill-fated expedition. The defeat was beyond logic, but the gods were no longer powerful enough to cause it. Greek culture eventually declined along with its gods. Indeed, the gods of nearby cultures died too, even the Roman gods. It took a while, but the religious needs of the populace were satisfied by accepting the new religion of Christianity, which itself was a more palatable version of Judaism. Christianity absorbed and co-opted what was useful in the old religions. Temples of the great Mother Goddess Cybele, for example, were converted into shrines of the Virgin Mary. The large taurobolium in Rome, where bulls were slaughtered while sinners sat in a pit to be baptized and to have their sins washed away by the blood that fell on them through a grating, is where St. Peter's Cathedral is now located.

The concept of God has always been fair game for rationalists who demand proof of his existence. St. Augustine (354–430 A.D.) knew about the purification of the heart through faith, but he also believed that "he who by true reason arrives at an understanding of what he had only believed in is in a better state of advancement . . ." His eleventh century disciple, St. Anselm of Canterbury, became famous for his statement "I do not seek to understand in order to have faith but I have faith in order to understand," and for his "ontological proof" of God's existence, which goes something like this:

I imagine God in my mind, and
I define God as that being which nothing greater can be
    thought, and since
Perfection is an attribute of God, and since
God's perfection can be manifested only if God exists
    because a non-existent
God cannot be perfect, therefore
God must exist.

Such wordplay may have philosophical and theological currency, but, as skeptics have noted, merely thinking of a dollar doesn't mean that you have a dollar in your pocket.

One standard "proof" of God's existence, the argument by design, views God as the master watchmaker who put together an orderly universe: "The heavens declare the glory of God; and the firmament shows his handiwork" (Ps. 19:1). In order for life to exist everything must be carefully balanced in a natural order that must have been designed by an intelligent creator, namely God. Further, design is associated with a final goal; according to St. Thomas Aquinas, "An orderedness of actions to an end is observed in all bodies obeying natural laws, even when they lack awareness . . . which shows that they truly arrive to a goal, and do not merely hit it by accident." The stock responses to this argument are many. Biological evolution depends on mutations that occur by chance. Many species of flora and fauna, not to mention stars, are continually becoming extinct, which isn't much of a goal. The human intestinal appendix serves no purpose other than to become inflamed at times. Order is a human construct: if a comet smashes into a planet, does this constitute order or disorder? Why would an intelligent creator design a world in which babies die and in which millions of innocents are slaughtered? Things are the way they are because that's the way things are. If things were different, then that's the way things would be.

Another standard "proof" is that every event has a cause, but that there must be a creator who set the chain of events into action and who is eternal, namely God. To this a skeptic might answer that perhaps the entire universe is eternal. It's just as easy (although less comforting) to believe that no one made the universe as it is to believe that no one made God.

Actually no one listens much to theologians or philosophers nowadays. Anything important about creation and the universe is much more likely to be reported by physicists. One physicist, Paul Davies, has tackled the question of God. Although he writes in simplified language, consideration of the points he makes and the questions he raises are guaranteed to precipitate migraine headaches. Consider the following: There is always an element of time between a cause and an effect. Yet time did not exist until the universe appeared. To say that God created (caused) the universe is meaningless because that creative act also created time. "If there was no "before" there can be no cause (in the usual sense) of the big bang, either natural or supernatural." What happened before the big bang to have caused it? There was no before; the notion of cause and effect cannot be applied to a state in which time does not exist.

God could not exist in time before the universe. But perhaps God could exist outside time and space, "above" the universe rather than before it. Unfortunately, a timeless God could not also be a personal God who thinks, plans, or intervenes in temporal affairs. A timeless God couldn't acquire knowledge (this takes time) but could know everything that ever was, is, or will be. If the outcome of each event is known in advance, however, then God would not be able to change an outcome and, therefore, would not be omnipotent. God's omnipotence is challenged also by the fact that rules of logic cannot be broken. God cannot make 2=3 or make a square a circle. God could create any universe that is logically consistent. "If there exists only one logically consistent universe then God would effectively have had no choice at all."

Complexity and organization are for physicists the two distinguishing features of living organisms. Since an atom within a living cell is exactly the same as an atom outside the cell, life cannot be reduced to a property of the components of an organism. Atoms don't need to be divinely animated to yield life, they simply have to be arranged in an appropriately complex way. Life emerges at the holistic collective level of structure, and spontaneous self-organization is characteristic of living matter (of lifeless matter too, e.g., the vortices in fluid flow). Likewise, mind, which has properties such as self-consciousness, ideas, and hope, is a holistic concept at a higher level of description. Individual brain cells do not inform us about the mind because the mind emerges only when all the brain cells are considered as a whole. "The brain is the medium of expression of the human mind. Similarly the entire physical universe would be the medium of expression of the mind of a natural God. In this context, God is the supreme holistic concept, perhaps many levels of description above that of the human mind."

THE NERVES OF GOD: THE STRANGE CASE OF DANIEL SCHREBER

Psychiatrists routinely encounter paranoid schizophrenics or manic-depressive patients who claim to be God or to have a unique relationship with God. They may identify with either an expansive, all powerful God or with the suffering, persecuted Jesus. Such delusions of grandiosity are attempts to reconstruct reality and to provide a meaningful context for their psychopathology. The most famous psychiatric case of grandiose paranoia was that of Daniel Schreber, a German judge, who published his *Memoirs of My Nervous Illness* in 1903. It begins, "The human soul is contained in the nerves of the body . . . The nerves of God are infinite and universal . . . [and can] transform themselves into all things of the created world; in this capacity they are called rays; and herein lies the essence of divine creation." Souls undergoing purification of their nerves after death learned to speak German because it was God's preferred language, the language of his chosen people. Schreber described "miracles" in which God was involved that included a terrifying plot to murder his soul and to transform his body into that of a female prostitute. The attacks on his body were horrendous. His skull was split open and "little men" placed in his feet attempted to pump out his spinal cord. He was emasculated and his body was saturated with female nerves of lust. He fought back with his own pure rays and the power of the Cosmic Order; his goal was to seduce God into impregnating him "by always playing the woman's part in sexual embrace with myself" and by "the cultivation of voluptuousness." His *Memoirs* conclude with a comparison of his torments with the crucifixion of Jesus and with a belief that "the spread of my religious ideas and the weight of proof of their truth will lead to a fundamental revolution in mankind's religious views unequaled in history." Schreber died in a mental hospital in 1907. In 1911 Freud published an analysis of the *Memoirs*. Freud's formulation was that Schreber's homosexual longing for his father and brother was displaced first on his physician and then onto God. His resistance to this longing was transformed into a delusion of persecution by those whom he desired to possess. He certainly couldn't possess his father or brother, and he thought it degrading to play the part of a female prostitute with his physician. His solution was to become God's mistress. From this lofty position he could participate in a great cosmic chain of events and even change the history of the world. Thus, from conflicts over homosexuality a delusion of persecution was formed which then was converted to a delusion of grandeur. Other psychoanalysts have interpreted Schreber's illness differently, and, at any rate, we now know that the association between homosexual conflicts and paranoid delusions is found in only a limited number of cases.

Few psychiatrists have concerned themselves profoundly with the question of God, especially in recent times. Among those who have, W. Meissner and Ana-Maria Rizzuto have distinguished themselves by proposing an understanding of the human experience of God based on individual development from infancy to old age. These modern approaches do not delve into speculations on the meanings of ancient myths or on the earliest stages of human existence. The following is an abbreviated version of Meissner's schema.

For the first few years of life a child's image of God is based primarily upon the image of its parents, although grandparents and siblings also may make an impact. The child's God lives in a sort of fairy tale world and at times may be loving and protective as well as fearsome and cruel. These characteristics of God are the same as those of the child's mother, who can provide warmth, nourishment, and security but who also sometimes may punish, withhold, and not be always on hand to gratify the child's wishes. A positive mother–child experience at this stage results in a basic sense of trust, which in later years may lead to a trusting faith in God, while a negative, insecure experience may distort the experience of God.

The child moves on to begin the process of separation and of becoming an individual with some independence (the so-called "anal stage"), learns that people make things, and asks endless questions about who made what and why and where. The child hears about something called God but lacks the capacity to understand what a spirit or a transcendent force is. To the child this God must be a big and powerful person since he made really big things like the sun and the earth. God must be like the most powerful persons that the child knows, namely both parents but especially the father, who tends to be the more aggressive or forceful parent.

Over the next few years the child comes to realize that his parents neither know everything nor are all powerful. The child then develops a somewhat romantic view of a perfect heavenly Father as well as a distorted view of his family. Both God and parents may be idealized as totally protecting or there may be a split into a good God and mean parents or into good parents and a mean God.

Between the ages of six and eleven the child begins to appreciate symbols, and the concept of God shifts from that of a concrete person to that of a still imperfectly understood spirit whose power must be revered but also feared. There is a certain magic about God, who, the child supposes, will exact punishment for every misdeed. In this, the "latency" stage, an immature obsessional religiosity emerges in conjunction with ritualistic behaviors.

At the beginning of adolescence the image of God becomes more personalized as "my Savior" or "my Father" and more connected to emotions and subjective attitudes such as love, obedience, trust, and fear. God is the ideal leader and advisor who points out the right path to take and who patiently and kindly listens to one's innermost problems and desires. However, Meissner warns, "Where adolescent realization is not tempered by a greater maturity of judgement and discretion, the figure of Christ can become a superhuman model and a repository for fanatical tendencies." As adolescents become moralists, the burden of sinfulness emerges, and they may engage in the extremes of either loose or puritanical behavior. Adolescents also often rebel against parental authority as they strive for independence; this rebellion may carry over to the religion that the parents practice as well as to the God whom the parents symbolically represent.

Adolescents who successfully master their many ambivalences step into adulthood. Choices now must be made about religion and God. Personal questions must be asked. Should I follow the religion of my parents, seek a different religion, or avoid religion altogether? It is thought that persons are not capable of acquiring a true religious faith that is based less on conflicts and more on mature understanding and acceptance until they are 30 years old. Throughout the rest of their lives, persons will encounter new experiences, friends, bosses, and children of their own. For some the inner representation of God will remain solid, for others it may change in many different ways, and for still others it may be rejected or replaced. God usually returns in old age, especially when death nears. "At that point," writes Rizzuto, "The God representation . . . will return to the dying person's memory, either to obtain the grace of belief or to be thrown out for the last time." A person's last breath may be an inspiration or an expiration.

Freud regarded belief in God to be a wish fulfillment. God softens our fears about the dangers of life; the moral world order that God promises instills hope that justice will be served; and belief in an after-life creates an ultimate setting for the fulfillment of our wishes. Thus, belief in God is an illusion that depresses the value of life, distorts the picture of the real world, intimidates the value of intelligence, and promotes a state of psychic infantilism.

As opposed to this exceedingly harsh view, modern formulations are quite different. Yes, God may be an illusion but not a pathological one. Rather, God is a benevolent illusion necessary for the growth and nourishment of both our mental and spiritual health. Psychoanalyst Donald Winnicott, in the 1960s and 70s, explored the concept of transitional objects and of phenomena whose origins lie in the earliest mother–infant interaction. First the mother's breast comforts the infant, then the infant's own hand, which is placed in its mouth, then other objects such as a baby blanket or a teddy bear. These objects become very special to the infant who assumes control over them, endows them with a unique vitality, gets upset if anyone changes them, cuddles them lovingly, and sometimes hates them. As the child matures, the special objects are neither mourned nor forgotten, but rather simply lose meaning. These "transitional" objects are the very stuff of illusion and exist mentally somewhere between inner subjective reality and outer objective reality. What the infant experiences is what Winnicott calls, for lack of a better word, "experiencing" itself. This illusory experience is "in adult life inherent in art and religion, yet becomes the hallmark of madness when an adult puts too powerful a claim on the credulity of others, forcing them to acknowledge a sharing of illusion that is not their own."

It is in the realm of "experiencing" that the capacity for symbolism is born as well as the capacity for artistic expression and appreciation. Both the audience and actors at a dramatic performance, for example, engage in what the poet Coleridge called a willing suspension of disbelief. The actors pretend they are the characters that they portray, and the audience agrees to this pretense. In Meissner's words, "All this is illusion willingfully entertained, maintained in a potential space that is neither wholly real nor entirely the product of the imagination." It is through illusion that we see reality more clearly, create things and ideas, use our imaginations, and express our inner life. "Winnicott's standard of psychic health is not the separation of the real and the wishful, as Freud might have had it, but rather their constant intermingling and exchange. It is through illusion, then, that the human spirit is nourished."

God is a special transitional object because God, unlike a teddy bear, does not lose meaning totally and because God "is uniquely connected to man's sense of himself, of the meaning and purpose of his existence and his ultimate destiny." God remains always available. Prayer, for example, is a transitional mental space where man meets God. God is an illusion that, if nurtured through each developmental crisis, can serve us well. Rizzuto concludes that "Men cannot be men without illusions. The type of illusion we select—science, religion, or something else—reveals our personal history and the transitional space each of us has created between his objects and himself to find 'a resting place' to live in."

Towards the end of the nineteenth century, the German philosopher Nietzsche told the story of a madman who cried out in the town square, "I seek God! I seek God!" Faithless townsmen laughed, "Is he lost? Is he hiding? Has he taken a trip?" The madman replied, "Where has God gone to? I will tell you: We have killed him—you and I . . . what are these churches if not the tombs and graves of God?" Many people, including modern theologians, have agreed with Nietzsche, especially after Auschwitz. How should we deal with God in the face of two world wars, countless slaughters, ethnic cleansing, and famine? According to Friedman some people turn to God for consolation, but many others feel that "God is not present and that humans are left on their own, responsible for their own fate . . . This century singularly has received the death of God as part of its legacy."

The world has always had prophets who proclaim the death of God. They have been correct in that specific gods do die, but then they are replaced by new or transformed gods. As long as babies are born the gods will survive. If history is a teacher then even Yahweh and Jesus will pass away too, although it's difficult even to imagine that this could occur. In a time when technology seems to know no limits and when science fiction no longer strains our imagination, what would a replacement God be like? Would it be real or virtual?

Would *deus ex machina* (God from a machine) no longer be just a literary or theatrical device? Would we be able to tune into God as easily as today we tune into a television program? Would we access God via a galactic Internet? Once the "power" button was pushed on, who would be able to turn it off?

ONCE UPON A TIME THE DEVIL...

CHAPTER 2

In 1149 A.D. an Irish monk wrote *The Vision of Tundal*, a wildly successful book that was translated into most of the languages of Europe. Tundal saw Satan in hell "blacker than a crow and shaped like a man except that it had a beak and a spiky tail and thousands of hands, each of which had twenty fingers with nails longer than knights' lances, and all of them squeezed unhappy souls. He lay bound with chains on an iron grid above a bed of fiery coals. Around him were a throng of demons. Whenever he exhaled he ejected the souls upward into Hell's torments. And when he inhaled, he sucked them back in to chew them again."

A few centuries later, Saint Brigit of Sweden saw a sinner tortured in hell. "The eyes seemed reversed, looking to the back of the head. The mouth hung open and the tongue was drawn through the nostrils. The teeth had been driven like nails into the palate and the skin seemed like a linen garment spattered with semen; it was icy cold and exuded a discharge like that which oozes from an infected ulcer, with a stench worse than anything in this world."

In 1850 visitors to New York City paid to see the "Infernal Regions" in a funhouse at Peale's Museum. Actors dressed as Satan and his demonic allies clanged chains, shrieked, and pranced around a pit of fire as they did their horrific best to amuse the customers.

In our time, the comedian Flip Wilson made the nation laugh when he put on a dress to become the character Geraldine, who explained her erratic behavior by joking that "The devil made me do it."

Life is never static, but the difference between Tundal's devil and Flip Wilson's is beyond remarkable. It is a difference in a basic worldview. In this chapter we examine the related concepts of hell, the devil, the Antichrist, evil, and sin. Once upon a time these words struck fear in the hearts of everyone. What they represented could be seen and smelled and touched. They were as real as the sun that orbited the earth. But slowly, surely, things changed. Reality became metaphor and metaphor became weary and outmoded. And here we stand, liberated from the old superstitions and mystified by the new ones.

SCALDING VOMIT: THE FATE OF SOULS

Heaven's an odd fish. We gaze upward to indicate its location, but because the earth spins, up can be down depending upon where we are in the rotation cycle. At any rate we usually imagine it's somewhere in the sky. Popular drawings of Christian heaven often contain billowy clouds, brilliant light, angels singing or playing musical instruments, a host of gaunt saints, and a kindly God who sits serenely while not doing much of anything. It's a cerebral, ethereal place that serves to foster hopes of being rewarded for living right and of meeting loved ones who have died and now reside there. It may seem that we're in heaven when dancing cheek to cheek or eating a pecan divinity, but the moment passes and it's back-to-reality time.

Hell, deep down in the earth, is a more familiar and intriguing place with far more dramatic possibilities. Infernal engines of destruction run riot through flickering flames. Horrible shrieks pierce the darkness. The stench of sulphur hangs heavy over neverending orgies of diabolical torture. Every newscast of a massacre or a disaster or a murder reminds us how much closer we are to hell than to heaven.

The writers of the Bible were surrounded by cultures with very different beliefs about what happens after death. The Babylonians believed that all mortals eventually traveled the road of no return to the world of the dead beneath the earth's surface. There they sat in silent darkness, ate dust and clay, and wore birds' feathers for garments. No one could escape this fate. The Egyptians, however, believed that virtue was rewarded and transgressions punished. Upon death a person's life-force (ka) and soul (ba) traveled in a celestial ferry to the Hall of Justice where the god Osiris judged the case while the god of wisdom, Thoth, prosecuted it. Each person was called upon to deny forty-two wrong doings such as "I have not committed theft . . . uttered falsehood . . . defiled another man's wife . . . violated sacred times and seasons . . . made haughty my voice . . . fouled water . . . thought scornfully of the god who is in my city." Then the person's heart was placed in a pan on a balance scale counterweighted by the feather of truth. If the sinful heart was heavier than the feather, the person was gobbled up by Ammit, a god with a crocodile head. In some versions, gods who felt offended could mete out punishment such as hacking the person into pieces and dumping him into a pit full of a lion's scalding vomit. This misery was not eternal; the offended god eventually ate the victim and ended his agony.

In Homer's *Odyssey* (eighth century B.C.) we encounter the classical Greek belief that the souls of the dead go to the shady land of Hades where they wander sorrowfully, bemoaning their situation. The gods punished most sinners while they were alive; in death they were left alone with their memories. A special section in Hades was reserved, however, for a precious few who had rebelled against the gods. For tricking Zeus, for example, Prometheus was chained to a rock while a vulture picked his liver clean. Each night his liver regenerated, providing a new feast for his hungry tormentor. By about 400 B.C. debate about the fate of souls was so serious that the playwright Aristophanes wrote a scintillating satire called *The Frogs*: a citizen of Athens traveled to Hades in order to effect the return to life of the poet Euripides because there weren't any good poets left. Aristophanes made fun of Hades (frogs, not monsters, guarded the entrance), mystery cults, politicians, and just about everyone else.

The Greek philosopher Plato (428–348 B.C.) made a determination that has greatly influenced theology to the present. He figured that the souls of the dead were met in Hades by a guardian spirit and judged by dead sons of Zeus at the Meadow of the Dividing of the Road. Those who were judged favorably went to the Isles of the Blessed. Those who lived neither well nor ill went to a lake in Tartarus where they were purified of their evil deeds and then received the rewards of their good deeds. Those who committed great crimes but repented were punished in Tartarus for a year and then, if mercy was granted by those who had been wronged, were released from the earthly prison. In contrast to these curable sinners, the incurable ones were punished eternally, "enduring forever the most terrible, painful, and fearful sufferings as the penalty of their sins—there they are, hanging up as examples, in the prison-house of the world below, a spectacle and a warning to all unrighteous men who come there." In his epic poem *The Aeneid* (19 B.C.), the Roman poet Virgil adopted Plato's categories. The dead entered the underworld through a cave near Naples. Some of those who led evil lives were rehabilitated through punishment, but those who had been truly evil were punished forever.

LIVING DOGS AND DEAD LIONS: NO GLORY IN DEATH

The Hebrews of the Old Testament saw no glory in death. Most believed what was stated in Deuteronomy: if you fly straight and obey the Lord then your life will be full of blessings. Do the opposite and your life will be a mess of scabs, boils, madness, famine. You'll be lucky to eat afterbirth for breakfast. Your wife will fornicate with other men. Your children will be sold into slavery. Your cattle will be stolen. There wasn't hell to pay, however, because hell didn't exist.

During your life you got what you deserved. When you died your soul and everybody else's went to a mass grave called Sheol, the equivalent of the Greek Hades (in fact, Sheol became Hades when the Old Testament was translated into Greek; the New Testament uses Hades). It was a silent, grim, ashen place, devoid of joy and full of worms. Everyone there was weary, weak, and constantly thirsty. They got no respect from the living, who regarded any contact with them as impure. The law against consulting with a dead soul was clear: "Give no regard to mediums and familiar spirits; do not seek after them, to be defiled by them: I am the Lord your God" (Lev. 19:31). The "normal" biography of a Hebrew would state that he or she lived about seventy years, had children, was buried in a tomb, and then went to Sheol. But just because existence in Sheol was everyone's natural destiny, it didn't mean that anyone wanted to go there. The author of Psalm 6 came up with a clever argument in asking God to save him from death: "Oh, save me for your mercies' sake! For in death there is no remembrance of you: In the grave who will give you thanks?" When his life was extended by fifteen years, Hezekiah thanked God and reminded him that "Sheol cannot thank you, Death cannot praise you" (Is. 38:18). Sheol was a place to be avoided for as long as it was possible: "A living dog is better than a dead lion" (Eccl. 9:4).

While most Hebrews accepted the concept of Sheol as described above, some biblical authors expressed a dissident view. They wondered, if Sheol offers equal opportunity housing and if everyone is treated the same there, why is it that during their lifetime some wicked persons prosper while some righteous persons are miserable? The poet of Psalm 73 was envious of the prosperity of the wicked; they don't have any fear but rather say "How does God know?" Ecclesiastes 9:2-3 noted, "One event happens to the righteous and the wicked; to the good, the clean, and the unclean; to him who sacrifices and him who does not sacrifice. As is the good, so is the sinner . . . This is an evil in all that is done under the sun: that one fate comes to call." It just wasn't fair. Job 21 stated things most clearly: "What is the point of our serving God?" The wicked live on easy street. They have power, bulls that breed without failure, children who dance. "How often does their destruction come upon them, the sorrows God distributes in His anger? . . . They say that God reserves a man's punishment for his children. No! Let him bear the penalty himself and suffer under it . . . When he is gone how can the fortunes of his house affect him?" According to scholar Alan Bernstein, "The story of Job is a call for compensatory discrimination in death . . . Job demands an end to the moral neutrality of the grave."

Among those who believed that God actually punished some of the wicked in Sheol were Ezekiel (about 590 B.C.) and Isaiah (about 540 B.C.). They were the first to delineate a map of the biblical netherworld, where special places were reserved for those who were especially wicked. There are other statements in the Bible that also indicate selective punishment after death. "Behold, the day is coming, burning like an oven, when all the proud and evil doers will be stubble. And the day which is coming will burn them up" and the righteous "shall trample the wicked, for they shall be ashes under the soles of your feet" (Mal. 4:1, 4). "Your hand will find all your enemies . . . You shall make them as a fiery oven in the time of your anger; . . . And the fire shall devour them" (Ps. 21:8–9). An earthly site, the ravine of Ge-Hinnon south of Jerusalem, came to be metaphorically regarded as the place in Sheol reserved for the wicked. Translated into Greek as Gehenna, it was the place where the Israelites had sacrificed their children in the fire as burnt offerings to Baal (Jer. 7:31). Even after Josiah destroyed the altar there, Gehenna remained an impure, deadly location and garbage dump for the corpses of animals. According to Berstein, "Because the corruption there resembled Ezekial's violent multitudes in graves of shame and Isaiah's image of corpses in heaps, [it] eventually took on the characteristics of the depths of the pit and came also to function as the fate of the wicked."

The historian Josephus (about 38–100 A.D.) wrote that the Jewish sect of the Essenes at the time of Jesus taught that good souls go to a place like the Greek Islands of the Blessed. "Bad souls they consign to a dark, stormy abyss, full of punishments that know no end . . . They tell these tales . . . in the hope of reward after death, and the propensities of the bad are restrained by the fear that, even if they are not caught in this life, after this death they will undergo eternal punishment." This eventually became the Christian position.

THE GREAT GULF FIXED: ONCE IN HELL, YOU'RE STUCK

St. Paul, the earliest New Testament writer, didn't think much of hell. He wrote that "the wages of sin is death" (Rom 5:6) and, therefore, only the souls of the elect who have received grace and have nurtured it through faith will exist forever in the kingdom of God on the Judgement Day. The good receive glory, honor, peace, immortality, and eternal life. Sinners, in contrast, receive wrath, fury, tribulation, and distress. Their main punishment, however, is exclusion from heaven.

The first reference in the Gospels to hell as we usually think of it is Mark 9:43–48, which states that if you have an offensive body organ you should destroy it because it's better to enter heaven maimed than to be cast whole into Gehenna, "where the worm does not die and the fire is not quenched." The Gospel of Matthew took this theme and beat it into the ground. Matthew was especially creative in reporting the parables of Jesus, many of which conclude that at the end of this age God will cast sinners "into the furnace of fire. There will be wailing and gnashing of teeth" (34:42). On the Day of Judgement those persons who fed the hungry, clothed the naked, took in strangers, and visited prisoners will go to heaven, but those who did not do these good deeds will be cursed and sent from God into the everlasting fire prepared for the devil and his angels (25:41). Over and over Matthew warns of the destruction of body and soul in hell, of the broad gate that opens into hell, of the hypocrites that cannot escape the condemnation of hell, of everlasting punishment, and that damned wailing and gnashing of teeth.

The rich man, poor man parable in the Gospel of Luke (16:19–31) contributed to the notion of hell. A rich man lived sumptuously, but a beggar starved while waiting for crumbs of food from the rich man's table. Both died. The rich man was tormented in the flames of Hades, while the beggar was carried by the angels to Abraham's bosom. The rich man pleaded with the beggar to give him some cool water, but Abraham reminded him that he had received good things during life while the beggar had been miserable. Now the tables were turned. "And besides all this, between us and you there is a great gulf fixed." You're in hell, we're in heaven, and you can't get here from there.

In the complicated Book of Revelation the resurrected Christ claims to have triumphed over death because he possessed the "keys of Hades and death." He speaks not only of a first resurrection but also of a second resurrection in which damned persons are consigned to an eternal lake of fire and sulphur along with the devil and his accomplices. Before this second resurrection the damned are pushed into a bottomless pit where they are stung by giant insects.

The Apocalypse of Peter, written about 140 A.D., was the first work to describe the nitty-gritty niceties of torture in hell. When Peter and the disciples ask Jesus about the last days, an incredible vision documentary appears before their eyes. The blessed ones look on as the evil ones pass away into darkness and fire. Judgement is passed, the General Resurrection takes place; let the horrors begin! The locale is full of cesspools, fiery rivers, melting stars, and precipitous cliffs. Blasphemers hang by their tongues over a steamy cesspool; adulterers hang by their feet with their heads in the cesspool. Idol worshippers are chained to the molten statues of the false gods that they worshipped. Women who had abortions are in pits full of feces, urine and bloody afterbirth up to their chins. They are understandably motionless while rays of fire shooting out from aborted fetuses penetrate their eyes. Parents who allowed their children to die of neglect are eaten by tiny flesh-loving beasts that form from the curdled milk that oozes from the mothers' breasts. Persecutors of Christians are tormented by a belly full of ravenous, restless worms. False witnesses against the martyrs suck on a flaming fire that pierces their guts; their lips are cut off so they can't stop the torture. Homosexuals and their women (!) are forced to jump off a cliff into a rocky gorge; demons beat their battered bodies back to the top of a cliff where they repeat the sequence for eternity. Disobedient children fall off of cliffs into ravines of fire, while disobedient slaves in a fiery pit endlessly bite their tongues. All in all, the vision was so heart-wrenching that both Peter and Jesus wept.

Hell, or rather the fear of it, was a presence in the lives of Christians from the early centuries through the Dark and Middle Ages. Theologians debated whether or not hell was truly eternal. Origen (185–254 A.D.) held that even the worst sinners would be rehabilitated through punishment and eventually united to God in heaven; he based this idea on Paul's statement that God will be all in all (1 Cor. 28). The Synod of Constantinople (543 A.D.) excommunicated Origen: "If anyone shall say or think that there is a time limit to the torment of demons and ungodly persons, or that there will even be an end to it, or that they will ever be pardoned or made whole again, let him be excommunicated." All sorts of tours of hell were published, the greatest being Dante's *Inferno* (1314 A.D.). However, the theological precision of the *Inferno*—punishment was proportional to transgression, illicit lovers were punished the least, traitors the most—was outweighed by its literary merit. Dante wrote as a poet and not as the beneficiary of a heavenly vision. The *Inferno*, along with the *Purgatorio* and *Paradiso*, were works of fiction. Their inspiration was human, not divine (Dante simply titled the trio "Commedia;" an enthusiastic editor in 1555 added the adjective "Divina"). Dante's fictional "vision" was so brilliant that it unintentionally eroded the public's belief in hell as a real presence in their lives. After Dante, hell became an allegory and thus was lost to future writers who wanted to depict reality. No one can mistake even Milton's *Paradise Lost* for anything other than a truly great imaginative poem.

Artists did a good job of bringing images of hell to church goers, most of whom were illiterate and therefore appreciative of visual representations. The most powerfully horrific scenes were often painted on the back walls, a last reminder to the faithful as they exited church. The most incredible and unforgettable scenes of hell were done by the Flemish painter Hieronymous Bosch (1460–1516 A.D.). Even though his paintings contain a great deal of undecipherable symbolism, there is more than enough riotous nudity, scatology, bizarre torture machines, and hideous demons to bemuse viewers. Pieter Bruegel and his sons jumped on the bandwagon and created their own fantastic hellish paintings. It couldn't go on forever. Artists became tired of depicting the bizarre. Death in and of itself offered more creative possibilities.

Besides, hell had lost its sting. Most Christians figured that at the worst they would end up in purgatory. From there it was a hop, skip, and a jump to heaven, especially if money was used wisely to buy indulgences. Then came Martin Luther (1483–1546), a no-nonsense reformer who despised the concept of indulgences. Even good works didn't signify much. With God's grace there is heaven, without it there is eternal damnation. Luther gave hell a boost. Not to be outdone, the Jesuits preached about hell too (this legacy lived on to the twentieth century, as witnessed in James Joyce's *Portrait of the Artist as a Young Man*). The Catholic Redemptionist order of priests was founded by St. Alphonso Liguori in 1732 for the express purpose of frightening the faithful into behaving properly and thus achieving salvation. Their weapons were vivid, blood-curdling sermons on hell. The great Protestant preachers in New England also became famous for their preaching of the terrors of hell.

In the long run all the raging sermons and witch hunts could not prevail against the force of what we call the eighteenth-century era of Enlightenment. In England Edward Gibbon blamed Christianity for causing the fall of the Roman Empire and described the ascetic St. Anthony as "a hideous, distorted, emaciated maniac, without knowledge, without patriotism, without natural affection, spending his life in a long routine of useless and atrocious self-torture, and quailing before the phantoms of his deluded brain." David Humes' *Dialogue Concerning Natural Religion* devastated the notions of supernaturalism, hell, and miracles. He described a trinity of Christianity, stupidity, and ignorance. In France, Diderot's *Encyclopedia* noted that hell was a product of the Bible that itself was a book of superstitions. Voltaire skewered religion mercilessly: "I never was in Judea, thank God, and I never will go there . . . men of all nations . . . describe the country as the refuse and rubbish of nature." In his *Philosophical Dictionary* he rejected hell because it seemed ridiculous that a poor chap should burn forever for stealing a goat although "I like my maid, my tailor, and especially my lawyer to believe in God because it's likely that I'll be robbed and cuckolded less often." In the United States, Thomas Jefferson and the Founding Fathers not only omitted hell but God as well from the Constitution, while the Declaration of Independence included only a benign statement about "the Laws of Nature and Nature's God."

Hell never recovered, although all the various Christian churches have done their best to keep it alive (only the Unitarian-Universalists have "unqualifiedly" rejected the doctrine of an eternal hell), and Pope Leo XXIII even issued a papal bill on the topic in 1879. The literal hell of the past is gone. Fear as a motivation of behavior is doomed to failure over the long haul. For most people nowadays hell is created by and for humans right here on earth. It is the wasteland of toxic dumps and alcoholic stupors, and in the Nazi concentration camps there was much wailing and gnashing of teeth. Jean Paul Sartre described hell as "other people." He had a point. Each of us, the living and the dead, are "other people" who impinge upon someone's sovereignty and freedom. It can't be helped else chaos reign. Hell is where the hate is and sometimes, alas, where the heart is too.

SATANEL: THE DEVIL ENTERS THE WORLD

Where does evil come from and why do we do evil things? One answer, at least according to Isaiah 45:6–7, is that evil comes from God: "I form the light and I create darkness, I make peace and create evil. I, the Lord, do all these things." Since we are created in God's image maybe, like him, we also create evil. Certainly God the Warrior commanded the Israelites to commit genocide and to slaughter children. This seems evil, but from God's point of view it was necessary and not sinful. On only two biblical occasions did God act sinfully: he incited David to take a census (2 Sam 24:1), and he deliberately gave the Israelites sinful laws, such as child sacrifice, weakly rationalizing "that I might make them desolate and that they might know that I am the Lord" (Ezek. 20:26).

With so many gods to choose from, the Israelite leaders, knowing the tendency of their people to backslide, decided to emphasize the goodness of the One True God. Evil, they reckoned, was present because of an archdevil called Satan and his band of little satans. Since it took many centuries for this notion to develop, the Bible presents differing views of the archfiend.

The Hebrew verb "satan" means to oppose or to obstruct and was used ordinarily to describe the actions of a person who acted as a prosecutor or who caused deviations in the lives of others. Eventually the term was applied to the actions of angels who served God by obstructing humans. As a noun, the satan referred to any angel who obeyed God's will and set obstacles in the paths of humans; in fact the Greek translation is *diabolos* (hence the English adjective diabolical), which means throwing something across the path. Sometimes a satan's obstructions were helpful; a satan caused the refusal of

Baalam's ass to move forward, thus saving Baalam's life (Num. 22:33). More often, however, God employed satans to make people miserable. In the book of Job (about 550 B.C.), the satan is described as one of the "Sons of God" who was "going to and fro on the earth, and walking back and forth on it" (1:6-7). Scholar Elaine Pagels likens the satan's activity to that of the secret police of the Persian King who roamed among the Jews looking for signs of disloyalty and dissent. God, giving in to the satan's challenge to subject Job to hideous torments, admitted that "you incited Me against him, to destroy him without cause" (2:3). Although satan may have incited God, he was still under God's control. In Zechariah (519 B.C.), satan began to show just the slightest movement toward independence when he opposed the appointment of Joshua as high priest because of his filthy clothes. God immediately rebuked him. David, according to the seventh-century B.C. book of Samuel, had been invited by God to take a census. Then Satan, for the first time, demonstrated his autonomy and in the revision of this story: it was he who "incited David to take a census of the Israelites" (1 Chron. 21:1). Satan didn't have very much power, but it was a beginning.

The concept of Satan with a capital S started to emerge during the second and third centuries B.C., especially as recorded in the apocryphal books of the Bible and other religious writings. Most of the time he was called Belial, the worthless one, but he was also called Mastemah (hostility), Gabriel (the death bringer), and Sammael (the angel of poison). In 2 Enoch 29:4 he originally was Satanel; when God flung him from heaven following a rebellion, the holy el (of god) was removed. As the personality of the archdevil developed over the centuries he was blamed for most of the unhappiness and ills of humankind. According to the Wisdom of Solomon, for example, "through the devil's envy death entered into the world" (2:24). The Old Testament stories were retold giving eminence to Satan. He was the serpent that cajoled Eve. He, not God, incited Abraham to consider the sacrifice of his son. He was the Daystar, eventually known as Lucifer, whom God cast from the heavens for thinking that he would set this throne higher than the stars of God (Is. 14:12-13; actually a satirical description of the king of Babylon). Most important, perhaps, he was named Semihazah and Asael and was identified as the leader of the strange "sons of God" who impregnated human woman. Unlike the bare description in Genesis 6:1-4, the nonbiblical literature emphasized the rebelliousness of these "sons of God" and the destructiveness of their demonic offspring. Many scholars have noted that Satan came more and more to resemble Ahriman, the Iranian mythical enemy of God who was introduced to the Hebrews during the period of Greek and Roman rule (starting in 332 B.C.).

FISHBAIT JESUS: SATAN IMPALED BY THE HOOK OF DIVINITY

During the time of Jesus and in the New Testament, the devil got his due. For starters he received some new names, such as the prince of demons, the ruler of this world, the tempter, the prince of the power of the air. Jesus called him Beelzebub (Matt. 10:25), but what that name means is unknown. Satan caused destruction of the flesh while inflaming marital infidelity (1 Cor. 5:5, 7:5). He took away God's message from men's hearts (Mark 4:15). He tempted Peter the Apostle, sifting him like wheat (Luke 22:31). He hindered Paul from visiting the brethren (1 Thess. 2:17). These are the behaviors of an Old Testament satan. The really powerful Satan derived his importance by being a larger-than-life cosmic force. The Essenes, authors of the Dead Sea Scrolls, were probably familiar to Jesus. Unlike most other Jewish groups, they elevated Satan to a prominent role as leader of the sons of darkness who battled against the Prince of Light and the sons of light. The battle was waged not only on earth but also in the universe. The cosmic nature of Satan can be seen in the book of Revelation: "So the great dragon was cast out, that serpent of old, called the Devil and Satan, who receives the whole world; he was cast to the earth, and his angels were cast with him" (12:9). Revelation looked back to the ancient Hebrew myth of primordial combat, when the world came into being and God killed or wounded a terrible dragon-monster called Leviathan or Rahab. Isaiah looked back to mythic times when Yahweh overcame Satan: "Awake as in the ancient days, in the generations of old. Did you not split Rahab in two, and pierce the Dragon through? Did you not dry up the sea, the waters of the great Abyss, to make the seabed a road for the redeemed to cross?" (51:9-10). And in the Psalms God's power "split the sea in two, and smashed the heads of monsters on the waters. You crushed Leviathan's heads ..."(74:13). By associating Satan with the mythic past greatness of the dragon-monster who challenged God, Revelation elevated Satan who, even though cast into the bottomless pit by an angel from heaven, supposedly would reemerge in a thousand years to lead yet another rebellion (20:1-3).

Satan's prestige was linked to his battles with Jesus. He tried temptations, but Jesus resisted. He stirred up the mob, but Jesus responded by telling a parable of the sons of the kingdom versus the sons of the evil one (Matt. 13:38). In another instance Jesus sent out seventy disciples to cities where Satan had power. "The servants returned with joy, saying, "Lord, even the demons are subject to us in your name." And He said to them, "I saw Satan fall like lightning from heaven"" (Luke 10:17–18). Retaliation soon followed: "Satan entered Judas Iscariot . . . . So he conferred with the chief priests and captains, how he might betray Jesus to them" (Luke 22:3–4). When Jesus was captured he spoke of "the power of darkness" (Luke 22:53).

Satan's greatest moment was the crucifixion of Jesus. It was the briefest of victories, however, because Christ overcame death. The victory really was God's, and he "delivered us from the dominion of darkness and conveyed us into the kingdom of his beloved Son . . . (who) having disarmed principalities and powers, made a public example of them, triumphing over them in [the cross]" (1 Cor. 1:13; 2:15). Christ's victory was both human and cosmic. A tradition even developed locating the site of the crucifixion atop the grave of Adam.

Paul wrote to the church members in Corinth that "You are not your own property; you were bought with a price" (1 Cor. 6:20). There has been much debate over the centuries about Paul's statement. The early Church Fathers believed that God had to pay a ransom to Satan in order to reclaim Christ's soul. Satan had claimed Christ's soul, it was thought, because he considered it blasphemous for Christ to say that he was the Son of God. Satan also claimed all human souls. In the words of the theologian Origen, "but to whom did He (Christ) give his soul as a ransom for many? Surely not to God. Could it, then, be to the Evil One? For he had us in his power, until the ransom for us should be given to him, even the life-soul of Jesus." In a later century, Pope Gregory the Great (540–604) announced that Satan, the giant sea-serpent, had swallowed up all the humans that had ever been born. He even swallowed Christ but did not realize that the human Christ was fishbait. When Satan devoured the bait, he was impaled by the hook of Christ's divinity. In the struggle Satan vomited up Christ's human body along with all the humans that Christ claimed.

CHILDREN OF THE DEVIL: JEWS AND HERETICS ATTACKED

Christ lived and died a Jew, and most of his early followers were Jewish. Being Jewish especially meant attending to the Hebrew scriptures that we now call the Old Testament, practicing circumcision, and eating only approved food. The new religion established in Christ's name needed to acknowledge its Jewish roots, yet it also needed to separate itself from the parent religion or else it would have been considered just another Jewish sect. Just how far to separate was a topic of heated debate in the early Church. In great part the debate was resolved by an unanticipated turn of events.

Paul, the Jewish mastermind of the establishment and growth of Christianity, opened the doors of the new religion to all comers: "There is neither Jew nor Greek, neither slave nor free, neither male or female; for you are all one in Jesus Christ" (Gal. 3:28). The new religion offered freedom from the "yoke of bondage" and "slavery," code words for Judaism. Circumcision counted for nothing. As for all the complicated rules of the Mosaic Law, Paul taught that the law is fulfilled simply by loving your neighbor as yourself (Gal. 5:14). The minds of the Jews were blinded by a veil when they read the Holy Scriptures, but Jesus took away the veil for Christians (2 Cor. 3:14). Except for a remnant, the Israelites have not attained the law of righteousness. The Gentile world benefitted from their fall and defection; Paul hoped to make the Jews envious of the Gentiles and in this way to save them (Romans 11:13–14). Paul's task was to win Gentile converts, and he was eventually more successful than his colleagues who evangelized among the Jews. In relatively short order the Christian Church became a predominantly Gentile one whose members did not feel bound by Jewish traditions.

While this process was taking place, many gospels were written. According to Elaine Pagels, the four that were eventually chosen for inclusion in the Bible were the most practical. They advised converts about fasting, diet, alms giving, prayer, and social organization; in Matthew 6, Jesus told converts to wash their face when fasting, to give alms in secret, and to say the "Our Father" prayer. Gospels that weren't selected often only offered general advice (e.g., in the Gospel of Thomas, Jesus said, "Do not tell lies, and do not do what you hate"). Also, they stressed sophisticated psychological concepts rather than pragmatic concerns. In Thomas, for example, Jesus said that "The kingdom is inside of you, and it is outside of you. When you come to know yourselves, then you will become known, and you will realize that it is you who are the sons of the living father." In the gospel of Philip, converts were told to "become not a Christian, but a Christ." In addition to being practical and relatively clear, the traditional four Gospels of the New Testament started a trend that has bedeviled Christianity ever since, namely the demonization of enemies, especially the Jews.

In Mark's Gospel, the earliest one written, Satan appears in the first chapter. The Holy Spirit had driven Christ into the wilderness for forty days, where he was tempted by Satan and ministered to by angels. Jesus then plunged into his ministry, but King Herod's men and the Jewish Pharisees plotted to kill him (3:6). Scribes came from Jerusalem and accused Jesus of being possessed by Satan because of his ability to exorcise demons. Christ's reply was, "How can Satan cast out Satan?" and he noted that neither a kingdom nor a house divided against itself can stand. Mark was not particularly hard on the Jews, but the battlelines were forming. Matthew's Gospel was written in great part to demonstrate that the life of Jesus recapitulated the history of Israel. Pagels, however, notes that in the Old Testament God delivered Israel from Egypt. In applying this item to Jesus, Matthew reversed things: Jesus fled from the land of Israel to Egypt because he was persecuted by the Jewish King Herod and not by Pharaoh. Matthew railed against the Jewish Pharisees who were his rivals for the hearts and souls of the populace. He has Jesus say that "unless your righteousness exceeds that of the scribes and Pharisees, you will never enter the kingdom of heaven" (5:20). In Chapter 23 Matthew's vituperation hit new highs. Seven times Jesus said, "Woe to you, scribes and Pharisees, hypocrites." Like whitewashed tombs, they were outwardly beautiful but inside were full of dead mens' bones and all uncleanliness. They were the sons of those who murdered the prophets. They were serpents, broods of vipers, and sons of hell. In the parable of the wedding feast (22:1–14), a king arranged a massive feast for his son, but those who were invited treated the king's servants spitefully, murdered them, and refused to attend. The furious king sent out armies, destroyed the murderers, and burned their city. Matthew here probably was implying that the destruction of Jerusalem was a punishment for rejecting God's son. When asked to judge Christ, Pilate the Roman declared himself "innocent of the blood of this just person (Jesus). You see to it." All the people answered and said, "His blood be on us and on our children." Matthew had the Jews curse themselves and their descendants. Soon it would get worse.

Both Mark and Matthew state simply that Judas betrayed Jesus. In Luke's Gospel, Satan entered into Judas, who then developed a plot of betrayal. Upon being captured Jesus said to the chief priest, captains of the temple, and Jewish elders, "This is your hour, and the power of darkness." In effect, they were Satan. In John's Gospel, written shortly after Luke's, anti-Semitism peaked. In a section of Chapter Eight, titled "Abraham's Seed and Satan's" in many editions of the Bible, John has Jesus say to the Jews, "I know that you are Abraham's descendants, but you seek to kill me, because my word has no place in you . . . You are of your father the devil, and the desires of your father you want to do. He was a murderer from the beginning . . ." (8:44). Despite theological attempts to minimize the impact of John's account, it has influenced the course of history.

The authors of the Gospels and the young Church itself weren't afraid of squaring off against the Jewish devils but were smart enough to back off when it came to the Romans, whose army was powerful and relentless. Indeed, the Gospels treat Pontius Pilate rather sympathetically, although an Egyptian Jew named Philo who lived at that time described him as inflexible, stubborn, and cruel; his administration of the Jewish provinces was characterized by "greed, violence, robbery, assault, abrasive behavior, frequent executions without trial, and endless savage ferocity." The only biblical book to demonize the Romans was Revelation, but the language was so confusing that to this day no one is absolutely sure of its meaning.

As Christians increased in number during the second century, they were persecuted horribly by the Romans. Christians were judged to be dangerous because they were atheists who, by refusing to sacrifice to the Roman gods, put the Roman Empire at risk of divine punishment. In truth, as noted by Pagels, "Christians did teach converts not only that the bonds of family, society, and nation are not sacred, but that they are diabolic encumbrances designed to enslave people to Roman customs that is, to demons." The Romans portrayed Christians as child-killers, cannibals, and participants in incestuous sexual orgies. These charges were based on a misinterpretation of the Eucharist and of the Agape (love-feast). In John's Gospel, Christ said, "Whoever eats my flesh and drinks my blood has eternal life . . . For my flesh is food indeed, and my blood is drink indeed" (6:54–55). The Romans believed that Christians used the blood of children when taking communion and that the love-feast communal meal was similar to a bacchanalian orgy complete with sacrifices. Christians, of course, defended themselves against these charges. Rome fell eventually (the Goths sacked the city in 410), while Christianity prospered. Then a strange thing happened on the way to the church: orthodox (straight-thinking) Christians turned these old charges against dissident Christians, who became known as heretics. What the Romans did to the Christians was, in turn, done by the Christians to the heretics among them who, in addition to being charged as socially disruptive, were also considered Satan's servants.

Heretics presented alternative interpretations of Scripture and refused to submit to the Church's priests and bishops. Some, such as Arius (he regarded Christ as a sort of demigod with a perfect human nature and the soul of an angel), argued fine points of theology. Others turned things topsy-turvy and held, for example, that the serpent in the Garden of Eden really was Christ or that the god called Yahweh was, in fact, a fallen angel. Still others, such as the followers of Valentinus, believed that it was possible for some believers to attain a profound level of personal spirituality outside the structure of the Church. These heretics were challenged by the great theologians who looked back to Paul's warning about "false apostles, deceitful workers, disguising themselves as apostles of Christ. And no wonder! For

Satan himself disguises himself as an angel of light. Therefore it is not strange if his servants disguise themselves as ministers of righteousness . . ." (2 Cor. 11:13–15).

Paul wrote that Satan had been destroyed through the death of Jesus (Heb. 2:14). Yet 1 Peter 5:8 warned Christians, "Be sober, be vigilant; because your adversary the devil walks about like a roaring lion, seeking whom he may devour." Despite this confusion, Satan, indeed, persisted, as did his assistant satans (some theologians thought that ten percent of all the angels had become satans). Ephesians 16:12 called them the "spiritual hosts of wickedness in the heavenly places," referring to their abode in the air above the earth.

The Church found a good use for Satan as it grew in power over the centuries. Heretical sects such as the Montanists, Paulicians, Bogomiles, and Waldensians were charged with being child-killers, cannibals, and participants in incestuous sexual orgies. New to the list of offenses was that of cultic Satan worshippers. By the time we reach the Middle Ages, cunning demons were lurking everywhere, ever ready to harass and trick Christians into committing sins (Norman Cohn's *Europe's Inner Demons* gives a masterful account). The demons sat on cabbage leaves and lingered in milk buckets; when ingested they cavorted in the bowels of their victims. Their leader, Satan, often appeared as a large black cat whom worshippers had to kiss under his tail. Satan could also appear as a giant toad or a pale, ice-cold man. He presided over gross orgies where anything could take place from bestiality and anal sex to the slaughtering of children and the drinking of their blood. Gregory IX's papal declaration, *Vox in Rama* (1233), aimed at heretical sects in Germany, provides all the exquisite details.

In the following centuries Satan was associated with ritual magic and witches. Fantastic stories derived from old folk tales and confessions extracted from heretics under torture were accepted as reality. In both religious and secular courts, straightfaced prosecutors told of nocturnal meeting, where witches flew through the night air, of pacts with the devil, of sexual intercourse with demons. At first heretics were the target, but soon witchcraft was suspected whenever a calamity or strange event took place. Women, especially those who were ugly, shrewish, or physically deformed, were suspect. Driven by religious zeal, priests and magistrates hounded the populace, especially in France, Germany, Switzerland, and Scotland. The great witch hunts peaked in the late 1500s and diminished towards the end of the next century.

The charges brought against witches were bogus. So how can we explain why so many educated and well-meaning persons let their fantasies run riot over their common sense? Norman Cohn suggests a psychological answer: "Unconscious resentment against Christianity as too strict a religion, against Christ as too stern a taskmaster." The response to the Christian exaltation of spirituality was the creation of an animalistic Devil who demanded to be kissed in unlikely places of his anatomy. Neurotic persons torn between conscious religious ideals and unconscious resentments conjured up all sorts of fantasies that seemed real to them. The victims of witch hunts were "scapegoats for an unacknowledged hostility to Christianity." Cohn's psychohistorical speculations may be correct. Why these factors came into play in certain locales at a specific time in history is still not understood clearly.

Reason and enlightenment paralyzed Satan for most people. We shall get back to this, but first we will consider a most peculiar form of satan, known as the Antichrist, who still has a following.

WHO EXACTLY IS THE ANTICHRIST?

The New Testament Epistle of John (not the same John who wrote the Gospel, but rather a member of the group who followed John's leadership) names a character who came to assume a significant role in history: "Children, it is the last hour. You heard that the Antichrist is to come; well, how many Antichrists have made their appearance, and this makes us certain that it is the last hour" (1 John 2:18). Bernard McGinn's masterful book, *Antichrist*, notes that "The history of Antichrist can be conceived as one way of writing . . . the history of the hatreds and fears of Christians." Not only have individuals been accused of being totally evil but also "groups of opponents and outsiders [have been] viewed as embodiments of evil, especially Jews, heretics, and Muslims." The Antichrist is the Final Enemy, a tyrannical, carnal, monstrous persecutor who seeks the destruction of Christianity. Belief in his existence stems from the prior belief that current battles between the forces of good and evil are preparations for the terrible time of devastation, the Apocalypse, when the world will be destroyed and the righteous saved. Every modern skirmish could be the prelude to the final battle. When it occurs, Christ will fulfill his destiny by destroying both Satan and the supreme human opponent of Christianity known as the Antichrist.

A series of Jewish books of revelations concerning the end of the world were written from about 250–150 B.C., when Greek influences were threatening to overturn the basic principles of traditional Hebrew religion. The apocalypse in Daniel 7–12 was the only one included in the Bible. Daniel was written in about 165 B.C., although the author describes historical events *as if* he were writing in the sixth century B.C. Thus, conflicts with the empires of Babylonia, Media, Persia, and the Hellenes—each is presented as a beast—are "predicted" even though they had already taken place. Daniel lived at a time when the ruler of the area was cruelly persecuting the Jews and forcing them to become Hellenized by adopting Greek ways. For Daniel this was the most evil of all empires:"It will devour the whole earth, trample it and break it in pieces" (7:23). The horrible leader of this empire was a sinister king, a horn growing from a beastly goat, who would destroy the holy people but who then would himself be destroyed by a messiah. A person reading the book of Daniel is led to believe that the prophecy of the then-current evil empire was made several hundred years earlier. In truth, the "prophecy" was composed at exactly the time that the prophesied historical events were taking place. The horrible ruler could even be identified as a living person, namely Antiochus IV.

The notion of an apocalypse surrounded Jesus, especially after his death. The Gospels of Mark (1:31-37), Matthew (24:1-24:46), and Luke (21:5-38) all give an account of what was to be expected. False Christs and false prophets will arise showing signs and wonders to lead the elect astray. There will be earthquakes, famine, and falling stars. Nation will rise against nation and kingdom against kingdom. There will be an abomination of desolation. And then Christ will return with power and glory to gather the elect. In Paul's version, the Enemy, the Son of Perdition, the Man of Sin will be revealed. His coming is the work of Satan. But he will be annihilated by Jesus. In the book of Revelation the Apocalypse takes center stage. A Beast arises from the abyss. It has a healed head wound. His number is 666 (13:18). He has seven heads which are the seven hills and seven emperors. "Five of them (heads) are already gone, one is here now, and one is to come" (17:9-10). He will be destroyed by the Lamb (Christ).

And who was the first person to be called the Beast? None other than Nero, Emperor of Rome from 64-68 A.D., the first great persecutor of Christians, slayer of Paul and probably Peter (as well as his own mother and his pregnant wife, Poppaea, whom he stomped to death during a temper tantrum). He falsely blamed the Christians for causing the great fire of Rome. According to the Roman historian Tacitus: "The result was a flood of summary trials, some victims ending their days as human torches to illuminate Nero's circus games." Hated by the Senate but well-liked by the average Roman, he stabbed himself to death at the age of thirty. Stories circulated that he had survived his suicide attempt and that he had fled to the Middle East, where he was forming an army in order to return to Rome and kill his enemies. A

section of the Jewish book called the Sibylline Oracles (actually written at the end of the first century A.D. but supposedly written in the
mythic time of Noah) predicted that an evil king would flee to the
East and then return to devastate Rome. A Christian adaptation of the
Oracles converted Nero into Beliar (Satan). The Beast of the book of
Revelation was both the Roman Empire (Rome is famous for its seven
hills) and its nefarious leader, Nero, who will be revived and climb up
from death to battle Christ who will step down from heaven onto the
earth. How does 666 come into play? The numbers signify letters of
the alphabet, a popular procedure in many ancient civilizations, and
spell the name "Nero Emperor."

The Church Fathers of the second and third centuries abandoned
Nero and developed other ideas about the Antichrist. Irenaeus determined that the Antichrist will be a Jew from the tribe of Dan because
Revelation 7 omitted this tribe from the list of "sealed" sons of Israel
and because Jeremiah 8:16 implicated the tribe of Dan in the destruction of Israel: "The snorting of his horses was heard from Dan. The
whole land trembled . . . for they have come and devoured the land
and all that is in it, the city and those who dwell in it." Hippolytus
wrote that the Roman Empire was only a precursor of the final kingdom of the Antichrist, which will appear in the year 500 A.D. At that
time Roman rule will be weakened and the Antichrist will rebuild the
city and the temple of Jerusalem. He will declare that he is God and
slaughter dissenters. Theologians from the Eastern branch of the
Church provided detailed descriptions of the Antichrist: bloodshot
right eye, two pupils in his left eye, large lower lip, eyebrows that
reach his ears, hair sticking up like arrow points, fingers like sickles,
a leprous spot on his hands, feet two yards long, "The Antichrist" written on his forehead.

Some Church Fathers took a totally different approach. Augustine,
for example, said that the Antichrist is "everyone who denies Christ
by his words." Gregory the Great, Pope from 590 to 604, said that
"Antichrist's work is done daily among the wicked." It is even possible to do the Antichrist's work without ever having known him. In the
Pope's words, "How many have not seen Antichrist and yet are his testicles because they corrupt the hearts of the innocent by the example of their actions."

The history of the Antichrist concept is so complicated that limited highlights must suffice. Because of the warfare in Spain between
Christians and Muslims, Muhammad was declared the Antichrist in
the ninth century. Since there were serious disagreements over the
need for Church reforms in the eleventh century, the German
Emperor established Archbishop Wiebert of Ravenna as an Antipope

and said that the reigning Pope, Gregory VII, was the Antichrist. Gregory said the same about Wiebert. For several centuries, Church reformers and Popes regularly exchanged Antichrist charges. One of the greatest exchanges was between Emperor Frederick II (1194–1250) and Pope Innocent IV. The Pope called for Christians to attack Frederick and to "destroy the name and the remains, the seed and the sapling of this man from Babylon! Let mercy forget him, since he is merciless and cruel without end." Frederick's supporters noted that the name Innocent the Pope could be converted to the number 666. In the late fourteenth century the English theologian John Wycliffe declared that "the multitude of popes, cardinals, bishops and their accomplices from the time of the Church's endowment" constitute a monstrous, composite Antichrist. Martin Luther wrote in *The Babylonian Captivity of the Church* (1520) that "the papacy is indeed nothing but the kingdom of Babylon and of the true Antichrist;" in *Against the Roman Papacy: An Institution of the Devil* (1545), he described the Pope as "the damned Antichrist" and used coarse language in associating the Antichrist with feces and flatus. His translation of the Bible into German was published (1535) with illustrations of the papal Antichrist. Luther's followers came to regard the menacing figure of the Turk as an Antichrist along with the Pope.

In America, Roger Williams (1603–1683), founder of Rhode Island, preached that the formation of a Christian state would play into the hands of the Antichrist. The authors of the hated Stamp Act were identified in 1776 as Beasts of the Apocalypse, and Americans were warned that they would "receive the mark of the beast" if they followed the Act's regulations. In Europe many persons considered Napoleon Bonaparte to be the Antichrist; a generation later his nephew, Napoleon III, received the title.

In modern times the concepts of Antichrist and of an imminent Apocalypse were spurred by the formation of a Jewish state in 1948 and by the great World Wars. Some people believe that the Apocalypse was forestalled when the Second Temple of Jerusalem was destroyed by the Romans in 70 A.D. With the new establishment of Israel and the return of the Jews to Palestine, the countdown to the Apocalypse had begun again. The devastation of the World Wars as well as the American offensive against Iraq have been interpreted as preludes to the End of Time, and the formation of the League of Nations and the United Nations, the European Common Market, and the Trilateral Commission have been interpreted as the final desperate revival of Rome (world government) leading to the Apocalypse.

A bizarre and sometimes amusing literature has developed on the topics of the Apocalypse and the Antichrist. Hal Lindsay's best seller,

The Late Great Planet Earth (1970) predicted that a Gentile dictator will help Israel rebuild the Temple of Jerusalem where he will proclaim himself God. In truth, he is the Antichrist as revealed by his recovery from a head wound. John Walvoord's *Armageddon, Oil and the Middle East Crisis* (1974, revised in 1990) predicted that the Antichrist as a leader of a group of circum-Mediterranean nations will force an Arab-Israeli peace and thus usher in the last seven years of the world. Jeane Dixon's *My Life and Prophecies* (1969) predicted that the Antichrist will come out of the closet in 1999. Among the persons identified by some Christian Fundamentalists as the Antichrist are Pope John Paul II, Mikhail Gorbachev (a deceptive peacemaker with a strange red birthmark on his head), Henry Kissinger, and Pat Robertson (accused by a fellow Fundamentalist, Constance Cumbey, because of his slick television style and his interest in the Middle East). Last, but certainly not least, is Ronald Wilson Reagan, whose three names contain six letters each and whose assistant, James Brady, was shot in the head! If you're into this sort of thing, a case could be made that Reagan's Alzheimer's disease is a form of head wound.

Revelation 13:16–17 relates that the Second Beast, the world leader of a false religion, will put a mark on the hand or forehead of his followers; "no one may buy or sell except one who has the mark of the name of the beast, or the number of his name." Based on this, Mary Stewart Rolefe's book *When Your Money Fails* (1991) stated that a "666 System" has been secretly encoded on credit cards, computer programs, and the bar codes on consumer products. She expected the Antichrist to imprint 666 on the foreheads of his followers soon. Her advice was to buy gold and cut up your credit cards.

Only really committed and strange people nowadays talk about and accuse others of being the Antichrist; their rantings can be heard sometimes on low-power AM radio stations late in the evening. Preachers of the imminent Apocalypse can be found in not a few Fundamentalist churches and in solitary sect living compounds. Two of the most infamous leaders have been Jim Jones and David Koresh; both brought an apocalypse of a sort on themselves and their almost one thousand dead followers in Guyana and Waco. Both were paranoid, hypersexual, and very persuasive.

The greatest American preacher of the Apocalypse was William Miller (1782–1849). He preached a version called premillenialism, the belief that Christ will return to earth to begin a thousand-year era of righteousness prior to the End of Time when all hell breaks loose. In 1741 he announced that Christ would return to earth in twelve years. He published a book about the second coming and held revivals under the largest tent in America. Supposedly more than a million people believed his biblical calculations. In January 1843 he predicted Christ's arrival between March 21, 1843, and March 21, 1844. When Christ didn't appear, he rechecked his math, uncovered an error, and pronounced that the new date of arrival was October 22, 1844. The excitement among his followers reached fever pitch. Needless to say, Christ did not materialize. This was known as the Great Disappointment. A large number of patients were admitted to mental hospitals in New England where the physicians attributed "excitement produced by Millerism" as a major factor in the need for hospitalization. The majority of the patients probably were schizophrenic or manic-depressive. Almost all were hospitalized *prior* to the Great Disappointment of October 1884. Most of Miller's followers simply repudiated him and went home. Among the few who kept the faith was Ellen Gould White, who went on to establish the Seventh Day Adventist Church.

HARD-HEARTED SINNERS

Long before the earliest portions of the Bible were written, the peoples of the Middle East had religious feelings and ideas. Knowing little about the physical, chemical, and biological operations of the natural world, they endowed it with spirits and spirituality. We have already seen how rocks and trees were considered gods. Words in the form of blessings or curses assumed a reality of their own. Individuals were bound to each other and to nature and to the gods by a chain of unseen, sometimes unfathomable, supernatural forces. Taboos that supposedly represented the desires of these forces were established in order to govern the orderly course of life. It is from the transgression of taboos that the concept of sin originated. Punishment such as exile or death was harsh and immediate, even for an accidental transgression. Vestiges of these notions can be found in the Bible; God's charge to Noah that "You shall not eat flesh with life, that is to say blood, in it" (Gen. 9:4) probably reflected an ancient taboo. Other examples are the swift exile of Cain the murderer (Gen. 4:13–14) and the necessity for a special offering to God for committing an unintentional sin (Lev. 4:2–3).

One of the most profound accomplishments of the Bible was the moral delineation of sin as a rebellion against the one, true God and its characterization as wicked, evil, and guilt-evoking. Despite protestations of innocence, no one was exempt: "Who can say, 'I have made my heart clean; I am pure from sin?'" (Prov. 20:9). Even great men such as David and Solomon were big-time sinners. Moses's sin prevented

him from living in the promised land. And Elijah prayed for death
because he was no better than his father (1 Kin. 19:4). Psalm 38
described how the wrath of God affected a sinner: "My wounds are
foul and festering . . . I go mourning all day long . . . I am feeble and
severely broken . . . my heart pants . . . the light of my eyes is gone
from me . . . my loved ones and friends stand aloof from my
plague . . . those who seek my hurt plan deception all day long . . . do
not forsake me, O Lord." In the old days a man's sin could lead both
to his destruction and to that of everyone and everything associated
with him: when Achan sinned by stealing instead of destroying some
accursed Babylonian treasures, he and his family and his animals and
his tent were stoned and set on fire (Josh. 7:20–26). Later on in history, God softened his position a little and said that he would visit the
iniquity of the fathers upon the children *only* to the third and fourth
generation (Ex. 20:5). More humanely, Jeremiah prophesied, "It shall
come to pass [that] . . . every one shall die for his own iniquity . . . In
those days they shall say no more: 'The fathers have eaten sour
grapes, and the children's teeth shall be set on edge'" (31:29–30).

The Old Testament writers did not elaborate about the origin of sin.
Demons weren't all that significant. The story of Adam not only didn't
use any words meaning sin but also was never central to ancient
Hebrew thought. Speculations involving the role of the "sons of God"
and their intercourse with women (Gen. 6) were late entries that told
more about the perpetuation of sin. The Old Testament writers took the
position that "The wicked are estranged from the womb; they go astray
as soon as they are born, speaking lies" (Ps. 58:3), and that man's corruption is the cause of sin. The human will was thought to be located
in the heart and each sinner follows "the dictates of his evil heart" (Jer.
11:8); "The Lord saw that the wickedness of man was great in the earth,
and that the thoughts in his heart fashioned nothing but wickedness all
day long" (Gen. 6:5). In the central portion of Second Esdras (a book
included among the Apocrypha of the Old Testament, written toward
the end of the first century A.D.) an angel taught the prophet Ezra why
the heart is evil: "A grain of evil seed was sown in Adam's heart from the
beginning and how much ungodliness it has produced until now, and
will produce until the time of threshing comes" (4:30). Who sowed the
evil seed and why is never clearly explained.

Although sin could not be totally avoided, each person could minimize its inevitability by adhering to the laws of behavior established
by God in his covenant with Israel. So many of these laws were given
directly to Moses by God during the exodus from Egypt that even the
addition of later laws came to be considered as part of "the Book of
the Law of Moses" (Neh. 8:1). The Ten Commandments (literally "ten

words") were central to the Law. Originally they all were brief state-ments that started with a negative particle; their present wording was written during or after the exile in Babylon in 598–530 B.C. (two commandments, honor the Sabbath and honor your parents, were probably changed from negative to positive). Laws presented as pro-hibitions—don't do this—allowed for a greater degree of personal freedom than laws that demanded exact behavior—you must do this.

The Covenant Code (Exodus 20:22–23:33), often paraphrasing Mesopotamian laws, dealt with property, slavery, bodily injury, interac-tions with neighbors and strangers, worship of God, covenant holi-ness, the Sabbath, and religious festivals. Most of these laws were quite precise: "If you buy a Hebrew servant, he shall serve six years; and in the seventh he shall go out free and pay nothing." A great number of laws were presented in the book of Deuteronomy, which is essential-ly a group of sermons supposedly given by Moses. It contains a second version of the Ten Commandments, a Covenant Code, and laws about marriage, social organization and welfare, and criminal justice.

When Jerusalem was destroyed along with the temple in 587 B.C. (by King Nebuchadnezzar) and some of its inhabitants sent into exile, Israel's fate was in doubt. The book of Lamentations described the pitiful conditions of hopelessness and famine that led compassionate women to cook and eat their own children; "The Law is no more, and her [Jerusalem's] prophets find no vision from the Lord" (2:9). During the exile in Babylon the Israelite priests composed the numerous laws found in the book of Leviticus on wide-ranging topics such as diet, sexuality, holy vows, and atonement rituals. When the exiled Israelites rejoined their brethren in Jerusalem, God had stopped com-munications both directly and through his prophets. What remained was the Law, and it eventually became the central focus of religious life. Malachi warned of the impending apocalypse when the proud and the wicked would burn up; salvation would come only to those who remembered "the Law of Moses . . . with the statutes and judge-ments" (4:4). In fact, it was Ezra, "a skilled scribe in the Law of Moses," who copied the Law and taught it to the Jews (Ezra 7:4).

The written Law was comprehensive but could not deal with all possible situations, such as how to cope with seductive Greek cus-toms and with Roman political rule. A tradition of oral laws devel-oped; some, called midrashic laws, were interpretations of the written Law of Moses, while others, called Mishnaic laws, were not based on Holy Scripture. These oral laws were codified during the first century A.D. and gave rise to a large new literature produced by rabbis who sought to interpret the laws and to link them with the Law of Moses. Jewish intellectual and religious concerns became engrossed with an ever-expanding and all-encompassing series of laws that came to be regarded as perfect, as a pillar of the universe, and even as existing in God's mind before the creation of the world. The living of life in such a legalistic system became both simple and incredibly difficult. Freedom from sin meant obeying every aspect of all the laws. However, from a practical standpoint, the thicket of laws was so dense that everyone was bound to take a wrong turn sooner or later. Even the greatest rabbis disagreed among themselves about how to interpret the laws. Also, strict attention to the laws could lead to an unfeeling, insecure rigidity of behavior and to an exaggeration of pious activities meant to impress others. What to do about sin and the law was a major problem for the founders of Christianity.

THE MEDIUM AND THE MESSAGE: JESUS AND THE LAW

Jesus was born and reared Jewish, yet the religion he founded eclipsed Judaism and even was antagonistic toward it. Was he for the law or against it? The answer is both. For two thousand years scholars have argued about this "on the one hand" and "on the other hand."

The Pharisees were guardians of the law. As told in Mark 7 they criticized Jesus about his "unclean" eating practices. Jesus ripped into them with a vengeance and said that they were the hypocrites about whom Isaiah (23:13) had prophesied: "This people honors me only with lip service, while their hearts are far from me. The worship they offer me is worthless, the doctrine they teach are only human regulation." Jesus then declared that all foods were fine to eat because it's what comes out of a man, rather than what goes in, that makes him unclean. As for sin, he listed fornication, theft, murder, adultery, avarice, malice, deceit, indecency, envy, slander, pride and folly: "All these evil things come from within and make a man unclean." No mention of the law here.

When Jesus' disciples picked corn on the Sabbath, the Pharisees had a conniption (Mark 2:23–28). Jesus challenged them with their own Scripture. Didn't David and his men eat consecrated bread when they were hungry? Jesus concluded that "The Sabbath was made for man, not man for the Sabbath."

A scribe tried to trick Jesus into declaring which was the supreme commandment. Jesus came up with two: love God and love your neighbor as yourself. Jesus didn't mention rituals and, in fact, he went on to warn about scribes in long robes who strutted in the marketplaces and took the front seats in the synagogues: "These are the men who swallow the property of widows, while making a show of lengthy prayers" (Mark 12:38–40).

It would seem that Jesus was intent on overturning the law. In Luke 12:57 he even suggested, "Why not judge for yourselves what is right?" And yet he said, "Do not think that I came to destroy the Law or the Prophets: I did not come to destroy but to fulfill" (Matt. 5:17). What did he mean? He went on to give some examples. He not only approved of the law "Thou shalt not kill," but he surpassed it by stating that it wasn't even permissible to be angry with another person (unless you had a darned good reason) or to call him a fool. Similarly he approved of the law about offering special sacrifices at the altar but added that you first have to be at peace with your fellow man. In these examples he made the law even more onerous. However, Jesus overturned the law allowing divorce (the phrase "except on the ground of fornication" was a later addition to Matthew). He also overturned the law "Thou shalt love your neighbor, and hate your enemy" and replaced it with "Love your enemies and pray for those who persecute you." In fact, there was no law about hating your enemy; Jesus' interpretation of Lev. 19:16–18 was off the mark but he was correct in picking up on Israel's historic hostility towards outsiders. In any event, his intent was clear.

It was a confusing situation. Jesus himself said that he didn't destroy the law, yet he did destroy some laws. He said that he came to fulfill the law, yet, like Moses, he was a lawgiver. Some theologians and scholars have tried to explain these contradictions with the lame argument that Jesus really meant to overturn the oral but not the written law. Others have held that Jesus really supported the old law but, upon his death, meant for a new law to take effect. This speculative argument is based on Matthew 5:18, "Until heaven and earth pass away, not an iota, not a dot, will pass from the law until all is accomplished."

Paul, himself a Pharisee before his conversion to Christianity, was conflicted about the law and its relation to sin. In some difficult lines (Rom. 5:12–14) he noted that "Sin came into the world through one man and death through sin, and so death spread to all men because all men sinned." Paul here meant that sin leads to death; this was true for Adam and for everyone since then. It wasn't because of Adam that we die. Adam just happened to be the first sinner, but each person who sins is responsible for his own death. (It's true that Adam and Eve sinned and were punished, but Genesis does not state that humankind would be punished for the sin of the first parents. In fact, nowhere in the Old Testament is there any direct statement linking human suffering with the transgression in the Garden of Eden. This linkage became popular in books such as Wisdom of Solomon and Ecclesiasticus in the first century B.C.) Paul then abruptly introduced another idea: "Sin indeed was in the world before the law was given, but sin is not counted where there is no law. Yet death reigned from Adam and Moses, even though their transgression, unlike that of Adam, was not a matter of breaking the law." For Paul, sin meant breaking the law. However, since there was no law before Moses, then logically no one could have sinned and no one should have died! Paul didn't explain things here but later developed extra-legal notions of sin as an alien demonic power that dwelled in a person's body and waged war with his mind (Rom. 7:22–23). In a complicated concept Paul explained that the law was holy and good but it led to death. "We know that the law is spiritual, but I am carnal . . . I serve the law of God with my mind, but with my flesh I serve the law of sin" (Rom. 7:14, 25).

Paul had once been so exceedingly zealous in his attendance to the law and observance of Jewish traditions that he persecuted Christians. He threw his past behavior away to the dogs—it was really garbage anyway he said—for the chance to know Christ (Phil. 3:6–8). Paul wrote in Galatians 2 and 3 that while Deuteronomy 27:26 cursed everyone who didn't obey the law, "Christ has redeemed us from the curse of the law . . . The law was our tutor to bring us to Christ that we might be justified by faith. But after faith has come, we are no longer under a tutor . . . For I through the law died to the law that I might live to God . . . for if righteousness comes through the law, then Christ died in vain."

Paul was the ultimate pragmatic evangelist. He recognized that Judaism was mired in the law. Its only remedy for inevitable transgressions was intensified dedication to the strict observance of rituals. Christianity offered converts something quite new, namely redemption through Christ who already had done the hard work by allowing himself to be crucified. If you've sinned, don't worry about the law; just keep the faith. Christ was both the medium and the message. Also, Paul saw that the future of Christianity was among the Gentiles, and they neither were reared in the tradition of the law (and so weren't terribly concerned about it), nor were they about to accept all sorts of strange dietary restrictions or rituals such as circumcision. In fact, after a short time the Church became predominantly composed of Gentiles, and all the furor over the law became a dim memory.

AWAY WITH ALL SIN: THE DECLINE IN PERSONAL RESPONSIBILITY

Many first-century B.C. Jewish theologians believed that from the moment of his creation, Adam had an evil inclination (*yetzer hara*) in him, a "grain of evil seed" that all subsequent humans also possess. Christian theologians developed their own ideas. Irenaeus imagined

Adam and Eve as literal "babes" during the childhood of the human race. They were created in the image of God but were too immature to avoid being led astray by Satan. Through Christ, man gained the possibility of maturing towards perfection. Origen held that all people were prone to sin by nature and that all souls were guilty of previous sins. Supposedly every soul existed before the creation of the universe. One of them, Satan, rebelled and was rejected by God. The soul-angels who sided with Satan were transformed into demons because they committed terrible crimes. The souls that remained weren't so culpable; God's punishment was to bind them to human bodies. Another theory was that of Saint Augustine, who eventually believed that Adam was a wise and perfect being; his "unspeakable sin" was a misuse of free will. Evil was not a distinct entity or thing but rather originated from goodness because God permitted it to do so. Adam was the root of humankind. His original sin infected his offspring, who became children of wrath: "In the faulty choice of that one man all men sinned in him; because all men were that one man, original sin affects everyone." Baptism removed the stain of original sin and Christ, the Second Adam, brought redemption, unlike the first Adam, who brought death.

For relief from the guilt of sin Judaism demanded increased adherence to the law, but Christianity offered something different: "If we confess our sins, he [Jesus] is faithful and just, and will forgive our sins and cleanse us from all unrighteousness" (1 John 8). The Epistle of 1 John, served to assist traveling evangelists in providing practical advice about the new religion. It warned about the Antichrist, for example, and advised, "Little children, keep yourselves from idols." It also divided sin into two categories, the sin unto death and the sin that is not unto death. The first became known as mortal and the second as venial sin. In Church tradition mortal sin turned persons from God by destroying the charity in their hearts; venial sin offended charity but allowed it to subsist. Thomas Aquinas listed blasphemy, perjury, homicide, and adultery as examples of mortal sin; he chose thoughtless chatter and immoderate laughter to exemplify venial sin. Augustine counseled against taking venial sins lightly: "If you take them lightly when you weight them, tremble when you count them . . . a number of drops fills a river; a number of grains makes a heap."

As for specific sins, the early Church turned to the Ten Commandments, to Jesus' Sermon on the Mount (Matt. 5:1-7:29), and Paul's lists (1 Cor. 5:10-11 and 6:9-10; Rom. 1:29-32; Gal. 5:19-21). By the third century the concept of the seven capital sins had emerged; they were envy, anger, pride, sloth, avarice, gluttony, and lust. John Cassion (360-435) deleted envy but added fornication and dejection. A final list that has endured was compiled by Pope Gregory the Great (540–604): pride (from which all the others derive), avarice, envy, wrath, lust, gluttony, and sloth.

Over the course of history, sin, like Satan and hell, has gradually withdrawn into the dim recesses of Western consciousness. In fact, the psychiatrist William Menninger's best seller *Whatever Became of Sin?* (1973) noted that, "Sin was no longer a topic of conversation, debate, argument, accusation, and public remorse." A new social morality had developed and old-fashioned sin had been reconfigured into either criminal behavior or a symptom of mental disorder. Menninger saw a negative side to this new social morality; the elimination of sin has effectively neutralized the importance of guilt and moral responsibility. We punish criminals with monetary fines or send them to a so-called penitentiary, but we no longer expect true atonement or repentance. Indeed, prisoners who claim to discover religion and to experience jailhouse conversions are nowadays regarded with cynical disbelief by most of us in the outside world. The fabulous affability and manipulative techniques of psychopaths have entered into the realm of common knowledge. Sadly, we have so lost our ability even to think in religious modes that we are now unable to identify and appreciate those instances—admittedly rare—when prisoners really do experience true religious conversion and repentance.

While our general cynicism may be relatively new (a result perhaps of media presentations of the foibles and character flaws of national leaders), disbelief has been around longer. The incredulous congregation in Nathaniel Hawthorne's *The Scarlet Letter* (1850) had already lost its ability to comprehend the heartfelt confession of their adulterous minister, "Ye, that have deemed me holy! Behold me here, the one sinner of the world." In 1838, Ralph Waldo Emerson had noted that "no man can go with his thoughts about him into one of our churches without feeling that what hold the public worship had on men is gone, or going. It has lost its grasp on the affection of the good and the fear of the bad." In *The Death of Satan*, Andrew Delbanco traced this loss of the world of spirit back even further. In 1724, a New England judge for the first time ordered a mental examination of a plaintiff in a witchcraft trial. A few years later, English law was recodified; witchcraft, formerly punishable by death, was redefined as the *pretense* of witchcraft, sorcery, or enchantment, and punishment was reduced to a year in prison. "One could no longer *be* a witch; one could only *pretend* to be one or delude oneself into thinking so."

In today's materialistic world where success is measured by the cost of one's toys, the seven capital sins don't seem very sinful. In fact, admirable capitalists are proud of their ability to squelch competition and to capture an ever growing share of the market. They are driven by avarice, are envious of others who are more successful, and channel their aggression towards the accumulation of wealth. Once rich, they can indulge their vices—lust, gluttony, even laziness or whatever else they might desire—without fear of public censure or the experience of guilt.

Max Weber's monumental *The Protestant Ethic and the Spirit of Capitalism* (1904-1905) argued cogently that the Reformation begun by Luther changed the course of history and facilitated the development of capitalism in such a way that morality and economics became interlinked. The new order encouraged the acquisition of property and the maximization of financial profit as an expression of God's will. The lines from Proverbs 22:29 took on special importance: "Seeth thou a man diligent in his business? He will stand before kings." John Wesley (1703-1791), the founder of the Methodist Church, wrote, "We ought not to prevent people from being diligent and frugal; we must exhort all Christians to gain all they can, and to save all they can; that is, effect, to grow rich." In the new ethic it was permissible to make tallow out of cattle and money out of men. However, along with this call to wealth came the serious admonition against enjoying it. Wealth entitled a life of sober simplicity and social responsibility.

With the decline of religion, especially in the twentieth century, only the economic aspect of capitalism flourished while its ascetic underpinning disappeared. The devastating American experience of a civil war in which both sides claimed God's support surely hastened the debasement of a belief in a beneficent Providence. The horrors of the Holocaust turned many people away from God. The evilness of the Nazis has been examined from many perspectives, but the concept of sin has rarely entered the discussion; the notion of moral responsibility has assumed a secular cast. We recognize evil but lack the capacity to discuss it in other than sterile terms.

In psychiatry, mind has replaced soul. Psychoanalysis offered explanations of behavior without recourse to the spirit world. So did behaviorism. Free will, a necessary ingredient of sin, became practically meaningless; we do what we do because of child-rearing patterns and social pressures. The latest explanatory force is biology; we do what we do because of chemical imbalances and faulty neuronal activity in our brains. The flaws of our parents and their parents before them through the generations are passed on to us genetically at the moment of conception. Original sin is nothing but a double-helix. Psychological and physical-chemical "mechanisms" have eclipsed supernaturalism and its panoply of sin and redemption, but these mechanisms provide few guidelines about how we are to lead our lives. Mushy spirituality and New Age psychologies have rushed in to fill the void, as have nostalgic calls for that old-time religion that supposedly sustained our forefathers. Do we really want to return to the past, when the mentally ill were flogged in order to chase away evil demons or when masturbation was considered both a mortal sin and a debilitating disease? As always, the past seems golden, but we can't go there anymore. If we could, we would certainly be most disappointed anyway. "Sin" has had its day, whether we like it or not. It's still around, of course, and manifests itself in the time-honored tradition of scapegoating (communists are gone, but homosexuals remain great targets, and there are always more than enough dark-skinned "devils" to meet the needs of moralistic bigots). The old Augustinian notion of sin as an ingrained tendency towards evil in everyone's soul resurfaces every so often. When the federal office building in Oklahoma City was bombed, we all suspected Arab terrorists; it has been difficult to accept the fact that home-bred Americans did it. We are all infected with sin. It's not pleasant, but it's what Abraham Lincoln and Martin Luther King preached. We shot them for their efforts.

What, you say? You've never harmed anyone, or, at least, never shot anyone. You are a good person. You harbor no ill-will towards human beings, whales, or trees. You even watch revivals on television (just for a few minutes, but it should count for something). You are not an assassin. Never was and never could be.

Never could be? I reply in psychiatric style.

That's right.

Right? I echo.

Yes!

Yes . . . Well then, good luck. Should you ever need me, just call for an appointment.

DON'T SPOIL THE SOUP:
WOMEN IN THE BIBLE

CHAPTER 3

Napoleon said that anatomy is destiny. Freud believed him. Because of their biological endowment men and women are supposed to do what each is supposed to do. Aside from the facts that men can never experience the dubious pleasure of childbirth and that women can never know what it's like to get kicked in the testicles, however, the two creatures are remarkably alike. Men are not neurally programmed to watch football nor are women genetically impelled to cook dinner. Yet it is historically true that men usually have ruled both roost and throne, and that women have been subservient.

There supposedly was a time when women were triumphant, at least according to the Swiss historian Jacob Bachofen (1815–1877). According to him Earth was the original mother whom human mothers have imitated. At the dawn of history the goddess Aphrodite reigned supreme in an era of unlimited freedom, promiscuous sexuality, nomadic existence, and the growth of vegetation. When men used their physical prowess to abuse women, there was a rebellion. Women became Amazon warriors and even cut off or cauterized their daughters' right breasts so that they could better handle weapons and draw their bows when shooting arrows. Men were kept for mating, and the Amazons dislocated the hips and knees of boys so that they could not fight when they matured. Eventually the goddess Demeter assumed control and allowed men to sow their seeds in Mother Earth, thus establishing marriage, agriculture, and religion. In time the god Dionysus became irresistible to women. He ushered in the age of paternal law, which reached its apotheosis in ancient Rome. Since then, women have tried to recapture the first fine, careless raptures of Aphrodite, but their bids for supremacy have failed. According to Bachofen, a return to the age of maternal power would be a regression to bestial sexuality and lawlessness.

Bachofen's theory has no substantiation in fact and is an example of the creation of a history justifying masculine domination. The world's literature, primarily the recorded thoughts of men until recent times, is top heavy with "wise" statements about women that support the superiority of men. Men's physical domination over women has been easy; any brute can swing a club. It's effective too, up to a point, but there's always a chance that while the man is sleeping, the woman might up and drive a tent peg through his head. Or, in the ultimate masculine nightmare, the woman might switch partners by finding a man with a bigger club. Psychological subjugation is far more difficult to achieve, but it has real staying power. Women rarely rebel when they are systematically made to believe that their inferiority is an expression of the laws of nature and that the gods want them to grim and bear it. True, they can make men's lives miserable at times by expressing what social scientists politely call "idioms of distress," such as hysteria, anorexia, depression, suicidal gestures, and cutting their skin, but, more likely than not, menfolk won't get the message anyway.

Charlotte Perkins Gilmore's *The Yellow Wallpaper* (1892) is a masterful story of well-intentioned masculine insensitivity. Its heroine is a married woman who feels suffocated at home and eventually goes mad. Her kind but overbearing husband is a physician who diagnoses her condition as a "temporary nervous depression—a slight hysterical tendency." His examination satisfies him that there is no real reason for her hysteria since she has a large home and him, a doting husband. With paternalistic concern he relegates her to bed. As her condition worsens, he locks her in the attic nursery. Now fully infantilized, she hallucinates a woman trapped behind the yellow wallpaper, yearning for freedom.

In the story, the heroine's husband threatened to place her under the care of S. Weir Mitchell, a Philadelphia physician. In real life the author had endured Mitchell's famous "rest cure" for her own "hysteria." He demanded complete obedience to his cure, which emphasized a minimum of intellectual life, "never touch pen, brush, or pencil as long as you live," an hour in bed after each meal, attention to domestic chores, and the constant companionship of her child. Gilmore noted that, "If I did but dress the baby it left me shaking and crying—certainly far from a healthy companion for her, to say nothing of the effect on me." A tedious month of the rest cure persuaded most women to abandon their symptoms altogether, but Gilmore had the opposite reaction. "I would crawl into remote closets and under beds to hide from the grinding pressure of that distress." A noncompliant patient, she divorced her husband, went to California with her child, and took on the life of a writer and feminist. For Mitchell, Gilmore's illness reflected her inability to cope with the inborn feminine position of dependency. He regarded the torments of nature as inevitable for women, while for men they were accidental and dependent on the chances of life.

Mitchell's beliefs were not unique to him. They represented thousands of years of tradition. "Woman" is a concept constructed predominantly by men. The way a woman is supposed to think and to act reflects the historical "reality" of male-dominated culture. The woman who refuses to think and act properly is a pariah, a bitch, a devil, or worse, a borderline (borderline personality disorder is a diagnosis predominantly given to impulsive women whose emotional life is like a roller coaster and who have the uncanny knack of making both themselves and others miserable and constantly on edge). Through "idioms of distress," however, women are able to express discontent without actually saying the words. I do not mean to imply that culture is the result of a conscious masculine plot, or that most women who "do the right thing" cannot find happiness of a sort. There is much to be said for church, children, and cooking. It just so happens that historically men have been on top of women. Perhaps this reflects a biological imperative since the propagation of humankind is accomplished most efficiently in the missionary position, but I rather think it is the result of historical vicissitudes and circumcision-stances.

SOMETHING LIKE AN ANIMAL

Unraveling the construction of Western woman is a complicated matter, but its primary foundations are Judeo-Christian and Greco-Roman. Hera, the sister and wife of Zeus, was the queen of heaven and the goddess of marriage. Her life was spent harassing and trying to kill her husband's many mistresses and children. She even murdered hundreds of innocent people living on the island of Aegina simply because it was named after one of Zeus' girlfriends. When angry over the birth of Athena, who emerged from Zeus' head, Hera became pregnant without the help of a male and delivered a son. Alas, he was lame so she threw him out of heaven like a piece of garbage. Moreover, Hera was narcissistic: when she lost a beauty contest judged by Paris, a Trojan hero, she used every trick in the book to ensure that the Trojans would be defeated in their war with the Greeks.

Athena was the virgin goddess of crafts, especially weaving. She protected her virtue with the spear and shield that she carried and often wore a helmet. She liked and helped handsome young men like Hercules and Perseus, but no man or god ever succeeded in breaking through her armor and seducing her. When Teiresias accidentally saw Athena bathing nude, she blinded him as a punishment. Gradually she came to be revered as the goddess of wisdom.

Aphrodite, the goddess of love, beauty, and fertility floated into existence from the foam created by the genitals of Uranus when they plopped into the sea as a result of his castration. With an entrance like that it is no wonder that she didn't spend her life tending children around her husband's hearth. In fact, she was unabashedly unfaithful to her husband and slept with anyone, man or god, who tickled her fancy. Aphrodite came to Greece from the Middle East, where she was called Ishtar and Astarte and where her female devotees had to serve as temple prostitutes. The Romans called her Venus, the ancestress of both Julius and Augustus Caesar.

These three great deities—Hera the goddess of marriage whose own marriage was a shambles, Athena the chaste goddess of wisdom, Aphrodite the seductress who always got what she wanted from a man—were not true archetypes but certainly present us with a glimpse into the classical concept of the female potential. Meanwhile, back on earth, the Greeks considered the first human woman to be Pandora. Her story is worth telling.

At a meeting between gods and men, Prometheus angered Zeus by tricking him into choosing inferior food at a banquet. Zeus then punished all mankind by withholding the gift of fire. Prometheus managed to steal some fire and bring it back to earth. This time Zeus devised the ultimate punishment; he ordered the creation out of clay and water of a woman so beautiful and sensual that no man could escape her snare. She was called Pandora because all the gods gave her gifts. Aphrodite endowed her with corrupting passion. Athena clothed her and gave her jewels. Hermes gave her the mind of a bitch, a talent for lying, and a thievish nature. It was easy enough to find a man willing to marry this gorgeous woman. Her dowry was a large jar filled with every imaginable evil and affliction. She lifted its lid and let loose ten thousand sorrows that filled the earth. According to the Greek poet Hesiod, "It was she who gave birth to the race of women; from her came this female sex, all manner of women who live among mortal men to bring them pain." This, then was "woman"—an artificially created being who was beautiful on the outside but, like the contents of her vase, evil within.

Beliefs in the natural deficiencies of women and in their legacy of misery were reiterated in classical plays and poems. We read in Euripides' *Andromache* that "The gods have sent medicines for the venom of serpents, but there is no medicine for a bad woman. She is more noxious than the viper, or any fire itself." Menander writes, "Nothing is worse than a woman, even a good one." Juvenal's *Satires* include, "Nothing is more intolerable than a wealthy woman," and "May the gods save us from a learned woman." Plutarch (about 50–99 A.D.), the champion of the partnership between Greek and Roman ideals, wrote many popular moral and educational treatises whose influence persevered in Europe for seventeen hundred years. His treatise on marriage called for a symbiotic intimacy between husband and wife, yet, as noted by the modern scholar Giulia Sissa, he compared the husband "to the sun, to a king, to a master, to a knight, while the wife is compared to the moon (or a mirror), a subject, a pupil, a horse. If a woman is active, if she takes the initiative, she is immediately accused of seduction, witchcraft, or shameful excesses. A woman must remain consenting and passive; she must adapt in every way to her husband's role." Plutarch warned that wives need to be taught by their husbands because they naturally "conceive many untoward ideas, low designs, and emotions."

In discussing gender differences, Aristotle (384–322 B.C.) held that women are inferior to men: "Females are by nature weaker and colder, and their nature must be considered naturally deficient." He noted that women had smaller muscles and brains, softer flesh, and high-pitched voices. Woman was a weaker organism because she lacked enough vital heat to "cook" (metabolize) blood. In men, blood supposedly was transformed into sperm through cooking, but in women blood was only partially cooked, the end result being menstrual blood. Sperm, the essence of being, contained the principles of soul, movement, and form. The uterus was an incubator and contained menstrual blood to assist the sperm in developing into the proper form. "The female is a passive element, and the man is an active element." The natural result of conception was a male child; females were conceived only when the sperm did not fulfill its potential. These ideas were codified by Aristotle but had been present in Greek thought for a long time. For example, in Aeschylus' *Eumenides*, written a century before Aristotle, the god Apollo says, "She who is called the child's mother is not its begetter, but only the nurse of the newly sown embryo. The begetter is the male, and she as a stranger preserves for a stranger the offspring, if no god blights its birth."

A woman's body lacked the grandeur of a man's, but at least the uterus was uniquely female. It is little wonder that when women presented with all sorts of illogical bodily complaints, men decided that their uterus was the culprit. The idea that perhaps women were using their bodies to complain about their social and psychological status never consciously crossed anyone's mind. Since distress in classical times evidently could not be expressed verbally by many women, it was expressed mysteriously and often symbolically in the language of bodily symptoms.

Had Charlotte Perkins Gilmore lived in classical times and encountered a physician of the Hippocratic school, her problems would still have been diagnosed as hysteria, a word that derives from the Greek term for uterus. She would have been told her uterus had dried up and that it was literally wandering about her body in search of moisture. If she gritted her teeth and had an ashen complexion, it meant that her uterus was clasping her liver. If she became anxious and nauseated, then her uterus was grasping her heart. If she felt a choking sensation and a lump in her throat, obviously her uterus was pushing up on her diaphragm. Headaches and lethargy indicated that her uterus had climbed into her head. Her chest palpitations, excessive perspiration, and irrational thoughts were caused by the movements of the uterus in its search for moisture. Had she been fortunate enough to have been under the care of the famous physician Aretaeus of Cappodocia, "the Latin Hippocrates," she would have been told that the uterus is an organ "closely resembling an animal" that can move left or right, up or down, inside of her body; "briefly stated, it is altogether erratic."

What about treatment? In order to entice Mrs. Gilmore's uterus to retreat downwards, foul-smelling substances such as burned hair, tar, or stale urine would have been placed under her nose while a pleasant perfume was placed between her thighs. The procedure was reversed if her uterus needed to be forced upwards. Like a little animal, her uterus could be attracted or repelled by appropriate odors. In Aretaeus' words, the womb "delights in fragrant smells, and advances towards them; and it has an aversion to fetid smells, and flees from them; and, on the whole, the womb is like an animal within an animal."

The problem with aromatherapy was its evanescence. Moreover, husbands probably didn't appreciate a smelly house. Far more to their liking was the definitive therapy suggested by male physicians. The only sure way to keep a uterus in place was to gratify its physiological needs by engaging in frequent intercourse. Hysterical widows and elderly virgins needed but to marry and their symptoms would disappear. It is doubtful that Mrs. Gilmore would have responded favorably to her physician as he patiently explained how her "little animal" would be tamed by her husband's penis with a resulting improvement in her health.

Of course, if she had in real life never met Dr. Mitchell but, instead, had been taken across the ocean to Vienna for a consultation with Dr. Sigmund Freud, she would have been told that her hysteria was the manifestation of a psychological conflict of a sexual nature. Perhaps he would have shared with her his satisfaction in discovering that his ideas went back to the very beginnings of classical medicine and that they revived a thought found in Plato's *Timaeus*: "The womb is an animal which yearns to generate children. When it remains barren too long after puberty it is distressed and sorely disturbed."

Hippocrates, Aretaeus, Mitchell and Freud were great physicians all, and well intentioned too. But they each would have driven Mrs. Gilmore deeper into the depths of despair had she accepted their explanations and followed their advice. They were unwitting captives of a patriarchal legacy, one of whose basic tenets is the crude fantasy that all a woman needs to cure what ails her is a romp in the hay.

THE CREATION OF EVE AND THE END OF INNOCENCE

In comparison with the classical, the Judeo-Christian tradition has been the more-potent force in defining the "natural" role of women. The unifying core of this tradition is the Bible, which provides numerous examples of proper and improper female comportment. Unfortunately the Bible was written and edited over the course of more than a thousand years so that no consistent "model" woman emerges. Additionally, for several thousand more years, rabbis, priests, and ministers in endless writings and sermons have provided endless and sometimes contrary interpretations of biblical statements about women. Many Orthodox Jews, for example, demand that a women's head should be practically bald and that wigs should be worn, while some Fundamentalist Christian groups demand long, uncut tresses on female members. St. Paul clearly states that women should cover their heads while in church; some congregations follow this thinking, others don't. If such diverse interpretations of the Bible exist on the simple matter of a woman's hair, then there is little chance that more significant and complex issues will be understood identically by all readers.

As noted by Phyllis Bird, the Old Testament is a "man's book, where women appear for the most part simply as adjuncts of men, significant only in the context of men's activities . . . The Old Testament is a collection of writings by males from a society dominated by males." The Judaic view of man's superiority is expressed tersely in the Shakarith service that includes the prayer, "Blessed are thou, O Lord, our God, King of the universe, who has not made me a woman." God is definitely masculine and is often described as a warrior, a husband, and a king. Only once is God metaphorically feminine. Zion complained of being forgotten by God, but God replied, "Can a woman forget her nursing child, and not have compassion on the son of her womb? Surely they may forget, yet I will not forget you" (Isaiah 9:15).

The first human was a man, Adam, who lived in the Garden of Eden. The implication in Genesis is that life there was lonely, perhaps even boring. His diet consisted of fruit and vegetables. He couldn't even contemplate his navel since he didn't have one. God, recognizing that "It is not good that man should be alone," created the birds and the beasts. Adam looked them over and, in the first act of human intelligence, gave each of them a name. He obviously started with aardvarks, worked his way through mudskippers and newts, and called it a day with yaks and zebras. Surely he lingered a little with the Labradors but, come night, he must have yearned for more than puppy love.

God then anesthetized Adam, removed one of his ribs, and closed the wound (most surgeons have since, either consciously or unconsciously, claimed divine kinship). With legendary virtuosity God double-helixed the rib, threw in a few curves, nipped and tucked around the edges, and voilà: a generic woman. Unfortunately, Adam's reaction upon awakening was not recorded, nor was the couple's subsequent behavior. Since they both were created as adults, they had no childhood, no memories of parents, no way of knowing how men and women were supposed to act. How they passed the time is anybody's guess. The only thing God told them was not to eat the fruit of a special tree. At any rate, the woman either out of restlessness or naivete was sweet-talked by a serpent into eating forbidden fruit with the promise of knowing both good and evil, just as God did. The woman could not have known anything about the concepts of "good" and "evil" because she lived in a natural paradise. Everything there simply was what it was. Nonetheless she ate the fruit and gave some to Adam, who ate it too. Whereupon God, angered by their act of defiance, cursed them all the way to hell and back again. It was a proper reaming and affected the couple curiously: they noticed that they were naked. In the first recorded act of human emotionality, Adam immediately became possessive and gave the woman a name, Eve, because she was now *his* woman.

With the end of innocence came many changes. God slaughtered some animals so Adam and Eve could dress decently. Nudity was out; fur and leather were in. Steaks and lamb shish kebab were added to their diet. Adam had to work for a living, while Eve was sentenced to painful, serial childbirth, to desire only her husband, and to submit to his rule (Genesis 3:16–21). Thus the primal platonic friendship of paradise was transformed into the dutiful, enmity-filled marriage of the real world.

Creation stories usually have great prestige in a culture. The story of Adam and Eve surely has enormous implications for male–female relationships, yet, once told, it is never mentioned again in the Old Testament except for a momentous interpretation in the apocryphal book of Ecclesiasticus (about 180 B.C.): "From a woman sin had its beginning, and because of her we all die. Allow no outlet to water, and no boldness of speech in an evil wife. If she does not go as you direct, separate her from yourself" (25:24–26). Ecclesiasticus appears in the Greek Orthodox and Catholic Bible but not the Protestant. Neither is it included in the Jewish Bible, although its exposition of traditional Hebrew wisdom and advice for men made it a favored text by many rabbis. What advice and wisdom about women were offered? From a woman's perspective the high point comes early in chapter 3: "Whoever honors his father atones for sin, and whoever glorifies his mother is like one who lays up treasure." Everything then rapidly goes downhill: "Do not give yourself over to a woman so that she gains mastery over your strength" (9:2); "Taking hold of an evil wife is like grasping a scorpion" (27:7); "Keep strict watch over a headstrong daughter lest, when she finds her liberty . . . she will sit in front of every post and open her quiver to the arrow" (26:10–12); "A wife's charm delights her husband, and her skill puts fat on his bones. A silent wife is a gift to the Lord . . . Like the sun rising in the sign of the Lord is the beauty of a good wife in her well-ordered home" (26:13–16); "He who acquires a wife gets his best possession, a helper for him and a pillar of support" (36:24).

THE MAIDEN, DEBORAH, DELILAH, RUTH, AND ESTHER

The portrayals of woman as a man's possession whose role is to cook, keep a neat house, and be silent and of woman as the seductive scorpion who can make men miserable are found throughout the "wisdom" literature of the Hebrews. This popular literature was developed by sages who spoke from experience; priests and prophets ended *their* comments with the definitive phrase "thus saith the Lord." The biblical book of Proverbs, several centuries older than Ecclesiasticus, contained many of the same ideas. "For the lips of an immoral woman drip honey, and her mouth is smoother than oil; but in the end she is bitter as wormwood, sharp as a two edged sword. Her feet go down to death, her steps lay hold of hell" (5:3–5); "The mouth of an immoral woman is a deep pit; he who is abhorred by the Lord will fall there" (22:14); "Do not give your strength to woman" (31:3). The virtuous wife (31:10-31) arises before dawn to prepare food, helps the poor, brings in money by investing in land and by selling the garments that she makes, is wise and kind, and does not eat the bread of idleness.

Because of Solomon's love of love, the Song of Songs has been attributed to him. It presents a unique biblical woman who is definitely neither silent nor a scorpion. This lovesick maiden burns with so much passion that she dreams of walking the streets of the city at night until she finds the man she loves, grabbing hold of him, and taking him home to bed (3:1-4). Her lips drip like a honeycomb that her lover devours; the roof of her mouth is like the best wine, and her lover imbibes. She invites her beloved to go with her out into the fields and into the vineyards and she seductively says, "Let us see if the vine has budded, whether the grape blossoms are open, and the pomegranates are in bloom. There I will give you my love . . . And at the gates are pleasant fruits, all manner, new and old, which I have laid up for you, my beloved" (7:12-13). Evidently her beloved had rented out his vineyard to the maiden's brothers, so she coyly describes herself as a vineyard and requests that he pay her brothers 200 silver coins for tending its fruit. Presumably business was taken care of, because the maiden then ardently says, "Make haste, my beloved, and be like a gazelle or a young stag on the mountain of spices" (8:14). This woman is unlike any other in the Bible. She has no hang-ups, no wifely duties, no children. She delights in her towering breasts and even shows concern for her small-chested sister (8:8).

The time of the Judges, 1200 to 1000 B.C., was a rough and tumble, cowboys-and-Indians era for the Israelites. In addition to lax morality there was plenty of lawlessness, treachery, and bloodshed. "In those days there was no king in Israel, all the people did what was right in their own eyes" (Judges 21:25). The various rulers fought both with each other and with their enemies, the Canaanites. Every time the Israelites seemed to get things together, they would backslide into the service of Baal and female goddesses. "So the anger of the Lord was kindled against Israel and he gave them over to plunderers who plundered them . . . Nevertheless the Lord raised up judges who delivered them out of the land of those who plundered them. And yet they did not listen to the judges but went a whoring after other gods" (Judges 2:14-16). The twelve Judges that saved Israel were a motley crew of leaders and not judges as we commonly think of them (with one exception). None succeeded in uniting the tribes or in preventing their people from self-destructive actions against God.

One of the most successful judges was a woman, Deborah, who also was that rare bird, a prophetess. She actually heard legal cases. However, her fame rested on her ability to inspire a military leader to destroy the Canaanite army. The Israelite general, Barak, found his courage only when Deborah agreed to accompany him to the battle-front. This sympathetic portrayal of a female was counterbalanced by the actions of Jael, an Israelite woman, into whose tent the tired Canaanite general found his way. He expected asylum because there was peace between him and Jael's husband. Jael covered him with a rug, told him to have no fear, gave him milk to drink, and then pounded a tent peg through his head. From the Israelite perspective, Jael was a heroine, but treachery is treachery, and her name was omitted from the list of those whose faith subdued kingdoms in the New Testament Epistle to the Hebrews (11:30–40). To be sure, Hebrews doesn't even mention Deborah, listing instead Barak, the military leader whom she propelled to victory.

Another woman, Delilah, played an important role in the life of the dull-witted, Mike Tyson-ish judge known as Samson. From the very beginning, Samson was something special. He was conceived only after his parents actually saw God. As he grew up the spirit of the Lord stirred in him and he was consecrated a Nazirite whose vows included no wine, no contact with dead bodies, and no haircuts. He broke all three vows, but a bigger problem was that he was driven to destruction by his brutish hormones.

His first faux pas was to fall in love with a Philistine girl who was as sweet as honey. There was wine at their wedding feast, and Samson livened the party by proposing a riddle to the guests. If they solved it he paid them 30 sheets and 30 garments, otherwise they had to pay him. No one had a clue about the riddle so the guests, Philistines all, threatened Samson's bride-to-be with death by burning unless she wheedled the answer out of her husband and gave it to them. She did as she was told. Samson was enraged, but a bet is a bet. He went to a nearby town, killed 30 Philistines and gave their sheets and garments to the wedding guests. He then sullenly went to his father's home without concluding the wedding ceremony. Meanwhile the embarrassed parents of his betrothed decided to give her in marriage to Samson's best man.

When Samson's hormones kicked in after the wheat harvest, he went back to consummate the marriage but discovered that he really wasn't married. He decided to punish the Philistines by attaching torches to the tails of 300 foxes; they went into the fields and set fire to the grain. The Philistines came after Samson but he slew a thousand of them using the jawbone of an ass as a weapon.

Samson then fled to Gaza, where he frequented a prostitute. The Philistines thought they had him trapped, but he arose at midnight, ripped out the gate of the city, and went to the valley of Sorak. There he took up with Delilah. The lords of the Philistines bribed Delilah with silver to discover the secret of Samson's strength. She agreed to the plan and certainly was straightforward in her intentions. She said, "Please tell me, Samson, wherein your great strength lies, and how you might be bound, that one could subdue you." Samson admittedly was a rogue and untruthfully told her to try binding him with seven fresh bowstrings. Perhaps he anticipated a little bondage. Who knows? She tied him up and said, "The Philistines are upon you," but Samson snapped those bowstrings quicker than a New York minute. Delilah tried again, as Samson suggested to her, with new ropes. Again he broke free. A third attempt failed, so Delilah applied a little guilt. "How can you say, I love you when your heart is not with me? You have mocked me these three times and haven't told me where your great strength lies." She kept after him night and day. You think he would have smelled a rat, but, no, he finally told her the truth. His strength was in his hair. This time the Philistines shaved his head, took him prisoner, gouged out his eyes, and imprisoned him. Their memories must have been short because they allowed his hair to grow back. While sporting with him in the temple of Dagon, they all died, including Samson, who used his superhuman strength to cause the temple to collapse.

By today's standards, Samson didn't have much going for him except muscle power. He was a none-too-bright womanizer, a vow breaker, an animal abuser, a hot-head who ended his own life. There is nothing particularly ennobling about his story. Yet he is a hero and Delilah lives in infamy ("Her name has become a synonym for deceit and treachery" according to *The Interpreter's Bible*). Biblical commentators over the ages have judged that the accomplishments of his death—the destruction of the pagan temple and a host of Philistines—outweighed the sins of his life.

Lawlessness during the time of the Judges was epitomized by the night-long fatal gang rape of a priest's concubine by men from the tribe of Benjamin (Judges 19:21). When the priest found her body, he cut it into pieces and "sent her throughout the kingdom of Israel." Incensed, the eleven tribes who received her body parts declared war on the Benjaminites and vowed never to give their daughters in marriage to any man of that tribe. Great slaughters ensued, but, come the light of day, the tribes lamented the fact that there would be one less tribe of Israelites. They spared 600 Benjaminite men, raided a village, and killed everyone except 400 virgins, whom they turned over to the Benjaminites for marriage. The other 200 men were allowed to capture the daughters of Shiloh while they danced at a festival; the girls' fathers and brothers were ordered not to interfere.

The period of the exile of many Jews in Babylon (587–538 B.C.) marks an important historical division. Before the exile, women, although subordinate to men, had a certain status. Along with concubines, slaves, precious metals, and animals, wives belonged to a man, but they could not be purchased or sold. Women could participate in religious ceremonies. They could be prophetesses or wise persons or sorceresses. They could be heroines, like Deborah, or agitators, like Jezebel, who advised her weak-willed husband, Ahab, to have a man killed in order to possess his vineyard: the Lord said that dogs shall eat both Jezebel and Ahab "who sold himself to do wickedness because his wife stirred him up" (1 Kings 25).

When the Israelites returned from their exile they were determined to avoid the circumstances that caused God to treat them so harshly. Their solution was a back-to-the-basics focus on purity, which meant keeping within the boundaries of divine order. There was a renewed emphasis on the covenant established between Abraham and God: "And you shall be circumcised in the flesh of your foreskins, and it shall be a sign of the covenant between me and you" (Gen. 17:11). Since circumcision was a male thing, females could enter into the covenant only through their relationship with men. Laws were developed to foster purity in every aspect of life. It was kosher, for example, to eat locusts, insects, and grasshoppers, "But all other flying insects which have four feet shall be an abomination to you" (Lev. 11:23–24). To emphasize the importance of sacrificial blood, which made atonement possible, other forms of blood were deemed impure. Thus a menstruating woman was unclean and so was everything she sat on. Slowly but surely, the social and religious status of women declined. A special court was constructed in the temple to keep women in their place away from the sanctuary. The period of a woman's impurity was seven days following the birth of a boy, but fourteen days after the birth of a girl. Ecclesiasticus noted that only one man in a thousand is wise, "But a woman among these I have not found" (7:28). A man could have a trial marriage with a female captive: "And it shall be, if you have no delight in her, then you shall set her free" (Deut. 21:14).

Ezra was so distressed by the iniquities of his fellow Jews that he tore his clothes and pulled out his hair. At a great assembly he said that the wrath of God would continue until they rid themselves of impure, pagan wives. Shechaniah spoke up: "Let us make a covenant with our God to put away all these wives and those who have been born to them, according to the advice of my master and of those who tremble at the commandment of our God; and let it be done according to the law" (10:3). Nehemiah was even more zealous: he slapped people around, cursed a lot, and forced them to swear by God that they would not intermarry (13:25).

The book of Ruth was a reaction against the movement forbidding intermarriage. Although the setting is during the olden time of Judges, it was written about six hundred years later, at least a century after the exile. It tells of Naomi, a widow, and her two sons who married pagan women. They were Moabites, (descendants of Moab, the son of the drunken Lot who was raped by his daughters). Wildness must have run in their blood, because Numbers 25 tells about the Israelites who "gave themselves over to debauchery with the daughters of Moab. These invited them to the sacrifices of their gods, and the people ate and bowed down before their gods." Yahweh was angry at the Israelites' worship of Baal, so he ordered Phineas the priest to kill them. While a son of Israel was fornicating with a Moabite princess who was probably a holy prostitute, Phineas seized a lance, followed them into an alcove, "and there ran them both through, the Israelite and the woman, right through the groin." Ouch!

After ten years, Naomi's sons died, and so she decided to return to Israel where food supposedly was plentiful. She counseled her daughters-in-law to find new husbands and to return to their families. One did so ("See, your sister-in-law has returned to her people and her gods") but the other, the Moabite Ruth, decided to travel with and care for Naomi, saying, "Entreat me not to leave thee, or to return from following thee: for whither thou goest, I will go; and where thou lodgest, I will lodge. Thy people will be my people, and thy God my God" (1:16). All's well that ends well; Ruth successfully set her sights on a kindly, middle-aged relative named Boaz. While he was sleeping on the floor of his mill, "she came softly, uncovered his feet, and lay down." His "feet" were, in fact, his genitals (that's what the Hebrews called them), so it's no wonder that "the man was startled." She asked that he spread his garment over her and take her under his wing; he agreed, providing that her closest male relative didn't want her. They spent the night together and he gave her six ephahs of barley as a present. To shorten the story, Boaz ended up acquiring Ruth in marriage, and she gave birth to a son. "They named him Obed; he was the father of Jesse, the father of David" (4:17). Ruth overcame her wild, ancestral streak and accepted Yahweh. The rehabilitation of Moabite women was so complete that Yahweh didn't object to the intermarriage. It's a delightful story with many folklorish sentiments and details. The kicker, of course, is that David, the greatest king of Israel, descended from Ruth, a foreigner. It is primarily because of this genealogical connection that the book was included in the Bible.

Esther (125 B.C.) is the other biblical book named after a woman. Interestingly, like Ruth, it supports intermarriage since Esther married a Persian king who didn't know that her uncle, Mordecai, had saved his life. The king's chief administrator vowed to kill Mordecai and all the Jews living in the kingdom, casting lots (purim) to set the date of the massacre. Esther confessed her Jewishness to her husband and carried through a plan in which the administrator was killed and the Jewish people saved. She accomplished this on her own; God is never mentioned. Even though the story was patriotic fiction, its godlessness was bothersome. In about 78 B.C., a new ending was added to the book. In it Esther removes all traces of her foreign identity. Off come her queen's robes. Instead of perfume she covers herself with ashes and dung. She abhors her crown "like a menstrual rag." Instead of personal strength, it is God who allows the plot to be successful. It just wasn't right for a woman to get credit for a smashing victory.

MOTHERS, WIVES, AND HARLOTS

Overall, women in the Old Testament were valued primarily as mothers. Some of the most poignant moments describe the grief of mothers for their dead children, especially their sons. "A voice was heard in Ramah; lamentation and bitter weeping, Rachel weeping for her children, refusing to be comforted for her children, because they are no more" (Jer. 31:15). After the Gibeonites hanged her sons, "Rizpah took sackcloth and spread it for herself on the rock, from the beginning of the harvest until the late rains poured from heaven on their bodies. And she did not allow the birds of the air to rest on them by day nor the beasts of the fields by night" (2 Sam. 21:10).

The process of childbirth was regarded by the prophets as so painful that it was often compared to the misery of a person who has been chastised by God. "Wail, for the day of the Lord is at hand! It will come as destruction . . . Every man. . . will be afraid . . . They will be in pain as a woman in childbirth" (Is. 13:6-9). Barren women could never fulfill their feminine potential, limited as it was, and often became desperate: "When Rachel saw that she bore Jacob no children, she envied her sister and said to Jacob, 'Give me children or else I die!' (Gen. 30:1). Other women made fun of them. Hannah's "rival provoked her severely, because the Lord had closed her womb" (1 Sam. 1:6).

Secondarily, women were valued as wives. In the early days polygamy was the norm. By the eighth century B.C., monogamy was standard and was a metaphor for Jewish acceptance of one God. Women could not file for divorce, but men had little problem: "When a man takes a wife and marries her, and it happens that she finds no favor in his eyes because he has found some uncleanliness in her," the husband merely had to hand her a written certificate of divorce (Deut. 24:1). Since a woman, even after marriage, owed some allegiance to her family of birth, the problem of divided loyalty was always present. Also, wives could become contentious, spiderlike, and even bovine. Amos 4:1 refers to them as cows. The presence of concubines—unmarried women who lived with the family at the pleas-

ure of the husband—undoubtedly made life easier in some ways by
taking the edge off things. The ultimate state of degradation into
which women might descend is depicted during a famine in Samaria.
One woman says to another, "Give me your son, that we may eat him
today, and we will eat my son tomorrow" (2 Kings 6:29).

In contrast to images of woman as mother and wife, the Old
Testament contains a bevy of prostitutes and adulteresses. Both were
reviled, but prostitutes were openly accepted as a fact of life, perhaps
even a necessity. When Tamar, for example, covered her face like a
prostitute and sat on the roadside, Judah calmly approached her as
Johns have been approaching Jills since the beginning of time and
said, "Please let me come into you" (Gen. 38:16). As in all patriarchal
societies, there was a double standard about sexuality, brides, but not
grooms, were expected to be virgins. In fact, it behooved a bride's parents to save the bloody honeymoon sheet in case the groom accused
the bride of not being a virgin. Absent the stained sheet, "the men of
her city shall stone her to death with stones; because she has done a
disgraceful thing in Israel, to play the harlot in her father's house"
(Deut. 22:21). In a hardly even parallelism, however, if the blood-
stained sheet was produced, then the accusing husband received two
punishments: a fine of 100 shekels and a life sentence of marriage to
his wife without the possibility of divorce.

As told in 2 Kings 9, Jezebel was a foreign queen. She was accused
of "harlotries and sorceries" and as she awaited her certain death, "she
painted her eyes and adorned her head, and looked out the window."
The term "a painted Jezebel" has come to mean a wanton hussy or a
whore with a lot of make-up. In fact, her "harlotries" refer metaphorically to her attempts to persuade the Jews to worship Baal. And there
was nothing sinister or lascivious about her use of cosmetics. As befits
a queen, she wanted to approach death regally. Too, she probably
shared the Persian belief that the body at the moment of death was
the body that a person had in the afterlife. Only a special kind of evil-
to-him-who-evil-thinks mentality could transform Jezebel into a tart.

The Israelites were intrigued by prostitutes. The expression "to
play the harlot" was used throughout the Old Testament to describe
the act of abandoning one's faith: "Yet they would not listen to their
judges, but they played the harlot with other gods, and bowed down
to them" (Judges 2:17). In a powerful metaphor, Israel, the bride of
God, became a harlot: "You have polluted the land with your harlotries and your wickedness . . . You have had a harlot's forehead; you
refuse to be ashamed" (Jer. 3:2–3). The greatest and sometimes confusing elaboration of this theme forms the drama of the book of the
prophet Hosea who was ordered by God, "Go, take to yourself a wife

of harlotry and have children of harlotry, for the land commits great harlotry by forsaking the Lord" (1:2). Hosea dutifully married Gomer, who might have been a sacred prostitute and whose name possibly means "perfect" or "fig cakes" or nothing at all. The couple had three children whose odd names were given to them by God. "Call his name Jezreel . . . and I will put an end to the kingdom of the house of Israel . . . in the valley of Jezreel"; "Call her Not Pitied, for I will no more have pity on the house of Israel"; "Call his name Not My People, for you are not my people and I am not your God" (1:4–8). Just as the married Gomer pursued her lovers, so too Israel pursued false gods, but just as Hosea reclaims his wife so too God will reclaim Israel. As usual, the female is the bad guy, and, as usual, the male comes to her rescue.

TOUCH ME, TOUCH ME NOT: MARY MAGDALEN

In the New Testament, Mark's Gospel, the earliest one written, plunges right into the ministry of Jesus where his dealings with women stirred up trouble. Jesus' first encounter with a woman was innocuous enough: he cured Peter's mother-in-law of a fever (1:30–31). His next encounter was tense. The Pharisees and the Herodians, upset at Jesus' comments about fasting and the Sabbath, plotted to harm him. Jesus left with the crowd but his mother and brothers called to him, probably out of concern for his safety. When the crowd informed him of their presence, he said, "Who is my mother or my brother?" Jesus then looked at the people sitting near him and said, "Here are my mother and my brothers! For whoever does the will of God is my brother and my sister and my mother" (3:31–34). The Jewish audience, familiar with the commandment to honor one's father and mother, must have been perplexed. Jesus didn't even acknowledge his mother, much less comfort her. His third encounter was a real zinger. A women with a vaginal flow of twelve years duration—the essence of Jewish uncleanliness—touched his robes saying, "If I touch even his garments, I shall be made well." Jesus' response was, "Daughter, your faith has made you well; go in peace and be healed of your affliction" (5:25–34).

Divorce was a hot topic. The laws of Deuteronomy allowed a husband to divorce his wife for whatever reason he saw fit. Of course, there was no question of divorce in the case of adultery because the wife would be stoned to death. When a man divorced his wife, he had to give her a written statement that she was free to remarry. The followers of Rabbi Hillel supported the traditional view; divorce was allowed even if a woman's major fault was that she spoiled her husband's soup. Jesus absolutely forbade divorce in Mark 10:" . . . and the two shall become one . . . what therefore God has joined together, let no man put asunder." However, in what scholars believe is a later addition to the Bible Jesus supposedly made an exception: divorce was forbidden except when a man's wife was unchaste (Matt. 5). Exception or no, Jesus' antidivorce stance elevated women's marital status by protecting them from the whims of their mates. It wasn't what most men wanted to hear.

Jesus had a few more surprises. Unlike other rabbis, he talked with women on the street (John 4:27), healed a woman on the Sabbath and referred to her as a daughter of Abraham (Luke 13:16), and let women accompany him and his male disciples (Luke 8:1-3). He harshly told the chief priests and elders of the Temple that "tax collectors and harlots go into the kingdom of God before you" (Matt. 21:31). In a traditional story that was added to John's Gospel, Jesus refused to condemn an adulteress to death but rather told her to "Go, and sin no more" (8:11). While at a private dinner party, Jesus allowed a sinful city woman to wash, kiss, and anoint his feet with oil and to dry them with her hair. He then said to his host, "You did not anoint my head with oil but this woman has anointed my feet with fragrant oil. Therefore I say to you that her sins, which are many, are forgiven for she loved much" (Luke 7:46-47). The host was scandalized that Jesus would let such a woman touch him.

What exactly was the sin of this woman and who was she? Many Christian scholars with a Jezebelian mind-set reckoned that she was a harlot. What's the evidence? She was a city sinner and everybody knows what goes on in the city. Her hair was unbound and no respectable Jewish woman would appear that way in public. She loved much and love is just another word for nothing left to lose. As to her identity, would you believe Mary Magdalen?

Everybody knows about Mary Magdalen (we'll refer to her as Mary M). Wasn't she the beautiful prostitute who repented and became one of the rare nonvirgin saints, revered for being the "beata dilectrix Christi" (Christ's blessed lover), the "castissima meretrix" (most chaste prostitute), patroness of the Dominican order of priests, and, according to legend, the bride of St. John the Evangelist whose wedding was celebrated at Cana? Having atoned for her sins for thirty years in a grotto in Southern France where she supposedly went after Christ's death, Mary M was sculpted by Donatello in the fifteenth century, scrawny, withered, cloaked by an animal skin and her long hair. Mary M, the voluptuous penitent, Venus of Divine Love, was painted repeatedly by Titian in the sixteenth century, her hair flowing like a necklace around her alabaster breasts, the naked representation of Truth and Repentance who burned with so much love of Christ that she could not stand to wear clothes. Mary M, who was very much in vogue as the subject of saintly portraits in the eighteenth century; the wives and mistresses of kings, even Lord Nelson's Lady Emma Hamilton, posed as models. Magdalen houses for the reclamation of prostitutes flourished in Victorian England. Mary M, amid palm trees and the song of the nightingale, a perfumed oriental beauty transposed by the French poet Theophile Gautier to a church foggy with incense, mysteriously close to Jesus. Mary M melting into the figure of Christ crucified by the great sculptor Auguste Rodin. Mary M in Nikos Kazantzakis' novel *Last Temptation of Christ*, stoned to death after Jesus was persuaded by a devilish angel to come down from his cross to mate with her. Mary M who erected Christ to life as Isis did for Osiris in D.H. Lawrence's novella *The Man Who Lied*. Mary M, the wife of Jesus, according to several modern scholars. Avast! Enough!

Just who is Mary M? It's a complicated story with a veritable mess of Marys. The Gospels of Mark, Matthew, and Luke vary in some details, but their stories are essentially similar. Mary M, out of whom seven demons had been exorcised, along with Mary (the mother of James the Younger and of Joses) and Salome (the mother of Jesus' disciples James and John) were among a group of women who ministered to Jesus from Galilee to Palestine. They viewed the crucifixion from afar and saw where Jesus was entombed. They returned to the tomb the next morning, where they encountered an angel who directed the women to tell the disciples that Christ had risen and would meet them in Galilee. They delivered the message; the disciples didn't believe it. Sometime in the first few centuries after Mark's Gospel was written, someone added verses 9–20 to form a new ending. In these verses the resurrected Jesus "appeared first to Mary Magdalen." In Matthew's Gospel the resurrected Jesus appeared both to Mary M and "the other Mary" (probably the mother of James and Joses) as they were rushing to deliver their message.

In John's Gospel, Mary the mother of Jesus and her sister Mary, along with the wife of Cleopos and Mary M, "stood by the cross" (19:35). The next day Mary M visited Christ's tomb, saw that it was empty, and ran to tell the disciples. They raced to the tomb, found only the linen cloths that had been used to wrap Jesus, and returned home. Mary M alone kept a vigil. A man appeared. She thought it was the gardener. When he called her name she recognized him as Jesus and said, "Master." He replied, "Don't touch me; for I have not yet ascended to my Father, to my God and your God" (20:17).

That's it. Mary M is honored in the Bible as the first person to see the risen Christ. The only information about her background is that

seven demons had been cast out of her. So how do we get from this
to Mary M the penitent prostitute? It took several centuries, but the
Church Fathers managed to accomplish this amazing feat as part of
their campaign in favor of celibacy.

The transformation of Mary M required a special mentality in
which the virgin and the whore were the basic female stereotypes.
The Virgin Mary, unsullied by pangs of the flesh, was created to represent extraordinarily high ideals. On a more human level, however,
another type of female model was needed, a model that offered hope
to even the most degraded women. Thus Mary M was created by turning her into a whore and then demonstrating the possibility of reclamation and salvation by converting physical desires into the spiritual
love of Christ.

Mary M was a good choice. The town she came from was a fishing
village on the lake of Galilee that had a reputation for sexual promiscuity. Too, she had been possessed by a whopping seven demons.
Now comes the tricky part (the key word is *anoint*). Since Mary M
went to Christ's tomb to *anoint* him, the Church Fathers looked back
at the city sinner who loved too much and *anointed* Christ's feet at
the dinner party (Luke 7:46–47). If the city sinner could be made out
to be a prostitute, she could also be made out to be none other than
Mary M! Since the woman dried Christ's feet with her loose hair,
Mary M came to be depicted with long, flowing tresses. If the association seemed a little weak, further evidence was found in John 12,
where Jesus went to Bethany. He stayed at the house of Lazarus
whom he had raised from the dead. While dining, Mary of Bethany
anointed Christ's feet with costly ointment. A disciple protested that
the ointment should have been sold and the proceeds given to the
poor, but Jesus said, "Let her alone: let her keep it for the day of my
burial." Who else could it be except Mary M (unless of course, she was
just plain Mary of Bethany)? Pope Gregory the Great made it official
in 591: the city sinner and Mary of Bethany really were Mary M. The
Pope said in his Twenty-third Homily that she had turned her sins—
perfuming her flesh in forbidden acts, coveting with earthly eyes, dis-
playing her hair to set off her face, speaking pridefully—to virtues
when she anointed Christ with costly oil, kissed and washed his feet
with her tears, and dried them with her hair. She did this "in order to
serve God entirely in penance."

What? The Pope's word isn't good enough? You demand even
more proof that Mary M was a whore? Go to John 4, where Jesus has
a conversation (the lengthiest in the New Testament) with a
Samaritan woman who had been married five times and currently
was living with yet another man. This women of poor morals was

declared to be Mary M. Now for the clincher. Remember the adulteress of John 8:11 whom Jesus refused to condemn to death? She was Mary M too!

The saga was advanced when Hippolytus (d. 235), a Roman priest and martyr, wrote a commentary on the only erotic book of the Bible, the Song of Songs. He interpreted the Bride seeking the Bridegroom as an allegory for Mary M seeking the body of Christ. The sensuality of this allegory as well as Mary M's reputation as a whore in the Old Testament tradition of Hosea's faithless wife, Gomer, intrigued people back then and has continued to do so. The second-century Gospel of Philip noted that Mary M was Christ's consort and that "Christ loved her more than the other disciples and used to kiss her often on the mouth." In his *Panarion* (375), Epiphanius, a bishop in Cyprus, wrote about a book called *Great Questions of Mary*, which supposedly asserted that Christ took Mary M aside to a mountain: "And he brought forth from his side a woman and began to unite with her, and so, taking his discharge, he showed that 'we must do so, that we may live'; when Mary fell to the ground abashed, he raised her up again and said to her: 'Why did you doubt, O you of little faith?'"

As noted in Haskin's scholarly study, in 1969 the Roman Catholic Calendar was changed to reflect the fact that Mary M was not the city prostitute or Mary of Bethany but rather was "Mary Magdala who, cured of her seven devils, became the devoted follower and witness of the resurrected Christ . . . In 1978 the epithets 'Maria poenitens' (penitent Mary) and 'magna peccatrix' (great sinner) were also deleted from the entry for Mary Magdalen in the Roman Breviary, thus officially removing the stigma which had been attached to her name for nearly two thousand years." Unfortunately, setting the record straight cannot undo the historical role of Mary M in the formation of our attitudes towards women and sexuality.

DRY FLEECE: THE VIRGIN MARY

Of all the women in the history of Christendom, none is greater than Mary, the virgin mother of Jesus. In her honor spectacular cathedrals have been built, sublime paintings painted, lyrical songs and poems written. She has inspired saints and sinners alike, male and female, to achieve the highest spheres of spirituality. Like Mary M, she is the product of wishes, fantasies, and propaganda, but, unlike Mary M, the brilliance of her myth often obscures its dark side from the faithful as they go to bed at night. It is not that we weren't warned: "A woman in the crowd raised her voice and said to him [Jesus], 'Blessed is the womb that bore you, and the breasts that you sucked.' His reply:

"Blessed rather are those who hear the word of God and keep it" (John 11:27–28). Thus saith Jesus.

What can we learn about Mary from reading the Bible? Nothing is written about her birth, her age, her family background, or her death. She is referred to as Miriam twelve times and Mary seven times. Paul's only reference to her is his statement that Jesus was "made of a woman" (Galatians 4:9). Acts 1:14 states that Mary, the disciples and their wives, and Jesus' brothers prayed together, probably in the temple, a day or so after Christ's ascension. That's all there is about Mary except for the Gospels.

Mark isn't very helpful. In 6:3 we read, "Is this not the carpenter [or son of the carpenter], the son of Mary, and brother of James, Joses, and Simon? And are not his sisters here with us?" In Mary's other appearance, recounted earlier in this chapter, Jesus didn't even acknowledge her presence when she and his brothers called out to him. Instead he said to the crowd that "Whoever does the will of God is my brother and my sister and my mother" (3:35).

Although John's Gospel never uses the word Mary, she appears twice. When provisions ran out at the marriage at Cana, she said to Jesus, "They have no wine." He replied brusquely, "Woman, what is it with you and me? It's not my time yet." She then said to the servants, "Whatever he tells you, do it" (2:3–5). Nothing more is said about Mary until the crucifixion. John places her at the cross along with three other women. Jesus said to her, "Woman, behold your son," and he entrusted her care to his beloved disciple.

The majority of the references to Mary occur in the Gospels of Matthew and of Luke. They focus on the birth of Jesus, but only Matthew states clearly that Mary was a virgin. Luke recounts that Mary and Joseph took the twelve-year-old Jesus to the temple in Jerusalem where they lost track of him for three days. Upon finding him listening and asking questions of the teachers in the temple, Mary said, "Son, why have you done this to us? Look, your father and I sought you anxiously." Jesus replied, "Why did you seek me? Did you not know that I must be about my father's business?" But neither parent understood what he said (2:48–49).

If it were possible to ignore centuries of traditions and beliefs and to focus solely on what is contained in the Bible, we would conclude that Mary's importance is that she gave birth to Christ. Nothing is said regarding her child-rearing practices except that she was traditional in that she had Jesus circumcised, presented him at the temple, and observed the Passover every year. It's a bit difficult to believe that a doting mother would have lost track of her twelve-year-old son for three full days, but that's what is written. She didn't play much of a role during Jesus' ministry except to tell him that there wasn't enough wine at a wedding reception. In fact, the few times that Jesus conversed with her, he was uncharacteristically detached in his attitude and somewhat rude in his speech. Only one Gospel places her at the cross, where no emotion is reported: Jesus simply saw her "standing near." She did not witness the risen Christ nor was she present at his ascension. Other contributors to the New Testament pretty much ignore her. Based on relatively scanty material, how did Mary come to achieve such an important position throughout Christendom and to be portrayed as the perfect woman of virtue whom all women should strive to emulate?

The key to understanding Mary's prominence is the mystery of the virgin birth, although in the earliest days of the church this was not a topic of much concern. Mark and John didn't mention it. Luke hinted about it in 1:34-35 but did not mention it in the lengthy birth and infancy narrative of 2:1-52, where Joseph was clearly identified as Christ's father. It didn't interest Paul, who could easily have written that Jesus was "made of a virgin" instead of "made of a woman." Only Matthew stated that Mary "was found with child of the Holy Spirit" (1:18) and "that which is conceived in her is of the Holy Spirit" (1:20).

Because so little about Mary was written in the Bible, a book was produced in Egypt around the year 100 to fill the void. It was called the *Book of James* and it enjoyed great success. James embellished the accounts of Mary found in Matthew and Luke with legends and bits of folklore. According to James, Mary was married at age twelve and pregnant at age sixteen. She was betrothed to Joseph, a widower, because a dove portentously flew from his rod onto his head. While Joseph was off constructing a building, an angel told Mary she would have a son called Jesus. When Joseph returned and found Mary pregnant, he was upset, but she claimed to be a virgin. A priest administered the water test for infidelity as described in the Old Testament Book of Numbers 5:26; both passed the test. Joseph declared that Mary was pregnant by the Holy Spirit. Right after Mary gave birth, a skeptical woman named Salome examined Mary's genitals. To her surprise she found that Mary's hymen was intact; for her disbelief, however, her examining hand caught on fire and fell off. These stories about Mary became quite popular, persisted over the centuries, and inspired many famous Renaissance paintings.

The concept of birth in which a human female was impregnated by a god was not unique to Christianity. The Greeks and Romans long believed that Zeus/Jupiter, for example, fathered many children. In order to differentiate Mary's experience from the classical pregnan-

cies, the Church Fathers determined that Mary did not have intercourse with the Holy Spirit or experience any sexual pleasure. Origen
(d. about 250) noted that since Jesus was the "word" (*logos*), it was
through the words of the angel Gabriel that Mary was impregnated.
In fact, many poets and artists over the ages have depicted Mary's
conception through her ear. The Holy Spirit, in a throwback to
Egyptian, Greek, and Roman symbols, usually has been depicted as a
dove who flew to Mary's ear or directly to her womb, where he
deposited an embryonic Christ. As expressed in the Apostle's Creed,
it was really the Holy Spirit who conceived Christ, while Mary's
womb provided lodging and nourishment until the child was born.
St. Thomas Aquinas held the view that Mary's most pure, virginal
blood contributed to the body of Christ.

The church added a special wrinkle to Mary's uniqueness by
claiming that she was a perpetual virgin: the act of childbirth did not
break her hymen, nor did she ever engage in intercourse. This notion
was justified by Salome's post-partum examination as reported in the
Book of James and by statements in the Old Testament that supposedly referred to Mary even though they were written centuries
before she was born. It was believed that her special conception was
alluded to by Numbers 17:8, which stated that "the rod of Aaron had
sprouted and put forth buds," and by Judges 6:36–40, in which
Gideon put a fleece of wool on the ground at night. In the morning:
"It was dry on the fleece only, but there was dew on all the ground."
The intactness of Mary's maidenhead was alluded to by verses such
as Song of Solomon 4:12, which declared "A garden enclosed is my sister, my spouse; a spring shut up, a fountain sealed," and by Ezekiel
44:2, in which the Lord said of the temple gate, "This gate shall be
shut; it shall not be opened, and no man shall enter by it, because the
Lord God of Israel has entered by it; therefore it shall be shut." The
debate over Mary's virginity was confounded by the debate over
Christ's human nature versus his godhood. At the Church Council at
Ephesus in 431, Mary was named mother of God. At the large
Ecumenical Council at Chalcedon in 451, she received the epithet
ever-virgin. And in 649, Pope Martin I officially made her perpetual
virginity a required belief of the Church.

One problem with Mary's perpetual virginity is that the Gospels
state that Jesus had brothers and sisters (Matt. 13:55–56; Mark 6:3).
Jerome (about 381) argued that the siblings in question were the children of Mary's sister who was also named Mary. This very complicated, brilliant, but flawed argument held that John 19:25 placed three
Marys at the cross, one of whom was both the Virgin Mary's sister as
well as the wife of Clopas (most scholars identify four Marys). She

was also the mother of James the Younger (Mark 15:40), who himself was an apostle called James the son of Alphaeus (Mark 3:16; Matt. 10:2–4; Luke 6:14–16). By this reasoning Christ's "brother" James was really his cousin. Similar arguments were used for the other brothers (no one cared much about Christ's sisters). However, the word "cousin" was not used by the writers of the Gospels. Also, if the word "brother" was used not to indicate a blood relative but rather to indicate a more general group of males who in this case were Christ's cousins *and disciples*, how can the statement in John 7:5, "For even His brothers did not believe in Him," be explained? Additionally, this argument would mean that the parents of the mother of Christ strangely gave the name Mary to two daughters. A better explanation of the sibling identity is that they were Joseph's children by a previous marriage. No data support this explanation; it is pure speculation.

The Gospels imply twice that Mary did have children after Jesus. Matt. 1:25 states of Mary that Joseph "did not know her till she had brought forth her firstborn son." Also, Luke's use of the term "firstborn son" (2:7) instead of "only son" or simply "son" leaves open the possibility that Mary may have had other sons. At any rate, the raging debate over this issue indicates that Mary's virginity was a crucial belief for the Church Fathers and that this belief was about more than Mary herself.

JUST SAY NO: BLESSED ARE THE BODIES OF VIRGINS

The young Christian Church was unified and strengthened by Roman persecution. The great theologian Tertullian, at the end of the second century, wrote to the Romans, "Nothing whatever is achieved by each more exquisite cruelty you invent; on the contrary, it wins men for our school. We are made more as often as you mow us down. The blood of Christians is seed (*semen est sanguis Christianorum*)." When the persecutions ended in the fourth century and the external enemy, the Romans, was vanquished, the Church concentrated on a very powerful internal enemy. This enemy lurked in the heart of every man and especially of every woman. The enemy was identified as lust. Exhortations that Christians accept death as martyrs were replaced by calls for asceticism and virginity. According to the scholar Marina Warner, in this campaign legends were altered to emphasize that female martyrs died defending their virginity as well as their faith: "But the particular focus on women's torn and broken flesh reveals the psychological obsession of the religion with sexual sin, and the tortures that pile up one upon the other with pornographic repetitiousness underline the identification of the female with the perils of sexual contact."

Virginity then replaced martyrdom as the unifying force in Christianity, and Mary assumed an importance out of proportion to her biblical role because she was the paragon of virginity. Unlike the Greek and Roman gods and goddesses, who could be very sexual at times, the Christian Father God, Son God, and Holy Spirit God were asexual and it was only fitting that the mother of the Son God also be asexual. Great legends were buttressed by Church doctrines to indicate the rewards of Mary's virginity, some of which were attainable to those faithful who followed her example. She became the exemplar of natural beauty, the Apocalyptic queen with a crown of stars. Her conception and her life, like that of Christ's, was proclaimed immaculate and unstained by sexual sin. She became Christ's virgin bride because she symbolized the glorious Church that was married to Christ "not having spot or wrinkle or any such thing, but that she should be holy and without blemish" (Eph. 5:27). Since she was pure, she did not have to wait until the Last Judgement for her body to be assumed into heaven. The milk from her breasts yielded superhuman sustenance and became in the Middle Ages a prized relic. In fact, so many shrines claimed to have little containers of her milk that the Protestant reformer, John Calvin, wrote: "There is so much that if the Holy Virgin had been a cow or a wet nurse all her life she would have been hard pressed to yield such a great quantity."

But as we are getting ahead of the plot, let us return to the Bible where Jesus started the arduous voyage to virginity by vehemently attacking traditional family values. He didn't mince his words, and he surely wasn't going to win a popularity contest. "If any one comes to me and does not hate his own father and mother and wife and children and brothers and sisters, yes, and even his own life, he cannot be my disciple" (Luke 14:26). He recognized that people marry but noted that "those who are considered worthy of participating in the coming age, which means in the resurrection from the dead, do not marry" (Luke 20:35). On the road to the crucifixion he said to the daughters of Jerusalem, "Behold, the days are coming when they will say, 'Blessed are the barren, and the wombs that never gave birth, and the breasts that never nursed an infant'" (Luke 23:29). He so shocked his disciples with his comments on divorce that they said, "If this is how it is in the case of a man and his wife, it is better not to marry." Jesus seemingly agreed by responding that there are castrated men who were born that way, and men who were castrated by others, and men "who castrated themselves for the Kingdom of Heaven's sake. If you are able to accept this advice, do so" (Matt. 19:12–13). Whatever the original intent of Jesus's words, they eventually came to be interpreted as condoning an ascetic, asexual lifestyle.

Paul never met Jesus nor could he have read Jesus' words in the Gospels (they were not written until after Paul's death). Yet he was able to develop a working theology based on his interpretation of the life of Jesus and his own development of the ideas of Jesus. Paul was convinced that the appointed time for the end of the world had grown short. His advice to the faithful was given so that they could prepare for the end of time when Lord Jesus with all his saints would appear. Had he known that the world would still be around for at least two thousand years more, perhaps his advice and ideas would have been different. This issue is not purely academic. Current Christians must decide if Paul's statements are as binding as those of Jesus.

Paul stated things clearly in 1 Corinthians 6 and 7:"The body is not meant for immorality, but for the Lord . . . Your bodies are the members of Christ. Shall I then take the members of Christ and make them members of a prostitute? Never! . . . Your body is a temple of the Holy Spirit; you are not your own . . . It is good for a man not to touch a woman. Nevertheless, to avoid fornication let every man have his own wife . . . I wish that all were as I myself am. It is good [for the unmarried and widows] if they remain single as I do. But if they cannot exercise self-control, they should marry; for it is better to marry than to be aflame with passion." He then related that it's better for virgins not to marry because married persons are concerned about pleasing their spouses. Since "the form of this world is passing away," single persons can attend upon the Lord without distraction. Go ahead and marry if your passions are strong, but "he who refrains from marriage will do better."

Paul died in about 60 A.D., but over the next century several letters appeared that were attributed to him and came to be included in the New Testament. *Ephesians* (about 90 A.D.) is not sour on marriage but rather in Chapter 5 orders, "Husbands, love your wives as Christ loved the Church and gave himself for her, that he might sanctify her . . . Husbands should love their wives as their own bodies. He who loves his wife loves himself. For no man ever hates flesh, but nourishes and cherishes it, as Christ does the Church, because we are members of his body. For this reason a man shall leave his father and mother and be joined to his wife, and the two shall become one." 1 Timothy (about 130–150 A.D.) says nothing of chastity but rather states that "Woman will be saved through bearing children" (2:15), that a bishop "must manage his own household well, keeping his children submissive and respectful in every way" (3:4), and that "I would have younger widows marry, bear children, rule their households, and give the enemy no occasion to revile us" (5:14). Obviously these later comments undo the original meaning of Paul's ideas and reflect a split within the church. The reformers lost. Paul's concept of marriage ruled the day and continued to prosper. Marriage was to be tolerated only if a person could neither control his passion for fornication nor exercise self-control. As expressed by the scholar Peter Brown, Paul's fatal legacy was that marriage came to be viewed "as no more than a defense against desire. In the future, a sense of the presence of 'Satan,' in the form of a constant and ill-defined risk of lust, lay like a heavy shadow in the corner of every Christian church." And, I might add, in the corner of many a bedroom.

The thrill of Paul's call for better living through abstinence was reflected in the second-century popular novel *The Acts of Paul and Thecla*. The virginal Thecla heard Paul preach: "Blessed are the bodies of virgins, for they shall be well pleasing to God, and shall not lose the reward of their purity." She was converted to virginity and to Christianity. Because she refused to marry her fiancé, the governor ordered a beating for Paul and death by fire for her. She escaped the flames during a ferocious thunderstorm and set out to find Paul, who also had escaped. Her trip was perilous. She barely avoided being raped, and she thwarted wild beasts by protecting herself through self-baptism. Paul finally commissioned her to preach the Gospel. For several centuries this book was regarded by Christians, especially those in Asia Minor, as belonging to the group of truly holy books that were to form the Bible. Although she never existed except as a character in a novel, she was named a saint; her cult was finally suppressed by the Catholic Church in 1969.

The Church Fathers established attitudes about sexuality and the nature of women that have greatly influenced Western thinking during the second, third, and fourth centuries. Tertullian (160–240), comfortable with the Roman stoic tradition that downplayed sexual pleasure as inferior to reason, wrote, "By continence you will buy up a great stock of sanctity; by making savings on the flesh you will be able to invest in the Spirit." He wrote texts such as *Exhortation to Chastity* and *On the Veiling of Virgins* in which he advocated abstinence from women and fasting as pathways to spiritual thinking because women were by nature seductive, "the Devil's gateway," and because full bowels led to an obsession with the toilet and then to lust. Origen (185–255) reinterpreted the Song of Songs to reflect not the joys of a human embrace but rather of an embrace by the Holy Spirit. Since the body was a temple of God and the soul was a priest of that temple, purity could be achieved only by emulating Christ the virgin who was conceived by a virgin. Stung by the charges of nonbelievers that he was sexually active with his female students, Origen voluntarily and secretly had himself castrated. Bishop Methodius (about 260–311) counterposed sexuality, the essence of being a mortal human, with spirituality, the essence of God and the angels. Virginity was the pathway to heaven. In the third century, Cyprian wrote that "Virgins do not fear the sorrows and groans of women; you have no fear about the birth of children, nor is your husband your master, but your Master and Head is Christ in the likeness of and in the place of a man; your lot and condition are the same as men's." In the fourth century, John Chrysostom noted that virgins didn't have to worry about being "split apart by labor pains and wailings" and that "the virgin is not obliged to involve herself tiresomely in the affairs of her spouse and she does not fear being abused." In 356 Athanasius wrote that virgins were the brides of Christ and that Jesus bestowed this benefit to Christians "that we should possess upon earth, in a state of virginity, a picture of the holiness of the angels." He argued that every Christian home needs a virgin "because the salvation of the whole house is that one virgin."

Towards the end of the fourth century, Gregory of Nyssa regarded procreation as a mental defense against the fear of death despite the fact that it resulted paradoxically in new births. Only through virginity could death be thwarted and the paradise of Eden regained. A virgin's marriage to Jesus was the true model for all marriages, and, far less problematic than sperm, virgins were impregnated by the spiritual seed of Christianity. With Jesus as husband, sexual intercourse with a man was adultery. Indeed, the Church Council of Ancyra in 314 declared that "All those who have consecrated their virginity and who have violated their promise ought to be considered bigamists"; it also upheld a ban on the cohabitation of virgins with continent men. In the Western Church, Ambrose, the bishop of Milan, gave glory to virginal integrity: "For in what does the chastity of a virgin consist, but in an integrity unexposed to taint from the outside?" Virgins were "subject to no man, but to God alone" and their model was the ever-virgin Mary. As noted by Brown, "In Milan and Rome, as in the great churches of the East, the virgins acted as nothing less than human boundary-stones. Their presence defined the Church basilica as a privileged, sacred space." Jerome, the translator of the Bible into Latin and a prodigious writer of letters, warned against the power of lust and barely accepted the notion of marriage. During a stay in a desert cell where he had condemned himself out of fear of hell, he described sensual fantasies that besieged him: "My only companions were scorpions and wild beasts [but] I often found myself surrounded by bands of dancing girls. My face was pale with fasting; but though my limbs were cold as ice, my mind was burning with desire, and the fires of lust kept bubbling up before me while my flesh was as good as dead." Jerome concluded that "all sexual intercourse was unclean," but he sweetened his advice to virgins with erotic hints: "Let the bridegroom [Jesus] ever sport with you within . . . When sleep overtakes you He will come and put his hand through the hole of the door and your heart shall tremble for Him; and you will awake, arise, and say, 'I am sick with love.' Then he will answer: 'A garden enclosed is my sister, my spouse; a spring shut up, a fountain sealed.'" Jerome also told mothers that they would become God's in-laws if they allowed their daughters to marry Christ.

The greatest of the Church Fathers was Ambrose's student, Augustine. He knew the joys of sensuality, having lived with a concubine for thirteen years and fathering a son. In his *Confessions* (397) he wrote about his sexual struggles and his youthful prayer: "Lord, give me chastity and continence, but not now." At the age of thirty-two he converted to Christianity and became both a bishop and one of the most influential theologians in the history of the Church. As his thoughts matured they became more morose because he determined that sexual desire was shameful and that death was unnatural yet inevitable. Had Adam and Eve not sinned, procreation would be blessedly passionless and men would sow their seeds as calmly as a farmer sets seeds into the furrow of a field: "Our ideal is not to experience desire at all." But because Adam and Eve sinned, all humans are conceived in sin, born between urine and feces with sin in their souls. They are helpless in the face of sexual arousal because human will is powerless when the genitals are excited. This, according to Augustine, was what Paul meant in Romans 7:14–24: "For I know that nothing good dwells within me, that is, in my flesh. I can will what is right but cannot do it. For I do not do the good I want, but the evil I do not want is what I do . . . I delight in the law of God in my inmost self, but I see in my members another law at war with the law of my mind and making me captive to the law of sin which dwells in my members." Adam's first spontaneous erection after his sin against God signified the beginning of man's loss of control over his body. When the tail wags the dog, so to speak, man stumbles through life barking up the wrong tree. Only through a life of chastity and neverending vigilance against the desires of the flesh can a person hope to undo the effects of original sin.

TEMPLES OVER SEWERS: WOMEN ARE THE DEVIL'S GATEWAY

The essential purity of virginity and the hint of shame that accompanies sexuality are themes that have permeated the Christian world since the early days of the Church. Although both men and women fell under the spell of Mary, virginity always seemed more suitable to women. The adjective "virgin" was given to female saints and martyrs but rarely to males. The virgins who were consecrated in special church ceremonies were female. Jerome, Augustine, the Desert Fathers and other men wrote openly of their sexual fantasies of women, especially untainted virgins. The religious literature written by women is decidedly smaller, but it does not contain sexual fantasies of men, virginal or otherwise, except for reveries about being married to Jesus, the passionate but asexual bridegroom.

The easy attribution of virginity to females was probably related to the anatomical fact that an unbroken hymen could be verified while men had to be taken at their word which, even in the olden days, wasn't worth much. Besides, men had special problems such as nocturnal emissions that usually were accompanied by lusty dreams and penises that became erect seemingly of their own volition. Also, female prostitutes and concubines were readily available. Why did men have such difficulty in controlling their sexual desires? The answer provided by many leaders of the Church was simple. Lust is the primary desire of the flesh that kept men in bondage to sin. Men lusted after women. Ergo, women were the problem.

Ambivalence was expressed in the need for women as well as in the fear and distrust of them throughout the Old Testament. Good women were caring mothers and subservient wives; bad women were seductresses who used their sexuality to overpower weak-willed men. Female sexuality was not only potent but also insatiable: "Four things never say 'Enough'; the grave, the mouth of the womb, the earth ever thirsty for water, and the fire which never says 'Enough'" (Proverbs 30:15-16). Once a woman opened her quiver god only knows how many arrows might find their way in. Harlots might have been despised, but they flourished because men patronized them. Another source of the fear of women was the normal process of menstruation, which made them ritually unclean.

In the New Testament, Jesus clearly elevated the status of women by letting a woman with vaginal bleeding touch him, by his stance on divorce, by including women in his traveling entourage, and by not only allowing Martha and Mary to sit at his feet while he taught but also by praising the more attentive sister (Luke 10:39-42). Also in parables such as the mustard seed and the leaven (Luke 13:18-21) and the coming of the kingdom (Luke 17:34-36), he included male and female subjects.

Continuing Jesus' intent, Paul wrote his exhilarating statement, "There is neither Jew nor Greek, there is neither slave nor free, there is neither male nor female, for you are all one in Christ Jesus" (Gal. 3:28). However, several lines later Paul reverted to the customary masculine form when he stated that Christ the redeemer came "that we might receive adoption as sons . . . therefore you are no longer a slave but a son, and if a son, then an heir of God through Christ" (4:5–7). This reversion is but a hint of Paul's inability to break with the past. Theologically he liberated women by acknowledging the worth of their souls, but socially he left them embedded where they always were.

Over the centuries the primary justifications for keeping women in a subordinate social position have been two statements by Paul in his first letter to the Church in Corinth. The first statement noted that the head of every man is Christ and the head of every woman is her husband, "but any woman who prays or prophecies with her head unveiled dishonors her head . . . for a man ought not to cover his head, since he is the image and glory of God; but woman is the glory of man . . . that is why a woman ought to have a veil on her head, because of the angels" (11:3–10). The fact that women prayed and prophesied in church was a break from Jewish tradition where women were silent and distant witnesses of rituals. The need for women to cover their heads during prayer was a Jewish custom that signified their association with sinful Eve and their inferior status in comparison with men. A veil was supposed to offer protection from not-so-angelic fallen angels who seduced and copulated with earthly women

The notion that only man was the glory and image of God derived from Genesis 1:27, "So God created man in His own image; in the image of God He created him; male and female He created them." If God created both "him" and "them" in his image, was God then a hermaphrodite? Of course not. Gnostic Christians in the second century, who searched for deeper meanings and sometimes secret knowledge from holy writings, believed that spirit and the potential for goodness was a male attribute while matter and the potential for evil was female. In order to achieve salvation, women had to become spiritual males. Some Church Fathers advised virgins to cut their hair and to wear men's clothing in order to facilitate a gender change; one measure of success was the withering of female breasts. Gnostics quoted from the Gospel of Thomas where Peter the disciple said to Christ, "Let Mary (Magdalen) leave us, for women are not worthy of life." Jesus replied, "I myself shall lead her in order to make her male, so that she also may become a living spirit like you males." Augustine settled things by declaring that man, either alone or when joined with his wife, is the image of God while woman alone is not.

Paul's second statement concluded that "The women should keep silence in the churches. For they are not permitted to speak but should be subordinate, as even the law says. If there is anything they desire to know, let them ask their husbands at home. For it is shameful for a woman to speak in church" (14:34–35). Since Paul previously had said that women pray and prophesy in church, the prohibition most probably represented his petulance at the troubled congregation in Corinth. Members there were taking grievances against each other to the secular courts instead of settling them in church. Paul also accused them of sexual immorality, arrogance, boasting, and associating with idolaters, drunkards, and robbers. One of his typically masculine solutions for these problems was for women to shut up so that religious services could be conducted decently and in order, "For God is not a God of confusion but of peace" (14:33). Unfortunately, blame-the-woman became a widespread attitude in Christianity, and Paul's words have been a major argument in denying women acceptance into the priesthood.

However, the primary and the ultimate reason, the alpha and the omega, for disparaging and even hating women was their descendance from Eve. Christian writers were quick to pick up on the Old Testament words of Ecclesiasticus, "From a woman sin had its beginning, and because of her we all die." Tertullian wrote to women: "Don't you know that you, too, are Eve? Even today God's judgement applies to all of your sex. You are the Devil's gateway: you consented to eat from his tree and were the first to renounce the law of God. Because of your first dessert, death, even the Son of God had to die."

Mary became the second Eve (and Christ the second Adam), a new mother for the human race, but her case was unique: she was not only Christ's mother but also his symbolic wife and a virgin to boot. The first Eve brought death, but the second Eve brought life. While mortal women might aspire to be like Mary, they are all sisters of the evil Eve. Thus, Jerome said, "Woman is the gate of the devil and the road to iniquity." From the desert St. Anthony wrote, "Her voice is the kiss of a serpent." St. John Chrysostom (347–407), bishop of Constantinople, was particularly vivid: "If men could see beneath the skin, the sight of women would make them nauseated. The whole of her bodily beauty is nothing less than phlegm, blood, bile, rheum, and the fluid of digested food. Since we are loathe to touch spit or dung with our fingertips, how can we desire to embrace such a sack of excrement?" Pope Gregory the Great (540–604) wrote that "Woman is the poison of the asp, and the hate of the dragon." St. Maximum (d. 662) said, "She makes a shipwreck of man, she is a tyrant who leads them captive, a lioness who holds them fast in her embrace, a siren decked out to lure them to destruction, a malicious evil beast." St. John of Damascus (657–749) described woman as "the daughter of lies, the sentinel of hell, the enemy of peace." The French Bishop Hildebert in the twelfth century wrote that "woman is a fragile thing, steadfast in nothing but crime and always harmful. Woman is a voracious flame, the utmost folly, man's intimate enemy . . . all consuming in vice she is consumed by all." And to St. Bernard (1090–1153) was attributed the sentiment that "a beautiful women is like a temple built over a sewer."

This brief litany of quotes is but an indication of the misogynistic roots of Christianity that were inspired by interpretations of the Bible. We have seen how women were blamed for stimulating men's appetite for lust. Women were also blamed for instigating and perpetuating religious heresies that challenged the authority of the church. They were accused of being witches and spreading social unrest.

At the end of the twelfth century, the Cathar heresy was picking up steam. Its goal was to replace the established Church clergy, which the Cathars considered to be corrupt, with its own "perfect" clergy. They set up an alternative Christian church complete with bishops and social programs. Pope Innocent III established the Dominican order of priests and charged them with winning over the Cathars. The Waldensian heretics won converts and chided the rich church by practicing extreme poverty. The Pope established the Franciscan order to answer this challenge. When these strategies failed, the Pope called for an armed crusade to destroy the heretics. Crusaders were rewarded with special forgiveness of their sins, tax breaks, and the possession of land owned by heretics. Fifteen thousand heretics in the French city of Beziers were killed in 1209 alone, but these slaughters stiffened the resistance of the heretics. Finally the church hit upon a winning plan in 1230 by forming a permanent Inquisition tribunal staffed by Dominican priests and given extraordinary powers to ferret out heretics.

The battle lasted several centuries during which countless heretics were tortured and killed. Women were especially at risk because they supposedly fostered heresy through their practice of witchcraft. In 1484 Pope Innocent VIII appointed the priests Henry Kramer and James Sprenger as Inquisitors in Northern Germany where "many persons have abandoned themselves to devils, incubi and succubi . . . and do not shrink from committing and perpetrating the foulest abominations and filthiest excesses." In 1486 these remarkable Inquisitors published *The Witches' Hammers* (*Malleus Maleficarum*), an erudite guide book to the detection and persecution of witches that influenced European witch trials for several centuries.

Using the Bible and authors such as Saints Jerome, Augustine, and Bernard as their authority, Kramer and Sprenger determined that the word Femina (woman) "comes from Fe (faith) and Minus, since she is ever weaker to hold and preserve the faith." Unlike men, women are apt to become witches. Their intelligence is like a child's. They are by nature carnal. Their tears are snares meant to deceive a man. They are liars by nature and, like Sirens, the sweet melody of their voices entices passers-by and kills them. They are imperfect because they were formed from the rib of Adam, which was bent in a contrary direction to man. "To conclude; all witchcraft comes from carnal lust, which is in women insatiable. See Proverbs 30; the mouth of the womb never says 'Enough.' Wherefore for the sake of fulfilling their lusts they consort even with devils."

The abominations that witches performed were legion and included causing death and sterility in men and animals merely by looking at them, devouring children, allowing themselves to remain silent during torture, turning men's minds to inordinate love or hatred, making horses go mad under their riders, and causing abortions. They could fly through the air on a chair or a broomstick that had been anointed with an unguent made from the limbs of children whom they had killed before baptism.

Kramer and Sprenger devoted a great deal of attention to male genitals. "God allows more power of witchcraft over the genital functions on account of the first corruption of sin which came to us from the act of generation, so also He allows greater power over the actual genital organ, even its total removal." While the devil can physically remove a man's penis, witches can delude a man so that "his imagination can really and actually believe that something is not present, since by none of his exterior senses, such as sight or touch, can he perceive that it [his penis] is present." By confusing a man's vision and by changing the mental images in a man's imagination, witches could make men report seeing penises, as many as twenty or thirty, collected by witches and placed "in a box or bird's nest where they move themselves like living members, and eat oats and corn." An anecdote was provided of a man who asked a witch to restore his lost penis. She told him to climb a tree and take the penis he liked best out of a bird nest. "And when he tried to take a big one, the witch said: 'You must not take that one' because it belonged to a parish priest."

NO FAT IN HEAVEN: ASCETIC WOMEN

The anthropologist Caroline Banks has written about a middle-aged woman named Margaret whose severe, deliberate self-starvation had been present for many years. Margaret's routine was to bathe after midnight and then to eat part of her supper. After another bath she completed her meal. She then took a third bath "to feel just immaculately fresh" before going to sleep at sunrise. Although she could afford better, she chose to eat food that was spoiled, rotten, or old. She described herself as a morally upright Fundamentalist Christian. She said that her friends told her she was too thin for men to like her, but she added that "it would never occur to me to be with a man." She was relieved that she had not had a menstrual period since age eighteen. She believed that true Christians do not really die and that their bodies turn into spirits that go to be with God: "The part of you that goes to heaven is really yourself because the body is nothing . . . anybody who believes in the Bible would believe in that as a matter of fact." She thanked God that she was in total control of her diet and confided to the anthropologist that "there is no fat in heaven."

In the Judeo-Christian tradition self-starvation has an obscure origin but a venerable history. Unlike Margaret's constant food restriction, however, biblical references point to time-limited fasting. In the early books of the Old Testament, fasting was usually an individual decision. King David, for example, impregnated the beautiful Bathsheba and then arranged for the death of her husband in battle. Because of these wrongdoings, the Lord struck her newborn love-child ill, whereupon David fasted. After seven days the child died, and David immediately resumed eating. He stated, "While the child was still alive, I fasted and wept; for I said, 'Who knows whether the Lord will be gracious to me, that the child may live?' But now he is dead; why should I fast? Can I bring him back again? I shall go to him, but he will not return to me" (2 Samuel 12:22–23). That David's servants were mystified at his fasting while the infant was still alive indicates that it usually was a mourning ritual. Earlier in the same book David and his men "mourned and wept and fasted every evening for Saul and for Jonathan his son and for the people of the Lord and for the house of Israel, because they had fallen by the sword" (1:11–12).

Another reason for personal fasting was to facilitate contact with the spirit world. Saul, for example, was frightened when he saw the Philistine army, so he tried to determine what God had in store for him. However, "The Lord did not answer him, either by dreams, by Urim, or by prophets" (Urim was a type of oracle). Saul then fasted for a day and a night so that he might communicate with the witch of En Dor (1 Samuel 28:7–20). Many centuries later Daniel fasted for three weeks and successfully had a vision of a man clothed in linen with a face like the appearance of lightning (Dan. 10:13–10). Christian theologians consider the man to represent the pre-incarnate Christ.

After the Jewish exile in Babylon, group fasting became established. Thus Mordecai and Queen Esther sent letters to all the Jews about the appointed time of Purim and "concerning matters of their fasting and lamenting" (Esther 9:31). However, the only general fast period according to the law was the Day of Atonement: " . . . you shall afflict yourselves [fast] and shall do no work; for on this day shall atonement be made for you, to cleanse you, that you may be clean from all your sins before the Lord" (Lev. 16:29–30). Fasting eventually became a widespread Jewish practice not only for specific events but also for general piety. Judith, being exceptionally devout, "fasted all the days of her widowhood" with just a few exceptions (Jud. 8:6).

In the book of Isaiah, Chapter fifty-eight is devoted to fasting. Isaiah was asked by his people why God did not value their fasts. The answer: God was put off by their phony displays of bowing down and covering themselves with sackcloth and ashes. In reality, they carried on with business and quarrels as usual during their fasts instead of doing God's work, which is to feed the hungry, clothe the naked, provide shelter to the homeless, and honor the Sabbath day. Although Jesus and his disciples rarely, if ever, fasted (Matt. 9:13), Jesus considered fasting along with charity and prayer to be major expressions of piety. His attitude toward fasting was similar to Isaiah's. Instead of fasting in public like hypocrites with ash-covered faces, Jesus told his followers to wash their faces and anoint their heads "that your fasting may not been seen by men but by your Father who is in secret" (Matt. 6:16–18).

The early Christian community practiced fasting. Acts mentions it three times. In fact, probably during the second century several verses were added to the original text of the New Testament in order to support the practice of fasting (see Matt. 17:21; Mark 9:15; Acts 10:30; 1 Cor. 7:5). A book called the *Didache* warned believers not to fast with the "hypocrite Jews" on Mondays and Thursdays: "You should fast on Wednesdays and Fridays." Food was necessary to sustain life, but there was something tainted about it. Wasn't the very first sin against God the eating of forbidden fruit? Didn't Esau sell his birthright for a bowl of lentils? Didn't Jesus tell people not to labor for food which perishes but for spiritual food which endures to everlasting life (John 6:27)? As with abstinence from sex, abstinence from food sharpened spirituality, purified both body and soul, and pleased God. To fast was both to undo the sin of the first Adam and to share in the suffering of Christ. And, according to Tertullian, thin bodies not only are preserved better in the grave but also resurrect more rapidly and pass more easily through the narrow gate into heaven.

Spiritual athletes such as the Desert Fathers as well as heroic nuns and Irish monks practiced severe asceticism highlighted by persistent, austere fasting. Common Christians followed the rules for fasting set by the Church. These rules were at first quite strict but gradually were relaxed to include fewer days and less-stringent dietary restrictions.

Fasting returned with a vengeance in the troubled times of the late Middle Ages. Secular and Church officials clashed over claims of temporal authority. Both kings and popes were labeled Antichrists. The costs of building cathedrals were so high that the Church became more mercenary. Epidemic diseases spawned fears of an impending apocalypse and preachers called for repentance. Amid this social turmoil the sweet simplicity of St. Francis of Assisi was a welcomed breath of fresh air and his fasting inspired others. Women especially were attracted to fasting. Unlike men they were not free to wander barefoot throughout the countryside and cities, but in the shelter of their cloisters they could starve themselves and mortify their bodies. This they did not only to achieve personal salvation but also to serve as models for all Christians.

With the Virgin Mary as the feminine ideal, women were in a difficult bind. Mary dutifully obeyed the dictates of God the Father by having a child, was venerated for her maternal sufferings (Our Lady of the Sorrows with seven swords piercing her breast), and was the idolized bride of her son as prefigured in the Song of Songs. All this she accomplished while retaining her virginity. The closest approximation a woman could come to this ideal was to become a nun, where, protected from the loathsome sexual demands of human marriage, she could enjoy the ecstatic embrace of Christ to whom she was ritually married. Thus, in the fourteenth century the pious Margery Kempe wrote what Jesus told her. He supposedly said that when she went to bed she could boldly "Take me as thy wedded husband, as thy dearworthy darling, and as thy dear son, for I will be loved as a son should be loved by the mother, and I will that thou lovest Me, daughter, as a good wife ought to love her husband." With dazzling virtuosity the virginal, ascetic Margery simultaneously became Christ's mother, daughter, and spouse!

But how to suffer like Mary? Female ascetics expertly developed stigmata, ate cat vomit and dead rodents, bound their bodies tightly with iron chains, burned their skin with hot wax, whipped themselves, and pressed thorns into their skin. However, the foremost method of suffering was self-starvation. Beyond emulating the Virgin Mary's sorrows, the deepest goal of all these behaviors was to share in Christ's Passion so thoroughly that he and the sufferer became one being. To facilitate this divine union, the ultimate fast consisted of a diet of consecrated communion wafers.

St. Catherine of Siena (1347–1380) was revered and quite famous throughout Europe for her extraordinarily pure lifestyle. As a child she experienced a vision of Jesus and his saints, secretly pledged a life of virginity to Jesus and Mary, and whipped herself with a knotted rope (even convincing her young friends to do likewise). She so vigorously resisted her family's efforts to find her a mate that her father finally relented, saying, "We know with certainty that you are moved not by the whims of youth but by the impulse of divine love . . . No one [in the family] is to bother my sweet daughter; no one is to try in any way to impede her; let her serve her Bridegroom as she pleases and pray ceaselessly for us."

Starting as a teenager, she began her life of austere asceticism in earnest. She ate only bread, water, and raw vegetables, wore a dirty, scratchy, wool garment, whipped herself with an iron chain for ninety minutes three times daily—for her sins, for the living, and for the dead—and supposedly slept only fifteen minutes a day. Following this regimen she lost half her body weight and spoke of evil spirits that attacked her. When taken by her mother to a healing spa, she found the hottest pool and deliberately scalded her body.

Catherine joined the Sisters of Penance, a lay order of older women, and lived at home. At the age of twenty-one, convinced that her terminally ill father was ready to die in peace, she prayed that his soul would go straight to heaven. At his death she received a vision of him among the saints, and she experienced a sharp hip pain that became chronic. Several years later Christ told her in a vision to go out into the world. She responded by eliminating bread from her diet and by caring for the sick. In order to overcome her revulsion at the oozing infected breasts of a woman with cancer, Catherine drank the pus that she collected from the woman's wounds. That night in a vision Christ invited her to drink the blood from his wounds. She then realized that her stomach could no longer function properly and that it had no need for food.

Despite her seeming position at death's door and accusations that her self-starvation was demonically caused, she gained strength upon a diet of water and the Blessed Eucharist. She actively engaged in high-level politics and advised both Popes and queens. When her efforts to save the Church from impending ruin failed (in part because Pope Gregory IX followed her advice), she resigned herself to death by refusing to drink water. Conscious of her failures and of the demons that attacked her, she offered her body to God as an anvil for his beatings. Dehydrated and depressed, she gave up the ghost after three months of agony. She was thirty-three years old.

BEWITCHED, BOTHERED, AND BEWILDERED
MEN RULE, WOMEN SUFFER

Unlike diamonds, the Bible is not a woman's best friend. The product of a patriarchal society, it proclaims male superiority and female inferiority as the natural order of the universe. God is to man as man is to woman. St. Thomas Aquinas noted, "Only the male represents the fulness of human potential, whereas woman by nature is defective physically, morally, and mentally. The male represents wholeness of human nature, both in himself and as head of the woman." As long as women accept this view of things, tend to their children, cook meals, and clean house, they will by and large be as content as cows chewing on their cud. In fact, married couples who endorsed the item "The Bible is the answer to all important questions" on a recent national survey reported fewer disagreements, higher levels of marital happiness, and more-positive spousal relationships then did couples with low religious fundamentalism scores. It is interesting that in the Bible the word for husband is actually "master," the word for wife is actually "woman," and the verb to marry is "to take." Thus, a man takes a woman from her father and becomes her master while a woman takes whatever she can get and follows a strict code of behavior. Consider the following rule: "If two men fight together, and the wife of one draws near to rescue her husband from the hand of the one attacking him, and puts out her hand and seizes him by the genitals, then you shall cut off her hand; your eye shall not pity her" (Deut. 25:11–12). Was this really such a big problem even back then? Was this a God-inspired idea? A statement about male sexual insecurity? Purity reduced to the absurd?

For over two thousand years biblical interpretation has convinced women not only of their inherent inferiority but also of the necessity for men to dominate and guide them. Women can't be trusted. Samson trusted Delilah to his ruination. Poor Ahab killed a man and sold himself to wickedness because his wife stirred him up. Women should feel guilty because Eve beguiled Adam into eating forbidden fruit, caused sin and death to enter into the world, and Christ to suffer and die on the cross. Women are filthy when they menstruate, and displeasing both to God and man. They deserve to suffer during childbirth; in fact, up until the mid-nineteenth century physicians in many Christian countries would not provide analgesics to women in labor for fear of clerical censure. Since the entrance to hell is found between every woman's legs, women should feel shame because they inspire lustful and sometimes irrational behavior in men. Masturbation by anyone is an unfortunate sin, but female masturbation additionally could give rise to a series of diseases beginning with hysteria and eventually leading to spinal irritation, epilepsy, idiocy, mania, and death. Sir Isaac Baker Brown, author of a widely used surgical textbook and president of the Medical Society of London in the 1860s, removed the clitoris of thousands of troubled women referred by their clergymen for the procedure.

These not-so-natural, supposedly God-inspired attitudes have impacted women enormously with resultant psychiatric morbidity. From an early age females are socialized to be passive, unassertive, and dependent. They learn to be helpless and to internalize frustration and anger. They generally view themselves as less competent than men, less in control over their lives, and less worthy of expressing their needs and desires. They are more critical of themselves than men and more apt to punish themselves and to feel guilt. It certainly can come as no surprise that women are more likely than men to develop certain types of mental illness and to engage in certain types of pathological behavior.

Depression affects women at least two or three times more than it does men. The ratios for skin-cutting and for suicide attempts, especially overdoses, are much higher. Women with agoraphobia, also known as the housewife's disease, are fearful of leaving their home and going into public places alone. An interesting dynamic often underlies this disorder: alone in the streets a woman just might indulge a sexual or aggressive desire, but agoraphobia provides an internal chaperone. Historically the disorder became prevalent only when Europe's streets became safe enough for women to walk unescorted. Anorexia nervosa, a disorder of deliberate self-starvation found almost exclusively in females, is regarded by many as a maneuver to establish ownership and control of one's body. Additionally it carries with it an aura of religious purity (unlike obesity with its connotation of sinful gluttony). Dissociation disorders such as amnesia, multiple personality disorder, and fugue states (a sudden, unexpected leaving of home with an inability to recall some or all of one's past) occur more often in females. They may represent attempts to blot out the memories of childhood sexual and physical abuse, to escape intolerable situations, and to engage in usually frowned-upon self-expression. Some women with traits of masochism and personalities heavy with dependency are at risk for battering by predatory men. Even mentally healthy women may find themselves trapped in abusive relationships; a devout Fundamentalist woman was married to an alcoholic who would boot her out of bed and tell her to sleep with their children while he had sex with women that he picked up in a bar. If she protested, he would beat her. He refused to seek help and threatened her if she did. After putting up with his behavior for over a decade, she shamefully approached her minister for advice. He told her that her husband philandered because she did not gratify him in bed. It was her Christian obligation to attend to her wifely duties and, by so doing, win her husband back to Jesus. The more her husband debased her, the harder she should try to please him. The harder he hit her, the quicker she should turn the other cheek. Since hers was the blame, hers was the punishment. Thus saith the Lord, said the minister. She became my patient after a serious suicide attempt.

Sexuality has been troublesome for some women who belong to Bible-based churches. Trying to live up to the standards of the ideal woman, Mary the Virgin Mother, is a crazy-making proposition. There is no way for a woman to be both a virgin and a mother. In the everyday world almost all women marry and have children. Since the Virgin Mary never had either carnal sex or an orgasm, even married women who would emulate her may feel guilt and shame about their sexuality. If they cannot refuse their husbands' demands, at least they can deal with the experience joylessly. The insistence of some religious groups that both birth control and abortion are sinful, that every act of intercourse should have the potential for pregnancy, and that divorce is forbidden robs women of control over their bodies and their fate. For some women, anorexia may signify a fear of magical oral impregnation and a rejection of female sexuality (severe anorectics do not have menstrual periods). However, for others, their emaciated bodies may be a caricature of the hopelessly slender models portrayed in fashion magazines. Like the Virgin Mary, such models are for looking, not for touching; there is no fat in heaven and big-bosomed Playboy bunnies go straight to hell.

Women are much more likely than men to seek spiritual help for their discontents. Although religion may pose a problem because of its negative and restrictive views of women, it also offers a partial solution. Through prayer to a powerful male God and faithful participation in his church services, women can aspire to healing their ills and improving their lot in life. Even if the procedures do not change things materially, they offer hope and the illusion of control. Sometimes God receives somewhat strange requests. I had as a patient an unhappily married Hispanic woman. Obedient to the social code of *marianismo* (women should behave like Mary, the mother of God), she was a virgin bride and a sexually unresponsive wife who denied herself in deference to the wants of her unappreciative husband and children. She had reached the status of a madonna. Then she fell in love with a married man and, according to the *marianista* code, became a whore. During attendance at a full nine-day spiritual novena at her church, she secretly prayed to the Virgin Mary and Mary Magdalen to intercede with God in killing both her husband and her lover's wife. Divorce was so unthinkable that heaven-caused death presented a more credible option!

Women are also more likely to come into contact with or to seek the help of physicians and psychiatrists. A small minority seem to find some sort of solace only when they are hospitalized or undergoing medical procedures or under constant care. They are skillful at feigning illnesses and symptoms; some thrive on surgical procedures, such as abdominal operations, while others may deliberately create lesions and symptoms in their children. However, for the vast majority of women, mental symptoms and illnesses—even those that have a significant genetic or biological component—are come by naturally and are not feigned. The psychological and social motivations underlying the behaviors may be understandable to the sensitive therapist but not to the involved actors. In the case of old-fashioned hysteria (now called conversion reactions because psychological conflicts are converted into physical symptoms), the symptoms often were symbolic: a bride who was fearful of sex developed a leg paralysis and was unable to walk to the altar. With the advent of psychology courses in schools and with psychologically sophisticated films and television shows, transparent hysterical symptoms are so easily recognized by most people that they are rarely seen anymore. In fact, the only places where they thrive are in settings where religious healings occur. The lame are made to walk and the blind are made to see amid shouts of "Praise Jesus" and the warm approval of onlookers.

Mrs. Charlotte Gilmore, whom we encountered earlier in this chapter, represented the conceptual evolution of single hysterical symptoms into hysteria as a temporary way of life. In the words of the psychiatrists Roland Littlewood and Maurice Lipsedge, the "hysteric provided a parody of the core social values; women's expected dependency and restricted social role . . . Hysteria was a conventionally available alternative behavior pattern for certain women, which permitted them to express dissatisfaction." Freud commented on the hysteric female in 1905: "Ill health will be her one weapon for maintaining her position. It will procure for her the care she longs for . . . It will compel him (the husband) to treat her with solicitude if she recovers; otherwise a relapse will threaten." Hysteria as a permanent way of life is enshrined in the official manual of psychiatric diagnosis as histrionic personality disorder. Almost always applied to women (although sometimes Anglo psychiatrists make the diagnosis in Latin men), the construct is a caricature of femininity gone amok. It is characterized by excessive and shallow emotionality, sexually seductive or provocative behavior, theatricality, suggestibility, constant attention seeking, intolerance of frustration, and a craving for novelty, stimulation, and excitement. The final touch is that the histrionic woman is often physically attractive, sexy, and, according to psychiatric legend, sexually frigid. Look on your works, O mighty men, and despair! Such are the daughters of Eve.

Undoubtedly the mental illness of a woman upsets the family applecart. An agoraphobic housewife, for example, can beg off certain responsibilities such as shopping or driving a child to school. The husband may be forced to perform many of her usual tasks and even may stop saying that he "works" while she "just stays at home all day." One mode of treatment for anorexia nervosa is family therapy; thus, the patient's illness could force an examination of how the entire family functions. In order to effect change a woman must sometimes get sick. As Littlewood and Lipsedge note, the sickness is not simply a self-punitive or manipulative ploy but rather represents the struggle of a powerless person who "is enmeshed in a situation which she cannot control, one which neither reflects her interests nor her perspective but which does afford room for maneuver by employing the dominant symbolism itself."

BOYS WILL BE BOYS
MARRIAGE, DIVORCE, AND TROUBLED PRIESTS

The most common type of marriage in the Bible is the patriarchal, kind in which the father/husband is the supreme authority as established in Genesis. God said to Eve, "In pain you shall bring forth children; your desire shall be for your husband, and he shall rule over you." David's and Solomon's many wives exemplify polygamy, although usually just two wives was more typical. By the eighth century, monogamy had become the prevalent form of marriage. The bride and groom entered into a covenant that involved not only them but also their families. On a larger scale monogamy represented the covenant between God and Israel. Isaiah's Chapters 61 and 62 compared the bride's and bridegroom's clothing with "the garments of salvation" and "the robes of righteousness" and promised that the desolate forsaken land of Zion would attain salvation through marriage with the Lord, "and as the bridegroom rejoices over the bride, so shall God rejoice over you." In 2 Corinthians 2, Paul betrothed the Church to Christ "as a pure bride to her one husband."

Marriage in Christianity has been somewhat problematic beyond the issue of the husband's domination over the wife. Although the Catholic catechism states that Jesus established marriage as a sacrament, most scholars disagree. In fact, both Jesus and Paul tolerated marriage but hardly gave it glowing reviews. Marriage for them was "a form of this world [that] is passing away" because the end of the world was approaching, "So that he who marries his betrothed does well; and he who refrains from marriage does better" (1. Cor. 7). That Jesus attended a wedding at Cana, where he performed his first miracle by changing water into wine, is not particularly significant. It would be a totally different story if he had consecrated the couple's marriage with a nuptial blessing.

The only biblical statement that could be used to argue that marriage is a sacrament is found in Ephesians 5:32-33. After quoting Genesis 2:24 about a man and a woman becoming one flesh, the author states: "This is a great mystery, and I take it to mean Christ and the Church; however, let each one of you love his wife as himself, and let the wife see that she respects her husband." There are several problems with this passage. The first phrase is really "This mystery is great," thus changing the meaning from the mystery being unfathomable to the mystery being important. The word mystery was translated by Jerome into Latin as "sacramentum," a word that could have meant either mystery or an oath of allegiance. Jerome's choice of words was fine, but centuries later some church officials mistakenly concluded that *sacramentum* meant sacrament. The allegorical use of the Adam and Eve story to represent the marriage between God and Israel was not a feature of Judaism, and its use here in a Christian context is somewhat strange. The phrase "I take it to mean" indicates the author's personal interpretation and implies that other interpretations can be made. The Christ–Church union differs from the husband–wife union; the former is neverending while the latter ends with death (poets and sentimentalists notwithstanding). Finally, the concept that a man should love his wife but that a woman should *respect* her husband doesn't quite jibe with the couple becoming one flesh.

With a few exceptions, the early Church Fathers were not terribly high on marriage. Ambrose wrote, "Even a good marriage is slavery. What, then, must a bad marriage be?" For Jerome, "Marriage is only one degree less sinful that fornication." The Church adopted the Roman concept that a valid marriage simply required the consent of the bride and groom. Marriage was a secular contract and the Church recognized the validity of all marriages, including those among slaves, that followed local civil laws. A priest could attend a marriage as a witness. At the Council of Elvira in 309 A.D., many rulings were made about the necessity for control over sexual matters; it was in this century that priests began to intrude cautiously into the marriage ceremony by blessing the newlyweds. In the sixth century, marriages were often associated with a mass but their validity was still based on a secular contract.

In the Eastern Catholic Church, marriage became a sacrament by order of the emperor in the ninth century; the only valid marriages were those performed by a priest who "crowned" the bride and groom. However, in the Latin church, the situation was different. Marriage reform was not stimulated until the Cathar heretic movement of the eleventh century challenged Church control of the social order. The heretics frowned on marriage because procreation resulted in children who would eventually mature and create even more children. This cycle of materiality had to be stopped so that a truly spiritual age would emerge (by all accounts the Cathars did indulge in nonmarital sex upon occasion, but this was not frowned upon as much as institutionalized marital sex). For regular Christians, including priests, marriage and divorce weren't solemn events, but, in part as a response to the heretics, the Church began moving slowly towards making marriage a sacrament. Pope Gregory VII (1073–1086) intensified the debate, and in 1215 the Fourth Lateran Council established a modicum of control by passing rules about the necessity of posting marriage bans and of holding public wedding ceremonies. It wasn't until the Council of Trent in 1563 that the church officially proclaimed marriage to be a sacrament. The current Catholic catechism states, "In the Latin Church, it is ordinarily understood that the spouses, as ministers of Christ's grace, mutually confer upon each other the sacrament of matrimony by expressing their consent before the Church."

In modern times just about all Christian churches, some more reluctantly than others, have modified their position on divorce because secular divorce is so prevalent. Even in those churches that might excommunicate persons who get divorced, members of the church usually will accept divorced persons as new members. The Catholic Church still has a hard-line policy about divorce, but each year new records are being set by couples who have their marriages annulled by the Church, sometimes on a flimsy pretext. Many parish priests do not withhold communion from remarried persons even though they technically are acting against Church policy. I might add that for a long time psychiatrists considered divorce a sign of emotional immaturity. However, when enough psychiatrists themselves split from their spouses, they changed their position. Now, divorce may indicate a mentally healthy action depending on the circumstances. Psychiatry reflects the times in which we live and the customs of the people.

Contraception has been problematic for the Catholic Church, whose traditional ban was based on Genesis 38:8–10. Onan was commanded by his father to marry the wife of his dead brother and "raise up an heir. But Onan knew that the heir would not be his; and it came to pass, when he went to his brother's wife, that he emitted on the ground, lest he should give an heir to his brother. And the thing which he did displeased the Lord; therefore He killed him also." Most scholars believe that Onan was killed because he refused to fulfill the obligations of the levirate marriage in which a man was duty-bound to marry his brother's widow and produce children if possible. This practice was a religious law that kept the widow within the family (no foreigner could marry her) and also kept the dead husband's lineage intact (the first-born son kept the name of the dead husband). However, the Church discounted the levirate law and instead ruled that Onan was killed because he practiced coitus interruptus. According to Augustine, "Intercourse, even with one's legitimate wife is unlawful and wicked when the conception of the offspring is prevented. Onan, the son of Judah, did this and the Lord killed him for it." For Augustine, the *only* acceptable role of intercourse was the generation of a child. "To seek the pleasure of the flesh in lying together, although within the limits of marriage; this has venial fault."

The Protestant churches did not protest the Catholic ban on contraception until 1930. As noted by Paul Johnson, at the Lambeth Conference the Anglican Church "reluctantly accepted artificial contraception, and shifted the moral theology to a consideration of whether the married couple's intention was selfish or not." Although the other Protestant churches eventually followed this position, the Catholic Church has steadfastly rejected contraception as sinful. Its only concession has been to allow the rhythm method, in which intercourse is allowed during the time of a woman's menstrual cycle when conception is supposedly physiologically impossible. Because of the imprecision of this method, it is often called "Catholic roulette." Nowadays many if not most Catholics practice birth control. This failure to follow official Church doctrine, according to Johnson, signaled the "general erosion of ecclesiastical authority, the assertion of lay opinion, the defiance of superiors, the spread of public debate among Catholics, the defection of many clergy and nuns, and the decline of papal prestige."

The defection of Catholic priests and nuns is often associated with issues of sexuality. Richard Sipe, a psychotherapist and Roman Catholic priest who is now married and retired from the ministry, has been collecting data and working with troubled clergy since 1960. His book *Sex, Priests, and Power* presents a great deal of sobering information. He estimates that on any given day twenty percent of priests are involved in a sexual relationship of some stability with a woman; eight percent are engaging in sexual experimentation; thirty percent have a homosexual orientation; one percent are transvestites (even St. Jerome, who died in 420, wore a woman's dress to a monk's choir); six percent have sexual activity with children (two percent with prepubescent minors and four percent with adolescents). If you think these numbers are high, consider that in a study by Murphy, sixty-two percent of priests who responded reported being sexually active; of these, fifty-eight percent had exclusively female sexual partners while thirty-two percent had exclusively male partners. Also, the respected sociologist Father Andrew Greeley estimated that four to eight percent of American priests have abused minors sexually. A study by Wagner in 1980 of fifty homosexual priests found that only four percent were celibate while the others averaged about 227 partners each.

As far back as 1973, a report of the Catholic Bishops' Committee on Priestly Spirituality stated about priests that "the institutional church fosters a pre-adolescent stage of psychosexual association with their own sex." Among the structural problems that underlie the current clerical crisis, Sipe identifies the designation of women as evil; the proclamation of a pure, dominant, powerful superior group of male virgins; the subjugation of "inferiors" by the pure group; justification of this subjugation by an appeal to nature or God's will; toleration and even encouragement of behaviors by the pure group that are condemned in others; and the necessity of violence in the establishment or retention of the system. Sipe goes as far as to state, "When I substitute *Jew* or *homosexual* for *woman* in the scheme, I am struck with how everything fits with Nazi theory and practice . . . Numerous parallels with the celibate/sexual power system make it chillingly familiar and force us to acknowledge that they both, system and power, spring from the same human impulses."

WAS WILL DAS WEIB? "WHAT DO WOMEN WANT?"

Akin to Catholicism, psychoanalysis provided not only an explanation for all human behavior but also, when things went awry, provided a form of salvation for all those persons who participated in its fifty-minute rituals. For about the first seventy years of the twentieth century, it was the dominant force in psychiatry and influenced American intellectual life in areas as diverse as child rearing and literary criticism. Like monks who bared their souls in confession and who studied the Bible in excruciating detail, psychoanalysts (most were men) in institutes bared their psyches during personal analyses and inter-preted the Freudian gospel. Those who challenged ideas and perhaps even started rival institutes were denounced as heretics. Analysts who trained applicants were like high priests. It was a patriarchal system whose authority rested on "science" instead of religion and whose holy texts, just as did the Bible, found women to be wanting.

Was will das Weib? What does a woman want? Freud said that this was "the great question that has never been answered and which I have not yet been able to answer, despite my thirty years of research into the feminine soul." The best he could come up with was that women wanted a penis of their own. He reckoned that early in child-hood girls are traumatized by the discovery that they lack a penis. They believe either that they, like their brothers, once had a penis but that it was chopped off, or that they were "born short." They develop penis envy, feel inferior ever after, and seek revenge against men for possessing what they lack, although, fortunately, the ability to pro-duce a child is for most women an acceptable compensation for their missing penis.

In *Analysis Terminable and Interminable* Freud wrote that women's desire for a penis was the source of acute attacks of depres-sion and that "their strongest motive in coming for treatment was the hope that they might somehow still obtain a male organ." He also felt that the superego (moral standards, sense of right and wrong, con-science) of women was inferior to that of men. For little boys the superego emerges from repression of their possessive yearnings for mother in accordance with the societal prohibition against incest. This repression in boys is driven by fear of castration. Little girls, alas, have much less fear of castration because they believe that it already has occurred; the result is a weaker superego. Also, little girls have sadistic fantasies that are driven by clitoral masturbation; these are turned inward because of penis envy and because of their growing awareness of the vagina as the central sexual organ. The result is the formation of female masochism and a desire for humiliation. Finally, Freud believed that at the age of thirty, men were ready for great accomplishments but that thirty-year-old women lost their capacity for intellectual and emotional growth: "It is as though the whole process had been gone through and remained inaccessible to influ-ence the future; as though in fact the difficult development which leads to femininity had exhausted all the possibilities of the individ-ual."

No person in their right mind, with the possible exception of those few minds which lean to the conservative extreme right, believe in these male chauvinistic ideas anymore. Back when they were in fashion, however, only a few brave psychoanalysts dared to confront them. In the 1920s and 1930s, Karen Horney pointed out that "woman has in motherhood, or in the capacity for motherhood, a quite indisputable and by no means negligible physiological superiority" and that men often have an "envy of pregnancy, childbirth, and motherhood, as well as of the breasts and of the act of suckling." In the 1940s, Clara Thompson refuted Freudian ideas with devastating clarity: "Childbearing is a sufficiently important biological function to have value for its own sake. Surely, only a man could have thought of it in terms of compensation or consolation." She felt that Freud erred by viewing his Victorian patients as universal women. What might have applied to them surely could not be applied to the women of today or to women in diverse cultural settings around the world. Thompson regarded penis envy as a metaphor for the envy women have of the greater freedom and opportunities that men have in Western culture: "the freedom to be, to force one's way, to get what one wants; these are the characteristics which a woman envies in a man." She noted that, "As long as a woman's sole opportunity for success in life was in making a successful marriage her career was made or lost by the age of thirty . . . Today there are many examples of women not dependent on their sexual value for security who remain flexible and capable of development." In short, Freud ascribed to biology processes that were primarily cultural, and he ascribed to women thoughts, emotions and fantasies that were primarily the creations of men.

Attempts by women to attain some of the freedoms enjoyed by men have almost invariably been stone-walled. There is, for example, an Old Testament ban against women dressing like men. Although several of the early Church Fathers condoned this behavior, especially for women with pretensions of saintliness, many Christian countries passed strict laws forbidding cross-dressing by women. In the famous historical case Jeanne d'Arc was burned as a heretic by her political enemies. The most damaging charge against her was her propensity to wear men's clothes. In fact, as described by the scholar Diane Owen Hughes, the regulation of women's fashion has been "an endless game of social negotiation."

The great theologian Tertullian (160–240 A.D.) looked back at Eve. If, at the beginning of time, he wrote, wool, silk, embroidery, pearls, gold, and mirrors had existed, "Eve would have coveted all these things, once she was banished from paradise and, in my view, already dead. A woman, therefore, if she hopes for rebirth in heaven, should not long for them now, or even know of them, since she did not possess them or know of them when she was truly alive in Eden. For all these things are the trappings of a woman who is damned and dead, arranged as if to lend splendor to her funeral."

When the plague devastated Europe, many priests scapegoated women; their decadent fashions supposedly resulted in declining morality that somehow facilitated the plague. The trains on gowns were like animal's tails and thus supposedly led to bestiality. Pointy headdresses were likened to horned devils. The expense of fashionable women's clothing made men leery of marriage. Bernardino of Siena cried out, "Because of this the population is down and sodomy is on the rise." In 1453 Cardinal Bessarion imposed a dress code on the city of Bologna in which only men, because they were more virtuous than women, could wear cloth of gold and silver. A noblewoman, Nieolosa Sanuti, rebelled: "Women are the ones who rebuild families, republics, indeed even the whole human race, and resolve what is high and immortal." She thus argued against Tertullian that women's clothing do not bespeak decay but rather virtue and refinement.

In today's developed world it is often considered chic, even sexy, for women to don "masculine" clothing. Such clothing holds a magical promise of the liberated sexuality usually reserved only for men; that is why many Christian fundamentalists oppose it. Also, the stigma of cross-gender behavior is not as great for females as for males. The diagnosis of transvestic fetishism is given to heterosexual men who dress like women (and who suffer significant social or occupational impairment because of this behavior). Gender identity disorder is diagnosed in a person with a strong and persistent identification with a member of the opposite sex; it is three times more common in males than females.

Western cultures generally have regulated the opportunities of men to behave like women. Theatrical performances in which men played female roles were common. In the seventeenth and eighteenth centuries the Catholic Church expanded and institutionalized a rather ghastly practice. Instead of allowing girls to sing, young boys were castrated to produce high-pitched voices for church services. In about 1600, Pope Clement VIII officially declared that the creation of castrati for church choirs was to be regarded *ad honorem Dei* (to the honor of God). Many of the castrati developed odd body shapes. Generally they were tall, but while some were spindly others were obese, like "melodious elephants." Casanova, however, in 1762 described a castrato who, when he appeared on stage dressed as a woman "was ravishing, a nymph, and incredible as it may seem, his breast was as beautiful as any woman's; it was the monster's chief charm. However well one knew the fellow's natural sex, as soon as one looked at his breast, one felt all aglow and quite madly amorous of him. To feel nothing, one would have to be as cold and impassive as a German." Pope Leo XIII put an end to the procedure in the late 1800s.

Great social changes took place in America in the 1960s, and even the conservative culture of psychoanalysis was affected. A series of books and papers were written on men's envy of the generative capacities of women. In this radical view women were no longer solely regarded as defective males, and the power of castration anxiety as a major motivation of men's behavior was diminished. It would have been a slap in the face of colleagues, even to the memory of Freud himself, if evidence had come from studies of Western patients, but there was no disrespect in new findings from exotic locales. Bruno Bettleheim, for example, studied ritual subincision among Australian aborigines in which the penis is sliced open along the urethra so that it somewhat resembled a vagina. He interpreted this ritual as a demonstration of men's desire to possess female sexual organs out of envy over women's creative and nurturing nature. Moreover, the native practice of periodically gashing the subincision site in order to draw blood was interpreted as menstruation envy.

As rulers of the planet, men had a tough time dealing with the fact that the earth was not at the center of the universe. As the supreme beings on the earth, men have had an even tougher time dealing with the fact that they evolved from apes. And now as the once-cocksure masters of women, men are struggling with the fact that anatomy is not really destiny.

WHAT (SOME) WOMEN WANT
THE WOMAN'S BIBLE AND FEMINISM

The twelfth chapter of Numbers has caused a lot of grief for a lot of people. It begins with Moses' sister, Miriam, and Aaron the priest speaking against Moses because he had married an Ethiopian woman. They then continue their griping and say to God, "Has the Lord spoken only through Moses? Has he not spoken through us also?" The Lord's anger was kindled, and he punished Miriam by inflicting her with a skin disease. Aaron wasn't punished; since all priests are descended from him it wouldn't do to ruffle his skin and make him impure. Miriam, the woman, not surprisingly took all the punishment. Although God was angry because Miriam was jealous of Moses, his scabrous response has been interpreted to mean that God would not speak through a woman. As if this wasn't bad enough, God's silence on the complaint about Moses' marriage to an Ethiopian woman has been used, especially in the United States, to justify religious condemnation of interracial marriage. In fact, Moses married a Cushite woman who probably came from Arabia, but since most translations use the term Ethiopian then Ethiopian she was. I suspect that this distinction probably wouldn't mean much to anyone who is opposed to interracial marriage anyway. Arab? Ethiopian? What's the difference? She wasn't white, as any damn fool could see, and God don't cotton to coffee-colored compromises.

If male biblical interpreters wouldn't let God speak through women, then women would have to speak for themselves. The United States, which had won its freedom from British tyranny, was a fitting locale for a new spiritual revolution. The first metaphorical shots were fired in South Carolina when Angelina and Sarah Grimke made a theological leap forward in the late 1830s. The sisters were staunch abolitionists who were able to move from a focus on the evils of racial slavery to the evils of the traditional masculine domination of women that was supposedly based on biblical precepts. They called upon women to become scholars who could offer more fair-minded interpretations of the scriptures.

A remarkable twenty-three-year-old woman named Elizabeth Cady Stanton rose to the challenge. In addition to fulfilling her domestic duties and rearing seven children, she studied classical Greek and law and organized a national convention in 1848 that urged women to spurn all false religious customs and beliefs that perpetuated their subordination by men. Stanton allied herself with abolitionists and suffragettes; in 1878, three resolutions passed by the National Woman Suffrage Association declared that religion had been used to subjugate women, that female self-sacrifice and obedience were self-defeating, and that women should claim "the right of individual conscience and judgement heretofore exercised by man alone."

Stanton gathered together twenty learned women in the 1890s and they published the first real document of the revolution, *The Woman's Bible*. It offered new interpretations of biblical texts. The first account of creation in Genesis, for example, states that God created male and female in his own image. Stanton interpreted this to mean that both men and women have equal dominion over every living thing; "not one word is said giving man domain over woman." The second account of creation relates to the creation of Eve from Adam's rib. The traditional interpretation was that man should rule over woman because Adam gave birth to Eve. Stanton retorted with a rhetorical question. Since women nowadays give birth to men, shouldn't man's place be one of subjugation? She preferred the first creation story in which both sexes were "created alike in the image of God—the Heavenly Mother and Father." Stanton chided her conservative critics; "Wipe the dew off your spectacles and see that the world is moving."

The world did move, but not very fast. It was not until the social ferment of the 1960s that feminism finally matured and women began their earnest, on-going attempt to liberate the Bible. Among the leaders of this effort are scholars such as Elizabeth Fiorenza, Anne Carr, R. Sharon Ringe, Elizabeth Johnson, Sallie McFague, Rosemary Ruether, Letty Russell, and Phyllis Trible. The feminist biblical literature is now quite large and impressive in its thoughtfulness. Trible, for example, has examined the texts of terror, the horrible biblical stories of rape, murder and sacrificial death of women, "in order to recover a neglected history, to remember a past that the present embodies, and to pray that these terrors shall not come to pass again." For Ruether, feminist critiques continue the tradition of the prophets who expressed God's will by passing judgement on injustices and the perversion of religion, and they call both for changes in the social order and the creation of a new era when wrong will be righted and God's peace will prevail: "This biblical principle of prophetic faith parallels the critical dynamic of feminism, which likewise examines structures of injustice toward women, unmasks and denounces their cultural and religious sanctifications, and points towards an alternative humanity, an alternative society, capable of affirming the personhood of women."

Fiorenza claims that feminist biblical interpretation is a mandatory political task because the Bible has been used to halt the emancipation of women and slaves: "Not only in the last century but also today, the political Right laces its attack against the feminist struggle for women's rights and freedoms in the political, economic, reproductive, intellectual, and religious spheres with biblical quotations and appeals to scriptural authority." She has developed a five-part feminist model of critical evaluation. First, all biblical texts should have a warning label stating, "Caution! Could be dangerous to your health and survival," and should be approached with suspicion. The Bible's patriarchal, oppressive, and destructive texts must be exposed, as must its sexist, racist, and anti-Semitic language. Second, biblical texts should be examined for their feminist liberating content and function both historically and in the present. The true Christian message must be distinguished from changing forms of cultural expression. Third, patriarchal authority texts should be denounced and replaced by texts that affirm equality. The psychological and political function of biblical interpretation must also be assessed. The biblical commandment of love and the model of Christ's suffering, for example, might be misused to foster acceptance of sexual violence. Fourth, since the Bible makes women invisible by subsuming them under linguistic masculine terms and by mentioning them only when they are exceptional or cause problems, the reality of women's participation in biblical history must be reconstructed. The memory of the struggles and victories of biblical women must be kept alive. Fifth, through the use of historical imagination, artistic recreation, and liturgical celebration, women should use a feminist perspective to "not only rewrite biblical stories but also reformulate patriarchal prayers and create feminist rituals for celebrating our foremothers."

Any compassionate, clear-thinking person must applaud the general goals of feminism, although some tactics and specific agenda items stick in the craw of many. The simple fact is that all social movements worth their salt are disruptive. Destabilization of the status quo is painful, especially to those persons and organizations who have the most status. Feminism is taking its toll on good-ole-boys clubs; sexual harassment, for example, is no longer accepted in the U.S. Congress. It's a sign of the times that the vast majority of both men and women just will not tolerate sexual harassment anymore. The tricky part is that the harassed woman must be man enough to press her case. The allied problem of physical abuse is a tougher nut to crack because the battered woman is often psychologically broken, especially when the club-wielding abuser is her husband. It is astounding how many battered women feel obliged to tolerate abuse because they believe it would be sinful to disavow the words of Ephesians: "Women, submit to your husbands as to the Lord" (5:22). It wasn't until 1992 that the National Conference of Catholic Bishops officially condemned the use of the Bible to condone spousal abuse.

It is unfortunate that the greatest success of the feminist biblical movement is also the easiest to deride. I refer to translations of the Bible that replace masculine references with gender-neutral ones and that also undo terms deemed to be racist or disrespectful of handicapped persons. The goal may be noble, but the outcome often leaves much to be desired. The latest entry is the Oxford University Press "inclusive version" of the New Testament and Psalms. In it words such as master, Lord, king and kingdom are nowhere to be found. " The blind" is changed to "those who are blind." The word "darkness" becomes "deepest night." When Mary and Joseph find the boy Jesus in the temple, he now says, 'Why were you searching for me? Did you not know that I must be in the house of my Father-Mother?' But they did not understand what Jesus said to them." Anthony Lane, a critic for the *New Yorker*, adds, "I bet they didn't." Lane's negative but perceptive and witty review also cites a book called *The Post-Modern Bible*,

essays written by the Bible and Culture Collective. It declares the
need to be liberated from the patriarchal oppression of racism, classi-
cism, and sexism, and states that "The attention paid to Jesus' death
diverts attention from that oppression." This is pretty hard-core stuff
and deserving of Lane's retort: "You wonder why they bother to read
the Bible at all. Tyndale (the first translator of the Bible into English)
was killed for trying to spread the Word; these guys make a living out
of deconstructing it to death." It's hard enough taking on a heavily
defended Holy Book as it is, but since it is written in the incredible
prose of the King James version the task seems almost impossible.
Biblical scholar Mary Ann Tolbert accurately has pointed out the par-
adox of feminist biblical interpretation: "One must struggle against
God as enemy assisted by God as helper, or one must defeat the Bible
as patriarchal authority by using the Bible as liberator."

Abortion is undoubtedly the most divisive social issue of our time.
Feminists, most of whom are pro-choice, believe that the issue of
woman's autonomy overrides all other concerns. The most avid anti-
abortionists, both male and female, object on religious grounds. Most
medical groups, including the American Psychiatric Association, are in
favor of female autonomy. What the politicians and judges will decide
is anybody's guess. It's an issue that stirs murderous passions.
However, one comment, made by whom I do not know, has struck
with me throughout the prolonged, fiery debate: If men could get
pregnant, abortion would be a sacrament.

COMME ÇA:
HOMOSEXUALITY AND THE BIBLE

CHAPTER 4

A Baptist minister in Topeka, Kansas, serves his God by leading church members through the streets and across college campuses. Like Jesus carrying His cross, they carry signs that are larger than life. Their message is short and bitter: "Faggots Burn in Hell," "AIDS is God's Revenge," and "Homos Should be Killed." The group has been known to travel thousands of miles to parade at the funeral services of well-known homosexuals and to taunt the bereaved family and friends. When asked why their message is so mean-spirited, the minister holds his Bible high and shouts that he is doing God's work as revealed in the Holy Book. With strident surety he says that God destroyed the "faggot Sodomites," and he recites chapter and verse from Leviticus: "Thou shalt not lie with mankind, as with woman kind; it is an abomination" (18:22); "If a man also lie with mankind, as he lieth with a woman, both of them have committed an abomination: they shall surely be put to death; their blood shall be upon them" (20:13).

Dio cane! There's no pussyfooting around this one. It's there in black and white, and all translations say the same thing. What more is to be said? As it turns out, plenty.

The list of prohibitions and abominations in Leviticus is long enough to gag a horse. Consider just a few: farmers are not allowed to plant crops every seventh year; men are prohibited from trimming their beards; fortunetellers should be stoned to death; when intercourse occurs while a woman is menstruating both she and her partner shall be cut off from their people; adulterers should be killed; garments made of a mixture of linen and wool can't be worn; a man who emits semen is unclean and needs to take a bath; pork, rabbit and shellfish are abominations and should not be eaten, nor should anyone touch a dead mouse.

Who but the most orthodox Jews follows the Levitical laws? Christians certainly don't. Why select only the homosexual prohibitions and neglect all the others? Even the early Church Fathers did not pick and choose Levitical laws to buttress their arguments about proper Christian behavior. According to the historian John Boswell "Most Christians regarded the Old

Testament as an elaborate metaphor for Christian revelation; extremely few considered it morally binding in particular details." He points out that pork, shellfish, and rabbit were dietary staples in the Greco-Roman world, and that Jewish laws were irrelevant to Gentiles. "The Old Testament strictures against same-sex behavior would have seemed to most Roman citizens as arbitrary as the prohibition of cutting the hair, and they would have had no reason to assume that it should receive any more attention than the latter." R.I.P. Leviticus.

GETTING TO KNOW YOU: THE STORY OF SODOM

The "faggot-bashing" minister also mentioned God's destruction of the Sodomites. Let's examine what the Bible says about this in Genesis 19. Two angels dressed as men came to Sodom in the evening. Lot offered them a warm meal and his home to sleep in. A large group of townsmen surrounded Lot's home and asked where the two men were. "Bring them out to us that we may know them." Lot was frightened by the mob. He told them to leave his guests alone and offered his virginal daughters in their place. The townsmen tried to break down the door but failed. The next day, God rained fire and brimstone on the city, killing all its inhabitants, although Lot and his family escaped.

Why was God so hot under the collar? It depends upon the definition and usage of the verb "to know." In fact, "to know" is used 943 times in the Old Testament; in only 10 places does it refer to sexual intercourse. Popular translations of the Bible, such as the King James version, translate the townsmen's request, "that we may know them carnally." The New English Bible says, "so that we can have sexual intercourse with them." Some scholars, however, refute these translations and state that the townsmen really wanted "to know" who the two foreign men were, i.e., their names and their reasons for coming to Sodom.

Lot himself was not a full citizen of Sodom. He became an object of suspicion because he let two strangers stay in the city at night without informing the proper officials and asking for permission. God destroyed Sodom because the city was inhospitable to strangers who, in this case, were really God's angels in mufti.

Can this be true? Would God pummel people's heads with boulders and choke them with poisonous sulfur gas just because of a social gaffe? It depends upon the God, I guess. Certainly Yahweh could be nasty at times. For example, he promised to afflict disobedient Jews with severe boils, tumors, scabs, an untreatable itch, madness, blindness, and such horrendous devastation that they would cannibalize their own children (Deut. 28).

The offering of hospitality was an important obligation in the Greek, Roman, and Jewish traditions. All the gods looked favorably on those persons who opened their homes and offered shelter to strangers, travelers, and guests. Even Yahweh, when he destroyed Jericho, spared the one hospitable person in the city, Rahab the prostitute, who took in Joshua's messengers (Josh. 6:17). The book of the Wisdom of Solomon warns about the terrible sufferings that befall those who refuse to receive strangers and who give aliens a hostile reception (Wisdom 19). In this context, if God judged the Sodomites rude to the two disguised angels that he sent, then, by God, they deserved what they got.

But how can we be sure that the Sodomites really were convicted for their rudeness rather than for attempted homosexual rape? Maybe the answer can be found in the 33 other Biblical references to Sodom. In one, Sodomites are described as giving themselves over to fornication and going after "strange flesh" (Jude 7). No one knows what is meant by "strange flesh," but it may refer to a Jewish legend that angels copulated with Sodomite women. None of the other references mention sex at all but focus instead on arrogance, pride, gluttony, sloth, and stinginess to the poor and needy. Ezekial wrote, "Look, this was the iniquity of your sister Sodom: She and her daughter had pride, fullness of food, and abundance of idleness; neither did they strengthen the hand of the poor and needy" (11:49). The next sentence, as often occurs in the Old Testament, restates the idea: "And they were haughty and committed abomination before me." In fact, Jesus himself linked Sodom not with any sexual problem but rather with inhospitality when he commanded his disciples to preach to the lost sheep of the house of Israel: "And whoever will not receive you nor hear your words, when you depart from that house or city, shake off the dust from your feet. Assuredly, I say to you, it will be more tolerable for the land of Sodom and Gomorrah in the day of judgement than for that city" (Matt. 10:14–15).

A biblical story based on that of Lot and Sodom uses a parallel plot and wording (Judges 19). A Levite priest and his concubine arrived at night in the city of Gibeah and could not find lodging. An old man offered them a warm meal and his home to sleep in. The townsmen surrounded the house and said, "Bring out the man who came to your house that we may know him." The old man was frightened by the mob. He told them to leave his guest alone and offered them his virginal daughter and the concubine. The townsmen raped the concubine so ferociously that she died. The Levite chopped up her body and sent the pieces to the tribes of Israel. He escaped to the city of Mizpah where he told an assembly of the tribes what the men of Gibeah did:"They intended to kill me, but instead they ravished my concubine so that she died." The similarity with the story of Lot is obvious, but few interpreters think that it contains any element of homosexuality. Like Lot's guests, the Levite feared for his life, not for his orifices.

A BUM RAP?

The exact nature of Sodom's sin has been debated for over 2,000 years. Were they or weren't they *comme ça*? The very earliest interpretations of the story focused on the Sodomites' arrogance and rudeness to strangers. In the second century B.C., the theme of sexuality started to emerge. Sodomites were linked with the giant "sons of God" (Gen. 6:1–4) and the sinful angels (2 Peter 2:4) who "went a-whoring with the daughters of men" (Jubilees 7:20–22). Hints of homosexuality cropped up, along with child-corruption. Philo of Alexandria, a Greek-educated Jewish historian of the first century B.C., blasted the Sodomites so harshly that they have been perceived as homosexuals and/or pederasts ever since by many Jews and Christians. He said that Sodomite men mounted men so lustfully that "little by little they accustomed those who were by nature men to play the part of women . . . and were corrupting the whole of mankind."

Some of the Church Fathers over the ages fully accepted Philo's depiction. Thus, Clement of Alexandria wrote about the Sodomites' "insane love for boys," Augustine about their desire to rape the male angels, John Chrysostom of their "barren coitus." Others, however, held fast to the rude hospitality and overall licentiousness notions. John Cassion wrote about the Sodomites' gluttony, while Origen claimed that Lot was spared on account of one thing only: "He opened his house to guests." Jewish rabbis writing about Sodom in the Talmud and the Midrashim generally did not mention homosexuality.

Sodom's lot was not a happy one. The very word Sodomite refers to a man who copulates with a man or with an animal. Did the Sodomites engage in homosexual behavior? Legends and stories indicate that they probably were an idle, wealthy, lusty bunch who liked to party and to engage in debauchery, including same-sex sex. Was homosexuality the *spécialité de la maison*? Probably not. Was the destruction of the city a punishment for their incivility to strangers? Probably yes. Since God destroyed Sodom, should Christians vilify homosexuals? No way. Not even in Topeka.

SOFT BY NATURE: PAUL ON HOMOSEXUALITY

If Leviticus is irrelevant and Sodom confusing, then let's turn to the New Testament for enlightenment. Christ's teachings on sexuality are brief: husbands and wives should not fool around outside the marriage, and, in fact, just thinking about it is sinful (Matt. 5:28); celibacy is fine if that's your cup of tea (Matt. 19:11–12); and don't be so quick to condemn adulterers unless you are without sin yourself (John 8:3–11). About masturbation, sex premarital and between unmarried persons, pederasty, and homosexuality, Jesus said nothing, offered no opinion, provided no guideline. Surely there were masturbators, hot-to-trot teenagers, pedophiles, and homosexuals back then. Jesus' silence is puzzling. Did it imply consent? Did it signify that these were such minor problems that divine commentary was not needed? Were his words on these issues accidentally omitted from the Bible?

Absent Jesus, we are stuck with St. Paul, the mastermind behind the survival and cultivation of Christianity. When it came to sex, Paul was hardly hell-bent for leather. Although he wished that everyone was celibate like him, he recognized the power of the gonads and advised that it was better to marry than to burn with desire. Procreation was not a concern because he believed that time was short until the end of the world. Why bother with sex when more urgent matters were at hand?

What Paul had to say about homosexuality depends upon which translation of the Bible you purchase and upon the interpretation you ascribe to a particular phrase. Let's look at translation first.

In 1 Corinthians 5:11, Paul warns Christians not to keep company with a brother "if he is guilty of immorality or greed, or is an idolater, reviler, drunkard, or robber." In the next chapter, he presents another list. This time he names the unrighteous who will not inherit the kingdom of heaven: thieves, greedy persons, drunkards, revilers, robbers, adulterers, idolaters, *malakoi* and *arsenokoitai*. The King James Bible translates the first Greek word as "effeminate," the second as "abusers of themselves with mankind." The Revised Standard Version collapses the two words into "homosexuals." The French edition of the Jerusalem Bible prefers "the depraved" and "persons of infamous customs," while the German edition prefers "sissies" and "child molesters." Whoa! Clearly we've got a problem here.

Malakos means "soft" (e.g., Matthew 11:8 describes clothing as *malakos)*. Boswell lists additional meanings: sick, liquid, cowardly, refined, weak-willed, delicate, gentle, debauched, licentious, loose, wanting in self-control, unrestrained, wanton. In its most common use by theologians, the word refers to masturbation. Philo, the

Alexandrine homophobe, had a lot of negative things to say about homosexuals, but he never described them as *malakos*.

Arsenokoitai is a compound word that cannot be found in Greek literature until Paul. The first half of the word means males; the second refers to active, vulgar sexual activity. Unite the two concepts and several possibilities emerge: men who do it with men; women who do it with men; or men who have it done to them. The most likely meaning is male prostitutes. One scholar, Robin Scroggs, argues that the word, in conjunction with several other words in Paul's list, constitutes a trio: "male prostitutes, men who lie with them, and slave dealers who procure them." None of the early Christian theologians treated the word as "homosexual."

As Greek cultural influence waned, Latin became the language of scholarship and religion. Theologians from the sixth century onward mainly utilized the Latin Vulgate text, where "male concubines" was the translation. They took their own liberties with "male concubines" and changed its meaning to pederasty and to heterosexual as well as homosexual anal sex. Seven centuries later St. Thomas Aquinas cited Paul's two words as definite Biblical disapproval of homosexuality, an interpretation that the King James translators, as well as many others, have accepted up to the present.

Paul's other reference to homosexuality occurs in chapter one of his Epistle to the Romans. Paul's major points here are that the just shall live by faith and that the worship of idols in the image of corruptible humans, birds, animals, and creeping things has resulted in God's wrath as manifested by decaying moral standards and vile passions. Paul then lists examples: same-sex sex *para phusin* (against or in excess of nature), sexual immorality, wickedness, covetousness, envy, murder, strife, deceit, evil mindedness, back-biting, hating God, violence, pride, boasting, inventing evil things, disobedience to parents, and being undiscerning, untrustworthy, unloving, unforgiving, and unmerciful.

Paul clearly disapproves of homosexual acts, but what does the phrase *para phusin* mean? In 11:24, Paul says that God could *para phusin* graft a wild olive tree onto a cultivated olive tree. God surely could not act immorally but he could, in Boswell's words, act in a way that is "unexpected, unusual, or different from what would occur in the natural order of things." Even the conservative Interpreter's Bible notes that Paul's purpose in this section "is to point not at sins, but to judgement." It is likely that Paul is not condemning homosexuality itself but rather mainstream Gentile men and women who had overstepped their normal sexual practices. In fact, St. John Chrysostom's fourth-century homily on Romans stated that Paul's disapproval of homosexual practices pertained only to people who fall in lust and not to those who fall in love. Quickies were sinful, but romance was another matter.

THE BIRDS AND THE BEES, THE HYENAS AND THE WEASELS: ACCUSATIONS OF HOMOSEXUALITY

What we call the Holy Land was considered a provincial backwater by the Greeks and Romans. Aside from the Temple of Jerusalem there wasn't much to attract tourists. Athens had the groves of academe, scrumptious statues, and dramatic hits. Rome had chariot races, the Forum, and triumphal parades. How did homosexuals fare in the bright lights of the big cities?

Perhaps unbelievable but nonetheless true is the fact that "homosexuality" did not exist in the Greco-Roman world. Of course, a multitude of men (and some women) engaged in same-sex sex, but they were not labeled as homosexuals because the concept of homosexuality had not yet been conceived. The love of a man for another man was as natural as his love for a woman. A man's inability to acknowledge and to feel desire for a good-looking, well-endowed male often implied crass insensitivity, maybe even a psychological hangup. In fact, some thought that men who cavorted only with women were likely to become effeminate! Hulk Hercules, a man's man if there ever was one, had at least a dozen male lovers. In the *Symposium*, Plato argued that barbarians disapproved of same-sex relationships, philosophy, and athletes, "since it is apparently not in the best interests of such rulers to have great ideas engendered in their subjects, or powerful friendships or physical union, all of which love is particularly apt to produce . . . wherever it has been established that it is sinful to be involved in love-gratifying relationships, this is due to evil on the part of the legislators, to despotism on the part of the rulers, and to cowardice on the part of the governed."

While the Greeks waxed eloquently about homosexual passion, the Romans went straight for the gusto without wasting words. Male prostitutes were readily available during both the Republic and the Empire, and the best ones commanded enormous fees. Taxes on male and female prostitution provided a great deal of revenue for the state. Famous Roman politicians such as Catiline and Sulla had male lovers. Julius Caesar was known as "every man's wife and every woman's husband," in reference to his indiscriminate philandering. The Emperor Tiberius loved to have young men swim between his legs in the blue grotto of Capri. Nero castrated Sporus, his favorite slave boy, to keep him from developing into an adult, and then married him.

The Romans did not idealize same-sex sex, they just enjoyed it and celebrated it in dozens of dirty little ditties. The poet Catullus, for example, wrote: "Just now I found a young boy/stuffing his girl,/I rose, naturally, and/with a nod to Venus/fell and transfixed him there/with a good stiff prick, like his own." As the inserter, Catullus was acting in a manly manner. The only taboo among the Romans was to be the insertee. Boswell notes the "popular association of sexual passivity with political impotence. Those who most commonly played the passive role in intercourse were boys, women, and slaves —all persons excluded from the power structure. Sexual passivity evoked a particular horror among Romans who prided themselves on control of the world around them." Even Julius Caesar, the most formidable of all Roman military leaders, was mocked by his troops as "the queen of Bithynia" because he supposedly uprumped for Nicomedes, the Bithynian king.

With the steady ascendancy of Christianity during the first five centuries, there was a parallel decline in classical Greek and Roman ways of thinking and doing things. Sexuality of any kind was devalued except as necessary for procreation. Semen was revered, but the orgasm that accompanied its ejection was reviled. Masturbation, logically, became sinful. Sexual continence for everyone became a virtue, and a husband who loved his wife "too much" was often considered an adulterer.

Homosexual acts, purely aimed at pleasure and without any pretense at procreation, were deemed repulsive and bestial. Indeed, an entire popular literature developed known as "bestiaries" in which animal behavior, anatomy, and physiology were described and sometimes related to homosexual behavior. Why did the Levitical laws forbid the eating of hares, hyenas, and weasels? According to the beastiaries it was because a hare develops a new anal opening each year; eat one and you might become a child molester. Hyenas change their gender annually; eat one and you might become an adulterer or seducer. Weasels conceive through their mouths; eat one and you might succumb to oral sex.

Over the next 600 years the tide of both popular and church opinion progressively turned against homosexual behavior. Then came a sea change. According to Boswell, from 1150–1350 "homosexual behavior appears to have changed, in the eyes of the public, from the personal preference of a prosperous minority, satirized and celebrated in popular voice, to a dangerous, antisocial, and severely sinful aberration." When King Philip the Fair of France wanted to destroy the noble Order of the Knights Templar, he prominently inserted accusations of homosexuality in his list of particulars. When the Laws of King Henry the First were recodified, the penalty of being buried alive was given to those who had sex with Jews, animals, or persons of their own gender. When St. Thomas Aquinas declared that homosexuality, like cannibalism and bestiality, was contrary to the natural law, he helped to solidify an antipathy toward homosexuality that has persisted to the present.

ENTER THE DOCTORS

From the fourteenth century on, physicians, theologians, and most everyone else considered homosexuality a moral crime against nature. Then, in 1621, Robert Burton wrote his massive masterpiece, *The Anatomy of Melancholy*. He catalogued all the causes of depression and added a new wrinkle. Sinful sex was a major category, headed by homosexuality where men go with other men and with "wanton-loined womanlings." (Other examples of sinful sex included women who go with beasts, men who go with goats or who ravish statues, and anatomy dissectors "who couch with beautiful cadavers.") Burton took a step back and determined that sinful sex itself was caused by "the onslaught of love's tyranny" on a person who was weak-willed and morally depraved. Raging love was madness itself, an incurable disease. But what caused raging love? Although medical scholars had cited lesions in the heart, liver, and testicles, Burton reckoned it "an injury in the brain and a lesion of the fancy."

Homosexuality came under sustained medical scrutiny starting with the last half of the nineteenth century. Case reports appeared in medical journals with discussions about its etiology. Was it an inborn tendency or a learned behavior? Did it require both an innate predisposition and the right environmental circumstances? The first true scientific students of homosexuality—Karl Ulrichs, Magnus Hirschfeld, and Havelock Ellis—all championed the inborn, biological point of view. Enter Freud, whose ideas about psychological functioning and about sexuality, like it or not, have influenced Western culture for much of the twentieth century.

Freud believed that every infant is innately bisexual and that, normally, a blending of (unknown) biological processes and childhood experiences caused heterosexuality. He then described differing, abnormal developmental patterns that could result in homosexuality. Central to these patterns was a boy's overly strong attachment to his mother; a secondary theme was a boy's fear of his older brother or of his father. Psychoanalysts modified some of Freud's patterns and came up with some new ones. But, always, homosexuality was regarded as a mental illness. The first American *Diagnostic and Statistical*

Manual (DSM) of Mental Disorders, published in 1952, reflected this position by listing homosexuality as a sociopathic personality disturbance.

In 1962, Bieber's book *Homosexuality: A Psychoanalytic Study of Male Homosexuals* reaffirmed the pathological status of the disorder. It featured the family dynamics of a dominant, overly intimate mother, a distant and hostile father, and a homosexual son upon whom the parent's psychopathology was focused and who was destined to a life of unstable, destructive relationships. In 1968, the second *DSM* was published and homosexuality was listed securely among the sexual deviations.

Five years later the American Psychiatric Association's Committee on Nomenclature voted to delete homosexuality from the list of pathological conditions. The Association's Council on Research and Development agreed, as did the Board of Trustees. A protest group led by some prominent psychoanalysts demanded that all the members of the Association be given a chance to vote on the issue. Of the 10,091 psychiatrists who voted, 58 percent affirmed the Trustees' decision. Homosexuality no longer was an illness. Just like that!

STOP IT! YOU'RE MAKING ME SICK
THE REASONS FOR PSYCHIATRY'S TURNABOUT

The decision to remove homosexuals from the sick role is a landmark in medical and social history. After two thousand years of oppression, homosexuality finally gained a measure of respectability. The reasons for psychiatry's total turnabout are complex and represent the culmination of decades of scientific studies and social changes.

Margaret Mead's books of the 1930s, *Male and Female* and *Sex and Temperament in Three Primitive Societies,* were immensely popular. Mead challenged the prevalent notion that masculine and feminine behavior was biologically fixed at birth. In New Guinea she found three tribes located within a hundred-mile area. In one, both men and women acted as Western women were expected to act, in a mild parental responsive way; in the second tribe, both acted like Western men, in a fierce initiating fashion; in the third, men acted like stereotypical Western women in being catty, curling their hair, and doing the shopping, while women were energetic, managerial, unadorned partners. She concluded that "certain human traits have been socially specialized as the appropriate behavior of only one sex, while other human traits have been specialized for the opposite sex. This social specialization is then rationalized into a theory that the socially decreed behavior is natural for one sex and unnatural for the other, and that the deviant is a deviant because of glandular defect, or developmental accident." She noted that problems arise when peoples' temperaments conflict with the gender-based expectations of the society in which they live.There is nothing inherently wrong with a homosexual temperament; difficulties occur only when society declares homosexuality inappropriate, sinful, or sick. Mead was sixty years ahead of her time.

The event that truly forced everyone to reconsider beliefs about sexuality was the publication in 1948 of Alfred Kinsey's *Sexual Behavior in the Human Male*. Kinsey's method was simple, the results unimaginable. In-depth interviews of a large, representative group of American men revealed that 37 percent had had orgasmic sex with another man, and that 10 percent had been exclusively homosexual for three years or more. Kinsey interpreted his results to mean that homosexual behavior was not a sign of mental illness, and that every individual had the capacity "to respond erotically to any sort of stimulus." Not since Darwin's *Origin of Species*, published 100 years earlier, did a book create such passionate responses. Psychiatrists took notice, but were unmoved about the basic pathology of homosexuality. Homosexuals took notice, too, were heartened, and started to organize.

In 1951, Ford and Beach's *Patterns of Sexual Behavior* examined data about homosexuality in seventy-seven, mostly noncomplex, societies. In 60 percent, homosexual behavior, in some instances exclusive homosexuality, was socially accepted. The book also reviewed data on animals. Homosexual behavior was common, especially among primates, the animals from whom we humans have evolved. Thus, although human homosexuality may transgress social rules, it is not "unnatural."The authors concluded that both exclusive heterosexuality and homosexuality are "extremes" and that the capacity for both expressions of sexuality constitutes our mammalian heritage.

It's all well and good to cite large samples, natives, and monkeys, but we psychiatrists were still unconvinced. The homosexuals that we encountered in the emergency room or in our clinics all seemed emotionally disturbed. We needed to discover "mentally healthy" homosexuals. Sure, some homosexual artists and actors and hairdressers *seemed* healthy, but what lurked in the deep, dark recesses of their minds?

One method of probing these recesses is the use of projective psychological tests in which a person is asked to comment on an ambiguous picture or an ink blot. The person's commentary is thought to reflect his unique mental functioning. A psychologist named Evelyn Hooker administered projective tests to 30 homosexuals and 30 matched heterosexuals. Two psychologists interpreted the results of the tests but were not told which were completed by the homosexual subjects. Surprise! The results were indistinguishable. Each group contained some mentally disturbed persons, but two-thirds of each group were functioning at least at an average level. Hooker examined the lives of the homosexual subjects and discovered that most enjoyed long-term same-sex relationships and that the majority of their abnormal behaviors and traits could be explained better as a result of social victimization rather than psychological pathology. Her findings stimulated psychiatric debate and emboldened homosexual groups for political protest.

And protest they did. Taking their lead from the civil rights activists of the time, they accused psychiatrists of denying them their right to be considered normal. They disrupted psychiatric meetings with shouting and catcalls. These in-your-face tactics were like nothing that psychiatrists had encountered before. During a panel discussion at the American Psychiatric Association meeting in 1973, as sedate psychiatrists debated the homosexual question, an activist yelled, "Stop it! You're making me sick!"

Unused to these assaults, many psychiatrists finally decided to listen to the arguments of the homosexual groups and of the small, but growing, cadre of distinguished colleagues who found no inherent psychopathology in the homosexual condition. The debate was intense but eventually a majority agreed that homosexuality was not a mental disorder. A number of well-functioning psychiatrists took the risk of jeopardizing their careers by openly declaring their homosexuality. Twenty years later the American Psychiatric Association elected a new president who referred to his male "beloved companion" in his inaugural address. There were no protests or catcalls.

MEANWHILE, BACK AT THE CHURCH

While organized psychiatry has set the issue of homosexuality to rest, the Christian churches still struggle with sexual and gender issues. The ordination of female priests has deeply divided many Christian communities. About homosexuals, the prevailing sentiment is to "love" the sinner but to condemn his sins. This approach, an uneasy proposition at best, opens acceptance to those homosexuals who refrain from acts against nature. The Biblical citations discussed in this chapter are used to justify this policy, along with the articulated fear that homosexuality is sterile because procreation is not its goal. No babies, no replenishment of church membership, perhaps eventually no more human race.

Is it fair, wise, realistic, or even merciful to ask homosexuals to be celibate? Would heterosexual persons remain Christians very long if they were required to place their genitals in storage? How well do Catholic priests deal with their vow of celibacy? A clue to the answer, perhaps, can be found in the statement of a priest as recorded in Richard Sipes' *A Secret World: Sexuality and the Search for Celibacy*: "Celibacy is like the unicorn—a perfect and absolutely noble animal . . . I have read eloquent descriptions of it and have seen it glorified in art. I have wanted desperately to believe in its existence, but alas, I have never been able to find it on the hoof."

The continual decrease in candidates for the priesthood is often attributed to an unwillingness to endure celibacy, and scarcely a month passes without some priestly sexual scandal being reported in the news. The problem certainly is not a new one. In 1538, according to Burton, King Henry the Eighth "inspected the cloisters of cowls and companies of priests and notaries, and found among them so great a number of wenches, gelded youth, debauchers, catamites, boy-things, pederasts, Sodomites, and Ganymedes, that in every one of them you may be certain of a new Gomorrah."

What's the big deal about celibacy? Why is it so esteemed? Many cultures esteem celibate priests and priestesses, but Jesus never really dealt clearly with the issue and never asked his apostles to abstain from sex. St. Paul chose celibacy when he was middle-aged, and St. Peter's family included his daughter, Petromilla, who was said to be quite saintly. Sipe writes that "the list of Popes who fathered future Popes reads like an Old Testament lineage recitation: Anastasius I (399–401) begat Innocent I (401–417); Hornisdas (514–523) begat Silverius (536–537);Sergius III (904–911) begat John VI (931–935)."At least seven more Popes were sired by priests. John XII (955–964) died at a young age while having sex with a married woman.

For the first thousand years of Christianity priests had wives, concubines, or the use of prostitutes, male and female. During the Middle Ages the Church really didn't consider homosexual activity by clergymen as a threat; a guide issued by Pope Gregory III, for example, specified three years of penance for priests who hunted animals but only a year for masturbation and homosexual acts.

The eleventh century was a turning point in the Church's stance towards celibacy. St. Peter Damian's *The Book of Gomorrah* was a savage attack against homosexuality in general and priestly homosexuality in particular. Damian identified four Sodomitic acts: individual and mutual masturbation, pollution between the thighs, and anal intercourse. He also coined the word *sodomia*, an event that influenced Christian theology forevermore. As noted by historian Mark

Jordan, the term "sodomy" established an essence. No longer did persons only participate in sodomitic behavior but, also, they now were Sodomites. "They are no longer persons who perform a few similar acts from a myriad of motives and in incalculably different circumstances. They are Sodomites doing Sodomy. The abstractive power of the word abolishes motives and circumstances." Damian charged that homosexual clerics not only polluted their flesh but also escaped detection and punishment by receiving absolution from homosexual confessors. What convinced the Church to demand celibacy was the realization that the widows and children of deceased priests were taking inheritance money and property for themselves. The Church was losing a great deal of revenue, so it acted in its own best interest. The Synod of Pavia in 1022 prohibited priests from taking wives or concubines, and priests' children were declared serfs. The ban was not terribly effective; a series of similar decrees were issued over the next four hundred years.

In order to succeed, the Church adopted a strategy of attacking the objects of priestly lust. The rhetoric of the early Church against women was resurrected. Once again they became parasites, deceivers, outwardly beautiful but inwardly rotten, and the opening between their legs was seen as the entrance to hell. Homosexuals, too, were savaged, often by declaring them heretics. Celibacy officially triumphed, but at what a cost! Women and homosexuals, the former more than the latter, are only now recovering from the drubbing, while wayward priests and nuns are in the headlines. It is ironic that economic concerns were the prime mover in the establishment of clerical celibacy, and today the huge financial payoffs to victims of priestly pederasts and seducers are rousing the Church to modify its protective attitude toward priestly perpetrators. Will the Church even return to its roots and eliminate the vow the celibacy for priests and nuns? Not in our lifetime, surely, but in the lives of our grandchildren . . . maybe.

THE BY-ROADS OF LOVE
SEXUAL DIFFERENCES AND HOMOPHOBIA

Sages from the West, wise men from the East, prophets, philosophers, poets, priests, and Ph.D.s have struggled to answer the question, "What is the meaning of life?" The many reasons offered—to praise God, to help others, simply to exist or to exist simply, to enjoy oneself or to really enjoy oneself, to prepare oneself for the afterlife, to suffer, to love and to work well—indicate that no one reason suffices entirely. How many people truly devote time and energy seeking the answer? Relatively few, I suspect.

The more fundamental question for everyone is much simpler: "Who am I?" The list of nouns, adjectives, and phrases that answers this question is vast, but among the most basic primal responses are "I am a male" or "I am a female." Much flows from our gender, the core of which is established during fetal life and is pretty well unchangeable several years after birth. The organization of our brains is determined genetically to produce a gender which, at birth, is declared as either male or female. Our parents then rear us as boys or girls so that we grow into our genders and conform to our society's expectations of males and females. Everywhere in the world most males assume an exclusively heterosexual identity while a minority, perhaps two to five percent, assume an exclusively homosexual identity.

The expression of our sexual identity is determined predominantly by social attitudes. Homosexual men as well as heterosexual men share the same potentials for all behaviors from playing football to writing poetry, from promiscuity to monogamy. The problem with masculinity is its fragility. Both boys and girls begin life intimately attached to their mother. Girls develop femininity naturally by identifying with mother. In order for boys to develop masculinity they must give up their maternal attachment, a painful task. Boys prize their penis, but after discovering that girls don't have one, they worry, according to psychoanalysts, that they might lose theirs. Dreaded castration anxiety takes hold; men undeniably compare penis size in the shower stalls. A woman can be a woman just by lying down, but a man must have everything in perfect working order to arise to manhood. Women cannot doubt their femininity when a baby is born, but men can only hope that their seed did the deed (blood tests can now determine paternity, but more men that you can shake a stick at, deep down, don't want to risk it). In Robert Stoller's words, "Masculinity in males is not simply a natural state that needs only to be defended if it is to grow healthy; rather, it is an achievement."

Just as the proof of a pudding is in the eating, so too must masculinity serve itself repeatedly to maintain this achievement. Men constantly self-engage the Kochian query, "How am I doing?" In this regard, the labeling of homosexuals as deviants serves an important function. All deviants help us define normality. If I don't do what homosexuals do, then I must be doing the proper masculine thing. It helps to stereotype homosexuals as effeminate or pretty boys or child molesters because it establishes the limits of normality. It matters not a whit that most homosexuals are neither effeminate nor pretty, nor that the vast majority of pedophiles are heterosexuals.

Mocking, condemning, and looking down on homosexuals also serve the purpose of making us heterosexuals feel good. In some way or another every group feels better about itself when it can identify a "flawed" group with which to compare itself. What is perceived as a flaw, of course, depends upon the perceivers. We seem to feel consoled knowing that no matter how miserable our lives are, there are others who are in less control over their lives. Even among the classical Greeks and Romans, the active inserter retained his masculinity while the insertee, the person at the bottom of the barrel, lost his dignity by accepting passively what was thrust at him.

Kinsey discovered that a significant number of men, almost a third even if we eliminate exclusive homosexuals, engage in homosexual behavior at one time or another. The motives of this phenomenon vary greatly. Some men may want to be adventurous and give it a try. Others, such as prisoners or seminarians, may simply lack access to females. An interesting dynamic occurs when a man feels that his masculinity is slipping away. Perhaps he is fearful of losing his job and of not being able to provide for his family. Perhaps he has been rejected by a woman. Magical thinking may come into play: "an "injection" of sperm, the very essence of masculinity, might provide a tonic boost. Many a male prostitute has benefitted financially from the patronage of middle-aged and elderly men eager to reclaim their failing manhood.

How can the intense, driven, irrational hatred of homosexuals by the Baptist minister from Topeka be explained? Since I never had the displeasure of conducting a clinical assessment, I cannot be sure. A glib answer would be that his behavior is an attempt to counteract his own secret attraction to the forbidden. If this be true, then he would be following in the steps of many others before him. The televangelists Jimmy Swaggart and Jim Bakker made a terrific living by preaching forcefully against sexual immorality, but ended up in disgrace because they got caught dipping into the cookie jar.

The minister was ordained in 1948 after graduating from Bob Jones University (he recently protested at his alma mater because homosexuals were allowed to visit the university's art museum in order to preserve the museum's tax-exempt status) in South Carolina. His theological training thus took place during the pre-civil rights era at a university where racial separation was enforced and in an area of the nation where blacks were traditionally looked down upon. Perhaps he had an overwhelming need to feel superior. In this cultural setting blacks were an obvious target but, in order to differentiate himself from the crowd, he chose homosexuals as objects of castigation. The depth of his hatred, however, surely seems to be pathological. The way in which he twists Scripture is perverse: for example, he cites Amos 4:11, "Just as a fag fuels the fire of nature, so does a sodomite fuel the fire of God's wrath." I am unaware of any major edition of the Bible that comes close to that translation. In fact, the standard translation is, "I overthrow some of your [Israelites], as God overthrew Sodom and Gomorrah, and you were like a fire brand plucked from the burning." Certainly the minister's aura of infallibility along with intensity of his personality and his ability to attract attention make him an attractive figure to some persons. I am surprised that his congregation numbers only sixty, many of them his own family members.

A gay activist wrote, "Why not regard homosexuality as merely a difference in the direction of the sexual instinct? Why not view the heterosexual life as the sexual super-highway, the homosexual as one of the by-roads of love?" It's a touching thought, and one that kindles cerebral nerve cells. It probably would have caused St. Paul to have a fit of apocalyptic apoplexy, but I rather think that Jesus would have approved of it, probably with a parable, something provocative that was a real sound bite on the Philistine's hides. Christ was very Christian, don't you know. He often had the strangest ideas, and said the darndest things.

GOD IN A BOTTLE:
ALCOHOL AND THE BIBLE

CHAPTER 5

In *The Varieties of Religious Experience* (1902), a proper William James wrote:"The sway of alcohol over mankind is unquestionably due to its power to stimulate the mystical faculties of human nature, usually crushed to the earth by the cold facts and dry criticisms of the sober hour. Sobriety diminishes, discriminates and says no; drunkenness expands, unites, and says yes. It is in fact the great exciter of the Yes function in man. It brings its votary from the chill periphery of things to the radiant core. It makes them for the moment one with truth. Not through mere perversity do men run after it." As we shall see, the devotees of the god Dionysus in classical Greece found a bit of heaven in their wine cups. Poets and artists often have lubricated their imagination with alcohol; especially revered in Paris was absinthe, the Green Muse. And for two millennia Christians have reenacted the mystical transformation of wine into Christ's blood. Psalm 104 praises God for vegetation that mankind "may bring forth food from the earth, and wine that makes glad the heart of man."

Alcohol seems a wondrous gift, yet James concludes on a somber note: alcohol is excellent early on but in the deeper mystery and tragedy of life it is a degrading poison. Men and women broken by alcohol populate skid rows in every Western city, ammunition for the Salvation Army. Ephesians 5:18 warns, "Do not be drunk with wine, in which is dissipation; but be filled with the spirit." Fundamentalists and Baptists, having heard the warning, disavow alcoholic spirits and, in their greatest political triumph, constitutionally banned them from an entire nation.

Attitudes among Christian groups towards drinking alcohol are sharply divided. Catholics drink, but Baptists don't. Episcopalians certainly drink, but Seventh Day Adventists don't. Since Christianity is a Bible based religion, what guidance about alcohol does the Holy Book provide? As might be expected from reading the conflicting previous quotes from the Psalms and from Ephesians, the Bible both condones and condemns drinking.

STRANGE AND PERVERSE THINGS
NO TO ALCOHOL

The clearest negative comment on drinking is found in Proverbs

23:29-33. "Who has woe? Who has sorrow? Who has strife? Who has complaining? Who has redness of eyes? Do not look at wine when it is red, when it sparkles in the cup and goes down smoothly. At the last it bites like a serpent, and stings like an adder. Your eyes will see strange things, and your mind utter perverse things."

In the Old Testament, wine is often linked with the cup of God's fury (Is. 19:24). When judging the nations, the God of Israel will say, "Drink, be drunk, and vomit. Fall and rise no more, because of the sword which I send among you" (Jer. 25:27). In the degradation of Zion, people will cook their own children for food, get drunk, and make themselves naked (Lam. 4:21). God promises to feed the oppressors of Zion with their own flesh, "and they shall be drunk with their own blood as with sweet wine" (Is. 49:26).

The first mention of wine comes in Genesis 9. Noah was stuck in an ark with his wife, sons, daughters-in-law, and a menagerie of animals for several months while the earth was flooded. Paintings of the ark and all its passengers are usually quite charming, but Noah must have toiled night and day to keep everyone entertained and fed, not to mention the problem of sanitation. Just keeping up with two elephants boggles the mind. When the ordeal was over, Noah built an altar, sacrificed some animals to the Lord, planted a vineyard, and made wine. Considering all he had been through, his behavior seems understandable. What thoughts must have gone through his head as he impatiently waited for the grape juice to ferment! When the wine was finally ready he went into his tent, got drunk as a skunk, and fell asleep. Either he drank in the buff or else took his clothes off after drinking. At any rate, his youngest son, Ham, saw him naked and told his two brothers. They modestly entered the test backwards to avoid the sight, and covered their father with a garment. When Noah awoke "and knew what his younger son had done to him" he praised the sons that had covered up his nakedness while he cursed Ham's own son whose name was Canaan. What exactly did Ham do to deserve having his son cursed? The footnote in *The Believer's Study Bible* states that "Noah could probably see in Canaan the same ungodly attributes that had surfaced in Ham." It really makes you wonder about Ham. Did he accidentally stumble into Noah's tent? Was he a peeping Tom? Did he simply view his father's nakedness or, as some scholars suggest, did he do something kinky? It's a tough one to figure out. To make matters worse, over the centuries both Ham and his son came to be regarded as black. Since all Africans supposedly have descended from Canaan's loins, they became an accursed race. Such an ugly belief, held by many god-fearing Christians, was used to justify slavery and discrimination. All this because Noah boozed the jib.

Another sorry story is that of Lot, who escaped to the mountains with his two daughters. Sodom and Gomorrah had just been destroyed. Lot was frightened, so he took his daughters to live with him in a cave. The daughters were worried because "there is no man on the earth to come into us as is the custom of all the earth." To remedy the situation they made their father drunk with wine and then each raped him. Although he didn't remember a thing afterwards, he must have performed adequately because both daughters became pregnant and gave birth to sons (Gen. 19:30–38).

1 Kings relates that King Elah of Israel was drunk when his servant killed him (16:8), and that King Ben-Hadad and thirty-two other Syrian kings were defeated in battle by the Israelites because they were drunk at the command post (20:16). Nabal, an alcoholic, was struck dead by God (1 Sam. 25).

Among the prophets, Isaiah saw nothing but woe for those who drink all day and night, men mighty at drinking wine and valiant for mixing intoxicating drink (15:11,22). He described Egypt as akin to a drunken man who staggers in his vomit (19:14). Intoxicated priests and prophets err in vision and stumble in judgement amid tables full of vomit and filth (28:7–8). Israel's leaders are irresponsible because they devote themselves to intoxicating drinks (56:12). Daniel and his four friends refused the delicacies and wine offered to students by the king of Babylon. Instead, they ate veggies and drank water; at the end of ten days "their features appeared better and fatter in flesh than all the other young men" (1:8–15). Hosea warned that "harlotry, wine, and new wine enslave the heart" (4:11). Joel called for repentance: "Awake, you drunkards and weep; and wail, all you drinkers of wine" (1:5). He warned of God's judgement on those who "sold a girl for wine, that they may drink" (3:3). Nahum said of his enemies that "while drunken like drunkards, they shall be devoured like stubble fully dried." In Habakkuk, a violent end was predicted for those who got their neighbors drunk in order to take sexual advantage (2:15).

Nazarites and Rechabites were special people who dedicated themselves to piety through special vows. The former vowed neither to drink anything produced by a grapevine nor to cut their hair (Num. 16), while the latter vowed neither to drink wine nor to build houses (Jer. 35). In the New Testament, John the Baptist probably took the Nazarite vow. Even before his conception an angel announced to his parents that John "will be great in the sight of the Lord, and shall drink neither wine nor strong drink" (Luke 1:15).

Jesus warned his followers to be alert and ready for the Day of Judgement: "Take heed to yourselves, lest your heart be weighed down with carousing, drunkenness, and cares of this life" (Luke 21:34). He also warned against being drunk at the time of his second coming (Luke 12:45, Matt. 24:49), a theme echoed by Paul (1 Thess. 5:7).

Finally, several lists in the New Testament cite drunkenness among the vices of those who will not inherit the kingdom of God (1 Cor. 6:10), who do not walk with Christ (Rom. 13:13), and who live doing the will of the Gentiles instead of God (1 Pet. 4:3). Bishops shouldn't drink (1 Tim. 3:3), and Paul advises that "It is good neither to eat meat nor drink wine nor do anything by which your brother stumbles or is offended or is made weak" (Rom. 14:21).

TO GOD AND MEN, CHEERS!: WINE A BLESSING FROM GOD

Rape, incest, vomit, death. These are the legacy of alcohol. But wait! There's another side to the story. Wine is often counted as both a staple of life and a blessing from God. In Deuteronomy, the Israelites are promised a productive land "that you may gather in your grain, your new wine, and your oil" (11:14) and are told that God "will bless the fruit of your womb and the fruit of your land, your grain and your new wine and your oil" (7:13). Isaac says of his son, Jacob, "May God give you of the dew of heaven, of the fatness of the earth, and plenty of grain and wine" (Gen. 27:29). Both Amos (9:13) and Joel (3:18) yearn for the restoration of Israel when "the mountains shall drip with wine." In Amos God says, "I will bring back the captives of my people Israel . . . they shall plant vineyards and drink wine from them" (9:14). Joel says that God will refresh the land of the children of Zion "and the vats shall overflow with new wine and oil" (2:24). Zechariah notes that when Judea and Israel are restored "their hearts shall rejoice as if with wine" (10:7).

The Song of Solomon extols the sensuousness of wine when The Beloved says, "Let now your breasts be like clusters of the vine . . . And the roof of your mouth like the best wine;" to which the beautiful Shulamite responds, "The wine goes down smoothly for my beloved . . . I would cause you to drink of spiced wine, of the juice of my pomegranate" (7:9; 8:2).

Judges 9:13 refers to wine "which cheers both God and men." Isaiah says that on a mountain God will make for all people a feast of choice food and wine (25:6). Proverbs 31:6–7 advises that while kings and princes shouldn't drink because they might forget the law and pervert justice, "Give strong drink to him who is perishing, and wine to those who are bitter of heart. Let him drink and forget his poverty, and remember his misery no more." The medicinal use of wine is also encouraged in 1 Timothy 5:23 "for the sake of your stomach and your frequent ailments."

TRANSFORMATION: ALCOHOL CHANGES BEHAVIOR

Although beer and fruit wines were produced in the lands near Israel, the Bible only mentions wine from grapes. "New wine" originally meant unfermented grape juice, but, except for a few clear instances (Micah 6:15, Is. 65:8), it refers to regular wine, especially that used in rituals. The alcoholic content of the wine probably was between nine and fourteen percent. It was usually drunk neat or mixed with spices. Christ on the cross was offered wine with myrrh to deaden his pain; he refused it.

Wine was an everyday drink in biblical times. Then, as now, the water supply was neither abundant in the area nor was it always pure enough for drinking. In addition to its ordinary nature, wine was both loved and feared for its ability to tap into the extremes of the human condition. It may bring woe or gladden the heart. It may sting like an adder or it may be good for what ails you. It may be used for devious ends or it may be a blessing from God. The Bible refers to wine as the "blood of the grape" (Gen. 49:11; Deut. 32:14; Rev. 14:20) and in its most glorious transformation it became the very blood of Christ.

At the Last Supper, Christ instituted the Eucharistic sacrifice. Its great moment occurred when he offered to his disciples bread and wine that he declared to be his body and blood. For the Christian believer this is not a symbolic statement but rather a truthful fact. By eating the bread-flesh and drinking the wine-blood, the disciples ingested their god. He became part of them and his immortality became theirs, an immortality available to all believers who partake of this sacrament.

The fullest explication of the sacrament is found in the Catholic Church. Vatican Council II declared that the Eucharist is "the source and summit of the Christian life . . . in which Christ is consumed, the mind is filled with grace, and a pledge of future glory is given to us." The sixteenth-century Council of Trent reaffirmed the Church's position "that by the consecration of the bread and wine there takes place a change of the whole substance of the bread into the substance of the body of Christ our Lord and of the whole substance of the wine into the substance of his blood . . . the same Christ who offered himself once in a bloody manner on the altar of the cross is contained and offered in an unbloody manner." Through communion, individuals devour what the Church calls "the medicine of immortality" to form a single body with Christ. The bread, the wine, and the communicant all undergo a process of transformation.

Bread is not commonly thought to be an agent of transformation, except when it is made with grain infected by the Claviceps fungus.

When eaten, the fungus may produce hallucinations; some scholars believe that participants in the Eleusinian Mysteries of classical Greece deliberately used it for this purpose. Epidemics involving the ingestion of infected rye bread have been common since the Middle Ages. This condition, known as ergotism, causes burning sensations in the hands and feet, convulsions, abortions, and gangrene, in addition to hallucinations and delirium. It is possible that ergotism played a significant role in the famed witchcraft experiences of New Englanders at the close of the seventeenth century.

Wine, of course, has the ability to transform the drinker. Many Greeks worshipped Dionysus, who supposedly invented wine on Mount Nysa in Libya and then carried vines with him throughout the known world. His religion was characterized by the release of almost bestial emotions at sacred rites that are better known by their Roman name, the bacchanalia. Women especially were attracted to these chaste orgies, where they were free to forget their domesticity, to dance ecstatically in the darkness of the mountains, and to transcend human cares and fears. With superhuman agility and strength they ripped apart wild animals and devoured them sacramentally, for they believed that each bloody morsel contained a bit of Dionysus himself. Edward Hyams writes that their joy was "not human at all [but rather was] the joy one observes in a cat or a fox at the kind of wild play which ends not in an embrace but in a killing . . . The Dionysian wine was dark and sweet and aromatic and thick; was powerful, pernicious, terrifying." The vine cult spread rapidly to areas as far apart as India and Britain. It also took hold in Palestine and Asia Minor where, according to classical scholar Robert Graves, the Dionysian orgy evolved into the Canaanite Feast of Tabernacles.

Were the intricate behaviors of the Greek women directly caused by the alcohol in their wine? The answer obviously is no. Were it yes, then we would expect most women to act as they did after a few drinks. True, alcohol does have typical physiological effects in many societies. An average person who takes two standard drinks (a standard drink is five ounces of dry wine or twelve ounces of beer) on an empty stomach in a two-hour time period usually experiences feelings of warmth and relaxation, slight dizziness, and a mild mood elevation. After four drinks, we would see an increased heart rate, slowed reaction time, slurred speech, and impairments in coordination, peripheral vision, and judgement. After eight drinks, judgement and coordination would be grossly impaired, and fatigue, sleepiness, depression, and emotional lability would be evident. After twelve drinks, we would encounter confusion, delirium, violent outbursts, and loss of control over behavior. Sixteen drinks in two hours often results in coma, shock, and even death. Chronic heavy alcohol drinking results in "alcoholism," an addiction.

However, the behavioral manifestations of alcohol ingestion depend very much on the setting of the drinking and the expectations both of the drinker and of the social group. In an important article on alcohol and culture, David Mandlebaum points out contrasting styles of drinking. The Kofyar tribe of Nigeria, for example, are preoccupied with beer drinking, yet very little aggressive behavior or pathological addiction is ever manifested. In many Central and South American societies men "drink steadily into a state of stupefaction . . . Though drinking is frequent and heavy, no problem of addiction arises. This pattern has been remarkably consistent through time and place. It was maintained by the peoples of the ancient indigenous civilizations, the Maya, Aztec, and Inca. It is followed in contemporary societies, both Indian and mestizo, from Mexico to Chile, in highlands and lowlands."

Many studies of North American Indian drinking demonstrate that drunken behavior can be turned off and on depending upon social cues. In describing one group, Lemert refers to "quick transitions from drunken to sober behavior and back again, depending upon the situation, particularly when a necessary task must be carried out, such as starting a motor or navigating a boat through dangerous waters." Drunkenness may provide what Westermeyer describes as "a social license to behave in ways that are unacceptable in the sober state." Hurt and Brown write that Native American "drunkenness is accepted as an excuse for aggressive and antisocial behavior by the men and for sexual license by the women," while Levy and Kunitz note that "Navajo men do not beat up their wives because they are drunk but they get drunk so that they may beat up their wives."

A major report of the British Royal College of Psychiatrists points out the variable effects of alcohol on feelings, thoughts, and personality. Alcohol may result in relaxation or in anxiety, in vivacity or depression, in communal harmony or irritable aggression, in shyness or sexual adventurousness. Alcohol induces a physiological change, but the specifics of the change are determined by culture. It is even possible to induce drunken behavior by administering a placebo in the right setting to a person who believes that he or she has drunk alcohol.

One group that has allowed drinking for thousands of years with minimal disruptive consequences is the Jews. According to Keller the basis of Jewish sobriety was set during the two-hundred-year period following the return of the Jews in 537 B.C. to Israel from their captivity in Babylon. Prior to this, the Bible contained many references to drunkenness, but none afterwards, even though the Jews continued to make wine, to drink it ritually and for pleasure, and to pour sacrificial libations.

The banishment of pagan gods whose rituals demanded heavy drinking was a factor. More important, however, was "the positive integration of drinking in religiously oriented ceremonials in the home and synagogue, including meals and rites of passage." It is during the period after the Babylonian captivity that local synagogues were established along with fixed religious practices including the use of wine. It became a rule, for example, that the Friday evening *kiddush* should be recited over a blessed cup of wine. Although only whole wine was used for libations, wine for drinking had to be diluted with water. Drunkenness disappeared as a social problem once wine came to be regarded as a substance that should be drunk with moderation and only in conjunction with food and holy rituals. Even the fear of drunkenness vanished, as evidenced by the scientifically unsound, medieval rabbinical ruling that since European wine wasn't as strong as the wine produced in biblical times it could be drunk undiluted.

Studies of Jewish-Americans consistently have yielded a low rate of alcoholism. Jewish culture has perpetuated an unambivalent attitude towards alcohol: it is to be drunk in a controlled manner. Further, a child learns to drink both at home and at the synagogue. Drunkenness and alcoholism are alien to Jewish identity, and are seen as characteristics of non-Jews; the Yiddish expression *shikker vie a goy* means "drunk as a Gentile." With the increasing loss of orthodoxy, however, Jewish alcoholism rates are slowly rising.

Unlike Judaism, where alcohol and religion mix well, some Christian groups—especially in the United States—are so troubled by alcohol that they forbid its use, even in a sacramental form. Although justifications for this practice can be found in the biblical passages cited earlier, its real roots rest in the unique experiences of American history where alcohol and religion have been uneasy bedfellows.

SUICIDE, DEATH, GALLOWS AND SIN

Benjamin Rush, the father of American psychiatry and a signer of the Declaration of Independence, published in 1785 a marvelous scale of temperance and intemperance labeled "A Moral and Physical Thermometer." In descending order, water was atop the scale, followed by milk and small beer. These drinks were equated with health, wealth, serenity of mind, reputation, long life, and happiness. Then came cider, wine, ale, and strong beer, which were paired with cheerfulness, strength, and nourishment when taken only at meals and in moderate quantities. Below zero on the scale we encounter punch, toddy, grog, flip, bitters infused in spirits, whiskey, brandy, and rum. The vices associated with these intemperate drinks start with idleness and proceed to fighting, obscenity, perjury, murder, and suicide. Associated diseases start with puking and morning tremors and proceed to red nose and face, jaundice, epilepsy, madness, and death. The course of punishments begins with debt and black eyes and goes on to the poor house, jail, whipping, and the gallows.

The good Dr. Rush was convinced that distilled spirits were the ruination of the new nation. Wine and beer in moderation were fine, but whiskey and rum were destroyers of health. In the 1780s the Methodists and the Quakers were like-minded in forbidding the drinking of hard liquor, the former because it interfered with religious practices and the latter because it interfered with self-control. Even the federal government got in on the act under the leadership of the Treasury Secretary, Alexander Hamilton. A high federal excise tax on hard liquor was imposed in order to reduce the consumption of these drinks and to bring in badly needed revenue. In fact, the tax accomplished neither goal. Americans were a free people who liked their liquor. They resented any governmental intrusion on their basic liberty to drink and get drunk. According to the historian W.J. Rorabaugh, in the early 1800s "Americans believed that whiskey was healthful because it was made of a nutritive grain, that it was patriotic to drink it because corn was native, and that its wholesome, American qualities ought to make it the national drink . . . The freedom that intoxication symbolized led Americans to feel that imbibing lustily was a fitting way for independent men to celebrate their country's independence." Group drinking gave way to individual binges and consequent delirium tremens, which was first reported in the 1820s.

The corrective response to widespread drinking came from the churches. Ministers in the Presbyterian church received directives from their General Assembly in 1812 "to deliver public discourses on the sin and mischief of intemperate drinking." In 1826 Rev. Lyman Beecher, a Presbyterian minister in Connecticut, delivered six sermons on intemperance that soon became a basic text for the American Temperance Society, which was founded in the same year. Beecher declared that "ardent spirits" (whiskey and other forms of hard liquor) corrupted morals, resulted in crime and neglect of education, and undermined the foundations of the nation. He stated that neither drunkards nor murderers shall inherit the kingdom of God, and he considered the sale of ardent spirits (but not wine and beer) as "a tremendous evil." Another minister, Rev. Justin Edwards, became

Secretary of the Temperance Society in 1829 and led a national pro-gram "for the purpose of removing that mighty obstruction which the using of intoxicating liquors as a beverage occasion to the efficacy of the Gospel and the means of Grace."

Local temperance societies mushroomed from 222 in 1827 to 8500 in 1834, and national leadership switched from Easterners, who accepted the moderate use of wine and beer, to conservative Westerners, who championed total abstinence from all alcoholic bev-erages. This shift can be seen in the Temperance Manual of 1836, which stated, "The Holy Spirit will not visit, much less will He dwell in him who is under the polluting, debasing effects of intoxicating drink. The heart and mind which this occasions is to Him loathsome and an utter abomination."

Even Catholics formed their own temperance societies. The official stance of Catholicism reflected the view of St. Thomas Aquinas, who wrote, "It is not unlawful to drink wine as such. Yet it may become unlawful accidentally." This opinion was based on Jesus' words, "Not what goes into the mouth defiles a man; but what comes out of the mouth, this defiles a man" (Matt. 15:11). Aquinas added, however, that abstinence was sometimes requisite if a person takes a vow not to drink, if a person gets drunk easily, or if drinking scandalizes others. Catholics worldwide rarely abstained, but in 1849 a priest name Father Matthew came to the United States from Ireland, where he had con-vinced half of that nation's alcohol-ravaged population to take the pledge of abstinence. He was extraordinarily well received by President Tyler and by the U.S. Senate. His Hibernian crusade netted several hundred thousand pledges as well as the enmity of Catholic bishops who disapproved of his fellowship with Protestant clergy.

The Eastern Protestant churches that helped establish the temper-ance movement were left behind by the growing popularity of evan-gelical frontier churches with their passionate revivals, camp meet-ings, and calls to be reborn in the Spirit. According to Rorabaugh, "When a man claimed grace, the minister looked for a visible proof of conversion, an indicator of true faith and allegiance, a token of renun-ciation of sin and acceptance of the Lord. One visible outward sign of inner light was abstinence from alcoholic beverages." Temperance was not enough to claim salvation; only total abstinence would do. Opposition came from Primitive Baptists who considered the absti-nence pledge blasphemy. They believed that "abstinence was sinful because God gave the spirit in the fruit of grain, and the ability to extract and decoct it, and then he gave them the inclination to drink." Indeed, most scholars credit a Baptist minister for discovering the process to produce bourbon.

While the older temperance leaders hoped to change the nation's drinking habits through moral persuasion, the new abstainers decided to push for a legal total prohibition of commerce in alcoholic beverages. State legislatures north of the Mason-Dixon line responded favorably but Southern legislatures, accurately perceiving the anti-slavery sentiments of many prohibitionists, did not. Thirteen states became legally dry. The laws led to civil contempt and within a decade were repealed.

The upheavals of the Civil War resulted in the temporary demise of concerns about alcohol. Then, in 1874, the Women's Christian Temperance Union was founded. Five years later, under the leadership of the indefatigable Frances Willard, this remarkable organization reached out not only to the nation but to the world. Willard and her cohorts at the World WCTU were at the forefront of social reforms such as the worldwide prohibition of alcohol, prostitution, child marriages, foot binding in China, the Japanese geisha system, and the sale of opium. The group championed voting rights for women, prison reform, child labor laws, unions and the right to strike, better treatment of natives in the Belgian Congo, a league of nations, a world court, vegetarianism, and world peace. These were interesting times for Christian idealism and for temperance. Many locales passed anti-drinking laws and new towns were established to advance temperance values, the best known being Palo Alto, California, the site of Stanford University.

The temperance forces could not muster much political support. Their Prohibition party was a dud and could not dent the powerful and well-connected alcohol industry of manufacturers, brewers, and saloon keepers. Saloons were where working men gathered to talk. They were poor men's clubs where regular customers made friendships, and for most it was the only show in town. Moreover, they were always open. A hard-working man couldn't be expected to sit in a crowded, tiny tenement apartment and stare at his wife and children all evening.

The dream of prohibition seemed doomed except for one man, a minister from Ohio named Howard Russell, who believed that God wanted him to "drive the satanic liquor traffic down to its native hell." He proposed an Anti-Saloon League in 1893. Two years later, under the leadership of clergymen, the League held a national convention and devised a strategy of establishing a branch in every church in the nation with a unified hierarchy of local, state, and national leaders. Its initial focus was the closing of all saloons and the shutting down of commercial alcohol production. Its method was political, not as a separate party but rather as a force that influenced established parties.

That the Catholics, Jews, Lutherans, and Episcopalians were not sup-
portive mattered little because there were more than enough devoted Christians to carry on the fight. The Salvation Army even proposed
transforming saloons into soda and juice bars.

The League was very pragmatic and very successful. It delivered
votes to any politician, drunkards and teetotalers alike, who supported its program. In 1913, despite the veto of President Taft, the League
was responsible for the passage of a national bill prohibiting the ship-
ment of liquor into dry states. Emboldened by the victory, the League
declared its real agenda, no alcohol for anyone anywhere. In the midst
of World War I both the Senate and the House of Representatives,
buoyed by patriotic feelings against beer-brewing German-
Americans, passed a prohibition amendment to the U.S. Constitution
in 1917.

The one person most responsible for the passage of the amendment was a Methodist bishop named James Cannon, whose influence
went beyond his home state of Virginia to include all the Southern
and border states. After securing prohibition he flexed his muscles in
1928 to defeat the Democratic presidential candidate Alfred Smith, an
anti-prohibitionist and a Catholic. Smith could not win without the
South, and the South was controlled by Cannon. With Herbert
Hoover's victory, Cannon's star rose so high that H.L. Mencken said he
was "the most powerful ecclesiastic ever heard of in America."

Once the religious right got the prohibition bandwagon in high
gear, many others, including the American Medical Association, busi-
nessmen, labor leaders, and liberal preachers of the Social Gospel
movement, climbed aboard. They demonized alcohol and focused on
it so intently that it became the cause of the nation's ills. They
believed that prohibition would result in economic prosperity, personal happiness, good health, and social stability. However, Bishop
Cannon's intense hatred of Catholicism and his drive to impose prohibition on the entire nation belied the sleazy underbelly of a
supreme moralist. In 1929 the charges against him came out fast and
furious. War profiteering. Illegal stock deals. Adultery. Corrupt political practices. His enemies reveled in this exposure of hypocrisy. With
Cannon's disgrace, the anti-alcohol crusade lost its greatest leader, and
the exposure of Cannon's weaknesses awakened the nation to the
weakness of prohibition itself. Clearly alcohol had been responsible
for many problems, but the prohibitionists had oversold it as an agent
of evil. In fact, prohibition resulted in widespread lawlessness and the
creation of a vast criminal underclass. Instead of prosperity, the nation
was hit by the great economic depression. Tired of austerity and nay-
sayers, Americans repealed prohibition in 1933.

THE LAST HOUSE ON THE STREET: ALCOHOLICS ANONYMOUS

The joy that greeted prohibition's end was quickly tempered by rising alcoholism rates. However, no one much cared. Churches, humiliated by the failure of "the great experiment," closed their doors to alcoholics; only the skid-row rescue missions, generally detested by alcoholics because of their singled-minded focus on salvation, and the surprisingly progressive Salvation Army, where drunkards merely had to sing for their supper, reached out. Physicians didn't know how to help. Psychoanalysis, the consuming passion of psychiatry, didn't focus much on alcoholism. Freud regarded alcohol as a substitute for sexual gratification, and Karl Abraham described alcoholics as suffering from an oral-dependent personality. In 1933 Sandor Rado dismissed alcohol's pharmacological effect as the major factor in alcoholism. For him, alcohol's pleasure was generated by its symbolic meaning; the alcoholic's mind was fixated at an early, oral stage of development and the bottle of booze really represented mother's breast. Alas, the repressed alcoholics who needed their nips and who fitted this formulation were not those likely to benefit from psychoanalysis.

Since the formal religious, medical, and psychiatric systems offered little hope, alcoholics were forced to turn inward for help. It was not a new idea. In 1840 a small group of alcoholics in Baltimore started the Washingtonian Movement, in which recovered alcoholics led group meetings to foster sobriety and rehabilitation. Despite initial success that bordered on the spectacular, the movement fizzled out in a few years. It's failure was due to criticism by religious temperance leaders who decried the Washingtonians' lack of interest in establishing ties with them. The temperance movement swallowed up the Washingtonians.

The new movement inward started in Zurich in 1931, where a wealthy American financier named Rowland H. was treated for alcoholism by the famous Swiss psychiatrist Carl Jung. Jung was a psychoanalyst much interested in spirituality and religion. After a year of failed treatment, Jung told his patient that since nothing else had helped perhaps he should place his hope in a spiritual experience. Rowland H. dutifully sought and found religion in the Oxford Group. Founded by a Lutheran minister, the Oxford Group was a nondenominational organization devoted to re-experiencing the dynamism of the early days of Christianity through inspirational talks, group discussion, and mutual support. Rowland's conversion and the process through which he achieved it was what one historian has called a "founding moment" of Alcoholics Anonymous.

Rowland then introduced his alcoholic friend Ebby to the Oxford Group. He too experienced a conversion (although he later reverted to drinking) and in 1934 tried to convince an alcoholic stock broker named Bill Wilson in New York that religion was the answer. Wilson responded by going on a bender. He then sought help from a psychiatrist, William Silkworth, who hospitalized him. Wilson went into a severe depression. He gagged on the notion of a greater power, but cried out in despair for God to show himself. "Suddenly the room lit up with a great white light. I was caught up into an ecstasy which there are no words to describe." He pictured himself on a mountain in a spiritual windstorm. "And then it burst upon me that I am a free man." As the ecstasy subsided he experienced "a new world or consciousness. All about me and through me there was a wonderful feeling of Presence and I thought to myself, 'So this is the God of the preachers.' A great peace came over me and I thought, 'No matter how wrong things seem to be, they are all right.'" Since he was neither a religious or spiritual person he feared that this ecstasy was the product of a brain damaged by alcohol, but the psychiatrist said no.

Wilson's life changed for good when he discovered William James' book, *The Varieties of Religious Experience*. In it he learned about the ecstasy that accompanies religious conversion and about the hopelessness that often precedes the change. James' book presented many case histories, including that of a homeless, friendless, dying drunkard who became an active and useful rescuer of alcoholics after his conversion. James also described the peculiar features of the "state of assurance" that comes with conversion: a sense that all is ultimately well, a sense of perceiving truths not known before, and a sense of clear and beautiful newness within and without. Wilson talked about the hopelessness of his condition and his subsequent conversion with his friend Ebby. From these talks he imagined "a chain reaction among alcoholics, one carrying the message and these principles to the next."

In 1935 Wilson was disconsolate while in an Akron, Ohio hotel. A business deal had failed and Mother's Day was coming up. He needed a drink. The hotel bar was just a few steps away. What to do? Maybe he would feel better if he could talk with a fellow alcoholic the way he had talked with Ebby. He called several ministers and finally was referred to a woman member of a local Oxford Group. She invited him to her home and introduced him to Dr. Bob Smith, a chronic alcoholic whose career as a surgeon was in ruins. Wilson talked and talked some more about his life and his drinking. In this one-sided conversation he discovered a truth: telling one's story can be therapeutic. He concluded by saying, "I needed you, Bob, probably a lot more than you'll need me. So, thanks a lot for hearing me out. I know now that I'm not going to take the drink, and I'm grateful to you." The sorry surgeon, who at times didn't even appear to be listening, responded by telling his story to Wilson. A relationship formed and a month later Wilson noted, "1935, June 10. Dr. Bob had his last drink. Alcoholics Anonymous founded."

AA is not exactly a religion, although it comes close and some critics have described it as a religion in denial. It isn't a Christian organization either, although its roots are. Its famous twelve steps, unconsciously recalling the twelve disciples, are powerful statements. Most people are surprised to learn that abstinence is not one of the steps.

1.   We admitted we were powerless over alcohol—that our lives had become unmanageable.
2.   Came to believe that a Power greater than ourselves could restore us to sanity.
3.   Made a decision to turn our will and our lives over to the care of God as we *understood Him*.
4.   Made a searching and fearless moral inventory of ourselves.
5.   Admitted to God, to ourselves, and to another human being the exact nature of our wrongs.
6.   Were entirely ready to have God remove these as defects of character.
7.   Humbly asked Him to remove our shortcomings.
8.   Made a list of all persons we had harmed, and became willing to make amends to them all.
9.   Made direct amends to such people wherever possible, except when to do so would injure them or others.
10.   Continued to take personal inventory and when we were wrong promptly admitted it.
11.   Sought through prayer and meditation to improve our conscious contact with God as we *understood Him*, praying only for knowledge of His will for us and the power to carry that out.
12.   Having had a spiritual awakening as the result of these steps, we tried to carry this message to alcoholics, and to practice these principles in all our affairs.

AA also has twelve traditions that are truly brilliant. They essentially maintain AA's neutrality on nonalcohol issues, its refusal to accept outside contributions or to endorse, finance or lend the AA name to any facility or enterprise, and a commitment to "remain forever nonprofessional." AA's independence has served it well, although it has hampered impartial research into its effectiveness. In most of the

Western world alcoholics can attend meetings free of charge where they can tell their stories and listen to the stories of others. This acceptance, provided only that the alcoholics have a desire to stop drinking, is present even when everyone else rejects them and has led to the description of AA as "the last house on the street."

Unconditional acceptance is a major factor in AA's effectiveness as identified by Edgar Nace in his highly regarded text on alcoholism. Another factor is the consistent debunking of denial that alcohol is a problem. At AA meetings, for example, each speaker starts with "My name is ——, I'm an alcoholic." The defenses of grandiosity and self-suffering are also addressed: alcoholics must admit that they are powerless over alcohol and that a power greater than themselves could restore their sanity and remove their shortcoming when "humbly" asked to do so. Nace also identifies positive aspects of group therapy present in AA fellowship: abstinent alcoholics provide hope by serving as role models; new social skills are learned; information is provided; there is opportunity for catharsis followed by a sense of group solidarity and cohesiveness.

The most detailed studies of AA dynamics are Ernest Kurtz's paper "Why AA Works" and book *Not God: A History of Alcoholics Anonymous*. The curious book title refers to the fundamental first message of AA: "The alcoholic's acceptance of self as human is founded in his rejection of any claim to be more than human." AA members must accept the limitation of their being; an alcoholic cannot drink alcohol safely. Formal religions take personal limitations as a problem that can be overcome by participation and belief in the mechanisms of salvation offered by a particular church. Religion aspires to perfection and contains what it considers to be absolute truths. However, organized religion promised too much for the founders of AA. When asked why AA separated from the Christian Oxford Group, Bob Wilson replied, "The Oxford Group wanted to save the world, and I only wanted to save the drunks."

BOOZE AND THE BOOZER

None of the Bible-based religions condones drunkenness. The Lutherans, Episcopalians, and Jews preach moderation as do the Catholics. They respect alcohol's power but do not blame it for causing alcoholism; the drinker creates his own problem. Some Protestants protest, however. Although Luther and Calvin called for temperate drinking, in 1739 John Wesley formulated a rule of abstinence for Methodists, a rule that has been relaxed only recently to allow for occasional social drinking. The Fundamentalist churches and the Baptists cling tenaciously to a total prohibition on alcohol. They have surrendered the idea of enforcing abstinence on a nation, but they demand it for their members. For them, alcohol is a destructive substance that must be avoided.

Since the Bible both condemns and accepts the drinking of alcohol, religious teetotalers offer several arguments based on scripture to defend their position. Man's first priority is to glorify God, but alcohol interferes with this capability. The human body is a "temple of the Holy Spirit" (1 Cor. 6:10) and Christians have an obligation to cleanse themselves "from every defilement of body and spirit, and make holiness perfect in the fear of God" (2 Cor. 7:1). Since alcohol adversely affects the body, it is a defilement. Christians should do not do anything that causes others to fall from grace:"Let us . . . decide never to put a stumbling block in the way of a brother . . . It is right not to eat meat or drink wine or do anything that makes your brother stumble" (Rom. 14:13, 21). Christians should be alert at all times in order to combat Satan:"Be sober, be watchful. Your adversary the devil prowls around like a roaring lion, seeking some one to devour" (1 Peter 5:8).

In a 1993 pamphlet distributed by the Christian Life Commission of the Southern Baptist Convention, the author states:"I perceive alcohol addiction not as an actual disease but as an authentic sin against God Almighty and against humanity made in God's image . . . I perceive alcohol consumption not as amoral but immoral, not as an inalienable right but as an unconscionable wrong, not as a social grace but as an antisocial disgrace . . . all drinking is irresponsible . . . the present qualifying, excusing, sweet-talking, soft-pedaling, pussyfooting approach to alcohol and alcohol problems is religiously hypocritical, morally reprehensible, social irresponsible, and culturally suicidal . . . abstinence is the only live option . . . just as moral stigma is properly attached to racism, child abuse, pornography, conspicuous waste, and planned obsolescence, so moral stigma [should be] properly attached to the consumption of alcohol."

Holy Glenfiddich! This boot-stomping hardcore stand on abstinence flies in the face of everyday experience. A glass or two of wine with dinner, champagne to celebrate a wedding, a few beers while watching the Super Bowl, a snifter of cognac on a chilly winter evening or a thimbleful of wine at communion surely do no harm. In 1864 a Scottish physician, Francis Anstie, felt that three drinks a day was a safe limit. In fact, most people drink alcohol without any adverse physical, mental, or social consequences. About one-third of Americans are light drinkers, one-third are moderate to heavy drinkers, and one-third are teetotalers. Amazingly only seven percent of Americans drink half of the alcohol (one-tenth of all drinkers). This group of alcoholics and problem drinkers creates havoc for themselves and others, but for ninety percent of drinkers alcohol usually is a benign substance.

While claims for the health-promoting effects of modest drinking are somewhat shaky, abstinence isn't necessarily beneficial. A review of data from several long-term studies indicates a consistently higher mortality rate for current abstainers than for current moderate drinkers. George Vaillant, an eminent alcohol researcher, offers two explanations for this finding: the group of current abstainers may include severe alcoholics in remission whose mortality rate is almost as high as active alcoholics, and in communities where drinking is common, abstainers may develop greater physical morbidity because of their tendency to manifest impaired mental health and interpersonal relations. Vaillant's own long-term study of 400 males contained 80 abstainers and 80 moderate drinkers. Comparison of the groups shows that abstainers were far more likely (by a 2 to 1 ratio in most categories) to be in a lower social class, to ever receive a psychiatric diagnosis, to use immature mental defense mechanisms, to never achieve independence from their families of origin, to never marry, and to have difficulties with spending time with friends and with taking enjoyable vacations. You abstain at your own peril.

CHRIST AND CLARET

There is something of the religious and spiritual in alcohol. When distilled spirits were created centuries ago, they were called *aqua vitae*, the water of life. The same phrase in Gaelic is *usquebaugh,* which gives us the word whiskey. In some ways it is a mystical substance so heavily endowed with symbolism that a leading scholar considered alcoholism as "the attempt to satisfy religious needs by nonreligious means—alcohol."

Blood, a fundamental ingredient of religion, can be symbolized by alcohol. The Bible, for example, calls wine the blood of the grape. Religious sacrifice is more than a sacred tribute; its essence is the communion between God and worshipers that results from carving the flesh and spilling the blood of the victim. Originally the meat and blood were devoured (they still are by Christians, although the practice has been spiritually sanitized), but over time the blood alone was invested with supernatural power. When the Jewish temple was destroyed and the Jewish people dispersed, animal sacrifice was displaced by wine offerings. Even in secular life some qualities of blood have been attached to alcohol, qualities such as life (the bleeding that accompanies birth, the distillation to produce *aqua vitae*), death (exsanguination from ruptured esophageal veins secondary to alcoholic liver cirrhosis), and impurity (menstrual blood, alcohol as an agent that defiles). Drinking together and "pledging in the cup" may substitute for the intermingling of blood to seal covenants between groups and individuals.

Alcohol's intoxicating "power to stimulate the mystical qualities of human nature" provides a core religious feeling of transcendence and can provide a sense of meaning in life for alcoholics. Alcohol's physiological ability to transform consciousness can, depending on the context, be interpreted as a transcendence of everyday experience, an entry into the cosmic world of spirituality that brings us nearer my God to Thee. Alcohol, however, comes to dominate the lives of alcoholics and slowly replaces a higher spiritual power with itself, an unholy comforter. Oates describes this as being "trapped in the idolatry of alcohol itself . . . [the alcoholic] looks to alcohol for redemption from the burden of his humanity, the power of his guilt, the threat of his insecurity." Bill Wilson himself said that "Before AA, we were trying to find God in a bottle."

Alcohol also satisfies what Clinebell identifies as the religious needs for experiences of trust and relatedness. By drinking, the alcoholic feels "a temporary but highly valued experience of unity." Alcohol provides an illusory closeness to others, at least during the early stages of intoxication, and it fosters a psychological regression. Just as infants expect mother to provide for them, alcoholics feel entitled to God's protection. Such narcissism is eventually rebuffed by reality with resultant feelings of despair. Unlike God, who doesn't always come through for everyone, much less alcoholics, alcohol always anesthetizes against despair and takes care of drunkards. It is their lifeline for a while, until it corrodes in the acid world, and they drown.

E.M. Jellinek, one of the greatest students of alcohol, claimed that milk, necessary for an infant's survival, and water, necessary for the continuance of life, are basic fertility symbols. Alcohol came "to displace water and milk as the ritual symbol par excellence of the stream of life" because of its psychological properties: "When we ingest an alcoholic beverage we have at least the illusion of the expansion of the chest; we feel stronger, more powerful, more self-confident." In the classical world fertility was associated with wine. Dionysus and his superabundant son, Priapus, were gods of crops and vegetation among other things; the latter was revered by some as the creator of the world, while the former was one of the rare gods who promised a better life after death. Dionysus had his orgies but he also was the Lord of Souls, his likeness painted on numerous sarcophagi leading drunken revelers to a happy hereafter. The notion that dead drunks can achieve a higher condition in the afterlife has, for Jellinek, some significance in understanding the psychology of addiction. "Drunkenness can be a kind of shortcut to the higher life, the achievement of a higher state without an emotional and intellectual effort." In truth, alcoholism is religion gone awry, a metabolic error of the religious impulse. Chronic drunkenness leads but to death; the rest is wishful elaboration.

Alcohol as master is an embalmer, each sip sapping the life force. But alcohol as servant cheers both God and man. There is room enough in the world for both Christ and claret. It's merely a matter of proportion. That is the message of the Bible.

CREEPING THINGS:
ANIMALS AND THE BIBLE

CHAPTER 6

Animals are important to our lives. Most days many of us pet one and eat one. Childhood experiences with puppies, kittens, and teddy bears provide us comfort long after we are weaned from our mothers' breasts. The elderly find animals more accessible and loving than their thankless children, and some chronic paranoids find them more worthy of trust because animals' motives are so transparent.

The Bible's only mention of a pet is 2 Samuel 12:1-31. King David arranged for the death of Uriah so that he could marry his wife, the beautiful Bathsheba. The Lord then sent Nathan the High Priest, who told David the following story about a rich man and poor man. The former had many animals but the latter had only a female lamb. "He raised it, and it grew up with him and with his children; it used to eat his own food, and drink from his cup, and lie in his bosom, and it was like a daughter to him." In order to feed a guest, the rich man killed the poor man's lamb. David's anger was great, and he said to Nathan, "As the Lord lives, the man who has done this deserves to die; and he shall restore the lamb fourfold, because he did this thing, and because he had no pity." Nathan retorted to David, "You are the man." David had lots of women, but his lust for Bathsheba caused him to kill an innocent man. The Lord threatened to take David's wives and give them to his neighbor who would sleep with them openly in the sunlight. David quickly repented, and the Lord relented. The new punishment was that the love-child of David and Bathsheba would die. The child became the scapegoat.

The Biblical Israelites used animals for the purpose of maintaining a proper relationship with God. In Leviticus 17:11, God made known his desire for animal sacrifice and offerings: "For the life of the flesh is in the blood, and I have given it to you upon the altar to make atonement for your souls; for it is the blood that makes atonement for the soul." The Israelites must have been a morose lot, because they were constantly atoning, and the Holy Temple was the greatest slaughterhouse in the history of the world. We're not talking a few chickens here or there but rather thousands of bulls, cows, sheep, and goats one after another. God usually got the lion's share and was particularly fond of cholesterolemic, fatty meat, while the priests ate the rest. They certainly needed the nourishment because, with the hungry yearning for atonement burning inside of them, they hacked night and day at the bellowing beasts.

Animals provided Biblical authors with material for marvelous similes. Proverbs 26:11 tells us that, "As a dog returns to his own vomit, so a fool repeats his folly." In Solomon's song the beloved man says of the lovely Shulamite maiden that her hair is like a flock of goats, her teeth like a flock of shorn sheep, and her breasts like two fawns. Admittedly it's difficult to relate to the goat and sheep images, but even today the fawns, all soft and cuddly and virginal, are a definite come-on.

For the psychiatrist the most important Biblical animal is that Satanic agent, the serpent. But if the serpent is so terrible, why is it on the seal of medical societies? We shall get to this matter shortly, but first let us consider man's beastly nature as illuminated by the stories of Daniel, Nebuchadnezzar, and werewolves at Harvard.

LYCANTHROPES AND WOLF-CHILDREN

Daniel defied King Darius' decree not to petition God and was punished by being penned overnight in a pit with a pride of lions. Fortunately, God sent an angel to close the lions' mouths. The troubled king didn't sleep well at all that night, and, come morning, he sorrowfully called down and asked Daniel if his God had saved him. Angel or no, Daniel was doubtless relieved to hear a human voice. With savvy, he shouted, "O king, live forever," and he told the lions' tale. The king freed him and in a tantrum then threw Daniel's accusers along with their wives and children into the pit, where they were crushed to death by the irascible pride. Daniel, understandably traumatized, counterphobically conjured visions of rams and goats and lions and terrible horned monsters that he tamed to become Beastmaster of the Lord.

Nebuchadnezzar, the Babylonian king who ruled over Jerusalem, was a dreamer, but his dreams were so unintelligible that he offered gifts and great honors to his court astrologers if they provided the correct interpretation. Those who got it wrong won the booby prize; they would be cut in pieces. No guts, no glory. No one volunteered. The furious king ordered them all killed. Luckily Daniel stepped forward and passed the test. Then Nebuchadnezzar had an ominous dream whose meaning, according to Daniel, was that he would be turned into a large animal. A year later, sure enough, as the king was boasting about his regal palace, he turned into a large animal. He was crazy as a loon, munching hay while his hair grew like eagle's feathers and his nails like bird's claws. After seven beastly years, his manhood was restored.

In many religions animals and gods co-mingle. Egyptians saw the sun god in the dung beetle and Anubis, the guardian of the dead, in the jackal. Dionysus was represented both as an almost effeminate youth and as a bull. Christ is the lamb, and kangaroos are the totem animals of Australian aborigines. But if animals gambol with gods by day, they root with Mother Earth at night. A veritable zoo emerges from the loins of the statue of multi-breasted Artemis, the goddess of fertility. At sacrificial rituals in honor of Zeus, Lykaios participants feasted by firelight on a stew of animal and human entrails. Those who wolfed wolf were transformed in a howling frenzy. Only if they refrained from eating human flesh for nine years might they become men again.

When mortals become beasts their nocturnal, lustful, hungry animal essence emerges. In Japan they become foxes, in Africa leopards, in Western cultures dogs and, more commonly, wolves or lycanthropes. Lycanthropy's heydays were in the late Middle Ages and in the sixteenth and seventeenth centuries, when hundreds of werewolves were slaughtered during epidemics of demon possession.

As far back as the third century, physicians limned lycanthropes as delusional, depressed persons who aped wolves in all things, lingered in graveyards at night, were pale skinned, feeble visioned, dry-eyed, thirsty, and had ulcerated legs. During an acute attack, treatment consisted of bleeding until the patient fainted, soothing baths, laxatives, and a wholesome diet.

In addition to depression, lycanthropy was thought to be caused by drugs such as belladonna, atropine, peyote, strychnine, mandrake root, nightshade, opium, and hashish. A third group of causes fell into the devilish category of magical spells and black magic. The disorder waxed and waned over the centuries until it disappeared from diagnostic compilations in the 1870s.

In recent years several articles have revived the condition. A 20-year-old schizophrenic took LSD while walking in the woods "and felt himself slowing turning into a werewolf, seeing fur growing on his hands and feeling it grow on his face. He experienced a sudden uncontrollable urge to chase and devour rabbits. He also felt that he had obtained horrible insight into the devil's world." A 37-year-old farmer with brain damage allowed his facial hair to grow and pretended it was fur, slept in cemeteries, howled at the moon, and said he was transformed into a werewolf. A 49-year-old married woman disrobed, adopted the female sexual position of a wolf, and offered herself to her mother. Later she growled, gnawed her bed, and said that the devil had entered her and that she was an animal. In the hospital she stated, "I am a wolf of the night, I am a wolf woman of the day . . . I have claws, teeth, fangs, and hair." She described her eyes: "one is frightened and the other is like the wolf . . . this creature of the dark wanted to kill." Gazing into a mirror, she saw "the head of a wolf in place of a face on my own body—just a long-nosed wolf with teeth, groaning, snarling, growling . . . with fangs and claws, calling out 'I am the devil.'" In 1988 a group of psychiatrists at Harvard found twelve cases of lycanthropy among 500 psychiatric patients treated at McLean Hospital in the previous twelve years. A man who growled like a Bengal tiger and another who hopped about the ward like a rabbit admitted that they could control their behavior. Of the remaining ten patients, "six apparently believed themselves to be, or acted like, wolves or dogs, two believed themselves to be cats; one patient believed himself a gerbil (he had raised gerbils as a hobby for six years); and one a bird." The authors concluded that lycanthropy is not specific to a particular mental disorder. The diagnoses of their cases included mania, depression, schizophrenia, atypical psychosis, cannabis intoxication superimposed on mania, and factitious disorder. The behavior has a generally favorable prognosis. Seven of the twelve patients, like King Nebuchadnezzar, had a complete remission of their primary disorder; three had a partial remission, two were unresponsive to treatment, including one man with the fixed delusion of being a cat. He lived with, had sexual activity with, and hunted with cats. His greatest love, unrequited alas, was a tigress in a zoo.

Men not only have worshiped weasels and throbbed with animal ferocity and passion, but also have suckled brutish breasts. In the prototypical "birth of a hero" folk tale, an endangered infant is placed in a basket and set adrift in a river to die but is serendipitously saved. Romulus and Remus, the founders of Rome, were set adrift as newborns on the Tiber River because their uncle wanted to kill them, the potential heirs to the kingdom. They floated to a river bank where a wolf, who descended from the hills to drink, discovered and suckled them until they were rescued eventually by a shepherd. Cyrus, the great Persian emperor, was reared by a dog. In the absence of his mother, even the great god Zeus was nursed by bees, doves, an eagle, a goat, a sow, and a cow.

In today's cynical world we might agree with the scholarly curmudgeons who say that the lupa, or wolf, that suckled Romulus and Remus was really the wife of the shepherd who found them. Lupa was Roman slang for prostitute. Similarly, the shepherd's wife who found Cyrus was named Spako, a bitch. For European romanticists, however, wolves' teats titillated. Philosophers and novelists like Rousseau and Chateaubriand adored the noble savage. Linnaeus, the great classifier of science, described the feral child who was hairy, mute, moved on all four limbs, and was reared in the wild by animals. Linnaeus' examples included the Lithuanian bear-boys (1661), the Hessian wolf-boy (1344), and the Irish sheep-boy (1672). Wild Peter of Hanover, a child captured as he ran naked in a German field, became a celebrity and savants discussed this "specimen of man in a state of nature," especially in regard to the origin of mankind and the concept of innate ideas. In 1774, Lord Monboddo effusively declared that the discovery of Wild Peter was more remarkable than then discovery of the planet Uranus.

In this sentimental environment the case of the Wild Boy of Aveyron (1799) was inevitable. Philippe Pinel, the famous French psychiatrist who struck the chains from the mental patients at the Salpetriere hospital, examined the "wild boy" and proclaimed him an incurable idiot (the old term for severe retardation). But Jean-Marc Itard, an ear doctor, devoted five years to working with the unfortunate youth. Although Itard's treatment ultimately failed, he is revered as the first modern child psychiatrist.

Other cases have been reported over the years, but the most interesting is that of Amala and Kamala, the wolf-children of Midnapore (India). In 1920, a visiting missionary, Reverend J.A.L. Singh, saw the two girls (eight years old and one year old) along with three grown wolves and several wolf cubs emerge from a tunnel near a gigantic ant-mound in the jungle. The girls had abnormally long and pointed canine teeth and they could see perfectly in the darkest places. They smelled meat at a great distance, and they ate and drank like dogs. They had "cultivated the animal nature and conditions of life almost to perfection in the animal world." The Reverend attempted to humanize them through behavioral techniques. Amala died in 1921 of dysentery, and Kamala died in 1924 of kidney failure.

Singh's diary was published in 1942 with a favorable commentary by an American anthropologist. Even Arnold Gesell, the highly respected Yale psychologist, published a romanticized account of Kamala's life and was quite impressed by her "slow but orderly and sequential recovery of obstructed mental growth." *Scientific American* published a report on the wolf-children (although a year earlier the scientific community had been defrauded by the case of a supposed South African baboon-boy). Bruno Bettelheim, a psychologist at the University of Chicago who devoted his career to treating severely disturbed children, felt that Reverend Singh was sincere but that his interpretations were false. Bettelheim himself had had fantasies about the histories of autistic children he had treated. His own speculations originated first in his narcissistic unwillingness to admit that these animal-like creatures could have had pasts similar to ours, and second, in his need "to find emotionally acceptable explanations for the nearly inexplicable and wholly unmanageable behavior of these children." The behaviors of the wolf-children of Midnapore were identical to those of the autistic children in Bettelheim's laboratory school. Once Dr. Singh and his gullible supporters convinced themselves that Amala and Kamala were reared by wolves, then the childrens' behavior was interpreted accordingly. What most likely happened: the impoverished villagers placed the children in the tunnel, led Rev. Singh to it, and duped him into taking them away and caring for them.

VIPERS VENOMOUS AND WISE

Animals abound in the Bible. Noah's Ark contained them all, every animal, every bird, every creeping thing that creeps on the earth. Most fascinating is the snake, and most paradoxical. Except for Balaam's donkey, the snake is the book's only talking animal, and the words that it spat out in the Garden of Eden had great consequences for humankind.

Biblical snakes surely are godly agents of bodily and spiritual death. "So the Lord sent fiery serpents among the people, and they bit the people; and many of the people of Israel died" (Num. 21:6). In the song of Moses, God threatened those who sacrifice to demons and to new gods with pestilence, bitter destruction, the teeth of beasts, and the poison of serpents (Deut. 32). Jesus said, "Woe to you, scribes and Pharisees, hypocrites . . . Serpents, brood of vipers! How can you escape the condemnation of hell?" (Matt: 23:29–33). In the Garden of Eden, God cursed the snake and said that he will put enmity between the snake's seed (the followers of evil) and Eve's seed.

But if snakes are so horrible, why did Jesus tell his twelve apostles to "be wise as serpents and harmless as doves" when they preached and healed the sick (Matt. 10:16)? And why are "the way of a serpent on a rock . . . and the way of a man with a virgin" things that are "too wonderful" (Prov. 30:19)? And why did the Lord tell Moses to put the image of a bronze serpent on a pole "and everyone who is bitten, when he sees it, shall live" (Num. 21:13)? And why did John (3:14–15) say, "As Moses lifted up the serpent in the wilderness, even so must the Son of man be lifted up, that whoever believes in Him shall not perish but have eternal life"?

Snakes are heady stuff. They kill and they heal. They are cursed and they are wise. They portend both damnation and salvation. Weston La Barre, an anthropologist, notes that more myths abound about snakes than any other animal. "The snake is both the ancestral or oedipal father, giver of life, God—and the phallic Devil, instrument of God . . . As the prime symbol used by human beings, the snake must always and everywhere be preoccupied with man's basic concern: the human body image and its life and death or immortality. The snake represents every modality of our body's guilt and needs."

To understand the serpent, our thoughts must wander serpentine paths. The earliest humans worshipped snakes, fascinated by their phallic shape and by their peculiar ability to rejuvenate themselves by shedding their skins each year. Snakes represented natural cycles such as the daily death and rebirth of the sun, the crops that fall in the Fall and spring to life in the Spring, the Nile that floods and recedes, the death that is followed by resurrection. The Egyptian kings used an image of the snake divinity, Uraeus, as their symbol, and Pharaoh, the divine king, was depicted by a snake hieroglyph. When Pharaoh demanded miracles, Moses told Aaron that his serpent-rod would devour the serpent-rods of the Egyptians. The Hebrews worshipped Moses' snake god until Hezekiah broke it into pieces (2 Kings 18:4), forevermore to be the enemy of the Lord, "that old serpent called the Devil" (Rev. 12:9). The ancient snake gods of Greece gave way to the Olympian gods, but their powers remained strong. Asclepius, the founder of medicine, healed through the power of his staff, the caduceus with the image of two snakes. Athena gave Asclepius two phials of blood from the Gorgon Medusa (a hideous creature with serpents for hair, to look at it was to die); with one he killed and with the other he raised the dead. The serpent gives death and life.

The serpent also is the most common symbol of the phallus, which produces water like the fertile rain-god and which repeatedly springs to life then dies a temporary petite morte in the endless cycle of reproduction. Barren women worshipped at the temple of Asclepius; if they dreamed of a snake, they would become pregnant, and the snake was considered the child's father. Greek gods often assumed the form of a snake when they seduced mortal women. The snake-phallus entices, knows pleasure (the fruit of the Tree of Knowledge was good to eat), erects and resurrects itself to create new life and immortality. Sexuality was created in the Garden of Eden. The exchange of immortality for sexuality might have been a bad bargain, but many are thankful that neither Eve nor Adam didn't just say no.

The God of the Hebrews vanquished but could not (or would not) completely destroy the older snake god who then assumed the role of the poisonous, phallic, Prince of Darkness, God's eternal enemy, the old serpent, Satan. The older snake god was not totally terrible and some of its attributes, such as healing and wisdom, were absorbed by the Hebrew God just as they were by the Greek gods. And that is why the serpent seems paradoxical in the Bible.

Although snakes are still venerated as village gods in India, most people nowadays don't care much for them. Ophidiophobia is a fancy name for the fear of snakes. Chimpanzees have an inherited fear of snakes, but humans don't. Our fears have a personal history; our fear of snakes is partly irrational because so few snakes are dangerous that the likelihood of encountering a poisonous viper is quite small. Some of our anxiety is probably stirred up by a snake's phallic shape.

What are we to make, however, of the Christian faithful who spend their weekends in church fondling and dancing with rattlesnakes? It is truly marvelous to behold men and women filled with the Holy Spirit toss rattlesnakes to each other and stare into unblinking serpent eyes. The text that moves them is found in the Gospel of St. Mark 16:17–18: "And these signs shall follow them that believe: In my name shall they cast out devils; they shall speak with new tongues; they shall take up serpents; and if they drink any deadly things, it shall not harm them, they shall lay hands on the sick, and they shall recover."

As chronicled by La Barre, the snake-handling movement began in 1909 in rural Grasshopper Valley, Tennessee. After a devotee was bitten and died, however, the cult moved to the mountains of Kentucky. In 1938, an article in the *St. Louis Post-Dispatch* described a snake-handling meeting of the group. "Cymbals, tambourines, foot-stomping, and hand-clapping provided the rhythm for the worshippers who, men and women both, passed serpents from hand to hand while jerking violently all over their bodies. One man thrust a snake before a seated woman holding a baby; the woman smiled, and the baby gravely reached forward and touched the snake. A dark-haired timberman opened the mouth of one rattler to show its intact fangs to the visitors; another man showed the scars of at least three bites on his hand and arm."

A 1995 newspaper report by Dan Sewell on a religious service in Kingston, Georgia, tells of "toe-tapping, hand-clapping, foot-stomping, hopping and dancing." The minister begins by saying, "We have serpents up here. There's death in them boxes." The participants throw the rattlesnakes and copperheads "over their shoulders, raise them over their heads, drop them down their shirts, let them coil themselves around their arms."The minister holds a snake to his face, stares into its eyes, and sees "the victory of faith over the devil's evil."

Despite or, perhaps, because of the persecution and laws against snake handling, the cult persists mainly in the economically impoverished rural regions of Appalachia and the South. Its members are usually poor, uneducated, sexually repressed, disaffected, unhappy souls with little hope of acceptance by affluent, mainstream American culture. They don't have many options in life. They could foment revolution, hunker behind barricades like the Branch Davidians in Waco and await slaughter. They could sink into depression and whistle Dixie until they give up the ghost. They could seek the consolation of psychosis and imagine themselves gods. Or they could turn to the Bible and discover that when the ancient Israelites felt abandoned by God and grumbled about not having even water and decent bread, they were pelted with fiery serpents (Num. 21:5-6). Why not surpass the Israelites, deliberately seek out fiery serpents, and put themselves in God's hands? With abundant trust in his love for the downtrodden, true believers tease, taunt, and overcome the serpent-devil. When you live in the pits, you're thankful when at least you get to pick your poison.

SOMETHING ABOUT THE BODY

CHAPTER 7

In *Thus Spake Zarathustra* the German philosopher Friedrich Nietzsche wrote: "The awakened and knowing say: body am I entirely, and nothing else; and soul is only a word for something about the body." Perhaps his statement has more than a touch of Teutonic overkill, perhaps it reflects the early signs of a syphilitic brain, but it contains some jot of concrete truth. Bones and blood, hair and guts are palpable things that can be coddled or tortured but cannot be willed away. What we do with our bodies in great part determines the fate of our souls.

The Judeo-Christian religions decry excessive bodily pleasures and demand control of the flesh in order to achieve salvation. The body as the metaphorical Temple of the Lord should be a place of holy sacrifice, but the body is also a place of sensuality and aggression and therein lies a lifelong dynamic tension. This tension is evidenced by the strange things that we do to our flesh in the name of religious inspiration. Taking our lead from the Bible, let us examine castration, skin-cutting, the stigmata, and circumcision. These topics hold more than a passing interest for the psychiatrist; skin-cutting especially is a most vexing clinical problem.

HOLY HARVEST: CASTRATION

"He whose testicles are crushed or whose male member is cut off shall not enter the assembly of the Lord" (Deut. 23:1). Why the warning? Who became eunuchs and what was so repulsive about them?

Livestock breeders and ranchers discovered long ago that castration made animals docile. Since it worked on animals, the next step in the advancement of civilization was easy, namely the castration of slaves. This early example of experimentation often failed, however, because of limp logic. Not all men are like animals. In fact, since castrated slaves did not have carping wives and children of their own to worry about, some were able to develop their mental capacities and to devote themselves to work. Free from the burdens of sexuality and heirs some eunuchs distinguished themselves as civil servants, generals, and, most importantly, priests.

A priesthood of eunuchs arose in Asia Minor where the most ancient supreme being was the Great Mother Goddess. She existed before the other gods were created and everyone worshipped her. The Babylonians knew her as Ishtar, the Semites as Ashtoreth. Around the Mediterranean Sea she became known as Astarte, Aphrodite, and Cybele.

Although the Great Mother Goddess epitomized desire and fecundity, she rarely consorted with men. Astarte, however, fell in love with Adonis. He was mutilated and killed by a wild boar. Through Astarte's tears he was resurrected. Cybele fell in love with Attis, but he was unfaithful. Driven by madness, he castrated himself. Later on, he was resurrected, too.

Astarte's grandest temple was in Hierapolis (Lebanon). At an annual festival, men desiring to devote themselves to the goddess castrated themselves. Carrying their sacrifice they ran through the streets and tossed their organs through the windows of a randomly chosen house whose fortunate inhabitants (good fortune being a relative concept) gladly provided the devotees with women's clothing to wear. Similarly, devotees of Cybele castrated themselves, not only would-be priests but also pious spectators who were overwrought by the frenetic music, the intense emotionality, and the flowing blood. They too wore women's clothes for the rest of their lives. After the Day of Blood came the Day of Joy to celebrate Attis' resurrection (March 25th). In secret ceremonies worshipers climbed into a pit (the taurobolium) where the blood of a slaughtered bull flowed through a grate onto them, washed away their sins, and granted them a new life. The taurobolium for this bloody baptism at Cybele's sanctuary in Rome was located in today's Vatican City near the site where St. Peter's Cathedral now stands.

As Mother of the Trojans who originally founded Rome, Cybele's statue was welcomed to the Eternal City in 204 B.C. Romans were generally tolerant about religious practices but Cybele's priests seemed beyond strange. They paraded around like women with long, bleached hair. They were fortunetellers, cross-dressers, trance dancers, and self-flagellators. The emperor Julian referred to their castration as "that holy harvest," but for most Romans it was Oriental bizarreness. They could not comprehend the ecstasy of priests who surrendered their manhood and lived like women in order to become one with a female goddess.

Jews denigrated eunuchs because of their impurity; they were imperfect men not fit to participate in communal life, especially religious rituals. During the exile, however, many Jews became eunuchs in the palace of the king of Babylon. Isaiah not only foretold this (Is. 39), but he also disregarded the earlier legal exclusion of eunuchs from the assembly of the Lord and welcomed them back into the fold.

In fact, God himself stated that eunuchs who kept the Sabbath and held fast the covenants would have both a place in the house of the Lord and a name "that shall not be cut off" (Is. 56).

In the New Testament, Jesus did not condemn castration but rather said, "After all, there are eunuchs who were born that way, and eunuchs who were castrated by others, and there are eunuchs who castrated themselves for the kingdom of heaven's sake. If you are able to accept this advice, do so" (Matt. 19:12). Perhaps his message was that eunuchs should not be discriminated against. Perhaps his metaphorical message was that a celibate person can better serve the Lord. Whatever his intent, some Christians have used his words to justify their self-castration.

In addition to sporadic individual self-castrations and to castrations by a group called the Valesians who, according to St. Augustine, "castrate both themselves and their guests, thinking that in this way they serve God," Christian castration was institutionalized by only one major group. The Skoptsi, or eunuchs, emerged in Russia from the Eastern Orthodox tradition and flourished in the eighteenth and nineteenth centuries.

Its founder cut off his testicles to help him keep a vow of sexual abstinence. He survived some sort of crucifixion, was regarded as Christ by his followers, and recognized one disciple as the Mother of God and another as John the Baptist. He achieved perfection by removing his penis, whereupon he called himself Tsar Christ Peter III.

The Skoptsi believed that Adam and Eve had no sexual organs until after the Fall when God grafted the forbidden fruit onto Adam as testicles and onto Eve as breasts. In order to return to the carefree days of yesteryear, Church members had to castrate themselves (women were encouraged to cut off their nipples or the glandular tissue of their breasts as well as the clitoris). A small offshoot of the sect, called the Twisters (Perevertysii), performed a type of nonsurgical vasectomy by twisting their spermatic cords in order to achieve physiological castration.

Propagation was impossible but the sect grew to a hundred thousand memberless members. The Skoptsi were master recruiters; one technique was to lend money at such high interest rates that some borrowers could meet their obligation only by paying the proverbial, albeit exaggerated, pound of flesh. Even though it was easy to identify Skoptsi men, typically chubby and beardless as a result of their hormonal changes, suppression of the cult was difficult. The Russian government tried imprisoning the Skoptsi in monasteries but a surprising number of Orthodox monks were converted by their prisoners. The last trial against the cult took place in the 1890s.

Self-castration as a result of mental illness is rather uncommon, but when it occurs everyone in the patient's psychological force-field feels unmanned. Thankfully, during their careers most psychiatrists encounter only a few such cases. Unlike eye enucleation, which is often influenced by the Bible (both Matthew 5:28–29 and Mark 6:22–23 offer counsel about tearing out one's eye), relatively few self-castrators nowadays attribute their motives directly to Scripture. They more often offer sexual reasons (e.g., to become like a woman, to avoid the temptation of being an inserting homosexual, to atone for sinful sexual behavior, etc). Except for transsexuals, who usually plan their castration carefully, most self-castrators are psychotic when they impulsively do the deed. Immediately afterwards they often are quite calm, suggesting that the act resolved some mental conflict at least temporarily.

A classic psychoanalytic theory holds that self-castration is the prototype of all self-mutilation and that when other organs are attacked they are unconscious representations of the genitals. Oedipus, for example, mutilated himself upon discovering that he had bedded his mother. Self-castration would seem the logical choice but, instead, he blinded himself by sticking the brooches from his mother's dress into his eyes. The eye–genital link may have its origins in the belief that visual rays are emitted by the eyes just as sperm is emitted by the penis. Thus, the glance of an eye may represent male sexual function. Many amulets, such as the red chili-horn, that counteract the force of the evils are symbols of the erect penis. Interestingly, while many myths and folk tales mention eye enucleation, clinical cases seem to be restricted to Christian culture areas. In contrast, deviant self-castration has a worldwide distribution.

SCARS AND STRIPES: SKIN-CUTTING

The prophet Elijah's first words in the Bible proclaimed a drought: "As the Lord God of Israel lives, before whom I stand, there shall not be dew nor rain these years, except at my word" (1 Kings 17). Times were so tough that the Israelites wavered in their faith. Elijah called them together and said, "How long will you falter between two opinions. If the Lord is God, follow Him, but if Baal, follow him." No one rose to the bait, so Elijah challenged 450 of Baal's prophets to a bull roasting contest. When his opponents couldn't rouse Baal to start a fire, Elijah taunted them to cry aloud and waken Baal from his nap. No luck. He didn't budge, "So they cried aloud, and cut themselves as was their custom with knives and lances, until the blood rushed out of them."

Self-mutilation comes in a variety of culturally sanctioned and deviant forms. Certainly ear and nose piercing have long been consid-

ered stylish in many cultures. Nowadays nipple and genital piercing
has become faddish and is not necessarily a sign of mental derange-
ment. Shiite Muslims flagellate themselves on the Festival of Husain,
and Saints Dominic, Peter Damian, and the early Franciscans were passionate self-whippers. In fourteenth-century Europe, itinerant bands
of flagellators were received as heroes by a public who prayed that
the bloody penitents would protect them from the plague. At various
Hindu festivals, men, women, and children pierce their tongues and
cheeks and attach decorated weights to their bodies with fish hooks.
The climax of the Sun Dance of the Plains Indians occurred when
skewers ripped open the back and chest muscles of the elite braves.
The Old Testament tells of pilgrims "with their beards shaved and
their clothes torn, and their bodies gashed" (Jer. 41:5). It links skin-
cutting with mourning: "Thou shalt not make any cuttings in your
flesh for the dead" (Lev. 19:28).

Of greater importance to psychiatrists are pathological self-
mutilators who cut and burn themselves. Their numbers are surprisingly large; the prevalence rate is at least 1,200 per 100,000 persons
per year (the suicide prevalence rate, in comparison, is about 12).
Some people episodically harm themselves, while others do it repeti-
tively. In fact, the first historical description of a repetitive self-mutilator is reported in Mark 5 when Jesus visited the Gadarenes. He met a
madman whom the villagers tried to control with shackles. He lived
in a graveyard; "And always, night and day, he was in the mountains
and in the tombs, crying out and cutting himself with stones." Jesus
immediately diagnosed possession by a multiple spirit called Legion
and performed a stat exorcism. The unclean spirits then entered into
a herd of 2,000 swine who promptly ran to the sea and committed
suicide by drowning. If Legion was an evil suicidal spirit, how did the
possessed man stave off self-destruction? What kept him alive? We
can't be sure but one fact is clear: he repeatedly cut himself. Could
the cutting have saved him?

That self-mutilation may be a morbid type of self-help is not such
a farfetched idea. Consider the Hamadsha, a group of Islamic, Sufi
healers in Morocco. They travel from town to town announcing their
arrival with music. Patients are brought out from their homes and
form a circle. As the musicians play trance-driving songs, the healers,
good Sufis all, psych themselves up by swallowing cactus spines and
drinking boiling water. They then dance and slash their heads. This is
the moment that the sick participants have awaited. They step forward, dip bread or sugar cubes in the freely flowing blood, and eat
the miraculous food in the belief that the power of healing resides
in the healers' blood. We usually associate self-mutilation with

patients, but here the therapists mutilate themselves to benefit the patients.

In fact, patients report that skin cutting and other acts of moderate or superficial self-mutilation provide rapid, temporary relief from distressing thoughts and feelings. The reasons they give are legion. Some say that skin-cutting releases enormous amounts of tension and compare it to lancing a boil or popping a balloon. Frightening episodes of depersonalization—emotional deadness, estrangement from the environment, altered perceptions of time, a sense of unreality—can be ended by cutting. Some females, fearful of the uncontrollable bleeding of menstruation, mistakenly believe that cutting diverts the blood from their genitals. For some persons self-mutilation is a "secret friend" that provides comfort, security, and relief from feelings of alienation. Dissatisfied persons, such as prisoners and scorned lovers, may use self-mutilation as emotional blackmail to force a change in their situation. In about half of multiple personality disorder cases one personality will mutilate another.

Repetitive self-mutilators often adopt an identity as a "cutter" or "burner," brood over their acts of self-harm, and describe themselves as being "addicted" to the behavior. Driven by impulsivity, they may switch symptoms (e.g., skin-cutting gives way to bulimia, or to episodic substance abuse or kleptomania, in all sorts of sequences and combinations). When the symptoms rage out of control, demoralization and suicide attempts are common.

At one level of analysis, self-mutilation represents an attempt to achieve personal reintegration and symptom reduction. At another level, however, the symbolism of the behavior suggests something profound, something that is embedded in elemental experiences of healing, salvation, and social orderliness. Without understanding why or how, some self-mutilators seem to tap into these experiences unconsciously, intuitively seeking to heal themselves and to restore order to their disordered minds and lives. Those salubrious facets of self-mutilation are exemplified by culturally sanctioned rituals and beliefs.

In shamanism, one of the most ancient systems of therapy, the healing of illness and reversal of misfortunes are affected by the shaman's personal contact with the spirit world. The high status of shaman is not easily attained. Would-be healers must survive an initiating sickness during which their body is dismembered, their flesh scraped to the bone, their visceral organs exchanged, and their blood renewed. Among the Dyak in Borneo, for example, their heads are opened, and their brains washed in pure water. Their eyes are packed with gold dust, the better to see any glimmering souls. Arrows are stuck into their hearts, the better to sympathize with the sick and suffering. The initiates cannot descend to hell to converse with demons nor ascend to heaven to be consecrated by god until they have been disassembled and reconstructed. That these horrifying experiences occur during trance and dream states does not diminish their significance. Through participation in the mutilative process, shamans emerge wiser, healthier, and more capable of healing both themselves and others.

The mutilative foundation of social order is encountered in the most prestigious of Indo-European myths, the creation of the cosmos. The basic Indo-European mythologem is that the sacrifice and mutilation of the primordial being resulted in the creation of the world. As told in the *Rigveda* of India, Perusa's body was dismembered; the sun was formed from his eyes, the moon from his mind, the sky from his head, the earth from his feet, the regions of the earth from his ear, birds and animals from his dripping fat. The same sort of story is attached to Gayomart, the Iranian primordial being, and to Ymir in the Scandinavian *Edda*. In a similar Asian myth, the Chinese giant, P'an-ku, was sliced up; his breath became the wind and clouds, his voice the thunder, his eyes the sun and moon, his limbs and fingers the earth and mountains, his blood the rivers, his sweat the rain, his skin and hair the plants and trees, his teeth and bones the metal and stoves, and the parasites in his body became human beings.

One incredible sentence in the Bible, expressed almost identically in the Old and New Testaments, has reverberated throughout the centuries to provide solace and hope: "By his wounds we are healed" (Is. 53:5) and "By his wounds you have been healed" (1 Peter 2:24). Isaiah describes the Suffering Servant, a metaphor for Israel, while Peter describes Jesus. Both the Servant and Jesus voluntarily accepted their wounds and provided evidence for the redemptive power of suffering. Edward Podvoll, a psychiatrist, noted that "the self-mutilator can incorporate into his actions patterns which, to a greater or lesser degree, remain unarticulated in most of us. That is, such patterns already exist in muted intensities within the patient's social field. As such, he may even perform a service to his culture in his dramatic expression of those patterns which are felt to be intolerable within the self. Still other patterns invoked are those which elicit silent levels of admiration and envy. The history of those images reaches at least as far back as the Passion of the Cross and has prevailed among some of the most respected members of our culture."

The scar-serried body of the self-mutilator is more than an artless artifact of twisted thoughts. Scar tissue is a natural mortar that holds us together when we become unglued and is a sign of healing. The singular human body mirrors the collective social body, and each continually creates and sustains the other. Mutilative rituals and individual acts of self-mutilation acknowledge disruptions and provide a mechanism for the reestablishment of harmony and equilibrium. Through the spilling of blood and the removal of limbs, the garden of relationships among humans, god, and nature is watered, pruned, and cultivated. The myths and personal dramas of dismemberment and reassembly, of wounding and healing, play out the eternal struggles between men and women, parents and children, friends and enemies, humankind and the environment, the world of the flesh and the world of the spirit.

PASSION MARKS: THE STIGMATA

Being a god isn't always wine and poses. As if dealing with rebellious angels isn't bad enough, interceding in the affairs of humans must be nettlesome at best, horrific at worst. The stiff-necked, slip-sliding Israelites certainly were a thorn in Yahweh's side, eternally questioning his power and his guidance and then counting on him to bail them out of predicaments. He finally sent his son to set things right. Jesus dutifully accepted the assignment, agreeing to adopt a human form and to be reviled, whipped, and crucified by those whom he had been sent to save.

Not all gods have shown such filial obedience. When Brahma ordered Siva to create humans, Siva was loathe to do his father's bidding. His anger became so ferocious that he turned it inward and castrated himself. His manhood fell to the ground, penetrated the netherworld, and then catapulted into the heavens as a burning pillar of flames. To this day, natural stones in the shape of Siva's severed organ are venerated by Hindus. A distinguished historian notes that the significance of these phallic stones for Siva worshippers is comparable to the holy cross for Christians, and when the stones have Siva's image cut into them they are kin to statues of Christ on the cross.

Although Christ's glory was the resurrection, Christians have long had a morbid fascination with his mortification, also known as the Passion. Artists have painted so many scenes of the Passion that it is among the most powerful images of the Western cultural tradition. Christ is seen tied to a column while his captors whip him. The wounded Christ is presented to the crowd while Pontius Pilate says, "Behold the man." Christ is nailed to the cross wearing a crown of thorns. Christ is crucified on the cross, his side punctured by the lance of the centurion, Longinus. Christ is lamented and his mother, Mary, is aggrieved. Christ, the Man of Sorrows.

A special genre of art evolved, called *Arma Christi* scenes, that depicted Christ's suffering by the arma (weapons) that he used to conquer death. These paintings display the whips and pincers used to torture Christ, the nails that pinned him to the Cross, a crown of thorns, the bloody knife of his circumcision, even Longinus' lance. In some scenes only the mutilated parts of Christ's body were shown. His wounded heart became a favorite devotional image, with the blood of grace gushing from it.

Paul equated the Church with the body of Christ, and both he and Peter urged Christians to share in Christ's sufferings. Paul, who was beaten and stoned in his travels, said that the marks, or stigmata, on his body were those of Jesus (Gal. 6:17). Many Christians heeded the call to suffer. The Christian Martyrs, especially in the second century, were lashed and torn with hooks, and tested by fire, sword, and beasts. Saint Anthony (251–356) led an exodus of Christians to the solitude of the Egyptian desert, where they refined the concept of mortification. Saint Simeon Stylites, for example, chained his foot to a rock and it became ulcerated and infested with worms. Whenever the worms fell to the ground, Simeon gently placed them back into the wound saying, "Eat what God has given you."

In the thirteenth century Saint Francis of Assisi lived a life of exaggerated suffering after contracting malaria while imprisoned as a youth for battling against Perugia. Upon release from jail he began to hear voices and act strangely, kissing the infected hands of a leper. After Jesus spoke to him he gave away his own money, as well as much that belonged to his father, to repair a decrepit church. When summoned to explain his behavior before the Bishop, he repaid his debts and announced that God was to be his father from then on. He stripped off his clothes and in bold nakedness declared that he intended to serve the Lord.

Francis attracted a group of followers who, like him, were devoted to privation. Even in the coldest weather they went barefoot, wore robes of scratchy wool, avoided the warmth of fires, and lived on the smallest possible rations of food and water. He developed a painful eye disease during a missionary trip to Egypt. By 1224 he was so emaciated that his body ached with pain and sores and he looked like a living cadaver. Then, on September 14, the feast day of the Holy Cross, while he prayed at a retreat, his misery was rewarded. As he fervently contemplated the Passion, he felt himself transformed into Christ. An angel in the form of a crucified man with fiery wings descended from heaven, and Francis saw the face of Christ. As the vision faded, Christ's bloody wounds were transferred to Francis' hands, feet, and side. They persisted until his death two years later, and he was officially proclaimed a saint.

All Europe marveled at the news. When a Dutch monk known as the Blessed Dodo was accidentally killed by a falling wall in 1231, his body bore the five wounds of Jesus. In 1237 a Dominican nun developed the stigmata on October fourth, the Feast of St. Francis. A few years later a Belgian nun named Elizabeth repeatedly reenacted imagined scenes from the Passion while in a trance, violently punching herself and beating her head on the floor. She, too, developed the stigmata, as did her contemporary, the German nun Lukardis, who imagined Christ's crucifixion so deeply that she pounded her palms with her finger tip and bored holes into her feet with her big toes until she acquired the stigmata.

Since St. Francis showed the way, about three hundred cases of the stigmata have been reported, the majority (271) in women. Although many cases are poorly documented, several have undergone medical scrutiny. One of the best known is that of Louise Lateau, who was examined by physicians under the auspices of the Belgian Royal Academy of Medicine.

While very seriously ill with throat abscesses at age eighteen, Louise had her first heavenly visions. A year later, in 1869, she developed the bleeding wounds of the stigmata. From then until her death at age thirty three (the age that Jesus was crucified), she experienced ecstasy and bleeding from her wounds every Friday. She allowed physicians to examine her and to perform experiments. They wrapped her hands with sealed leather gloves and bound her feet in shoes to prevent her from touching the sites of her wounds. When they removed the wrappings the signs of the stigmata were present. They then immobilized her right arm and hand in a glass cast with tight rubber and wax seals. Still the wounds appeared. The physicians noted that when blood was present, Louise was in a state of deep contemplation that often changed to sadness, terror, and contrition. During these periods of ecstasy she claimed that all the scenes of the Passion passed before her eye. The medical conclusion was that the wounds and bleeding appeared spontaneously and were not self-inflicted or caused by other persons.

In the twentieth century, Therese Neumann of Bavaria had stigmata that bled on Fridays for thirty-six years. Blood also fell from her eyes. Since she had a history of episodes of blindness, deafness, and paralysis that suddenly remitted, and since the physicians who examined her overnight were put off by "her frequent manipulations behind the raised coverings," her stigmata were judged to be caused by hysterical psychopathology.

The twentieth century has seen other stigmatics. Padre Pio, an Italian monk, developed lesions in 1918 that stayed open for fifty years until his death. Cloretta Robinson, an eleven-year-old African-American student from Oakland, California, bled from stigmatic wounds for nineteen days during the Easter period in 1972. In 1985 Jane Hunt, a bus driver's wife in England, developed the stigmata while grocery shopping.

What are we to make of this bloody business? Twelve centuries after the Crucifixion, St. Francis was honored by God and given the stigmata. Then, up to current times, sporadic cases have appeared. In his popular book, *The Bleeding Mind*, Ian Wilson examined the phenomenon and concluded that a "profound inner mechanism" is at work. This mechanism is activated by extreme stress: "A recurring feature of stigmatics' case histories is some severe shock such as a serious fall, a near fatal illness, or the death of one or both parents. There also recur the extremes of fasting and mortification which many stigmatics have inflicted on their bodies."

A second feature is a dramatic tendency for altered states of consciousness during which stigmatics see visions and hear voices which usually are traceable to personally familiar religious stories. Their fantastic faith and intense religious beliefs allow them to experience the visions and voices as real. True ecstasy is realized when Christ himself is seen and heard. In this setting the mechanism automatically causes the stigmatic's skin to develop lesions, some of which "have been precisely positioned to conform with the wounds of a stigmatic's favorite crucifix."

Alfred Lechler, a German psychiatrist, wrote a marvelous, little-known book about his experiences in 1932 with a patient named Elizabeth K. As a teenager she suffered from involuntary trembling of her head and limbs. She was paralyzed on her right side following four days of unconsciousness. Her mouth became so distorted that she refused to eat and had to be force-fed. She was intermittently incontinent of urine and feces.

Dr. Lechler hired her to work as a maid in his home while he treated her with hypnotherapy. On Good Friday, after hearing a sermon on Christ's crucifixion, she told Lechler that she could feel the pains of nails being driven into her hands and feet. Knowing the case of Therese Neumann, he implanted a suggestion under hypnosis that Elizabeth concentrate on real nails being hammered into her extremities. The next morning, violá, wounds appeared.

Elizabeth was frightened, but Lechler explained the power of hypnotic suggestion, and she agreed to participate in more experiments. While she was fully conscious he asked her to attend to her daily chores but also to concentrate on photographs of Therese Neumann showing bloody tears flowing from her eyes. Within hours, Elizabeth's face was covered with blood from inside her eyelids. Lechler then suggested that the bloody tears stop flowing. He watched as his suggestion took hold, and Elizabeth's eyes returned to normal.

So there we have it. The skin is a remarkably complex psychosocial organ, although anatomically simple. It functions not only to separate the self from the outer world but also to send inner messages to the outer world when it blushes in embarrassment, flushes in anger, or blanches in fear. Through intense, focused concentration which may be self-induced as well as induced by others, suggestible persons can create all sorts of images and lesions on their skin from the mark of the beast to a rosy crucifix.

The stigmatic's creation of wounds is not necessarily willful. When the creation is the work of the unconscious mind, the result may be surprise and bafflement. Still, it is also probably fair to say that a large proportion of stigmata cases are bogus, a pathetic conscious attempt at fame and glory.

THE FORESKIN SAGA

Male circumcision surely ranks among the behavioral oddities of the world. Men and psychoanalysts, ever fascinated by penises, have tried to understand these admittedly quirky organs but have not been able to explain the why of circumcision. Why do men assault their penis with knives? Why carve out even the smallest portion when there isn't that much to start with?

There are rational explanations aplenty, but none ring true. For cleanliness? Perhaps, rarely. As a form of birth control? Not at all effective. Philo of Alexandria, a first-century philosopher, said that it curbed sexual desire, but we all know better. The real reason, maybe, is that the penis provokes seemingly irrational behavior because it seems to have a mind of its own. It arises at odd times, during sleep or a church service or a football game, whenever it likes. Or it may lay low despite the impassioned pleas of its so-called master to rise to the occasion. It can be most disrespectful when it wants to be.

By understanding the nature of the organ, the origin of circumcision during the childhood of the human race can be explained somewhat reasonably. Let us imagine the dawn of human existence when the primal horde of middle-aged men were faced with the dilemma of the unruly penis. As they bonded around a campfire in the forest beating on their drums, they sang sophomoric songs and shared sad stories about how their penis let them down. Since they were both primitive and men, their repertoire of remedial possibilities was limited. The fire's sparks inflamed their primal minds and violent talk erupted. One man, a therapist perhaps, certainly a genius in those times, listened attentively as he idly whittled a branch with a sharp rock. Then a prodigious idea popped into his consciousness. Just as unruly women and children must be scared into submission, so too must the penis. With the sharp rock in one hand and the whittled branch in the other, he gazed at his loins and the solution became clear. We can tame the little brute by whittling its tip. We'll bloody its nose, so to speak, and teach it a lesson it will never forget. And we'll nip it in the bud when our sons are young, before the penis has a chance to become headstrong. In such a transcendent moment circumcision may have been conceived, and the rest is history.

The Bible provides religious explanation for circumcision among the Jews, although Jeremiah (9:25) states that other Semitic groups—Edomites, Ammonites, Moabites—were circumcisers. All the Semites probably learned about the practice from the Egyptians, who had been gashing their foreskins since 4000 B.C. both singly and en masse. A stone marker from the twenty-third century tells of about 120 men who were circumcised at the same time. A stone relief on a tomb of that period shows a priest removing a boy's foreskin and saying to an assistant, "Hold him and don't let him faint."

The most widely known account of the origin of Jewish circumcision appears in Genesis 15–17. Abram, the great-grandson of Noah, was promised land by God as a reward for doing his bidding but was upset because he had no child as an heir. God told him that he would have lots of children. Abram demanded proof, so God instructed him to cut a heifer, a goat, and a ram in two pieces. This done, God made a covenant with him and gave his descendants all the land between the Nile and the Euphrates Rivers. Abram, at age 86, sired a son. A decade later, Abram spoke again with God and learned of a second covenant: his name would be changed to Abraham (father of a multitude), kings and nations would be among his offspring and they would have perpetual possession of the land. In return, all of Abraham's male descendants as well as their slaves ought to be circumcised. Circumcision was a sign of the agreement: "My covenant shall be in your flesh for an everlasting covenant." That very day Abraham, his son, his male relatives and all their slaves were circumcised, and so have most Jewish lads ever since.

As noted in an essay by Erich Isaac, Judaism has never allowed bodily modification or mutilation; even tattoos and scarification are forbidden. Circumcision goes against the grain of the religion, and it was not unique to the ancient Jews anyway. Exactly why God chose the procedure is unclear although the parallels between the two covenants with Abraham suggest that slicing serves the paradoxical purpose of binding things together. "Even today we cut silk ribbons when inaugurating bridges and highways: we thereby symbolize the joining together of places that were previously separate."

The Abraham story appears early in the first book of the Bible. A reader might assume that it is the earliest written piece on circumcision. However, the story was written and inserted into Genesis in the fifth century B.C. by Jewish priests who codified the Bible. They were familiar with Hittite and Greek ceremonies in which agreements were bound by marching between divided animals. The process was a symbolic warning: those who failed to keep the agreement would end up like the slaughtered animals. The priests made circumcision a sign rather than an integral part of God's covenant. It was a mark that identified those who would benefit from the covenant, but it did not necessarily exclude the uncircumcised. According to Jewish law it is not necessary to be circumcised in order to be a Jew (although it surely doesn't hurt one's chances); any child of a Jewish mother is automatically a Jew.

The earliest biblical reference to circumcision, written in the tenth century, is the difficult story in Exodus 4. Moses, his wife (Zipporah), and his children were traveling back to Egypt. God ordered Moses to tell Pharaoh that all firstborn Egyptian sons will be killed. Then, "The Lord met him and tried to kill him." Zipporah, a quick thinker and model crisis intervention expert, saved the day by immediately cutting off her son's foreskin. She cast the bit o' flesh at Moses' feet and said, "Surely you are a husband of blood to me because of the circumcision." So God let him go. Most of the fuzzy interpretations of the brief episode consider the "him" that God wanted to kill as Moses. If so, then God's murderous motive is difficult to divine and Zipporah's words are unintelligible. A recent interpretation is that the "him" refers to Moses' son who was to share the fate of the Egyptian sons since his mother was not Jewish but rather Midianite. In her native language the word for circumcision was the same as the Hebrew word for husband. She said of her son, "You are mine, circumcised with blood," thus saving him from death. As if this story isn't confusing enough, shortly afterwards in the text God orders Moses to tell Pharaoh to let the children of Israel out of his land. Whereupon Moses laments, "The children of Israel have not heeded me. How then shall Pharaoh heed me, for I am of uncircumcised lips?"

Undoubtedly the strangest circumcision story is told in 1 Samuel 18. David wanted to marry the daughter of King Saul, but sour Saul was violently jealous of David's popularity. David was definitely the crowd favorite, and even cheerleaders sang songs about him. Saul tried every trick to prevent David from becoming his son-in-law, but

David persisted, not knowing that Saul had an ace up his sleeve. In Peckinpaugh-ish delight he told David that a dowry wasn't necessary. Instead, he told him to "bring me the foreskins of one hundred Philistines." He reckoned that the procuring of a hundred enemy foreskins would not exactly be a piece of cake. David and his men not only came back with a hundred foreskins, but also brought a hundred extra as icing! David got his wife, but in the bargain Saul become David's enemy. There probably is a lesson to be learned from this, some moral for the ages but, unfortunately, neither Talmudic scholars nor Christian allegorists nor I have any idea what it is.

Circumcision as dirty pool is found in the Genesis story of Jacob's daughter, Dinah. Shechem, the son of a Hivite prince, loved her, chatted her up, maybe even strummed his lyre to amuse her while she cooked, and ended up raping her. Jacob's anger was not assuaged even when Shechem asked to marry Dinah, and he devised a fiendish plot. Shechem would be allowed to marry her, and other Hivites would be allowed to marry women in Jacob's camp, but only if they agreed to be circumcised. The hot Hivites agreed to the procedure. On the third day, while they were recuperating and weak with pain, Dinah's brothers killed them all.

We have encountered circumcisions as a sign of a covenant, a price to be paid for a bride, and as a vengeful ploy. The Old Testament also figuratively applies it to unspecified fruit (what possibilities!) and to various body parts. After planting trees, the fruit should not be eaten right away. "Three years it shall be uncircumcised to you. It shall not be eaten" (Lev. 19:23). Mention has already been made of Moses' uncircumcised lips, but ears, too, can be affected: "To whom shall I speak and give warning, that they may hear? Indeed their ear is uncircumcised, and they cannot give heed." (Jer. 6:10). But prize of place, after the penis, goes to the heart: "And the Lord your God will circumcise your heart and the heart of your descendants, to love the Lord your God with all your heart and with all your soul, that you may live" (Deut. 30:6).

Enter Alexander the Great, conqueror of much of the known world, and with him Greek culture. Alexander died in 323 B.C., but Greek culture flourished brilliantly. Many Jews, especially those of the upper social class, adopted the Greek language, Greek names, and Greek customs, especially sports. Released from the stifling demands of Jewish law, they reveled in their new-found freedom. Jason, the Jewish high priest, even built a gymnasium in Jerusalem where naked men and boys worked out, bulked up, and played games.

A Syrian dynasty won control of the area and its leader, Antiochus IV, looted gold from the Jewish temple in Jerusalem in order to finance his war against Egypt (171 B.C.). Some Jews fought back, and Antiochus responded by outlawing the Jewish religion and circumcision. He forced the populace to worship Greek gods, burned all copies of the Mosaic law, and built an altar to Zeus in Jerusalem's temple. These high-handed tactics stirred a full-scale Jewish revolt under the leadership of the Maccabees, who defeated the superior Syrian forces and established a friendship treaty with Rome.

The Maccabees forced a return to traditional values, especially circumcision, and they even forcibly circumcised Jewish boys whose families were Greekified. In the traditional procedure, known as *milah*, only the tip of the prepuce was cut off. Many circumcised Jews who either converted to paganism or simply emulated Greek customs tried to conceal evidence of the *milah* through a blistering process that enlarged the remaining foreskin. Disembarrassed, these Adonis wannabes proudly strutted their stuff in the gym. The Maccabean revolt put an end to such nonsense. From then on the entire foreskin was removed during circumcision and the frenum was split. This new periah circumcision was permanent and beyond the capacity of plastic surgeons to repair.

Jesus referred to circumcision only once. When he sensed that an angry conservative crowd might murder him because he had performed a healing on the Sabbath, he told them that if they allowed circumcision on the Sabbath then surely they should allow healing (John 7:19–23).

Jesus' silence reflects his underestimation of circumcision's divisive potential. Shortly after his death the small band of believers discovered that the formation of a new religion was no easy task. They had neither a literature (the Gospels had not yet been written), nor a comprehensive theology, nor temples, nor priests. They didn't even have a name for their religion. Yet they understood that their movement would be dead in the water without converts from the pool of Jews and Gentiles. In short order, however, the flabby foreskin became a bone of contention.

Jewish converts believed that Jesus did not overthrow the old law but rather fulfilled it; since Jesus himself was circumcised, so too must every man who desired to become a Christian. Gentile converts regarded Judaism as a tribal or regional religion and were put off by the strange complexities of Jewish law. They certainly were not going to put their penises on the chopping block.

Peter and Paul led small groups of recruiters among the Jews and the Gentiles. They attempted to preach Christ crucified, but this was a stumbling block to the Jews, who asked for signs, and foolishness to the Gentiles, who sought wisdom. Sooner or later, everywhere they went, the issue of circumcision vexed them. The Jewish converts' insistence that all Christians must be circumcised threatened to destroy the new religion as it was aborning. If their position won out, then the large Gentile population probably would have dismissed Christianity as just another Jewish sect without universal relevance.

The issue had to be settled, and so the very first Church council was held in Jerusalem in 49 A.D. Peter, Paul and Barnabas attended, as did the apostles and church elders. Emotions ran so high that the Bible contains two contradictory accounts of what happened. In Paul's version (Gal. 2), written a few years after the council, neither circumcision nor any adherence to the old law of Moses was determined to be necessary. In the version reported in Acts 15, written more than a decade after the council, a compromise was reached: Gentiles didn't need to be circumcised, but they did need to follow some precepts of the old law such as abstinence from certain foods, from idolatry, and from sexual immorality.

In fact, the circumcision problem continued to fester, and Paul admonished its proponents. He warned that those who circumcised in the belief that they could be justified by holding to the law really were estranging themselves from Christ: "For in Christ Jesus neither circumcision nor uncircumcision avails anything, but faith working through love" (Gal 5:6). He railed against those persons who desired to circumcise others "that they may glory in your flesh" (Gal. 6:13). He warned against dogs and evildoers who mutilate the flesh "for we are the circumcision who worship God in the spirit, rejoice in Christ Jesus, and have no confidence in the flesh" (Phil. 3:2-3). He argued that Abraham, the father of circumcision, was blessed and justified by faith *before* he was circumcised. At one point Paul was so angry at the agitators who were turning Christians against each other over this issue that he wished they would castrate themselves (Gal. 5:12)!

Despite these harsh words, Paul softened his tone at times in order not to alienate the pro-circumcisers totally. He said that men who already were circumcised shouldn't try to remove the mark of the procedure (Cor. 7:18), and that the Jews profited from circumcision because God entrusted them with "oracles" (a reference probably to the Old Testament scriptures) (Romans 3:1-2). On one occasion he even had his companion, Timothy, circumcised, in order to make him more acceptable to the Jews that they were trying to convert (Acts 16:3). Paul was the ultimate pragmatist: "To the Jews I became as a Jew, in order to win Jews . . . I have become all things to all men, that I might by all means save some" (1 Cor. 9:18-22).

Paul's beliefs prevailed and, over time, circumcision lost its sting. Christianity left the Jews behind and progressed into the larger

Roman world where circumcision was not culturally acceptable. In fact, the Roman emperor Hadrian punished the Jews for their revolt (132–135 C.E.) by forbidding them to circumcise their non-Jewish slaves. Circumcision then dropped out of the historical news except for odd snippets. In the seventh century, for example, the Spanish Visigoths passed a law that punished circumcisers with death by stoning or burning alive. In the Middle Ages, Christians, hoping to gain support for the Crusades, accused the Turks of horrible deeds: "For they circumcise Christian boys and youths over the baptismal fonts of churches and spill the blood of circumcision right into the baptismal fonts and compel them to blaspheme the name of the Holy Trinity." Jesus' foreskin was claimed as a true relic by no less than a dozen churches. Cloistered nuns during the fourteenth century had visions of the foreskin; St. Birgitta saw the Virgin Mary hold it in her hand, and St. Agnes saw herself swallowing it every January first, the day of the Feast of Jesus' circumcision.

When two male infants in New York City died shortly after their ritual circumcision, Paul Weiss performed a worldwide survey of the current practice of ritual Jewish circumcision in 1962. He described the historical progression from *milah* to *periah* and, finally, to *metsitsah*. In this last procedure, developed in the Talmudic era (about the sixth-century A.D.), the circumciser sucks blood from the infant's newly circumcised penis into his mouth. Although widespread and currently practiced among some Orthodox Jews, *metsitsah* was not universally adopted.

Jewish circumcision is a religious ritual that is performed typically on the infant's eighth day of life by a mohel (a male ritual circumciser). In nineteenth-century Europe, reform rabbis agitated to improve the hygiene of the procedure, but these advances were delayed in the United States because of the shortage of mohalim, many of whom were itinerant. In addition to death from hemorrhage, a mohel sometimes passed tuberculosis to the infants, probably by the bloodsucking procedure.

In 1914, a Board of Milah was established in New York City and a pamphlet produced in conjunction with the city Department of Health. Sanitary procedures were recommended (e.g., "Sucking the wound with the mouth is absolutely prohibited and any mohel found resorting to this practice will be barred from the certified list"). In fact, the procedure for *metsitsah* had slowly been changing: a glass tube was used to draw blood. That the issue still burns is attested to by a meeting of the Los Angeles Rabbinate in 1988. A Hasidic mohel wondered if traditional *metsitsah* was still to be practiced during these times of AIDS. Since "whoever observes a commandment will not experience evil," he argued that the traditional practice should not be altered. After much scholarly discussion, a common sense recommendation was made to discontinue *metsitsah* during the present AIDS dilemma.

Psychoanalysts have made wondrous speculations about the meaning of circumcision. On the one hand, it stems from primal fathers who castrated their sons in jealousy; on the other hand, it stems from bisexual yearnings (cutting off the foreskin symbolically results in a person who is more like a female). From a religious standpoint, the gods demand sacrifices. The earliest gods demanded human sacrifice. Later gods, often associated with phallic worship and fertility cults, demanded "sacrifice" of only the genitals either through castration or through sexual orgies that left the phallus limp. Finally, the One God demanded only a sign, namely circumcision. In this respect, one God was an evolutionary advance; Abraham did not have to sacrifice his child, only nip his foreskin.

Freud felt that anxiety about castration occurs when people think of Jews because "even in the nursery little boys hear that a Jew has something cut off his penis . . . and this gives them a right to despise Jews." This castration anxiety, the deepest unconscious root of anti-Semitism, arises out of two unconscious fears: if the Jew is "castrated," then maybe I will be castrated, and the Jew who is mutilated by circumcision may seek revenge by mutilating me.

Medically there is no reason for circumcision. Even Dr. Spock writes that "there is no excuse for the operation—except as a religious rite. So, I strongly recommend leaving the foreskin alone." It isn't a terribly pleasant surgical procedure, especially since no anesthesia is used. Some adult men claim that circumcision results in a dry and less-sensitive tip of the penis. This is true in theory but doesn't seem to make much difference in the heat of grappling. Among circumcised homosexuals there is a small group with such a passionate desire to regain their lost foreskin that they are willing to undergo reconstructive surgery. This procedure requires not only four operations spread out over a year but also a lot of counseling. It hurts a lot, both physically and financially.

A far greater problem is that of female circumcision. About it I will say little except to note that it was practiced in the age of the pharaohs and has been perfected in modern Egypt, Sudan, and other African nations. The term pharaonic circumcision refers to a harsh procedure in which a young girl's clitoris is removed, the labia scraped, and the vagina sewn shut except for a little opening. The virginity of the girl and the purity and cleanliness of her womb are protected, but the cost in pain and physical morbidity is high. A faux pas in the translation of religious materials unwittingly fostered the practice among the Kikuyu tribe in Kenya at a time when the British government and Presbyterian missionaries were struggling to prohibit it. It seems that the Kikuyu word for virgin refers to a girl who has been circumcised. If the procedure is so terrible, reasoned the natives, why do Christians praise virgins in general, and the Virgin Mary in particular, when they had been clipped, scraped, and closed up? The African anecdote is not all that quaint. Centuries earlier, some European devotees of Mary believed that the events of her life duplicated those of Jesus. Since Jesus had been circumcised, they reasoned, so too had Mary.

PRAISE THE LORD AND PASS THE MEDICATION:
HEALING AND FEELING GOOD

CHAPTER 8

Long, long ago, when bison roamed Europe and hairy humans sought shelter in caves, the healing of disease and the reversal of misery were entrusted throughout much of the world to spiritually powerful men and women known as shamans. Biology and science did not exist then. Illness and ill-fortune occurred when a person's soul left the body accidentally or due to a spiritual transgression or was stolen by an enemy, or when a body was invaded and possessed by a malign spirit, or when a person was the object of a sorcerer's magic. The shaman's job was to retrieve lost souls, to pacify and exorcise spirits, and to provide counter-magic, often by supposedly sucking out harmful stones and animal parts from a person's body. These were not tasks for the dull-witted or squeamish, for they could be accomplished only by contact with the frightening realm of the supernatural. Shamans had to be adept not only at dealing with spirits, but also at convincing tribal members that their diagnostic and healing practices were useful and based on reality.

As civilization slowly developed, the bison were slaughtered and humans climbed out of their caves into huts and houses. Formal religion was established, and shamans were transformed into healing priests and priestesses. Most priests gradually specialized in inserting themselves between gods and humans, leaving physicians to deal with new-fangled scientific notions about the causes and treatment of disease.

Long before the modern era, when spirits and diseases were still connected, healing the sick was central to the ministry of Jesus. He encouraged his apostles to preach and to heal. Let's examine what the Bible has to say about disease and treatment, for there are many unanswered questions. What happened to all the demons that Christ encountered? Should priests be doing more healing? Can patients be cured by incantations? How can pseudo-healers be identified? Do Prozac and prayers mix well? Is suffering from disease truly a blessing or a punishment from God?

MY SON, THE DOCTOR

Although Jewish doctors have made enormous contributions to medicine in general and to psy-

243

chiatry in particular, the ancient Hebrews did not believe in professional physicians. They had midwives with whom God dealt well because they defied Pharaoh's order to kill all newborn Jewish boys (Exodus 1:16-20). They had healers who splinted broken bones (Ezek. 30:21), prescribed mandrake root for infertility (Gen. 30:14) and balm for wounds (Jer. 46:11), but if they wanted a real doctor, they would have needed to travel to Egypt.

Egyptian physicians were either general practitioners, exorcists, or specialists. Poor people received inexpensive treatments such as bandages, honey dressings (quite effective for preventing germ growth), and incantations. Royalty and wealthy people paid for the best medical care, which often consisted of sophisticated enemas to stimulate the cardiovascular system and to rid the body of harmful feces. Egyptians were quite finicky about putrefaction, so they embalmed corpses to prevent the decay of the dead body and constantly cleaned their bowels hoping to prevent the decay of the living body.

Perhaps the Hebrews didn't need physicians, because they were basically healthy and lived long lives. Old man Methuselah, for example, supposedly lived to the truly ripe age of 969 years. But in Psalms 90:10, a more reasonable seventy years is presented as a lifetime. Then comes old age, which really isn't much fun: pleasure in living is lost, terrors come upon us, desire fails, and people that look in through the windows grow dim as our eyesight dwindles (Eccl. 12:1-5).

Didn't the Hebrews get sick? Of course they did. Leprosy is described prominently in the Old Testament. It was a catchall phrase for a variety of skin conditions including eczema, psoriasis, vitiligo (patchy depigmentation), and ringworm as well as true leprosy (Hansen's disease). Among other conditions mentioned are gonorrhea (Numbers 5:2), dysentery (2 Chronicles 21:18-19), spinal column deformities, poliomyelitis (2 Samuel 4:4), bubonic plague (1 Samuel 5-6), stroke (1 Kings 13:4), malingering (1 Samuel 21:12-15), sciatica (Gen. 32:22-32), blindness, pituitary tumor (causing "giants" such as Goliath), senility and possible syphilis (King David), and intestinal cancer (2 Maccabees 9:5-27). King Saul was manic depressive and Nabal alcoholic (1 Samuel 25:36-38).

The Old Testament attributes most disease to God's retribution. In Deuteronomy God threatened the disobedient with consumption, severe burning, fever, inflammation, mildew, boils, tumors, scabs, untreatable itch, madness, blindness, and confusion. In God's own words, "I kill and I make alive; I wound and I heal...I will render vengeance to my enemies." This is not a touchy-feely God! Obey him and you get blessed, disobey him and you get blasted. The rules were clear enough. Then we meet Job, who suffered and tried to reason with God since mortals were both forgers of lies and worthless physicians. God allowed Satan to strike Job "with painful boils from the sole of his foot to the crown of his head." Here disease was part of God's plan and had nothing to do with any transgression, although all of Job's acquaintances shunned him because they assumed that he must have been a big-time sinner. Even his wife urged him to "Curse God and die." There's no point in second guessing or, heaven forbid, battling with the Lord. All that any man can do is trust God's judgement, accept unjust suffering, keep the faith, and repent. That's what Job did, and he lived to be a rich old man, the proud possessor of 14,000 sheep, 6,000 camels, 1,000 yoke of oxen, 1,000 female donkeys, seven sons, three beautiful daughters, and a passel of grandchildren.

Since God caused diseases, it seemed only logical to look to God for cures. Exodus 15:17 is the definitive Old Testament statement on God the healer: "If you diligently heed the voice of the Lord your God and do what is right in his sight, give ear to his commandments and keep all his statutes, I will put none of the diseases on you which I have brought on the Egyptians. For I am the Lord who heals you." Unfortunately, the stiff-necked Hebrews didn't always turn to God for healing.

Sick persons sometimes sought help in heathen temples. Ahaziah, for example, sent a messenger to Baal-Zebub to ask if he would recover from a fall. This action angered Elijah, who said, "Is it because there is no God in Israel that you are going to inquire of Baal-Zebub?...You shall surely die." (2 Kings 1:1–4). The sick must have sought help from spiritualists too because God clearly warned them to avoid soothsayers, sorcerers, interpreters of omens, practicers of witchcraft, spell conjurers, mediums, and those who call up the dead (Deut. 18:10–11). Healers (sometimes translated as "physicians") also were used by the sick, but the results were not good. When King Asa of Judah developed a severe foot disease, "he did not seek the Lord, but the physicians" (2 Chron. 16:12). As might be expected, he died. Asa possibly had gout or, strange to say, a disease of his sexual organs which the Hebrews euphemistically referred to as "feet."

Probably the most common acceptable "treatment" for sick Hebrews was prayer. The model for this approach was Hezekiah who, ill and near death, turned his face to the wall, cried and prayed to the Lord. God responded, "I have heard your prayer, I have seen your tears; surely I will add to your days fifteen years" (Is. 38:1–5). Another route for healing was to consult a prophet. Elisha's medical abilities were formidable, although he couldn't cure his own baldness (2

Kings). He did mouth-to-mouth resuscitation on a boy, detoxified a poisoned stew, and purified foul water. He told Naaman to wash himself seven times in the Jordan River to cure his leprosy. Naaman followed the advice and "his flesh was restored like the flesh of a little child, and he was clean." A third option was to visit a holy temple as did Hannah. She was infertile, but after her trip to the temple at Shiloh, God granted her petition and she became pregnant (1 Samuel 1). King David received a very special treatment (1 Kings 1:1–4). It was his obligation to invigorate through his fertility both his subjects and their crops, but he was frosty with old age and everyone was worried. An impotent king had to abdicate his position. David's servants tried to warm him with covers, but he remained limp. Next, they searched the entire territory of Israel for the most ravishing female of all. Their choice was Abishag the Shunamite. Her job was to "excite him and lie with him" (the King James Bible says "let her care for him and let her lie in your bosom"). She "served him: but the King did not know her." Once Abishag blabbed, word must have gotten around pretty fast because in the very next sentence David's son, Adonijah, exalted himself and declared, "I will be king."

The Hebrews led a spiritualized life in which God's handiwork was implicit in every event. Today we understand drought to be a natural environmental disaster, war a social calamity, family break-ups an interpersonal crisis, illness a biological event, but the Hebrews would have viewed God as the prime mover in each of these incidents. We disassociate mind from body but the Hebrews dealt with the entire person, almost always in a religious context. The primary metaphorical body organ in ancient Israel was the heart, which was regarded as the center of emotions, intellect, memory, thought, sense of morality, and personality. Thus the heart can be sad or glad, hardened or pure. When God promised to renew Israel he said, "I will give you a new heart and put a new spirit within you; I will take the heart of stone out of your flesh and give you a heart of flesh" (Ezek. 36:26). When David lost his potency, his subjects became disheartened; the time had come in God's plan for new kings to lead Israel.

Because they diminished God's position, formal medical practice and magic were disdained by the early Hebrews. In order to remain healthy and to have a good heart, the best approach was to follow God's rules as written in the code of Moses. Many of the rules were, in fact, incidentally beneficial to public health. Rest one day a week. Eat vegetables with impunity but avoid pork (pigs probably were sacred to some Semitic group; Moses didn't know that pork is often infested with parasites). Don't pollute the water supply. No incest.

Wash frequently. Bury human excreta. Obey these rules and you not only stay on God's good side but you also decrease the possibility of getting sick.

Things started to change in about the fourth century B.C. after the Hebrews returned from their exile in Babylon. The priestly writers who re-edited the Bible put such an emphasis on purity that physically "impure" humans, such as lepers, the blind, and the lame, were treated badly and excluded from the Holy Temple (Lev. 13–14; 2 Sam. 5–7). Perhaps it is purely coincidental, but the attitude towards physicians began to change as handicapped and chronically ill persons were increasingly stigmatized by the priests. By 180 B.C., Jesus the Son of Sirach wrote that physicians are needed and should be honored (Ecclesiasticus 38). Likewise, sensible persons should take medicines that heal and take away pain. When you are sick, you should pray to the Lord for healing, but "There is a time when success lies in the hands of a physician."

CHRIST CURES: NO QUESTIONS ASKED

Jesus wasn't your typical rabbi. His distinctiveness is nowhere more apparent than in his approach to the sick, many of whom were disenfranchised from full participation in Temple activities. He actually *welcomed* the sick as well as a lot of socially marginal and even despised persons such as the blind, eunuchs, hunchbacks, dwarfs, cripples, tax collectors and prostitutes. He probably even would have welcomed lawyers and telemarketers had they existed back then, as sure a sign as any of his godliness.

He healed people on an "as needed" basis without any hocus pocus or ritual fol-de-rol. The sick didn't need to make an appointment because he was always on call, even on Wednesday afternoons and the Sabbath. He didn't take a medical or social history, didn't do a physical examination, didn't order laboratory tests or a wallet biopsy, and didn't require confessions or a therapeutic relationship. Perhaps most important, he didn't blame the sick for being sick, a truly revolutionary attitude. This is clearly portrayed in John 9:2 when his disciples asked him about a man: "Rabbi, who sinned, this man or his parents, that he was born blind?" Although this really was an inane question because the man would have had to sin while a fetus, Jesus nonetheless replied that "neither this man nor his parents sinned, but that the works of God should be revealed in him."

So central was healing to Christ's ministry and self-identity that when the imprisoned John the Baptist sent two disciples to ask him if he was the Messiah, he told them to tell John that "The blind see again and the lame walk; lepers are cleansed and the deaf hear; the dead are raised, and the poor have the good news preached to them" (Matt. 11:4-5). Although it is unlikely that Christ actually said these exact words, the episode tells us that the early Christians accepted Christ as the Messiah in great part because he healed the sick, thus accomplishing what had been foretold in the Old Testament.

Almost twenty percent of the Gospels are devoted to Christ's forty-one healing encounters with individuals and with groups. His usual technique was to say a few words while he touched the sick person. Sometimes he just spoke, while on two occasions he just touched. He applied his saliva to the tongue of a deaf mute and to the eyes of a blind person (Mark 7:33-34, 8:23); once he applied a mixture of saliva with mud to another blind person's eyes (John 9:6-7). A woman with vaginal bleeding of twelve year's duration was cured by touching his robe (Mark 5:25-34). Jesus obtained rapid results on the first try, except for the blind man at Bethsaida who needed two treatments (Mark. 8:22-25).

What types of illness did he heal? The list includes the fever of Peter's mother-in-law, eleven lepers, a man with palsy and one with dropsy or edema, the severed ear of the High Priest's servant who had arrested him, a crippled man, a boy and a girl on the brink of death, the woman with vaginal bleeding, a man's withered hand, a centurion's paralyzed servant, the dead son of a widow, four blind men, the blind and the lame in the Temple, a blind, mute man, and a veritable dumpster of demons.

The list of healings is impressive and contains triumphs over both physical and spiritual/psychological disorders. In comparison with the Old Testament, however, disproportionate attention is given to demons. It seems that every time Christ turned around, he bumped into a demon. Where did they all come from?

THE DEVIL YOU SAY: THE RISE OF DEMONS

In the oldest notion, a demon or daemon was equivalent to a god whose power was also regarded as a spirit. When a spirit entered a body, where did it reside? Its most obvious abode was the lungs because breath equals life. At death, when we expire for the very last time, it was thought that our air and our spirit left our lungs and exited out the mouth and nose. This connection still exists linguistically; the Greek word *phren* refers both to the mind, as in schizophrenia, and to the diaphragm, the muscular partition between the chest and abdomen that participates in respiration.

Loose in the world, evil spirits were like ill winds that brought proverbial bad luck, bad news, and bad air (such as mal-aria). Good spirits, on the other hand, brought blessings and good fortune. The single Hebrew God turned the good spirits into angels but reserved for himself a mighty Holy Spirit that ever since has intervened in the lives of the righteous.

A motley group of demons (evil spirits) populate the Old Testament, but they never really dominate events. Representative demons such as the night creature (Is. 34:15), the ghoul, a.k.a. the leech (Prov. 30:15), and the king of terrors (Job 18:14) are fairly forgettable in the great scheme of things. Psalm 91:5-6 lists four demons: the terror in the night, the arrow that flies in the day, the pestilence that walks in darkness, and the midday demon. It's all a bit confusing because proper names and common names seem to be used interchangeably. The terror in the night, for example, probably refers to a particular demon named "Terror," but it also might mean exactly what it says. Whether name or noun it was advisable to avoid contact with demons through fumigation (Lev. 16:12-13), wearing clothes with a blue thread (Num. 15:38), and placing cylinders with demon-keep-away-from-my-door messages at the entryway of houses. Even the well-known Passover story in which the Lord promised not to kill anyone who smeared lamb's blood on their doorpost is a historical revision and a rationalized account of an identical ancient practice to frighten away evil spirits during the spring barley harvest. Some of the original version is evident in Exodus 12:13 when the Lord says that he will pass over the houses with the blood, and the plague demon "shall not be on you to destroy you when I strike the land of Egypt."

When the Israelites were captives in Babylon they encountered a powerful and popular religion founded by the old prophet Zoroaster, or Zarathustra. They learned about the never-ending conflict between the Good God with his angels and the Evil God with his devils. It made sense to blame adversity on legions of evil spirits, but the Jewish priests weren't about to grant them a godlike status. Some believed that they were angels of destruction sent by God to punish sinners, or that they were rebellious angels whose leaders were Satan, Belial (Beelzebub), Azazel, and Mastema.

If hard times, fear, divisiveness, neurosis, and cruelty are demons or are caused by demons, then Christ's world had to be infested with them. The valiant Maccabean revolt resulted in Roman control of the area and with it came tyrannical rulers. The Book of Daniel, full of horrible visions, was the talk of the town. The progressive Pharisees and the conservative Sadducees had at each other, the Zealots attacked the Romans, while the Essenes escaped to the desert. Belief that the woeful Last Times had started made everyone jittery. Even Jesus preached about earthquakes, arrests, wars, beatings, false prophets, falling stars, and the destruction of the Temple (Mark 13).

When the center no longer holds and nature fragments, when people sense that control over their destiny is slipping, when the Hotel California becomes a metaphor for life, that is when demons rush from the wastelands of the mind into consciousness. In Christ's time disease and distress were not thought to originate within the minds and bodies of humans but were perceived as demonic attacks from outside. They struck suddenly, sapping the vitality from vulnerable people. They assaulted brains and chests, causing strokes, seizures, and heart attacks. They gripped bowels. They struck people deaf, mute, blind, and dead. They besieged and paralyzed with fear. They assailed sensibilities and pounded heads until they ached.

Christ gave his twelve disciples as well as all believers the power to cast out unclean spirits (Mark 16:17; Matt. 10:1, Luke 9:1). Once Paul used his power to remove a demon from a slave girl who earned money for her masters by telling fortunes. Without her demon she couldn't see the future anymore. Her masters became enraged. Paul paid the price for his own lack of foresight; he was beaten and thrown into prison (Acts 16:16–24).

In the early centuries of Christianity both clergy and laypersons performed exorcisms, and the Western Church even established an ordained, minor order of exorcists. In the Greek Orthodox Church exorcisms were quite common for the evil eye, a powerful force motivated by jealousy that caused a host of psychological and physical symptoms in persons who were afflicted by it. St. Basil (300–379) and St. John Chrysostom (347–407) helped to develop special prayers: "I exorcise you by Jesus Christ ... by God Pantocreator ... Depart, unclean and abominable demon! Infernal, abysmal, deceptive, shapeless, visible because of your shamelessness, invisible because of your hypocrisy, foul-smelling, greedy, fornicating ... God, take away from your servant every working of the Devil, all sorcery, witchcraft, drugaddiction, idolatry, astrology, horoscopy, necromancy, passion for pleasure, eros, wrath, instability, and every evil fancy." Additionally, exorcists often made the sign of the cross, laid hands on their subjects, and encouraged them to exhale their demons, while water made pure and holy by exorcism was used in a blessing.

For about five hundred years most demons went into hibernation. They were aroused in the eleventh century when the calmness of European social order during the Middle Ages was shattered by conflicts between church and state. The Popes declared their superiority over kings and their intention to rule over the temporal as well as the spiritual world. "Rebellious" kings were humbled by excommunication and were called Antichrists. People's loyalties were pulled in opposite directions. The kings had might on their side, but the Popes had an army more deadly and more vicious, an army of clerical lawyers. For every theologian at the papal court, there were supposedly twenty lawyers. The exquisitely detailed codification of canon laws in 1140 allowed Popes to intervene in the affairs of everyone. All roads led to Rome because the Christian world, according to the Popes, was their church.

The social order was in flux. Monasteries that once offered spiritual respite now entered into the bustling world of commerce. Bishops and religious orders sued each other for financial gain. Thomas Becket was put to death, a supposed martyr, because he argued that criminal priests should not be punished by the English king but rather by the Church, and that "princes should bow their heads to bishops rather than judge them." The papacy moved from Rome to Avignon, and two Popes claimed supremacy at the same time. One obviously was not the real Pope, but which one? Crusaders marched to battle Moslems but slaughtered Jews as well as fellow Christians. Mob violence was rampant. Groups who sought to purify the Church were labeled heretics, captured, and put to death. Bubonic plague killed hundreds of thousands of people. Flagellant cult members whipped themselves in the streets. Prophets proclaimed the end of the world. Repent before it's too late.

No self-respecting demon could sleep through such times. Fed by human fear, natural and unnatural disasters, hysteria, and religious fervor, the demons of Christ's time roamed the earth again. St. Bernard of Clairvaux (1090–1153) was one of the first to confront them. Just before saying mass he saw a demon-possessed little girl. He dipped his fingers into his chalice and put some wine on the girl's lips. "Immediately Satan, scalded, could not endure the virtue of this infusion. Thanks to this urgent remedy from the Cross he came forth hastily, all trembling, in a stinking vomit."

Demons were especially fond of priests and nuns. When they invaded the sedate Ursuline convent at Aix-en-Provence in 1611, all Europe took notice. A forceful social climber named Father Louis Gaufredi seduced a young girl who was then sent to the convent. She developed convulsions, saw visions of demons, and even defiled a crucifix. Clearly she was possessed, and soon another young nun in the convent became possessed as well. They publicly announced the names of all the demons within them: the archfiend Beelzebub, Leviathan, Asmodeus, Astoroth, Baalbirith, Verrine, Grisel, Sonnillon, and 6,661 others! Gaufredi was put to death on the recommendation of the Inquisitors who tried his case. Alas, the two nuns did not benefit by his death; the first was cured for a while but was then imprisoned for witchcraft, while the second remained possessed for the rest of her life.

NOT A GOOD TIME FOR SATAN: THE FALL OF DEMONS

It was not until the end of the eighteenth century that demons finally met their match. They were conquered by the Age of Reason (although some Fundamentalists might argue that "reason" is itself a terrible demon). In this enlightened period the *Encyclopedia* of the French philosopher Denis Diderot (1713–1784) presented new interpretations of ideas and events. The providential trinity of Father, Son, and Holy Spirit was supplanted by Nature, Reason, and Humanity. Voltaire's motto, "Crush the Infamous," was an attack on religious and political tyranny. Baron Holbach's *Good Sense* (1722) stated that: "Almost always fascinated by religious fiction, poor mortals turn not their eyes to the obvious causes of their misery; but attribute their vices to the imperfections of their natures, and their unhappiness to the anger of the gods. They offer up to heaven vows, sacrifices, and presents, to obtain the end of their sufferings, which in reality, are attributable only to the negligence, ignorance, and perversity of their guides, to the folly of their customs, to the unreasonableness of their laws, and above all, to the general want of knowledge; let justice govern them; and there will be no need of opposing to the passions such a feeble barrier as the fear of the gods." The bond between God and man was weakened by a new emphasis on what Jean Jacques Rousseau (1712–1778) called the social contract. He proclaimed that liberty resulted from fulfilling one's obligation to society, and he railed against an exclusive national religion: "Tolerance should be given to all religions that tolerate others, so long as their dogmas contain nothing contrary to the duties of citizenship." There can be no Christian republic; "The terms are mutually exclusive. Christianity preaches only servitude and dependence ... True Christians are made to be slaves, and they know it and do not much mind; this short life counts for too little in their eyes." In such an environment Satan and his legions were sent scuttling for cover.

The watershed year for demons was 1775, when two commissions met in Germany to examine the immensely popular healings performed by the Catholic priest Johann Gassner. He believed that the devil could make people ill by the power of sorcery, by imitating medical disorders, and by possession. Gassner's methodology seemed quite reasonable by traditional standards. He diagnosed demonic illness by calling upon demons to produce or exacerbate a patient's symptoms. A negative response to this entreaty resulted in a referral to a physician, but when the response was positive Gassner would perform an exorcism. His success was phenomenal but his critics smelled a rat. There *must* be an alternative, scientific explanation for the cures, but what was it?

The answer was provided by Franz Anton Mesmer, a physician who made a startling discovery in 1774 when treating a woman with confusing, multiple symptoms. Since Mesmer's doctoral dissertation studied planetary influences on human illness, he attempted to predict the flux of symptoms in his patient. Obviously he could not influence celestial bodies, but he decided to experiment by producing an "artificial tide" in his patient's body through the use of magnets placed on her stomach and legs. Her symptoms, indeed, floated away for a while as she experienced the movement of internal fluid streams. Mesmer was puzzled by this response until he hit upon a unique interpretation: the healing force was really a special, invisible fluid that came from him! He named this force animal magnetism.

Like Gassner, Mesmer effected many cures, but he invoked a "scientific" explanation instead of demonology. He testified to the Commission that Gassner's ability to heal was due to the tremendous amount of animal magnetism that he possessed in his body. He concluded that Gassner's cures were real, but his spiritual explanations were false.

Although Mesmer eventually came to be regarded as a quack and his theory as bogus, he had succeeded in demystifying the dramatic cures of exorcists. No longer was it necessary to consider demonic influence as an explanation for illnesses. Psychiatry and psychology emerged from the morass of invisible animal magnetism as exciting new disciplines that developed explanatory models based on an invisible organ known as the mind.

Of course, belief in demons and spiritual influences did not disappear totally among the general populace. In the 1890s, for example, an attractive Swiss medium named Helen Smith was quite popular for her ability to reveal information about people's lives. She claimed that she had led past lives as a fifteenth-century Indian princess, as Marie Antoinette, and as a Martian. A psychologist, Theodore Flournoy, demonstrated that Smith had a romantic "subliminal imagination." Her so-called past lives were simply expressions of her unconscious wishes, and her so-called Martian language was really a mish-mash of fractured Hungarian words and French grammar. Flournoy's findings, published in 1900 in his book *From India to the Planet Mars* broke her spirits in more ways than one. She ended her life as a solitary, religious artist.

A case that exemplifies the shift away from demonology was recorded by the greatest of French psychiatrists, Pierre Janet. In 1890 he encountered a businessman who became depressed upon returning from a brief trip. The patient cursed God and the Virgin Mary and then said, "It is not my fault if my mouth says these horrible things ... It is the devil who drives me." He openly conversed with the devil but would not speak to anyone else, so Janet handed him a pencil and addressed "the devil." The patient automatically and dutifully wrote answers to Janet's questions. Playing on the devil's vanity, Janet asked him to put the patient into a hypnotic state. While in this condition, the patient confessed that he was ashamed of a sexual transgression he committed on the business trip. He told about frightening, morbid dreams of being dead, of being whipped by goblins who also drove nails through his eyes, and of Satan taking possession of his body. The dream had so overcome him that he believed it to be real. Janet diagnosed the illness as "remorse" and regarded the patient's belief in demon possession as a secondary elaboration. He suggested to the patient that his wife would forgive him. Taking the suggestion to heart, the patient "hallucinated" the presence of his wife granting him a pardon and was cured. Janet wrote, "In a few days he had made sufficient progress to laugh at his devil and he explained his illness by saying that he had read too many story books."

It has taken almost two thousand years for us to laugh at devils, yet there is a sizeable minority who still cling to old beliefs. The Catholic Church retains its formal, rarely used rite of exorcism, although one or more simple exorcisms are routinely pronounced over every candidate during baptism. Many hard-core Fundamentalist ministers perform exorcisms. A female patient of mine, for example, stopped taking her antipsychotic medication and made bizarre noises during religious services. When the congregation couldn't stand it anymore, she was taken to the church basement where the minister and a group of church women forcibly tried to drive the devil out of her with sticks and prayer. It didn't work. She became so frightened that she punched her way to freedom and fled.

Among sophisticated faith healers the current trend is to distinguish between demonic possession (rare) and demonic oppression (common). Without appearing nostalgic, the simple truth is that there just aren't enough old-fashioned, mangy, foulmouthed, guttersnipe, stinky-smelling, hideous-to-behold, breath-sucking, maggot-infested demons to go around any more. However, there is more than enough alcoholism, drug abuse, binge eating and purging, gambling, and self-harm to satisfy everybody's needs. What these "oppressive" behaviors share are elements of compulsivity, impulsivity, and resistance to treatment. Self-help groups, usually modeled after the Alcoholics Anonymous twelve-step program, get a major portion of the action. Mental health professionals get their share too. But that still leaves a multitude for faith healers who have promoted a marvelously clever interpretation of impulsive behavior. To the person who lacks inner discipline, who seems unable to overcome incessant urges for self-gratification, who bemoans that "I couldn't help myself," there comes a fresh, old reply: "Perhaps the devil made you do it."

When you get down to brass tacks, the impulsive disorders really are a giant pain in the neck for everyone involved. They make afflicted persons miserable, therapists cringe, and ministers tremble. Since no treatment is particularly efficacious, practicality will out. For some people a dollop of Prozac (thank God for Prozac!) helps, for others a self-help step-along provides comfort, for still others it takes an exorcism to turn the tide, provided that certain rules are followed.

Consider the following well-conceived program of exorcism described in the book *Healing* by Francis MacNutt: First, the prayer for deliverance from oppressing demons should be performed in private with a team of healers. It starts with a prayer for protection from evil forces for everyone present, followed by a prayer that the force and power of any demons lose their power to resist what follows. The patient is then asked to provide the name of the demon (e.g., the spirit of lust or alcohol), to renounce any sin associated with it (such as harming others), and to forgive those persons who have harmed him or her. The patient alone should try to cast out the demon. If this doesn't work, then the healer prays aloud: "In the name of Jesus Christ I command you, the spirit of ——, to depart anyone in this house, or anyone anywhere else, and without creating any noise or disturbance, and I send you straight to Jesus Christ that he might dispose of you as he will."

According to MacNutt, the patient experiences a sense of joy and freedom when the demon departs. If there is a struggle and the demon throws the patient to the floor or comes out in a fit of coughing or vomiting, the healer cuts short the exhibition by commanding the demon to keep quiet!

So far, so good. But there's a rub. Following the deliverance, "If there is no follow up, chances are the condition of oppression will return." The follow-up consists of an immediate prayer to fill the person with God's love and grace, and the patient is also "taught to break the habitual behavior patterns that originally led to the demonic infestation." The patient should then adopt a regular schedule of prayer, reading the Bible, and receiving the sacraments of communion and penance. Finally and ideally, the person should then become an active member of a Christian community.

From a psychiatric perspective MacNutt's program is pretty darn good. The healer and the patient share an explanatory model. Shifting blame onto a demon relieves the patient of guilt, but the patient retains responsibility for participating actively in the cure. The team lends support and authority to the exorcism, and the drama heightens expectations for a cure. The key to any success rests with the follow-up. Teaching the patient to break habitual behavior patterns is easier said than done, as every therapist knows. MacNutt doesn't present any specifics, except for a mention of "some kind of spiritual discipline," and this is the weakest link in the program. Having the patient engage in a regular schedule of beneficial activities, in this case religious ones, means that less time is available for harmful activities. Regularly receiving appropriate sacraments reinforces the patient's original decision to participate in a cure. Membership in a special community is a major element of the best support groups such as AA. Unfortunately, the definition of a Christian community is unclear and may vary drastically among churches.

No one knows if MacNutt's treatment is effective for impulsive disorders. Theoretically, it very well might work. In comparison, the lucrative, generic exorcisms of televangelists—"Someone out there is oppressed by the demon of alcoholism. In the name of Jesus I command this demon to depart. Yes, I can feel that the demon is departing even as we pray. Praise Jesus. Call the 800 number flashing on your screen if you have just been liberated from a demon of oppression"—are pale imitations and doomed to failure.

The notion of demonic oppression is intellectually more acceptable than possession because it can be understood as a metaphor. Unfortunately, it also loosens boundaries. Although demonic oppression best refers to specific cases of impulsive behavior, it opens the door for belief in Satanic influence over events and persons. As a background theme this is a core Christian belief. As a foreground theme in the modern world it becomes a travesty and a cause of hysterical epidemics.

Nothing gets my blood boiling faster than media reports of devil worship, horrible deeds done in the night, Black Masses, children ripped from their mother's breast, fornication, arse-kissing, blood spilled and drunk like wine, milk carton photos of abducted boys and girls, expensive wards in private mental hospitals set up to receive those persons driven by Satan as well as their victims, itinerant ministers roaming the countryside sounding the alarm. Lock up your pet black cats and your blue-eyed blonde daughters, devil worshipers are on the prowl!

Drivel, drivel, drivel. Unadulterated hogwash. Evidence of demonic activity? There is none except for an occasional mutilated cow, a fanciful spread in Playboy, rumors of rumors, "re-creations" especially done for television. Today's witches tend to be mild-mannered, gentle souls with Birkenstocks for broomsticks; today's Satan worshippers tend to be solitary schizophrenics, drugged teenagers playing make-believe, or persons receiving psychological "help" from a Christian therapist. Mainstream persons don't much talk about evil and demons but rather of criminality and mental illness. This just isn't a good time for Satan. The Star Trek generation much prefers explanations based on strange encounters with extraterrestrial bogeys, hairless shriveled aliens who perform nasty secret operations on our brains and sexual organs.

The only survivor, a minor one at that, is the demon of excess. It has found its niche in the realm of multiple personality disorder. The literary prototype of this disorder is *Dr. Jekyll and Mr. Hyde*, one person with two distinct personalities. It's dramatic stuff, but when you're competing with spaceship Satans, the more personalities the merrier. The bizarre theatricality of multiple personalities is sometimes reminiscent of the glory days of demon possession. This has impressed some Christian healers and mental health professionals so much that they have reclaimed Beelzebub, Leviathan, Asmodeus, and their evil companions. While no person has even come close to 6,661 personalities, the numbers are rising, usually in direct proportion to the cleverness, prurience, and directing skills of the "therapist."

Mainstream psychiatry recognizes multiple personality disorder as a bona fide, rare condition. It afflicts persons who are highly suggestible and who experience sudden, temporary changes of personality function. The fact that multiple personality patients can be hypnotized easily points to an underlying biological flaw that facilitates the splitting off of personality components that are usually integrated together. A normal person retains a single identity even while expressing differing behaviors such as coyness or aggressivity or sexuality. In the multiple personality patient each of these behaviors may be expressed as the distinguishing feature of a distinct personality. The goal of treatment is to reintegrate the components into one personality through the clarification and resolution of the patient's many psychological problems. The histrionics of an exorcism only make things go from bad to worse for these patients, like setting off a fragmentation grenade in a war zone.

SAVE THE SOUL, CURE THE FLESH

Jesus cured every sick person that he encountered, saints and sinners alike, without dense elaborations about the causes of sickness. It was all quite simple. Then Paul came along and, as theologians frequently do, complicated matters. Jesus regarded sickness as an evil in itself, but Paul regarded sickness as a consequence of humankind's enslavement by sin and death, by demonic principalities and powers, by idols and false gods, by all the hosts of wickedness in the universe. Consider the following Biblical examples.

Some Corinthian church members ate well, drank well, and were joyous when they gathered together for the evening meal. They were following the example, perhaps, of the apostles who daily attended the Temple together, broke bread in their homes and partook of food with glad and generous hearts (Acts 2:46). Paul took a dim view of this behavior. For him, the evening meal should be a sober commemoration of the Last Supper. Because the Corinthians did not eat and drink as he thought they should, Paul told them, "That is why many of you are weak and ill, and some have died."

A married couple sold one of their possessions with the intention of giving all the money from the sale to the church. They were greedy, however, and kept some of the proceeds. Because Satan had filled their heart, they lied to the Holy Spirit. Then they both dropped dead (Acts 5). It seems like a pretty harsh penalty, but the story makes a practical as well as a theological point: you dip into the collection basket or cheat the church only at deadly peril.

Paul reclaimed the old Jewish concept that sick persons are transgressors. Although this unChrist-like concept has permeated Christianity ever since, it has been weakened in modern times among mainstream believers. Moralistic Bible-thumpers, however, selectively cling to the judgmental theory of sickness; when they or their family members are sick it is at best a natural illness, at worst a trial akin to Job's, but when homosexuals get AIDS, prostitutes syphilis, and alcoholics cirrhosis of the liver, they truly get what they deserve.

Presumably as a punishment for his early persecution of Christians, Paul himself was blinded for three days (Acts 9). He also suffered from another illness, perhaps epilepsy, that he called a thorn in his flesh (2 Corinthians 12). Paul's interpretation was that God used Satan as an agent who then sent the illness as a messenger. It's a bit convoluted, but Paul declared that the purpose of the illness was to harass him into humility. He asked God to cure him three times, but was turned down. According to Paul, God then said, "My grace is sufficient for you, for my power is made perfect in weakness." This was truly a brilliant, new idea: a handicap was transformed into an asset by perceiving it so. Instead of regarding an infirmity merely as a defect or liability, declare it an opportunity to receive the power of Christ and make the most of it. The upside of this reformulation is the enhanced sense of self-worth that it provides to the disabled and chronically ill. The downside is the potential for persons to accept their infirmities with passivity or even to harm themselves deliberately in pursuit of a higher, spiritual goal.

Church members ought to live the life of Christ who suffered, died, and was resurrected because they are literally and metaphorically the body of Christ (1 Corinthians 2). Paul said that believers must suffer for Christ's sake and expect persecutions. He invited them to share in Christ's sufferings (2 Timothy 1:8). Suffering produces endurance which produces character which produces hope, "and hope does not disappoint us, because God's love has been poured into our hearts through the Holy Spirit" (Romans 5:3–5). Like Christ, we must endure bodily sufferings, "for whoever has suffered in the flesh has ceased for sin ... those who suffer accordingly to God's will do right and entrust their souls to a faithful creator" (1 Peter 4). Bodily decay renews our spiritual nature.

The redemptive value of suffering was poignantly expressed in Isaiah's description of the suffering servant (a metaphor for the people of Israel): "Ours were the sufferings he bore, ours the sorrows he carried ... and through his wounds we are healed." Centuries later Christ became the suffering servant: "He himself bore our sins in his body on the tree, that we might die to sin and live to righteousness. By his wounds you have been healed" (1 Peter 2).

The glorification of suffering has influenced Christian attitudes towards illness for almost two thousand years, aided by a mistranslation of a key word in the Bible. Clearly the early Church encouraged healing of sickness. It certainly impressed people and made recruitment to the new religion easier. In the battle for people's minds, the Church promised resurrection of the body, but Greek philosophers, especially Plato, and cultists droned on and on about souls and shadows. Intellectuals and many theologians became hooked on Plato, but common folk with common sense became hooked on Christ, the God who assumed a human body just like theirs.

The first apostles performed healings of people who were blind, crippled, feverish, demon-possessed, and diarrheic. A second-century prophet named Hermas even considered it sinful not to cure the sick. As long as Christians were persecuted by the Romans, healing was a common occurrence. After the Edict of Milan in 313 stopped the persecutions and gave the Church legal status, however, healing of the body was infrequent. For several centuries the text from James 5:13-16 had served as the model for healing. James wrote that sick people should call the elders of the church to pray at their bedside and anoint them with oil in the name of the Lord. They should confess their sins to one another and pray for one another, and they will be "healed." Then, in about 400 A.D., St. Jerome translated the Bible into Latin. In translating James, however, one word was changed. Instead of "they will be healed," Jerome wrote "they will be saved." By this alteration, spiritual salvation displaced the healing of illness as the central focus of James's text.

Jerome's error is a reflection of the man himself. He was dyspeptic and ill-tempered. He found sex thoroughly disgusting and human company disagreeable. His happiest years, or to be more accurate, his least miserable ones, were spent with his library in a desert cell: "There I sat solitary, full of bitterness; my disfigured limbs shuddered away from my sackcloth, my dirty skin was taking on the hue of the Ethiopian's flesh; every day tears, every day sighing: and if in spite of my struggles sleep would tower over and sink upon me, my battered body ached on the naked earth." To such a man the body was little more than a cesspool of passions, a festering burden that pulled humans away from God. Jerome had no love of healing and saw little use for it. Far better was it to be saved.

Jerome's heroes were the Desert Fathers, holy Christians who retreated to the deserts of Egypt and the Middle East in the fourth and fifth centuries. They lived in solitary cells, unwashed, dressed in rags, constantly fasting and contemplating God, punishing their flesh and disavowing the wickedness of the world. As athletes of God they were lionized for their seemingly bizarre feats. St. Simeon Stylites lived the last thirty years of his life atop a sixty-foot pillar on a small platform. St. Anthony (251-356) was celebrated in a biography that stunned the Christian world and inspired imitators. He lived in an isolated deep pit for twenty years wearing a course animal skin for clothing. Back then, he and the other Desert Fathers were tourist attractions. The deserts were flooded by persons seeking a glimpse or a whiff of them. Some Fathers did perform healings, usually exorcisms, but as much as possible they desired to be alone in their suffering. Neither cleanliness nor the integrity of the body was their concern.

BONES AND DYMPNAMANIACS: RELICS AND HEALING SHRINES

Christianity's neglect of healing can be seen by examining the works of St. Thomas Aquinas (1225-1274), the most comprehensive and, along with St. Augustine, the most influential of Church philosophers.

As a member of the Dominican Order of priests, he vowed to defend the Church and Christian doctrine. His massive *Summa Theologica* examined every theological idea deemed important by the Church and contained most everything that could be contained about Christian doctrine. His arguments and "proofs" were based on biblical texts and scholastic reasoning. He was familiar with the tremendous emphasis on healing in the Gospels, yet he wrote very little about it. It is doubtful that he consciously decided to avoid the topic, and there is nothing in the story of his life to suggest a neurotic streak. It simply seems to have been unimportant for him, an attitude that probably reflected the spirit of the times.

The antagonism of the Church towards medicine and healing picked up steam in the twelfth century. Since the Bible says that King Asa of Judah died after consulting physicians, medical treatment was deemed unworthy by leading clerics. At the Second Lateran Council (1139), priests were censured for neglecting the welfare of the soul by making "themselves physicians of human bodies." At the Fourth Lateran Council (1215), physicians, under threat of excommunication, were ordered to seek and accept advice from a priest in treating patients. Because the Church abhorred the shedding of blood, surgery and dissection were frowned upon and often forbidden. Medical books were not allowed in many monasteries.

Physicians were ridiculed for the splendor of their dress and the ignorance of their knowledge. The great Italian poet, Petrarch (1304–1374), wrote a letter to Pope Clement VI: "I know your bedside is beleaguered by doctors, and naturally this fills me with fear ...They learn their art at our expense, and even our death brings them experience: the physician alone has the right to kill with impunity. Oh, Most Gentle Father, look upon their band as an army of enemies." Physicians were stigmatized as magicians, atheists, and even worse, Mohammedans (many of the best medical texts were written by Moslems). Jewish physicians, among the best in Christendom, were consulted secretly by many top church and state officials but were publicly derided. Even in the seventeenth century the clergy in Wurtenberg, Germany, protested the issue of a medical license to a Jew, stating, "It is better to die with Christ than to be cured by a Jew doctor aided by the devil."

When medicine is devalued and formal religious healing is forgotten, when the living cannot be solaced by the living, it is only natural to turn to the dead. If quick priests, Popes, and bishops would not do the job, there was already in place a legion of dead saints awaiting the call. Although entombed for centuries, these saints lived in the hearts of the faithful through the glorious stories of the miracles they had performed. That these were not just fairy tales was evidenced by the palpable bits and pieces of the saints themselves that were on display for all to see.

The cult of relics consumed Christianity for almost a thousand years. St. Ambrose, the bishop of Milan who gave the movement impetus in the fourth century, could not have anticipated the results of his actions. Relics—mainly the bones and other body parts of saints— often were the most precious possessions of cities and towns. Rome became the center of Christianity in great part because it possessed the bodies of Peter and Paul. Every locale in Christendom vied for relics to attract pilgrims and the economic prosperity that they brought.

The Church encouraged devotion to relics and assigned saints to specific organs or diseases. St. Apollonia, a martyr whose teeth were knocked out, became the patron of persons with toothaches; St. Vitus was the patron of those with a movement disorder known as chorea; St. Giles was the patron of cripples. St. Lucy enucleated her eyes to calm the ardor of an unwanted suitor who had praised their beauty and, thus, she became the patron of persons with eye diseases. And then there was St. Fiacre, a marvelous gardener who was falsely accused of witchcraft. While waiting for several days to be interviewed by his Bishop, he sat near the church on a large stone where the outline of his posterior miraculously was imprinted. He became the patron of hemorrhoid sufferers, who were supposedly cured by sitting on the stone.

Churches made large sums of money by charging the sick to touch relics with healing powers. For pilgrims as well as for those sick persons who couldn't travel, the churches made available healing potions such as bottles with water used by St. Bernard to wash his hands, and water into which the hair or bones of a saint had been dipped. In fourteenth century Pope Paul II sold pieces of wax made from Easter candles stamped with the figure of a lamb. These Agnus Dei (Lamb of God) fetishes were consecrated as protection from shipwrecks, lightning, and difficult childbirth. In 1517, Pope Leo X sold paper fetishes with the picture of a cross and a message: "This cross measured forty times makes the height of Christ in his humanity. He who kisses it is preserved for seven days from falling sickness, apoplexy, and sudden death."

It is difficult for us to appreciate the mindset of the enormous crowds that traveled to be near the bones of a saint. For them, relics were not just lucky charms but rather objects of intense devotion. The relics radiated the actual presence of the saint and were thought to be capable of performing miracles. Shrines were built around relics, and the sick in both spirit and body came in droves. Some shrines were for general healing while others specialized.

Relics lost their power to heal when medical practice became more scientific and effective. The myriad healing shrines faded into obscurity and today attract only local partisans. One major exception is the relatively new French shrine at Lourdes, where St. Bernadette had her visions of "the lady" in 1858. "The lady" was identified as the Virgin Mary by local enthusiasts. Although Bernadette died of tuberculosis at the age of thirty-five and never stated that "the lady" would cure anything, the shrine at Lourdes was promoted by mercantile interests as a place for healing. Several million visitors from around the world travel there each year, including many desperate persons whose illnesses have not responded to medical treatment.

A true cure of a true illness such as malignant brain tumor or end-stage kidney failure would truly be a miracle, as would the regeneration of an amputated leg. Many travelers go to Lourdes hoping for a miracle, but the odds against it are staggering. The Catholic Church has certified less than a hundred miraculous cures. The forest of discarded crutches that adorn the shrine are not necessarily the testimonials to miraculous activity that a discarded glass eye or peg leg would be. Alas, none of the latter have ever been found.

Lourdes has an official medical bureau for the certification of miracles. An English scholar, Donald West, examined the files of certified miracle cures and found them lacking. Most of the cases involved women with chest disorders. Evidence for a cure, such as biopsies of affected areas and appropriate x-rays, was not documented. West did find evidence, however, of passionate and politically apt case pleading by the priests who accompanied the patients to Lourdes. Interestingly, people who live in the town of Lourdes have rarely received any health benefit from their location.

So why do the crowds keep coming, and why do people return home uncured but feeling better? The power of the Holy Spirit could be invoked as an explanation. Or one could argue reasonably that patients benefit from the support of the family members who accompany them on their pilgrimage, from sharing expectations for improvement with thousands of like-minded patients, from participation in emotionally charged and spiritually uplifting ceremonies that include fervent praying, hymn singing, and a formal parade of children, priests, nuns, bishops, nurses, and physicians, and from a sense of expectant excitement. In the words of Jerome and Julia Frank, ".... the improvement probably reflects heightened morale, enabling a person to function better in the face of an unchanged organic handicap. Fully documented cures of unquestionable and gross organic disease are extremely infrequent—probably no more frequent than similar ones occurring in secular settings." Improvement seems to be linked with the intensity of the faith of patients. According to Cranston, those who feel better are "almost invariably simple people —the poor and the humble; people who do not interpose a strong intellect between themselves and the Higher Power."

None of the saintly relics or shrines were dedicated to the mentally ill, with the exception of St. Dympna's shrine in Geel, Belgium. Since its origins, Christianity had made provisions for widows, orphans, captives, even lepers, but not for the mentally ill who were either left alone or shunned as demon possessed. As the Middle Ages progressed the treatment of the mentally ill, regressed. The churches, both Catholic and Protestant, held that all diseases were Satanic in origin. With the rapid advances in medicine in the sixteenth century, however, diseases were slowly being understood in scientific terms. With each medical discovery, the churches further lost their grip on the populace, but mental illness defied medical understanding. In fact, religiously driven persecution of the mentally ill and of witches escalated. Thousands of witches, many of whom were mentally ill, were killed in accordance with the biblical admonition, "Thou shalt not suffer a witch to live," while persons identified as mentally ill were chained in "towers of fools" and whipped in order to scare the devil out of them. The whippings were undoubtedly done in good faith. Had not the Desert Fathers purified themselves through bodily mortification?

Indeed, many of the saints and mystics were strange characters who abused their bodies. Pope Benedict XIV (1675–1758) wrote: "With the exception of the martyrs, the Church venerates and gives the sanction of her authority to the sanctity of those only whom she finds to have been zealous in the mortification of the flesh and senses." One such person was Heinrich Suso, a German mystic who wrote a third-person account of his mortification: "He shut himself in his cell and stripped himself naked, and took his scourge with the sharp spikes, and beat himself on the body, arms, and legs until blood poured off him. One of the spikes was bent like a hook, and whatever flesh it caught tore off. He beat himself so hard that the scourge broke into three pieces. He stood there bleeding and gazed at himself. It was such a wretched sight that he was reminded of the appearance of the beloved Christ when he was fearfully beaten."

St. Dympna was an Irish princess. Her father, the king, became distraught following the death of his beautiful and beloved queen. He turned to his daughter, Dympna, for consolation, which then turned to lust. She fled to Belgium with her confessor, St. Gereburnus, but was caught by her father in Geel. Head over heels in love, he begged her to marry him, but she refused his incestuous demands. The reward for her virtue was decapitation. Centuries later, in about 1250, her bones were unearthed and a church was built in her honor. Because her death had vanquished the demon that had driven her father to insanity, she became the patron spirit of the mentally ill who traveled to her church, where they lived for nine days and underwent daily exorcisms. So popular was Dympna's appeal that the church was flooded with patients. Appeals were made for local lodgings and, since many patients desired to remain near the church, a foster-care boarding system was developed. The patients benefitted by this arrangement and were required to perform chores alongside the members of their host families, most of whom were farmers. Soon patients were sent to Geel by civil authorities who paid the families to take them in. It was a cheaper and probably more humane method than keeping the patients chained in an institution.

The French revolutionary army closed the Church of St. Dympna in 1797, but the boarding system was allowed to continue and to grow. As a cost cutting measure the mental hospital in Brussels was closed in 1803 and its hundred patients were sent to Geel. By 1850, there were nine hundred patients living there, and the Belgium government took control of the operation, a significant event signaling the victory of medicine over religion in regards to mental illness. The Geel colony persists today as the State Psychiatric Hospital-Center for Family Care. The story of St. Dympna is now regarded as a mere legend, and she is no longer a driving force in people's lives.

HAPPY DAYS ARE HERE AGAIN: THE REVIVAL OF FAITH HEALING

As we have seen, the greatest era of healing occurred during the first few centuries of Christianity. Once the Church was established, however, it focused on spiritual salvation, and physical suffering came to be regarded as a worthy avocation for believers. The Protestant reformers held similar attitudes. In fact, the power to heal by touching a sick person reached its high point in Protestant England, but it was the King who did the touching and not priests. Mental illness with its connections to demon possession was the one condition Christianity held onto until it was challenged by enlightened attitudes during the Age of Reason.

Church authority was undermined in the nineteenth century by a host of developments including Darwin's theory of evolution, new approaches to Bible scholarship, and the establishment of psychiatry and psychology as academic and clinical disciplines. Had I written this book a hundred years ago, it probably would have pointed to a bleak future for Bible-based healing. Who could have foreseen the current explosion of Christian healing activities and the rebirth of a tradition that had been moribund for over fifteen hundred years?

The first glimmer of the rebirth was localized in New England. Especially in the Boston area during the years surrounding the end of the nineteenth century, interest in religion and in mind cures was quite high. Harvard professor William James published in 1902 his masterpiece *The Varieties of Religious Experience*. He wrote that during a special state of mind known only to religious persons, "what we most dreaded has become the habitation of our safety, and the hour of our mortal death has turned into our spiritual birthday. The time for tension in our soul is over, and that of happy relaxation, of calm deep breathing, of an eternal present, with no discordant future, has arrived. Fear ... is positively expunged and washed away ... Religion becomes an essential organ of our life, performing a function which no other portion of our nature can so successfully fulfill."

James noted that the mind-cure movement aimed to replace the morbid Christian hell-fire theology with healthy-minded attitudes. Thus, doubt, fear, and worry are replaced by courage, hope, and trust. A person can choose to vacate hell and to rise heavenward. "The whole matter can be summed up by one sentence: *God is well, and so are you.* You must awaken to the knowledge of your real being."

Mary Baker Eddy underwent a "mind cure" treatment and proceeded to found the Christian Science movement and to write its central text, *Science and Health* (1875). In it she stated that Christian Scientists do not have doctrinal beliefs, but they do take the inspired word of the Bible as their guide to eternal life, acknowledge Jesus' crucifixion and resurrection, and "solemnly promise to watch and to pray for that Mind to be in us which also was in Jesus Christ." She believed that since God is mind and infinite, then everything is mind. "Sickness is a belief, which must be annihilated by the divine Mind. Disease is an experience of so-called mortal mind. It is fear made manifest on the human body. Christian Science takes away this physical sense of discord, just as it removes any other sense of moral or mental disharmony." She considered medication, material hygiene, mesmerism, hypnotism, theosophy, and spiritualism to be examples of false beliefs and mortal illusions. Needless to say, Eddy's ideas were beyond the ability of most people to comprehend, although Christian Science has persevered to the present.

A small group of highly educated ministers and physicians lead by Elwood Worcester, the pastor of the Emmanuel Church in Boston, undertook the treatment of "nervous sufferers." The group believed in the power of the mind over the body, in medicine, in good habits, and in a wholesome regulated life. Using the Bible as their foundation and Jesus as their guide, they understood and treated mental illness with kindness, common sense, and psychological insights. They believed that trust in Jesus "draws together the scattered forces of the inner life, unifies the dissociation of consciousness created by guilt and remorse, soothes the wild emotions born of sorrow and despair, and touches the whole man to finer issues of peace and power and holiness. By the sweet constraint of such a faith, the jarred and jangled nerves are restored to harmony." Although Worcester's book *Religion and Medicine* (1908) has a remarkably modern feel to it, the Emmanuel movement was too sophisticated to catch on.

The real rebirth of Christian healing took place far from Boston and the rarified environment of Harvard. At about the same time it may have occurred among Christians in Bombay, Armenia, the Camp Creek Baptist Church in the hills of North Carolina, and, most importantly, in Topeka, Kansas, on New Year's Eve, 1900, at 7P.M., in the Bible school of Rev. Charles Parham.

Rev. Parham, a Methodist minister, was disappointed in his ministry, especially when he compared it to Biblical accounts of the earliest days of Christianity. Back then there were miracles and healings and the challenge of winning new converts. He yearned to recapture the religious excitement that Paul and the first Christians must have experienced. The more he thought about it, the more he was convinced that the answer had something to do with baptism and with the Holy Spirit. He opened up a Bible school and asked his forty students to study the accounts of baptism in Acts. They found five instances, namely at Pentecost, and in Samaria, Damascus, Caesarea, and Ephesus. On three occasions baptism was associated with speaking in tongues, and a fourth occasion involved Paul, who spoke in tongues later in his life. Was speaking in tongues the key?

The group prayed for this gift but nothing happened. Then a student named Agnes Ozman suggested that Rev. Parham place his hands on her head as they prayed because the biblical accounts had references to this practice. On New Year's Eve he did as she requested, and she responded as they all had desired, by uttering incomprehensible words. Although Mormons, Quakers, Shakers, and especially Methodists had stumbled upon speaking in tongues many decades earlier, they had abandoned the practice. The deliberate, successful attempt to experience it in Topeka was a most significant event. Soon all the students spoke in tongues and, on January 3, twelve ministers invited by Parham were baptized in the Holy Spirit and they immediately spoke in tongues too.

Parham was overjoyed and probably a little starstruck. He set off on a grand tour of the United States and Canada to spread the news, but at the first stop, in nearby Kansas City, he was clobbered by reality, ridiculed by the press, and run out of town by the clergy. Everything fell apart and Parham became an itinerant preacher without a church, a congregation, or a school.

He made his way to El Dorado Springs, a small Missouri town known as a health spa, and preached to whomever would listen. Since many of the people visiting the spa had health problems, Parham tried his hand at healing. It was a logical step because he believed in the "full Gospel" and it clearly is written in Mark 16:17 that believers will not only speak in tongues but also will lay hands on the sick who will recover.

After Parham cured a women with eye problems, she invited him to her home town of Galena, Kansas, where he was welcomed warmly. His success was rapid and remarkable. A reporter from a Cincinnati newspaper wrote that in just three months Parham had healed more than a thousand persons. Riding high, Parham left the prairie and opened another Bible School in Houston, Texas.

An African-American minister, W. J. Symour, attended Parham's school and soon became its greatest ambassador. He went to Los Angeles and led a revival at a building on 312 Azusa Street in 1906. The joyfulness of the revival and the tremendous excitement of speaking in tongues took the area by storm. Thousands came to the services, and newspaper reporters had a field day. Before long people arrived from all over the continent for the Azusa Street experience. The revival continued daily for three years!

Once the word got out, similar revivals with speaking in tongues popped up all over the nation. A number of Christians left their staid churches and became Pentecostals (Pentecost refers to a day described in Acts 2 when all the apostles were filled with the Holy Spirit and spoke in tongues). The established churches did not take kindly to the loss of members and attacked the Pentecostals as uneducated primitives who spoke gibberish and did not appreciate the solemnity of Christianity. To be sure, most Pentecostals were blue-collar types along with a sprinkling of middle and upper social class members intrigued by the happenings on the other side of the tracks. For many decades the tongues-speaking, highly emotional, Holy Spirit power-driven, hands-on healing Pentecostals were loved by no one but themselves. They whooped it up in their clapboard churches and were generally looked down on by fellow Christians with condescension, bemusement, and embarrassment.

OLIVE OIL, SPICE & PICNIC TABLES
SCAM ARTISTS & SUBDUED HEALERS

The American Midwest proved to be an especially congenial cultural setting for Pentecostal faith healing. By some accounts a Fundamentalist preacher named William Branham got his act together in Jeffersonville, Indiana, in the 1940s and started the shameless trend of faith healing as show business. Flamboyant preachers like Billy Sunday and Aimee Semple McPherson discovered that people would pay big bucks for a hot sermon. Rev. Branham, operating on a smaller scale, added the promise of a health cure to attract audiences. He must have been terrific because lots of imitators tapped into his promotional genius. Rex Humbard in nearby Akron, Ohio, was the first to see the tremendous possibilities of television for a healing ministry in 1952. A few years later Oral Roberts, a most controversial healer, had his own television show. A true rogue's gallery of healers such as A.A. Allen, Peter Popoff, W.V. Grant, Pat Robertson, and the bizarre Willard Fuller soon followed.

Sinclair Lewis' novel *Elmer Gantry* and the Steve Martin film *Leap of Faith* have satirized the phony, hypocritical, money grubbing aspects of modern so-called faith healers, while television news magazines and newspaper reporters have exposed specific, real hucksters. The most complete and well documented study is James Randi's *The Faith Healers*.

Let's look at the character of these characters, courtesy of Randi:

Asa Alonso Allen: Stripped of his ministry by the Assemblies of God Church in 1955 after forfeiting bail on a drunk-driving charge. Regularly developed a miraculous cross of blood on his forehead during tent revivals. Established his own community in Arizona and became the top-dog healer of the late 1960s. Peddled holy water from his Church pool with the message: "People are being healed constantly while they sip it as an act of faith." Displayed dead animals in bottles as "disease demons." Boasted that he sent out 55 million pieces of mail a year. Grossed about 4 million dollars a year. Died in 1970 of alcoholic liver cirrhosis.

Granville Oral Roberts: Perfected television showmanship to become the greatest fundraiser in faith healing history. Created his own university, medical school, hospital, and half-a-billion-dollar evangelistic complex in Tulsa, Oklahoma. Suffered disastrous financial losses. Promised to raise the dead and to facilitate healing cures for persons who sent money to his special tower where an always on-call team of specialists prayed for miracles (the greater the donation, the lengthier the prayer). In 1980 came "face to face" with Jesus Christ, who was 900 feet tall. Threatened that God would "call me to heaven before my time" unless he received millions of dollars. Peddles "Expect a Miracle" coffee mugs, jigsaw puzzles of himself on horseback, and small sacks of cornmeal to be used for baking communion wafers. Refined the seed-faith concept: send him money and the money that you have left will grow, but only if you have enough faith.

Walker Vinson Grant: Operates from his Eagle's Nest cathedral in Dallas. Once heard prophecy from a young deer while attending a health spa for his obesity. Falsely claims to have been a great high school football player and to have graduated from college. Peddles a Bible course to subscribers, who get an honorary Doctor's Degree, a license to preach, and a diploma as a "Reverend." Heals all illnesses and, in a testimonial, even replaced the reproductive organs of a woman who had had a hysterectomy. Collected money to support several thousand Haitian orphans, but only forty received aid. Best soul-less scam: holy paper liners supposed to cure foot problems when cut out and placed in the sufferer's shoe.

Peter Popoff: Particularly unscrupulous (and that's saying a lot considering his peers) master of begging letters and staged crises. Californian. Peddles anything and everything including holy shower caps, mustard seeds, handkerchiefs with his sweat on them, and anointing oil from the Holy Land (actually olive oil mixed with Old Spice cologne).

Pat Robertson: Marvelously slick, very well-organized ruler of the Christian Broadcasting Network and would-be politician. Cleverly claims to heal at a distance but does not deal much with specific persons. Once claimed the healing of an elderly man in the television studio audience; the man died ten days later.

Willard Fuller: A Floridian who specializes in the regeneration of teeth and the miraculous filling of dental cavities with silver, gold, or porcelain. He claims that Jesus rearranges the atoms in a person's mouth. What more is there to say?

How can this be, you ask? Are people so easily talked out of their money? Are they so blinded by their faith that they can't spot a fraud? Can they be tricked over and over again? Yes, yes, and yes.

The really rich faith healers are superb actors with a well-rehearsed plan and a god-given talent for feigning sincerity. Cloaked in a mantle of religiosity, they manipulate the emotions of the faithful, especially those who are sick, to their advantage. The combination of religiosity, television celebrity status, and a glowing presence near an altar surrounded by a choir creates an aura of credibility that melts normal skepticism.

One reason for their success is the sheer volume of printed material they send. In this material they offer God's blessings and promise miracles for cash. They invite the reader to participate in a holy cause. When one healer was investigated by the IRS and other government agencies, he wrote to everyone in his mailing list: "When Jesus Christ hanged down from the cross at 33 years of age, people didn't lose their faith and respect for him. The government is what killed him, the same thing they're trying to do to me, the same thing they would try to do to you." He sought funds by writing: "I believe that some of you have something in land, in cars, in houses, and your savings accounts, money that you were going to use for something else. You're going to loan it to Jesus now, and God's going to give it back to you many, many, many times over." The mailings are often personalized with handwritten notes begging for money to help resolve some sort of crisis in the ministry. It all can be very flattering to the lonely, the lost, and the needy. Randi discovered that many letters with specific requests from the faithful are relieved of their cash and tossed in the garbage.

A trick uncovered by Randi involves a faith healer's ability to identify members of an audience and then to provide details about their lives. This "gift of knowledge" is bogus. As people enter the auditorium, the healer's cronies often strike up conversations and then let the healer know where specific persons are seated. The information may be passed on by hand signals or by electronic messages sent to a tiny receiver in the healer's ear.

What about people who get out of wheelchairs and walk? The truth is that many such participants can walk fine but are placed in a wheelchair by the staff and then rolled down the aisle before an expectant audience and television cameras. It would take a remarkably strong person to proclaim a fraud in such a situation.

Leg-lengthening miracles are a staple of the faith healer's repertoire. Randi notes that this is a variation of a carnival act called "The Man Who Grows," in which a man scrunches down into a tight-fitting suit so that it seems to fit well. When the person stands tall and expands his chest, the suit becomes too small, giving the illusion that the person has grown. In the leg-stretching "miracle," the healer simply repositions the person's shoes (loose cowboy boots are best) to create the illusion. An alternative method is to swing the person's legs to one side so that, from the audience's perspective, one leg appears shorter. By swinging the legs back into line with the person's body, they seem to have grown.

A sure and simple broadcasting technique relies on probabilities; shoot into a crowd and a few people will always be hit. When Pat Robertson, for example, calls out an illness before a television audience of millions and then announces a cure, it is likely that some viewers in the vast audience will have this illness and will naturally be recovering from, say, terrible headaches, stomach pains, vaginal bleeding, marital problems, etc. When these viewers call in to present testimonials, they make Robertson look genuine and, of course, they get on a valuable mailing list. Some mailing lists follow a person to the grave and beyond. Unknown to me, my mother evidently sent a donation to an evangelist at some time in her life. Eighteen years after her death she still was receiving pleas for donations. Miraculously, they were sent to her at my new address in a state that she had never visited!

Although it hardly balances the scale, there is a less spectacular, calmer group of modern Christian healers. They mainly come from the traditional churches and talk more about inner healing than miracle cures. Agnes Sanford, a quiet and modest woman, introduced the concept of spiritual healing to the Episcopal Church in the 1940s. Her books, especially *The Healing Light*, were best sellers with a simple message: "Christian love is a powerful, radiant and life-giving emotion, charged with healing power both to the one who yearns to love and the one who is loved." She believed that it is every Christian's duty to pray for self-healing as well as the healing of others. Since God is present in every person, those who are sick may be healed by allowing God to accomplish perfection in their spirits and bodies, and by accepting medical help they cooperate with God. "Being sick, therefore, I gladly call upon my best friend and advisor, the doctor. He not only helps my body, he also helps my mind. His cheerful assurance strengthens my faith, and his diagnosis calms my fears. I should not have fears, true. But I do have, and there is no fear so destructive as the fear of the unknown. No one can pray with power while thinking, oh dear, I do feel awfully queer. I wonder if something terrible is wrong with me?" No tent shows for Agnes, by golly, and no strident calls for money. Her sugary notions about physicians are enough to gag a modern reader, but she was a pioneer.

Ruth Carter Stapleton, the sister of President Jimmy, came along in the 1970s with a more sophisticated approach to spiritual healing that "attempts to bring authentic principles of psychology under the guidance and inspiration of the Holy Spirit." Her therapeutic discovery is that negative memories can be replaced with God-inspired reconstructions of those memories. She calls this method "faith imagination." An example from her book, *The Experience of Human Healing*, demonstrates the process: A woman attempted suicide out of total despair over her husband's infidelity. She was unaware that her extreme reaction stemmed from the death of her father when she was two years old. His death had sensitized her to being rejected and deserted by men. "During counseling the woman was able to see and deal with this fear. Through the miracle of the timeless ministry of Jesus, she went back to her father's death. By faith imagination she was a little girl of two as she sat beside me, looking at her daddy in the casket. But Jesus, who stood beside her, touched her father as He did the widow's son whom He resurrected in the City of Nain centuries before. The father arose from the casket and took his little daughter in his arms—she had her daddy again ... In the new confidence that all men are not deserters, a new relationship could now begin with her husband."

This is powerful stuff, a truly Christian psychotherapy. With the right sort of patient there is no doubt in my mind that it would prove effective. Unfortunately, it also requires the right kind of therapist, a person with psychological as well as spiritual sensitivity, a person who does not expect miracle cures, a caring person who does not wield righteousness like a cudgel. Carter wrote: "Jesus told Simon Peter, 'Feed my sheep.' He didn't say 'Mold and manipulate my untrustworthy people.' Heavy handed religious organizations and leaders inhibit free spiritual growth toward unique identity." I wonder if these comments would make sense to Oral, Pat, and the rest of the gang? They all profess to be Christians, but I wonder if they could distinguish spiritual growth from Shinola.

The Catholic Church, after a lapse of sixteen hundred years, rediscovered healing during Vatican Council II in the 1960s. Anointing of the Sick was a sacrament based on the text of James. Over the centuries, however, it became known as the Last Anointing, or Extreme Unction, and was administered to the dying. Although it always had an element of possible healing, its primary purpose was spiritual, namely to prepare a dying person for the afterlife. In countless Catholic households for countless generations, the appearance of a priest at a sick person's bed was usually followed by a call to the mortician.

Vatican II abolished the term Extreme Unction in favor of the original Anointing of the Sick. No longer reserved only for the dying, the sacrament now can be administered "as soon as anyone of the faithful begins to be in danger of death from sickness or old age." In this ritual the priest prays for God to send the Holy Spirit from heaven onto the oil:"May your blessing come upon all who are anointed with this oil, that they may be freed from pain, illness, and disease and made well again in body, mind, and soul. Father, may this oil, which you have blessed for our use, produce its healing effect, in the name of Lord Jesus Christ." Unlike the old Extreme Unction, which was administered in private because dying persons had to confess their sins, the renewed Anointing of the Sick can be administered publicly as a liturgical and communal celebration. The actual words said at the moment of anointing are, "Through this holy anointing may the Lord in his love and mercy help you with the grace of the Holy Spirit. May the Lord who frees you from sin save you and raise you up." The use of "save" goes back to St. Jerome's translation and really means "heal," while "raise you up" means up from the sickbed. The sacrament also implies the forgiveness of sins and increased valuation of the recipient's suffering "by configuration to the Savior's redemptive Passion."

Vatican II not only confirmed the healing practices that were already taking place in many local parishes, albeit usually in church basements, but also contributed to their spread. By 1978 the *New York Times* reported that 2,500 Catholic and Episcopal churches had regular spiritual healing services, often associated with the "charismatic renewal." Although speaking in tongues and uttering prophecy are part of this renewal, the healing practices have remained relatively subdued and, with a few exceptions, have been free of scandalous behavior and financial greed.

Francis MacNutt, a Catholic who left the priesthood for marriage, is the person most responsible for the vigor of the reputable spiritual healing movement. He is located in Florida with close ties to an Episcopalian church and works with a dedicated group of colleagues. Although he is quite photogenic, articulate, and educated, he is not a tent performer or televangelist. Instead, he and his group run seminars for health professionals and ministers as well as patients. His newsletter contains order forms for books and tapes (the most expensive item I could find was a ten-tape series on "Dealing with depression" for fifty dollars) and requests for donations ("We are still hopeful of the gift of a picnic table to place outside in the Spring"). A picnic table! Holy Toledo! Are we dealing with some rube here? A naive country bumpkin? Or a diabolically clever con artist who has developed an as-yet-impenetrable picnic table scam?

In fact, MacNutt is on the side of the angels. His books, *Healing* and *The Power to Heal*, are sophisticated and scholarly. He describes three types of interrelated sickness (spiritual, emotional, and physical) whose remedies include repentance, penance, prayer for inner and physical healing, sacramental Anointing of the Sick, psychiatric and spiritual counseling, and medical care. For "demonic" disorders a prayer of deliverance may be used or, more rarely, a formal exorcism. MacNutt claims that spiritual healing works by speeding up the natural recuperative forces of the body through prayer. He downplays the notion of miracle cures and feels that people usually are not completely healed by prayer but rather are improved. He traces the root of most deep emotional problems to childhood and suggests that when delving into the psychological origins of illness, "an hour is a good amount of time: 45 minutes to talk and 15 to pray." Francis, take it from a psychiatrist: you'll never get rich spending an hour with a patient.

YOU MEAN I'VE BEEN HEALED? PERCEPTIONS OF HEALING

According to the Bible, the cure of pathological conditions by spiritual means occurred in Old Testament times, during Jesus' life, and for several decades after his death. Jesus gave his disciples the power to heal all kinds of sickness and disease (Matt. 10:1; Luke 9:1). He also gave this power to all believers in Mark 16:17–18 (although this verse was added in the second century). James established that spiritual healing can occur if certain procedures are followed. Paul also cited healing as one of the gifts of the Holy Spirit that is apportioned to persons as the Holy Spirit sees fit.

What about modern times? Does spiritual healing occur today? The answer in large part depends on semantics and mindset.

The evidence that organic, biological, and structural changes occur in diseased body parts as a result of a spiritual intervention is meager indeed. Data from the medical bureau at Lourdes are highly suspect. Randi's book attempts to certify claims of spiritual healing, but, alas, proof of healing never materializes. In a marvelous story, Randi wondered why photographs of discarded braces and crutches on display at the Sanctuary of Chimayo in New Mexico differed over time. He discovered that a local orthopedic surgeon reclaimed the orthopedic devices periodically and returned them to the poor patients who, believing themselves to be healed, had left them but now needed them again!

Another story involves Peter Popoff, who, on his television show in 1986, spoke of a girl in Florida. Supposedly she had severe migraine headaches because of an inoperable, malignant brain-stem tumor as confirmed by CT scans of her head. Her grandmother sent a prayer request for healing to Popoff, and miraculously the tumor disappeared. The grandmother herself appeared on the show. Unfortunately for Popoff, a Dr. Gary Posner obtained the girl's medical records and spoke to the physicians on the case. The results? The scan shown by Popoff neither showed a tumor nor was it a CT study of the brain stem. The girl's physicians did not suspect a tumor. The actual case took place two years prior to the broadcast, and the girl was still alive and still had bad migraines. The voice of the girl's grandmother was really that of another woman.

Kathryn Kuhlman, a popular faith healer from Missouri, allowed a surgeon named William Nolan to work as a volunteer during one of her healing performances and to contact participants for a follow-up. She was absolutely convinced that she was curing people. Nolan was captivated by the religious fervor of the large audience and Kuhlman's truly charismatic abilities. The crowd expected miracles, and when she called out for people in the balcony to come forward and claim their healing of a specific illness (cancer, bursitis, headache, etc.), they were happy to oblige. In his book Nolan noted that "No one wanted to let Kathryn Kuhlman down, no one wanted to embarrass her." Kuhlman quoted extensively from the Bible as she explained her miracle healings to Nolan, who took notes. "When I tried to check out these references, I was unable to find any of them in the Bible." On follow-up interviews with 23 people who claimed cures at the performance, none was objectively better several weeks later. Nolan concluded that Miss Kuhlman was a sincere, dedicated, devout woman who believed fervently that she was doing the Lord's will. Unfortunately, she failed to cure anyone, although for a brief time many people felt better.

A seminal study of forty-three Fundamentalist-Pentacostals in Seattle who experienced seventy-one faith healings was published in 1973 by Pattison, Lapins, and Doerr. The healings were for disorders that ranged from leukemia and cancer to peptic ulcer and ruptured intervertebral (spinal) discs to warts and backache. A few persons prayed by themselves for their healing, while most participated in rituals such as anointing with oil and laying-on of hands.

Half reported instantaneous healing and half reported gradual healing despite the fact that the original symptoms were unchanged! The subjects reported that they rarely experienced worry, anxiety, restlessness, depression or anger, yet they demonstrated these behaviors during an interview and denied or minimized them when questioned directly. Psychologically the subjects had a strong need for social acceptance and affiliation and used so much denial and repression that major disruptive life events went ignored. They felt that healing had occurred not because of any change in symptoms but because it affirmed their conviction that they were living a proper, righteous life. After experiencing healing, their belief in God and in their religious convictions were markedly increased. "Thus, faith healing is not an exercise in the treatment of organic pathology but an exercise in the treatment of life style." If you believe that disease is the devil's work and that God looks after the faithful, then you had better experience healing in order to maintain membership among the faithful. Failure to do so would be an admission of unatoned sin.

The claim of healing despite any objective change is not unique to Fundamentalists. One of the most successful new spiritual movements is known as "A Course in Miracles." It started in 1965 when Helen Schucman and Bill Thetford, medical psychologists at Columbia University, had some uncanny mystical experiences. Late one night Helen began hearing an inner sound that said, "This is a course in miracles. Please take notes." Helen had no visions, no alteration of consciousness, no bizarre signs or symptoms. She took notes, dictated them to Bill, and finally produced a 1,500 page manuscript in 1975. Unlike most channeled literature (books in which the earthy author is merely a channel for the "real," otherworldly author), the *Course* has remained popular for several decades and is discussed in study groups. It basically is an updated version of Christian Science with intimations that Helen was a channel for Christ. The *Course* states that "Sickness is but a faulty problem-solving approach, it is a decision. And if it is a decision, it is the mind and not the body that makes it ... Who is the physician? Only the mind of the patient himself. The outcome is what he decides that it is ... Healing is always certain. It is impossible to let illusion be brought to truth and keep the illusion." In the section on "Should healing be repeated?" this unJesus-like language goes beyond the pale: "... *to doubt a healing because of the appearance of continued symptoms is a mistake in the form of trust...* Doubt not the gift and it is impossible to doubt the result." In plain words, you are healed if you believe that you are healed even should you die from your illness.

PRAY TELL

Prayer has many reasons, but the Christian tradition that comes directly from the New Testament often emphasizes asking God for something. Paul states it is kosher to make all sorts of requests: "Be anxious for nothing, but in everything by prayer and supplication, let your requests be known to God " (Phil. 4:6). Among the most common requests are those for self-healing and the healing of others. Let's suppose that God-fearing, church-going, hard-working, devout parents pray in Jesus' name for the recovery of their child who is dying of leukemia. What is God supposed to do? The scriptures say, "Whatever things you ask in prayer, believing, you will receive" (Matt. 21:22); "Ask, and it will be given to you" (Luke 11:9); "Whatever you ask the Father in My name He will give you" (John 16:23).

It would seem that God is obligated to save the child, but, more likely than not, the child will die. One could argue that God can't be expected to honor frivolous requests: "Lord, please don't let the Dodgers leave Brooklyn" (I tried this one as a child), or "Lord, please let me win the super-lottery" (I tried this one as an adult). But the life of a child hardly seems frivolous. Maybe the parents really didn't have enough faith or say the right words or pray long enough? Malarkey! These are heartless rationalizations. Fortunately for believers, the Bible comes to the rescue because there is another passage (there always is another passage if you search diligently enough) that explains things. When Jesus prayed in the garden of Gethsemane prior to his betrayal and capture, he said: "Father, all things are possible for you. Take this cup away from me, nevertheless, not what I will, but what you will." No one clearly understands what the cup is. It's a red herring; the meat's in the last phrase. God's will takes precedence over a person's will, even if that person is Jesus.

Whatever will be, will be, because whatever happens is God's will, a.k.a. divine providence. Should the dying child recover "miraculously," one can't suppose that the parents' prayers had anything to do with it. Miracles are a human convention and really are exclamations of wonderment at unexpected changes in the course of events. From a providential perspective, what happens is what is supposed to happen and cannot be unexpected. Jesus couldn't change God's mind, so what chance has a mere mortal? If you ask, the Gospels notwithstanding, you won't necessarily receive unless God already planned for you to receive. But Jesus promised, you might argue. That's between you and him, I would answer.

Would our hypothetical, devout parents have had better luck by taking their sick child to a faith healer? Even the most narcissistic healers do not claim to be gods, at least not publicly, but rather claim to have special spiritual "gifts" that signify an ability to intercede with God or, things get a little murky here, to tap into God's will. MacNutt, who at least tries to discuss the matter seriously, distinguishes between an ordinary Christian's prayer of petition and the gifted healer's prayer of command. The former involves speaking to God while the latter "already knows in some mysterious way the mind of God, and so can speak in his person ... Be healed. Amen. I see it being done

... It is as if the person praying were standing *with* God and speaking for him." Even if we assume that some healers actually do speak for God, they cannot assume God's power to heal, just as a press secretary can speak for the president but cannot assume presidential authority. The special connections of faith healers are either imaginary or gossamer things. The Christian God is not a puppet. Maybe the healers reflect God's will, but so can anyone. It's really quite simple: *whatever* happens must be part of God's plan.

What about those occasions when a disease process actually is changed following prayers for healing? A rational view would be that the timing of the prayer and of the disease change is coincidental. Not all diseases are progressive. In some, such as epilepsy, migraines, gastric ulcers, multiple sclerosis, and manic depressive illness, symptoms may remit for extended periods of time as the disease process become quiescent. Also, medicine has always recognized the rare spontaneous remission of some diseases, especially cancers. In fact, fourteenth-century Saint Peregrine is associated with cancer regression; the cancer in his leg bones supposedly regressed following his prayers and dream of a cure. He was spared an amputation and lived for sixty more years. Spontaneous cures of biological lesions do occur, however, both with and without prayer. Mental illnesses also often get better with or without prayer, although it is difficult to quantify or measure "lesions" in these cases.

Demoralized, sick persons who psychologically give up may accelerate their moment of death, but participation in a prayer-healing ceremony and prayers for healing foster hope and positive feelings that may help persons feel better. This in turn may energize a sick person's natural recuperative powers, perhaps by affecting the immune system or by increasing motivation to participate in a rehabilitation program. Prayers may help but not necessarily through a supernatural process. The only way to disprove the previous statement is to demonstrate that prayers can produce results when the sick person being prayed for has absolutely no knowledge of the event. Even those people who associate with the sick person must be kept in the dark, too, because they might act in a hopeful manner and influence the sick person's psyche. Such an experiment must also clarify if a total cure is the desired result, or perhaps a temporary improvement will do. "Healing" is a very ambiguous term that ranges from slam-dunk dramatic reversals of illness to a drawn-out process of barely perceptible therapeutic gains.

A small number of prayer-at-a-distance studies have been carried out in which a group of prayed-for patients were compared to a similar group of control patients. The results generally have been negative, with a few equivocals. Studies of 18 leukemic children and of 38 patients with either "chronic stationary or progressively deteriorating psychological or rheumatic disease" demonstrated no advantage either to the prayed-for or control groups. A poorly designed, pseudo-scientific-experiment popularized in the book *Prayer Can Change Your Life* studied 45 neurotic volunteers who were placed in either a psychotherapy group, a prayer for self-healing group, and a prayer therapy group. The prayer therapy group supposedly showed 72 percent improvement, the psychotherapy group 65 percent; the self-healing prayer group was a washout. Despite the impossibility of sorting out what variables were doing what, the experimenters could only claim a 7 percent advantage to the prayer therapy group. That's not very much to crow about.

Perhaps the best known study, published in 1988 by Byrd, compared a control group (201 patients) with an experimental group (192 patients) who were prayed for by born-again Christians. All the patients were on the coronary care unit of San Francisco General Hospital. A good hospital course was reported for 85 percent of the experimental group and for 73 percent of the controls, and a bad course for 14 percent of the experimental group and for 22 percent of the controls. In addition to the author's religious bias (in the acknowledgments he thanks God for responding to the prayers), there is no information about either the psychological characteristics of the subjects or the treatment practices of the various health care teams. Any of these factors could account for the 12 percent difference in the good course and the 8 percent difference in the bad course. In order for strict scientific requirements to be met, no one involved with the study should have known which patients were in the control and prayed-for groups. However, the coordinator of this study not only knew the names of the patients in each group but also was responsible for keeping detailed records of all the patients. Additionally, the first version of the paper describing the study was returned with a request for a revision by the editor of the journal to which it had been submitted. The selection of criteria about what constituted good or bad hospital courses by the patients was reconstructed by the author after he knew which group each patient was in.

Some modern scientists attempt to displace the traditional prayer model with a rational-spiritual one. The new model, explicated in Larry Dossey's *Healing Words*, holds that prayers don't need an external God as an intermediary: "If God is present to some degree in all individuals, the Divine Factor in prayer is internal, not external to everyone." Further, since prayers are inherently infinite in both time and space, they don't go anywhere, and yet they are able to affect not only the present and the future, but also the past!

The underpinning of the new model relies on observations made by physicists working in the bizarre field of quantum theory. I use the word bizarre because quantum physics often overturns the basic concepts of reality on which most people rely. In the quantum world effects don't necessarily need to have a cause; atoms can have either a location or a motion but not both; an observer generates atomic reality and can even influence the past; and alternative worlds exist in parallel to one another. No, quantum physicists are not psychotic, they just seem to be. In any event, the relationship between the quantum world and the world of everyday experience is unclear at best.

Dossey's new model also takes into account a strange experimental literature demonstrating the effect of prayer on fungi, bacteria, yeast, moth larvae, plant seeds, vegetables, enzymes, cells in test tubes, and various physiological tests in rats. He concludes that open-ended invocations such as "Thy will be done" or "Let it be" are prayers that might get results. "They are more like an invitation for prayer's effect to manifest and show up."

I am reminded of Mesmer's displacement of demonic forces by his concept of animal magnetism two centuries ago. Mesmer, however, was able to produce "cures" in humans, while Dossey can only cite "changes" in seeds, germs, and laboratory rats. Unless a spectacular breakthrough comes along (doubtful), Dossey will have to be content with an interesting book.

The major problems in trying to *prove* anything that involves spirituality or the supernatural are that "god" is a limitless concept, and the human mind-set determines the interpretation of results. Let us suppose that a well-done experiment demonstrates an overwhelmingly high cure rate in a prayed-for group of patients and a low cure rate for a control group. The believer will say that the facts speak for themselves and that prayer works, while the nonbeliever will say that there must be a rational, scientific explanation, even if such an explanation is not readily apparent as yet. Reverse the results and the nonbeliever will stand on the facts, while the believer will say that the experiment was flawed, the prayers were not offered properly, God should not be tested, etc. Rational discourse cannot be applied to the supernatural and vice versa.

The tension between the rationalist and the supernaturalist is nicely presented in *Divine Healing and Cooperation Between Doctors and Clergy*, a 1956 publication by the British Medical Association. The physician authors reported to the Archbishop's Commission on Divine Healing that, "We can find no evidence that there is any type of illness cured by 'spiritual healing' alone which could not have been cured by medical treatment." The conclusion of the Commission, however, stated that, "Scientific testing can be a valuable corrective of rash claims that healing, ordinary or extraordinary, has occurred and it may bring to light natural healing virtues in religious rites; but it is idle for the Church, or anyone else, to appeal to science to prove the reality of supernatural power or the truth of theology or metaphysics."

QUESTIONS ANSWERED

Several questions were posed in the beginning of this chapter. Now they can be answered.

What happened to all the demons that Christ encountered? Christ didn't kill any demons; he just cast them out of sick people. They continued to kick up a fuss for a few centuries, and then most of them crawled under rocks for a thousand-year nap. When they awoke they caused all sorts of illness, especially the mental kind. In the late 1700s they lost much of their appeal and powers and were emasculated by reasonable-for-the-times scientific explanations of illness. Currently, the old-fashioned, brutish demons of possession have given way to impulsive demons of oppression. Metaphors these, to most people, but still real to some believers. Modern-day versions of demons are found in psychoanalytic object relations theory. This theory holds that good and bad "objects" are introjected by the ego. According to the well-known psychoanalyst, W. Fairbairn, "It is to the realm of these body objects ... that the ultimate origin of all psychopathological developments is to be traced; for it may be said of all psychoneurotic and psychotic patients that, if a True Mass is being celebrated in the chancel, a Black Mass is being celebrated in the crypt. It becomes evident, accordingly, that the psychotherapist is the true successor to the exorcists, and that he is concerned not only with the 'forgiveness of sins,' but also with 'the casting out of devils.'"

Should priests be doing more healing? Can patients be cured by incantations? Priestly healing rituals and prayers do give some patients encouragement and may foster the will to be healed and to live. Hands-on "healing" can have a tremendous emotional impact and may be beneficial as long as patients are not dissuaded from seeking medical help or reduced to penury by unscrupulous "healers." While supernatural mechanisms can never be disproved (anything is possible in the realm of the supernatural), natural psychological mechanism, are utilized in faith healing. Incantations have a venerable history going back to the early shamans. Done properly, even hocus-pocus and abracadabra can mobilize movements towards health. Done crassly, they can prove harmful.

How can pseudo-healers be identified? Usually by their luxurious cars and large choirs. If they peddle artifacts and gizmos made in China, watch out! Vocal twangs used to be a dead giveaway, but not anymore. A final tip: if you are promised a miracle or feel like applauding, turn tail, get away as fast as possible, and check for pickpockets.

Do Prozac and prayers mix well? There can be no doubt that medications, Prozac among them, are extremely helpful in the treatment of mental illness. No one knows if medications actually cure these illnesses, but, at the least, they often relieve symptoms. With symptom relief, patients can continue functioning and may then be able to deal with deeper troublesome issues. Without relief, patients are often too tired, nervous, paranoid, or confused to seek and participate in healing.

Some religious fundamentalists distrust psychiatry and psychology. They regard mental illness as either demonic or a sign of sinfulness or the result of a weak will and flawed faith. This misguided approach needlessly adds to suffering and may lead to demoralization, despair, and suicide. Fortunately most Christians today regard medication and therapy as consonant with God's will. Prozac and other medications may help Christians to participate more actively in congregational life and to broaden their prayers from repetitive petitions for health to include prayers of thanksgiving, praise, etc.

Is suffering from disease a Christian blessing? For the suffering servants, the nation of Israel and Jesus, atonement and suffering were redemptive. Their suffering, however, was not caused by illness, and Jesus intervened on every occasion to stamp out the suffering attached to illness. The tribulations that Christians are expected to endure, according to the Bible, are those that stem from political and social persecution, not from illness. The notion that sick people are somehow blessed because they share in Christ's suffering is a rationalization, an attempt at making something horrible appear meaningful. It is an understandable rationalization given that in the past, medical treatment was not very effective and the church had forgotten how to heal. In today's world medical suffering is usually both unnecessary and nonproductive. That is not to say that medical suffering sometimes can't be beneficial. Some (not all) alcoholics, for example, may need to hit bottom before they get better, and the shock of illness may induce a healthful change in lifestyle and the reordering of relationships in some persons.

Is suffering from disease a punishment from God? The answer depends upon what section of the Bible you turn to. The Old Testament God clearly used disease and suffering as a punishment, while the New Testament God did not. From the beginning of time it has been observed that some nasty sinful people lead a good life and die painlessly at an old age, while some wonderful, sinless people lead a miserable life and die young. Christianity holds that everlasting hell probably awaits the former, while the latter probably will go to heaven. In today's materialistic world, where success is often measured by the size and expense of one's toys, I suspect that given a choice most people would opt for hedonism over spiritual suffering and would hope for divine charity instead of divine justice. Only those with a truly impeccable sense of timing, however, can trust in a deathbed confession and atonement to mitigate a life of profligacy.

Isn't it possible that spirituality might contribute to healing? Yes, it is both possible and probable, depending, of course, upon what we mean by spirituality. In regards to prayers for the sick, William James wrote that it should be encouraged as a therapeutic measure because "in certain environments prayer may contribute to recovery." James understood prayer to be the movement of the soul to a point of personal contact with a mysterious power (God) and not the mere repetition of sacred formulas. A result is that "energy . . . is by prayer set free and operates in some part, be it objective or subjective, of the world of facts." The modern psychiatrist, Andrew Weil, suggests the use of religious practices in medically hopeless cases because they do no harm and might activate healing responses. We'll examine spirituality in greater detail in the next chapter.

TRUE, FALSE AND USEFUL:
THE SPIRITUAL MARKETPLACE, RELIGION & PSYCHIATRY

CHAPTER 9

The various modes of worship which prevailed in the Roman world were all considered by the people as equally true; by the philosopher as equally false; and by the magistrate as equally useful." Edward Gibbon, *The Decline and Fall of the Roman Empire* (1776–1788).

Perhaps because they confront so much seemingly senseless suffering and death, physicians traditionally have been skeptical about religion. Thus the ancient proverb, "Three doctors, two atheists." However, in recent years, the popular press has featured articles with titles such as "The new faith in medicine" and "Believing in God may be good for your health." A nationally distributed newspaper commissioned a poll of a thousand adults and reported that "56 percent say that their spiritual faith has helped them recover from illness, injury or disease." The article quoted a well-known physician, Herbert Benson, as saying, "To put it simply, we're wired for God." Also quoted was Albert Ellis, the psychologist who developed rational emotive therapy. He told the reporter, "This whole field is off its rocker." These divergent views reflect a confusion about the concept of spirituality.

The spectrum of spirituality is exceedingly broad. At one end there is the religious spirituality found in the quiet, prayful practices of monks and nuns. Hardcore Christian spirituality is best exemplified by Pentecostal worship, the most rapidly growing branch of Christianity, whose origins go back to the eighteenth-century Methodist renewal and the nineteenth-century North American holiness movement. As described by religious historian Steven Land, the Pentecostal movement's impetus was kindled and spread by an outpouring of the Spirit accompanied by attesting gifts and signs at revival meetings. It was believed that the biblical prophecies about the Holy Spirit were coming to fruition and that the apostolic church was being restored with faith and not man-made creeds, with authority based on the Spirit and the Word instead of human organization, and with power to proclaim the Gospel and demonstrate the presence of God.

In Pentecostal worship, emotions and physical activity are in high gear and serve as "proof" that the Holy Spirit is present.

Examples include hand clapping, arm waving, dancing in the Spirit of heavenly victory, swaying in the Spirit's wind, laying on the floor over-come by God's presence (slain in the Spirit), marching around the church until the walls of spiritual resistance collapse (the Jericho March), episodes of uncontrollable laughter, and laying on of hands and anointing with oil for healing purposes. Of course, there is much singing, witnessing, giving testimony, praying aloud, and speaking in tongues so that "the congregation becomes a temple of stereophonic praise though it may seem a cacophony to the uninitiated." The spiri-tuality is marked by spontaneity and enthusiasm. As participants are filled with the Spirit, and baptized by the Spirit they believe them-selves to be resurrected into God's kingdom and it is for this that they shout praises and battle against evil.

At the other extreme is soft-core spirituality. It is informed by "New Age" thinking and epitomized by phenomena such as suppos-edly ethereal music, auras, astrological influences, contacts with aliens, close encounters of the third kind, psychic readings (although television ads note "for entertainment only"), past-life regressions, channeling, near-death experiences, and being touched by angels. Let's examine the last two.

Neath-death experiences or something like them have a lengthy and widespread tradition. In *The Republic,* Plato described the hero Er who was slain in battle and carried home for burial. Twelve days later his body, surprisingly unaffected by decay, was placed on a funeral pyre. Er then came to life and reported that his soul had left his body and gone on a journey with a great company to a mysterious place where the souls of the dead resided. He saw a rainbow-colored col-umn of light extending through heaven and earth and scenes of judge-ment that were both terrifying and joyful. Descriptions have been found in Buddhist and Islamic texts and in Chinese, Siberian, Finnish, and North and South American accounts of out-of-body experiences in which a person's spiritual body experiences a bright light accompa-nied by joyful peace and meets with ancestors and departed friends after crossing the border between the living and the dead. In a study of deathbed visions among 875 terminally ill patients, 7 percent of Americans saw Jesus, while 24 percent of Indians saw a Hindu deity.

Raymond Moody's *Life After Death* (1975) contains 150 inter-views with persons who had near-death experiences. It was the best seller that brought attention to this phenomenon. Near-death experi-ences occur when persons are in a state of what appears to be death (they may even be pronounced dead by a clinician) but then are revived. Many report that during the period of not-quite-life and not-quite-death they are out of their bodies looking down at themselves and feel themselves moving through a dark tunnel peacefully and quietly. Their lives are reviewed as in a panorama. They see a glowing light with a human shape, cities of light, and a border from which there is no return. They meet deceased relatives and friends. They may hear doctors or spectators who pronounce them dead, but they are rescued from death by a spirit.

People who survive a near-death experience clearly endow it with a spiritual interpretation. As emphasized in Betty Eadie's popular books *Surprised by the Light* and *Touched by the Light,* the perception of a light often results in a more-spiritual understanding of life and existence. Many religious traditions associate darkness with hell and the forces of evil, while light epitomizes heaven, goodness, and God. In *The Divine Comedy*, perhaps the greatest literary evocation of God in Western literature, Dante in paradise sees both a cross that brilliantly "flames forth Christ" and God, "the eternal light." The light in the near-death experience supposedly has some association with heaven and with God.

Even if the reports of near-death experiences are accurate, it is possible to provide more earthy interpretations. Biological processes can cause mystical, religious, and otherwise strange perceptions. Some epileptic seizures, for example, are associated with religious hallucinations and mystical experiences. In fact, epilepsy was known as "the sacred disease" until the time of Hippocrates. A person whose painful leg has been amputated may still perceive pain as if the leg was present. This phantom-limb pain starts at the limb stump and persists in the sensory centers of the brain. Another type of experience, known medically as an autoscopic phenomenon, is often associated with epilepsy and migraine headaches; it consists of the sudden and brief perception of a person's own face or body as a colorless, transparent phantom that imitates the person's actions. The German poet Goethe described a likely autoscopic experience: while horseback riding he saw an approaching horseman who was his double and who then rapidly disappeared.

Remarkable similarities exist between the reports of near-death survivors and by users of hallucinogenic and other drugs. Patients recovering from anesthesia, for example, may recall words spoken by the operating team during surgery. Bright lights and tunnel imagery can occur when drugs that mimic the effects of light on the retina stimulate the central nervous system or when the threshold for light perception is lowered so that bright lights are seen surrounded by darkness. Published statements from hallucinogenic drug users describe "bright colors not like here on earth but just indescribable . . . I could see a city, a city of light . . . There are tall structures all

around me in all colors . . . It seems like I'm getting closer and closer to the sun and there's a geometric network or lattice in the distance." Even the panoramic, rapid review of a person's life has been
described by users of drugs that excite the central nervous system.
Such excitation may also be induced by fever, exhaustion, and psychological processes associated with dying (decreased sensory input
from failing body organs, a turning inward of attention and a blocking
out of the environment, reminiscence, and a fear of death that may
trigger both comforting fantasies and dissociative mental states). A
fanciful theory is that the near-death experience is so traumatic that
it kindles the memory of birth trauma when the infant travels
through the vaginal tunnel towards light. Yet another theory is that all
our memories are stored, but most are suppressed by new experiences that create more memories. In situations such as the near-death
experience, new input is markedly decreased, thus allowing the old
memories to be released and to be psychodynamically experienced
as hallucinations, dreams, or fantasies. When faced with imminent
death a person's thoughts often turn to God, heaven, and associated
culturally accepted religious images.

Unfortunately some near-death experiences are not so splendid. In
various studies, up to 22 percent have been described as hellish and
terrifying with a sense of being condemned to a barren void for eternity or falling into a demon-filled deep pit.

Our own death is not an easy thing to accept. Freud considered
belief in immortality to be a denial of death and a refusal to accept
annihilation. We long for proof of life after physical death and of an
everlasting spiritual existence. After ingesting special plants, shamans
say that they encounter the gods and the souls of their ancestors; we
regard the shaman's claims as hallucinations. When Westerners take
hallucinogens the door of perception is opened; what is perceived
may be multicolored, rapturous visions or hellish, terrifying ones. The
visions of the near-death experience are probably caused by biological processes and mediated by cultural expectations. Scientists were
surprised to discover that the human brain contains receptor cells for
the tranquillizer Valium, which means that we naturally produce a
Valium-like substance. It is possible that we also naturally produce a
hallucinogenic compound that is activated or processed only under
certain conditions, near-death being one of them.

ANGELS: THE SOCIAL WORKERS OF THE UNIVERSE

Angels occupy a prominent position in soft-core spirituality, and
almost everywhere we turn we seem to bump into angels or things

angelic. We eat angel food cake and use angel placemats. Angel wall-paper is popular, especially in bedrooms. We sing songs about *Teen Angel, Earth Angel*, and *Johnny Angel*. We watch movies about angels, most of which are godawful, such as *Michael*, or saccharine tear jerk-ers, such as *It's A Wonderful Life*. *Angels in America*, a play about angels and AIDS, received a Pulitzer Prize. The female "angels" on the popular television show *Charlie's Angels* were gorgeous to behold, as are the lovely models for Victoria's Secret angel bras.

All the world's major religions have angels. Judeo-Christian angels and stories about them derive from earlier religions and folklore ,where they are portrayed as fairies, guardians of welfare, demons, phantom hosts, lower gods, heavenly bodies, sphinxes, and winged intercessors. In the Old Testament books about the kings and patri-archs of Israel, angels were primarily God's agents. They carried his messages to human beings, protected the faithful, and sometimes punished sinners and the faithless. In Genesis, for example, an angel announced to Hagar that she was pregnant with Ishmael (16:11) and an angel ordered Abraham not to sacrifice his son (22:11-12). An area of some confusion in the Bible centers on the appearance of enigmat-ic persons such as the commander of the army of the Lord seen by Joshua near Jericho (Josh. 5:13-16) and the man who wrestled with Jacob (Gen. 32:24). It is not always clear if these persons are angels or God himself. In the oldest stories they were God, but as the religion developed and God became more transcendent and distant, the enig-matic persons were transformed into messenger angels. Christians have traditionally regarded some of the persons as the preincarnate Christ (before he took on human flesh). Another area of confusion is the Hebrew belief that angels were one group among a larger num-ber of celestial beings, all of whom were fairly similar. The infamous "sons of God," for example, were celestial beings who cohabited with human women (Gen. 6:1-4).

Those old notions about angels changed markedly after the Jewish exile in Babylon, as exemplified in apocryphal biblical books such as Tobit, Baruch, and Susanna, in the Dead Sea Scrolls, in Jewish books such as Enoch and Jubilees that were not included in the Bible, and in the biblical book of Daniel. Among the fallen angels Satan and his band of satans emerge (although some satans served God as destroy-ers and angels of punishment). Guardian angels now interceded with God on behalf of righteous persons. A hierarchy of angels was devel-oped; it included an army that was prepared to wage apocalyptic war. Angels were given individual names. Many of the traditional functions of angels continued in the New Testament, and Jesus warned against despising children because "in heaven their angels always behold the face of my Father who is in heaven" (Matt. 18:10). He also stated that all persons who acknowledged or denied him before men will themselves be acknowledged or denied before the angels of God (Luke 12:8–9).

The Bible contains some warnings about angels. Job 4:18 notes that God puts no trust in his servants and charges his angels with error. Paul told the Colossians not to be beguiled by a cult leader who preached self-abasement and angel worship (2:18). Acts 23:8 notes that the Sadducees, an aristocratic Jewish group at odds with the Pharisees, "say that there is no resurrection and no angel or spirit."

Fascination with angels is first recorded in the Jewish book of Enoch, a compilation of sometimes contradictory religious writings produced probably in the first century B.C. All sorts of angels received names, a practice that went amok. Gustav Davidson, author of *A Dictionary of Angels*, relates that in his search for angels the book of Enoch led him to many texts: "apocalyptic, cabalistic, Talmudic, agnostic, patristic, Merkabah [Jewish mystic], and ultimately to the grimoires, those black magic manuals, repositories of curious, forbidden, and by now well-neigh forgotten lore." By the fourteenth century, cabalists declared that there were exactly 301, 655, 722 angels! It is all very confusing. Sammael, for example, was variously regarded as the chief of the satans, the angel of death, Esau's guardian angel, the disguised-as-a-serpent seducer of Eve and father of Cain, and the enigmatic person who wrestled with Jacob (other angels nominated for this honor include Gabriel, Michael, Uriel, Metatron, and Chamuel). His mates included the four angels of prostitution, Eisheth Zenunim, Naamah, Agrat bat Mahlat, and Lilith, who was notorious also as Adam's first wife (supposedly she gave birth to a hundred children daily) and as the screech owl/night hag described in Isaiah 34:14. Theologians vied to name the most angels. Techniques included renaming gods and demons (the Greek god Hermes, for example, became the angel Hermesiel), adding the holy suffixes "el" or "irion" to a word (*hod*, the word for splendor, became the angel Hodiel, while *gevurah*, the word for strength, became the angel Gevirion), and playing around with the alphabet until a likely cryptic word was formed. Cabalists were hopelessly up to their neck, in angels. Catholics, fond of the notion of intercessors with God, made use of angels in elaborate church decorations. Protestant reformers, however, tossed the gilded angels out of churches and taught that intercessors weren't necessary since each person could read the Bible and communicate directly with God.

Modern interest in angels can be traced to Billy Graham's best seller, *Angels: God's Secret Agents* (1975). In this slim volume Graham states, "I believe in angels because the Bible says there are angels . . . because I have sensed their presence in my life on special occasions . . . they provide unseen aid." Possibly influenced by the American experience in Vietnam, Graham described angels as "God's dynamite" and noted that "Satan's BB guns are no match for God's heavy artillery . . . If your valley is full of foes, raise your sights to the hills and see the holy angels of God arrayed for battle on your behalf."

In recent years so many books about angels have been written that some bookstores provide them with a separate section. A common approach is to consider angels responsible for the unexpected good things that happen to people. *Time* magazine featured angels in its Dec. 27, 1993 issue and quoted the editor of *AngelWatch* newsletter: "Each of us has a guardian angel. They're nonthreatening, wise and loving beings. They offer help whether we ask for it or not. But mostly we ignore them." One book even describes angels as "social workers of the universe" and offers a twelve-step program to assist readers in linking up with their angels.

What with warm and fuzzy angels hovering above us and mini-resurrections from near death, not to mention a Harvard University professor of psychiatry writing seriously about abductions by aliens, it was only a matter of time before a work of New Age fiction would triumphantly burst upon the scene. I refer to James Redfield's highly successful *The Celestine Prophecy* and its companion workbook in which the heroic forces of pure energy, vibrations, intuition, and cosmic confluence of events lead to spiritual evolution and the salvation of humankind. The author even tells the reader: "Your own willingness to take time to study *The Celestine Prophecy* is part of the evolutionary process . . . the amount of consciousness you bring to the evolutionary process is part of your contribution." Whenever I meet people who tell me how meaningful Redfield's book is, I want to rap them on the snout with my old but trusty neurological hammer. Hello! Is anyone there? For God's sakes, you're talking about fiction. If you want to read a novel go get *Moby Dick* or *The Scarlet Letter*. In a perceptive essay on modern irrationality, Wendy Kaminer makes the point that pop-spirituality books offer intensity of personal belief as evidence of truth, and they substitute a good attitude for good works. They foster childlike passivity and habits of unreason while denigrating skepticism and rational thinking as forms of denial.

PSYCHOSPIRITUALITY

What lies between religious and New Age spirituality is a vast area occupied by psychospirituality. In 1984 the California State

Psychological Association's Task Force on Spirituality and Psychotherapy defined this form of spirituality as "the courage to look within and to trust. What is seen and what is trusted appears to be a deep sense of belonging, of wholeness, of connectedness, and openness to the infinite." Psychospirituality holds great appeal for many persons, especially for the spiritually homeless. Dissatisfied with their church and religious life, these persons seek spiritual direction, physical and emotional healing, and a sense of wholeness and well-being.

How have we arrived at this condition of disaffection with traditional church life? Many forces are probably influential. People have to work harder to make ends meet, and many family members hardly see each other during the course of a week. For them the thought of getting dressed up to attend church and listen to a sermon isn't all that appealing. Who needs another "meeting"? Televangelism has contributed to the situation. People who desire a religious message can simply turn on the television rather than attend a church. Also, revelations about the scandalous behavior of some prominent televangelists and their seemingly ceaseless requests for "faith offerings" have devalued religion, as have scandals, especially sexual ones, concerning local clergy. Churches that stress authoritarian, orthodox positions towards issues such as homosexuality, abortion, and even birth control are now often regarded as intolerant, unjust, mentally unhealthy, and out of touch with the increasingly liberal values of many persons. Other factors that undoubtedly have contributed to disaffection are a trend towards religious relativism (all the major religions share common and valid truths) and the loss of sectarian distinctiveness (Catholics and Protestants sometimes worship together; clergy from different denominations are invited to conduct services). Little wonder that the fastest growing churches are nondenominational. The decline of faith in the basic goodness of secular authorities from Presidents to child-abusing parents has spread to include religious authorities.

In the psychospiritual marketplace related to healing there is an array of more or less respectable therapies. Certainly AA's twelve-step program with its emphasis on a "Power greater than ourselves" (a.k.a. *God as we understand Him*) and upon a spiritual awakening is well accepted. Twelve-step programs are now being used indiscriminately by all sorts of groups for all sorts of conditions and situations from sexual "addiction" to self-mutilation. Clergy who have undergone formal training in pastoral counseling are often associated with hospitals, where they may be members of a clinical team, although usually they are undervalued and underutilized except when a patient is dying. Some areas they commonly focus on in counseling are the soul, the imminence of God in everyone, forgiving and being forgiven for trespasses, the importance of prayer and of grace, and healing as a manifestation of divine love. A few psychiatrists pray with their patients; sometimes it may be appropriate, often it is not. An agitated, acutely psychotic patient was asked by his psychiatrist to recite an "Our Father" together. The patient was temporarily calmed, but later that night slashed his hands and feet with a razorblade. He claimed that his Father in heaven would love him only if he cut himself to be like Jesus on the cross. In another case, a depressed woman who had been abandoned by her husband sought help from a psychiatrist. Just minutes into the session he suggested that they pray to Jesus to give her the courage to attend a weekend seminar offered by a well-known pastor on healing the hurt of failed relationships. The woman bolted from the psychiatrist's office in deepening despair. As a child she had been sexually molested over a three-year period by the pastor of her church.

A number of secular psychotherapies include a spiritual component. Jungian therapy, for example, attempts to reveal the "God within" and to achieve self-healing through contact with the universal unconscious. Psychosynthesis, a therapy developed by the Italian psychiatrist Roberto Assagioli, utilizes meditation, prayer, and visualization of religious symbols to help patients evolve past the force of biological drives to the superconscious realms of transcendence. In his book on *Spiritual Presence in Psychotherapy*, David Steere claims that the empathic understanding, respect, and genuineness of client-centered therapy (made popular by Carl Rogers) has a spiritual presence. A biblical precedent can be found, perhaps, in Philippians 2:4-11. In these difficult verses Paul tells the Philippians to look beyond their own interests and to consider the interests of others. He urges them to be of one mind with Jesus who "emptied himself" into a human form. Steere writes, "In this way members of the early Christian community viewed themselves as participating in the empathic identification of God in Christ with humankind."

The words "spiritual" and "religious" are not synonymous. A person who attends a church service every Sunday and participates in church rituals may be considered religious, but if the behaviors are simply motivated by habit the person may lack spirituality. A person who does not attend church but who volunteers at a soup kitchen and is active in environmental causes may be deeply spiritual but not religious. In 1990, psychologist David Elkins outlined the values of spiritual persons. These include belief in "a greater self" or a personal God, a sense of purpose in life and a quest for meaning, acceptance of the sacredness of nature and of all human experience, knowledge that ultimate fulfillment is found in spirituality and not in material things, altruism, idealism, awareness of suffering and death, and leading a life that has a positive effect on people, nature, and their relationship "with whatever they consider to be the ultimate and transcendent reality." This list would seem applicable to both spiritual and religious values. In the case of Christianity, however, the list would need to contain specific beliefs about Jesus Christ as the savior of humankind, personal salvation as the ultimate goal of life, participation in church activities and rituals, and acceptance of the Bible as the sacred book of Christianity, which is the one true religion. Consideration would then have to be given to sectarian beliefs such as obedience in spiritual matters to a church hierarchy, reservation of the priesthood for men, and nonacceptance of homosexuality as a potentially sacred experience.

These orientations can be confusing. One would suppose, for example, that what the media have labeled "the new soul movement" would be primarily religious, yet most of the many new books about the soul aren't. Consider the following advice about six ways to feed one's soul from Keen's popular book *Hymns to an Unknown God*: "1) Slow down, breathe and allow the marvels of ordinary things to saturate your mind; 2) Listen to the subtle messages of your body, and then follow them; 3) Start your day gently by taking fifteen minutes to contemplate your dreams and think of the day ahead; 4) Follow your bliss by seeking happiness in your work, free time, and relationships; 5) Tell a story, savoring the particulars and the mysteries; 6) Create a ritual to involve something you wish to give birth to, to celebrate something in your life or to mourn something you have lost." There's nothing particularly religious about this pleasant generic advice. It's good horoscope material.

Modern popular references have less to do with the New Testament immortal soul than with the ancient Hebrew notion of an animating principle that is the essence of a living person. The Old Testament recognized that the life principle of a body is found in blood (thus the prohibition against ingesting blood), but the life principle of a living person is the soul. In fact, the word "soul" was used to indicate a person; in genteel newspaper articles we still read occasionally about the souls who perished in a tragic accident. For the Hebrews the soul did not exist apart from the body, and so it experienced joy and sorrow, strength and weakness, love and hatred. It could be energized by God's spirit and could be metaphorically expressed as the heart, but it was not considered an independent entity or immortal until Greek philosophers got hold of it. Their influence is evident in the apocryphal biblical book Wisdom of Solomon (written about 30 B.C.), where we read that "a perishable body weighs down the soul" (9:15), that the soul exists before the body is created ("As a child I was by nature well endowed, and a good soul fell to my lot." 8:19), and that "the souls of the righteous are in the hands of God, and no torment will ever touch them. In the eyes of the foolish they seemed to have died . . . their hope is full of immortality" (3:1-4).

The New Testament (King James Version) contains the famous verse, "For what shall it profit a man, if he gain the whole world and lose his own soul" (Mark 8:36). Most modern Bibles translate the verse ". . . if he gain the whole world and forfeit [or ruin] his life." The Greek word *psyche* here means both soul and life, just as it does in Matt. 6:25, where Jesus teaches, "Do not to be anxious about your *psyche*, about what you shall eat or what shall drink, nor about your body, what you shall put on. Is not *psyche* more than food, and the body more than clothing?" This use of *psyche* reflects the Old Testament concept. What is new in the New Testament are the ideas that the soul exists as an independent entity separate from the body and that the soul is immortal. Thus Jesus said, "Do not fear those who kill the body but cannot kill the soul" (Matt. 11:28).

The ancient Greeks believed that every person possessed a *psyche*, or a second self that manifested itself only during dreams and ecstatic states. Unlike the body, which has a visible shape, the *psyche* is an invisible image. The "psych" in psychiatry and psychology derives both from Greek and biblical concepts, although redefined as "mind." In the Bible, Paul developed a complicated theory of personality that made distinctions between the soul, the spirit, the body, the flesh, the mind (or reason), and the conscious ego (Rom. 7:7-25; Gal. 5:16-24). The flesh and the body were associated with desire and with sin, and they worked to confuse the mind. The decision to follow God or the flesh must be made by the conscious ego. Fortunately, by the grace of God through Christ, the Spirit can assist the ego to make the proper decision: "If you live according to the flesh you will die, but if by the Spirit you put to death the deeds of the body you will live" (Rom. 8:13); "The Spirit helps us in our weakness; for we do not know how to pray as we ought, but the Spirit himself intercedes for us with sighs too deep for words" (Rom. 8:26).

For Paul the flesh clearly was the enemy, "and those who belong to Jesus Christ have crucified the flesh with its passions and desires" (Gal. 5:24). He provided a list of the benefits that come from being led by the spirit: love, joy, peace, patience, kindness, goodness, faithfulness, gentleness, and self-control (Gal. 5:22-23). That good physical health isn't listed should not be surprising. Paul was ever distrustful of the flesh and said, "I take pleasure in infirmities, in reproaches, in needs, in presentations, in distresses, for Christ's sake. For when I am weak, then I am strong" (2 Cor: 12:10). A case even might be made that for Paul, a vigorous, healthy body could be problematic in being more likely and able to pursue carnal pleasures. Jesus, however, certainly didn't have a problem with healthy bodies and took the time to cure people whenever the opportunity arose.

Paradoxically, the current, uncritical rush to spiritual healing is in part a result of the success of biomedicine. The explosion of scientific medical discoveries and efficacious treatments has raised expectations so high that nothing short of rapid cure is acceptable. Such expectations are unreasonable. Biomedicine doesn't have all the answers, especially for those persons who now live longer than ever and are prone to developing disorders associated with aging. Hucksters have made a good living peddling snake oil, magic bracelets, and the like over the ages. Some faith healers, too, have acted as predators, although, hiding behind the Bible, they are able to ply their trade with relative impunity.

LET THE BUYER BEWARE: THE PLACEBO EFFECT AND GOD

Only time will tell if the boom in spiritual healing is merely a fad. Certainly testimonials and case reports have outpaced controlled clinical studies, although the mechanisms of spirituality can never be studied. However, secular spirituality can be studied and has been, although it has been lost in the emphasis on biomedicine. In the past secular spirituality was known as the placebo effect (a placebo is a physiologically inert treatment whose effectiveness is based on a recipient's expectations of getting better). In fact, until the midnineteenth century, a great deal, perhaps most, of medical therapeutics lacked specificity, yet many patients got better because they and their physicians enjoyed a positive relationship and each shared the belief and expectation that the treatment being offered would help. The efficacy of placebos has been well documented. In the case of angina pectoris (severe paroxysmal chest pain associated with an inadequate blood supply to the heart), useless treatments such as vitamin E and surgical ligation of the internal mammary artery not only were seventy to ninety percent effective in providing relief from pain but also increased patients' ability to exercise and reduced their use of nitroglycerine (a physiologically effective treatment). Among the other disorders or conditions in which placebos have been demonstrated to be significantly effective are bronchial asthma, duodenal ulcer, pain, headaches, seasickness, the common cold, and nausea during pregnancy.

The current major champion of the placebo effect's efficacy is Dr. Herbert Benson, President of the Mind/Body Medical Institute of Harvard Medical School and Boston's Deaconess Hospital. He does not advocate the use of inert pills or sham procedures, which are, after all, deceptive practices, but rather emphasizes warm and sympathetic doctor–patient relationships in a setting of mutual positive beliefs. Benson claims that sixty to ninety percent of patient visits to physicians have stress-related and psychosomatic components. In his popular book *The Relaxation Response* (1975) he advocated a rather benign form of meditation to counteract the body's flight-or-fight hyperarousal response to stress. In fact, meditation can slow down heart and respiratory rates as well as relax muscles. Through this simple technique many infertile women achieve pregnancy, patients use less medication to control their pain, and insomniacs fall asleep more easily. In *Timeless Healing: the Power and Biology of Belief* (1996) Benson jumped on the spirituality bandwagon. He holds that belief in an "Infinite Absolute" is a result of our "genetic blueprint" and counterbalances our unique propensity to contemplate our death. He then reasons that since faith in a medical treatment can be wonderfully therapeutic in up to ninety percent of the most common medical problems, then "faith in an invincible and infallible force carries even more healing power." Benson provides some evidence, although hardly conclusive, to support his claim: among a group of chronically ill patients whose health improved while practicing meditation, those who also felt close to God improved even more.

If the mechanism for improvement is faith alone and faith in medical treatment is termed a placebo effect, then faith in an Infinite Absolute must also be a placebo effect. But maybe another mechanism is at work. Maybe the enhanced improvement is a result of prayers being answered. However, as discussed in the preceding chapter, it is impossible to draw any conclusion about spiritual matters because the results of any experiment will be interpreted according to one's beliefs. A positive finding in the study of the efficacy of prayer could be interpreted by a nonbeliever as the result of a not-yet-understood natural phenomenon; a negative finding could be interpreted by a believer as a result of a flawed procedure (not enough prayers or faulty prayers) or a not-yet-understood divine purpose. There is scant evidence that prayers are answered and certainly not ninety percent of the time. And then there are always the lingering hard questions: Why aren't the prayers of parents for the healing of their dying, innocent infant answered? Why weren't the prayers of the Holocaust victims answered? A response to this last question that still sends shivers down my spine was given to me by an intensely fanatical born-again Christian: "Maybe the prayers of the Jews weren't answered because they didn't pray to Jesus." I angrily replied that his was the most unchristian comment I had ever heard. He smugly answered that he would pray for my soul.

The richest merchant in the spiritual marketplace is the Indian-born endocrinologist-mystic, Deepak Chopra. He is a master communicator who radiates slick sincerity and offers the hopes of an ageless body and a timeless mind, of growing younger, and of reversing diseases. More a master marketer than an innovator, his therapeutic approach primarily consists of meditation, massage, herbal remedies from India, testimonials from celebrities, and a marvelous mishmash of grandfatherly advice, literary allusions, and spiritual pap: "All of us are connected to patterns of intelligence that govern the whole cosmos. Our bodies are part of a universal body, our minds an aspect of a universal mind." He is a star from the East who understands the West.

Far more substantive is the American psychiatrist, Andrew Weil, whose book *Spontaneous Healing* (1995) has a large following. His message is that the body's natural healing mechanisms are more effective when a person eats a proper, low-fat diet, stops smoking, uses herbal remedies, slows down, takes the time to meditate, approaches life passionately ("apathy may be the major emotional obstacle to spontaneous healing"), and uses mental imagery to influence the body. Weil has identified seven strategies of patients who have experienced spontaneous healing, and he believes that if other patients adopted them then there would be a dramatic rise in the incidence of spontaneous healing. The strategies are: don't accept the opinion of a physician who says that there is no possibility of getting better, keep searching actively for help, seek out persons who have experienced healing, form constructive partnerships with health professionals who believe in your ability to heal yourself, be willing to make radical life changes, regard your illness as an opportunity for personal growth, and surrender to a higher will by accepting yourself and the circumstances of your life.

Weil's book contains a chapter on alternative medicine with brief commentaries on approaches from acupuncture to therapeutic touch. He notes that Indian Ayurvedic herbal remedies are inexpensive in India but quite costly in the West (Deepak Chopra owns an Ayurvedic herbal company; he and his colleagues once offered an expensive herbal mix described as "pure knowledge pressed into material form"). Weil's one paragraph on religious healing concludes, "Since religious practices can clearly activate healing responses and cannot cause direct harm, there is no reason not to use them as adjunctive or primary treatments in cases of medically hopeless disease." It's hardly a ringing endorsement but certainly is reasonable. The popular media place Weil with the spiritualists, but he really belongs to the conservative wing of physicians in the alternative medicine movement. He clearly gives scientific medicine its due but counsels a healthy lifestyle and a more active participation by patients in their treatment. Bernie Siegel, a surgeon at Yale University, has written several bestsellers on self-healing. His shtick is simple and inspirational: love heals. He claims that the most powerful stimulant of the body's immune system is unconditional love and that miracle cures happen to patients who have the courage to love and to work with their physicians to influence their recovery. Siegel is so optimistic and enthusiastic that it's difficult to chide him when he gets carried away with himself:"If we choose the path of love we save ourselves and our universe."

The spiritual marketplace is vast, and it would take an entire book to examine all that is offered to persons in search of healing. You want reincarnation? How about past-life regression? Tibetan meditation? Pyramid power? I do feel somewhat compelled to call attention to the immensely popular book *You Can Heal Your Life* by Louise Hay, a Science of Mind minister (don't ask, I don't know what a Science of Mind minister is either). The book contains some pop psychology statements such as, "When we are very little, we learn how to feel about ourselves and about life by the reactions of the adults around us." It also contains outlandish statements:"I believe that we choose our parents." And provocative statements:"I bless with love each and every bill that comes into my home . . . If you pay with resentment, money has a hard time coming back to you." But most of all it contains a lot of hogwash, namely a list of "probable mental problems that create illnesses in the body." Thus, cancer of the breast results from resentment of the mothering process. The heart lovingly pumps joy throughout our body; when we deny ourselves joy and love, the heart shrivels and becomes cold, our blood gets sluggish, and we end up with anemia, angina, and heart attacks. Bladder problems result from being "pissed off," usually at a partner. Varicose veins represent standing in a job or place that we hate. Knee problems result from self-righteousness and a refusal to bend. A person with birth defects chooses to come into the world that way. Brain tumors are a result of stubbornness and refusing to change old patterns. And, best of all, hernias are caused by ruptured relationships. As proof, Hay states that many people working in alternative healing therapies "find that the mental causes run 90 to 95 percent true." Lord love a duck! This book is unadulterated folly, yet over three million copes have been sold.

Where's the spirituality in telling a person dying of a brain tumor, "If only you hadn't been so stubborn," or in saying to parents that their newborn child chose to be born with a cleft palate or a deformed body?

The Jericho march. Alien abductions. Angels as social workers of the universe. Cosmic vibrations. Follow your bliss. Expensive Indian herbs. Love can save the universe. God is a placebo. Spirituality sure can be confusing. Let the buyer beware.

RELIGION: PSYCHIATRY'S LAST TABOO

In 1874, John Draper published his *History of the Conflict Between Religion and Science*. He claimed that "Roman Christianity and Science . . . cannot exist together; one must yield to the other; mankind must make its choice—it cannot have both." Protestant Christianity, however, could be reconciled to science but only if it permitted the intellectual liberty that accompanies "the right of private interpretation of the Scripture." Twenty-one years later Andrew White, the first president of Cornell University, published his *History of the Warfare of Science With Theology in Christendom*. He wrote that the interference of religion into science resulted in dire evils for both, while the investigations of science into religion resulted in the highest good for both. He declared that "Science had conquered Dogmatic Theology based on biblical texts," and that science now could accommodate a religion based on a love of God and neighbor and on "a power in the universe which makes for righteousness" without creeds and dogmas. Both authors chronicled the struggles over astronomy in the seventeenth century, physics in the eighteenth century, and biology in the nineteenth. In 1873, Thomas Huxley, a defender and popularizer of Darwin, wrote that there could be no reconciliation "between free thought and traditional authority. One or the other will have to succumb after a struggle of unknown duration."

Sigmund Freud burst onto the scene at the turn of the twentieth century with his discovery of psychoanalysis. One of his favorite philosophers was Spinoza (1632–1677), a Jewish outcast who held that free will does not exist and that, because everything in the universe is part of God, we can attempt to understand our actions but we cannot determine them. Another favorite was Ludwig Feuerbach (1804–1872), who defined religion as "the dream of the human mind." It is "an illusion whose effect on mankind is utterly pernicious" and must be destroyed by reason.

Freud regarded religion as an infantalizing, neurosis-producing, tyrannical force, while psychoanalysis was liberating and healthy. Religion is an illusion, psychoanalysis is not: "But it would be an illusion to believe that we could get anywhere else what it cannot give us," wrote Freud. Most psychoanalysts followed their founder's hard line on religion, with the prominent exception of Karl Jung, but even when they said something positive about religion they managed to find a rankling counterbalance. Ernest Jones, for example, wrote about the "enormous civilizing influence of Christianity" and "sublimated homosexuality" in the same sentence.

Roman Catholics vigorously opposed psychoanalysis. They charged it with an exclusive focus on humankind's animalistic qualities, with glorifying sexuality at the expense of spirituality, and with undermining the concept of free will. In a 1953 address at the Fifth International Congress of Psychotherapy and Clinical Psychology, Pope Pius XII said that "the natural and supernatural knowledge of God and worship of Him do not proceed from the unconscious or the subconscious, not from an impulse of the affections, but from the clear and certain knowledge of God by means of His natural and positive revelation." In an article, "The Pope on psychoanalysis," a Jesuit priest contended that participation in psychoanalytic treatment by Catholics was a mortal sin.

Psychoanalysts claimed that the adult behavior was determined by childhood experiences, by instinctual drives, and by associations of ideas and emotions. Behavioral psychologists such as Ivan Pavlov and John Watson claimed that behavior simply was a response associated with a stimulus and that it was predictable. Anatomists and physiologists demonstrated that neurons in the brain were interconnected and that behavior was determined by electrochemical impulses that passed among associations of neurons. On a larger scale, Karl Marx proposed that behavior was determined by an inevitable process based on interactions among social classes. A major effect of these new understandings was a decline of belief in free will. If our behavior is determined by a multitude of forces, then our ability to act freely is diminished. Without free will, the concepts of sin and moral choice become fairly meaningless, and religion itself loses some of its reason for being.

Attempts have been made to reconcile psychoanalysis with religion. Oskar Pfister, a Swiss Protestant pastor, was Freud's friend. Their correspondence makes for fascinating reading. In 1918, Freud wrote: "Quite by the way, why did none of the devout create psychoanalysis? Why did one have to wait for a completely godless Jew?" Pfister replied that Freud was neither a Jew nor was he godless, "for whoever lives in God, and whoever battles for liberation of love remains according to John 4:16, in God . . . A better Christian never was." As noted by historian Peter Gay, "Like Pfister, Freud had explicitly likened the eroticism of psychoanalysis to the love at the heart of pastoral care." Indeed, in 1906, Freud told Karl Jung that psychoanalysis was "essentially a cure through love." R.S. Lee, an Anglican minister, wrote *Freud and Christianity* and praised psychoanalysis for showing that Christian freedom and love cannot be produced by "Superego religion, with its emphasis on sin, guilt, and punishment—its castration complex." In a 1951 article on Catholicism and psychoanalysis, Choisy pointed out that authentic morality exists "only when man is completely free. As long as he is neurotic, he is not responsible. In this is not psychoanalysis in accord with theology which teaches us that it is necessary to be fully conscious in order to sin? . . . A little psychoanalysis separates us from God; a great deal of psychoanalysis brings us closer to Him." Vanderveldt and Odenwald's *Psychiatry and Catholicism* differentiated between objectionable psychoanalytic concepts and acceptable aspects of psychoanalytic treatment.

Although Freud was reared a Jew and all the first Viennese psychoanalysts were Jews, the portrayal of psychoanalysis as a "Jewish science" is flawed. In fact, Martin Buber, the great Jewish theologian, consistently attacked psychoanalysis, as have many conservative Jews. Kushner's *Freud: A Man Obsessed* denounced "the priesthood of Freud's cult" and its "whitewashing of sexual perversions." Amsel's *Rational Irrational: Man, Torah, Psychology* denounced psychoanalysis as unethical, while Klein's *Psychology Encounters Judaism* attacked Freud's antireligious views: "Arbitrarily he attributed many social problems to religious causes and actively fought against the religious convictions of his clients." Among the few Jewish supporters of Freud was Joshua Loth Liebman, rabbi of the Reform Temple Israel in Boston. He was a nationally known radio preacher and author of *Peace of Mind*, a 1946 bestseller that went through forty printings. His upbeat messages included praise for Freud as a person who "really had a spiritual purpose, even though he may have not been aware of it." Gay's assessment of Liebman's cheery, self-help platitudes and view that all troubles can be cured is that they constitute a softly psychological religiosity that is the antithesis of Freud's science.

Psychiatry's antipathy towards religion predates psychoanalysis. Certainly there is a long medical tradition of conflict with religion (as well as of cooperation especially in regards to hospitals established by religious orders). Starting with Hippocrates, who established epilepsy as a biological and not a divine illness, physicians have provided naturalistic explanations for pathological conditions once thought to be caused or influenced by the supernatural. Mental illness was the last category of disorders to be freed from demonology, although the current epidemic of massive child sexual abuse supposedly associated with satanic rituals and cults has kept the issue of demonology alive. There is now an impressive literature showing that false memories of satanic abuse are mainly the result of flawed interview techniques—including the implantation of false memories—by flawed clinicians, law enforcement personnel, and social services workers. Accusations of satanism despite lack of evidence have provided grist for the mill of some Fundamentalist ministers who spread the fear of God among the members of their congregation. La Fontaine writes that the traumatized victims are unfortunately received in the churches "with acclaim as 'trophies of grace,' living manifestations of God's power to rescue souls from the grip of Satan." Childhood abuse may represent devilish depravity, but claims of satanic rituals including the killing of babies, eating their flesh, drinking their blood, and using young girls as brood mares are the products of disturbed minds. Recently the courts have awarded multimillion dollar settlements against psychiatrists caught up in this folly. In one case a patient was told to imagine memories of familial sexual abuse and of satanic rituals with cauldrons of dead babies; in another case the psychiatrist was accused of implanting false memories during hypnosis and of misdiagnosing the patient as having 120 separate personalities including those of a duck, Satan, and angels who talked to God.

Although Western religion positively emphasizes that our behavior should be motivated by love of God and neighbor, it also uses a powerful negative system of sin and guilt to regulate our thoughts, feelings, and actions. The Ten Commandments, for example, contain only one that is expressed positively, do honor your parents—while all the others are expressed as don'ts—don't commit murder, don't steal, etc. We are told to honor the Sabbath and then told not to work. As pointed out by psychiatrists, this negative, guilt-evoking aspect of religion often contributes to clinical depression. One particularly troublesome commandment in this regard prohibits coveting a neighbor's wife or possessions. It is one thing to prohibit an action, but it is quite another thing to prohibit a thought or fantasy. Most psychiatrists believe that it is fine to have fantasies, sexual and otherwise, as long as they fall within a range of normality (incest fantasies, for example, are a no-no), are not consuming, and are not acted upon. Psychiatrist Nancy Andreasen notes that sincerely religious persons experience some pain from their religion and that moments of remorse and spiritual anxiety along with moments of fulfillment and joy "are so pervasively described by religious writers that they are apparently interwoven into the very fabric of religious experience and are quite compatible with normality." True enough, but too often normal remorse can escalate into pathological guilt, despair, depression, and even suicide. It cannot be denied that many of the paintings and statues in Catholic churches are quite morbid, and that hell-and-brimstone revivalists are masters at scaring the heck out of everyone, especially children.

Another reason for psychiatry's traditionally jaundiced view of religion is the observation that religious rituals and obsessive-compulsive behaviors share many commonalities. In 1907, Freud noted that obsessional neurosis outwardly seems to be a tragic-comic travesty of a private religion, but on deeper examination it operates in the same way as religious rituals. They are both driven by guilt, for example, and the behaviors must be performed in a precise manner or else they are invalidated and cause anxiety or pangs of conscience. Freud wrote, "The protestations of the pious that they know they are miserable sinners in their hearts correspond to the sense of guilt of the obsessional neurotic; while the pious observances (prayers, invocations, etc.) with which they begin every act of the day, and especially every unusual undertaking seem to have the significance of defensive and protective measures." He also noted the importance of washing rituals on the one hand to cleanse the soul from sin and on the other to cleanse the body from germs.

A study by two anthropologists has shed light on the topic. Their understanding is that people engage in religious rituals and obsessive-compulsive behaviors in order to simplify the world by reducing many varied concerns and actions to fewer, more regular, orderly, concentrated and schematic ones. Ambiguity and complexity are replaced by certainty about a few simple, crucial distinctions. The concentration of multiple types of significance onto a few acts and beliefs gives rituals and ritualistic acts their mysterious power. When these acts and beliefs are shared by people and are used for culturally formulated purposes, they are called rituals. These rituals serve such purposes as dealing with misfortune and facilitating a right relationship with God. "But in some people, organic damage, physiological imbalance, or sociopsychological trauma apparently causes hyperactivity of this ritual mechanism." Such affected persons perform their ritual actions alone and idiosyncratically. Their personal rituals resemble culturally constructed rituals in form and content, but they differ importantly by lacking any shared meaning or collective legitimacy.

The historical reasons for psychiatric distrust of religion are based not only on psychological but also on biological concepts. Henry Maudsley, the most influential English psychiatrist of his time, wrote, "The corporeal or the material is the fundamental fact—the mental or the spiritual only its effect" (1918). In applying this dictum to psychopathology, the deranged brain causes mental as well as spiritual symptoms. Negative attitudes toward religion by the early leaders of psychiatry had a marked influence on its development. Studies have demonstrated consistently that psychiatrists are not as religious as the general population. Belief in God is endorsed by 90 percent of the American population, but by only 43 percent of psychiatrists and 5 percent of psychologists in surveys done in 1975–76. In a 1993 survey of psychiatrists in London, only 27 percent reported a belief in God.

It is likely that many persons who chose to enter psychiatry are attracted by its historical bias against religion. It is also likely, however, that contact with mentally ill persons influences psychiatrists to develop prejudiced attitudes (in my experience, psychiatric nurses are not nearly so affected, perhaps because the nursing tradition emphasizes caring for patients more than trying to understand the nature of their illness). Psychiatrists are trained not to accept things at face value but rather to look for what is beneath the surface. All too often they discover that people are not really what they seem to be. The kindly person may secretly harbor murderous rage, the children's advocate pedophilic desires, the moralist a love of pornography. Grand public figures may be nasty brutes at home. Decorous corporate executives who make difficult decisions all day may grovel before a domineering mistress at night. It is little wonder that psychiatrists tend to be cynics. This cynicism is aroused especially in considering persons such as politicians or religious leaders who attract attention to their supposedly superior ideas or personal traits. It is also aroused when considering institutions such as religion that are thought to put a damper on rational thoughts, freedom of sexual expression (even within marriage), and women's "rights," and to foster excessive feelings of guilt and conformity, dependency on the "saved" group, and intolerance. In fact, the outspoken psychologist Albert Ellis has gone so far as to declare that religion is a mental sickness "that must make you self-depreciating and dehumanized" (1975).

RELIGION AND MENTAL HEALTH

Whatever all the reasons are, psychiatrists have not taken religion seriously. A study of 2,348 articles in major psychiatric journals from 1977–1982 revealed that only 59 contained a quantified religious variable, usually a simple listing of a patient's denomination such as Protestant, Catholic or Jewish. Such a static variable is next to useless. In fact, attempts to determine significant religious variables are at least as problematic as determining significant mental health variables. Is mental health merely the absence of the psychopathological symptoms listed in psychiatric textbooks, for example, or does it

imply happiness, contentment, tranquility, spontaneity, the capacity to
love and to work, the maintenance of a right relationship with God,
and the fulfillment of one's intellectual potential? Is mental health the
ability to criticize authority or is it healthier to submit to authority?
To be independent or to be dependent upon family and friends?

It really is difficult to define religion succinctly. It generally refers
to belief in a supernatural, creative God and in the practice of rituals
that serve to appease, glorify, or relate better to this God. For some
persons, religion is an ongoing, self-actualizing quest for holiness,
while for others it is an achievable destination. Religion provides a
stable orientation and a moral compass. Since at least 21 variables
have been identified as components of religiosity, the selection of
appropriate ones to include in scientific studies is problematic.

Just as there is mental health and mental illness, so too there are
different types or kinds of religion and religiosity as described in the
religious studies literature. Committed religiosity is healthy, while
consensual religiosity involves shallow, restrictive thinking and a simple, conformist orientation to life. Functional religion furthers freedom and advances a person's potential and development, while dysfunctional religion is dogmatic, limits freedom, distorts reality, separates people, and arouses fear and anxiety. Humanistic religion stresses self-realization, while authoritarian religion is controlled by a deity
that demands reverence, worship, and obedience. There is healthy
religion and neurotic religion, moral involvement and calculative
involvement. The most useful delineation of religious orientation is
probably Allport and Ross's intrinsic and extrinsic types. Intrinsic religion implies a sincere commitment to one's beliefs which are internalized and serve as the guiding motivation of behavior. Its best measure on the Religious Orientation Scale is "My whole approach to life
is based on my religion." Extrinsic religion implies the use of religion
to obtain status, security, self-justification, and sociability. Its best
measure on the Scale is the statement, "I go to church mainly because
I enjoy seeing people I know there."

So what is the relationship between religion and mental health?
Psychiatric studies have either neglected the topic or treated it superficially, while religious studies are great in number but with questionable results. It is possible to find studies supporting every relationship
possible. In Gartner's review (1983) of 18 studies relating religion and
self-esteem, for example, eight showed no relationship, while six
showed a positive and four a negative relationship. Sample selection
is a major issue. College students and church goers are overrepresent-
ed, while nonbelievers are rarely considered: a few small-scale studies
have found lower anxiety levels in nonbelievers. One study found low

levels of psychological distress both in persons with strong religion and in persons with no religion; a review of this and other studies noted that,"It appears that certainty of belief, or lack of conflict, may be more important to well-being than religion per se. Other authors have noted that persons with high intrinsic religion as well as nonreligious individuals often score similarly on various measures of mental health." The relationship between religion and mental health may depend in part on the intensity of a person's religious convictions, yet this variable has not been well studied. A serious problem with most studies is that they merely correlate findings. The fact that elderly persons who attend church demonstrate better mental health than those who do not, for example, may simply mean that elderly church goers are in good enough physical health to make the trip to church. Since there is a strong positive relationship between physical and mental health, church attendance in this group may signify good physical health and may have little to do with mental health. Another research shortcoming is that most studies report on material gathered at only one point in time; what would be more helpful are studies that gather information on subjects over a long time span. Also, religious studies rely too heavily on self-reports as opposed to objective measures. And, always, the issue of differing definitions both of religion and of mental health remains. High religious fundamentalism is often correlated with self-reports of mental happiness. Humanists and feminists might reply that in fundamentalist households, women are conditioned to be so subservient to their husbands that they are unable to express themselves freely or to fulfill their potential intellectually. Like animals kept inside a barn, they may think that they are happy, but they are deluding themselves.

No meaningful general conclusions can be made at this time about the impact of religion on mental health. A 1983 review of studies found no relationship in 30 percent, a positive relationship in 47 percent, and a negative relationship in 23 percent. A 1994 review of the relationship found that 12 percent of studies were neutral, 72 percent were positive, and 16 percent were negative (this material was presented at a seminar and has not undergone the scrutiny of the peer review editorial process). One of the most conceptually sound studies, published in 1997, examined 1,902 female twins in Virginia over six years. The major finding was that except for a possible lower level of depression, there is "little overall evidence for a relationship between religiosity and current psychiatric symptoms or lifetime psychopathology."

In the Project on Religion and Coping, comprehensive batteries of religious coping measures were administered to several hundred

members of Protestant churches and of Roman Catholic parishes in
the United States who had experienced major stressful events within
the past year. Based on the results as well as on a thorough review of
the literature, the author concluded that, "On the face of it, people
appear to be able to cope as effectively without religion as with it."
Religious rituals in times of crisis were helpful in 40 percent of cases
and harmful in 23 percent. Religion seemed to be especially helpful
to more-religious persons who have less access to material resources
and power, such as the "elderly, poorer, less educated, blacks, wid-
owed, women." Further, "Those studies that have compared religious
forms of treatment to nonreligious counseling have yielded mixed
results." It is true that some persons who experience a religious conversion, often during a time of crisis, report positive psychological,
behavioral, and social changes. However, these reports occur after the
conversion and "in the process of telling this tale, it may be all too
easy for the converts to exaggerate the troubles they had before the
conversion and to exaggerate the happiness they experienced after."
There is a question, too, about how long the positive effects of conversion really last. A study of converts to ultra-orthodox Judaism
showed that while mental problems abated temporarily, they had re-
emerged on examination several years later.

While it is true that psychiatry's modern history has had an anti-
religious bias, by the middle of the twentieth century Western culture
had become quite psychologized. Psychiatrists and psychologists led
the charge of triumphant therapy, claimed the territory that once was
exclusively held by theologians, and even assumed quasi-priestly
roles. This environment was captured by a satirical couplet quoted in
Gross' book *God and Freud* (1959):

Jesus loves me, this I know,
My psychiatrist told me so.

Psychologists such as Erik Erikson and Rollo May dispensed spiritual wisdom in their books far better than priests did from their pulpits. Theology was becoming secularized in many ways, and a religious historian in 1967 wrote that the theologian was "faced with the
question whether he has anything distinctive to say that could not be
said as well or better by other interpreters of the meaning of existence." Having achieved the high ground, most psychiatrists treated
religion with neglect rather than active antipathy.

The growth of the community mental health movement in the late
1960s and 1970s, along with the development of the first effective
psychotropic medications, marked the beginning of the decline of

psychoanalysis. The new movement called for psychiatrists to work with natural caretakers, such as clergy, teachers, bartenders, funeral directors, and policemen, who were in a position to influence the mental health of large numbers of people. Although the movement lost much of its steam after a decade of exhilaration, psychiatrists no longer thought it unseemly to work with willing allies in the clergy.

Psychiatry in the last decade has primarily focused on patients with major mental illness, such as schizophrenia, major depression, and manic-depressive illness, and with other debilitating conditions such as borderline personality disorder and severe obsessive-compulsive, panic, and generalized anxiety disorders. Pharmacotherapy has become a major therapeutic modality both because it is effective and because insurance companies are insisting upon it. As a result, psychiatrists spend less time talking with patients. In such an environment psychiatrists are welcoming all the assistance they can obtain in helping their patients to get better, and they have come to realize the importance of the churches in providing psychological support and of the congregation as a healing resource. Ezra Griffith, for example, has demonstrated the therapeutic psychological benefits of rituals, especially in black churches. For their part, most clergy now accept the usefulness of psychiatric treatment, although there are still some fundamentalists who regard psychiatrists as agents of Satan.

The anti-religious bias of psychiatry is pretty much a thing of the past. Patients are encouraged by psychiatrists to attend churches where they will be helped and discouraged from attending churches where they will be treated as outcasts or where their illness is interpreted as a sign of demonic possession, weakness of character, or retribution for their sins. Psychiatric journals have published a number of articles in recent years urging attention to the spiritual life and needs of patients, incorporation of a religious perspective into clinical practice, and research on religion as it pertains to mental health and illness. This turnaround in psychiatric attitudes is not based on an upsurge of religious beliefs or acceptance of supernatural forces but rather reflects the pragmatic realization that spiritual and congregational support may help patients. Even psychiatry's official *Diagnostic and Statistical Manual* has found room for spiritual and religious problems and has decreased its emphasis on the use of symptoms with religious content in describing psychopathology. While these new attitudes are laudable, it should not be forgotten that the ultimate purposes of religion are not mental health and positive emotions but rather salvation and the quest for holiness.

BACK TO GOD AND THE BIBLE:
JOY AND SUFFERING

CHAPTER 10

Usually for the better but sometimes for the worse, the Bible has influenced the global course of human events more than any other book. Judaism and Christianity are Bible-based religions; neither could have survived only by oral tradition. The impact of Judaism on the world mainly has been through the brilliant accomplishments of individual Jews. Christianity's impact has been greater because of its evangelistic zeal and its good fortune in becoming the predominant religion of the European continent. European soldiers, merchants, settlers, explorers, and priests boldly advanced throughout the world bringing their Bibles and their religion with them.

Unfortunately the Bible cannot provide an answer to every specific question about life's vicissitudes. Although the priests who codified the book of Leviticus tried to cover all the important areas, rabbis still are debating about what constitutes proper behavior. Even the Ten Commandments can pose problems. "Thou shall honor thy mother and father" seems clear enough, but shall a physically and sexually abusive parent be honored? And didn't Jesus say, "A man's enemies will be those of his own household" (Matt. 10:36)?

Surely no book, even the Bible, should be expected to anticipate every nuance of historical and technological change. Holy Scripture, for example, doesn't mention automobiles or atomic bombs. However, while things change, human nature surely doesn't and one might reasonably expect the Bible to provide insight on proper comportment. The difficulty here is twofold: not a few Christian religious leaders and followers historically have behaved in a seemingly most unchristian-like way, and "human nature" itself is a troublesome construct.

There is no need to recite the litany of unchristian behavior by people who should have known better throughout history. Of note, however, is a current trend of repentance for historical acts. In 1994, the Evangelical Lutheran Church in America confessed its dismay that Martin Luther's "anti-Judaic diatribes" continue to be used to foster anti-Semitism. In 1995, Pope Paul II apologized while in the Czech Republic for the Church's complicity in the Catholic-Protestant wars that devastated much of Europe several hundred years ago. In 1992, he acknowledged that the Church was wrong to condemn Galileo Galilei, and, during a trip to Africa and to Latin America, the Pope apologized for the Church's involvement with slavery and the exploitation of indigenous peoples. In 2000 at a Mass of Pardon in Rome, he offered a general apology to all those people throughout history who had been wrongfully harmed by Catholics. Unlike a person who in confession must enumerate each sin, the Pope did not specify the wrongdoings which, in any case, he attributed to individual Catholics and not to the Church itself. In 1995, the Southern Baptists publically apologized to African-Americans for endorsing slavery, and in 1997, the bishops of the Anglican, Lutheran, Methodist, and Roman Catholic churches in South Carolina issued a statement confessing to the sin of racism and asking for forgiveness. The International Reconciliation Council, founded in 1992, has sponsored a number of events, such as a conference in Atlanta where a woman from a former slave-owner family held the hand of a slave's great-grandson and said aloud: "In the name of Jesus, I ask forgiveness for the sin of slavery, for buying human beings like animals, for saying they had no soul, for raping the women, for separating families, for tearing arms off of fathers who were holding their children, for beating them bloody." Several responses to this trend were recorded in an article by John Dart (1995): the editor of *The Christian Century*, a major traditional Protestant journal, noted that "The idea of later generations repenting a historic evil does not seem meaningful," while the chairman of the committee that promotes the annual American National Day of Prayer said that "There is no wholesale agreement that repentance can somehow mysteriously break the spiritual impact of past violations."

Surely these criticisms are too harsh, and it would be remiss not to point out the many historical and current beneficial achievements of Christianity. The point remains, however, that when religious leaders and followers engage in noxious behaviors for extended periods of time, it is difficult to argue that the religion itself is uninvolved and the victim of faulty interpretation. Books such as Deblassie's *Toxic Christianity*, Milam and Harris' *Serpents in the Manger: Overcoming Abusive Christianity*, and Booth's *The God Game: It's Your Move* make powerful indictments. The authors claim that Christianity often has been used to manipulate believers through threats of eternal damnation, the use of prayer as magic, the fostering of an unhealthy dependency on rituals, religious leaders who claim to speak for God, and promises of a divine right to heaven only if one bows appropriately and follows the rules of the Bible as interpreted by one's church. In his famous *Autobiography* (1873), John Stuart Mill told of the surprising enmity that his father had towards Christianity. His father, educated in a Scottish Presbyterian seminary, came to regard Christianity as "the greatest enemy of morality" because it established fictitious excellences, such as belief in creeds, devotional feelings, and ceremonies, and substituted them for genuine virtues. In fact, he considered the ultimate wickedness of Christian belief to be a God "who would make a hell—who would create a human race with the infallible foreknowledge, and therefore with the intention, that the great majority of them were to be consigned to horrible and everlasting torment."

The concept of "human nature" is hardly natural. There is only human behavior, which is wondrously variable depending upon latitude, longitude, and time. Through Christianity the Bible has contributed to a notion of human nature in which certain attitudes and behaviors are deemed natural while others are sinful, deviant, or barbaric. One example is the love of a mother for her child. While neither the Bible nor Christianity has a monopoly or even first dibs on mother love, the images of Mary holding the infant Jesus and then the limp, crucified Jesus are very powerful. They are the essence of natural mother love (although the Bible says nothing directly about Mary's love for her child and contains no account of her holding him either alive or dead). Anthropologists note the practice of infanticide among some non-Christian groups. Historians, too, have recorded the behavior in functional societies without any attribution by the parents of sin or deviancy. Mother love is surely wonderful, but it is not necessarily human nature any more than is sadness at the death of a loved one. In fact, in addition to behaviors related to basic biological needs, there are few universals that are glaringly present. One is an incest taboo, about which we will not comment; another is a religious impulse and belief in God, about which much of this chapter will concern itself.

THE OBJECT OF OUR HEART'S DESIRE:
THE SACRED, THE MYSTICAL, AND GOD

Jesus endorsed the words of Deuteronomy 8:3 that "Man shall not live by bread alone; but man lives by every word that proceeds from the mouth of the Lord." Throughout history people have sought some sense of understanding about the purpose and meaning of life, the world, and the cosmos. This quest for understanding has invariably led to a belief in some sort of divine power or process that is called God, the Holy, or the Sacred. In his book with the telling title *Religion*

Without Revelation Julian Huxley noted that "Not only does the normal man have this capacity for experiencing the sense of the sacred, but he demands its satisfaction."

In 1917, Rudolph Otto published an influential study on the Holy. He considered the Holy to be so special a category that neither it nor the human experience of it can be denied; it can only be evoked and awakened in the mind. In the presence of the Holy a person is filled with emotions that Otto labeled in Latin *mysterium tremendum et fascinosum*, eerie, sublime, numinous, astounding feelings of wonder and dread. These feelings supposedly are primary, unique, underived from anything else, and they comprise the basic factor and basic impulse underlying the entire process of religious evolution. The Holy, however, is foreign terrain beyond our apprehension and comprehension. God is "inherently holy other, whose kind and character are incommensurable with our own."

In his *Systematic Theology* (1951), the Protestant theologian Paul Tillich expanded Otto's notion and asserted that the sense of the numinous presence of the Holy is really an awareness of ultimate reality. For Tillich the ultimate reality is God who is being itself and not a being. In fact, "It is as atheistic to affirm the existence of God as to deny it." Apart from being or existence, there is nothing and nonexistence. Every person who ponders why anything exists must face the possibility of personal annihilation and experience existential anxiety. Psychiatrists can treat neurotic anxiety, but existential anxiety can be dealt with only by encountering God, the ground of being. For Tillich, true wisdom does not depend on philosophical discussion but rather on a religious experience, "a saving transformation and an illuminating revelation not of a personal God but rather of a God upon whom everything is dependent." This is the God above God. The leading modern Catholic theologian Karl Rahner equates being with knowing and asserts that mind is ultimate reality. For him God and self come together in "the mysticism of everyday life, the discovery of God in all things; there is the sober intoxication of the Spirit, of which the Fathers and the liturgy speak, which we cannot reject or despise, because it is real."

On a voyage to the world of full-fledged Judeo-Christian religious mysticism one would encounter fabulous people. Moses de Leon (1250–1305), for example, published *The Zohar*, the basic text of Jewish mysticism (Kabbalah). *The Zohar* is a compilation of esoteric materials collected since the second century A.D. It deals with the ten emanations of God and the secrets hidden within the text of the Torah. One would also surely encounter the greatest German mystic Meister Eckhart (1260–1328), who taught that "the just soul is to be like God, by the side of God, exactly his equal and neither above or beneath." Because of his notion of the God-man and his teachings that "incite ignorant and undisciplined people to wild and dangerous excesses," he was declared a heretic.

Mystical states are sudden, brief altered states of consciousness during which all things are experienced as interrelated. They often occur during periods of deep moral and psychological conflict, and they may be cultivated by the self-discipline of appetites, desires, and thoughts, by breath regulation, and certain drug experiences. In religious conversions or illuminations, the mystical state may be perceived as extraordinarily meaningful, creative, and coherent. The personal self expands to a close contact with God. Inner peace prevails and may give rise to a vision or special message.

While theologians and religious mystics themselves explain these special states as linkages to God, behavioral scientists have offered more mundane explanations such as an integration of left (logical) and right (holistic) hemispheric brain functioning, or a physiological change in the usually automatic regulation of sensory perceptions, or a response to opium-like chemicals (endorphins) that are naturally produced by the brain, or a psychological regression to the earliest stage of life when the infant has not yet developed a sense of self and feels connected and even fused with the environment. It is probably too great a leap of conjecture that the Garden of Eden represents life in mother's womb, but it does seem reasonable to identify the origins of consciousness in the earliest communal unity of infant with mother. In the process of growth and development, it is necessary for this unity to recede as the self emerges. We are led through this process by our brains and by our experiences with living things and inanimate objects, although many persons retain a connection with the primal unity as manifested by brief "complex affective-cognitive states such as awe, wonder, the numinous, states of creative insight, eureka experiences, and mystic states."

Freud in 1930 theorized that the mystical oceanic experience was a regression to the infant-mother unity. In Chapter Two we examined Meissner's and Rizzuto's development of this theory. An even more sophisticated psychoanalytic approach is that of Christopher Bollas, who stresses the importance of the earliest stages of being when infants record their first experience of mother not through language or mental representations but rather through bodily sensations and emotions. Through cumulative experiences based on this form of knowing, the infant is transformed into a self. In these acts of creation mother is experienced as a process of this transformation. Adults carry the memory of this process as evidenced by their search for a person, place, event, or ideology that promises to transform the self.

We revere objects that may transform us and may consider them to be sacred. We are religious beings because we carry within us the potential to be reborn and to recreate ourselves. These experiences are regressive in a positive sense because they foster transformation and restructuring of the self; they are not the regressions associated with psychopathology. The original creation of our self can be expressed not by easily understood words but rather by terms such as mysterious, unknowable, numinous, and transcendent that are used to describe the sacred. From this perspective our experience of God is ultimately based in the transformative potential of creating our self. The act of creation, however, cannot occur in a vacuum. It depends upon a relationship with another being. It is possible for dependency and relationship to be configured as wholly human, but it is also possible to imagine a broader dependency and relationship on what Tillich called "the ground of being" itself, namely God.

For most anthropologists, religion, or sacred culture, is a projection outwards of human wishes and represents a way of coping with anxieties. La Barre (1972), for example, describes all religions as a group dream that originated historically "in the dream, trance, 'spirit' possession, epileptic 'seizures' REM sleep, sensory deprivation, or other visionary state of the shaman-originator." Indeed, Moses and Aaron in the Old Testament are presented as shaman rivals of Pharaoh's magicians. The Bible reports that Moses was able to reconfigure his staff into a snake, to part the sea, to send plagues upon his enemies, and to find water by striking a rock. Some might consider these to be miraculous acts, but to anthropologists they represent ancient shamanic magic grown larger over time and embroidered by mythology. Yahweh is seen as the deified Moses and, in truth, it is often difficult to distinguish the voices of the two. According to La Barre, Christianity's God is the deified Jesus who, like Moses, was also a shaman-messiah. Historically and psychologically Yahweh was a more primitive God. His recurring paranoid-like statement that "I am a jealous God" reflects the fact that he is a mental projection of Moses. The compelling, uncanny, mysterious, awesome force of religion and of the sacred is so perceived because it resonates with the private wishes of Everyman to be special, to live eternally, to experience power and protective love.

These theories explain God as a creation of the human mind. Another interpretation is that they only explain how we come to experience, appreciate, and acknowledge God. The same may be said of biochemical theories that focus on the use of hallucinogenic mushrooms and cacti, substances that have been used to induce mystical states, to experience contact with God, and to make users feel godlike.

(Karl Marx's famous metaphor involved narcotics:"Religion is the sigh of the oppressed creature, the heart of the heartless world, just as it is the spirit of a spiritless situation. It is the opium of the people." Similarly in 1848 the British Christian Socialist Charles Kingsley wrote that "We have used the Bible as if it was . . . an opium dose for keeping beasts of burden patient while they were being overloaded.")

Donald Tuzin, an anthropologist, points to the importance of sound as a link to the sacred. We talk to God through prayer, and in the Old Testament God not only talked to his chosen people but also created the universe through speech. Drumbeats facilitate the production of ecstatic states found in many religious activities. We experience "sacred sensations" when listening to liturgical chants of the Roman and Eastern churches, and the experience of hearing Tibetan monks who repeatedly chant the sacred word "Om" is "so unbelievable . . . as to seem hallucinatory." In psychoanalytic studies Theodore Reik fancifully claimed that the sound of the shofar (a ram's horn) used in Jewish religious ceremonies stirs up unconscious memories of the primal father as he was murdered by his sons and arouses the listeners' anxiety and guilt, while Derek Freeman examined thunder-gods and claimed that thunder evokes fear and reverence because it represents the fearsome father. Tuzin notes that the parental voice may be the prototype for all sacred sounds through mechanisms of primary process thinking (the earliest type of mental functioning) "interwoven with the ineffable memories of pre-verbal childhood." He goes on to examine infrasonic sound waves, which can produce high-intensity sound pressure in the absence of perceived sound. They affect the vestibular system rather than the auditory nerve. A loud noise gets our attention because it is processed in the reticular activating system, which connects to other brain structures such as the temporal lobe of the cortex.

The temporal lobe is an intriguing brain structure. Lesions in it are associated with such symptoms as hallucinations, delusions, illusions, compulsive laughing and crying, déjà vu experiences, and hyperreligiosity. We are brought to a state of alertness and identify the source of the noise. Infrasonic sounds in the low hertz range are perceived and processed in the brain, but because they cannot be heard or their source identified ("their acousticity is an eery miming of audible sound") they have a mystifying, anxiety-provoking effect on a person. The most common natural occurrence of infrasonic waves consists of the inaudible sounds of distant thunder, which cause a person to have a quiet before the storm feeling, a quite distinct, vaguely disturbing sensation of the uncanny, of the something-about-to-happen. Tuzin believes that the mystery of this experience in combination with the mystery of temporal lobe processing results in the human interpretation of the event as "a dreadful, majestic, wholly other reality that defies ordinary experience and understanding, yet is always there to haunt us." In other words, we bind the anxiety engendered by the mysterious event by identifying it as a religious experience, namely contact with the sacred. Drumbeats and chants facilitate religious experience not by what can be heard but rather by what cannot be heard, namely subauditory infrasonic sound waves. The implication of Tuzin's theory is that religious feelings may be "natural emanation or proclivities of the brain itself."

The concept of God defies definition and consequently poses limitless problems for anyone who strives to understand or comprehend "him." Most serious strivers would probably agree that God might be best described as some sort of cosmic consciousness or the essence of existence or the creative and sustaining force of the universe. The impersonality and aloofness of such descriptors have little meaning for any except a few deeply involved devotees. The greatest allures of Christianity are the personalization of God in Jesus; the use of biblical concepts that portray God as a king, a father, a shepherd, a mighty warrior; and visual depictions of God/Jesus. It may be emotionally uplifting to regard God as "my shepherd," but it is also intellectually inane. Metaphors about God clearly are human inventions that tell us about ourselves.

So what are we to believe? Is God an objective or a subjective reality? From what I can make of it, the answer is "both." It seems reasonable that the personal God to whom we pray, the God who consoles us, the God whose voice speaks from Sunday pulpits, is the subjective fabrication of human experience. This is the heartfelt God within us, the God that we can briefly and deeply experience in moments of intense crisis or sublime beauty. It also seems reasonable that an objective, indescribable God . . . words cannot suffice . . . "is." This is the impersonal sustaining cosmic force or consciousness or principle that cannot be understood by a metaphor or moved by a petition. This is the God that does not exist because this God is existence itself. Even the word "God" is merely a human convention that imposes limits and therefore misses the mark. This God is beyond human understanding but not beyond human appreciation, although few of us ever reach this stage. The German philosopher Immanuel Kant wrote that "Two things incline the heart to wonder, the moral law within and the starry sky above." In some way I believe that he was describing the inner subjective God and the outer objective God.

THE BIBLE RECAPTURED: COMING TO GRIPS WITH JESUS

In the dullness of a fool the Bible can seem foolish. In the grips of a zealot it can suffocate the human spirit. In the hands of a psychopath it can rationalize greed, lust, and all the antisocial vices. In the eyes of a narcissist it can promote self-glorification. It has been used to justify religious wars, slavery, racism, self-castration, anti-Semitism, and myriad odd behaviors. The seventeenth-century English Quakers, for example, were inspired by Old Testament prophets to run naked through the streets; their leader, George Fox, said it was "a sign amongst you before your destruction cometh, that you might see that you were naked and not covered by the truth." Also inspired by the ancient prophets but with the addition of New Testament Holy Spirit enthusiasm, eighteenth- and nineteenth-century Presbyterian revival participants in Appalachia and the South wept, prayed, shouted, and engaged in special bodily exercise such as growling, snapping, and barking like dogs while gathered around a tree on their hands and knees ("treeing the devil"). But artists, authors, architects, and composers have been moved by the Bible to produce some of the most sublime, beautiful, and marvelous works ever created by humankind. Countless deeds of mercy and charity have been performed over the centuries in the pursuit of biblical holiness and in imitation of Christ. And for more than two millennia the Bible has provided solace and hope to the vexed and the hopeless.

Because the Bible is so vast and complicated it can be interpreted to suit many purposes. If it were an easy text there would not be so many divisions among both Christian and Jewish groups. Catholics believe that correct biblical interpretation can only be made by a select group of the Church hierarchy. Believers are spared the onerous task of trying to make sense of difficult biblical passages. In theory, this approach makes some sense. In practice, however, it makes both for passivity and a disinclination to actually read the Bible. Also, the Catholic Church is a huge institution with economic and political interests. It would be naive to believe that these interests have not affected or do not continue to affect the Church's behavior, including biblical interpretation. Protestants believe that every person has the capacity to interpret the Bible accurately. In theory, this approach also makes some sense. In practice, however, most persons neither take the time nor possess the cognitive tools to study the Bible. They may turn to their ministers for guidance, but with little assurance that the ministers themselves really know much about the Bible. The variability among ministers is astounding and ranges from the superbly trained to those whose training is obtained from correspondence

courses or even just from attending a church. The centralized authority of the Catholic approach offers an unquestioning stability, while
the decentralized authority of the Protestant approach allows more
spontaneity. Fortunately, at least in current times, each of these great
traditions shows signs of accommodating some of the best features of
the other. Many more Catholics now are reading the Bible, and in a
number of parishes there is tolerance of charismatic activities.
Protestants are flocking to megachurches, some with more than ten
thousand members, where Bible study with more or less standardized
interpretations is offered.

In the ken of a reasonable person, the Bible offers rich and truly
wondrous rewards. It is a book that deserves to be studied and not
merely accepted in a superficial manner as the "gospel truth." To
study the Bible means looking at all reasonable points of view. It may
mean changing one's thoughts and abandoning cherished notions in
the light of scientific and scholarly findings. And it should always be
remembered that the Bible is about holiness and salvation; as St.
Augustine noted fifteen hundred years earlier, it is not a scientific
textbook. Consider, for example, the biblical account of human creation and descent from Adam and Eve. This powerful account has had
profound implications for Western male–female relationships and
should be studied. As a scientific fact, however, it is poppycock. In
1996, at a meeting of the Pontifical Academy of Sciences, the Pope
finally acknowledged that the human body has developed through
the biological, evolutionary process, although the soul is a creation of
God. Creationist spokespersons, some of whom are quite intelligent
but all of whom are totally unreasonable, talk disparagingly of human
evolution "from pond scum through the apes to the present so-called
dignified position." Their ideas are promulgated by The Institute for
Creation Research, which was founded in California in 1975 with the
mission of bringing people "back to Genesis." One of their silliest
notions is that the earth is only a few thousand years old, despite
incontrovertible scientific evidence that the earth was created over
four billion years ago. The use of the Bible to defend the indefensible
is a mindless perversion. Pat Buchanan, a presidential candidate in
1996, stated on television that he wasn't descended from monkeys
and that parents "have a right to insist that Godless evolution not be
taught to their children." Mr. Buchanan's comments won him neither
votes nor respect. Going back to Genesis for scientific information is
intellectual genocide.

The greatest task of Christian reader-students of the Bible is coming to grips with Jesus. No God has had such an enduring and worldwide significance. Over the centuries each culture encountering

Jesus has reconfigured him to meet its needs. Thus, medieval monks cloistered themselves for love of Jesus. Mystics made Jesus the Bridegroom of the Soul. In the Renaissance he became the universal man. In nineteenth-century romanticism he became an ideal of beauty and sublimity. He has been used as a symbol of opposition to injustice and oppression by such diverse reformers as Martin Luther King, Mahatma Gandhi, and "liberation" priests in Central and South America. These culturalized Christs, readily accessible through examination of art, literature, architecture, and Christian creeds, are glorious tributes, but they do not wholly satisfy the desire to know what sort of a person Jesus really was and what things he really said and did.

Jews don't seem to be concerned about Moses the man, but Christians, especially in current times, seem to be preoccupied with stripping off the layers of devotional debris and discovering the essential, pristine Jesus. This modern quest for the historical Jesus began in eighteenth-century Germany, where a professor of Oriental languages, Hermann Reimarus, attempted to differentiate between what the Gospel writers said about Jesus and what Jesus actually said about himself. It was no accident that this and much succeeding scholarship on Jesus and the Bible occurred in Germany, where Martin Luther protested against the orthodoxy of the church. Biblical scholars were attempting to uncover Jesus' original teachings in order to arrive at a pure, nonorthodox Christianity. In 1835, David Friedrich Strauss' *Life of Jesus Critically Examined* caused a tremendous furor by differentiating between biblical material about Jesus that was historical and that which was created by the faith of the Gospel writers. The next step in the quest came with textual analysis demonstrating that the Gospel of John was independent of the closely linked Gospels of Mark, Matthew, and Luke. John portrayed the Jesus of faith while the other Gospels were thought to be more accurate historically. Mark was determined to be the oldest Gospel and, thus, the closest to the historical truth. Further analysis showed that Matthew and Luke shared common material, known as the Q source, which probably was passed on by early Christians orally or in writing and consisted of a collection of the sayings of Jesus.

In 1906, Albert Schweitzer reviewed all available material and published his famous *The Quest of the Historical Jesus*. Schweitzer turned to Paul's Epistles, the earliest written material in the New Testament. He reckoned that Paul, who clearly expected the world to end soon, must have reflected the belief of Jesus and the early Christians. Christ died. The world did not end. What were Christians to make of the situation? According to Schweitzer, the Gospel writers stepped in, reevaluated things, and composed their books about Jesus so as to present him in a favorable light, even though it meant distorting some facts and inventing others. "The Jesus who came forward publically as the Messiah, who preached the ethic of the Kingdom of God, who founded the Kingdom of Heaven on earth and died to give His work its final consecration, never had any existence. He is a figure designed by rationalism, endowed with life by liberalism, and clothed by modern theology in an historical garb." Although despondent over his conclusion, Schweitzer claimed that the mighty spiritual force of Jesus continues to flow through the world. "It is not Jesus as historically known, but Jesus as spiritually arisen within men, who is significant for our time and can help it." Schweitzer abandoned theology for medicine and established a hospital in the depths of the African jungle. For the next seventy years little scholarly interest was shown in the historical Jesus. Leading theologians such as Karl Barth and his student, Rudolf Bultmann, emphasized the importance of faith and derided those persons who dared to question the credibility and historical accuracy of the Gospels.

Since the 1990s there has been such an incredible upsurge of interest in the historical Jesus that he has regularly been featured on the cover of magazines such as *Time*, *Newsweek*, and *U.S. News and World Report*. Scholarly books about Jesus that were once neglected by the popular press have become the focus of attention. The sociological reasons for this trend are not totally clear, but it comes at a time when scholars believe, based on new interpretative methods and on evidence from the Dead Sea Scrolls and other recently discovered artifacts, that we understand the world of Jesus better now than has anyone except the early Christians themselves.

What emerges from the new scholarship is not a Sunday-school, embellished-from-the-pulpit, or Sistine-Chapel Jesus. For John Crossman he was a cynical, Mediterranean, Jewish peasant and a champion of outcasts who used demon possession as a metaphor of Roman oppression; the virgin birth, the resurrection, and most of the Gospel stories about him are myths. Many of these conclusions are based on nonbiblical sources such as the Gospel of Thomas and the Secret Gospel of Mark. Burton Mack paints a similar picture, although he turns to the Q source for his evidence. For John Spong, Mary's conception was the result of a rape, and biblical accounts of Jesus really represent not historical facts but rather the attempts of early Christians to make sense of his life and message (especially by forging links with statements from Jewish Scripture). For Stephen Mitchell, the history of Jesus is legendary but his teachings are not; he worked through his feelings about being an illegitimate child by coming to grips with God the Father. For Marcus Borg, the historical Jesus was a wise teacher, a social prophet, the founder of a Jewish revitalization movement, and a person who experienced the reality of God but did not consider himself to be a messiah or believe that the world would end in his time. The "post-Easter Jesus" is a construct of his followers who experienced the risen Christ as a spiritual reality: "So it has been ever since. The living risen Christ of the New Testament has been an experienced reality (and not just an article of faith) from the early days of Easter to the present. Thus, in the experience, worship, and devotion of Christians throughout the world, the post-Easter Jesus is real."

The Five Gospels: The Search for the Authentic Words of Jesus by Robert Funk and the group of scholars collectively known as the Jesus Seminar has created a great deal of controversy. Funk is an outspoken advocate of the view that Jesus needs to be liberated from the scriptural and creeded prisons in which he has been entombed. The Jesus Seminar Scholars aver that 82 percent of the words ascribed to Jesus must be separated from the mythic Christ, and that Jesus was not the first Christian, although his devoted followers made him to talk like a Christian. Funk has been quoted as saying that "Jesus was perhaps the first stand-up Jewish comic" and that Christianity needs to be reinvented with a new understanding of Jesus because it is anemic and wasting away. Although Funk has been called Satan and a huckster, especially by conservative Christians, the work of the Jesus Seminar is presented in a sober, clear manner and is essential reading.

Of course, there are some modern scholars who defend traditional understandings of Jesus. Gregory Boyd, for example, writes that the only Jesus of history that we can know "is the disturbing Jesus reflected in Paul's epistles and Mark's Gospel . . . The earliest followers of Jesus proclaimed him to be the Son of God, and basic historiographical reasoning suggests that they were right." Luke Johnson's *The Real Jesus* is a feisty, blistering critique of the new scholarship and a defense of biblical accuracy. Johnson attacks present worldly wisdom as expressed in "individualism, narcissism, preoccupation with private parts," while he champions the wisdom of the cross as "the most profoundly countercultural message of all." He admits that the claims of the Bible about Jesus cannot be demonstrated logically or proved historically, but they can be validated by the experience of authentic Christians: "The Jesus who truly challenges this age, or every age, is the one who suffers in obedience to God and calls others to such suffering service in behalf of humanity. This is the real Jesus that classical Christianity has always proclaimed; this is an understanding of discipleship to which classical Christianity has always held."

It is easy to sympathize with traditionalists who feel threatened by current portrayals of Jesus, but traditionalists tend to glorify the best of the past while conveniently minimizing the worst and forgetting the drab, unhygienic in-between. It is doubtful that modal Christians have historically or are presently engaged in suffering service on behalf of humanity. And Jesus has been recreated numerous times over the millennia. The power of Jesus to be meaningful is enhanced by the sketchy outline of his life and contradictory accounts of the Bible because it allows believers to fill in the blanks. Too much knowledge would deter the ability of Jesus to swell in our imagination and to provide counsel uniquely matched to our needs. The Jesus of the aristocrat differs from the Jesus of the peasant in personal details. He hears different prayers and offers different solutions. It is not that Christ is a chameleon but rather that he is often perceived differently by men and women, children and adults, conservatives and liberals, Protestants and Catholics. Traditionalists might argue that the Jesus of their parents is an anchor in a world that is changing so rapidly that even last year's computer is already obsolete. Modernists, however, could point to the marked decline in the size of traditional congregations and in the number of persons declaring a religious vocation. Modernists might agree with Funk that Christianity has become anemic and that its revitalization demands a truly contemporary recreation of Jesus. In our brave new world of virtual reality and relentless advertising puffery, the new recreation of Jesus is taking shape as a search for an authentic Jesus who is naturally constituted without preservatives or artificial coloring, the real thing. In an accommodation to science, the recreated Jesus of the twenty-first century may be unresurrected except in our hopeful hearts (there's room for hope even in science). And, who knows, in five hundred years, science may find a way to resurrect the body, in which case the risen Jesus will return victorious and choirs will sing "Hallelujah! I told you so!"

FAITH AND RELIGION, JOY AND SUFFERING

The concept of faith in the Old Testament is expressed by the group trust of the descendants of Abraham that if they believe in, fear, and keep the laws of the one God Yahweh, then he will deliver them from their enemies and cause them to flourish and to pursue holiness. Faith in action is accompanied by signs and wonders such as those shown by the Lord when he brought the Israelites out of bondage (Deut. 7:20–23). Faith in the New Testament is expressed by the individual conviction that salvation is possible through Jesus the Messiah in whom is contained all the promises of God, and by a personalized relationship with Jesus. In his Epistle to the Romans, Paul explains that faith is a gift from God; it can't be earned or learned but may be given to believers who are open to receiving it. Matthew, Mark, and Luke show that faith can produce mighty works and miracles, while John shows that those who witness mighty works and miracles may develop faith.

Secular life would grind to a halt or be severely restricted without some faith. When we cross a busy street, we have faith that automobile drivers will stop at a red traffic light. When we enter an airplane, we have faith that it will actually fly and take us to our destination. In performing these acts of faith, however, we are expected to exercise prudence. In fact, life involves a constant balancing of faith, trust, prudence, and caution. Trusting persons are commonly taken advantage of by the unscrupulous.

In religious life, faith seems simple enough but really is rather complicated. What does it mean to believe in the Bible? The books of the Bible have been edited many times, and there is no original text. Translations differ markedly, and after thousands of years of learned debate there is no unanimity about what many passages mean. Those persons who believe that every word in the Bible is true are stubborn, wrong, and lazy. The stubbornness of their faith may be quaintly admirable, but it is blind to reality. The Holy Book of Judaism and Christianity should be studied and not accepted passively. It surely is unrealistic to expect readers of the Bible to learn Hebrew and Greek and then to pour over centuries of tomes on interpretation of the Scriptures, but those who take the Bible seriously should know more about it than what is told to them from the church pulpit or provided to them in simplistic pamphlets. Study of the Bible means exposure of its warts as well as its glories and serious consideration of differences in interpretation. Just as Moses and Jesus took on enormous hardships, the faithful should be willing to struggle with the Scriptures. It's a pale imitation of heroic labors, but at least it is something. The faithful who engage in this process and who learn to love the Bible despite its flaws will emerge with an authentic, deeper, more abiding faith. Those whose faith is diminished by this process had little to begin with. The Bible can be appreciated as literature or mined for its wisdom, but as a living document and a guide to life it requires study based on faith, trust, prudence, and caution.

Historians refer to periods of religious revival as Great Awakenings and have identified several such periods in America. Robert Fogel believes that each Great Awakening ushers in a three-generation cycle of intensified religious beliefs and a new or reinvigorated focus on ethics that precipitate powerful political programs and movements. A cycle ends when the ethical and political programs come under attack and the religious awakening declines. The First Great Awakening, which began in 1730 with the introduction of revival meetings, led to attacks on the British for their moral and political corruption and helped to establish an ideological foundation for the American Revolution. The Second Great Awakening started in about 1800 with intensified revivals and camp meetings. The desire to cleanse the nation of corruption in preparation for the Second Coming of Christ resulted in antislavery and temperance movements as well as the formation of the Republican Party. In 1890, the Third Great Awakening began as the nation tried to deal with mass immigration, labor strikes, and urbanization. The belief that poverty was a personal failure and the wages of sin was replaced by the Social Gospel, which held that poverty was a social failure that could be corrected by governmental efforts to redistribute income and equalize opportunities for advancement. These efforts spawned Social Security and the welfare state, labor reforms, the civil rights movement, and the early feminist programs. We may be in the midst of a Fourth Great Awakening that started in about 1960 with an upsurge of "enthusiastic" religions that stress spiritual intensity linked to conversions. Depending on the study, participants in enthusiastic religions range between one-fourth to one-third of the population. Most are Fundamentalist, Pentecostal, and Protestant Christians, but the movement also includes a large number of mainline Protestants, nearly five million Mormons, and four to six million "born again" Catholics. These religious enthusiasts have taken a strong stance against abortion, sexual promiscuity, and indulgence in alcohol, tobacco, and drugs. Politically the movement gave rise to the Moral Majority (which collapsed in 1989) and to the Christian Coalition (whose leader, Ralph Reed, resigned in 1997). Both directly and indirectly, the movement has influenced right-to-life groups, welfare and immigration reform, the "Just Say No" anti-drug campaign, anti-homosexuality attitudes (keep gays out of the military and out of religious vocations, and block or repeal laws affording gays a special status), harsher penalties for drunk drivers and drug users, and attending to family values.

It is too early to know if, indeed, we are in a cycle of a Great Awakening. Was the change in our national motto from "E Pluribus Unum" to "In God We Trust" a harbinger or simply an isolated fact? A major recent study of American religious orientation found that only 26 percent of persons classify themselves as conservative, while 44 percent are moderate, and 30 percent are liberal (or refuse to be classified). Amazingly, 65 percent participate in religious services less than four times a year. The key to the future is held by moderates who may accept certain sociopolitical programs but reject others, such as anti-abortion and homophobic initiatives. Will the push to break down the barriers between church and state succeed or result in a major backlash? Will the ridicule accorded fundamentalists for their anti-science views erupt into hatred as attempts are made to force schools to teach creationism? Americans who are increasingly intolerant of governmental influence in their lives may become even more irate at perceived religious interference.

The historian Arthur Schlesinger Jr. has called all forms of fundamentalism the scourge of modern times. Fundamentalists consider themselves above morality. They kill heretics without compunction and engage in whatever is necessary to advance their cause since they are absolutely sure that they are the anointed carriers of a sacred gospel. Secular fundamentalists claim to execute the will of history, while religious fundamentalists claim to execute the will of God. The totalitarian faiths of fascism and communism have collapsed, but religious fundamentalism is "now busting forth in all righteous and murderous rage . . . Unrebuked and unchecked, fundamentalists of all faiths will continue to believe that they are serving God by mayhem and murder."

Those persons who claim divine objectivity for their own fragmentary perceptions are presumptuous if not egomaniacal. Schlesinger cites the American theologian Reinhold Niebuhr, who warned about "the depth of evil to which individuals and communities may sink, particularly when they try to play the role of God in history." However, public disgust over the assassinations and massacres inspired by religious fundamentalists in the Middle East and India could create distrust of American religious fundamentalists who, with the rare exceptions of bombings and shootings at abortion clinics, are nonviolent. Unfortunately, the Bible offers no consistent advice. On the one hand it counsels turning the other cheek, but on the other hand it glorifies the annihilation of one's enemies. Jesus displayed anger when he overturned the tables of the money changers in the Temple of Jerusalem, and he certainly cursed the scribes and Pharisees, yet he achieved his greatest victory by passively allowing himself to be crucified.

The enthusiastic religions are growing in great part because they uplift people's emotions. Surely over the centuries people have wanted to feel good, but the current desire to do so has a driven quality. Surely there are many sociocultural reasons for this trend, but there also might be a psychiatric one. Robust, clear-cut epidemiological data indicate a marked worldwide increase in major depression. The lifetime prevalence of this disorder in the United States is 38 percent, and the disorder is now being identified in children. The World Health Organization reports that 200 million persons suffer from major depression. It is unlikely that these high figures are solely the result of better case finding, overly sensitive diagnostic criteria, or a psychiatric plot. The causes for this global increase in depression are unclear. Are we being punished by God? Is the shock of truly rapid modernization to blame? Is some environmental toxin, tentatively labeled Agent Blue, affecting us? Since American popular culture has been exported throughout the world, can we fault television sitcom reruns or confusing messages on T-shirts or tainted cola drinks? Whatever the causes, the phenomenon is real. The incredible rise in the use of antidepressant medications is neither frivolous nor self-indulgent.

It's possible that to some extent the popularity of feel-good religions is a social response to epidemic depression. I am not insinuating that participants in these religions are necessarily depressed or even more depressed than any other group. However, depression is so ubiquitous that there are few persons who do not personally know of a relative, friend, or colleague with this illness. With so much depression around us, it seems reasonable to expect that feel-good organizations would prosper, as would feel-good behaviors. Unfortunately, activities that make us feel good can have negative consequences. Physical fitness enthusiasts frequently injure themselves and some even drop dead. Cocaine and methamphetamine users feel terrific for a moment.

Since depression drags us down, sometimes into the pit of despair, then we should welcome emotionally uplifting religious experiences. But do emotional highs have a downside? In the condition known as manic-depressive illness, the dysfunctional symptoms of depression can switch poles to become the dysfunctional symptoms of mania which include inflated self-esteem or grandiosity, pressure to keep talking, increased activity, and agitation. Manic individuals cannot be reasoned with; some feel exalted and euphoric. The behaviors of many participants in intensely emotional religious services—feeling filled with the power of the Holy Spirit, talking in tongues, prophetic utterances, impulsive ejaculations, falling down, unrestrained laughter and tears of joy, waving arms, mock battles with Satan, an absolute sense of certitude—share many references with and at times come perilously close to manic behaviors. True mania is uncontrolled and idiosyncratic, however, while enthusiastic religious behaviors are shared and performed in a controlled environment. These behaviors are not necessarily pathological but they may appear to be so to uninformed, nonbelieving observers (as Paul noted in 1 Corinthians 23).

Regularly intense uplifting religious practices are perceived to be authentic and desirable by those who experience them but are usually perceived to be a little crazy and suspect by nonbelievers or moderate Christians and Jews who witness them. These contrasting views reflect our ambivalence about joyful emotionality. No doubt we all like to feel good, but emotions can overcome us, get the better of us, and cloud our thinking. To feel good is wonderful, but the experience is so short-lived that the pursuit of it can become an end in itself. In religious life there is a superficiality in the unending quest for joy. Although a modicum of joy may exist in the heart, its deep experience is reserved for special occasions in both the Jewish and Christian traditions. Intense uplifting emotions are suspect because they are as evanescent as incense. They don't stick to the bones or endure in the way that suffering does.

The quintessential images of the Bible are the Suffering Servants, Israel in the Jewish Scripture, Jesus in the Christian Scripture. It is from past and continued tribulations that Judaism has extracted holiness. It is in Christ crucified that Christianity has found salvation. As a guide to religious life, the greatest message of the Bible is that worship without sacrifice is as meaningless as Israel without Egypt or Jesus without a crown of thorns.

NOTES

INTRODUCTION

The quote from Deuteronomy, "Hear O Israel: the Lord our God, the Lord is one" are among the most sacred words in Judaism: "Shema Israel, adonai eloheynu adonai ehad" (see John Bowker's *The Religious Imagination and the Sense of God*). The historian who condensed Christian history as being a series of facts that have about nothing in common but the name is Arthur Lovejoy.

Babylon conquered Jerusalem in 597 B.C. The Jewish temple was looted and the king, Jehorachin, along with his family members and leading citizens (including the prophet Ezekiel) were exiled as captives to Babylon. According to 2 Kings 24:14, "None remained except the poorest people of the land." This probably is an overstatement. In fact, many Jewish cities in the area prospered under Babylonian control and luxurious artifacts found in burial caves that were used during that time period indicate that wealthy persons lived there. (See *The View From Nebo* by Marcus).

The quote about the 1966 standard Greek New Testament text is from Fox, and that about Luther's Bible is from *The Interpreter's Bible*.

Jaraslav Pelican's *The Reformation of the Bible*, *The Bible of the Reformation* contains a series of technical, important essays that complement the photographs and discussions of an exhibit held at Southern Methodist University. Pelican is one of the great students of religion. He has written many books for the general reader but this one was meant for his scholarly colleagues.

The quote from M. Jarvis about the New Testament is from his entry on New Testament Texts in *The Interpreter's Dictionary of the Bible*. Martin Luther is one of the most complicated personalities in religious history. Erik Erickson's *Young Martin Luther* examines his formative years from a psychoanalytic perspective. His chronic irritable bowel syndrome is well documented, as is the fact that he was sitting on the privy when he achieved the insight that salvation depends on faith alone. He was a voluminous writer and prone to nasty, scatological invective. Norman Brown's *Life Against Death: The Psychoanalytic Meaning of History* notes that "the anal character of the Devil is sensuously perceived and sensuously recorded by Luther (in his *Table Talk*) with a gross concreteness that latter-day Protestantism cannot imagine and would not tolerate."

329

When bothered by the Devil, Luther told him to "kiss my ass" and to "shit in his pants and hang them around his neck." He threatened to "shit in his [the Devil's] face" and to "throw him into my ass, where he belongs." Scatological drawings are frequently found in publications of Luther's works. One of the most infamous is *The Depiction of the Papacy* (1545), a pamphlet which contains nine crude drawings of the Antichrist pope in association with defecation. Luther, of course, was a genius who changed the course of history. His anality made possible the Protestant revolution and, although Luther did not plan it, the consequent rise of capitalism, an economic approach that psychologically represents repressed anality and regards an accumulation of money (filthy lucre, feces) as a sanctified activity. For more on this see, in addition to Brown, R.H. Tawney's *Religion and the Rise of Capitalism*, E. Troeltsch's *The Social Teaching of the Christian Churches*, and M. Weber's *The Protestant Ethic and the Spirit of Capitalism*.

Desiderius Erasmus (1466–1536), one of Tyndale's teachers, was a Catholic theologian, a truly great humanist and scholar, a religious reformer, and a champion of simplicity. He revered the Bible and believed that every person should read and interpret it without the assistance of the clergy. In fact, he felt that many theologians reached faulty conclusions based on their use of flawed biblical texts. He detested rigid orthodox pronouncements and championed minimalism. Aside from a few basic Christian truths, he believed that "everyone should be left to follow his own judgement, because there is great obscurity in these matters." He had little use for the theory of predestination but rather preached about the Greek and Roman virtues and the necessity of good deeds as well as abundant faith. He agreed with the basic ideas of Luther's reform but would not support Luther's tactic of inflaming nationalistic wars. Luther responded by calling him a "a piece of shit" and a pedophile. Erasmus called upon the Pope to stop the Inquisition, to allow priests to marry, and to establish a sweet concord among Christians by tolerating differing views on debatable issues. For his troubles Erasmus, who once turned down an offer to become a cardinal, was labeled a heretic after his death and Pope Paul IV encouraged the burning of all his books. In 1546 at the Council of Trent, the Catholic Church cursed and banned his translation of the New Testament.

Augustine's warning about citing the Bible as evidence for natural phenomena is from his *On Genesis According to the Literal Sense*. Augustine followed the lead of the theologian Origen of Alexandria in understanding that the Bible was inspired by God but written by men who were permitted to compile their narratives in their own style. God inspired but did not dictate each word. The sentiment and intent of the biblical writers was more significant than phraseology. The Bible was absolutely truthful on matters of importance such as faith, salvation, and the resurrection but was not necessarily accurate in matters of little consequence such as animal husbandry or botany.

The quote about the Bible being not a scientific text but rather "a living instrument serving God for the proclamation of the message of salvation" is from Gerrit Berkouwer, a twentieth-century Dutch theologian. See *The Authority and Interpretation of the Bible* by Rogers and McKim for more on Berkouwer and other major modern theologians.

William Keller's *The Bible As History* (2nd revised version, 1991) is a more accurate title than that of the first edition, *The Bible is Right*. Keller strives to put a positive spin on things but, in fact, presents very little evidence that the Bible is historically accurate. Readers who want to believe that the Bible is right seem to find sustenance in the book but only at the cost of suspending their critical faculties.

All the biblical characters prior to Abraham were clearly mythic. He appears to be the first historical person, although there is no evidence outside of the Bible that he truly existed. If he was a single person (he might represent a small tribe), he probably lived about 2000 B.C. Stories about him circulated for a thousand years before they were written down. A thousand years is a long time, and it would be naive to believe that oral stories would not be influenced by the events of time. Some would be forgotten, some embellished. And when they were written down they were then edited over hundreds of years by the various authors of the Torah. The J writer stressed that Abraham would be a father of many nations, and he wrote about the covenant in which God gave the land to Abraham's descendants. The E writer added other material such as the expulsion of Hagar and her son Ishmael (Abraham had obeyed his wife's wishes and impregnated her maid, Hagar; when his wife had a child of her own, she convinced Abraham to boot the maid and her son out of the camp), the treaty with Abimelech, and the famous story when God tested Abraham by ordering him to kill his son and burn him as an offering. The P writer added stories such as Abraham's meeting with Melchizedek, the purchase of the plot of land called Machpelah, and Abraham's death. In the historical books of the Bible, Abraham is mentioned only once in Joshua (24:2-4), once in 1 Kings (18:36), and once in 2 Kings (13:23). What we have is a patchwork of material that casts doubt on the historical truthfulness of the biblical accounts about Abraham. Even the changing of his name from Abram to Abraham appears to have been invented by the P writer who, perhaps, wanted to emphasize the role of Israel as a leader of all the nations.

The derivation of the word Hebrews presented in the chapter seems reasonable although there are other possibilities. The verb '_bar means "to cross over" or "to cross beyond"; a Hebrew might be a person who crossed over the Jordan or Euphrates Rivers. A weaker argument links the Hebrews to the Eberites who descended from Shem's grandson, Eber. Hebrew is an old term that was used mainly in the time before King David. At one time there was a distinction between the larger groups of Hebrews and a subset of this group known as Israelites. For example,1 Samuel 14:21 notes that "the Hebrews who had been with the Philistines . . . turned to be with the Israelites," and in 29:3 the Philistines who were preparing to battle the Israelites refused to let David fight on their side because he was identified as a Hebrew.

Sigmund Freud wrote *Moses and Monotheism* shortly before his death from cancer at age 83. In it he wrote, "There was no place in the framework of the religion of Moses for a direct expression of the hatred of the faith." Some psychoanalysts believe that the book's thesis represents Freud's attempt to assuage his guilt over his part-loving, part-hateful feelings towards his deeply religious father, Jacob. Freud resented Moses/Jacob and so Moses was murdered in Freud's book just as Jacob was murdered in Freud's fantasy. Freud also identified himself with Moses, who created the new faith of Judaism just as Freud had created the new science of psychoanalysis. By claiming that Moses was Egyptian, Freud stripped him of his Jewish identity. Though identification with Moses, Freud stripped himself of the Jewish identity given to him by his father. *Moses and Monotheism* was Freud's act of liberation. In fact, when he was told that Ernst Sellin, the scholar who first suggested that the Jews had murdered Moses, no longer believed that this was true, Freud reportedly shrugged his shoulders and said, "It might be true all the same." See M. Robert's *From Oedipus to Moses: Freud's Jewish Identity*; Rice's *Freud and Moses*; Yerushalmi's *Freud's Moses*; Allan Young's review essay "The return of the return of the repressed"; and Paul's *Moses and Civilization*.

The Hebrews were deeply impressed by the power of words. Yahweh created the universe through speech, and Isaiah wrote that God's word accomplishes whatever God pleases (55:110–11). When the early biblical prophets referred to the word of God, they meant the inspiration of God, which could be in the form of either words or visions (words were preferred over visual images, which smacked of idol worship). The book of Amos combined the two: "The words of Amos . . . which he saw concerning Israel . . ." After the exile God's word came to mean not only what he said to the prophets but also what was revealed in the law. Jesus began his explanation of the parable of the sower, "Now the parable is this . . . The seed is the word of God" (Luke 8:11), and throughout the New Testament his disciples preached the word of God. In his Gospel John wrote, "In the beginning was the Word, and the word was with God, and the word was God . . . And the Word became flesh and dwelled among us" (1:1, 14). Thus, Jesus personified the word of God. There is another reference to Jesus as the Word in the New Testament letter of 1 John: "For there are three that bear record to heaven, the Father, the Word, and the Holy Ghost; and these three are one" (5:7). Some Bibles include this verse while others don't because it cannot be found in any old Greek manuscript. It first appeared as a quote in a text by the Spanish theologian Priscillian (died in 385) and eventually became integrated into Jerome's Latin Vulgate Bible.

Reverence for the word of God is especially found in Islam. The text of the Koran was, according to Muslim belief, revealed to the prophet Muhammad from 610 to 632 A.D. He spoke these revelations to his followers, who wrote them down. These writings were brought together into a finalized text within several decades. Every word is considered to be the direct word of God, and no changes have been made to the Koran over the centuries (this is the official view, but scholars have found discrepancies in various manuscripts). Bowker (1978) cites a classic Muslim theological formulation: "The Koran is the speech of God, written in the copies, preserved in the memories, recited by the tongues, revealed to the prophet. Our pronouncing, writing, and reciting the Koran are created, but the Koran itself is uncreated." Muhammad's followers record that at times he sweated, was red in the face, or seemed to be overwhelmed with grief when he uttered the words of God. According to one tradition, Muhammad was asked how revelation came to him. He replied, "Sometimes it comes to me like the clanging of a bell, and that is heaviest upon me; then it leaves me and I remember what he has said; and sometimes the angel comes to me resembling a man and speaks to me and I remember what he says." During Muhammad's lifetime several men tried to create their own holy book; they were quickly exposed as false prophets. In fact, the Koran issues a dare: "If you are in doubt concerning what we have sent down on our servant, then produce a sura [section] like it, and summon your witnesses beside God if you are true. But if you cannot—and certainly you cannot—then fear the fire whose fuel is men and rocks, prepared for those who refuse belief" (ii 22).

The Christian Bible includes Daniel among the prophetic books, but the Hebrew Bible places in among The Writings. Daniel is somewhat of a puzzle. No one knows why it switches from Hebrew to Aramaic at 2:4 and back to Hebrew at chapter 8. Scholars are sure that the book was written in about 165 B.C., yet the author pretended that he had written it in about 530 B.C., that he lived during the exile in Babylon, and that he was an active participant in the royal activities of the Babylonians (King Nebuchadnezzar), the Medes (King Darius), and the Persians (King Cyrus). Calculations of time are confusing: In 12:11, 1,290 days is written, but the next verse lists 1,335 days. The book notes that Nebuchadnezzar was changed into a beast for seven years, but historical reports from that time make no mention of any interruption in the king's reign. The Greek Septuagint Bible contains material about Daniel, such as the Song of the Three Holy Children, Susanna, and Bel and the Dragon, not found in the Hebrew Masoretic biblical text.

The figure of Daniel appears to be a literary invention derived from ancient history and legends such as that of the king named Dnil who was noted for his righteous decisions in the six-thousand-year-old Ugrit culture on the Syrian coast. The authors of the book of Daniel wrote during a time when Antiochus, the foreign ruler of the area, was persecuting the Jews. He desecrated the Jewish holy temple, demanded that the Jews worship Zeus, and claimed divinity for himself. He tried to force Jews to eat pork. The book of Daniel was written to bolster the spirits of the oppressed Jews by creating a hero. Daniel wouldn't eat the king's food, yet he thrived. His friends refused to worship a golden idol yet survived being tossed into a fiery furnace. Daniel was thrown into the lions' den because he prayed to God and not to the king but was saved by an angel. A boastful king was punished by being transformed into a beast. And in a final maneuver, Daniel offered hope to the Jews that God would not allow the reign of terror to endure. He prophesied that in just three and a half years it would end. Not only would evil persons be punished but, a new idea for Jews, the righteous will be rewarded with everlasting life and will shine like the stars forever and ever (12:2–4). The Mesopotamians, Egyptians, and Greeks all had ideas about life after death, but no concept like the resurrection in Daniel. Claims that other Old Testament passages refer to resurrection are misguided. In this instance, Daniel is unique.

The Song of Songs, Ecclesiastes, Proverbs, Psalms 72 and 127, and the apochryphal Wisdom of Solomon have all been attributed to Solomon who reigned as the third king of Israel from 962–922 B.C. The prophet Nathan named him Jedidiah (the Lord's beloved), but he was called Solomon by his parents, King David and Bathsheba. As David lay dying, Bathsheba, Nathan, and others managed to have Solomon named king instead of Adonijah who was the legitimate heir. Adonijah was disappointed but swore allegiance to Solomon. When he foolishly asked for the woman, Abishag, who had been assigned to keep David warm in his deathbed, Solomon had him executed. Solomon embarked on an immense building program of palaces, armories, fortifications, stables, ore refineries, and the temple of Jerusalem. So ambitious were his plans that he drafted 30,000 Israelites to work alongside 153,600 alien captives. He supposedly had 1,000 wives and concubines, although many wives came from political alliances. After making a treaty with the Egyptian Pharaoh and marrying his daughter, Solomon sacrificed a thousand burnt offerings to God. That night God appeared in a vision and said, "Ask! What shall I give you?" Solomon asked for "an understanding heart . . . that I may discern between good and evil." Pleased that Solomon had not asked for riches or honor or a long life, God gave him "a wise and understanding heart, for there has not been anyone like you before you, nor shall any like you arise after you." He also gave him riches, honor, and (if he kept God's laws) long life (1 Kings 3:5–14). He was a wise judge and became famous for his proverbs, his musical compositions, and his ability to solve the riddles that the Queen of Sheba asked him. With such a record it's understandable that so many books were attributed to him. Alas, all did not end well for Solomon. His grandiose programs brought strife and economic hardship upon the people, and his love of foreign women (he even built places of worship for their gods) angered God. God raised up an adversary, Jeroboam, so that the end of Solomon's forty-year reign was troubled by revolution.

Ecclesiastes has a bit of something for everyone, especially when brief statements are taken out of context. An interesting verse that has come to refer to a futile act is "Cast your bread upon the waters, for you will find it after many days. Give a portion to seven, or even to eight, for you know not what evil may happen on earth" (11:1-2). There have been many interpretations of this verse. One of the most probable is that the word "for" really means "yet" or "nevertheless"; thus, even if a person engages in a seemingly futile act, things might turn out alright (even the bread that is thrown on the water might be recovered), but it's better to play it safe and to invest one's efforts in seven or eight ventures. The custom of casting bread onto the water most likely refers to a ritual concerning the god Adonis. His followers put vegetable seeds in baskets. When sprouts appeared the baskets were thrown in lakes or the sea in the hope that this would result in a rich harvest.

Jesus is the name of the central character in the Gospels. Christ is an honorific title meaning "anointed" and signifying messiahship. The list of his apostles appears in Mark 3:14-19, Luke 6:12-16, Matt. 10:2-4, and Acts 1:13-14. Paul also considered himself to be an apostle along with James, the brother of the Lord, Barnabas, Andronicus, and Junias. John (21:2) counts Nathanael of Cana as an apostle. Judas Iscariot, the betrayer of Jesus, was the treasurer of the apostle's group, and according to John 13:23, seems to have sat next to Christ during the Last Supper. Matthew relates that Judas repented and tried to give the betrayal money paid by the priests back to them. When they refused he hanged himself. Acts 1:18-19 records that Judas used the money to buy a field and suffered a most unlikely spontaneous disembowelment: "falling headlong, he burst open in the middle and all his entrails gushed out." Iscariot derives from the word "assassin" (*sicarius*), a term used by the Romans to describe the religious Zealots who rebelled against them in 66-70 A.D. Peter, a fisherman, was the leading apostle despite his many failings, especially his denial of Jesus (Mark 14:66-72). In Matthew, Peter identifies Jesus as the Christ who then says "You are Peter, and on this rock I will build my church . . . I will give you the keys of the kingdom of however, and whatever you bind on earth shall be bound in heaven, and whatever you loose on earth shall be loosed in heaven" (16:18-19). The Catholic Church bases its concept of papal authority upon these verses, but there has been much acrimonious debate about them. Why don't the other three Gospel writers mention the scene? Why does the word church (ecclesia) appear only here and in Matt. 18:17 and not in any of the other Gospels? Since Jesus mentions the church only in Matthew, is the entire scene Matthew's invention? Did Jesus have the idea of a Pope in mind, or did he pass on his authority to all the disciples and to any two or three believers who are gathered in his name (Matt. 8:18-20)? Although John 21:18-19 predicted Peter's martyrdom, no one really knows where, when, or how Peter died. It seems likely that he went to Rome at the end of his career and was martyred. St. Peter's church probably is located in the area where he was killed.

Mark 14:32-52 are odd verses about Jesus in the garden of Gethsemane. Jesus takes three disciples (Peter, James, and John) and asks them to stand watch. They fall asleep, and Jesus returns to them three times. Later on, Peter will deny knowing Jesus three times. Jesus spends three hours on the cross and was resurrected in three days. The story is stirring, but the emphasis on "three" does not ring true. While the disciples sleep, Jesus speaks some memorable words. To God the Father he says, "Not what I will, but what thou wilt." To Peter, a sleeping apostle, he says, "Could you not watch one hour? Watch and pray that you may not enter into temptation; the spirit indeed is willing, but the flesh is weak." A major problem with the scenario is that since the apostles were sleeping, who recorded what Jesus said? At any rate, Jesus was taken prisoner and the disciples "all forsook him and fled." Then a young man wearing a linen tunic followed Jesus, "and they seized him, but he left the linen cloth and ran away naked." Who was this naked youth? Many annotated Bibles state that he was none other than Mark himself, although there is little substance to this interpretation. Most likely the naked youth was Mark's invention, a link to the Old Testament book of Amos where it is written that when God judges Israel "The most courageous men of might shall flee naked in the day" (2:16).

Why exactly was Christ crucified? This question has been problematic over the ages. Biblical accounts of Christ's trial differ in important details. Raymond Brown's *The Death of the Messiah* is the most exhaustive study on this topic. Brown writes, "Christians have misused the crucifixion to blame Jews and to persecute Jews." He notes that not all Jews, but rather only a few leaders were responsible for the crucifixion. Their decision was based on economic reasons (Christ's negative prophecies about the temple of Jerusalem threatened the livelihood of many persons) and religious reasons (among other things, Christ claimed that he could forgive sins). Matthew has the Jews say, "His blood be on us and on our children." Brown does not regard this as an everlasting self-condemnation, but rather as a statement of responsibility by the Jewish leaders of that time for passing a death sentence that they believed was justified.

During the time of Jesus, Jews were buried in caves for a year or so in order for the flesh to dry and flake off of the skeleton. The bones were then placed in an ossuary (a small limestone box) for permanent burial. In around 1976, an Israeli bought an ossuary on the antiquities market; in 2002, a French professor translated the Aramaic inscription on the box as "James, son of Joseph, brother of Jesus." Indeed, the Bible does cite James as brother of Jesus. Historians figure that James was stoned to death between 60–70 A.D. by the Romans at the instigation of the Sadducee Jews. Heated scholarly debate about the inscription abounds. Some claim it is a forgery or that it refers to a family other than that of the biblical Jesus. Clearly, the inscription is not authentic. However, the importance of the ossuary is overblown since most reasonable people do believe that Jesus did actually live; it is the events of his life that are problematic.

Chapter 1: GOD BLESS THE GOD WHO HAS HIS OWN

Linwood Urban's *A Short History of Christian Thought* condenses an enormous amount of material, and his book was especially useful to me in my treatment of the Holy Trinity, the Incarnation, and attempts to prove the existence of God. Another indispensable book is Karen Armstrong's *A History of God*.

Especially helpful in dealing with the names and images of God are *The Interpreter's Bible* and Homer Smith's *Man and His Gods*. The quotes by Freud come from his 1923 article "A seventeenth century demonological neurosis." His theory of the primal horde was developed in *Totem and Taboo*. The quote about Jung is from Victor White's *God and the Unconscious*.

Jack Miles' *God: A Biography* and Richard Elliott Friedman's *The Disappearance of God* were my main sources for tracing the development of God by following the narrative story of the Bible. It is a commentary on our times that two books published in the same year dealt with the retirement of God. Miles traces God's development through the books of the Old Testament Friedman deals more with the end stage of the story (where God disappears) and then focuses on the death of God. It makes for somber reading.

The literature about Jesus is overwhelmingly vast. Among the many books that I have read, several that are informative and not overly technical are Jaroslav Pelikan's *Jesus Through The Centuries*, John Bowker's *The Religious Imagination and the Sense of God*, and John Robinson's *The Human Face of God*.

Charles Sandford's *The Quest For Paradise* states, "More than almost any modern nation the United States was a product of the Protestant Reformation, seeking an earthly paradise to perfect a reformation of the Church." The European colonizers thought that New England would become "a kind of heaven on earth," and they were impressed that Georgia lay "in the same latitude with Palestine herself, That promis'd Canaan, which was pointed out by God's own choice, to bless the Labours of a favorite

People." Many considered the American Indians to be remnants of the ten lost tribes of Israel.

America, alas, was not quite the paradise people had hoped for. Life was hard and sometimes strange behavior erupted. I am indebted to Professor Raymond Prince of McGill University for calling my attention to the following incident. In 1642, William Bradford, the first governor of the Plymouth Plantation in Massachusetts, wrote about a sixteen-year-old servant lad who was "detected of buggery, and indicted for the same, with a mare, a cow, two goats, five sheep, two calves and a turkey." The youth was convicted and executed, but only after witnessing the killing of all the animals that he buggered. Justifying the sentence of death, Bradford cited the biblical verse, "And if a man lie with a beast, he shall be put to death: and ye shall slay the beast" (*Of Plymouth Plantation: 1620-1647*). About fifty years later in Salem, Massachusetts, the "witch bitches" (that's what they were called) were put on trial. Nineteen persons were hanged and an eighty-year-old minister was pressed to death by stones placed on his chest because he refused to cooperate with the authorities.

The Prophet Joseph Smith founded the Mormon Church, a uniquely American institution, in the 1830s. The Church started in the East and ended in Utah. Smith's *Book of Mormon* tells the fantastic story of the flight from Jerusalem of an Israelite family to the New World (North America). The family was divided into the virtuous Nephites and the corrupt Lamanites who constantly fought not only among themselves but also against the nefarious Gadianton Bands. When the Nephites and Lamanites united and peace came to the New World, Jesus Christ himself came for a visit in 34 A.D., after his resurrection! In about 200 A.D., the people started turning to sorcery, lying, robbery, and all manner of wickedness. Eventually, the civilization was destroyed and all the gold and silver artifacts were stolen by robbers and witches. It is truly a testimony to faith that today's Mormons believe that a great civilization existed for hundreds of years in America despite a total absence of historical or material evidence. With this one significant exception, the Mormons actually are ardent historians and maintain the world's largest genealogical data bank. Many books have documented the history of the Mormon Church in excruciating detail, while John Brook's *The Refiner's Fire* examines its complicated intellectual origins. After the assassination of Joseph Smith, the Mormons made an exodus to Utah from Illinois, where they had been persecuted for practicing "celestial marriage" (polygamy), counterfeiting money, and robbing the locals. Their leader at that time was Brigham Young, a man with a tremendous appetite for power, money, and wives. When federal officials in Utah charged and arrested him for lewd and lascivious cohabitation with sixteen wives, Young rallied his supporters: "Trust to God, keep your powder dry, and don't fail to have on hand a good supply of fixed ammunition." He died in 1877, and an article in the *New York Times* (August 30,

1877) noted, "Cruel, bloody, and vindictive though this man doubtless was, he must be credited with the possession of abilities of a superior order." The *Times* predicted that his death would "shatter the monstrous fabric of Mormonism." Although buried in Salt Lake City, his birthplace, a farm in Vermont, is marked with a stone tablet erected by pious Mormons.

It reads:

Brigham Young
Born on this spot in 1801
A man of much courage and superb equipment

There also is a cult of Jesus in Shingo, Japan, which claims that Jesus studied theology in Japan for eleven years beginning at the age of twenty-one. He supposedly returned, after a stop in Monaco, to Judea where the Romans mistakenly crucified his brother. Jesus then traveled to Siberia and finally settled in Shingo, where he married and had three daughters. He died there at the age of one hundred and six years, but left behind a secret testament scroll, written in Japanese, that was unearthed at a temple in the 1930s. Alas, the original scroll was destroyed during World War II, but old photographs of it do exist which show, among other things, that Genghis Khan was Japanese. Pilgrims come to visit Christ's grave and the YMCA conducts "holy wedding" specials. See Quentin Hardy's article.

Tom Driver's article "Sexuality and Jesus" takes on a touchy subject respectfully yet provocatively. He notes that the Gospels are mute about Christ's sexuality and that the equation of sex and the fall of mankind is not biblical but rather a creation of the early Church Fathers. He points to one of the first heresies, namely that Jesus only appeared to be a man (this heresy was called Docetism, from the Greek word for "appearance"), and states that almost every age has espoused its own kind of Docetism. "In our day it may be suggested that a Docetism lingers with regards to Jesus' sexuality . . . A sexless Jesus can hardly be conceived to be fully human . . . somehow above masculinity or femininity." Even back in the first centuries of Christianity there have been those persons who attributed sexuality to Jesus, especially in his relationship with Mary Magdalen. Modern Mormons still do. In our time, D.H. Lawrence's *The Man Who Died* tries to return "Christianity to a pre-Christian state in which natural sexuality is elevated into a religious and sacramental act." The man who died was Jesus, and in the story his resurrection was cold and incomplete until Mary Magdalen awakened his sexual desires. Lawrence writes:

He crouched to her, and he felt the blaze of his manhood and his power
  rise up in his loins, magnificent.
"I am risen."

This is anti-Docetism taken to the extreme and misses the mark. It is neither an authentic episode in the life of Jesus nor does it add or subtract from his divinity unless one believes that all sex is sinful.

Sexuality is neither some sort of cosmic force nor is it a pollution, neither a pure, spiritual blessing nor an impure, demonic power. Christ had a human nature and therefore was a sexual being. Driver argues that only when mythology is stripped away from sexuality can a truly Christian ethic of sex be constructed. Wouldn't we all have been better off if Christianity had heeded the advice offered in the second-century Gospel of Philip: "Do not fear the flesh nor love it. If you fear it, it will gain mastery over you; if you love it, it will devour and paralyze you"?

It isn't very difficult nowadays to certify as insane a person who claims to be God (the situation becomes touchier, however, when that person has a large-enough following). It probably was just as easy in Christ's time, but, since psychiatrists and mental hospitals didn't exist back then, the case was handled by the legal system. Was Jesus mentally ill? At the beginning of this century, several authors considered Christ a paranoid on weak evidence. In 1971, Raymond Lloyd published a lengthy, two-part article, "Cross and psychosis," in which he made the diagnosis of manic-depressive disorder.

Lloyd argues that Christ's basic personality traits, such as concern for others, emotionality, enthusiasm, and hard work, match those of persons with a tendency to mania when heavily stressed. Further, Christ's dependency traits (as shown by his idealization of the Father, his rejection of matrimony, his selection of dull disciples, and his undue emphasis on service and love) match those of persons with depressive tendencies. Lloyd considers the ecstasy of Christ's baptismal experience, followed by his decision to make a prolonged fast, followed by the grandiose temptations in the wilderness as evidence of hypomania. Christ's mental breakdown and full-blown mania probably was precipitated by Herod's persecution. Not only did one Herod want to kill the baby Jesus, but when Jesus was an adult another Herod said to his servants about Jesus, "This is John the Baptist himself, risen from the dead." Herod had chopped off John's head. After Peter identified him as "The Christ of God," Jesus' mania was manifested by his transfiguration on the mountain where "the appearance of His face was altered" and Moses and Elijah "were speaking of his death which he was to accomplish in Jerusalem."

Lloyd agrees that it was not necessarily psychotic for Jesus to preach about the coming of the Kingdom or about resurrection, ideas that the Pharisees generally accepted. What was psychotic, however, was Christ's self-expansive claims that he would usher in the Kingdom of God and that he would be resurrected. In typical manic style, he said that he would rise from the dead in only three days. The manic person's total disregard for money was evidenced by Christ's unjustified attack upon the money-changers in the temple. Other examples of Christ's mania are his expectations of finding fruit on a fig tree out of season and his forecast that the Kingdom of God was at hand. Christ's descent into the depressive phase of his illness is illustrated by the poverty of answers at his trial and meeting with Pontius Pilate. Total depression was evident when he said, "My God, my God, why have you forsaken me?" while on the cross. His rapid death is explained by the exhaustion of his manic period and the despair of depression.

It's bad enough when psychiatrists try to make diagnoses and formulations based on inadequate data, but it's god-awful awful when laymen give it a go. Lloyd's arguments are lacking from a psychiatric perspective. Given the political climate of Christ's time, the blood-lust of the crowd, and the lack of Roman protection, I suspect that a psychiatrist would have declared Christ sane and then run for his life. Even with an objective mental examination, I suspect that Christ would not have been judged psychotic. At any rate, the data from the Bible are so limited and probably biased that any attempt to make a meaningful diagnosis would be beyond speculation.

Schonfield's contention that Jesus consciously acted out his fate does not necessarily diminish his godhood (Christ's, not Schonfield's), at least up until the resurrection caper. A noted novel about Christ's survival is George Moore's *The Brook Kerith*. In Moore's book, Jesus, posing as a shepherd, meets up with Paul who, of course, had never met him before. As Paul spoke about Jesus, Jesus felt great pity. "Were I to persuade him that there was no miracle, his mind would snap, Jesus said to himself, and he figured Paul wandering demented in the hills." Jesus never told the truth about himself to Paul, although he did provide him with some good ideas that he learned from Indian monks during his travels.

The theme of god's resurrection from the dead was a feature of many Near Eastern religions, but mere mortals could be resurrected too. The Roman author Flavius Philostratus (170–245 A.D.) wrote about a contemporary of Jesus named Apollonius who raised a girl from the dead. She had died during her marriage ceremony. Apollonius happened upon her funeral. "He touched her and pronounced something inaudible over her. All of a sudden the young woman woke from what looked like death . . . Whether Apollonius detected some spark of life in her that those caring for her had not noticed . . . or whether she was really dead and Apollonius warmed her and raised her up has become an inexplicable phenomenon, not just to me, but alas to those who happened to be there at the time . . . This is reminiscent of Alcestis when she was brought back to life by Hercules." The author's reference is to the Greek legend of Alcestis, who willingly died so that her husband might continue living. When Hercules was later helped by the husband, he went to Hell and forced Hades to let Alcestis return to life.

Morton Kelsey's *Tongue Speaking* is an easy-reading, sympathetic account of the charismatic experience. It also provides brief but interesting accounts of what may be glossolalia over the centuries in both Western and Eastern Christianity, e.g., the "little prophets of Cevennes" were children in Southern France whose "tongue-like" utterances and prophecies in about 1700 turned into a political revolutionary movement. Cyril Williams' *Tongues of the Spirit* is a scholarly and critical review of historical, religious, linguistic, and psychological aspects of glossolalia. Williams also examines kindred phenomena such as the mysticism of sound. Along with unintelligibility, for example, repetition is a feature of glossolalia. Some Islamic Sufi groups repeatedly murmur the syllable "Hu," which represents the h at the end of the word Allah. In Indian tradition the sacred sound of OM is revered as the "seed-syllable of the universe, a medium of concentration, and a means of inner unification." Maloney and Lovehin's *Glossolalia: Behavioral Science Perspectives on Speaking in Tongues* is an exceptionally thorough review of just about everything important that has been published on glossolalia. The authors' somewhat unclear conclusion points out the difficulties of trying to understand glossolalia: "We affirm the stance of 'phenomenological numenalism' whereby human needs, transcendent reality, and religious experience are all assumed to be substantively real and worthy of serious study." Although the authors are "unable to isolate a glossolalia effect," they still believe that it causes personality, value, and behavioral changes in members of social groups.

Ernest Jones' *Essays in Applied Psychoanalysis* contains several chapters on religion, including "The Madonna's conception through the ear" and "A psychoanalytic study of the Holy Ghost concept." I have tried to compress a lot of material and to simplify concepts, so I urge those who are astounded, offended, or intrigued by Jones' ideas to read his essays in their entirety. He proposes, for example, a six-stage process of sublimation involving intestinal gas: 1) disagreeable smells are deodorized and replaced by aromatics and incense; 2) odor is replaced by an interest in sounds such as music and speech; 3) sound is replaced by silence and an interest in moisture (baptism, rain, purification); 4) moisture is replaced by dessication and an interest in fire and internal warmth; 5) warmth is replaced by cooling and an interest in wind and breath; 6) wind is calmed down so that all "material grossness" is now purged. All that remains of the original gas are "such lofty thoughts as those of the rational soul, universal ether, and world-consciousness." Jones also mentions a well-known episode in the life of Martin Luther, who had significant bowel problems. During a ferocious bout of diarrhea and gas, Luther said, "Get thee behind me, Satan!" He was expressing the belief that the devil could be driven away by a loud noise. Sweeter sounds, such as hymns, are used to attract and please God.

As strange as Freud's ideas seem about the killing of the father and the adoption of animal totems to replace him, it should be noted that the Israelite clans' association with animals may reflect an ancient totemism. The

Leah tribes, for example, were linked to antelopes, the Rachel tribes to lambs, and the Manasch tribe to asses.

A lengthy and complicated psychoanalytic article on the development of ethical monotheism by Andrew Peto is worth mentioning. Peto contends that Yahweh had a demonic nature and castrated his victims. He was a tyrannical, jealous father and his sons, the Israelites, were forced to give up all other relationships, especially that with mother, if they wanted to stay on his good side. He demanded all their love exclusively for himself. His demand for circumcision was a warning that he could cut off a lot more flesh if his wishes weren't met. The son-people decided that the best way to avoid the father's wrath was to abandon the male role completely. By adopting a feminine identification, the son was no longer a rival but rather became a desired love partner for father. Thus, the prophets said that Yahweh and Israel would be bound together forever as bride and bridegroom. This passive homosexual solution was made easier by the fact that the unconscious fantasy life of the sons regarded mother herself to be a castrating, malignant figure. This is demonstrated by the oldest biblical circumcision story, when the wife of Moses symbolically castrated their son, cast the bloody foreskin "at his feet and said, 'Surely you are a bloody husband to me.'"

Yahweh and Israel were husband and wife, but then Israel turned to Baal in adultery. In the book of Hosea the God-husband responded with renewed passion to woo his woman. "Therefore, behold, I will allure her, will bring her into the wilderness, and speak to her heart. I will give her vineyards . . . She shall sing there as in the days of her youth, as in the day when she came out of the land of Egypt. And when that days comes—it is Yahweh who speaks—she will call me 'my husband' . . . I will betroth you to myself forever, betroth you in righteousness and justice, in tenderness and love; I will betroth you to myself with faithfulness, and you will known Yahweh" (2:14–20). Hosea went on to say, "Assuredly I desired *chesed* (love, mercy, *pietas*) and not sacrifice; knowledge of God more than burnt offerings" (6:6). Thus, sexuality became sublimated into devotion. According to Peto, Hosea's *chesed* became one of the most important pillars of Western civilization. Then came Isaiah, who deepened the concept's of God's universality and love and who managed to expunge the evil connotations of the word "holy." Israel drew closer to Yahweh and, no longer burdened with excessive castration anxiety, sublimated the love of God and extended it into love of man, animals, nature, and eternal peace (Isa. 2:4).

The trustful unification of God and man, of husband-father and bride-son, was raised to an even higher level by the prophet Jeremiah. No more fear, no more secrets. Mankind could be open and honest with its father and ask all sorts of troublesome questions. Why do the wicked prosper? Why are treacherous persons happy? God invites his sons to "call upon me and pray to me, and I will listen to you. And you will seek me and find me." Alas, familiarity breeds contempt. The closeness to their father, no matter how ethically sublimated, was too intense for the sons to endure. In order to control their heightened anxiety, they added to sublimation the mental defense mechanism of denial. Yahweh became more imperceptible, less imaginable as an entity in any definite place. He was, in fact, unseen but was still everywhere and had become a universal God.

For more on this area I recommend Bruno Bettleheim's *Freud and Man's Soul*, Paul Vitz's *Sigmund Freud's Christian Unconscious*, Erich Fromm's *Psychoanalysis and Religion*, Carl Jung's *Psychology and Religion*, James Jones' *Contemporary Psychoanalysis and Religion*, and Paul Pruyser's *A Dynamic Psychology of Religion*.

Robert Coles, a prolific scholar and fine writer, has authored a number of books from a psychoanalytically informed perspective. *The Spiritual Life of Children* is a wonderful and very informative study in which children of differing social groups reveal their spirituality and religious beliefs and concerns. In *Harvard Diary: Reflections on the Sacred and the Secular,* Coles confronts personal and professional spiritual issues.

D.W. Winnicott's books include *Collected Papers: Through Pediatrics to Psychoanalysis*, *The Maturational Process and the Facilitating Environment*, and *Playing and Reality*. Judith Hughes' *Reshaping the Psychoanalytic Domain* examines Winnicott's work as well as that of Charles Rycroft, Harold Gruntrip, and others who have influenced Meissner and Rizzuto.

Paul Davies' *God and the New Physics* is a fascinating, provocative book that succeeds in bringing clarity to two fuzzy fields, namely theology and quantum physics. It contains suitable quotes from a wide array of sources, such as the physicist Niels Bohr's, "Anyone who is not shocked by quantum theory has not understood it." In a relatively simple manner (I had to read the book three times), Davies examines the major arguments for the existence of God in the light of modern physics. He is as equally at ease with Aquinas, Hume, and Kant as he is with oscillating universe theory, the Poincaré cycle, and quarks. Highly recommended no matter what your position is on the existence of God.

Evidence of Purpose: Scientists Discover the Creator, edited by John Templeton, is astonishing in its own way. It is a collection of essays by well-known scientists who believe in the existence of God based on the concept of purpose: "The fact that [the universe] is as it is, and that its form is linked so intimately with our own existence, is powerful evidence that the universe exists for a purpose, and that in our small yet significant way, we are part of that purpose." The problem is that only God knows what that purpose is. Presuming, of course, that there is a God. Purpose itself is a purely human notion; it's comforting to think that our lives have meaning. But what's the purpose of dead babies? It simply won't do to say that it's one of God's mysteries.

The developmental psychological model of man's experience of God presented in the chapter is about where we stand today in understanding the phenomenon. Eighty years from now we might find it as quaint or objectionable as some early psychoanalytic studies now seem. Meissner, himself a Catholic priest, carefully notes that "A psychology of religious experience does not concern itself with the suprahuman—the supernatural or divine elements that may be intermingled with the human experience in given religious context or manifestation. The psychology of religious experience in fact must pass over the suprahuman because it has no resources even to attempt to understand that loftier dimension." This is a reasonable enough statement that implies to me that a person can maintain both religious faith and belief in scientific truths.

My chapter concludes with the suggestion that any new god who might appear is likely to have technological roots. My thinking was stimulated by Frank Tipler's *The Physics of Immortality: Modern Cosmology, God and the Resurrection of the Dead.* Let me start by saying that anyone who claims to understand this book completely is lying. Tipler states that "Science now tells us how to go to heaven." He claims that there must exist in the past, present, and future "a Person Who is omnipotent, omniscient, omnipresent, Who is simultaneously both transcendent and yet immanent in the physical universe of sphere time and matter . . . The physics shows the Person to have a 'point-like' structure in the ultimate future, so I will call Him/Her the Omega Point . . . the completion of the finite existence." Tipler holds that future information processing machines will be able to create "a sufficiently perfect simulation of a living being who would be alive." The Omega Point will possess enough computer capacity to simulate our present day world by brute force and to create an exact simulation of all logically possible variants of our world. The dead will be resurrected when the computer capacity of the universe becomes exceedingly large. "Since the information storage capacity diverges to plus infinity roughly at t^{-1} in proper time near the final Omega Point singularity at t=0, resurrection will occur between $10^{^{-10^{10}}}$ seconds and $10^{^{-10^{123}}}$ seconds before the Omega Point is reached." A person's soul won't exist since it is not naturally immortal. "When you're dead, you're dead until the Omega Point resurrects you." Amazingly, no subjective time passes between the moments of death and of resurrection, although trillions of years may pass. Sir Isaac Newton supposedly knew this when he wrote:" . . . ye resurrection is to them that sleep and perceive it not, a moment." Mohammed knew this too because the House of Imran Sura in the Koran states: "Count not those who were slain in God's way as dead, but rather living with the Lord."

Tipler goes on to state that he is an atheist and that "I do not yet even believe in the Omega Point . . . The only evidence in its favor at the moment is theoretical beauty." The problem of the simulation of Jesus' risen body could be accommodated by the master computer. He concludes, "Science can now offer *precisely* the consolations in facing death that religion once offered. Religion is now part of science."

Say what? In *The End of Science,* John Horgan assesses Tipler to be "perhaps the most bunkrapt scientist I have ever met."

Chapter 2: ONCE UPON A TIME THE DEVIL...

The chorus of frogs in Aristophane's play repeatedly chanted "Brekekekek, coax, coax, brekekekek coax." Yale University students adopted this as a cheer at football games. Plato's description of what happens after death can be found in his *Phaedo* and *Gorgias* (my quote is from section 525). Alan Berstein's *The Formation of Hell* is an important scholarly treatise on the ancient and early Christian eras. Also see Alice Turner's less scholarly but entertaining *The History of Hell.*

Abraham's bosom created problems for medieval theologians. How could Abraham be in heaven since souls could not go there until after the Judgement Day? An exception was made for Elijah who "went up by a whirlwind into heaven" (2 Kin. 2:11). Enoch, the father of Methuselah, possibly was in heaven too although the evidence is skimpy: "And Enoch walked with God; and he was not, for God took him" (Gen. 5:24). Later on the Virgin Mary was assumed into heaven, though not on biblical evidence. Even after Judgement Day, Abraham couldn't go to heaven because it was reserved for Christians. One solution was to create a location that bordered heaven. It was called limbo, and it was where the souls of unbaptized babies and worthy pre-Christians resided. The parable in Luke, however, seems to place Abraham in heaven. When Jerome translated "the breast of Abraham" into Latin, he used the phrase "in sinu Abrahai"; since "in sinu" literally means "in the fold of a garment," many artists painted Abraham with a cloth across his chest with saved people in it.

The horrors of the *Apocalypse of Peter* reflected the violence exacted by the Romans upon Christian martyrs. The *Acts of the Martyrs* by the Bollandists comprises fifty large folio tomes in which the lives of the martyrs are recorded. St. Agatha had her breasts cut off with shears. St. Catherine of Alexandria was ripped to death by a spiked wheel. St. Eustace was stuffed inside the red-hot statue of a brazen bull.

James Joyce's *Portrait of the Artist as a Young Man* devotes many pages to the fearsome descriptions of hell by priests: "The blood settles and boils in the veins, the brains are boiling in the skull, the heart in the breast glowing and bursting, the bowels a red hot mass of burning pulp, the tender eyes flaming like molten balls." In a recent article by Robert Boynton the well-known art critic Robert Hughes described his childhood indoctrination session with a Jesuit priest: "Now, you boys know what its like to be kicked in a certain place when you're playing football? It's agony, isn't it? You roll on the ground and wish you could vanish off the face of the earth. Gradually, it passes and you feel O.K. But when you are in *Hell* you're *never* going to feel O.K., because a big demon with a great, horny clawed foot will be kicking you in that place twenty times a minute, sixty minutes an hour, twenty-four hours a day, *for all eternity*."

The ancient Hebrew myth of primordial combat between God and the monster-dragon probably derives from an even older Babylonian myth in which the hero Marduk slew Tiamat, the sea-dragon who lived in the waters of chaos. The Canaanites had a similar combat myth in which Baal bested Yamm (the sea).

Christ's victory over Satan was symbolized by the Cross of the Crucifixion. Although not in the Bible, Christians early on made the sign of the cross as a means of identifying themselves and as a defense against demons. The fourth-century Roman emperor Julian wrote of Christians: "You adore the wood of the cross and draw its likeness on your foreheads and engrave it on your house fronts." The Cross disappeared, but three crosses supposedly were rediscovered in Jerusalem by Saint Helena. Which was the True Cross? Simple: Helena touched a corpse with all three; only the True Cross revived the dead body. She built the Church of the Holy Sepulcher on the site, enclosed part of the Cross in a silver case, and sent the rest to her son, the Roman Emperor Constantine. No fool, he enclosed the cross inside a large statue of himself, and out of the nails that supposedly pierced Christ's wrists he had a helmet and bridle-bits made for his use as leader of the army. The discovery of the True Cross by his mother was celebrated on May 3 by the Catholic Church until 1960 when the Second Vatican Council dropped it from the calendar.

Among the pagan critics of the church, the greatest was Celsus. His *The True Word* (written 179–180) was the first comprehensive anti-Christian polemic. He argued that Christians not only were troublemakers who threatened the stability of Roman rule, but also that they were ignorant blasphemers for believing that their God's capacity to do good was constrained by a hostile, imaginary adversary called the devil. For more on this see Elaine Pagels' *The Origin of Satan*.

Ephesians 6:11–12 is quite interesting: "Put on the whole armor of God that you may be able to stand against the wiles of the devil. For we do not wrestle against flesh and blood, but against principalities, against powers, against the rulers of the darkness of this world, against spiritual hosts of wickedness in the heavenly places." I have heard people interpret this in political terms. They associate *principalities* and *powers*, for example, with municipalities and governments. In some Bibles, "heavenly places" is translated "high places," which becomes associated with high political office. In fact, the principalities and powers noted in Ephesians are astrological allusions to two groups of spirits that supposedly influence human behavior. The *rulers of this world* are none other than pagan gods; the descriptive adjective used here indicates that they are sun-gods. The *heavenly* or *high places* is a reference to the location of Satan and his band of fallen angels; they lived in the atmosphere above the earth. Augustine wrote that the Devil and his angels were cast down from high "into darkness, that is to say into our atmosphere, as into a prison."

The Church was not alone in associating its enemies with the devil. The Knights Templar was a small religious order established to help crusaders and to fight for control of the Holy Land against Moslems. The organization became tremendously wealthy through banking and commerce. When Moslems took control of the Holy Land in 1290, the Knights Templar didn't have much to do other than to accumulate money (although a small force continued to fight in Spain against Islam). King Phillip IV of France had a poor treasury and great dreams of expanding his rule. In 1306, he expelled all Jews from France and confiscated their money. Next he moved to confiscate the funds of the Knights Templar. He accomplished this by accusing them of kissing black cats under the tail, engaging in orgies that often included sodomy, renouncing Christ, and worshipping idols of Satan that were anointed with the fat of roasted infants. Phillip's propaganda was awesome. He convinced some willing bishops to imprison and murder a number of Knights as heretics. Confessions were obtained through torture. By 1314, Phillip's victory was complete. The order was destroyed, and the king got his money. The full story is told in Norman Cohn's scholarly study *Europe's Inner Demons*.

After Nero's death, several men claimed to be him. One, in the Parthian Empire where Nero supposedly was hiding, almost succeeded in precipitating a war between Rome and the Parthians. Although most early manuscripts list 666 as the number of the Beast, several manuscripts list 616. Gematria is the technical term given to the use of numbers as symbols for letters. Bernard McGinn's *Antichrist: Two Thousand Years of the Human Fascination with Evil* was my primary text for the section on Antichrist and contains the references for quotes that I have used. For more information on William Miller, see *The Disappointed: Millerism and Millenarianism*, edited by Ronald Numbers and Jonathan Butler, and Ronald and Janet Numbers' "Millerism and Madness." The Millenium Watch Institute in Philadelphia publishes a monthly Millennial Prophecy Report that "presents excerpts from the publications of Christian Churches, Jewish sects, UFO believers, New Age groups, and extremist and fringe books difficult to classify."

May 14, 1948, was a great day for believers in the Apocalypse and the Antichrist because it was the birth of the state of Israel and supposedly marked the beginning of the Final Days. The establishment of a Jewish state was a long time in the making. The Jews actually were latecomers to the area, which had been inhabited for several thousand years before the Canaanites, who probably lived there for a thousand years until the Israelites dispossessed them. When King David conquered Canaanite Jerusalem in the tenth century, it wasn't much of a city. David brought the ark of the covenant to Jerusalem, and his son, King Solomon, built the great temple there. The city became a major religious and political center until it was destroyed in 587 B.C. by King Nebuchadnezzar, who exiled some of its inhabitants to Babylon. The prophet Ezekiel, one of the exiles, described Jerusalem as the "most glorious of all lands" (20:7), "the most holy place" (41:4), "the place of [God's] throne and the place of the soles of feet" (43:7). He noted that one man, Abraham, got possession of the land, "but we are many; the land is surely given to us to possess" (33:24). The land referred to by Ezekiel included not only Jerusalem but all the territory extending north to Syria, east to Palmyra, south to Egypt, and west to the Mediterranean Sea. The city and temple of Jerusalem were rebuilt in 520-515 B.C., but both were destroyed again, this time by the Romans in 70 A.D. The Romans left the ruins of the temple untouched but constructed a statue of Emperor Hadrian there. They built a new city out of the rubble and called it Aelia Capitolina in an attempt to stamp out even the memory of Jerusalem. They also transferred the administrative seat of the area to the lovely, rebuilt coastal city of Casaerea. By the second century A.D., Casaerea had become the dominant Jewish city in the region. It also had a sizeable Christian population, whose bishop had a higher rank than the bishop of Jerusalem. Jerusalem did not thrive again until the fourth century, when Christians reestablished its position as a major religious center. See Robert Wilken's *The Land Called Holy* for the fabulous early history of the Holy Land.

Although Jews were scattered throughout the world, they never relinquished their hope of returning to Jerusalem. They were especially sustained by the promise of God in Deuteronomy: "Many of you are driven out to the farthest parts under heaven, from there the Lord your God will gather you, and . . . will bring you to the land which your fathers possessed, and you shall possess it. He will prosper you and multiply you more than your fathers" (30:4-5).

In 1897, Theodor Herzl convened the first Zionist (Zion is the poetic name for both Jerusalem and the land of Israel) Congress in Basle, Switzerland, and called for the creation of a Jewish homeland in Palestine. The immediate precipitating cause of Herzl's action was the anti-Semitism that swept through France following the Dreyfus Affair (Dreyfus, a Jewish military captain in the French army, was accused falsely of selling military secrets to the Germans). In 1896, Herzl had written an essay, *The Jewish State (Der Judenstaat)*, in which he wrote, "Shall we choose Palestine or

Argentina? We shall take what is given us, and what is selected by Jewish public opinion." In fact, most Jews selected Palestine, but many pragmatists thought that other temporary areas would be acceptable until it was actually possible to get to Palestine. When the Turks (who controlled Palestine until 1918) refused Herzl's request, other "Jewish Territory" proposals were considered; the British suggested a site in Uganda. A small Jewish settlement was established in Argentina. Shortly before his death in 1904, Herzl gave a rousing speech at the Sixth Zionist Conference where he recited Psalm 137:5; "If I forget you, O Jerusalem, let my right hand wither away." Jerusalem it would be, but not until more than four decades of political intrigue had passed.

The Ten Commandments were literally stuck into Exodus 20:1-17. They are not linked to the verses that precede or follow them. Chapter 19 concludes with Moses speaking to the people. Then come the Ten Commandments with no explanation; Moses is not mentioned at all. The people saw lightning and a smoking mountain, and they heard thunder and a trumpet blast, whereupon Moses talked to them with no mention of the Commandments!

During the time of Jesus, the majority of those living in the Holy Land were just plain folks struggling to get by. Known as "people of the land" ('Am Ha' arez), they were looked upon with contempt by religious leaders who were people of the Law. They were second class citizens because they didn't study or observe the Law of Moses. Many welcomed the opportunity to change their status by joining the new, more egalitarian group of Christians who preached a simple form of brotherly love—entertain strangers, be kind to prisoners, share your possessions, exhort each other to love and good works. In fact, all the complexities of the Law were reduced to one concept: "Owe no one anything except to love one another, for he who loves another has fulfilled the law" (Rom. 13:8). Potential converts were told that Jewish scripture itself prophesied a new covenant in which every person, from the least to the greatest, will truly know God (Jer. 31:31-34); the old covenant and all its rituals had become obsolete and had been replaced by the sacrifice of Christ and the establishment of Christianity (Heb. 8-9).

The twentieth-century theologian Reinhold Niebuhr is one of the most thoughtful students of sin. For him, Adam's Fall is not an historical fact but rather an allegory of what all humans endure in dealing with our inherent inclination to evil. Humans cope with insecurity and anxiety by falling into pride: I don't depend on God; I am superior to others; I am Number One. I can indulge myself in any way I see fit. For Niebuhr, all sins derive from the egoism of self-love, and "the selfishness of man and nations is a fixed datum of historical science." Though egoism is inevitable, we are still responsible for mastering it. The failure to do so is original sin. Niebuhr finds relief through Christian love "in which regard for the self is completely eliminated." This is the message of 1 Corinthians 13:4-7: "Love suffers long and is kind; love does not envy; love does not parade itself, is not puffed up; does not behave rudely, does not seek its own, is not provoked, thinks no evil; does not rejoice in iniquity, but rejoices in the truth; bears all things, believes all things, hopes all things, endures all things.'"

The seventeenth-century French philosopher Blaise Pascal wrote: "There are only two kinds of men, the righteous who consider themselves sinners; the rest are sinners who consider themselves righteous." The notion of a self-less love that does not seek its own sounds good, an antidote for those of us living in an age of narcissism. However, everyone has and needs a narcissistic core of self-worth. Paul was incomplete when he focused on loving one's neighbor; Jesus advised that "You shall love your neighbor as yourself." In fact, lack of self-love may lead to depression, masochism, and, especially in women, a vulnerability that attracts predatory men. As summarized by Linwood Urban in his discussion of sin, St. Bernard of Clairvaux (1090–1153) defined three stages of love of God. The first is the stage where most people stay, loving God for what he can do for us. The second stage, achieved by some, is loving God for God's own sake. The third and highest stage, attained by precious few, is loving ourselves for God's sake. Urban concludes that "The heart of sin seems best described as seeing the world only from one's own perspective. Contrarywise, true right mindedness is best described as the ability to see the world and one's place in it from God's point of view—that is, to see it as it really is." The problem, alas, is to comprehend God's point of view. The comprehension is different in Rome and in Shreveport. In her drug-addled lyrics, even that wonderful singer Janis Joplin knew that if you couldn't find love in Dee-troit, it's unlikely that you'd find it in Katmandu.

Karl Menninger's *Whatever Became of Sin?*—written during a period of great social activism—called for doctors in general and psychiatrists in particular to become moral leaders. The community mental health movement came to life at that time with two agendas. The first was to allow patients to lead their lives outside of mental institutions; the second was to treat society as a patient and to change our world view of war, racism, poverty, and other social ills. We overshot the mark on item one; many patients do live in the "community," which too often consists of a residential care facility, while others who *should* be in an institution have nowhere to go. Item two was a humbling experience for psychiatrists. We actually thought that we could impact social ills with our good hearts and wise words. Talk about narcissism! But at least we tried.

Mohandas Gandhi, the Hindu pacifist who freed India from British rule, composed a modern version of the seven deadly sins: politics without principle, wealth without work, commerce without morality, pleasure without conscience, education without character, science without humanity, and worship without sacrifice. England didn't stand a chance against a man like Gandhi.

Finally, I highly recommend Andrew Delbanco's *The Death of Satan: How Americans Have Lost the Sense of Evil*. It is a felicitously written book that synthesizes hundreds of items from literature, science, theology, history, and popular culture. It helped me to gain a better perspective on the general topic of this chapter.

Chapter 3: DON'T SPOIL THE SOUP: WOMEN AND THE BIBLE

The oldest known representation of a human being is an 11-centimeter-high sandstone statue made in Austria some 20,000 years ago. As cited in Richard Lewinshon's *A History of Sexual Customs*, one of its discoverers reported, "It represents a fat, over-blown woman, with large lactating glands, a prominent belly, and full hips and thighs, but not actually steatopygous." Named the "Venus of Willendorf," the statue is thought by some to portray a fertility goddess. However, Lewinshon states that "never has any form of art, realistic or stylized, produced a woman as monstrous . . . This Venus was no more than a lump of fat . . . no fertility symbol but a matron deformed by childbearing," and that she probably was a portrayal of "particularly unprepossessing local type" of woman. It is, perhaps, more an omen than an irony that the oldest representation of a woman is so repulsive. The bracelets on her arms are a pathetic attempt to appear attractive. Of course, we know nothing of her personality. She may have been, forgive me for saying so, udderly charming. If we fast-forward many thousands of years to the literary portrayals of the first woman—Pandora in Greek mythology, Eve in Jewish mythology— we can appreciate the slow and limited progress of man's mentation. Both Pandora and Eve were gorgeous on the outside but not so nice on the inside.

The reference to Giulia Sissa is her chapter "The sexual philosophies of Plato and Aristotle." For a fuller discussion of Bachofen's theory of maternal law, see Stella Georgoudi's chapter "Creating a myth of matriarchy."

There were several Greek theories about the production of sperm (See *The Origins of European Thought About the Body, the Mind, The Soul, World, Time and Fate* by R. Onion). Sperm was considered the essential ingredient in the formation of an embryo. Pythagoras (500 B.C.) wrote that sperm derives from marrow in the spinal cord which, in turn, derives from the brain. As stated by Diogenes Laertius, "Sperm is a drop of brain." Plato adopted this idea in his *Timaeus*. In this theory both males and females produce sperm; the sex of the child was thought to depend upon factors such as the quantity of either male or female sperm, the temperature of the uterus and of the sperm, and the location of the fetus in the left or right side of the uterus. The second major theory held that sperm was formed by all the organs of the body in both men and women. The Hippocratic school of physicians held that male and female contributions were equal and that a child must resemble each parent in some respect. However, the theory that had the most support was that sperm came from cooked blood and that only males had enough body heat to produce it (the cooked blood of woman turned into menstrual blood). This was Aristotle's position. Galen (120–200 C.E.) modified this theory and held that women's ovaries produced sperm, but they are thinner, colder and less perfect than that produced by men. The two types of sperm supposedly met in the uterus, where the female sperm served as food for the male sperm, which really formed the embryo. Galen's approach was the predominant one in Western culture for over a thousand years.

The question of sperm arises in a New Testament text. Hebrews 11:11 states that Abraham's barren wife, Sarah, had enough faith to produce sperm and, thus, to conceive a child. It's a sentence that has challenged interpreters. The King James translation is, "Through faith also Sarah herself received strength to conceive." Pieter Van Den Horst's chapter "Sarah's seminal emission," states that the author of Hebrews meant exactly what he said, and that there is evidence in the Talmud and Midrashim to support the influence of this Greek concept on rabbinic embryology. Van Der Horst also cites an eleventh-century biblical scholar, Theophylactus, who wrote that, "because those who have studied these matters in detail say that a woman too, in a sense, produces seed of her own, perhaps the words 'for a seminal emission' should be taken to mean this: so that she [Sarah] herself too could emit semen."

Much of the material on hysteria is referenced in Ilza Veith's fascinating book *Hysteria: The History of a Disease*. Also see *The Culture of Pain* by David Morris. The Greek notion of hysteria was borrowed from the Egyptians. The words used in Freud's imaginary encounter with Mrs. Gilmore are taken from his *Autobiographical Study*. The Roman prescription for the treatment of hysteria was "Nubat illa et morbus effugiet" (let her marry and the sickness will disappear).

The quote by Phyllis Bird comes from her chapter "Images of women in the Old Testament" in Rosemary R. Ruether's *Religion and Sexism*. This book contains many scholarly chapters on the images of women in the Jewish and Christian traditions. In *God: A Biography*, Jack Miles states that in Malachi 2:13–16, "We hear God's first completely unequivocal and unmistakable reference to himself as a female . . . In Isaiah, God was the husband and Israel the wife of his youth, rejected but then taken back with merciful tenderness. Now, God is the wife, and Israel is the husband." This interpretation is at odds with just about all other scholars. *The Interpreter's Bible*, for example, notes that the Hebrew of verse 13 is "ambiguous," that verse 15 "is one of the most obscure verses in the entire Old Testament," and that verse 16 "also is corrupt in the Hebrew and the versions render it very differently." The usual interpretation is that Malachi charges the Jews with being unfaithful to their wives and of divorcing old wives in favor of younger ones. Malachi's statement, "for I hate divorce, says the Lord God of Israel," was written five centuries before Jesus' hard stand against divorce.

Esther is regarded by all reputable scholars to belong to the genre of patriotic fiction. The name Esther derives from the Babylonian goddess of love, Ishtar; Mordecai derives from the chief Babylonian god, Marduk. The purpose of the book seems to be to provide a historical basis for the Jewish festival of Purim, which had been very popular centuries before Esther. Purim was, and remains, a somewhat secular, joyful holiday. It had no place in the holy festivals of the Mosaic Law. Over the centuries, Esther's triumph has assumed special meaning for the Jews because of the oppression that they have faced. Martin Luther didn't care for it at all; in *Table Talk* Luther felt so hostile to II Maccabees and to Esther that he wrote, "I wish they did not exist at all; for they Judaize too much and have much heathen perverseness." Moses Maimonedes, the great medieval Jewish philosopher, felt that Esther and the Law would endure beyond all other Biblical books. Only after the additions were made to emphasize Esther's reliance on God did the book become acceptable for inclusion in the Bible.

Regarding concubines, *New York Magazine* (Aug. 7, 1995) published an article about the Shalom Bayis Organization, an Orthodox Jewish men's rights group in New York City. In order to bring about household peace (*shalom bayis*), the group encourages the return of concubines, which are supposedly legal under Jewish law. The concubine, however, must be a Jewish woman who observes the female purity laws, remains monogamous, and lives at home with the man's wife and family. According to the group there are many benefits of concubinage: men won't be sexually frustrated when their wives are menstruating, wives will be selected on the basis of character instead of good looks, unmarriageable women will have a relationship with a man, wives will know with whom their husbands are sleeping, and the spread of sexually transmitted diseases will be prevented. According to the article, a rabbi from another Orthodox group stated: "What day is this? What planet am I on? They're crazy, fanatic idiots. They have nobody of heavy rabbinic stature behind them. Not even anyone mediocre."

A basic, concise, and balanced reference for information about women in the Bible is the section on "Women" in Metzger and Coogan's *The Oxford Companion to the Bible*, which contains articles by Elizabeth Achtemeier, Mary Joan Winn Leith, Sidnie Ann White, and Valerie Abrahamsen. Also see the entry on "Feminism and the Bible" by Katharine Doob Sakenfeld.

Christ's encounter with an "uppity" Gentile woman has embarrassed Christian scholars. The story told in Mark 7:24–30 and in Matthew 15:21–28 differs in some aspects but basically tells about a Gentile woman who pestered Christ because she wanted him to heal her demon-possessed daughter. He replied that he was sent only to the Jews and added, "It's not fair to take the childrens' bread and throw it to the dogs." His reference to Gentiles as dogs didn't put off the quick-witted woman, who one-upped Christ: "Yes, Lord, but even the dogs eat the crumbs that fall under the table." He rewarded her "for this saying" and for her faith by healing her daughter.

The account in John 8 of Jesus and the woman taken in adultery is a "floating story." Depending upon the manuscript used, it appears in various places in the Gospels (see Luke 21:38). It certainly was not part of the original Gospel of John and *The Interpreter's Bible* notes, "It is significant that no Greek writer for a thousand years after this Gospel has written comments upon this story."

The most informative source for material on Mary Magdalen is Susan Haskins' *Mary Magdalen: Myth and Metaphor*.

The commentary by Hippolytus on the Song of Songs is confusing at best. He referred to Mary M as both Martha and Mary!

The single best book about the Virgin Mary is Marina Warner's *Alone of All Her Sex: The Myth and the Cult of the Virgin Mary*. The "immaculate conception" refers to the conception of Mary by her mother and not, as many people believe, to the conception of Jesus by Mary (although it too was "immaculate"). The notes in Warner's chapter on this topic contain a joke that the poet W.H. Auden was fond of: "When the woman taken in adultery was brought to Jesus, he said 'Let he who is without sin cast the first stone.' All was silence, and the Pharisees began drifting away in shame, when suddenly a stone whizzed past Jesus' ear. Without turning, and in a tone of deep irritation, Jesus cried out: 'Mother!'"

Readers interested in sexuality and the early centuries of the Church should turn to Peter Brown's encyclopedic *The Body and Society: Men, Woman and Sexual Renunciation in Early Christianity* and Elaine Pagels' *Adam, Eve, and the Serpent*.

Kramer and Spanger's *Malleus Maleficarium* is a fascinating read and an entry to the mind-set of the inquisitors. The story of the mens' sexual organs eating corn and oats can be found in Part Two, Chapter 7 (page 121 in the Dover edition).

Major books about religion and self-starvation are Rudolph Bell's *Holy Anorexia* and Caroline Bynum's *Holy Feast and Holy Fast*. A particularly instructive article is Rebecca Lester's "Embodied voices: Women's food asceticism and the negotiation of identity." For a history of self-starvation see *From Fasting Saints to Anorexic Girls* by W. Vandereycken and R. Van Deth. Also see the two-part article "Anorexia multiforme: Self-starvation in historical and cultural context" by Vincenzo Di Nicola.

The chapter "Religion and the mental health of women" by Robert Bridges and Bernard Spilka is an excellent review. Some specific articles and books that support my comments are S. Nolan-Hoeksema, *Sex Differences in*

Depression; H.K. Singer, *The Sexual Desire Disorders*; S.A. Wallington, Consequences of transgression: Self-punishment and depression; M.B. McGuire, *Religion: The Social Context*. E. Howell and N. Bayes, *Women and Mental Health*; V. Franks and E.P. Franks, *The Stereotyping of Women*. For information on Sir Isaac Brown, female genital mutilation, and skin-cutting see Favazza's *Bodies Under Siege*. The relationship among culture, psychopathology and biomedicine is brilliantly examined in R. Littlewood and M. Lipsedge's "The butterfly and the serpent." Nada Stotland's "Domestic abuse and the misuse of religion" presents the travails of a woman who struggled to free herself from a husband who used biblical injunctions to dominate and control the activities and beliefs of family members.

For material on feminist religious studies, I found two edited books to be quite helpful: Letty Russell's *Feminist Interpretation of the Bible* and Rosemary Radford Ruether's *Religion and Sexism*. Newsom and Ringe's *The Women's Bible Commentary* contains scholarly essays on every book in the Bible. Other recommended readings are Phyllis Trible's *Texts of Terror* and Elizabeth Schüssler Fiorenza's *In Memory of Her: A Feminist Theological Reconstruction of Christian Origins*. The review article "Scripture rescripted" by Anthony Lane appeared in the *New Yorker*, Oct. 2, 1995, pages 98–100.

A 1993 *New York Times* article by Dirk Johnson deals with Mormon feminists who, according to a male church leader, posed a threat to the faith along with homosexuals and "so-called intellectuals and scholars." Feminists were upset that females were excluded from many church activities while boys as young as twelve years old could distribute the sacrament and become deacons (an office within the priesthood). Six leading feminists were recently excommunicated and their names removed from church rolls. One reason for the action was the feminist version of the "Our Father" prayer, which adds "and Our Mother." Evidently a popular Mormon hymn written in 1843 by Eliza Snow and often sung in today's church contains the verses "In the Heavens are parents single? No, the truth makes reason stare. Truth is reason. Truth eternal tells me I've a Mother there." A male teacher at Brigham Young University was excommunicated after claiming that Mormon leaders continued their polygamous way from 1890 to 1904, although the practice officially ended in 1890 (the "Great Accommodation") in order to facilitate Utah's bid for statehood. The teacher also wrote an article claiming that in 1843, Joseph Smith, the founder of Mormonism, accepted women into the priesthood through a ceremony called "Endowment in the Temple." Also see Maxine Hanks' *Women and Authority: Re-emerging Mormon Feminism* and Jan Shipps' *Mormonism: The Story of a New Religious Tradition*. Burgoyne and Burgoyne point out the psychiatric morbidity of Mormon women as a result of paradoxes in their belief system. Education, for example, is encouraged, yet women with advanced degrees never get to use them because of the belief that they should stay at home." . . . Mormon women are often in conflict and depressed. But in church they are told that they are happier and healthier than most other women." In therapy, attacking the paradoxes often result in a worsening of symptoms. The patient feels obligated to adhere to Church beliefs when the psychiatrist is also a Mormon "whom she feels will judge her church allegiance. If her doctor is a non-member, she must adhere as a good example, perhaps even fantasizing that she will convert him."

For information on the problematic issue of marriage as a sacrament, see Rodorf's "Marriage in the New Testament and in the early Church." The rulings of the Council of Elvira are described in S. Laeuchli's *Power and Sexuality*. The quotes of Paul Johnson are from his brilliant *A History of Christianity*. Richard Sipe's *Sex, Priests and Power* was published in 1995. I recommend it highly. Also see S. Murphy, *A Delicate Dance: Sexuality, Celibacy, and Relationships Among Catholic Clergy and Religions* and R. Wagner's *Gay Catholic Priests*. The estimation by Greely was published in "A view from the priesthood," *Newsweek*, Aug. 16, 1993. Also recommended is R. Curb and N. Manahan's *Lesbian Nuns: Breaking Silence*. It contains the autobiographies of forty-six lesbian nuns who tell the stories of their struggles with spirituality and sexuality.

The quote from Karen Horney can be found in her article "The flight from womanhood"; that from Clara Thompson can be found in "Cultural pressures in the psychology of women." Both articles as well as other pertinent ones have been collected in *Psychoanalysis and Women*, edited by Jean Baker Miller. The reference to Diane Owen Hughes is her chapter "Regulating women's fashion." Enid and Richard Peschel's article on castrati is a good source for information. Bruno Bettleheim's book is *Symbolic Wounds*. Also see Jaffe's "The masculine envy of woman's procreative function," Hogbin's *The Island of Menstruating Men*, and Lidz's "Male menstruation."

Another area of interest is couvade, a term that refers to male behaviors that resemble what woman experience during pregnancy and labor. Although a British anthropologist, Edward Taylor, provided the name in 1865 and studied the phenomenon, it had been described by the ancient Greeks and Romans. Marco Polo in the thirteenth century described a custom in Turkestan:, the husband stays in bed with a newborn infant, "and his wife, as soon as she has given birth to her child, gets up from bed as soon as she can and does her household duties and serves her Lord, taking him food and drink while he is in the bed, as if he himself had given birth." Many anthropologists have studied couvade. In an American study, 22.5 percent (60 of 267 men) developed pregnancy-like symptoms during their wives' pregnancy. The symptoms included nausea, vomiting, loss of appetite, diarrhea, constipation, sties, abdominal pain, skin conditions, faintness, lassitude, and leg cramps. Despite numerous visits for medical attention and multiple diagnostic tests and procedures, no medical condition could be found to explain the symptoms. See *The Use and Abuse of Medicine* by deVries et al. The usual psychiatric interpretation is that couvade symptoms reflect envy of the woman's ability to give birth, identification with the pregnant woman, and/or ambivalence about the pregnancy with repressed hostility. Also see Trethowan's "The couvade syndrome."

Chapter 4: COMME ÇA: HOMOSEXUALITY AND THE BIBLE

Mercenary female prostitutes were active throughout the Bible. Often they were accepted as part of the social landscape, especially if they were not Israelites. There is no mention in the Bible of mercenary male prostitutes. Many religious groups in the area had sacred prostitutes, male and female, who performed their duties at holy shrines especially in association with the god Baal and the goddess Ishtar (Asherah). Their intercourse was thought to stimulate the gods and goddesses to sexual activity, which promoted the growth of crops and the fertility of animals and humans. The allure of these fertility cults was a threat to the Hebrews. A law in Deuteronomy 23:17–18 states: "There shall be no cult prostitute of the sons of Israel. You shall not bring the hire of a harlot, or the wages of a dog, into the house of God in payment for any vow" (holy male prostitutes were referred to as dogs). 1 Kings 14:23–24 describes an evil scene in Judah during the reign of King Solomon's son: "For they built for themselves high places, and pillars, and temples to Asherah on every high hill and under every green tree; and there were also [cultic] male prostitutes in the land." When King Asa instituted his reforms "He put away the male cult prostitutes out the land, and removed all the idols that his fathers had made" (15:12). King Josiah also "broke down the houses of the cultic male prostitutes" (2 Kings 23:7). The female prostitutes serviced men, but little is known about the activities of the male prostitutes, although it is generally accepted that they also serviced male devotees. Certainly there was biblical condemnation of cultic male prostitution. In a controversial book, Peter Gomes, a Harvard professor of Christian Morals, writes: "The biblical writers never contemplated a form of homosexuality in which loving, monogamous, and faithful persons sought to live out the implications of the Gospel with as much fidelity to it as any heterosexual believer. All they knew of homosexuality was prostitution, lasciviousness, and exploitation."

John Boswell's *Christianity, Social Tolerance, and Homosexuality* is a scholarly tour de force and the primary reference in the area. Robin Scroggs' *The New Testament and Homosexuality*, John McNeill's *The Church and the Homosexual*, and Mark Jordan's *The Invention of Sodomy in Christian*

Theology are excellent resources. Ronald Bayer's *Homosexuality and American Psychiatry* provides the details of the amazing process in which homosexuality was deleted from the official list of pathological conditions.

Robert Stoller's *Presentations of Gender* covers the concepts of masculinity and femininity. The book's last chapter, coauthored by Gilbert Herdt, discusses a fascinating tribe in New Guinea that believes that maleness is not innate or natural. In order to become a male, boys must ritually fellate adult men and swallow as much semen as possible. No other type of homosexual behavior is practiced. When a boy finally becomes an adult male, he will marry a woman and practice exclusive heterosexuality except, of course, when he fulfills his duty to boys by offering his semen.

Richard Sipe's *A Secret World: Sexuality and the Search for Celibacy* is a comprehensive study of Roman Catholic priests and their problems in dealing with celibacy.

The thorough and thoughtful article, "Human sexual orientation: the biologic theories reappraised," by W. Byne and B. Parsons notes that "the appeal of current biologic explanations for sexual orientation may derive more from dissatisfaction with the present status of psychosocial explanations than from a substantiating body of experimental data."

Starting in the 1940s, a theory emerged stating that homosexuals had low levels of the male sex hormone, testosterone. This theory persisted for forty years even though "treatment" with testosterone could not change a homosexual's orientation, and even though twenty studies found no lowering of testosterone levels in homosexuals; three studies found a low level, while two studies found elevated levels. See Meyer-Bahlburg's "Psychoendocrine research on sexual orientation."

Newer hormonal theories have evolved. One holds that all fetal brains have an intrinsic female "pattern" and that the development of a male "pattern" depends upon the production of androgen hormones. Certainly formation of the male external genital organs depends upon the production of androgens, but it is not so certain that brain development follows a similar course. Nonetheless, in this theory homosexuality in males (and heterosexuality in females) is the result of a female brain pattern caused by exposure to low androgen levels during fetal development. Conversely, homosexuality in females (and heterosexuality in males) is caused by exposure to high androgen levels. Laboratory evidence for this notion comes from mating behaviors of rodents exposed to high and low prebirth androgen levels.

Although men can be real rats sometimes (sons of bitches too, and even worse), it takes a true leap of faith to equate rodent and human sexuality. The chemically prepared male rodent who adopts a female sexually receptive posture is considered homosexual by the scientists, but the normal male rodent who mounts his companion is considered heterosexual! The Romans would have appreciated this distinction, but it just doesn't make sense. Also, rodent sexual responses are fairly fixed and repetitive, while human responses can flip-flop depending upon where and when the flipping and the flopping take place.

A few anatomical studies suggest that the size of some brain structures may be related to sexual orientation. S. LeVay reported that a clump of cells known as the third interstitial nucleus of the anterior hypothalamus was smaller in male homosexuals. However, his 19 homosexual subjects all died of AIDS, a condition that may have affected the results. Allen and Gorski found that a structure known as the anterior commissure was larger in homosexual men. However, not only did many of the subjects have AIDS, but also the commissure size in almost all the homosexual men overlapped the bottom of the range of the heterosexuals.

After reviewing the literature, Byne and Parsons delineated five lines of reasoning and associated problems dealing with biology and sexual orientation: 1) Humans and mammals are alike, but brain anatomy is not identical in all mammals, and "sexual orientation" may not be a meaningful concept when applied to nonhuman mammals; 2) childhood gender nonconformity, a fairly reliable prediction of adult sexual orientation, must be inborn because it appears so early in life, but infants are assigned a sex at birth and are reared on the basis of this assignment; 3) sexual orientation is so resistant to change that it must be inborn, but during the first few years of life children are not only socialized as boys and girls, but also their brains grow enormously; 4) some behavioral scientists are discontent with psychosocial explanations of sexual orientation, but biological explanations have at least as many flaws; 5) the discovery of a biological difference would reduce the social stigma of homosexuality, but "the undisputed innateness of skin color does not appear to have a mitigating influence on racism."

The authors propose a model in which genes or hormones influence *personality* traits (rather than sexual orientation). These traits, in turn, influence the way in which persons interact with their environment to develop a sexual orientation. Thus, the emergence of sexual orientation is dependent upon temperamental and personality traits, some of which are developmentally influenced by either hormones or heredity. Sexual orientation is the culmination of a complex synthetic process that ultimately involves the highest level of mental functioning in the cerebral cortex rather than only the hypothalamus or other simpler brain structures.

I suggested that the homophobic minister's rigid and exceedingly zealous behavior may be his way of keeping in check his attraction to homosexuality. In this case the attraction would reside in his unconscious mind, which, by definition, means that he would be totally unaware of it and would deny it vehemently. The more vehement the denial the more likely that this interpretation might be correct. Of course, once I invoke his unconscious, he has lost the battle. Were he aware of an attraction, which seems most unlikely, then he would simply be a hypocrite like the televangelists that I cited. A study by Adams et al. exposed homophobic and non-homophobic men to erotic, explicit heterosexual, male homosexual, and lesbian videotapes. "Only the homophobic men showed an increase in penile erection to male homosexual stimuli: The groups did not differ in aggression. Homophobia is apparently associated with homosexual arousal that the homophobic individual is either aware of or denies." This would seem to support the reaction formation theory, although it is possible that the tumescence was a result of anxiety over a perceived threat rather than due to sexual arousal.

The problem with the concept of reaction formation is that, while it is often observed in clinical practice, it cannot be tested in the usual scientific manner. No matter what actions the minister takes, I can still claim victory.

There is yet another possibility. Is it possible that the homophobic minister is simply acting out God's will? There are many Old Testament examples of God's brutish behavior, and several of the prophets engaged in strange behavior. Had the minister lived in biblical times, would he have been accepted as a prophet? Or a false prophet? In today's world most people regard him as a cranky, repulsive person who dishonors religion.

Chapter 5: GOD IN A BOTTLE: ALCOHOL AND THE BIBLE

Basic references are P. Conley and A. Sorenson's *The Staggering Steeple: The Story of Alcoholism and the Churches*, W. Oates' *Alcohol: In and Out of the Church*, W. Rorabaugh's *The Alcoholic Republic*, L. Bennett and G. Ames' *The American Experience With Alcohol*, S. Barrows and R. Room's *Drinking: Behavior and Belief in Modern History*, and J. Ewing and B. Rouse's *Drinking: Alcohol in American Society*. William James' *The Varieties of Religious Experience* was published in 1902.

Mark 15:23 states that the Roman soldiers offered Christ wine mixed with myrrh to deaden the pain of his crucifixion. *The Interpreter's Bible* notes that "It was a pious Jewish custom to give a condemned man unmixed wine or wine with an opiate in it to make him unconscious." Matthew writes that Christ was given sour wine mixed with gall, not myrrh, in order to conform to the prophecy in Psalm 69, "They also gave me gall for my food, and for my thirst they gave me vinegar to drink."

The transformation of bread and wine into Christ's body and blood is known as transubstantiation. See the *Catechism of the Catholic Church*. Psychiatrist Carl Jung discusses this matter in great detail in his *Psychology and Religion, West and East*. He notes that at the moment of consecration the priest speaks the scriptural words "This is my body" and "This is my blood" to signify that Christ himself is present.

The Aztecs in Central America had a god-eating rite that was described clearly by the Catholic priest Bernardino de Sahagún. The seeds of a poppy were crushed into a paste and then molded into a figure of the god Huitzilopochtli. The god was then killed by a high priest who pierced the figure's side. The figure was dismembered and eaten. "And of this which they ate, it was said: 'The god is eaten.'" The parallels to Christian communion, according to Jung, "caused much consternation among the worthy Spanish Fathers at the time."

A Christian ritual wafer and tiny cup or sip of wine do not induce changes in the communicant as a result of any pharmacological activity. However, many psychoactive plants have been used in religious rituals throughout the world because of their ability to induce changes in perception, thought, and mood when eaten (in the case of the ergotism, the effect is due to toxicity). These plants, when used in the proper cultural context, allow the partaker to enter the world of the supernatural.

Epena, a hallucinogenic snuff, is used by shamans of tribes in the interior Amazon River area. It allows them to send their souls on magical missions and to communicate with the hekula spirits. The snuff is blasted through a blowpipe into the shaman's nostrils. The San Pedro cactus, boiled in water and drunk by shamans (and sometimes patients) in Peru and Ecuador, is used in healing rituals. Those who drink it feel detached from their bodies and can then fly around the universe and consult with spirits. Teonanactl, a sacred mushroom, was called "god's flesh" by the Aztecs who ate it in order to gain insights into the synchrony between the past and the future. Its active ingredient is the chemical psilocybin. The peyote cactus or mescal buttons (mescaline is the active chemical) are used by Indians in Mexico and the United States to induce beautiful, vibrant visions and to communicate with god. The Native American Church regards its use as a sacrament. For information on these and other plants, see R. Schultes and A. Hoffman's *Plants of the Gods* and P. Furst's *Flesh of the Gods*.

E. Hyams' *Dionysus: A Social History of the Wine Vine* presents a complete picture of the bacchanalia. M. Marshall's *Beliefs, Behaviors and Alcohol Beverages* as well as his chapter, "Four hundred rabbits: An anthropological view of ethanol as a disinhibitor" in R. Room and G. Collins' *Alcohol and Disinhibition* provide an enormous cross-cultural bibliography of studies on alcohol.

The citation on Jewish drinking is "The great Jewish drink mystery" by Mark Keller. He cites comments about Jewish sobriety made by the philosopher Immanuel Kant in Germany and by the sociologist Emile Durkheim in France. In a 1944 doctoral dissertation at Harvard, R.F. Bales found that Irish drinkers enjoyed the pharmacological effect of alcohol, while Jewish drinkers avoided it. He attributed the Jewish approach to cultural practices in which alcohol was not used primarily for fun. C.R. Snyder's *Alcohol and the Jews* reaffirmed Bales' findings and is a classic study in this area. Also see the chapter on "Jewish-Americans and Alcohol" by B. Glassner and B. Berg.

In 1957, a group of African-Americans from Chicago who believed that they were the authentic descendants of the biblical Israelites moved to Liberia and then to Israel. A leader of these Black Hebrews declared that "the appointed time has come for us to stand up and claim our land, our language, and our culture." The Israeli government was not amused and placed restrictions on the group, which responded by defensive structuring. They developed solid boundaries, a highly centralized authority structure, and a strict code of morality. In order to remain vigilant against possible attacks, the group placed strict limits on drinking. Only weak, home-brewed wine was allowed; individual drinking was prohibited, as was drunkenness; only adults could drink, and women had to drink in the company of men. See M. Singer's "The function of sobriety among Black Hebrews." Singer draws an analogy to the Mormon ban on alcohol, which became mandatory in the late 1860s. The completion of the transcontinental railroad at that time brought an influx of outsiders to Utah. The Mormon response was defensive structuring. "Mormon abstinence, it would appear, became institutionalized as a means of ethnic boundary maintenance during a period of external threat. Abstinence continues to serve this function in the Mormon community today."

My primary sources for material on temperance and abstinence in the United States are listed at the head of the notes for this chapter. Interesting biographies include V. Dabney's *Dry Messiah: The Life of Bishop Cannon*, and J. Bland's study of Father Matthew titled *Hibernian Crusade*.

The literature on AA is not as large as one might suppose because AA steadfastly maintains its independence and the anonymity of its members, thus making research difficult if not impossible. See P. Beebington's "The efficacy of AA: The elusiveness of hard data." The General Service Office of Alcoholics Anonymous in New York City is the only source of official AA publications. See also M. Rodin's "Getting on the program: A bicultural analysis of AA," E. Kurtz's "Why alcohol works," and H. Tiebout's "Therapeutic mechanisms of AA." For information on the Vie Libre (Free Life), a French ex-alcoholics association, see S. Fainzang's "When alcoholics are not anonymous." The best history is E. Kurtz' *Not God: A History of Alcoholics Anonymous*.

Many disorder-specific groups have appropriated AA's twelve steps, e.g., Overeaters Anonymous, Gamblers Anonymous. The American membership of AA is about one and a half million persons (about half a million more worldwide), many of whom sport bumper stickers on their cars with the slogan, "One Day at a Time." Overcomers Outreach, founded in 1985 by an alcoholic minister in California, utilizes the twelve steps but in a totally Christian context. It should be noted that although AA is not supposed to be aligned with any particular religious persuasion, most group meetings include a recitation of the Lord's Prayer. This Christian flavor is a turn-off for some alcoholics, especially Jews. Rational Recovery, founded by a social worker, disavows the higher power concept and focuses on alcoholics' irrational beliefs. It caters to AA drop-outs and claims one thousand groups in the United States.

Books on alcoholism are plentiful. For an authoritative clinical text see E. Nace's *The Treatment of Alcoholism.* A brilliant longitudinal study and clinically informed book is George Vaillant's *The National History of Alcoholism: Causes, Patterns, and Paths to Recovery.*

My major sources for the confluence of religion and alcohol are H. Clinebell's "Philosophical-religious factors in the etiology and treatment of alcoholism," and E. Jellinek's "The symbolism of drinking." Also see S. Klausner's "Sacred and profane meanings of blood and alcohol," and Sorenson and Cutter's "Mystical experience, drinking behavior, and the reasons for drinking."

An important National Institute of Mental Health funded study, *Alcohol Problems: A Report to the Nation*, was published in 1967. As discussed by Conley and Sorenson in *The Staggering Steeple*, the report called for an alteration in American drinking practices and referred to the great differences in alcoholism among ethnic and cultural groups, e.g., the Jews and the Irish. It proposed a national alcohol policy to reduce the emotionalism associated with alcoholic beverages, to clarify and emphasize the distinctions between acceptable and unacceptable drinking, to discourage drinking for its own sake and encourage the integration of drinking with other activities, and to assist young people to adapt themselves realistically to a predominantly drinking society. The report was well received by most religious groups. An editorial in *The Christian Century* (Nov. 8, 1967), for example, called it "a must for all Americans interested in solving the nation's increasing alcoholism problems," and noted that "the study discovered that problem drinkers are produced primarily by two groups of people—those who view alcohol as sinful and those who view drinking as a sign of maturity." A negative response appeared in *Christianity Today* (Nov. 10, 1967), which declared that the report's proposals "are enough to drive church goers to drink . . . It is irresponsible folly to relax deterrents to alcoholism . . . the Gospel of Jesus Christ is the only sure cure for alcoholism and every other sin."

In September 1968, a Methodist Bishop, James Matthews, addressed a plenary session of the 28th International Congress on Alcohol and Alcoholism. He concluded that "alcohol alone is not the problem; man alone is not the problem; but alcohol is a problem to man because man is a problem to himself. This is the new stance of the churches."

Similar thoughts are contained in the perceptive book *Alcohol: In and Out of the Church* by Wayne Oates, a Baptist minister. He describes three dimensions, based on the New Testament, of a creative attitude toward sin in relation to alcohol and alcoholism:"First, alcohol is a part of creation, and our task is to find God's intention for its use that it can bless and not curse human life . . . Second, any approach to the alcoholic as a sinner must begin with a confession of our own faults . . . Third, this attitude toward sin involves an appreciation of the compulsive, irrational, violent nature of human beings. Even as the alcoholic becomes compulsively addicted to alcohol, so the over pious religious person can become addicted to self-righteousness and be lost in the power of his pride." In his acknowledgements Oates thanks the Christian Life Commission of the Southern Baptists Convention for making it possible for him to state his ideas. He also thanks the graduate students at Southern Baptist Theological Seminary who helped him develop his ideas in a seminar. Back in the 1960s freedom of expression was possible. Since then conservative forces have gained control. The results are exemplified by the 1993 pamphlet cited in this chapter, which calls drinking immoral and alcoholism a sin. Oates refers to this attitude as "an unchristian kind of bigotry."

Chapter 6: CREEPING THINGS: ANIMALS AND THE BIBLE

The concept of the scapegoat is found in Lev. 16:1–34. On the yearly ritual Day of Atonement the high priest presented two goats to God. One was sacrificed while the other, the scapegoat, was sent into the wilderness after the high priest had confessed all the sins of the Israelites over its body. The Hebrew text does not use the word scapegoat but rather the goat "for Azazel" (an evil spirit like Satan). The ritual was probably very ancient but it and the Day of Atonement were officially established only after the exile in Babylon. David's child died for his father's sins. In Christianity Jesus died for mankind's sins.

Nebuchadnezzar's story as well as that of Daniel in the lion's den is told in the Book of Daniel 1–4. The third century A.D. physician who wrote the first clinical account of lycanthropy was Marcellus; his work was popularized by Paul of Aegina (625–690 A.D.). Walter Burkert's *Homo Necans* discusses werewolves in ancient Greece. The cases of the 20-year-old schizophrenic and the 37-year-old farmer are from Surawicz and Banta's "Lycanthropy revisited." The case of the 49-year-old woman is from Rosenstock and Vincent's "A case of lycanthropy." Other recent articles are Jackson's "Another case of lycanthropy," and Coll, O'Sullivan, and Browne's "Lycanthropy lives on." The Harvard study is found in Keck et al.'s "Lycanthropy alive and well in the twentieth century." These articles have been published in Richard Noll's *Vampires, Werewolves, and Demons*. Other references include Jackson's *Melancholia and Depression* and C.F. Ohen's *A Dog Man*.

A full review of the feral children literature can be found in Favazza's arti-cle and chapter. The book by A. Gesell is *Wolf-Child and Human-Child*. Favazza and Eppright reported the case of a man who was involuntarily hos-pitalized during a manic episode for menacingly barking like a dog. Hospital staff and patients were frightened until the discovery that the man had belonged to a college fraternity with a secret signal; members barked to alert their brothers that they were in distress and needed help.

The key book on the snake handling cult is Weston LaBarre's *They Shall Take Up Serpents*. Also see E.R. Dodds' *The Greeks and the Irrational* and B. Schwarz's "Ordeal by serpent, fire and strychnine." About 75 persons have died from snake bites during church services. Many more worshippers have been bitten, some more than a hundred times. Those who die usually praise the Lord and say that they must not have had enough faith at the time of the bite. Snake handling rituals may occur in isolated Pentecostal Holiness churches. Appalachian migrants have brought the ritual with them to sites throughout the nation, although it tends to be more secretive in urban areas.

Chapter 7: SOMETHING ABOUT THE BODY

Homer Smith's *Man and His Gods* provides a good introduction to the mutilative rituals of the Great Mother Goddess. Maarten Vermaseren's *Cybele and Attis* is the leading work on the myth and the cult. See also Bernice Engle's "Attis: A Study of Castration." Hasting's *Encyclopedia of Religion and Ethics* has informative articles on eunuchs in general and on the Skoptski (listed under Sects, Russian). Also see R. Battey's "Practice of Scoptzy in Roumania," and B.Z. Goldberg's *The Sacred Fire*.

In the Eastern Roman Empire castration became a big business; about six thousand eunuchs a year were sold as slaves and lust objects from the sev-enth to the ninth centuries. Since Byzantine emperors often chose eunuchs for high political positions, some noblemen voluntarily were castrated in order to obtain a prestigious job (climbing the corporate ladder never has been easy).

Muhammad reportedly said, "He who castrates himself or another does not belong among my followers, for castration in Islam may consist only in fasting." Muslims, especially during the thirteenth-century Mamaluke period in Egypt and the fourteenth-century Ottoman Empire in Turkey, purchased eunuchs to serve as harem keepers. Some eunuchs rose to the highest ranks of leadership and even married. Christian monasteries in Egypt castrated slaves for financial gain, as did barbers, monks, and physicians in large cities, especially Khartoum.

For information about clinical cases of self-castration and other forms of self-mutilation, see Favazza's *Bodies Under Siege*.

Vincent Crapanzano's *The Hamadsha* is an in-depth study of these Sufi healers. Christian flagellation cults are discussed in Norman Cohn's *The Pursuit of the Millenium*. For material on shamanism see Mercea Eliade's *Shamanism* and *Rites and Symbols of Initiation*. The mythological mutilative foundation of social order is discussed in Bruce Lincoln's "The Indo-European myth of creation."

The story of Jesus among the Gadarenes was a cause celebre in nineteenth century England. Thomas Huxley, a free-thinking bona fide intellectual, was charged with being an infidel and a cowardly agnostic at a church congress in 1888. He responded by publishing an article on the ridiculousness of both the demon possession concept in general, and the flight of demons from a man to a herd of swine in particular. The English Prime Minister, Gladstone, entered the fray by asserting that since Gadara was a Jewish city, the swine-keepers should not have been raising pigs. The drowning of the demonic pigs was God's punishment! The two great men carried on their spirited debate in mutually antagonistic articles. Huxley, ever the bulldog, lost all sense of perspective when he declared the "final judgement of the Gadarene tale" will determine whether Christianity will revere the ethical-ideal of Israel or an ideal "foul with savage superstition and cankered with false philosophy, to which the theologians have bound it."

See Stella Kramish's *Manifestations of Shiva* for photographs and commentary on Shiva lingam stones. The devotional image of Jesus' heart was inspired by the image of the Aztec death god's heart that diffused from Mexico to Europe. See A.B. Kehoe's "The Sacred Heart."

Ian Wilson's *The Bleeding Mind* offers the best general overview of the stigmata and contains a chronological list of all known stigmatics from St. Francis to the present day. Important references on this topic are Herbert Thurston's *The Physical Phenomena of Mysticism*, F.A. Whitlock and J.V. Hynes' "Religious stigmatisation," E. Warlomont's *Louise Lateau*, R.W. Hyneck's *Konnersreuth: A Medical and Psychological Study of the Case of Therese Neumann*, and Aldous Huxley's *The Devils of Loudon*.

The bogus stigmatic's quest for glory reminds me of a bogus tale. The Bible recounts that the devil tempted Jesus three times, even offering Jesus authority over all the kingdoms of the world if he would worship him. Jesus, of course, refused. The editors of the Bible, however, did not tell the rest of the story. It seems that the devil tempted Jesus a fourth time. "If you worship me," he said, "I promise to have you crucified for all the world to see." This offer was too good to refuse.

The most sublime fictional account of a stigmatic is Ron Hansen's *Mariette in Ecstasy*. It is the account of a novice at a convent in upstate New York in 1906. Did Mariette create her wounds? Was she a victim of hysterical self-deception? Was she truly touched by God? Each reader must decide.

Probably the best general book about male circumcision is Edward Wallerstein's *Circumcision: An American Health Fallacy*. Erich Isaac is a cogent religious scholar; his essay on "The Enigma of Circumcision" appeared in 1967. The newspaper article on "AIDS and Circumcision" was written by Rabbi J.S. Cohen in 1988. For psychoanalytic material see Jules Glenn's "Circumcision and Anti-Semitism" and Howard Schlossman's "Circumcision as Defense." The full text of the spurious letter of Alexius Comnenus to Count Robert of Flanders imploring his aid against the Turks in the late eleventh/early twelfth century can be found in John Boswell's *Christianity, Social Tolerance and Homosexuality*. For a culturally sensitive view of female circumcision see Helen Boddy's "Womb as Oasis:The symbolic context of pharaonic circumcision in rural Northern Sudan." The *Hosken Report on Genital and Sexual Mutilation of Females* and A. El Dareer's *Women Why Do You Weep?* present the darker, morbid side of female circumcision. Julian Huxley's *Africa View* tells the complete story of the confusion among the Kikuyu over the translation of "virgin."

Certainly female genital circumcision is a major public health concern in many African countries. Its most severe form results in a host of medical complications such as urine retention, urinary tract and chronic pelvic infection, implantation cysts, injured urethral and anal tissue, problems during childbirth, and painful intercourse. Although Muslims are the greatest followers of the practice and often give religious justifications for it, female circumcision is definitely not a part of Islam. Some Africans who immigrate to Europe and the United States continue to circumcise their female children. Many Western countries are considering laws to ban the procedure.

The mildest form, removal of the clitoris, was actually utilized in mid-nineteenth century England. Sir Isaac Baker Brown, President of the Medical Society of London and author of a widely used surgical textbook, performed the operation on hundreds of women. He believed that female masturbation caused a progression of pathological conditions starting with hysteria, then epilepsy, then idiocy, mania, and death. Clitoridectomy offered a rapid cure. He was soundly reprimanded by his colleagues and booted from all medical societies. As one of the most revered surgeons in England, he was devastated by his fall from grace. An editorial in the *British Medical Journal* (1867) concluded: "So severe a punishment as this has not fallen upon any man holding a respectable position in our profession in the memory of any of us. It is impossible not to feel pity and deep regret for the man who thus suffers. . . . The fault has been great; the punishment severe." For a full account see J.B. Fleming's "Clitoridectomy:The disastrous downfall of Sir Isaac Baker Brown."

Chapter 8: PRAISE THE LORD AND PASS THE MEDICATION: HEALING
AND FEELING GOOD

Arturo Castiglioni's massive *History of Medicine* is a basic text. *The Healing Hand* by Guido Majno is a wonderfully written and illustrated book about medicine in the ancient world. Simon Levin's *Adam's Rib: Essays on Biblical Medicine* is a delightful read and full of astute observations and entertaining guesses, e.g., both Noah and Samson may have been albinos. Also see A. R. Short's *The Bible and Modern Medicine* and C. R. Smith's *The Physician Examines the Bible*.

In Mesopotamia both physicians and sorcerers practiced medicine but neither were regarded very highly by patients. Great use was made of herbs, oils, and other materials. These were mixed to form mushes that could be eaten, inhaled, put in an enema, or applied externally. It was fairly primitive stuff. Herodotus described the situation in Babylon: "They bring out the sick to the market place, for they do not use physicians. People who walk by and have suffered the same illness as the sick man's, or seen others in like case, come near and advise him about his disease and comfort him, telling him by what means they have themselves recovered of it, or seen others to recover."

In contrast, Egyptian medicine was quite advanced and specialized. Proctologists were in great demand because decay was associated with elimination. About the anus, Majno writes: "The Egyptians soothed it, refreshed it, smoked it . . . and they became all-time experts on enemas." They believed that blood vessels centered in the heart but had a secondary center in the anus where feces could create havoc by invading the bloodstream.

Saul's erratic behavior (1 Samuel) probably would be diagnosed as manic-depressive illness with psychotic features. He had episodes of severe depression, delusions of persecution, and ended up committing suicide. Levin, however, makes a case for the diagnosis of a slow-growing pituitary tumor and acromegalic gigantism based on Saul's notable height and strength, headaches, and poor vision (at close range he hurled his javelin twice at David but missed both times). Levin, in a real stretch, also attempts to diagnose Paul as having a form of muscular dystrophy known as dystrophia myotonica. He bases this diagnosis on Paul's weak bodily presence and speech defect (2 Corinthians 10:10), eye problems (Acts 9:9, 18) and mental disturbances (Acts 18:9; 26:24). Other symptoms such as baldness, bow legs, and a long nose are not attributed to Paul in the Bible but do appear in *The Acts of Paul and Thela*, a popular second century romance.

The record of Jesus' healings can be found in Mark 1:30 (fever); Mark 1:40 and Luke 17:11 (leprosy); Matt. 9:2 (palsy); Luke 14:1 (edema); Luke 22:51 (severed ear); John 5:6-8 (crippled man); John 4:49 and Mark 5:41 (children at death's door); Mark 5:25-34 (vaginal bleeding); Mark 12:10-13 (withered hand); Matt. 8:5-13 (paralysis); Luke 7:14-15 (dead boy); Mark

8:22, Luke 18:35, Matt. 9:27 (blindness); Matt. 21:14 (the blind and the lame); Matt. 12:22 (blind, mute man); Mark 1:39, 7:25–30, 9–14, Matt. 8:28, 9:32, Luke 8:2, 13:11, 13:32 (demons).

Recommended readings on demons and exorcism are S. E. Nauman's *Exorcism Through The Ages*, Kramer and Sprenger's *Malleus Maleficarum*, M. Eliade's *Occultism, Witchcraft, and Cultural Fashions*, R. Robbins' *The Encyclopedia of Witchcraft and Demonology*, E.M. Pattison's "Psychological interpretations of exorcism," and W. Fairbairn's *An Object Relations Theory of Personality*.

The evil eye refers to the belief that a force may be emitted from the eye of a human or an animal in order to cause disease, damage, or injury. Proverbs 23:6 states, "Eat not the bread of him that hath an evil eye," while Mark 7:22 lists the evil eye as one of the evil things that come from within and defile a man. Isaiah 13:18 notes that God will stir up the Medes and "Their eye will not spare children." Among the disorders attributed to the evil eye are disrupted social relationships, diarrhea, vomiting, anorexia, insomnia, impotence, sudden death, depression, hypochondriasis, headaches, fevers, malformed fetuses, epidemics of plague and cholera, and even crop damage. The fourth-century Council of Elvira in Spain prohibited Jews from looking at the fields of Christians for fear that the crops would wither. In fact, a German word for evil eye is *Judenblick*, or Jew's glance. Those who are particularly susceptible to the evil eye are pregnant women, nursing mothers, children, and the wealthy. Those most likely to possess an evil eye are strangers, hunchbacks and others with a physical deformity, and jealous persons. Amulets such as the red chilihorn and red ribbons supposedly offer protection. Participation in rituals can remove the evil eye; an afflicted person drops oil in water and says, "Who fascinated you? The eye, the thought and the evil desire? Who will remove the fascination? The Father, the Son, and the Holy Ghost." See C. Maloney's *The Evil Eye* and E. Foulks' "The Italian evil eye."

Morton Kelsey's *Healing and Christianity* and Francis MacNutt's *Healing* and *The Power to Heal* are excellent sources, as is A. White's *A History of the Warfare of Science with Theology*. For more on Mesmer, Gassner, Fluornoy, and Janet see H. Ellenberger's *The Discovery of the Unconscious*. H. Waddell's *The Desert Fathers* is a classic book on the topic. For more on shrines see *Christian Pilgrimage in Modern Western Europe* by Mary and Sidney Nolan. Perhaps the best book on Lourdes is D. West's *Eleven Lourdes Miracles*; also see Jerome and Julia Frank's *Persuasion and Healing* and R. Cranston's *The Miracle of Lourdes*.

J.L. Sherill's *They Speak With Other Tongues* presents a brief history of the modern charismatic healing movement. In addition to James Randi's *The Faith Healers,* also see G. Straub's *Salvation for Sale* and W. Nolen's *Healing: A Doctor in Search of a Miracle*. D. Fry's *Can God Fill Teeth?* is about the ministry of Willard Fuller.

For materials on Catholicism see A. Flannery's *Vatican Council II* and the *Catechism of the Catholic Church*.

The studies mentioned in the chapter are Pattison et al., "Faith healing," J.P. Collipp's "The efficacy of prayer," Joyce and Welldon's "The objective efficacy of prayer," R.C. Byrd's "Positive therapeutic effects of intercessory prayer in a coronary care unit," and Parker and St. Johns' *Prayer Can Change Your Life*. A rather complete bibliography on prayers and healing, including material on the effects of prayers on nonhuman living things, can be found in Larry Dossey's *Healing Words*. Also see Favazza's "Modern Christian healing of mental illness." For critical commentaries on Byrd's often-cited study see articles by Posner, Sloan et al. Tessman and Tessman, and Witmer and Zimmerman.

Chapter 9: TRUE, FALSE AND USEFUL: THE SPIRITUAL MARKETPLACE, RELIGION & PSYCHIATRY

Ronald Siegel's article "The psychology of life after death" presents information on near-death experiences from various sources such as cinematography, science fiction books, turn of the century psychical investigations, physics, evolutionary biology, ethology, anthropology, individual reports, and modern studies. In 1908, British scientists determined that the human soul weighs roughly one ounce based on the immediate loss of weight at time of death. Although Moody's description of the typical near-death experience is the best known, other descriptions have been derived from studies of hallucinations (Klaver), of religious movements and of folklore (Holck), of psychic communications received by mediums (Crookall), of physicians and nurses who observed dying patients (Osis), and of deathbed visions (Osis and Haroldson). Depersonalization experiences as a reaction to life-threatening danger have been studied by Noyes and Kletti, who note that mystical elaborations of the experience may include a feeling of rebirth and visions of hoped-for future events. Siegel provides multiple examples of statements made by hallucinogen users that parallel those made by persons who have undergone a near-death experience. For more on the topic in general, see Gabbard and Twenlo;, Ring; Greyson; Pasricha and Stevenson; Zaleski; Roberts and Owen; Appleby; and Greyson and Bush. Schroter-Kundardt lists many non-English language references. Stevenson examines research into the evidence of survival after death. Freud's comment about our denial of death is from his 1915 essay on "Thoughts for the times on war and death."

The insipid description of angels as the "social workers of the universe" comes from *Ask Your Angel* (Daniel, Wyllie, and Ramer). The authors report reassuringly that "We were given an angel to help us in the creation and writing of this book." Sophy Burnham's *A Book of Angels* takes the position that encounters with angels are often unnoticed because angels may disguise themselves as a dream, an energy, a person, or just about anything "so as not to disturb" the recipient of their interventions. The popular television show *Touched by an Angel* features two angels disguised as kindly women who tell individuals beset by problems (drugs, suicidal thoughts, and the like) that God loves them and wants to enter into their lives. In the Old Testament, God did send angels to interact with persons. The angels were almost always disguised as men, however, and their visits usually weren't sugar-coated. Following the visit of two angels to Sodom, the entire city was destroyed.

The book about persons who believe that they have been abducted by aliens is John Mack's *Abduction*. He claims that these persons do not exhibit much psychopathology and that they communicate their experience "sincerely." Sincerity, of course, counts for something, but fixed delusions typically are experienced sincerely. Since Mack is a full professor and protected by tenure, there wasn't much that his colleagues at Harvard could do except express their embarrassment, chide him for his approach to the topic, and speculate about his personal intrapsychic problems.

Spiritual Dimensions of Healing by Kippner and Welch contains a great deal of information on the topic with an extensive bibliography. *Habits of the Heart: Individualism and Commitment in American Life* by Bellah reports about people who describe themselves as spiritual but not religious; many are attracted to the relatively formless and whim-guided New Age forms of spirituality as opposed to the spirituality associated with traditional churches, clergy, and rites. Also see Fuller's *Alternative Medicine and American Religious Life* and Numbers and Amundsen's *Caring and Curing: Health and Medicine in the Western Religious Tradition*.

Thomas Moore's *Care of the Soul: A Guide for Cultivating Depth and Sacredness in Everyday Life* and *Soul Mates: Honoring the Mysteries of Love and Relationship* are thoughtful wisdom literature books. Rohde's *Psyche* is the classic study of the cult of souls and belief in immortality among the ancient Greeks. The rather mundane advice about six ways to feed your soul is more than matched by the five habits of highly effective prayers from Castelli's *How I Pray*: clear your head in the morning, collect your thoughts, and set a daily goal and priorities; use cues to remind yourself of spirituality (one Catholic bishop prays every time he opens the refrigerator or car door); take a few seconds to reflect before any confrontation; stimulate reflection by daily reading, e.g., the Bible, spiritual readings, or The One-Minute Manager; make notes about the ideas, insights, and goals that come in a flash during reflection. The audacious combination of the Bible and The One Minute Manager in the same sentence is a sad commentary on modern religious sensibility.

The "father of clinical pastoral education" is Anton Boisen, a Presbyterian minister, who unfortunately developed schizophrenia in 1920. Some well-known books on pastoral care include those by Campbell, Capps, Hiltner, Holifield, Oden, and Purvis.

In addition to Benson's writings on the placebo response (he proposes renaming it "remembered wellness"), which contain more than adequate bibliographies, a few specific instructive readings are Beecher's "The powerful placebo," Butler and Steptoe's study of asthmatics, and Archer and Leier's "Placebo treatment in congestive heart failure." The best book on the topic is Shapiro's *The Powerful Placebo*. Meditation figures significantly in many modern spiritual hearing programs. West's *The Psychology of Meditation* is a good book to consult. Davidson's *Trust the Force* deals with the use of meditation in psychotherapy.

Even Christian Science, which has been practically dead for half a century, is making a minor comeback. It holds that health is the natural expression of personhood and that illness is an illusion. Its founder, Mary Baker Eddy, believed in Christ's words, "For indeed, the kingdom of God is within you" (Luke 17:21). Thus, "Prayer cannot change the Science of being, but it tends to bring us into harmony with it."

Hans Kung, the somewhat controversial Dutch Catholic theologian, has written a book titled *Religion: The Last Taboo*. Two major sources for this section are Peter Gay's *A Godless Jew: Freud, Atheism, and the Making of Psychoanalysis* and John Burnham's "The encounter of Christian theology with deterministic psychology and psychoanalysis." The quote by Freud is from his *The Future of an Illusion*. In 1916, Adolph Meyer, the great psychiatrist at Johns Hopkins University, wrote that psychiatry and religion need not be allies because psychiatry was "absolutely coextensive with all the life interests of our patients."

Don Browning's "The Protestant response to psychiatry" covers the work of William James, Anton Boisen, Seward Hiltner, Rheinhold Niebuhr, Paul Tillich, and Paul Ricoeur. Marie McCarthy's "A Roman Catholic perspective on psychiatry and religion" covers the pre- and post-Vatican II periods. The Jesuit priest who linked psychoanalysis with mortal sin was Gordon George. Gay regards Lee's book, *Freud and Christianity*, as "perhaps the most convincing (or least unconvincing) attempt to bring Freud and Christ together." Gay also provides a thorough story of Freud's Jewishness. He concludes that "Freud was a Jew but not a Jewish scientist" and that "his Judaism was inessential, not to Freud, but to his creation, psychoanalysis." He cites a letter from Freud to Ernest Jones: "If someone should reproach you with my Fall into Sin, you are free to reply that my adherence to telepathy is my private affair, like my Jewishness, my passion for smoking and other things, and the theme of telepathy—inessential for psychoanalysis" (March 7, 1926). Gay also concludes that "the claims for the Jewishness of psychoanalysis based on its materials or its intellectual inheritance have proved to be without foundation."

Recommended readings on the satanic ritual child abuse nonsense are Wright's *Remembering Satan*, Nathan Snedeker's *Satan's Silence*, and Ney's *True and False Allegations of Child Sexual Abuse*. For a British perspective on the topic see Britt-Krause's "Devil's worship or a devilish psyche?" and La Fontaine's reply, which includes the quote I included in my chapter as well as a note that Members of Parliament who are pushing the satanic abuse notion belong to the Movement for Christian Democracy, a cross-party organization that aims to increase Christian influence in the House of Commons. Loftus and Ketcham's *The Myth of Repressed Memory* provides much evidence that people can believe they experienced something that never really happened. Freyd's *Betrayal Trauma* takes the position that "children who suffer abuse at the hands of a trustful caregiver end up repressing memories." Interestingly, Freyd's mother is the founder of the False Memory Syndrome Foundation, a support group for persons falsely accused of childhood abuse. My information on the court cases comes from Grinfeld's "Memory theories still abound: psychiatrists suffer huge verdicts in retractor suits."

In the course of my clinical practice I have seen a consistent decrease in the number of patients with guilt of a religious nature. This may simply reflect a change in my sample of patients, but even in psychiatric articles and meetings the topic is rarely discussed. If anything, we are encountering persons with too little guilt and no sense of remorse or pangs of conscience.

Delaney and Fiske authored the study on religious and obsessive-compulsive rituals. Greenley examined obsessive-compulsive symptoms in Jewish patients and he concluded that "religious patients have religious compulsions just as religious psychotics have religious delusions, in that their religious commitment is merely incorporated into the presenting problem rather than being a causal factor." Actually, current research in obsessive-compulsive disorder has focused almost exclusively on biology. Lesions in the brain's basal ganglia, defects in brain serotonin levels, and even childhood exposure to bacterial infection have been implicated.

The study of English psychiatrists' religious attitudes as well as references to other studies is by Neelemen and King. Research on religious variables in psychiatric journals is found in the article by Larson et al. Psychiatrists are generally cynical, so also are police officers, but because their lives are literally in danger on a daily basis they have a healthier respect for religion. An example of a cynicism moment for me was the admission by a troubled priest whom I was treating that he masturbated on the mornings that he said Mass and did not wash his hands. He was angry with the Church's ban on marriage for priests and experienced a perverse sense of comfort in administering the communion wafer to women.

The 21 factors of religiosity were proposed by King and Hunt. Allen and Spilka described committed and consensual religiosity, Spilka functional and dysfunctional, Fromm humanistic and authoritarian, Pruyser healthy and neurotic; Allbrook focused on moral commitment versus calculated involvement.

Rokearch and Kemp found lower anxiety levels in nonbelievers. The study showing low levels of psychological distress in persons with strong religious beliefs and in persons with no religion is by Ross; the commentary on it is by Masters and Bergin. The relationship between church attendance and subjective health has been examined by Levin and Markides. For factors affecting the religion–mental health relationship in the elderly see Koenig. The 1983 review of the relationship between religiosity and mental health is by Bergin; the 1994 review is by Larson and Larson. The study of female twins in Virginia is by Kendler et al. Subjects were interviewed three times over an average of 5 years. They were assessed for current and lifetime diagnoses of mental illness (using well-accepted criteria), religiosity (self-reports about "personal devotion" such as frequency of private prayer, of seeking spiritual comfort, and of church attendance, and about "personal conservatism" such as belief that God rewards and punishes people and that the Bible is the literal word of God), institutional conservatism (Fundamentalist Protestants were ranked the most conservative, followed in order by Baptists, Catholics, mainline Protestants, and other or unaffiliated), and history of stressful life events. Although no relationship was found between religiosity and mental health except for possible lower rates of depression associated with stressful life events (Gartner et al. also found lower depression in their 1991 review), religiosity was related to lower use of alcohol and drugs. One limitation of the study was that the subjects all were female; gender differences may affect the relationship between religiosity and mental health.

For a sociological view of the secularization of theology see Berger. Beardslee was the historian who questioned whether theologians had anything distinctive to say. Anderson has written about the congregation as a healing resource. For articles urging psychiatrists to attend to the religious concerns of patients and to engage in research on religion see Kehoe and Gritheil; Kroll and Sheehan; Sims; King et al.; Crossley; Nealeman and Persaud; and Dein. Lukoff et al. wrote about psychiatry's Diagnostic and Statistical Manual and its accommodation of psychospiritual and psychoreligious problems. Galanter et al. have examined the small group of practitioners who refer to themselves as Christian psychiatrists. Koenig's *Is Religion Good For Your Health?* contains an extensive and useful list of references on the topic. The author is quite optimistic about the health benefits of religion throughout the book but weakly concludes, "If further evidence continues to show that these [religious effects on health] are indeed positive, then we will need to actively encourage cooperation and collaboration between mental health care providers and the clergy."

The Project on Religion and Coping is detailed in Pargament's large and well-reasoned *The Psychology of Religion and Coping.* The book certainly attempts to make a positive case for the unique contributions of religious processes during struggles with coping, but it also fairly presents data that clearly indicate neutral or negative results. It also covers situations that have given religion a bad name. Religious subterfuge or self-deception, for example, have been used to justify social oppression. During the American Civil War, the Vice President of the Confederacy, Alexander Stephens, declared: "To maintain that slavery is in itself sinful, in the face of all that is said and written in the Bible upon the subject, with so many sanctions of the relation by the Deity himself, does not seem to be a little short of blasphemous! It is a direct imputation upon the wisdom and justice, as well as the ordained ordinances of God." An example of an error of religious explanation is the contention that AIDS is the just dessert of homosexuals who engage in perverse, ungodly practices (see Chilton). The error is that biological, social, and psychological factors that play a significant role in the AIDS epidemic are shortchanged; "the end result is a nasty form of religious scapegoating." An error of religious moderation is the excessive use of corporal punishment of children based on biblical texts; Greven's *Spare the Child* is a sobering read. The study of converts to ultra-orthodox Judaism is by Witztrum et al.

Chapter 10: BACK TO GOD AND THE BIBLE

By human nature, we usually mean the way people behave or are expected to behave in our culture. Clearly there are biological constraints on behavior (see Melvin Konner's *The Tangled Wing*), but any anthropology textbook or issue of *National Geographic* attests to the variability of normal behavior across cultures. The best historical examples of infanticide in a highly functional society are found in ancient Greece. Since the Spartans valued strength and bravery, newborns judged defective by their fathers and by governmental inspectors were thrown from a cliff to their deaths. In Athens, fathers were permitted to place newborns deemed weak, deformed, or illegitimate in a clay pot usually located in a temple or public place. Such children were rarely rescued; most died of exposure. In Book Five of *The Republic,* Plato described the ideal eugenic policy: "the offspring of the inferior, or of the better when they chance to be deformed, will be put away in some mysterious, unknown place, as they should be." As for mother love, consider Colin Turnbull's *The Mountain People.* The African tribe known as the Ik live in an area where semi-starvation due to limited resources is the rule.

Turnbull describes how mothers grudgingly nurse their infants and while foraging for food place their children on the ground "almost hoping that some predator will come along and carry it off. This happened once while I was there—once that I know of, anyway—and the mother was delighted."

The literature on mysticism is large and often muddled. The material in my chapter defining mystic states is from what I consider to be the best work on the topic, namely "Religions and creative states of illumination: A perspective from psychiatry" by Philip Woollcott and Prakesh Desai. These authors provide an extensive bibliography and differentiate between creative and regressed mystic states. Creative states are characterized by a paradoxical combination of intense perceptual clarity, a profound sense of integration and interconnectedness, and highly developed moral behavior. The brevity of the mystical states is described in the sixteenth-century masterpiece *The Interior Castle*. In it St. Teresa of Avila relates that God "would come upon me unexpectedly so that I could in no way doubt He was within me or I totally immersed in Him . . . the union never lasts for as much as a half hour." Pathological regressed states are characterized by pseudoreligious ecstasy, paranoia, and disturbed ethics such as self-righteousness, omnipotent grandiosity, and destructive hatred of a scapegoat. Films of Hitler addressing Nazi rallies vividly display fanaticism and regressed merger states.

According to *The Zohar*, God sent a light beam into the empty space that he had occupied. The excess light cascaded to form the universe and the ten emanations of God. This concept was evoked at a recent meeting of astrophysicists and cosmologists on the possible compatibility of religious and scientific ideas regarding the creation of the universe. Keter, the first emanation, symbolizes God's infinite creative potential and is similar to "eternal inflation," the pre-Big Bang bubbling potential of the universe. Hokhman, the second emanation, is like the Big Bang itself and symbolizes the transformation of potential energy into physical existence. Binah, the third emanation, is like the formation of space, time, and matter and symbolizes the female womb where creation expands. The meeting was held in May, 1997, at the Center for Theology and Natural Sciences in Berkeley, California.

Meister Eckhart, an assiduously devout Christian, advised, "Love God whether he is loving or not, and certainly not because he is loving, for he is non-loving, being above love and affection." Incredibly, Alfred Rosenberg, the philosopher of German National Socialism, declared that Eckhart provided the spiritual basis for Nazism!

In 1927, Freud sent his *The Future of an Illusion* to the great French humanist and novelist Romain Rolland. In his response Rolland chided Freud for emphasizing the illusory nature of religion at the expense of its real core which was "a sensation of the eternal . . . a rich and beneficent energy . . . [an experience] as if oceanic." In *Civilization and Its Discontents* (1930), Freud developed the concept of an oceanic experience as the essence of mystical states and explained it as an adult regression to the earliest undifferentiated state of infantile life. Readers might be interested in looking at Laski's *Ecstasy: A Study of Some Secular and Religious Experiences*, Diekman's "Biomodal consciousness and the mystic experience," and Prince's "Religious experience and psychosis" and "Shamans and endorphins." Hardy's *The Spiritual Nature of Man: A Study of Contemporary Religious Experiences* and Hay's *Exploring Inner Space: Scientists and Religious Experience* report on some of the more than 4,000 examples collected by Oxford University's Religious Experience Research Unit. The older classic books in this area are Brucke's *Cosmic Consciousness* and James' *The Varieties of Religious Experience*.

The connection between the temporal lobe of the brain and religious feelings is well accepted by neurologists. Some of the religious leaders who *may* have had temporal lobe epilepsy are Buddha, Mohammed, St. Ignatius Loyola, St. Theresa of Avila, and St. Paul (see Lennox and Lennox). The Russian novelist Dostoevsky probably had a different kind of epilepsy, although the character, Prince Myshkin, in *The Idiot* described an aura just prior to a seizure as a moment for which "one might give one's whole soul." In that moment, "his soul was flooded with intense inner light." In his 1928 essay "Dostoevsky and parricide," Freud argued that the Russian author suffered from hysterical pseudoseizures.

Saver and Rabin's "The neural substrates of religious experience" is an excellent review. The authors note that there is no unique organ of religious perception and that religious joy, love, fever, and awe are analogues of ordinary emotions, the only difference being that they are directed to a religious object. Thus, our apprehension of the divine is mediated by the same brain systems that are involved in our perception of touch, sight, sound, and smell.

Religious interpretations are likely to be placed on epileptic seizures because they are "paroxysmal, riveting, and unexpected—sudden intrusions of unanticipated and often extraordinary experience into the ordinary daily flow of consciousness." In addition, partial complex seizures in the brain's temporal lobe are often associated with psychic auras of fear, auditory and visual hallucinations, and sensations of *déjà vu* and *jamais vu*. Less commonly (about 25 percent), the auras may be of dreamy states, depersonalization, derealization, and double consciousness (normal consciousness combined with a new and different perception of reality). Autoscopy—seeing a double of one's self or an out-of-body experience—is also found in temporal lobe seizures, as are feelings of ecstasy. Morgan reported the case of a patient with a temporal lobe tumor whose seizures consisted of feelings of bliss, a bright light described by the patient as the source of knowledge, and the vision of a Jesus-like figure. After the tumor was removed, the ecstatic seizures ceased. Six patients who underwent dramatic religious conversions immediately following intense temporal lobe seizures were reported by

Dewhurst and Beard. Some seizures are followed a day or so later by elevat
ed mood, grandiose thoughts, and psychosis. About a fourth of post-seizure
psychoses have a religious content (see Kanemato et al.). A substantial sub-
group of temporal lobe epileptics demonstrate hyperreligiosity and intense
philosophical and cosmological concerns. Saver and Rabin list the core qualities of religious and mystical experiences as a sense of having touched ultimate reality, the incommunicability of the experience, and a sense of unity,
timelessness, peace, joy, and positive affect. They suggest that the primary
neural substrate of these experiences is the limbic systems of the brain and
note that temporal lobe-limbic epileptic discharges can produce each of the
components of these experiences in fragmentary or complete forms. Also
see Carmody and Carmody; Hardy; D. Hay; D.A. Miller; and Roberts and
Guberman.

Contemporary Psychoanalysis and Religion by James Jones is a highly
recommended, intellectual tour de force, albeit somewhat difficult reading
for persons unfamiliar with psychoanalytic history and concepts. Jones
makes a case that "the structures of our selfhood are the transmutations of
our interactions." By this he means that we internalize from our interactions
in the world. If our psychology is inherently relational, then maybe reality is
also relational: "There is nothing childish about acknowledging connection
to a self-sustaining universal matrix."

George Rosen's *Madness in Society* contains a marvelous chapter on religious psychic epidemics. Medieval dance frenzies occurred throughout
medieval Europe and were attributed to demon possession or excess enthusiasm upon visits to certain shrines such as that of St. Vitus. The fifteenth-
century Bohemian Adamites and the Anabaptists a century later often wore
no clothes as a sign of purity. The twentieth-century Doukhobors in Canada
have done the same. The Shaking Quakers trembled, jumped up and down,
shuddered, and sang under the power of God to express their indignation
against sin. See Ronald Knox's *Enthusiasm: A Chapter in the History of
Religion*.

The World Health Organization's *World Health Report 1995* notes that
half a billion people suffer from neurotic, stress-related, and psychological
disorders that present with physical symptoms. Mood disorders, primarily
depression, affect 200 million persons, mental retardation 83 million, demen-
tia 22 million, and schizophrenia 16 million. By the year 2020 it is estimated
that mental disorders, especially depression, will top the list of causes of illness morbidity.

I did not mention Scientology, an amalgam of pseudopsychology and
some quite bizarre religious beliefs, in the chapter. It's founder, Ron
Hubbard, was a science fiction writer. Scientology's creation myth concerns
Xenar, a cruel ruler in outer space who banished groups of souls called
Thetans to earth 75 million years ago. Today's humans supposedly have trou-

blesome repressed memories or "engrams" of Thetan life that cause all sorts of problems, including mental illness. With the aid of a device call an "e-meter" (a simple meter that measures skin resistance to an electrical charge and that was used many decades ago as a primitive type of lie detector) engrams can be audited and eventually "cleared." In a scathing cover article, *Time* magazine (May 6, 1991) called Scientology "the cult of greed" and exposed many financial scams run by the organization. According to *Time*, dentists, chiropractors, podiatrists, and veterinarians appear to be primary targets of Scientology recruiters. It's a scary organization.

As explained by the theologian Harvey Cox (1995), the "religious right" is not monolithic but rather contains several groups that frequently disagree with each other. Almost forty percent of Americans claim to be born-again and to have personally experienced Jesus. Like Billy Graham, evangelicals recognize the special authority of the Bible and a duty to share their faith with others in addition to having a personal experience with God. Fundamentalists are like evangelicals but insist that every word in the Bible is absolutely correct. Pentecostals also are like evangelicals but place a primary emphasis on "an immediate encounter with the Holy Spirit in a style of worship that is exuberant and even ecstatic." Charismatics are persons in Catholic and Protestant Churches who practice a Pentecostal form of worship. Cox visited Regent University, established by televangelist Pat Robertson, and was surprised by the lively discussion of issues. One area of controversy was Robertson's claim, based on Genesis 1:2–8, that God gave Adam and Eve dominion over every living thing that moves on the earth. Robertson explained this doctrine in *The New World Order*: "There will never be world peace until God's house and God's people are given their rightful place of leadership at the top of the world. How can there be peace when drunkards, communists, atheists, New Age worshippers of Satan, secular humorists, oppressive moneychangers, revolutionary assassins, adulterers, and homosexuals are on top?" Cox was disturbed that a theologian named Rousas John Rushdoony has refined the dominion concept by proposing the killing of adulterers, homosexuals, blasphemers, witches, and teachers of false doctrines. It's not much to be thankful for, but at least he spared the drunkards, moneychangers, and assassins.

In the Introduction of this book I noted my Catholic upbringing. It is the world's largest religion, yet it is sometimes difficult to appreciate why people have stuck with it. I find incense to be a mind-deadening toxin. For every beautiful church painting or statue there are ten thousand garish, ugly ones. I still am amazed at believers who fall on their knees when confronted by the "miracle" of a weeping statue of the Virgin or the image of Jesus on a taco crust. Modern chemists utilizing fourteenth-century knowledge have even simulated the liquefying blood of the Neapolitan Saint Januarius (by producing a thixotropic gel of iron hydroxide: see Epstein and Garlaschelli). In fact, in a marvelous essay, Catholic priest and sociologist Andrew Greeley notes the persuasive case that can be made against Catholicism. The Church is repressive, discriminates against women and homosexuals, tries to regulate the bedroom behavior of married couples and to impose its anti-abortion policy on everyone, preaches against birth control in poor, overcrowded nations, controls its finances with little input from the lay congregation, covers up sexual abuse by priests, and makes priests unhappy by a ban on marriage. So why do Catholics stay in the Church? Greeley answers that Catholics like their heritage because it has great stories and "at the center of its heritage is sacramentalism, the conviction that God discloses Himself in the objects and events and persons of ordinary life." Thus, all the stories of angels, saints, and souls in purgatory, all the rosaries and medals and stained glass windows, and "the whole panoply of images and devotions that were so offensive to the leaders of the Reformation." Catholicism also is attractive because it has rich ceremonial Sacraments that embrace the human life cycle. Because of the stories, Greeley contends, Catholics are more likely to have a "gracious" image of god as a Mother, Lover, Spouse, and Friend as opposed to a Father, a Judge, a Master, a King. The most powerful image is that of Mary.

Greeley concludes with a story told to him by some nuns that sums up why people stay Catholic:

Jesus was touring heaven when he noticed certain new residents who should have been serving time in purgatory. He stormed to the pearly gates and chided St. Peter:

"You've failed me again."

"What have I done now?" was the reply.

"You let a lot of people in that don't belong." "I didn't do it."

"Well, who did?" asked Jesus.

"You won't like it."

"Tell me anyway."

"I turn them away from the front gate and they go around to the back door and your mother lets them in!"

The French encyclopedist, Diderot, said that religious superstition is immortal. Thomas Edison said that religion is all bunk. Greeley likes the stories. Maybe he's right, but even if he's wrong, it's a charming ending to a long book.

BIBLIOGRAPHY

Adam H, Wright L, Lohr B: Is homophobia associated with homosexual arousal? *J Abnormal Psychology* 105:440-445, 1996

Allen LS, Gorski RA: Sexual orientation and the size of the anterior commissure in the human brain. *Proceedings National Acad Sciences* 89:7199-7202, 1992

Allen RO, Spilka B: Committed and consensual religion. *J Scientific Study of Religion* 61:91-206, 1967

Allport G: *The Individual and His Religion*. New York: MacMillan, 1950

Allport GW, Ross JM: Personal religious orientation and prejudice. *J Personality Social Psychology* 5:432-443, 1967

Amsel A: *Rational Irrational: Man, Torah, Psychology*. New York: Feldheim Publishers, 1976

Anderson H: The congregation as a healing resource. In *Religion and Ethical Factors in Psychiatric Practice*, Browning DS, Jobe T, Evison IS (editors). Chicago: Nelson-Hall, 1990

Andreasen N: The role of religion in depression. *J Religion and Health* 11:153-166, 1972

Appleby L: Near death experience: Analogous to other stress induced psychological phenomena. *Brit Med Journal* 298: 976-977, 1989

Archbishop's Commission on Divine Healing: The Church's Ministry of Healing. London: Church Information Board, 1958

Archer TP, Leier CV: Placebo treatment in congestive heart failure. *Cardiology* 81:121-133, 1992

Armstrong K: *A History of God*. New York: Knopf, 1993

Ashbrook JB: The relationship of church members to church organizations. *J Scientific Study of Religion* 5:397-419, 1966

Assagioli R: *Psychosynthesis*. New York: Viking Press, 1965

Banks C: There is no fat in heaven. *Ethos* 24: 107-135, 1996

Barrows S, Room R: *Drinking: Behavior and Belief in Modern History*. Berkeley: University of California Press, 1991

Barth K: *The Knowledge of God and the Science of God*. New York: Charles Scribner's Sons, 1939

382

Battey R: Practice of Scoptzy in Roumania. *Atlanta Med Surg J* 11:483-487, 1873

Bayer R: *Homosexuality and American Psychiatry.* Princeton: Princeton University Press, 1987

Beardslee WA: *America and the Future of Theology.* Philadelphia: Westminster Press, 1967

Beebington P: The efficacy of AA: The elusiveness of hard data. *Brit J Psychiatry* 128:572-580, 1976

Beecher HK: The powerful placebo. *J Amer Medical Assn* 159:1602-1606, 1955

Bell R: *Holy Anorexia.* Chicago: University of Chicago Press, 1985

Bellah RN: *Habits of the Heart: Individualism and Commitment in American Life.* Berkeley: University of California Press, 1996

Bennett L, Ames G: *The American Experience With Alcohol.* New York: Plenum Press, 1985

Benson H: *Timeless Healing: The Power and Biology of Belief.* New York: Scribner, 1996

————. *The Relaxation Response.* New York: Morrow, 1975

Berger P: A sociological view of the secularization of theology. *J Scientific Study of Religion* 6:3-16, 1967

Bergin AE: Religiosity and mental health: A critical reevaluation and meta-analysis. *Professional Psychology* 14: 170-184, 1983

Berstein A: *The Formation of Hell.* Ithaca: Cornell University Press, 1993

Bettleheim B: *Freud and Man's Soul.* New York: Knopf, 1982

————. *Symbolic Wounds.* New York: Collier Books, 1971

Bieber I: *Homosexuality: A Psychoanalytic Study of Male Homosexuals.* New York: Basic Books, 1992

Bird P: Images of women in the Old Testament. In *Religion and Sexism*, Reuther R (editor). New York: Simon and Schuster, 1994

Bland J: *Hibernian Crusade.* Washington, DC: Catholic University Press, 1951

Boddy H: Womb as oasis: The symbolic context of pharaonic circumcision in rural Northern Sudan. *Am Ethnologist* 9:682-698, 1982

Boisen A: *Religion in Crisis and Custom.* New York: Harper and Row, 1945

————. *The Exploitation of the Inner World.* New York: Willet, Clark and Co., 1936

Bollas C: *The Shadow of the Object.* New York: Columbia University Press, 1987

Booth L: *The God Game: It's Your Move.* Walpole: Stillpoint, 1994

Borg M: *Meeting Jesus Again for the First Time.* San Francisco: HarperSanFrancisco, 1994

Boswell J: *Christianity, Social Tolerance, and Homosexuality.* Chicago: University of Chicago Press, 1980

Bowker J: *The Religious Imagination and The Sense of God*. Oxford: Clarendon Press, 1978

Boyd GA: *Cynic, Sage, or Son of God?* Wheaton, Il: Bridgepoint, 1995

Boynton RS: The lives of Robert Hughes. *The New Yorker*, May 12, 1997, 48-53.

Bradford W: *Of Plymouth Plantation*: 1620-1647. New York: Modern Library, 1981

Bridges R, Spilka B: Religion and the mental health of women. In *Religion and Mental Health*, Schumaker J (editor). New York: Oxford University Press, 1992

Britt-Krause I: Devil worship or devilish people? *Brit Med Anthro Review* 3 (1): 83-89, 1995/96

Brooke J: *The Refiner's Fire*. Cambridge: Cambridge University Press, 1994

Brown LB: *The Psychology of Religious Belief*. London:Academic Press, 1987

Brown N: *Life Against Death:The Psychoanalytic Meaning of History*. New York: Random House, 1960

Brown P: *The Body and Society: Men, Women and Sexual Renunciation in Early Christianity*. Cambridge: Harvard University Press, 1989

Browning D: The Protestant response to psychiatry. In *Religious and Ethical Factors in Psychiatric Practice*, Browing D, Jobe T, Evison I (editors). Chicago: Nelson Hall, 1990

Browning D, Jobe T, Evison D: *Religious and Ethical Factors in Psychiatric Practice*. Chicago: Nelson-Hall, 1990

Bucke, RM: *Cosmic Consciousness*. New York: Dutton, 1901

Bultmann R: *Existence and Faith*. Cleveland:World Publishing Co., 1960

Burgoyne RW, Burgoyne RH: Conflict secondary to overt paradoxes in belief systems: The Mormon woman example. *J Operational Psychiatry* 8 (2):39-45, 1977

Burkert W: *Homo Necans*. Berkeley, University of California Press, 1983

Burnham J: The encounter of Christian theology with deterministic psychology and psychoanalysis. *Bulletin Menninger Clinic* 49:321-352, 1985

Burnham S: *A Book of Angels*. New York: Ballantine, 1992

Burton R: *The Anatomy of Melancholy*. New York:Tudor, 1938 (orig. 1621)

Butler C, Steptoe A: Placebo response:An experimental study of asthmatic volunteers. *Brit J Clin Psychology* 25:173-183, 1986

Byrd RC: Positive therapeutic effects of intercessory prayer in a coronary care unit. *Southern Med J* 81:826-829, 1988

Byne W, Parsons B: Human sexual orientation: The biological theories reappraised. *Archives General Psychiatry* 50:228-239, 1993

Bynum C: *Holy Feast and Holy Fast*. Berkeley: University of California Press, 1985

Campbell A: *Rediscovering Pastoral Care*. Philadelphia:Westminster Press, 1981

Capps D: *Biblical Approaches to Pastoral Counseling.* Philadelphia, Westminster Press, 1981

Carmody DL, Carmody JY: *Mysticism.* New York: Oxford University Press, 1996

Castiglioni A: *History of Medicine.* New York: Knopf, 1947

Catechism of the Catholic Church. Liguori: Liguori Publications, 1994

Chilton D: *Power in the Blood: A Christian Response to AIDS.* Brentwood, TN: Wolgenmuth and Hyatt, 1987

Choisy M: Psychoanalysis and Catholicism. *Cross Currents* 1:75-90, 1951

Chopra D: *The Path to Love.* New York: Harmony Books, 1997

———. *Boundless Energy.* New York: Harmony Books, 1993

———. *Ageless Body, Timeless Mind.* New York: Harmony Books, 1993

Clinebell H: Philosophical-religious factors in the etiology and treatment of alcoholism. *Quart J Studies Alcohol* 24:473-488, 1963

Cohen JS: *AIDS and Circumcision.* The Jewish Press, April 22, 1988

Cohn N: *Europe's Inner Demons.* New York: Basic Books, 1975

———. *The Pursuit of the Millennium.* New York: Essential Books, 1958

Coles R: *The Spiritual Life of Children.* Boston: Houghton Mifflin, 1990

———. *Harvard Diary: Reflections on the Sacred and the Secular.* New York: Crossroad, 1988

Coll P, O'Sullivan G, Browne P: Lycanthropy lives on. *British J Psychiatry* 147:201-202, 1975

Collipp PJ: The efficacy of prayer. *Medical Times* 97 (5): 201-204, 1969

Conley P, Sorenson A: *The Staggering Steeple: The Story of Alcoholism and the Churches.* Philadelphia: United Church Press, 1971

Cox H: The warning visions of the religious right. *Atlantic Monthly*, Nov. 1995, 59-69

———. *The Seduction of the Spirit: The Use and Misuse of People's Religion.* New York: Simon and Schuster, 1973.

Cranston R: *The Miracle of Lourdes.* New York: Popular Library, 1955

Crapanzano V: *The Hamadsha.* Berkeley: University of California Press, 1973

Crookall R: *The Supreme Adventure: Analyses of Psychic Communications.* London: James Clark, 1961

Crossan JD: *The Historical Jesus: The Life of a Mediterranean Jewish Peasant.* San Francisco: HarperSanFrancisco, 1991

Crossley D: Religious experience within mental illness. *Brit J Psychiatry* 166:284-286, 1995

Csordes TJ: Prophecy and the performance of metaphor. *Am Anthropologist* 99:321-332, 1997

———. *The Sacred Self: A Cultural Phenomenology of Charismatic Healing.* Berkeley: University of California Press, 1994

Curb R, Manahan N: *Lesbian Nuns: Breaking Silence.* New York: Warner Books, 1985

Dabney V: *Dry Messiah: The Life of Bishop Canon*. New York: Knopf, 1949

Daniel A, Wyllie T, Ramer A: *Ask Your Angels*. New York: Ballantine, 1992

Dart J: Christians repenting sins in history. *Los Angeles Times*, July 16, 1995

Davidson G: *A Dictionary of Angels*. New York: The Free Press, 1967

Davidson T: *Trust the Force: Change Your Life Through Attitudinal Healing*. Northvale, NJ: Jason Aronson, 1995

Davies P: *God and the New Physics*. New York: Simon and Schuster, 1983

Deblassie P: *Toxic Christianity*. New York: Crossroad, 1992

Deikman AJ: Bimodal consciousness and the mystic experience. In *Understanding Mysticism*, Woods R (editor). New York: Doubleday, 1980

Dein S: Religion and mental health. *Brit Medical Anthropology Review* 3: 40–49, 1996

Delbanco A: *The Death of Satan: How Americans Have Lost the Sense of Evil*. New York: Farrar, Straus, and Giroux, 1995

deVries M, Berg R, Lipkin: *The Use and Abuse of Medicine*. New York: Praeger, 1982

Dewhurst K, Beard AW: Sudden religious convulsions in temporal lobe epilepsy. *Brit J Psychiatry* 117:497–507, 1990

DiNicola V: Anorexia multiforme: Self-starvation in historical and cultural context. *Transcultural Psychiatric Research Review* 27:165–196, 245–286, 1990

Divine Healing and Cooperation Between Doctors and Clergy. London: British Medical Association, 1956

Dodd E: *The Greeks and the Irrational*. Berkeley: University of California Press, 1951

Dossey L: *Healing Words*. San Francisco: HarperSan Francisco, 1993

Driver T: Sexuality and Jesus. *Union Theological Quarterly Review* 20: 235-246, 1965

Dulaney S, Fiske AP: Cultural rituals and obsessive-compulsive disorder. *Ethos* 22:243–283, 1994

Dupre L, Saliers D: *Christian Spirituality*. New York: Crossroad, 1989

Eadie B: *Surprised by the Light*. Placeville, CA: Gold Leaf Press, 1992

Eddy, MB: *Science and Health With a Key to the Scriptures*. Boston: The Christian Science Publishing Society, 1875

El Dareer A: *Women Why Do You Weep?* London: Zed Press, 1982

Eliade M: *Occultism, Witchcraft, and Cultural Fashions*. Chicago: University of Chicago Press, 1976

———. *Rites and Symbols of Initiation*. New York: Harper and Row, 1975

———. *Shamanism*. Princeton: Princeton University Press, 1974

———. *Myth and Reality*. New York: Harper and Row, 1963

Elkins DB: On being spiritual without necessarily being religious. *Assn for Humanistic Psychology Perspective*, June: 4–5, 1990

Ellenberger H: *The Discovery of the Unconscious*. New York, Basic Books, 1970

Ellis A: Psychotherapy and atheistic values. *J Counseling Clinical Psychology* 46:635 639, 1980

———. The case against religion: A psychotherapist's view. In, *Counseling and Psychotherapy*, Ard B (editor). Palo Alto: Science and Behavior Books, 1975

Engle B: Attis: A study of castration. *Psychoanalytic Review* 23:363–372, 1936

Epstein M, Garlarschelli L: Better blood through chemistry: A laboratory replication of a miracle. *J Scientific Exploration* 6:233–246, 1992

Erikson E: *Young Man Luther*. New York: Norton, 1958

Ewing J, Rouse B: *Drinking: Alcohol in American Society*. Chicago: Nelson-Hall, 1978

Fainzang S: When alcoholics are not anonymous. *Med Anthropological Quarterly* 8:336–345, 1994

Fairbairn W: *An Object Relations Theory of Personality*. New York: Basic Books, 1954

Favazza A: *Bodies Under Siege: Self-Mutilation and Body Transformation in Culture and Psychiatry*. Baltimore: Johns Hopkins University Press, 1996

———. Feral and isolated children. *British J Medical Psychology* 50:105–111, 1977

———. Feral and isolated children. In *Mental Health in Children*, Volume One, Sanker DVS (editor). Westbury: PJD Publications, 1975

Favazza A, Eppright T: Understanding the meaning of a symptom. *American J Psychiatry* 144:1620, 1987

Finke R, Stark R: *The Churching of America*. New Brunswick NJ: Rutgers University Press, 1992.

Fiorenza ES: *In Memory of Her: A Feminist Theological Reconstruction of Christian Origins*. New York: Crossroad, 1983

Flannery A: *Vatican Council II*. Northport: Costello Publishing, 1992

Fleming JB: Clitoridectomy: The disastrous downfall of Sir Isaac Baker Brown. *J Obstetrics Gynecology* 67:1017–1034, 1960

Fogel R: The fourth great awakening. *Wall Street Journal*, Jan. 9, 1996

Ford C, Beach F: *Patterns of Sexual Behavior*. New York: Harper and Brothers, 1951

Foulks E: The Italian evil eye. *J Operational Psychiatry* 8 (2):28–34, 1977

Fox G: *The Journal of George Fox*. Cambridge: Cambridge University Press, 1952 (orig. 1652)

Fox RL: *The Unauthorized Version: Truth and Fiction in the Bible*. New York: Knopf, 1992

Frank J, Frank J: *Persuasion and Healing* (third edition). Baltimore: Johns Hopkins University Press, 1991

Franks V, Franks EP: *The Stereotyping of Women*. New York: Springer, 1983

Freud S: *Moses and Monotheism*. Standard Edition 23:7–137. London: Hogarth Press, 1964 (original 1939)

————. *The Future of an Illusion*. Standard Edition 21:5-56. London: Hogarth Press, 1962 (original 1927).

————. *A Seventeenth Century Demonological Neurosis*. Standard Edition 19:72-105. London: Hogarth Press, 1961 (original 1923)

————. *Civilization and Its Discontents*. Standard Edition 21:64-145. London: Hogarth Press, 1961 (original 1030).

————. An Autobiographical Study. Standard Edition 20:1-74. London: Hogarth Press, 1959 (original 1935)

————. Obsessive actions and religious practices. Standard Edition 9:117-129. London: Hogarth press, 1959.

————. Dostoyevski and Parricide. In *Collected Papers*. New York: Basic Books, 1959 (original 1928).

————. Thoughts for the times on war and death. In *Collected Papers*. New York: Basic Books, 1959 (original 1915).

————. *Totem and Taboo*. Standard Edition 13:1-161. London: Hogarth Press, 1955 (original 1913)

Freud S, Pfister O: *Psychoanalysis and Faith* (edited by Meng H, Freud E.) New York: Basic Books, 1963

Friedman RE: *The Disappearance of God*. Boston: Little Brown, 1995

Fromm E: *Psychoanalysis and Religion*. New Haven: Yale University Press, 1950

Fry D: *Can God Fill Teeth?* Lakemount: CSA Press, 1970

Fuller RC: *Alternative Medicine and American Religious Life*. New York: Oxford University Press, 1989

Funk R: *Honest to Jesus*. San Francisco: HarperSanFrancisco, 1996

Funk RW, Hoover RW: *The Jesus Seminar: The Five Gospels*. New York: Macmillan, 1993

Furst P: *Flesh of the Gods*. New York: Prager, 1972

Gabbard GO, Twemlow SW: *With the Eyes of the Mind: An Empirical Analysis of Out-of-Body States*. New York: Praeger, 1984

Galanter M, Larson D, Rubenstone E: Christian psychiatry: The impact of evangelical belief on clinical practice. *Am J Psychiatry* 148:90-95, 1991

Gallup G: Religion in America. *The Public Perspective*, Oct-Nov 1995, 1-8

Gartner J: *Your Better Self: Psychology, Christianity, and Self-Esteem*. New York: Harper and Row, 1983

Gartner J, Larson DB, Allan GD: Religious commitment and mental health: A review of the empirical literature. *J Psychology Theology* 19:6-25, 1991

Gay P: *A Godless Jew: Freud, Atheism, and the Making of Psychoanalysis*. New Haven: Yale University Press, 1989

Geertz C: Religion as a cultural system. In, *Anthropological Approaches to the Study of Religion*, Bantom M (editor). New York: Praeger, 1966

George G: The pope on psychoanalysis. *America 88* (Oct. 4), 1953

Georgoudi S: Creating a myth of matriarchy. In *A History of Women: From*

Ancient Goddesses to Christian Saints, Pantel P (editor). Cambridge: Harvard University Press, 1992

Gesell A: *Wolf-Child and Human-Child*. New York: Harper and Brothers, 1940

Glasmer B, Berg B: Jewish-Americans and alcohol. In *The American Experience With Alcohol*, Bennett L, Ames G (editors). New York: Plenum Press, 1985

Glenn J: Circumcision and anti-Semitism. *Psychoanalytic Quarterly* 29:395–399, 1960

Goldberg BZ: *The Sacred Fire*. New York: Horace Liveright, 1930

Gomes P: *The Good Book: Reading the Bible With Mind and Heart*. New York: William Morrow, 1997

Graham B: Angels: *God's Secret Agents*. New York: Doubleday, 1975

Graves R: *The Greek Myths*. Baltimore: Penguin Books, 1955

Greeley AM: Because of the stories. *New York Times Magazine*, 38–41, July 10, 1994

Greenley D: Are religious compulsions religious or compulsive? *Am J Psychotherapy* 38:524–532, 1984

Grever P: *Spare the Child: The Religious Roots of Punishment and the Psychological Impact of Physical Abuse*. New York: Knopf, 1991

Greyson B: A typology of near-death experiences. *Am J Psychiatry* 142:967–969, 1985

Greyson B, Bush NE: Distressing near-death experiences. *Psychiatry* 55:96–110, 1992

Griffith EEH: The impact of sociocultural factors on a church based healing model. *Am J Orthopsychiatry* 53:291–302, 1983

Griffith EEH, English T, Mayfield V: Possession, prayer, and testimony: Therapeutic aspects of the Wednesday night meeting in a black church. *Psychiatry* 43:120–128, 1980

Griffith EEH, Mabry GE: Psychological benefit of spiritual Baptists mourning I. *Am J Psychiatry* 141:769–773, 1984; II. *Am J Psychiatry* 143:226–229, 1986

Griffith EEH, Young JL, Smith JL: An analysis of the therapeutic elements in a black church service. *Hosp Community Psychiatry* 35:464–469, 1984

Grinfeld M: Memory theories still abound: Psychiatrists suffer huge verdicts in retractor suits. *Psychiatric Times*, April, 1977.

Gross L: *God and Freud*. New York: David McKay, 1959

Guirdham A: *Christ and Freud*. London: Allen & Unwin, 1959

Guntrip H: *Psychoanalytic Theory, Therapy, and the Self*. New York: Basic Books, 1971

Hammon N, Scullard H: *The Oxford Classical Dictionary*. London: Oxford University Press, 1970

Hanks M: *Women and Authority: Re-emerging Mormon Feminism*. Salt Lake City: Signature Books, 1992

390 BIBLIOGRAPHY

Hansen R: *Mariette in Ecstasy*. New York: Harper Collins, 1991

Hardy A: *The Spiritual Nature of Man:A Study of Contemporary Religious Experience*. Oxford: Clarendon, 1979

————. *The Biology of God*. New York:Taplinger, 1975

Hardy Q: Newest Testament: Japan is the land of the rising son. *Wall Street Journal*, Oct. 11, 1993

Harris R: *The World of the Bible*. New York:Thames and Hudson, 1995

Harris S: *Understanding the Bible*. Palo Alto: Mayfield, 1980

Hasting's Encyclopedia of Religion and Ethics. New York: Scribner, 1961

Hay D: The biology of God. *Intl J Psychology Religion* 4:1-23, 1994

————. *Exploring Inner Space: Scientists and Religious Experience*. Harmondsworth: Penguin, 1982

Hay L: *You Can Heal Your Life*. Carson, CA: Hay House, 1984

Hiltner S: *The Christian Shepard*. Nashville:Abingdon Press, 1959

————. *Preface to Pastoral Theology*. Nashville:Abingdon Press, 1958

Hogbin HI: *The Island of Menstruating Men*. Scranton: Chandler, 1970

Holck FH: Life revisited: Parallels in death experiences. *Omega* 9:1-11, 1978-1979

Holifield E: *A History of Pastoral Care*. Nashville:Abingdon Press, 1983

Hooker E: Male homsexuality in the Rorschach. *J Projective Techniques* 22:33-54, 1958

Horgan J: *The End of Science*. Reading, Mass:Addison-Wesley, 1996

Horney K: The flight from womanhood. *International J Psychoanalysis* 7:324-339, 1926

Hosken: Report on Genital and Sexual Mutilation of Females. Lexington, Women's International Network News, 1970

Hoskins S: *Mary Magdalen: Myth and Metaphor*. New York:Harcourt Brace, 1993

Howell E, Bayes N: *Women and Mental Health*. New York: Basic Books, 1981

Hughes DO: Regulating women's fashion. In *A History of Women: Silences of the Middle Ages*, Klapiach-Zuber C (editor). Cambridge: Harvard University Press, 1992

Hughes J: *Reshaping the Psychoanalytic Domain*. Berkeley: University of California Press, 1989

Hurt WR, Brown RM: Social drinking patters of the Yankton Sioux. *Human Organization* 24:222-230, 1965

Huxley A: *The Devils of London*. London: Chatto and Windus, 1952

Huxley J: *Africa View*. London: Chatto and Windus, 1971

————. *Religion Without Revelation*. New York: Harper, 1957

Hyams E: *Dionysus:A Social History of the Wine Vine*. New York: Macmillan, 1965

Hyneck RW: Konnersreuth:*A Medical and Psychological Study of the Case of Therese Neumann*. New York: Macmillan, 1932

Interpreter's Bible (The). New York:Abingdon Press, 1951

Interpreter's Dictionary of the Bible (The). New York:Abingdon Press, 1962

Isaac E:The enigma of circumcision. *Commentary* 43:51-56, 1967

Jackson P:Another case of lycanthropy. *American J Psychiatry* 135: 134-135, 1978

Jackson S: *Melancholia and Depression*. New Haven:Yale University Press, 1986

Jaffe DS:The masculine envy of women's procreative function. *J American Psychoanalytic Assn* 16:521-548, 1968

James W: *The Varieties of Religious Experience*. New York: Modern Library (original 1902)

Jellinek E: The symbolism of drinking. *J Stud Alcohol* 38:849-866, 1977

John D: As Mormon Church grows, so does dissent from feminists and scholars. *New York Times*, Oct. 2, 1993

Johnson CA: *The Frontier Camp Meeting: Religion's Harvest Time*. Dallas: Southern Methodist University Press, 1995

Johnson P: *A History of Christianity*. New York:Athaneum, 1979

Jones E: *Essays in Applied Psychoanalysis*. London: Hogarth, 1951

Jones JW: *Contemporary Psychoanalysis and Religion*. New Haven: Yale University Press, 1991

Jordan M: *The Invention of Sodomy in Christian Theology*. Chicago: University of Chicago Press, 1997.

Joyce C, Welldon RM: The objective efficacy of prayer. *J Chronic Disease* 18:367-377, 1965

Jung C: *Psychology and Religion*. New Haven:Yale University Press, 1938

Kaminer W:The latest fashion in irrationality. *Atlantic Monthly*, July, 1996

Keck P, Pope H, Hudson J, McElroy S, Kulick A: Lycanthropy alive and well in the twentieth century. *Psychological Medicine* 18:113-120, 1988

Keen S: *Hymns to an Unknown God:Awakening the Spirit in Everyday Life*. New York: Bantam Books, 1994

Kehoe AB:The sacred heart. *Am Ethnologist* 6:763-771, 1979

Kehoe NC, Gutheil TG: Neglect of religious issues in scale-based assessment of suicidal patients. *Hosp Community Psychiatry* 45:366-369, 1994

Keller M:The great Jewish drink mystery. *Brit J Addictions* 64:287-296, 1970

Keller W: *The Bible As History*. New York: Morrow, 1991

Kelsey M: *Tongue Speaking*. New York: Crossroad, 1981

————. *Healing and Christianity*. New York: Harper and Row, 1973

Kendler KS, Gardner CO, Prescott CA: Religion, psychopathology, and substance use and abuse. *Am J Psychiatry* 154:322-329, 1997

King M, Hunt R: Measuring the religious variable. *J Scientific Study of Religion* 14:13-22, 1975

King M, Speck P, Thomas A: The Royal Free Interview for religious and spiritual beliefs. *Psychological Medicine* 25:1125-1134, 1995

Kingsley C: *Letters to the Chartists*. London: JW Parker, 1848

Kinsey A: *Sexual Behavior in the Human Male*. Philadelphia: Saunders, 1948

Klausner S: Sacred and profane meanings of blood and alcohol. *J Social Psychology* 64:27–43, 1964

Klein J: *Psychology Encounters Judaism*. New York: Philosophical Library, 1979

Kluver H: Mechanisms of hallucinations. In *Studies In Personality*, McNemar Q, Merrill MA, (editors). New York: McGraw Hill, 1942

Knox R: *Enthusiasm: A Chapter in the History of Religion*. Oxford: Oxford University Press, 1950

Koenig HG: *Is Religion Good for Your Health?* New York: Haworth Pastoral Press, 1997

————. *Research on Religion and Aging*. New York: Greenwood Press, 1995

————. Research on religion and mental health in later life. *J Geriatric Psychiatry* 23:23–53, 1990

Konner M: *The Tangled Wing*. New York: Holt, Rinehart, and Winston, 1982

Kramer H, Sprenger J: *The Malleus Malificarum*. New York: Dover, 1971 (original 1486)

Kramish S: *Manifestations of Shiva*. Philadelphia: Philadelphia Museum of Art, 1981

Krippner S, Welch P: *Spiritual Dimensions of Healing*. New York: Irvington, 1992

Kroll J, Sheehan W: Religious beliefs and practices among 52 psychiatric inpatients in Minnesota. *Am J Psychiatry* 146:67–72, 1989

Kung H: *Religion: The Last Taboo*. Washington, DC: American Psychiatric Association Press, 1986

Kurtz E: Why alcohol works. *J Studies Alcohol*: 43:38–80, 1982

————. *Not God: A History of Alcoholics Anonymous*. Minnesota: Hazelden Educational Services, 1979

Kushner M: *Freud: A Man Obsessed*. Philadelphia: Dorrance, 1967

La Fontaine J: A reply to "Devil worship or devilish psych?" *Brit Med Anthro Review* 3(1):86–88, 1995/96

La Barre W: *Culture in Context*. Durham: Duke University Press, 1980

————. Hallucinogens and the shamanic origins of religion. In *Flesh of the Gods*, Fuerst P (editor). New York: Praeger, 1972

————. *They Shall Take Up Serpents*. New York: Schocken Books, 1969

Laeuchli S: *Power and Sexuality*. Philadelphia: Temple University Press, 1972

Land S: Pentecostal spirituality. In *Christian Spirituality: Post-Reformation and Modern*. Dupre L, Saliers D (eds). New York: Crossroad, 1989

Lannert J: Resistance and countertransference issues with spiritual and religious clients. *J Humanistic Psychology* 31:68–76, 1991

Larson DB, Larson SS: The forgotten factor in physical and mental health: What does the research show. Am Independent Study Seminar. Rockville, MD: National Institute for Healthcare Research, 1994

Larson DB, Pattison EM, Blazer DG, Omran AR, Kaplan BH: Systematic analysis on religious variables in four major psychiatric journals, 1978–1982. *Am J Psychiatry* 143:329-334, 1986

Laski M: *Ecstasy: A Study of Some Secular and Religious Experiences.* Bloomington: Indiana University Press, 1961

Lawrence DH: *The Man Who Died.* London: M. Secker, 1931

Lee RS: *Freud and Christianity.* New York: AA Wyn, 1949

Lemert EM: The use of alcohol in three Salish Indian tribes (1958). In *Alcohol and Native Peoples of the North*, Hamer J, Steinbrig J (editors). Lanham, MD: University Press of America, 1980

Lennox W, Lennox M: E*pilepsy and Related Disorders.* Boston: Little, Brown, 1960

Lenski G: *The Religious Factor.* New York: Anchor Books, 1963

Lester R: Embodied voices: Women's food asceticism and the negotiation of identity. *Ethos* 23:187-222, 1995

LeVay S: A difference in hypothalamic structure between heterosexual and homosexual men. *Science* 253:1034-1037, 1991

Levin JS, Marksides JS: Religious attendance and mental health. *J Scientific Study of Religion* 25:31-40, 1986

Levin S: *Adam's Rib: Essays on Biblical Medicine.* California: Geron-X, 1970

Levy JE, Kunitz SJ: *Indian Drinking: Navajo Practices and Anglo-America Theories.* New York: Wiley & Sons, 1974

Lewishon R: *A History of Sexual Customs.* New York: Harper, 1958

Lidz R, Lidz T: Male menstruation. *International J Psychoanalysis* 58:17-31, 1977

Liebman JL: *Peace of Mind.* New York: Simon and Schuster, 1946

Lincoln B: *The Indo-European myth of creation.* History Religion 58:17-31, 1977

Littlewood R, Lipsedge M: The butterfly and the serpent. *Culture, Medicine and Psychiatry* 11:289-335, 1987

Lloyd R: Cross and psychosis. *Faith and Freedom* 24:13-29, 67-87, 1971

Loftus E, Ketcham K: *The Myth of Repressed Memory.* New York: St. Martin's Press, 1994

Lovejoy A: *The Great Chain of Being.* Cambridge: Harvard University Press, 1936

Lukoff D, Lu F, Turner R: Toward a more culturally sensitive DSM-IV: psychoreligious and psychospiritual problems. *J Nervous Mental Disorder* 80:673-682, 1992

Mack B: *The Lost Gospel.* San Francisco: HarperSanFrancisco, 1993

Mack J: *Abduction.* New York: Scribner, 1994

MacNutt F: *The Power to Heal.* Notre Dame:Ave Maria Press, 1977
————. *Healing.* Notre Dame:Ave Maria Press, 1974
Majno G: *The Healing Hand.* Cambridge: Harvard University Press, 1975
Maloney C: *The Evil Eye.* New York: Columbia University Press, 1976
Malony HB, Lovekin AA: *Glossolalia: Behavioral Science Perspectives on Speaking in Tongues.* New York: Oxford University Press, 1985
Mandlebaum D:Alcohol and culture. *Current Anthropology* 6:281-293, 1965
Marcus AD: *The View From Nebo.* Boston, Little Brown, 1998.
Marshall M: *Beliefs, Behaviors, and Alcohol Beverages.* Ann Arbor, University of Michigan Press, 1979.
Masters KS, Bergin AE: Religious orientation and mental health. In *Religion and Mental Health*, Schumaker J (editor). New York: Oxford University Press, 1992
Maudsley H: *Religion and Realities.* London: John Bale, Sons and Danielsson, 1918
McCarthy M:A Roman Catholic perspective on psychiatry and religion. In *Religion and Ethical Factors in Psychiatric Practice*, Browing D, Jobe T, Evison I (editors). Chicago: Nelson Hall, 1990
McGinn G:*Antichrist:Two Thousand Years of the Human Fascination with Evil.* San Francisco: HarperSanFrancisco, 1994
McGuire MB: *Religion:The Social Context.* Belmont:Wadsworth, 1987
McNeill J: *The Church and the Homosexual.* Boston: Beacon Press, 1993
McNemar R: *The Kentucky Revival.* New York: Edward Jenkins, 1846
McNichol T: The new faith in medicine. *USA Weekend*, April 5-7, 1996
Mead M: *Male and Female: The Classic Study of the Sexes.* New York: W. Morrow, 1996.
————. *Sex and Temperament in Three Primitive Societies.* New York: New American Library, 1950.
Meier JP: *A Marginal Jew: Rethinking the Historical Jesus.* New York, Doubleday, 1991
Meissner W: *Psychoanalysis and Religious Experience.* New Haven: Yale University Press, 1984
Menninger W: *Whatever Became of Sin?.* New York: Hawthorn, 1973
Metzer B, Coogan M: *The Oxford Compansion to the Bible.* New York: Oxford University Press, 1993
Meyer-Bahlburg H: Psychoendocrine research on sexual orientations. *Progress in Brain Research* 61:375-388, 1984
Milam M, Harris J: *Serpents in the Manger: Overcoming Abusive Christianity.* New York: Barricade Books, 1994
Miles J: *God:A Biography.* New York: Knopf, 1995
Miller DA: Neuropsychology and the emotional component of religion. *Pastoral Psychology* 33:267-272, 1995

Miller JB: *Psychoanalysis and Women*. New York: Brunner/Mazel, 1973

Mitchell S: *The Gospel According to Jesus*. New York: HarperCollins, 1991

Moody R: *Reflections on Life After Death*. New York: Bantam, 1977

————. *Life After Death*. New York: Bantam, 1975

Moore G: *The Brook Kerith*. New York: Liveright Publishing Corporation, 1969 (originally published in 1916)

Moore T: *Soul Mates: Honoring the Mysteries of Love and Relationship*. New York: Harper Collins, 1994

————. *Care of the Soul: A Guide for Cultivating Depth and Sacredness in Everyday Life*. New York: Harper Collins, 1992

Morris D: *The Culture of Pain*. Berkeley: University of California Press, 1991

Morgan H: Dostoevsky's epilepsy: A case report and comparison. *Surg Neurology* 33:413–416, 1990

Murphy A: *A Delicate Dance: Sexuality, Celibacy, and Relationships Among Catholic Clergy and Regions*. New York: Crossroad, 1992

Nace E: *The Treatment of Alcoholism*. New York: Brunner/Mazel, 1987

Nathan D, Snedeker M: *Satan's Silence*. New York: Basic Books, 1995

Nauman SE: *Exorcism Through the Ages*. New York: Philosophical Library, 1974

Neeleman J, King MB: Psychiatrists' religious attitudes in relation to their clinical practice. *Acta Psychiatrica Scandinavia* 88:420–424, 1993

Neeleman J, Persaud R: Why do psychiatrists neglect religion? *Brit J Medical Psychology* 68:169–178, 1995

New Larousse Encyclopedia of Mythology. New York: Prometheus Press, 1968

Newsom CA, Ringe SH: *The Women's Bible Commentary*. Louisville: Westminster/John Knox Press, 1992

Ney T: *True and False Allegations of Child Sexual Abuse*. New York: Brunner/Mazel, 1995

Niebuhr R: *The Nature and Destiny of Man*. New York: Charles Scribner's Sons, 1943

Nolan M, Nolan S: *Christian Pilgrimage in Modern Western Europe*. Chapel Hill: University of North Carolina, 1989

Nolan W: *Healing: A Doctor in Search of a Miracle*. New York: Random House, 1974

Nolan-Holksema S: *Sex Differences in Depression*. Palo Alto: Stanford University Press, 1990

Noll R: *Vampires, Werewolves, and Demons*. New York: Brunner/Mazel, 1992

Noyes R, Kletti R: Depersonalization in the face of life threatening danger: a description. *Psychiatry* 39:19–27, 1976

Noyes R, Kletti R: Depersonalization in the face of life threatening danger: an interpretation. *Omega* 7:103–114, 1976

Numbers R, Amundsen D: *Caring and Curing: Health and Medicine in the Western Religious Tradition*. Baltimore: Johns Hopkins University Press, 1986.

Numbers R, Butler J: *The Disappointed: Miller and Millenarianism*. Bloomington: Indiana University Press, 1987

Numbers R, Numbers J: *Millerism and madness*. Bulletin Menninger Clinic 49:289-320, 1985

Oates W: *Alcohol: In and Out of the Church*. Nashville: Broadman Press, 1966

Oden T: *Pastoral Theology*. San Francisco: Harper and Row, 1983

————. *Kerygma and Counseling*. Philadelphia: Westminster Press, 1966

Ohen C: *A Dog Man*. Chicago: University of Chicago Press, 1991

Onion R: *The Origins of European Thought About the Body, the Mind, the Soul, World, Time and Fate*. Cambridge: Cambridge University Press, 1951

Ornstein RE: *The Psychology of Consciousness*. San Francisco: WH Freeman, 1972

Osis K: *Deathbed Observations of Physicians and Nurses*. New York: Parapsychology Foundation, 1961

Osis K, Haroldsson E: *At the Hour of Death*. New York: Avon Books, 1977

Otto R: *The Idea of the Holy*. New York: Oxford University Press, 1958 (original 1917)

Pagels E: *The Origin of Satan*. New York: Random House, 1995

————. *Adam, Eve, and the Serpent*. New York: Random House, 1988

Pargament KI: *The Psychology of Religion and Coping*. New York: Guildford, 1997.

Parker WR, St. John E: *Prayer Can Change Your Life*. New York: Prentice Hall, 1986

Pasricha S, Stevenson I: Near-death experiences in India. *J Nervous Mental Disease* 174:165-170, 1986

Pattison EM: Psychological interpretations of exorcism. *J Operational Psychiatry* 8(2):5-21, 1977

Pattison EM, Lapins, NA, Doerr HA: Faith healing. *J Nervous Mental Diseases* 157:397-400, 1973

Paul R: *Moses and Civilization: The Meaning Behind Freud's Myths*. New Haven: Yale University Press, 1996

Pelikan J: *Jesus Through The Centuries*. New Haven: Yale University Press, 1985

————. *The Reformation of the Bible, The Bible of the Reformation*. New Haven, Yale University Press, 1996

————. *Jesus Through The Centuries*. New Haven: Yale University Press, 1985

Peschel E, Peschel R: Medical insights into the castrati in opera. *American Scientist* 75:578-583, 1987

Peto A: The development of ethical monotheism. In *The Psychoanalytic Study of Society*, Vol. 1., Wensterberger WM, Axelrad S (editors). New York: International Universities Press, 1960

Podvoll E: Self-mutilation within a hospital setting. *Brit J Med Psychology* 42:213-221, 1969

Posner GP: God in the CCU? *Free Inquiry* 10(2): 44-45, 1990

Prince R: Shamans and endorphins. *Ethos* 10:409-429, 1982

———. Religious experience and psychosis. *J Altered States of Consciousness* 5:167-181, 1979

Pruyser P:The seamy side of current religious beliefs. *Bull Menninger Clinic* 41:329-348, 1977

———. *Between Belief and Unbelief.* New York: Harper and Row, 1974

———. *A Dynamic Psychology of Religion.* New York: Harper and Row, 1968

Purvis A: *The Search for Compassion.* Louisville: Westminster Press, 1989

Rahner K: *A Rahner Reader*, edited by McCool G. New York: Seabury Press, 1975

Randi J: *The Faith Healers.* Buffalo: Prometheus Books, 1989

Redfield J: *The Celestine Prophecy: An Experiential Guide.* New York: Warner, 1995

———. *The Celestine Prophecy.* New York:Warner, 1994

Reiff P: *The Triumph of the Therapeutic: Uses of Faith After Freud.* New York: Harper and Row, 1966

Reik T: *Ritual: Psychoanalystic Studies.* New York: International Universities Press, 1946 (original 1919)

Rice E: *Freud and Moses.* Albany: State University of New York Press, 1990

Ring K: *Heading Toward Omega: In Search of the Meaning of the Near-Death Experience.* New York:William Morrow, 1984

Rizzuto AM: *The Birth of the Living God:A Psychoanalytic Study.* Chicago: University of Chicago Press, 1979

Robbins R: *The Encyclopedia of Witchcraft and Demonology.* New York: Crown, 1959

Robert M: *From Oedipus to Moses: Freud's Jewish Identity.* New York: Anchor Books, 1976

Roberts G, Owen J:The near-death experience. *Brit J Psychiatry* 153:607-617, 1988

Roberts J, Guberman A: Religion and epilepsy. *Psychiatric J Univ Ottawa* 14:282-286, 1989

Robertson P: *The New World Order.* Boston: G.K. Hall, 1992.

Robinson J: *The Human Face of God.* Philadelphia:Westminster Press, 1973

———. *A New Quest of the Historical Jesus.* London: SCM Press, 1959

Rodorf M: Marriage in the New Testament and in the Early Church. *J Ecclesiastical History* 20:192-210, 1969

Rogers J, McKim D: *The Authority and Interpretation of the Bible.* New York: Harper and Row, 1979

Rohde E: *Psyche.* New York: Harper and Row, 1966 (original 1925)

Rokeach M, Kemp CG: Open and closed systems in relation to anxiety and childhood experience. In *The Open and Closed Mind*, Rokearch M (editor). New York: Basic Books, 1960

Roof WC: *A Generation of Seekers: The Spiritual Journeys of the Baby Boom Generation*. San Francisco: HarperSanFrancisco, 1993.

Room R, Collins G: *Alcohol and Disinhibition*. Washington, DC: NIAAA, 1983

Rorabaugh W: *The Alcoholic Republic*. New York: Oxford University Press, 1979

Rosen G: *Madness in Society*. Chicago: University of Chicago Press, 1980

Rosenstock H, Vincent R: A case of lycanthropy. *American J Psychiatry* 134:1147–1149, 1978

Ross CE: Religion and psychological distress. *J Scientific Study of Religion* 29:236–245, 1990

Royal College of Psychiatrists: *Alcohol and Alcoholism*. New York: Free Press, 1979

Ruether R. *Religion and Sexism*. New York: Simon and Schuster, 1994

Rushdoony RJ: *The Roots of Reconstruction*. Vallecito CA: Ross House Books, 1991

Russell L: *Feminist Interpretation of the Bible*. Philadelphia: Westminster Press, 1985

Rycroft C: *Psychoanalysis and Beyond*. London: Hogarth, 1985

————. *Imagination and Reality*. New York: International Universities Press, 1968

Sandford C: *The Quest for Paradise*. Urbana: University of Illinois Press, 1961

Saver J, Rabin J: The neural substrates of religious experience. *J Neuropsychiatry Clinical Neurosciences* 9:498–510, 1997

Schlesinger A: The worst corruption. *Wall Street Journal*, November 22, 1995

Schlossman H: Circumcision as defense. *Psychoanalytic Quarterly* 35:340–356, 1966

Schonfield H. *The Passover Plot*. New York: Geis/Random House, 1965

Schroter-Kunhardt M: A review of near-death experiences. *J Scientific Exploration* 7:219–239, 1993

Schultes R, Hoffman A: *Plants of the Gods*. New York: McGraw Hill, 1979

Schumaker J: *Religion and Mental Health*. New York: Oxford University Press, 1992

Schwarz B: Ordeal by serpent, fire, and strychnine. *Psychiatric Quarterly* 34:405–449, 1960

Schweitzer A: *The Quest of the Historical Jesus*. London: A. & C. Black, 1926 (original 1906)

Scroggs R: *The New Testament and Homosexuality*. Philadelphia: Fortress Press, 1983

Shapiro AK, Shapiro E: *The Powerful Placebo*. Baltimore, Johns Hopkins University Press, 1997

Sherill JL: *They Speak With Other Tongues.* New Jersey: Revell Spire Books, 1977

Shipps J: *Mormonism: The Story of a New Religious Tradition.* Champaign: University of Illinois Press, 1985

Short AR: *The Bible and Modern Medicine.* London: Paternoster Press, 1953

Siegel B: *Love, Medicine, and Miracles.* New York: Harper and Row, 1986

Siegel R: The psychology of life after death. *Amer Psychologist* 35:911-931, 1980

Sims A: Psyche-spirit as well as mind? *Brit J Psychiatry* 165:441-446, 1994

Singer HK: *The Sexual Desire Disorders.* New York: Brunner/Magel, 1995

Singer M: The function of sobriety among Black Hebrews. *J Operational Psychiatry* 11:162-168, 1980

Sipe R: *Sex, Priests, and Power.* New York: Brunner/Mazel, 1995

————. *A Secret World: Sexuality and the Search for Celibacy.* New York: Brunner/Mazel, 1990

Sissa G: The sexual philosophies of Plato and Aristotle. In *A History for Women: From Ancient Goddesses to Christian Saints*, Pantel P (editor). Cambridge: Harvard University Press, 1992

Sloan RP, Bagiella E, Powell T: Religion, spirituality, and medicine. *Lancet* 353:664-667, 1999.

Smith CR: *The Physician Examines the Bible.* New York: Philosophical Library, 1950

Smith H. *Man and His Gods.* Boston: Little Brown, 1953

Smith WC: *The Meaning and End of Religion.* London: SPCK, 1978

Snyder CR: *Alcohol and the Jews.* New Brunswick: Rutgers Center for Alcohol Publications, 1958

Sorenson A, Cutter H: Mystical experience, drinking, behavior, and the reasons for drinking. *J Stud Alcohol* 43:588-592, 1982

Spilka B: Functional and dysfunctional roles of religion. *J Psychology and Christianity* 8:5-15, 1989

Spong J: *Resurrection: Myth or Reality?* San Francisco: HarperSanFrancisco, 1994

————. *Born of a Woman.* San Francisco: HarperSanFrancisco, 1992

Steere D: *Spiritual Presence in Psychotherapy.* New York: Brunner/Mazel, 1997

Stevenson I: Research into the evidence of man's survival after death. *J Nervous Mental Disease* 165:152-170, 1977

Stoller R: *Presentations of Gender.* New Haven: Yale University Press, 1985

Slotland N: Tug of war: domestic abuse and the misuse of religion. *Am J Psychiatry* 157:692-702, 2000

Straub G: *Salvation for Sale.* Buffalo: Prometheus Books, 1986

Surawicz F, Banta R: Lycanthropy revisited. *Canadian Psychiatric Assn Journal* 20:637-642, 1975

Tawney RH: *Religion and the Rise of Capitalism*. London: Murray, 1926

Templeton J: *Evidence of Purpose: Scientists Discover the Creator*. New York: Continuum, 1994

Teresa of Avila: *The Interior Castle*. New York: Paulist Press, 1979 (original 1557)

Tessman I, Tessman J: Efficacy of prayers. *Skeptical Inquirer* 24(2):31-33, 2000

Thiede CP, D'Ancona M: *Eyewitness to Jesus*. New York: Doubleday, 1996

Thompson C: Cultural pressures in the psychology of women. *Psychiatry* 5:331-339, 1942

Thurston H. *The Physical Phenomena of Mysticism*. London: Burns Oates, 1952

Tiebout H: Therapeutic mechanisms of AA. *Am J Psychiatry* 100:468-473, 1943

Tillich P: *The Courage To Be*. New Haven: Yale University Press, 1952
————. *Systematic Theology*. Chicago: University of Chicago Press, 1951.

Tipler F: *The Physics of Immortality: Modern Cosmology, God, and the Resurrection of the Dead*. New York: Doubleday, 1994

Trethowan WH: The couvade syndrome. In *Modern Perspectives in Psycho-Obstetrics*, Howell J (editor). New York: Brunner/Mazel, 1971

Trible P: *Texts of Terror*. Philadelphia: Fortress Press, 1984

Trip E: *The Meridian Handbook of Classical Mythology*. New York: New American Library, 1974

Troeltsch E: *The Social Teaching of the Christian Churches*. London: Allen & Unwin, 1931

Truehart C: Welcome to the next church. *Atlantic Monthly*, 37-56, August, 1996

Tucker DM, Novelly R, Walker P: Hyperreligiousity in temporal lobe epilepsy. *J Nerv Mental Disease* 175:181-189, 1987

Turnbull C: *The Mountain People*. New York: Simon and Schuster, 1972

Turner J: *Without God, Without Creed: The Origins of Unbelief in America*. Baltimore: Johns Hopkins University Press, 1985

Turner A: *The History of Hell*. New York: Harcourt Brace, 1993

Tuzin D: Miraculous voices: The auditory experience of numinous objects. *Current Anthropology* 23:579-596, 1984

Urban L: *A Short History of Christian Thought*. New York, Oxford University Press, 1995

Vaillant G: *The Natural History of Alcoholism: Causes, Patterns, and Paths of Recovery*. Cambridge: Harvard University Press, 1983

Van Der Horst P: Sarah's seminal emission. In *Greeks, Romans and Christians*, Balch E, Gerguson E, Meeks W (editors). Minneapolis: Fortress Press, 1990

Vandercychen W, Van Deth R: *From Fasting Saints to Anorexic Girls*. New York: New York University Press, 1994

VanderVeldt J, Odenwald R: *Psychiatry and Catholicism*. New York: McGraw-Hill, 1952

Veith I: *Hysteria: The History of a Disease*. Chicago: University of Chicago Press, 1965

Vermaseren M: *Cybele and Attis*. London: Thames and Hudson, 1977

Vitz P: *Sigmund Freud's Christian Unconscious*. New Haven: Yale University Press, 1987

Waddell H: *The Desert Fathers*. Ann Arbor: University of Michigan Press, 1957 (original 1936)

Wagner R: *Gay Catholic Priests*. San Francisco: Institute for Advanced Study of Human Sexuality, 1980

Wallace ER: *Freud and Anthropology*. New York: International Universities Press, 1983

Wallerstein E: *Circumcision: An American Health Fallacy*. New York: Springer, 1980

Wallington SA: Consequences of transgression: self-punishment and depression. *J Personality Social Psychology* 28:1-7, 1973

Walsh R, Vaughan F: *Paths Beyond Ego*. New York: G.P. Putnam's Sons, 1993

Warlomont E: *Louise Lateau*. Paris: Balliere, 1875

Warner M: *Alone of All Her Sex: The Myth and the Cult of the Virgin Mary*. New York: Random House, 1976

Weber M: *The Protestant Ethic and the Spirit of Capitalism*. London: Allen & Unwin, 1930

Weil A: *Spontaneous Healing*. New York: Knopf, 1995

Weiss C: A worldwide survey of the current practice of Milah. Conference on Jewish Social Studies, 30-48, 1962

West D: *Eleven Lourdes Miracles*. London: Duckworth, 1957

West M: *The Psychology of Meditation*. Oxford: Clarendon Press, 1987

Westermeyer J: Options regarding alcohol use among the Chippewa. *Am J Orthopsychiatry* 42:398-409, 1972

White A: *A History of the Warfare of Science With Theology in Christendom*. New York: Braziller, 1955 (original 1895)

White V: *God and the Unconscious*. Cleveland: World Publishing Co., 1961

Whitlock FA, Hynes JV: Religious stigmatisation. *Psychological Medicine* 8:185-202, 1978

Wilkens R: *The Land Called Holy*. New Haven: Yale University Press, 1992

Williams C: *Tongues of the Spirit*. Cardiff: University of Wales Press, 1981

Wills G: *Papal Sin*, New York: Doubleday, 2000

Wilson I: *The Bleeding Mind*. London: Weidenfeld and Nicolson, 1992

Winnicott DW: *Playing and Reality*. New York: Routledge, 1971

————. *The Maturational Process and the Facilitating Environment*. London, Hogarth, 1965

————. *Collected Papers: Though Pediatrics to Psychoanalysis*. London: Tavistock, 1958

Witmer J, Zimmerman M: Intercessory prayer as medical treatment? *Skeptical Inquirer* 15(2):177–180, 1991

Witzum E, Greenberg D, Dasberg H: Mental illness and religious change. *British J Medical Psychology* 63:33–41, 1990

Woods R: *Understanding Mysticism*. New York: Doubleday, 1980

Woollcott P, Desai P: Religious and creative states of illumination: A perspective from psychiatry. In *Religious and Ethical Factors in Psychiatric Perspective*, Browning D, Jobe T, Evison I (editors). Chicago: Nelson-Hall, 1990

Wright L: *Remembering Satan*. New York: Knopf, 1994

Wurthnow R: *Sharing the Journey: Support Groups and America's New Quest for Community*. New York: Free Press, 1994.

Yandell DW: Epidemic convulsions. *Brain* 4:339–350, 1881–1882

Yerushalmi Y: *Freud's Moses*. New Haven: Yale University Press, 1991

Young A: The return of the return of the repressed. *Transcultural Psychiatric Research Review* 29:235–243, 1992

Zaleski CG: *Otherworld Journeys: Accounts of Near-Death Experience in Medieval and Modern Times*. New York: Oxford University Press, 1987.

SCRIPTURE INDEX

INDEX

ABOUT THE AUTHOR

Armando Favazza was born and reared in New York City. He received his undergraduate degree from Columbia University, his medical degree from the University of Virginia, and his Master of Public Health Degree from the University of Michigan where he completed his psychiatric residency training. He is a co-founder of the Society for the Study of Psychiatry and Culture, past-president of the Missouri Psychiatric Society, and a Fellow of both the American College of Psychiatrists and of the American Psychiatric Association. He has authored several hundred chapters, articles, reviews, and essays especially in the area of cultural psychiatry. His best known book, *Bodies Under Siege: Self-Mutilation and Body Modification*, is considered a classic in the field. He has lectured widely both nationally and internationally at conferences, hospitals, and more than fifty medical schools, including Emory, Harvard, Karolinska, Mayo Clinic, McGill, Michigan, New York University, Toronto, UCLA, Virginia, Washington, and Yale. He is a professor of psychiatry at the University of Missouri-Columbia and has served three terms as chair of his medical school's Faculty Affairs Council; a resolution of the Missouri Senate commended and applauded "his unparalleled record of service, support, and leadership" at the university. In addition to several teaching awards he has received the prestigious George B. Kunkel Award for Advances in Medical Science. He has had much media exposure including several appearances on the television show 20/20 and interviews on National Public Radio and the BBC, and has been cited in numerous newspapers and magazines, including *Time* and the *New York Times Magazine*. He is an avid, competitive tennis player and has been ranked in the 5 state Missouri Valley region. His son, Terry, is a urologist and his daughter, Laura, is a lawyer. His wife, Christine, has a Ph.D. in Education and served for thirteen years as assistant athletic director for academics at the University of Missouri. He and his wife enjoy preparing great meals, playing with their Cairn terriers, and tending to their spectacular garden.